ENCYCLOPEDIA OF NATIVE AMERICAN RELIGIONS

UPDATED EDITION

AN INTRODUCTION

ARLENE HIRSCHFELDER
PAULETTE MOLIN

Foreword by
Walter R. Echo-Hawk

☑®

Facts On File, Inc.

This work is dedicated to Dennis for his unwavering support.

—A. H.

This work is dedicated with love to my family, especially to Larry,

and to the memory of my father and brother.

—P. M.

ENCYCLOPEDIA OF NATIVE AMERICAN RELIGIONS, UPDATED EDITION

Updated Edition copyright © 2000 by Arlene Hirschfelder and Paulette Molin
First Edition copyright © 1992 by Arlene Hirschfelder and Paulette Molin
Foreword copyright © 2000 by Walter R. Echo-Hawk

Facts On File, Inc.
11 Penn Plaza
New York, NY 10001

Library of Congress Cataloging-in-Publication Data

Hirschfelder, Arlene B.
   Encyclopedia of Native American religions.—Updated ed.
      p.   cm.
Written by Arlene B. Hirschfelder and Paulette Molin.
   Includes bibliographical references (p.   ) and index.
   ISBN 0-8160-3949-6
   1. Indians of North America—Religion—Encyclopedias. 2. Indians of North American—Rites and ceremonies—Encyclopedias. I. Molin, Paulette Fairbanks. II. Title.
E98.R3H73 2000
299'.7'03—DC21   99-21586

Facts On File books are available at special discounts when purchased in bulk quantities for businesses, associations, institutions or sales promotions. Please call our Special Sales Department in New York at (212) 967-8800 or (800) 322-8755.

You can find Facts On File on the World Wide Web at http://www.factsonfile.com

Text design by Evelyn Horovicz

Cover design by Cathy Rincon

Printed in the United States of America

VB Hermitage 10 9 8 7 6 5 4 3 2 1

This book is printed on acid-free paper.

CONTENTS

FOREWORD

—Walter R. Echo-Hawk, Senior Staff Attorney
Native American Rights Fund

Encyclopedia of Native American Religions is a major reference work on an important but too often overlooked subject. Religion is a basic attribute of humanity cherished by mankind in all ages, races, and cultures. This mark of humanity includes America's 500 Indian tribes and 2 million Native peoples. Columbus was wrong when he wrote in his diary, on his first day in this hemisphere, that Indians should easily be made Christians because they have no religion. On the contrary, North America is teeming with diverse Native American religions that rank among the world's religious traditions for their rich spirituality, profound beliefs, practices, and traditions.

Based upon centuries of close observations of the natural world, these unique religions bring depth and beauty to America's religious and cultural heritage. Beyond the religious sphere, America's Native religions contain environmental ethics and teachings that are sorely needed by industrialized society, which has converted some parts of the world into uninhabitable polluted wastelands. To the art world, the sacred symbols, music, art, and religious objects that accompany Native American religions are prized cultural patrimony and intellectual property coveted by museums for their intrinsic beauty. For Native peoples, cultural survival depends on the traditional religions that have been the glue holding Indian tribes and Native communities together in the face of great adversities over the centuries.

It has been more than 500 years since Columbus's arrival and the religions of Native peoples still remain a mystery to most Americans. Little is known about Native American religions by citizens or policy makers in the United States. Ignorance in religious affairs is usually harmful. The history of Native American religious liberty is a case in point that is pockmarked by European intolerance, military confrontations, government bans, and government-sponsored proselytization. More recently, Native worship has been possible only through a patchwork maze of legislation, litigation, and government regulation that demonstrates an inability to adequately incorporate the basic needs of indigenous worshipers into the social, legal, and political fabric of our nation.

Native American religions enjoy surprisingly little legal protection. Courts have experienced inordinate difficulty applying First Amendment principles to Native American worship, as seen in such extraordinary and troubling opinions as *Badoni v. Higginson* (1977), *Lyng, Secretary of Agriculture, et al. v. Northwest Indian Cemetery Protective Ass'n. et al.* (1989), and *Bowen v. Roy* (1986). The judiciary had such difficulty that it finally abandoned the task altogether in *Employment Division, Department of Human Resources of Oregon et al. v. Smith et al.* (1990) in a sweeping exit that left protection of American worship—regardless of religion or race—up to the political process. Yet when politicians took up the task and passed the Religious Freedom Restoration Act of 1993, the Supreme Court declared that effort unconstitutional in *City of Boerne v. P. F. Flores* (1997)!

While federal lawmakers passed the American Indian Religious Freedom Act Amendments of 1994 to protect the religious use of peyote, no other Native American religious practices enjoy significant legal protection.

At this century draws to a close, Native American religious liberty is a pressing human-rights concern to Indian tribes. Under watchful government eyes, worship is committed to the discretion of government administrators without meaningful judicial review. Fundamental Native American religious observances, such as access to sacred sites and use of religious sacraments and religious objects, are heavily regulated by federal agencies. In some quarters, ancient tribal religious practices continue to be viewed with antagonism by intolerant right-wing groups, uninformed administrators and lawmakers; in other quarters, religious patrimony and related intellectual property have become commodities for commercial exploitation or expropriation by uninformed non-Indians. Under these conditions, survival of Native religious traditions is clearly endangered.

For all of the above reasons, it is important to understand Native American religions and safeguard their survival into the future. It should not be difficult for a democracy that prides itself on protecting human rights to allow Native religious diversity. Yet this task remains a pressing human-rights challenge that might only be achieved through public education that changes the hearts and minds of the next generation.

This book is a bridge between cultures. It compiles introductory overviews of many traditional Native American religious beliefs, practices, and histories. The data show that Columbus was wrong. Indians have religions on a scale that far surpasses Middle Eastern religious diversity, including more numerous traditional holy places that predate the writing of the Old Testament. Organized in a handy encyclopedia format, the material is often presented in the context of closely related social, legal, and political issues. This book is warranted, overdue, and should be helpful to students, scholars, teachers, policy makers, and the interested public at large.

PREFACE

The public knows or understands little about Native religions in North America, despite all the Native American religious issues that frequently make the news. The 1990 Supreme Court ruling permitting state prohibition of sacramental peyote use captured national attention. So have the issues of Indian burial ground desecrations and the debates over repatriation to Indian tribes of Indian skeletal remains and associated burial objects. It makes news when museums return sacred War God statues to the Zuni people or when they return sacred wampum belts to the Iroquois. It makes news when state legislatures pass laws that make it a felony to desecrate Indian burial grounds, when the federal government passes legislation requiring federal officials to respect the religious freedoms of Indian peoples and when law requires the National Museum of the American Indian to return identifiable bones to requesting tribes. It makes news when the Hopi village of Shungopavi prohibits non-Indians from viewing the Snake Dance or when a Santa Fe newspaper is sued for invasion of privacy for printing photos of a Santo Domingo religious ceremony taken from a low-flying plane without permission. It makes news when tribes in Canada and the United States oppose U.S. Forest Service efforts to commercialize Medicine Mountain and Medicine Wheel in Wyoming or when tribes in northwestern California protest the building of a logging road through the tribes' sacred area in the Six Rivers National Forest. It makes news when the first Navajo is consecrated as a bishop in the Episcopal Church. And it makes news when the pope canonizes Native Americans.

Yet despite all this, the North American public remains ignorant about Native American religions. And this, despite the fact that hundreds of books and articles have been published by anthropologists, religionists and others about Native beliefs in spirits, the Native American Church, peyote religion, Plains Sun Dances, Navajo chants, Pueblo ceremonialism; guardian spirits and vision quests, Inuit masks, Iroquois thanksgiving rites, shamanism, and medicine objects. Little of this scholarly literature has found its way into popular books about Native American religion in the United States.

This book responds to this lack of reliable information about Native American religion in conventional reference books about religion in North America. North American Native religions should not be consigned to the margins of study of religions. Indian country in North America is still home to hundreds of religious traditions that have endured, despite a long history of persecution and suppression by government and missionaries. These traditions are intrinsically interesting and are important as religious expressions. *Encyclopedia of Native American Religions* tries to accord these Native sacred traditions the respect, status, and rightful place they so richly deserve among other great spiritual traditions, correcting the misimpressions that Indian religions are quaint curiosities, exotic, strange, or even nonexistent. Native American sacred beliefs are as dignified, profound, viable, and richly faceted as other religions practiced throughout the world. Native sacred knowledge has not been destroyed or lost but in fact lives on as the heart of Native American cultural existence today.

The entries in this book cover the spiritual traditions of Native peoples in the United States and Canada before contact with Europeans and Americans, the consequences of this contact on sacred traditions, and contemporary religious forms. We debated over what information to include from the numerous published works about Indian religions. Some of these works tell far too much, some far too little; some parade Western bias, others convey appropriate and respectful information.

Although there are many sacred sites located in the United States and Canada, we have not identified them all here. Undisturbed sacred sites are essential to Native American practices and revealing their locations jeopardizes their private nature. We have included, however, information on sacred sites that have been involved in public disputes and litigation. For example, there is information about the San Francisco Peaks, a site sacred to Hopi and Navajo who tried to prevent the expansion of a ski resort in the peaks. There is information about the Chimney Rock area of the Six Rivers National Forest, a region sacred to Yurok, Karok and Tolowa who opposed Forest Service plans to build a road through the sacred area. And there is information about the right of New Mexico Zuni pilgrims to cross a rancher's land in order to make a pilgrimage to Kolhu/wala-wa, a sacred site located in Arizona. We also omit information (as well as photographs) about detailed rituals and ceremonies and the contents of sacred altars and medicine bundles. Though this information can be found in published works available to any reader, much of it simply should never have been published. Scholars too often broke trust with Native people who shared their spiritual practices on condition that descriptions of their rites not appear in published form.

Some anthropologists have admitted their indiscretions. Elsie Clews Parsons, who wrote volumes about Pueblo ceremonialism, tells how she "harass[ed] the old chap with my questioning," while he was making prayersticks. She also bought 140 paintings by an Isletan artist, some of which depicted religious rites. The paintings were sent to her clandestinely, and although the artist pleaded for anonymity because of fear of punishment, his paintings were published, his name revealed after his death, and his relatives condemned by Isletan people. Matilda C. Stevenson, who wrote about Zuni religious practices, tells that "while the [Zuni] priests and other high officials favored photographing the ceremonials . . . the populace were so opposed to having their masks and rituals carried away on paper that it was deemed prudent to make but few ceremonial pictures with the camera, and the altars and masks were sketched in color by the writer without the knowledge of the people." By this method, in 1904 Stevenson was able to document the largest and most valuable collection of ceremonial items, especially of sacred objects and sacred vessels, ever secured from any of the pueblos. In his work about the Snake cere-

monial at the Hopi village of Walpi, J. Walter Fewkes brags that "several secret rites took place in the kivas which are here published [in 1894] for the first time." Apache practitioners objected to having their medicine objects scrutinized and touched, but this did not stop John C. Bourke from convincing the owners to allow him glimpses of the sacred objects that they wore.

Many Indian religious practitioners resent discussions about the specifics of their spiritual traditions, which they consider private, sacred, and powerful legacies of their people. They feel certain concepts and vocabulary are not always communicable. They are deeply concerned that sacred information that becomes public will lose its power or that it will be misused, which can be detrimental not only to Indian people but to all people. We have tried to include enough material for readers to gain an understanding and appreciation of spiritual traditions but have also tried to avoid the specific descriptions that would offend Native peoples.

This volume includes entries based on published information. We have included information on important ceremonies of Native groups. There are not, however, descriptions of every corn dance, round dance, eagle dance, deer dance, or war dance but rather representative descriptions that suggest the nature of religious worship. Examples from various tribal groups suffice to illustrate the basic outline of a rite or ceremony. The book emphasizes contemporary rituals although there are discussions of important early ceremonies that are believed to have been discontinued as a result of forced removals, destruction of natural environments, and pressures to assimilate. Since entire books have been written about one ceremony of a group, it is important to stress that entries in this book only introduce and outline a ceremony. The extensive bibliography at the end of the book suggests works that provide in-depth material. We have highlighted the interrelatedness of Native cultures, religion, and land, or as Walter Holden Capps suggests in an essay about Native American religion, "the harmonious combination of nature and religion that . . . impresses every outsider." Another religion scholar has pointed out that there are "inextricable linkages . . . between religion and culture, and between religion and land" in Native American cultures.

This book also contains biographies of Native American religious practitioners. Some prefer anonymity and choose not to talk about their spiritual knowledge, especially with outsiders; others choose to share their knowledge. Either choice should be respected. Some practitioners revealed information to adopted members of the tribe. Others revealed information on condition that the material be published after the practitioner's death. Practitioners without successors have chosen to reveal sacred knowledge because they want it to survive for future generations. Some

Native peoples are now using computers, tape recorders, and videotape to ensure that cultural traditions survive and to prevent further loss of knowledge. We have included information on religious figures only from published writings or about whom information is available in biographies or autobiographies.

Many biographies of Catholic and Protestant missionaries who influenced Native American religious traditions are included here as well. Native American people have demonstrated a remarkable resiliency despite almost 400 years of exposure to European and American missionaries who tried to suppress Native religious practices and to damage or prohibit access to sacred places. Missionaries preached against traditional Native practices such as dancing, potlatching, and those associated with mourning ceremonies. They encouraged governments to pursue misguided, shortsighted, and devastating policies that tried to eradicate Native beliefs and convert Indians to the "true faith." They supported the persecution and jailing of Native American religious practitioners. They trivialized diverse religious beliefs by labeling Indians as *heathens, conjurers, pagans,* and *primitives,* terms that persist to the present. We have also included biographies of some historic figures who, though not religious practitioners, affected the development or practice of Native religion.

There is also information here about disease and Native medicine. Many Native American groups believe that many ailments are caused by spiritual forces and therefore can be cured only with spiritual aid. Illness is often defined as disharmony of spirit, mind, and body, and wellness as harmony of spirit, mind, and body. Illness can be caused by violating sacred taboos, by the presence of "pains" or "strengths," by ghost sickness, by witchcraft, or by other influences that vary from group to group. The book describes some curing ceremonies that heal these spiritual illnesses, as well as religious ceremonies that attempted to heal entire communities devastated by upheavals and epidemics stemming from Euro-American and Euro-Canadian contacts.

The book also contains information about ceremonial races, games, and sacred clowns and their integral roles in Native American ceremonies. These subjects, which are not customarily mentioned in connection with religious rites, are indeed closely associated with Native religious traditions.

This book has limits as well. There are no systematic descriptions of tribal cosmologies, stories about deities, tales of lower (under-) worlds where beings predating Indian people originated, or similar topics. Each of these subjects alone could fill many volumes. The book does not include texts or discussions of the countless sacred oral stories, chants, prayers, songs, and poetry that address questions about the creation of the world or the origins of human, plant, and animal life. (The bibliography lists a few of the countless books that deal with North American oral traditions.) Nor does this volume describe in a systematic way each tribe's major deities, spirit beings, and culture heroes. Those entries that describe those deities and culture heroes are included because they figure prominently in the spiritual traditions of the respective Native groups.

Finally, this volume reflects the state of published research. Since the spiritual traditions of some tribes have been more extensively documented than others, the book reflects the state of the literature, and contemporary descriptions are not always available for every group. In the entries on ceremonies, sacred sites, practitioners, religious societies, and so on, the authors do not reveal any information that has not been previously published.

Over the centuries, spellings of the names of Native American nations have varied considerably and still do. In most instances, the authors have tried to use spellings preferred by Native groups. For example, Navajo have declared a preference for that spelling (over *Navaho*). The Blackfeet have expressed similar declarations of preference for *Blackfeet* over *Blackfoot.* The authors have selected current spellings for *Abenaki* (Abnaki), *Athabascan* (Athabaskan), and *Shoshone* (Shoshoni). Other tribal spellings selected for this volume also conform to modern usage.

Tribal names have varied as well as tribal spellings. For consistency, the authors have chosen *Ojibway* (Ojibwa) over *Chippewa,* another name for the same people that call themselves Anishinabe, the traditional name by which they have always known themselves. The authors also use *Mississauga* and *Saulteaux* for two Canadian Ojibway groups. A reserve near London, Ontario, in Canada, which has been known for years as Oneida of the Thames, is now known as Onyota'a:ka. The people formerly called Papago have officially declared a preference for Tohono O'odham, their own language name. The people formerly known as the Winnebago of Wisconsin officially renamed themselves Ho-Chunk, their traditional name for themselves, but the Winnebago of Nebraska have not made the change.

Sioux, the popular name for the Dakota, Nakota, and Lakota peoples, is often used in treaties and book titles. The authors use *Dakota, Nakota,* and *Lakota* to differentiate, when possible, eastern groups (Dakota) from western groups (Lakota) from groups in-between (Nakota). In 1993, the people formerly called the Sisseton-Wahpeton Sioux Tribe adopted as its official name *Sisseton-Wahpeton Dakota.*

Although many Navajo routinely call themselves Dineh (Diné) their traditional name in their own language, the group continues to call itself the Navajo Nation. Twice, in 1992 and 1994, the Navajo Nation Council rejected proposals to change the tribal name to Diné.

Many people popularly called Eskimo prefer to call themselves Inuit, meaning "the people" in the Inuit language. In Canada, the word *Eskimo* has practically disappeared. But in Alaska, there are two language and culture groups, the Inupiat and Yupik. While the word *Inuit* exists in the Inupiat language, it does not exist in Yupik, the most widely spoken Native language in Alaska. People prefer to be called "Yupik" or "Yupik Eskimo," the designation of the Eskimo of southwestern Alaska, or "Inupiat," the indigenous people from northwestern Alaska.

In Canada, the preferred collective name for Native peoples is First Nations. In the United States the terms *Native Americans* and *American Indians* tend to be used interchangeably.

Note: In the text, words in SMALL CAPITAL LETTERS denote cross-references.

ABISHABIS ("Small Eyes") *(fl. mid-1800s) Cree* The principal prophet of a religious movement that spread among Cree in the Hudson Bay region from Churchill, Manitoba, to Albany, Ontario, from 1842 to 1843. Abishabis, said to be influenced by words in hymns written in the Cree syllabic system devised by the Methodist missionary JAMES EVANS, applied the name of "Jesus" to himself, while a companion became known as Wasiteck, or "light." The two men were believed to have visited heaven and returned with blessings and teachings for the people. They claimed the ability to draw "The Track to Heaven" on paper or wood, using the map or chart they created to convey their prophetic message. Abishabis and Wasiteck warned against the ways of the whites while pointing out the promise of game and other heavenly rewards for those who followed their teachings. In mid-1842, activities associated with the religious movement were recorded in Churchill and Severn on the western coast of Hudson Bay. By fall of that year, a large group of Cree in Severn were reportedly occupied in "psalm singing and painting books" and "making the woods to ring . . . with musick." There is evidence that the activities eventually spread and gathered strength throughout the area. As his influence as a prophet grew, Abishabis was given gifts and clothing and other goods by his supporters. An elderly woman referred to as a "priestess" helped gain acceptance for the religious movement by carrying its message eastward from York to Albany.

The religious movement had roots in both Native and non-Native cultures. In 1840 Cree syllabic writings started circulating among Native people in the area. Evans, who promoted Christianity with the system, encouraged those he taught to teach others. As the teachings written in Cree syllabics traveled, Indians, such as Abishabis and Wasiteck, could have added their own interpretations to the texts. Besides taking words from hymns for their names, the two men were said to have introduced observance of the Sabbath as part of their religious teachings. Although they used fragments of Christianity, the religious movement of Abishabis and Wasiteck was rooted in their own culture as well. It is likely that the symbolic writings and drawings reminded the Cree people of those used in MIDEWIWIN scrolls and other sacred texts. The messages of the prophets also placed an emphasis upon returning to Native ways.

The religious movement declined as a result of white opposition to it and because of the waning popularity of Abishabis himself. As he sought more goods for his followers, his support diminished and he returned to his earlier poverty. By mid-1843 he was suspected of robbing and killing a York area Indian family. Abishabis subsequently fled to Severn, where he was temporarily detained by a Hudson's Bay Company officer. During his detention he was seized by area Indians, who killed and burned him. Abishabis was believed to have become a windigo, a dreaded cannibalistic being of Cree and other northern Algonquian belief, which

1

would endanger the people if it was not destroyed. Although it is not known how long the religious movement persisted, it is believed to have lasted for a time after the death of Abishabis. The movement was written about by GEORGE BARNLEY, Methodist missionary to the James Bay area, and in the Hudson's Bay Company post records.

ACCEPTANCE OF THE DRUM CEREMONY *Osage* A ceremony conducted in connection with the transfer of a sacred drum to a new drumkeeper during the course of the four-day I'N-LON-SCHKA CEREMONIAL DANCE in June. The drumkeeper is always an eldest son, for in Osage belief such a child is considered a special blessing. The drumkeeper is assisted by family members in carrying out the extensive responsibilities associated with the role, the most important of which is the care and protection of the sacred drum belonging to his community. Each of the three Osage communities in Oklahoma possesses its own drum. Features of the ceremony include an announcement of acceptance of the drum by the new drumkeeper and his family, the public honoring and thanking of individuals for past service, the presentation of gifts to honored persons and the giving of formal speeches. The gift-giving signifies the new drumkeeper's acceptance of the honor and responsibility of caring for the sacred drum. His first act as the official drumkeeper is generally to open the dance by striking the first drum beat. The first drumkeeper of the I'n-Lon-Schka was BEN MASHUNKASHAY. (See also PASSING OF THE DRUM CEREMONY.)

ACORN FEAST *Hupa* An annual observance that sanctified the first eating of acorns each fall to ensure the continuing supply of this food. People celebrated in autumn when nuts began to fall from tan oaks. An officiant collected the acorns and ritually cooked them, repeating lengthy ritual texts, saying prayers, and executing sacred acts. After the procedures were completed, people were allowed to eat the acorns. An acorn feast was held in November 1989 at the Hostler Rancheria for the first time in more than 50 years. (See also FIRST SALMON RITES.)

ACT FOR THE PRESERVATION OF AMERICAN ANTIQUITIES (Act of June 8, 1906, c. 3060, & 1, 34 Stat. 225 [codified at 16 U.S.C. & 431–433, 1976]) *(1976)* This federal act, which became law on June 8, 1906, makes it a criminal offense to appropriate, excavate, injure, or destroy historic or prehistoric ruins or monuments or objects of antiquity located on lands owned or controlled by the United States government. The Antiquities Act, which provides a permit requirement for those conducting archaeological research and excavations in areas under federal jurisdiction, was found to be unconstitutionally vague in *UNITED STATES*

V. DIAZ (1973) because it did not define significant statutory terms. The statute's weakness was also noted in *UNITED STATES V. JONES* (1978), when charges were dismissed against defendants seen digging among ruins and arrested with American Indian artifacts in their possession. Another federal law, the ARCHAEOLOGICAL RESOURCES PROTECTION ACT OF 1979 was passed by Congress to correct deficiencies in the Antiquities Act. However, problems persist in protecting Native American remains, gravesites, and burial offerings from exploitation under these laws.

ADOPTION STRING *Tutelo, Six Nations Reserve, Canada* During the Tutelo SPIRIT ADOPTION CEREMONY, the person adopted wears a long single loop or chain of white Tutelo WAMPUM beneath the shirt. The wampum passes over the left shoulder and down the right side to the waist. The chain symbolizes the return to life of a deceased Tutelo person as revived in the personality of the adopted person who becomes the living representative of the deceased. At the end of the ceremony, the string of Tutelo wampum is removed from the adopted person and safeguarded until the next adoption rite.

AFRAID-OF-BEARS *(fl. late 19th c.) Kiowa* Feather Dance Priest. Afraid-of-bears, who had suffered a serious illness as a youngster, was assisted in his recovery by a Ghost Dance adherent. He later experienced a vision in which he saw a performance of a sacred dance he named the FEATHER DANCE. A reinterpretation of the GHOST DANCE OF 1890, it included the ordination of 10 priests, the use of a symbolic yellow cross and cedar tree, the gift of an eagle feather to members who generally wore them upright during the ceremonies, and prayers to the Creator. The dance itself followed the instructions received from SITTING BULL, the Arapaho apostle, who had introduced the Ghost Dance to the Kiowa. Afraid-of-bears served as a missionary, spreading a message of hope among his Kiowa followers. The federal government, which considered the Ghost Dance one of the "heathenish" customs it opposed, sought to eradicate the religious dance among the Kiowa between 1890 and 1916. The Office of Indian Affairs withheld tribal rations and lease funds from the Kiowa people until they agreed, in a statement signed in 1916, to no longer hold the sacred dance.

AFTERWORLD See SOUL

AIR SPIRIT *Inuit* Called *sila* by most Inuit people, this term has an extensive range of meanings. It is a spiritual power or force permeating the universe, nature, the air, the wind, the weather, and open sky. The beliefs of individual peoples vary. The Chugach, southernmost Alaska Natives, believe *sila* signifies the universe, controls the weather and air, and is an omnipresent power in the world. The Koniag regard *sila* as the highest power that created sky and earth, ruling air and light and having power to create earthquakes. The Copper Inuit perceive *sila* as the lower regions of the sky, responsible for good weather. A major deity in some regions, his (the masculine pronoun is employed by Inuit with the exception of Caribou groups) power includes giving life and healing the sick.

ALLIS, SAMUEL, JR. *(1805–1883)* Presbyterian missionary who worked among the Pawnee people under the auspices of the AMERICAN BOARD OF COMMISSIONERS FOR FOREIGN MISSIONS (ABCFM). Allis was born on September 28, 1805, in Conway, Massachusetts, to Congregationalist parents. He began learning the saddle and harness trade when he was 17 years old, eventually working at it for four years. Allis later joined the Presbyterian Church in Ithaca, New York, and turned to religious work. In 1834 he accompanied the Reverend JOHN DUNBAR west to establish a mission among the Flathead or Nez Perce people. Their plans changed en route, and they instead began working among the Pawnee in present-day Nebraska. After arriving in the fall, the two missionaries settled with different bands until the following spring. After acquainting themselves with the people and selecting a mission site, the work was delayed because of a number of circumstances. The tribal population was devastated by smallpox, starvation, and war. A mission was eventually established and "civilizing" programs started. Allis was married to Emeline Palmer on April 23, 1836, and she joined him in his work among the Pawnee.

In 1841 Allis received an appointment to serve as government teacher to the Pawnee. The mission was abandoned in 1846 because of repeated raids against the tribal group by their Lakota enemy. Allis then operated a boarding school for Native children in what is now Bellevue, Nebraska, for two years. He farmed in Iowa from 1851 to 1857, also serving as an interpreter for the government. Allis moved to Fremont, Nebraska, in 1857 and remained there until his death in 1883. His book *Forty Years among the Indians and on the Eastern Borders of Nebraska* was published in 1887.

ALLOUEZ, CLAUDE JEAN *(1622–1689)* French Jesuit missionary and explorer. Born in France, Allouez became a Jesuit novitiate in 1639 at the age of 17 and was ordained in 1655. Three years later, he went to Canada and started his work among Huron and eastern Algonquian peoples. Father Allouez mastered both the Huron (an Iroquoian language) and Algonquian languages, eventually preparing a prayerbook in the Illinois (an Algonquian language) and French languages. His fluency in these Native languages earned him prestige among the different Indian nations. It is reported that he preached to more than 22 different tribes and baptized an estimated 10,000 Indians in the present-day states of Michigan, Minnesota, and Wisconsin during his 24 years of missionary work. In 1663, he was appointed vicar general of the part of Quebec that now constitutes the central part of the United States. He established missions at Saint Esprit on the south shore of Lake Superior, at Green Bay on Lake Michigan, and at Sault Ste. Marie. He explored thousands of miles of lands unknown to the French and penned the earliest published accounts of Illinois Indians, people he preached to after 1676. He died in present-day Michigan.

ALL-SMOKING CEREMONY *Blackfeet* A sacred ceremony and religious society among the Blackfeet. The ceremony is generally initiated after a request is made, according to the appropriate ritual procedure, to an individual qualified to lead it. When an agreement is reached to have the ceremony, preparations begin. Ritual elements include the singing of sacred medicine songs by their owners, the preparation of an offering to the Sun, the symbolic painting of the person who made the vow along with family members, ritual smoking, and consecration. The all-smoking ceremony concludes with a feast of berry soup after offerings and prayers are made. (See also BLACK-TAILED DEER DANCE; CROW-WATER SOCIETY; STICK GAME DANCE.)

ALTHAM, JOHN *(1585–1640)* English Jesuit missionary. Altham was born in Warwickshire, England. It is believed he became a Jesuit missionary in 1623. In 1633, Father Altham joined Father ANDREW WHITE, another Catholic missionary, on a colonizing expedition to the present-day state of Maryland. Although his constituency was the Catholic residents at St. Mary's Fort in Maryland, he was interested in work among the Indians. He preached and converted several chieftains before he died at St. Mary's.

AMANTACHA *(1610[?]–c. 1636)* *Huron* Huron aide to Jesuit missionaries. Amantacha was born in Huron country, in Canada. He was educated in Rouen, France, by Jesuits and baptized as Louis de Sainte-Foi in the cathedral at Rouen. In France where he remained for two years, he learned to read and write the French language. In 1629 he returned to Huron country, where he assisted explorer Samuel de Champlain and other Jesuits in their relations with the Huron people. Amantacha made raids into Iroquois country in order to gain prestige with his own people as a warrior. In 1636, on one such raid, he was captured and believed to have been killed.

AMERICAN BOARD OF COMMISSIONERS FOR FOREIGN MISSIONS (ABCFM)

A society founded in Massachusetts by the Congregationalists in 1810 to support Christian missionary efforts among nonbelievers. It supported the efforts of Presbyterians and Congregationalists. Its first mission to American Indians was initiated in the Cherokee Nation by the Reverend Cyrus Kingsbury in 1816 and began with the founding of Brainerd Station near Chattanooga, Tennessee. (See Subject Index for missionaries affiliated with the board who are included in this volume.)

AMERICAN INDIAN MISSION ASSOCIATION

A missionary society founded by the Reverend ISAAC MCCOY in 1842. McCoy believed that overseas missions received more funding from the Baptist Foreign Mission Board than did missions for American Indian groups. He further believed that a separate organization would garner more support for Native missions. However, the Baptists failed to adopt the American Indian Mission Association at a triennial convention held in 1844. The following year McCoy's association was included in the work of the newly organized Baptist Board of Domestic Missions of the Southern Convention.

AMERICAN INDIAN RELIGIOUS FREEDOM ACT AMENDMENTS OF 1994 (P. L. 103–344, 108 Stat. 3125) (1994)

On October 6, 1994, President Bill Clinton signed historic legislation guaranteeing American Indians the right to use the sacrament of peyote in traditional religious ceremonies throughout the United States. The year before, on November 16, 1993, President Clinton signed the RELIGIOUS FREEDOM RESTORATION ACT OF 1993 (RFRA) reversing the Supreme Court's 1990 ruling in *EMPLOYMENT DIVISION, DEPARTMENT OF HUMAN RESOURCES OF OREGON, ET AL. V. SMITH ET AL.* The Court held that Native Americans who use peyote in their religious ceremonies were not exempt from the narcotics law that applies to everyone else. RFRA prohibited any unit of government from substantially burdening a person's exercise of religion unless the government demonstrates that the application of the burden to the person is in the furtherance of a compelling governmental interest and is the least restrictive means of furthering that governmental interest. RFRA restored the "compelling interest" requirement wherein governments would have to show an overriding public interest was being served by interfering with a religious practice, the requirement removed by the Supreme Court in the Oregon peyote case. On June 25, 1997, the U.S. Supreme Court declared RFRA unconstitutional in *CITY OF BOERNE V. P. F. FLORES.*

At the time Congress considered RFRA, it also considered another bill—the Native American Free Exercise of Religion Act of 1993 (NAFERA)—that aimed to protect traditional forms of worship practiced by Indian peoples. After working with the Clinton administration, tribes, and leaders of the AMERICAN INDIAN RELIGIOUS FREEDOM COALITION on extensive amendments to NAFERA, in the summer of 1994, Senator Daniel K. Inouye (D-Hawaii) introduced new legislation that included cultural protection as well as religious protection. This act specifically protected sacramental use of peyote, sacred sites, prisoners' rights, and ceremonial use of eagle feathers and other animal parts. No action was taken on the bill due to mounting concerns regarding sacred sites.

Congressional inaction led to the formation of an unprecedented coalition of Native American Church (NAC) leaders, tribal leaders, and Native American Rights Fund attorneys that came together to develop a strategy for the enactment of separate peyote legislation. The group focused its efforts on H.R. 4230, introduced by Representative Bill Richardson (D-N.Mex.), that aimed to amend the American Indian Religious Freedom Act of 1978 and provide for the traditional use of peyote by Indians for religious purposes. Throughout the campaign to enact H.R. 4230, the group worked closely with officials of the Drug Enforcement Administration (DEA) and U. S. Department of Justice. Representatives of the DEA testified at a House hearing that religious use of peyote by Indians was not related to the nation's drug problem.

Technically, Public Law 103–344 is an amendment to the AMERICAN INDIAN RELIGIOUS FREEDOM ACT OF 1978 (AIRFA). It amends AIRFA by adding a new Section 3 with provisions to protect the religious use of peyote by Indians. The intent of the law was to overturn the Supreme Court decision in the Oregon case.

Section 3(b)(1) provides that: (1) the use, possession, or transportation of peyote by Indians for religious purposes is lawful and shall not be prohibited by any state or by the federal government; and (2) no Indians shall be penalized or discriminated against for such use, possession, or transportation, including the denial of otherwise applicable benefits under public assistance programs.

Consistent with these protections, section 3(b)(2) and (3) of the law preserve the existing authority of the DEA and the state of Texas, where peyote is harvested, to reasonably regulate the cultivation, harvest, and distribution of peyote by Indians (considered to be those with at least one-quarter degree Indian blood) for religious purposes. The sole change to Texas law is that "Indians," as defined in the statute may use peyote for religious purposes in Texas without regard to the one-quarter degree blood requirement. As defined in the law, "Indian" means "a member of an Indian tribe."

Section 3(b)(5) clarifies the intent of NAC leaders that the bill does not require federal or state prison authorities to permit the use of peyote by Indian inmates, even though such authorities may allow such use at their discretion.

Section 3(b)(4) and (7) requires that any public safety regulations limiting Indian use of peyote must: (1) be reasonable; (2) be done in consultation with religious leaders; and (3) be subject to the religious freedom "compelling state interest" balancing test of RFRA. This section, requested by the Clinton administration, applies to "safety sensitive" jobs, law enforcement, and jobs in federal public transportation. The NAC asserted this was a nonissue because members do not go to work in an impaired condition or drive while taking peyote. See also PEYOTE AND PENTAGON RULE.

AMERICAN INDIAN RELIGIOUS FREEDOM ACT OF 1978
(P.L. 95–341, 92 Stat. 469., 42 U.S.C. 1996) *(1996)*
Act designed to officially guarantee constitutional First Amendment protection of freedom of religion for Native Americans. The legislation protects and preserves the inherent right of "American Indians, Eskimos, Aleuts and Native Hawaiian" people to believe, express, and exercise their traditional religions, including the "access to sites, use and possession of sacred objects, and freedom to worship through ceremonials and traditional rites." The act requires federal agencies to respect the customs, ceremonies, and traditions of Native American religions and makes amends for the federal government's previous suppression of Indian ceremonial life. The act's second section directs federal departments and agencies to review their policies, procedures, and practices with the intent of making changes to correct the historical legacy of persecution, intolerance, and insensitivity. However, AIRFA has been viewed as more of a policy statement rather than a mandate giving Indian people legally enforceable rights. Subsequent to the negative Supreme Court decision in *LYNG, SECRETARY OF AGRICULTURE, ET AL. V. NORTHWEST INDIAN CEMETERY PROTECTIVE ASS'N. ET AL.* (1988), Indian tribes, national Indian organizations, and certain senators and representatives have been trying to strengthen the act by amending it. They are trying to improve notice and consultation procedures, legal courses and action, and other aspects of AIRFA. (See also AMERICAN INDIAN RELIGIOUS FREEDOM ACT AMENDMENTS OF 1994; Subject Index for legal decisions involving Native American religious practices included in this volume.)

AMERICAN INDIAN RELIGIOUS FREEDOM COALITION
An association of the United States's major mainstream religious denominations, human-rights groups, environmental organizations, Indian tribes, and national Indian organizations that tried to overturn the Supreme Court's ruling in *EMPLOYMENT DIVISION, DEPARTMENT OF HUMAN RESOURCES OF OREGON, ET AL. V. SMITH ET AL. Smith* not only stripped Native Americans of First Amendment protections for traditional worship and created a crisis in Indian country, it also seriously weakened religious liberty for all Americans and forced the courts to treat other religious practitioners like the Indians in *Smith.*

The decision produced an enormous public outcry by the American religious community and constitutional law scholars. The ruling had a profound impact on the concept of American religious liberty in general, and in particular, narrowed the religious liberties of Americans from many different faiths and religious backgrounds. After *Smith,* the constitutional right of religious freedom was reduced to a statutory right and the goodwill of legislators. Citizens of all religious persuasions turned toward Congress to restore their human right of worship.

In 1991, Senator Daniel K. Inouye (D-Hawaii), a champion of Native rights in the U.S. Senate, sponsored a national leaders' forum in Denver, Colorado. Out of this forum was born the American Indian Religious Freedom Coalition, co-chaired by President Peterson Zah of the Navajo Nation and Patrick Lefthand of the Confederated Salish and Kootenai tribes of the Flathead Nation. The coalition held its first national conference in Albuquerque, New Mexico, on November 22, 1991. Over the course of the next two years, the coalition grew to more than 100 members from the nation's major mainstream religious denominations, human-rights groups, environmental organizations, Indian tribes, and national Indian organizations.

The coalition aimed to develop and support federal legislation to overturn the *Smith* Supreme Court decision and restore Native Americans to the protections of the First Amendment. The coalition drafted, lobbied for, and ultimately secured the passage of the RELIGIOUS FREEDOM RESTORATION ACT OF 1993.

AMERICAN INDIAN RITUAL OBJECT REPATRIATION FOUNDATION
Founded by Elizabeth Sackler and headquartered in New York City, the American Indian Ritual Object Repatriation Foundation (AIRORF) assists in the repatriation of ceremonial material to Native nations, clans, or families who are the rightful owners. The loss of ceremonial material has prevented many American Indians from passing tribal knowledge to future generations, consequently destroying traditions of prayer, medicine, and rites of passage. AIRORF is an intercultural partnership also committed to ridding the art market of inappropriate sales of Native ceremonial items.

Sackler's efforts in repatriation began in the spring of 1991. The Hopi and Navajo Nations requested Sotheby's auction house in New York City to remove three ceremonial masks from its annual Fine American Indian Arts auction.

Sotheby's refusal, on the grounds that the NATIVE AMERICAN GRAVES PROTECTION AND REPATRIATION ACT OF 1990 (NAGPRA) was inapplicable to the auction house, received national media coverage. Because art auction houses, dealers, private collectors, corporations, and other nonfederally funded institutions are not bound by NAGPRA, they are not required to notify Native nations of potentially repatriatable materials in their collections. Nonetheless, Native nations regularly learn of materials in these kinds of collections that they would like to have returned. Though individuals and institutions in the private sector are under no legal obligation to repatriate these materials, there have been a number of occasions in which they have done so.

Moved to action, Sackler attended the May 21 auction and purchased the masks in order to return them to the Hopi and Navajo. The event began Sackler's commitment to the repatriation of traditional Native American ceremonial material that is inappropriately displayed and sold on the art market. She wrote that she began AIRORF when she "realized that an opportunity existed for an intercultural partnership addressing issues of exploitation of Native Peoples by the art market."

The foundation assists in repatriation from the private sector by acting as a liaison, introducing the individual collector to Native representatives and assisting in the transfer of material directly from the collector to the Native nation or individual. It serves as a conduit, legally and physically accepting title and possession of an object from a donor, and then transferring title and possession to the tribe/clan/individual. When requested, it assists Native nations, museums, and collectors with federal and other repatriation policies and serves as a clearinghouse for information about the Native American Graves Protection and Repatriation Act, sales, and private sector repatriation strategies. AIRORF communicates with dealers, auction houses, collectors, and the general public, through magazine articles and interviews with the media, about the importance of repatriation and ethics in the art market.

The foundation, which neither grants funds nor purchases ceremonial objects, is a nonfederally funded, public, nonprofit organization that makes it possible for collectors to obtain tax deductions allowable by law on repatriated objects. According to Sackler, the foundation's "Board of Trustees determined that purchasing objects supports the art market; our mission is not to participate in the marketplace but to transform it."

Examples of AIRORF's endeavors include:

- donation of 11 Anasazi pots to the Southern Ute Indian Cultural Center in 1992

- successful negotiations for the donation of three sacred False Face masks to the organization for return to the Tonawanda Band of Seneca owners in November 1993
- successful negotiations for the donation of a Mountain Spirit headdress, Crown mask, and two Lightning Wands by the City of Willcox, Arizona, to the White Mountain Apache in May 1994
- successful negotiations for the donation of a ceremonial mask to the organization for return to the Eastern Band of Cherokee Indians by Continental Casualty Company in February 1997

The foundation's involvement in education has resulted in publications such as *Mending the Circle: A Native American Repatriation Guide* (1996, revised in 1997) as well as newsletters. Besides Sackler, who serves as president of the Board of Trustees, board members include cofounder Anne Bleecker Corcos; Vine Deloria, Jr. (Standing Rock Sioux), professor of History, University of Colorado; Michael Haney (Seminole/Sioux), executive director, American Indian Arbitration Institute; Oren Lyons (Onondaga), professor of History, SUNY Buffalo; Carol Master, M.D., Harvard Hillel Children's School; Franc Menusan (Creek/Métis), educator; Sheri Sandler, exhibition research and development, Cooper-Hewitt National Design Museum; and Marilyn Youngbird (Arikara/Hidatsa), holistic health practitioner. See also MASK [Iroquois] MOUNTAIN SPIRIT DANCERS.

ANAWANGMANI, SIMON ("He Who Goes Galloping Along") *(c. 1808–1891) Dakota* An early convert to Christianity and a licensed preacher of the Dakota presbytery. He attended the mission school established by Dr. THOMAS S. WILLIAMSON at Lac qui Parle in Minnesota Territory. Anawangmani was one of the signers of the Treaty of Traverse des Sioux in 1851 in which the eastern Dakota bands ceded millions of acres of their ancestral lands in the Mississippi valley to the U.S. government. He served as a church elder from 1854 to 1863 and was a member of the Hazelwood Republic that PAUL MAZAKUTEMANI, a Dakota convert, had helped organize for tribal members who had adopted farming and accommodated to the changes promoted by Williamson, STEPHEN RETURN RIGGS, and other mission workers. During the Dakota War of 1862, fought between Santee Dakota and Euro-American forces, Anawangmani favored peace. He helped to protect the missionaries in the area, took a female captive and her children to Fort Ridgely in Minnesota, and served as a scout in Colonel Henry H. Sibley's military campaigns against rebel Dakota until 1865. Anawangmani received his license to preach from the Dakota presbytery in July 1866. In 1875 he resettled on the Sisseton Reservation in South Dakota and died there in 1891.

ANDERSON, GEORGE *(c. 1875–?) Delaware (Lenni Lenape)* A leader and missionary of the PEYOTE RELIGION and missionary in the area of Dewey, Oklahoma. Anderson was the nephew of JOHN WILSON, the Caddo-Delaware originator of the Big Moon peyote ceremony. Anderson's first experience with peyote occurred at the age of 14 when Wilson gave it to him as treatment during an illness. It was not until several years later, however, that he began learning more about peyotism. He and his brother, John Anderson, both became recognized leaders who professed the religious doctrines of their famous uncle. Anderson eventually spread peyotism among other tribal groups, including the Osage and the Seneca. He provided an account of Wilson's religious conversion to the ethnologist Frank Speck, published in 1933, and his own practices were described a year later in another publication. The Anderson brothers were identified as very pious adherents who considered it almost sacrilegious to talk about peyote. (See also ELK HAIR; THOMAS, WILLIE; WASHINGTON, JOE.)

ANIMAL DANCES *Pueblo* Ceremonies held during winter variously named after buffalo, deer, antelope, or other game animals and having many different functions. The dances dramatize the relationship between Indians and the game animals that furnish their wintertime food. Some dances are meant to lure animals from the mountains and plains to sacrifice their lives, to propitiate the spirits of animals, and to encourage an increase of animals offering themselves to hunters. Some dances are prayers for rain, snow, and well-being. Some dances are enacted for healing (there are many versions of this dance). Some dances may include numerous deer or buffalo; other dances may have two buffalo, one or two buffalo mothers, a hunter, a chorus of singers and drummers, or pairs of deer, antelope, elk, and mountain sheep. Dancers may be masked or unmasked, and some may portray a great deal or little, if any, impersonation of animal behavior. The dancers dress to represent the animal, wearing headdresses, horns, and antlers. The dances begin at dawn when the "animals" come in from the hills surrounding a pueblo to perform their dance.

ANOINTING THE SACRED POLE CEREMONY *Omaha.* A ceremony held to commemorate the origin of the SACRED POLE and to give thanks for the buffalo. It was conducted annually during the summer, although it was once customary to anoint the pole twice a year. The ceremony, including pre-

liminary activities, lasted several days. All travel came to an end until the observance was completed.

The Sacred Pole symbolized different aspects of Omaha life in the two-part ceremony. In the first part, officiated by a man, the pole stood for the governing authority of the tribe and the unity of the people. During the second part of the ceremony, conducted by a woman who represented motherhood and prayed for the people to continue and prosper, the pole was symbolic of the men as protectors and providers of the home. The religious observance included the performance of ritual songs, ceremonial offerings, the smoking of the pipe belonging to the pole, symbolic charging of the pole, and anointing of the pole with a mixture of buffalo fat and red paint symbolizing abundant life. The songs had to be sung in the proper sequence; a ceremony of contrition was required if a mistake was made.

With the decimation of the buffalo, essential to the religious observance, the ceremony became more and more difficult to continue. During the late 1800s the Omaha requested permission from the Department of the Interior to use funds to purchase cattle for use in a feast. They hoped to bring about the return of the buffalo and to restore blessings to the people through the performance of their traditional rite. Although ceremonies were held, conditions remained the same and opposition developed, both by the government and within the tribe, against future expenditures for that purpose. In 1888 the Sacred Pole was turned over by the keeper SHU'DANACI to Harvard's Peabody Museum for safekeeping, and 101 years later, in 1989, it was returned to the Omaha tribe. (See also MON 'HIN THIN GE.)

APACHE CEREMONIALISM Ceremonies are conducted by people who are channels for spiritual power for healing, locating an enemy, finding lost persons and objects, diagnosing illness, protecting from illness, and improving luck. The rites may be conducted by a shaman for a particular individual in need, or they may be more traditional ceremonies. Healing ceremonies last one, two, four, or eight nights. Shorter ceremonies are held for diagnostic reasons with longer rituals aimed at eliminating the illness. Curing ceremonies have discrete elements, including masked dances, chants, prayers, stylized gestures, and the use of ritual paraphernalia and sand paintings. In the case of illness, the shaman sucks at the afflicted spot with a tube and administers herbs or special foods. At the rite's conclusion, the shaman is paid. Vital rituals are also associated with an individual's life cycle. These rites include a cradle ceremony, a ceremony when children begin to walk (PUTTING ON MOCCASINS), and a HAIR-CUTTING CEREMONY. At puberty, girls participate in another elaborate rite. Observances for boys at puberty are less formal. (See also APACHE POWER CONCEPTS; GIRL'S PUBERTY RITE; LONG LIFE CEREMONY.)

APACHE POWER CONCEPTS In traditional Apache belief, there is spiritual power that pervades the universe and can be utilized for human purposes by ritual procedures known to priests or shamans. The sources of power can help or harm as they wish, depending on whether they are pleased or offended by human conduct. Some powers can be called in to diagnose, cure, and protect against illness. Besides aiding its owner in performing specific tasks, power also provides protection against adversity.

Power must be conveyed through some channel or spiritual helper, like a plant, animal, rock, celestial body, or any created thing. Power can only be transmitted through the helper to a receptive and responsive believer. If the individual accepts the invitation from a spiritual power, he or she is put through an initiation to test courage and then undergoes years of training under the guidance of an established shaman who is paid for his services. Acquisition of power at some point in life is considered normal for some Apache males. The power is acquired through instruction or by a vision in which the power presents itself voluntarily and is imparted.

Regardless of how power is acquired, it is controlled with a set of chants and prayers "belonging" to the power. The ability to dispense power depends on the ability of a person to learn and retain chants and prayers. Once a power has given some part of itself to a seeker, the person determines what it is capable of doing through him. He learns what it can accomplish, through trial and error, when correctly used. Owners must maintain appropriate behavior toward sources of power and the channeling power of the shaman can be withdrawn any time the power is displeased. Failure to observe effective contact with a power engenders hostility or results in sickness if taboos surrounding objects from which power emanate or reside are violated. (See also APACHE CEREMONIALISM.)

APES(S), WILLIAM *(1798–?) Pequot* A Methodist missionary and author who worked among the Mashpee people of Cape Cod. Born on January 31, 1798 near Colrain, Massachusetts, his father was a mixed-blood and his mother a descendant of the Wampanoag leader King Philip. As a child William's parents, basketmakers, were often away, and he stayed with his grandparents, who treated him brutally. After his grandmother broke his arm when he was five, he was rescued by an uncle and a neighbor. Apes lived with whites until he was 15, then ran away and enlisted in the army. After his military discharge, he married a white woman and became a

minister. Unable to obtain a license from the Methodist Episcopal Church, he joined the Methodist Society and was ordained in 1829.

A few years later Apes visited the Mashpee and found them in need of community services and leadership. Although a missionary had been appointed to the local Native peoples by Harvard College and had obtained several hundred acres of land, he was working instead among neighboring whites. Apes not only became a member of the Mashpee tribe but assumed a leadership role as well. He encouraged the Mashpee people to adopt a number of measures, including the dismissal of the white missionary and overseers. Apes also forbade the whites to cut wood on tribal land and was later arrested after forcibly reclaiming wood from a man who had challenged the order. Charged with inciting to riot, he received a 30-day jail sentence. The case received widespread attention, and the legislature later acted favorably on a petition presented by the Indians stating their grievances. Apes filed libel suits against his opponents, compelling them to apologize.

Apes was the author of several publications: *A Son of the Forest* (1829), an autobiography; *The Experiences of Five Christian Indians* (1833); *Indian Nullification of the Unconstitutional Laws of Massachusetts Relative to the Marshpee Tribe: or, the Pretended Riot Explained* (1835); and *Eulogy on King Philip* (1836). Apes later added an *s* to his surname.

APIATAN See WOODEN LANCE

ARCH, JOHN *(Atsi) (?–1825) Cherokee.* A missionary assistant and interpreter who helped establish Creek Path Mission among the Chickamauga Cherokee in 1820. Because he knew English, which he had learned earlier, Arch became an invaluable assistant to the missionaries after they admitted him provisionally to the Brainerd mission school in 1818. He arrived at Creek Path, near present-day Warrenton, Alabama, with the Reverend DANIEL SABIN BUTRICK in March 1820. After constructing a building, they began their missionary efforts. Besides assuming responsibility of elementary instruction, Arch itinerated among the people and served as an interpreter. His linguistic work included a Cherokee translation of the third chapter of John. Arch, who was in his twenties during the brief time he was at Creek Path, died of tuberculosis on June 18, 1825 at Brainerd Mission. (See also BUTLER, ELIZUR; WORCESTER, SAMUEL AUSTIN.)

ARCHAEOLOGICAL RESOURCES PROTECTION ACT OF 1979 (P.L. 96–95, 93 Stat. 721., 16, U.S.C. &&470aa–470ll [Supp. IV, 1980]) An act of Congress designed to protect archaeological resources and sites on public and American Indian lands from "uncontrolled excavation and pillage." This legislation attempted to correct deficiencies, including vague statutory terms, found in the ACT FOR THE PRESERVATION OF AMERICAN ANTIQUITIES of 1906. The Archaeological Resources Protection Act prohibits any person from excavating, removing, damaging, or otherwise altering or defacing any archaeological resource on lands under its jurisdiction unless a permit for such activities has been obtained. Archaeological resources are defined by the act as:

> . . . any material remains of past human life or activities which are of archaeological interest, as determined under uniform regulations promulgated pursuant to this chapter. Such regulations shall include . . . : pottery, basketry, bottles, weapons, weapon projectiles, tools, structures, or portions of structures, pit houses, rock paintings, rock carvings, intaglios, graves, human skeletal materials, or any portion or piece of the foregoing items.

The statute also requires that an item be at least 100 years old to be considered an archaeological resource.

Under the Archaeological Resources Protection Act, an applicant seeking a permit to work on Indian lands must obtain the consent of the Indian landowner or Indian tribe with jurisdiction over the area. The act also includes a provision concerning tribal religious or cultural sites located on public lands. Where there is reason to believe that archaeological activities could result in harm to a site, the tribe or tribes considering the area religiously or culturally important must be notified before a permit is issued. Mandatory terms and conditions for permits include those specified by Indian landowners having jurisdiction over sites where an applicant seeks to work. Other provisions of the Archaeological Resources Protection Act address the custody of recovered objects, with the emphasis upon preservation, not repatriation.

Penalties for violating the Archaeological Resources Protection Act are stiffer than those under the 1906 antiquities legislation. They include initial fines of up to $10,000 and imprisonment for up to one year. The penalties are higher when restoration costs and the value of the archaeological resource removed or damaged exceeds $5,000. Further violations may result in fines of up to $100,000 and imprisonment of up to five years.

One limitation of the legislation is that it does not protect objects created less than 100 years ago. Another is that it does not affect anyone who lawfully possessed archaeological resources before October 31, 1979, when the act was passed. Therefore, the problem for Native Americans of reacquiring objects taken before that date still remains. (See also AMERICAN INDIAN RELIGIOUS FREEDOM ACT OF 1978.)

ARTHUR, MARK K. (Kul-Kul-Stu-Hah) *(1873–1947) Nez Perce* An ordained Presbyterian minister who worked among the Nez Perce people. Arthur was born near present-day Whitebird, Idaho. After his father was killed in Montana at the Battle of Big Hole in 1877 and his mother captured a short time later, Arthur and other tribal members fled to Canada. There, the Native exiles included SITTING BULL, the Lakota holy man. Upon his return to the Nez Perce, Arthur was converted to Christianity and attended the school of SUSAN LAW MCBETH, the Presbyterian missionary. He was reunited with his mother after the tribal members who had been sent to Indian Territory (present-day Oklahoma) as captives were returned home. Following studies for the ministry, Arthur was ordained in 1899 by the Walla Walla presbytery. His ministerial posts in Idaho included the Spalding Presbyterian Church from 1899 to 1921 and then an assignment in Kamiah until his retirement. Arthur also served as a delegate, representing both Indians and non-Indians, to the general assembly of the Presbyterian Church.

ASPENQUID *(?–c.1682) Abenaki* Aspenquid was born in the present-day state of Maine in the late 16th century. He was one of the first American Indian people to be converted to Christianity by French missionaries. He then traveled extensively throughout northern New England and eastern Canada preaching to Indian peoples. After his death in Maine, sometime after 1682, the town of Halifax, Nova Scotia, honored his memory with an Aspenquid Day.

ATHABASCAN CEREMONIALISM Traditional religious practices of the Athabascan people revolve around funeral and memorial potlatches, which are community and family expressions of grief. When a person dies, he or she is given two potlatches. One is held at the funeral, in which the body is burned, and the second, a memorial POTLATCH, is usually conducted one year later, at which time the family releases the spirit of the deceased. An essential ingredient of the potlatch ceremony is that a young man from the family of the deceased provides moose meat that is shared with the whole community. Often moose used ceremonially must be obtained outside the established season. The state of Alaska, delegated authority to manage the fish and game resources on federal lands by the Alaska National Interest Lands Conservation Act of 1980, has criminally prosecuted Athabascan people who have taken moose for funeral and memorial potlatch ceremonies outside of established seasons. In 1978, the Alaska Supreme Court ruled in FRANK V. ALASKA that taking a potlatch moose for a funeral potlatch was a religious practice protected by the free exercise clause of the U.S. Constitution. Alaska has continued, however, to jail Athabascans taking moose for potlatch ceremonies outside the established hunting seasons. (See Subject Index for other cases involving Native American religious freedoms included in this volume.)

AUBERY, JOSEPH *(1673–1755)* Jesuit missionary. Father Aubery was born in Gisors, Normandy, France. In 1690, at the age of 17, he became a Jesuit novitiate. He was transferred to Canada and ordained at Quebec in 1700. Father Aubery directed the Abenaki missions at St. François for 47 years.

AUPAUMUT, HENDRICK (Captain Hendrich) *(1757–1830)*
Mahican   An influential chief, translator, missionary, Indian agent and diplomat who promoted Christianity and the adoption of Euro-American ways among his people. Aupaumut was born in Stockbridge, Massachusetts, where the Reverend JOHN SERGEANT had established an Indian mission community. Several years before Aupaumut's birth, his grandfather Hendrick and a group of 90 Mahican had joined other tribal members as well as Indians from other tribes at the settlement. Aupaumut, a member of the third generation of his family to embrace Christianity and an heir to political leadership, received a mission school education at Stockbridge. Influenced by Christianity and Euro-American culture from birth in the unique settlement, he promoted the adoption of the new ways among Native Americans as the best means to survive. He served as an assistant and translator under Sergeant and became an influential spokesman of missionary efforts. By Aupaumut's time, the Muhheakunnuk or Mahican Indians had become known as the Stockbridge. A staunch supporter of the colonial Americans, he enlisted in 1775 to serve in the Revolutionary War and was later promoted to the rank of captain by General George Washington. Aupaumut subsequently served as an emissary of the secretary of war among western tribes, served with General Anthony Wayne at the Battle of Fallen Timbers, helped negotiate treaties at Fort Wayne, fought under General William Henry Harrison against Tecumseh's resistance movement, and participated in the War of 1812 against the British.

Besides his efforts for the colonial Americans, Aupaumut continued to work among his own people as a chief, emissary, and agent. In 1808 he represented the Tuscarora in Washington, D.C., when they sought compensation for land losses they had sustained during the Revolutionary War period, and he was also appointed as a federal Indian agent to the Delaware (Lenni Lenape) in Indiana. After the removal of his tribal group from Massachusetts, he bought land in Madison County, New York, for the establishment of New Stockbridge in 1783. It was located next to another Christian community, the Brotherton settlement of the Oneida. When the government failed to uphold President Thomas Jefferson's promise of land in Indiana Territory, the Stockbridge tribe eventually settled on land purchased in Wisconsin. Aupaumut's son, Solomon, who continued the family's legacy of leadership by serving as chief, led the resettlement effort. Aupaumut, who lived to be over 70, suffered from alcoholism at the end of his life. In 1791 he wrote *History of the Muhheakunnuk Indians*, which includes information about the traditional religious ways of his people. Aupaumut is often referred to as Captain Hendrick.

B

BADGER-TWO MEDICINE *Blackfeet* This sacred site of the Blackfeet and other tribes, which borders the Blackfeet Reservation on the west, is located in the Lewis and Clark National Forest in northwest Montana. Named for two rivers that begin in the snow fields and glaciers of the Continental Divide, Badger Two-Medicine is also a key biological region in the Bob Marshall wilderness ecosystem.

After the "Starvation Winter" of 1883–84, the Blackfeet, in utter desperation to survive, agreed to negotiate with federal government agents who offered food and money in exchange for land. In the 1896 agreement with the U.S. federal government, the tribe ceded the mountain strip on the western edge of the reservation, which some believed to be rich in gold and other precious metals. In 1910, one-third of the ceded strip, Badger-Two Medicine, became part of the Lewis and Clark National Forest.

The tribe has retained treaty rights to religious use of the area. For centuries, the Blackfeet have carried out practices in this sacred region that are vital to the Blackfeet culture and people. They have built sweat lodges near Badger Creek, conducted Sun Dances, and other ceremonies, buried their dead, gathered tipi poles, collected medicinal herbs and roots, and climbed the peaks to conduct fasts and to seek visions and communicate with the Creator.

The Blackfeet PIKUNI TRADITIONALISTS ASSOCIATION has been fighting since 1986 to keep the U.S. Forest Service from allowing oil and gas drilling in the 130,000-acre region. They have argued that oil and gas development will make sacred rites impossible, destroy the region's spirituality, and violate their First Amendment rights.

During 1981 and 1982, Chevron USA and Fina Oil and Chemical Company purchased mineral leases to thousands of acres in the Badger-Two Medicine area for approximately one dollar per acre. Although a Forest Service environmental impact statement said the chance of discovering oil or gas in the area was less than 1 percent, both companies have wanted to drill and develop oil and natural gas wells in the region. Interior Secretary Bruce Babbitt placed a temporary moratorium on exploration in response to extensive public support for protecting the area. The moratorium was renewed annually, then automatically extended until the completion of a review to decide whether the site is eligible for the National Register of Historic Places. The moratorium prohibits any new leasing in the Badger-Two Medicine area, although existing leases remain valid. In the absence of congressional protection, negotiations have been under way to exchange existing leases for drilling opportunities elsewhere.

BADONI V. HIGGINSON (455 F. Supp. [D. Utah 1977]) *(1977)* A suit brought by Navajo religious leaders against federal officials to allow private worship at RAINBOW NATURAL BRIDGE, a traditional sacred site in Utah, and to have the area managed in a reverent manner by the National Park Service.

In 1910, Rainbow Bridge had been designated a national monument by executive order and separated from the Navajo Reservation without tribal consent or compensation. Although this remote site was initially accessible only by foot and horseback, by 1963 access had become easier with the Bureau of Land Reclamation's completion of Glen Canyon Dam and Lake Powell around the monument. The National Park Service provided boat and dock service for tourists, who were then able to walk in the vicinity of the arch. The Navajo plaintiffs in 1977 contended that alterations of the natural site, started with flooding of sacred deities, threatened the sanctity of the area and public intrusion interfered with religious practices. They requested a prohibition against beer drinking at Rainbow Bridge and asked that the monument be closed to tourists during Native ceremonies. The district court ruled that Navajo lack of title precluded remedies and that public interest outweighed their claim.

In 1980, the Tenth Circuit Court, while rejecting the land ownership argument, agreed with the lower court's finding that the public's interest in low-cost electricity and tourism superseded religious rights of the plaintiffs. It ruled that accommodating Navajo religious practices would be a violation of the Establishment clause of the First Amendment, contending that Rainbow Bridge would become a shrine managed by the federal government. Although the provisions of the AMERICAN INDIAN RELIGIOUS FREEDOM ACT OF 1978 were considered, accommodation of the Navajo plaintiffs was denied. In June 1981, the U.S. Supreme Court refused to review the lower court decisions. (See SACRED SITES for similar cases in this volume. See also Subject Index for other legal decisions regarding Native American religious freedoms included in this volume.)

BALD AND GOLDEN EAGLES PROTECTION ACT OF 1940

(16 U.S.C. 668–668d) *(1940)* Under this federal act, the Fish and Wildlife Service of the United States Department of the Interior issued regulations restricting the taking, possessing, and transporting of bald and golden eagles or their parts. These regulations continue to affect Native people who consider the eagle sacred and use it, or its parts, for religious purposes. Arrests have been made, including those of Cheyenne and Arapaho in the 1970s in Oklahoma, on charges of violating provisions of the act. The Fish and Wildlife Service has formulated policies aimed at easing the impact of the regulations on Native religious practitioners. For instance, it maintains a depository for storing confiscated or accidentally killed eagles and American Indians may apply for such eagles or their parts through a federal permit system. In addition, the secretary of the interior issued a policy statement in 1975 that states in part that American Indians "may possess, carry, use, wear, give, loan or exchange among other Indians, without compensation, all federally protected birds, as well as their parts or feathers." According to some practitioners, the government's role in establishing a formal permit system for American Indians to obtain eagles or their parts has re-

sulted in a lack of separation of church and state. Other difficulties include lengthy delays in the federal processing of requests for eagle feathers and other eagle parts, the handling and condition of the eagles at the depository, the restriction on selling feathers and other parts when some exchanges or transfers between Native religious practitioners occur by ritual purchase and issues related to the law's enforcement. The 1940 act initially protected the bald eagle, but it was amended in 1962 to include the golden eagle. (See also AMERICAN INDIAN RELIGIOUS FREEDOM ACT OF 1978; ENDANGERED SPECIES ACT; MARINE MAMMAL PROTECTION ACT; MIGRATORY BIRD TREATY ACT.)

BARAGA, FREDERICK *(1797–1868)* Roman Catholic missionary. Born into a wealthy family in Austria, Baraga was ordained a priest in 1820. After serving Austrian parishes for seven years, he came to America in 1830. He started a mission at present-day Grand Rapids in 1833, but he was transferred in 1835 to Lake Superior after he antagonized traders by denouncing the liquor traffic they carried on with tribes. He arrived at LaPointe on Madeline Island, opposite Bayfield, Wisconsin, and built a church there about 1837. He traveled by canoe in summer and snowshoe in winter to visit tribes. In 1843, at L'Anse, at the foot of Keweenaw Bay, Michigan, he began a mission and soon moved there. In 1853, he was consecrated a bishop of Upper Michigan and lived at Sault St. Marie. From there, he visited former missions of Lake Superior. He died in Marquette, in northern Michigan, and was buried in a cathedral he had built two and a half years earlier. After learning the Chippewa language, he published *Theoretical and Practical Grammar of the Otchipwe Language* (1850) and *Dictionary of the Ojibway Language* (1853), works still used by Chippewa scholars. He also authored numerous devotional works in Ottawa.

BARNLEY, GEORGE *(c. 1817–?)* A Methodist missionary who worked among the Cree of James Bay in Canada. Barnley, a native of England, was sent to Moose Factory, Ontario, in 1840 by the Wesleyan Methodist Missionary Society, which had its headquarters in London, England. Barnley's tenure in the area was brief, as he left in 1847. While drilling Native people in Methodism he was known to use a stick as a memory-assisting device to remind them of the number of persons needed to recite a given prayer or lesson. He also attempted to devise a writing system but later adopted the syllabary devised by JAMES EVANS after it was introduced into the area by two Indians from Fort Severn. Barnley's departure may have stemmed from his wife's ill health, discouraging results in attempting to Christianize the Cree people, and a conflict with the Hudson's Bay Company's chief factor Robert Miles. It was not until 1851, when missionary JOHN HORDEN arrived, that Christianization efforts at Moose Factory were resumed.

BASKET DANCE *Tewa Pueblos* This dance held in late January, early February takes its name from the food baskets used during the ceremony. The baskets symbolize those things they normally contain—food that preserves the life of the people. The dance promotes fertility in plants and human beings by the symbolic power of baskets and the women who carry them. An equal number of women and men dance. Once held in early spring, the Basket Dance is now performed in winter because the early Catholic missionaries did not want ritual dancing during Lent.

BATHING *Nootka* Also called washing, this ceremony celebrated a loved one's escape from death, or it was enacted to speed up a full recovery. The basis of the ceremony was the idea that by giving away material possessions to others, one gains physical and spiritual health. The ceremony serves as a form of ritual cleansing.

BATTEY, THOMAS C. *(1828–1897)* Quaker teacher and Indian agent in Indian Territory. Battey was born on February 19, 1828, to Joseph and Rebecca (Starbuck) Battey in Starksboro, Vermont. After growing up on his uncle's Vermont farm, he attended a Friends school in Westtown, Pennsylvania. Although Battey wanted to study medicine, a lack of funds forced him to change his career goal to teaching. He eventually moved to Iowa, where he lived on a farm located near the town of Viola and taught school. In 1871 he began working among Native people at the Wichita Agency in Indian Territory (present-day Oklahoma). Battey and the agency's superintendent, A. J. Standing, were both employed under the peace policy of President Ulysses S. Grant. They constructed a school and began teaching Caddo children. After receiving an appointment as field agent and teacher at the Kiowa Agency near Fort Sill (present-day Oklahoma), Battey settled among Kicking Bird's band in 1873. A year later the Red River War between southern Plains groups and the U.S. military broke out, and he subsequently played a significant negotiating role during the conflict. He eventually convinced Big Tree, White Bear, and other Kiowa leaders to attend a peace commission meeting at the Wichita Agency. A short time later, Battey left Indian Territory and returned to his family and farm in Iowa. After his second wife died in 1887, he eventually moved to Ohio and remarried. He was the author of *A Quaker Among the Indians,* first published in 1875. Battey, known as Thomissey to

Native people, died in October 1897 in Middleton, Ohio. (See also GRANT'S PEACE POLICY.)

BEAN, GEORGE WASHINGTON *(1831–1897)* A pioneering Mormon missionary and interpreter. Bean was born on April 1, 1831, in Adams County, Illinois. In 1841, at the age of 10, he was baptized into the Mormon faith after his family had been converted by an elder they had sheltered in their home. The Beans moved to Nauvoo, Illinois, in 1845 and George, then 14, was initiated into the Mormon hierarchy by being named a "Seventy," an official of the Mormon Church. The following year, at 15, he traveled to a Mormon camp at Council Bluffs, Iowa, then went to Missouri with his father to work. By the time he was 17, Bean had traveled to Utah, arriving there in 1847.

Although his parents reached the area the following year, George soon left on an assignment, helping establish a new Mormon settlement at Fort Utah, presently Provo, in the region of the Ute Indians. Armed conflicts occurred as the Ute fought to protect their resources from encroachment, and Bean joined the militia formed to protect the Mormons. During a premature explosion while on duty he sustained severe injuries that required one of his arms to be amputated. While recuperating he studied the Ute language and assisted in trading with the Indians. Bean also became a deputy U.S. marshal. During this period, the young Mormon married and became a father.

Unlike other denominations, the Mormons sent missionaries to the field for a limited time. Bean began his service in 1855 at the Mormon Indian mission in Las Vegas, Nevada. His missionary group consisted of 33 men who had a number of challenges to overcome. Besides struggling to maintain themselves in the desert, they anticipated problems with the Native people they wanted to convert. Bean, who served as interpreter, began learning the Paiute language. As the mission became established, Mormon influence grew. One writer reported more than 50 Indian baptisms. Besides religious work, the missionaries explored the territory for ways to serve and expand Mormon interests.

In 1856 Bean returned to Provo, where he continued to receive civil appointments. In 1865 he served as an interpreter at treaty negotiations with the Ute. Two years later he became a lieutenant colonel of cavalry for the Mormons in Utah's Black Hawk War. One of his last references to Indians occurred in 1872 when he wrote about helping to get Ute who wanted to return to their traditional homeland back to the Uintah reservation. A practicing polygamist, Bean married two more women in 1856. Thirty children, 26 of whom survived to adulthood, were born to his three wives.

Bear Butte. A Cheyenne and Lakota sacred site near Sturgis, South Dakota. *Photograph by Paul Conklin.*

BEAN CEREMONY (Green Bean, Stringbean) *Iroquois* A one-day ceremony honoring cultivated foods during the first week of August when the green beans mature. This food spirit ceremony is directed to beans, considered one of three sacred foods along with corn and squash, and other plant spirits in order to thank them for past bounties and to entertain them, with OUR LIFE SUPPORTER DANCES, ceremonies addressed to cultivated foods, so they will continue to bear fruit.

BEAN DANCE *Hopi* See POWAMU CEREMONY

BEAR BUTTE   Cheyenne and Lakota sacred site. Bear Butte is a mountain near Sturgis, South Dakota, at the eastern edge of the Black Hills, that is considered sacred by Native American peoples. For thousands of years, both Lakota and Cheyenne peoples have conducted their most important religious practices in the Black Hills, including vision quests, prophesying, and the SUN DANCE. Called Noaha-vose by the Cheyenne people, the mountain is believed to be the site where the religious covenant between MAHEO, the Creator, and SWEET MEDICINE, the Cheyenne prophet, was made.

Called Paha Wakan or Mato Paha by the Lakota, the mountain has for generations been the site of prayers and fasts, vision quests, and spiritual inspirations where adherents feel directly connected to the Creator.

Today Bear Butte continues to draw Indian people from across the United States and Canada who go there year-round for ceremonies and vision quests, and prayer flags and offerings to the Great Spirit cover the sides of the mountain. Located in a South Dakota state park, the mountain has been disturbed in recent years by the construction of a tourist facility that now draws more than 100,000 visitors annually. The tourists frequently interfere with Native religious practitioners whose prayers require solitude and privacy. Roadways, parking lots, and a viewing platform have transformed the pursuit of religious practice into a spectacle. In 1980, the Interior Department leased the Black Hills for coal and uranium mining and nuclear power development. Nearby tribes have filed lawsuits against mining companies and the state whose conduct threatens their rights to practice their religion at Bear Butte and in the Black Hills in general. (See also *FOOLS CROW V. GULLET*; SACRED SITES for similar cases in this volume.)

BEAR CEREMONIALISM The tradition of beliefs, stories, and rituals centering on the bear was practiced by a range of cultures in Europe and in North America, particularly the Algonquian Indians of eastern Canada and the United States. Among the oldest forms of religious practice, bear hunting was conducted according to complex religious procedures. Rites, which varied from group to group, involved ritual appeasement and ceremonial disposal of a slain bear so that other bears would feel honored to be caught and killed. Hunters apologized for having to kill the bear, accomplished with clubs or knives. After the kill, the bear was dressed in fine clothing. Some tribal groups erected a pole upon which the bear skull, ears, and muzzle were hung, together with offerings. Butchering was done according to ritual prescription. At all times, the hunters showed respect for the slain bear and for the "owner" guardian spirit of this animal species. (See also BEAR DANCE; HUNTING RITUALS.)

BEAR DANCE *California* Held in the fall or winter, bear dances, short and intense, have been held to bring the beneficent aspects of bear power into a community. Depending on the group, ritual dress might include a bear skin that possessed power from the spirit of the bear who once wore it, bear claws strung as a necklace, or bear paw mittens. People who "become" bears by putting on bear skins have had remarkable powers to do good or harm.

BEAR DANCE *Ute* A traditional dance among the Ute people. One version of its origin states that it first appeared to a man in a dream. During this dream, the man saw a bear dancing back and forth from a pole. When he awoke, the man decided to search for the bear, eventually finding it in the mountains and receiving spiritual instructions from it. After the man had learned the Bear Dance, he returned to his people and taught it to them. Early dances took place in late February or early March, signifying seasonal changes and lasting about a week to 10 days. The elements of the ceremony included the selection of a dance chief and his assistants, the participation of men and women dancers in line dances, the use of wooden musical rasps, the announcement that the girls' puberty rituals had been completed, the construction of menstrual lodges for females, the participation of visitors from other tribal bands in the area, and the provision of a feast by the sponsoring community. Although modifications occurred during the reservation period, the Bear Dance retains many of its earlier features. Performances are held not only on the Ute reservations but in other Native communities in the region.

BEAR DOCTOR *California* Medicine men whose GUARDIAN SPIRIT is the bear are recognized over most of the state.

They are "transformed" into bears as soon as they put on their hides. In some tribes, they exhibit their curing powers and in others, they guard them from observation.

BEAR RIBS V. GROSSMAN (C.D. Cal) *(1979)* A California state case in which the denial of a request by Indian inmates to build a sweat lodge for religious use at a federal prison in Lompoc, California, led to the filing of a class-action suit. On April 18, 1979, a consent judgment and decree permitted the plaintiffs access to a sweat lodge in support of their First Amendment claim. (See also AMERICAN INDIAN RELIGIOUS FREEDOM ACT OF 1978; Subject Index for other cases in this volume.)

BEAR SOCIETY *Iroquois* A private medicine society of men and women whose object is to cure its members and candidates of diseases by ritual chanting and dancing. Curing ceremonies are conducted at the MIDWINTER CEREMONY in the longhouse, or throughout the year in private houses. Rites are held only for certain illnesses that the Bear Society can cure. A person cured by the ceremony becomes a member of the society. (See also MEDICINE SOCIETIES [Iroquois].)

BEAR SOCIETY *Keresan Pueblos* A society of medicine men that assigns great curing powers to the bear. Deriving their power from bears, the medicine men, also called bears, are powerful healers who can cure illness caused by witchcraft. These societies are also charged with the task of bringing rain and guarding the community from misfortune.

BEARSHIRT V. THE QUEEN *(1987)* 2 C.N.L.R A Canadian legal case in which Phillip Bearshirt, a Blackfeet, asked to keep a prayer bundle in his cell at the Edmonton Remand Centre in Alberta. The Crown objected to his application on the grounds that the bundle might contain items used to injure prison officials, other inmates, or the accused himself. Cited as potentially dangerous objects were leather thongs, a necklace "made of some kind of animal tooth," and the bundle wrapping. Bearshirt's religious adviser testified that a believer would not misuse the bundle or its contents. Bearshirt also testified, indicating the significance of the prayer bundle and his belief in Native religion. The finding of the Alberta Court of Queen's Bench on January 20, 1987, was that the applicant was entitled to have the prayer bundle in his cell. The ruling indicated that, since Bearshirt was incarcerated in a single cell, the authorities would encounter no undue difficulty in letting him keep the bundle and that, if they wished to search him, one of the Native officers could do so. If he was moved to a cell with more than one inmate, the ruling stated, the issue might have to be reconsidered. The court concluded that depriving Bearshirt of the prayer bundle offended his religious freedom. (Other important Canadian religious freedom cases include *JACK AND CHARLIE V. R.* and *REGINA V. MACHEKEQUONABE*.)

BEAR-TRACK *(c. 1790–c. 1880) Salish-Kootenai (Flathead)* A famous shaman and prophet among the Salish-Kootenai people. His spiritual gifts were said to enable him to locate buffalo, to warn against approaching horse thieves, to foresee battles and their outcomes, to tell the location of friendly or unfriendly camps, and to locate missing persons and articles. Crow and Blackfeet tribal members were said to fear him, fleeing when they heard his drum. In 1854 the holy man's portrait was sketched by artist Gustavus Sohon. Bear-Track lived to be more than 90 years old, dying sometime in the 1880s. He is also referred to as Bear Tracks, Grizzly Bear Tracks or Grizzly Tracks.

BEAST GODS *Zuni* Beast gods headed by POSHAYANKI are associated with prey animals, who control long life and give medicine, and with the six directions: north is symbolized by the mountain lion; west, the bear; south, the badger; east, the wolf; above, the eagle; and below, the gopher or mole. Beast spirits, who make their home in the sacred place Shipapolina, are invoked and impersonated by CURING SOCIETIES during societies' retreats.

BEDELL, HARRIET M. *(1875–?)* Episcopalian deaconess. Bedell began her missionary career among the Southern Cheyenne in Oklahoma in 1911 and later worked with Alaskan Natives before settling among the Florida Seminole. She received her appointment to the Seminole people in 1932 and established a small mission near Everglades City after her arrival. Bedell named it Everglade Cross Mission after an earlier Protestant Episcopal mission founded by Bishop WILLIAM CRANE GRAY. She started an arts-and-crafts program, emphasizing quality and authenticity, and sought markets for the work produced. Advocating the use of traditional materials and designs, her influence became evident in Seminole basketry, dolls, patchwork, and other articles. Glade Cross Mission was destroyed in 1960, when Hurricane Donna struck the area. Bedell's advanced age, 85, and a lack of support prevented her from reestablishing the mission. Glade Cross Mission then closed, ending the deaconess's 27 years of work among the Seminole people. (See also GODDEN, WILLIAM J.)

BEGGING DANCE *Lakota, Blackfeet, Ojibway, and other groups* One account of the Teton Lakota Begging Dance identified it as an appeal to the Creator to have the people who prospered give to the needy. Gifts were not sought by the dancers for themselves but to help other people. The Begging Dance also emphasized that those who shared their prosperity with the poor and helpless would be treated kindly by the Creator. The 19th-century artist George Catlin painted such a dance in the 1830s among the Teton people. A later account compared the dance to a serenade, with a group of men and women going from tipi to tipi and performing at each place until the resident, praised in song, appeared with a contribution. The Begging Dance was often performed to obtain food donations for a tribal society, council meeting, or other gathering. It is also referred to as the Beggars' Dance. (See also SEVEN SACRED RITES OF THE LAKOTA.)

BELVIN, B. FRANK *(b. 1914) Choctaw* A Baptist missionary and minister to the Creek and Seminole people in Oklahoma. Born in Boswell, Oklahoma, he was educated at Ottawa University in Kansas and at the Eastern Baptist Theological Seminary. Belvin's publications include *The Status of the American Indian Ministry, War Horse Along the Jesus Road,* and *The Tribes Go Up.* Besides his ministerial work, he has served as the chairman of the Oklahoma Human Rights Commission and has participated in the National Congress of American Indians.

BEMO, JOHN *(fl. 19th c.) Seminole* Missionary for the Presbyterian and Baptist denominations in Indian Territory. Bemo, a nephew of the great Seminole leader Osceola, was captured as a youth by federal troops when the Second Seminole War broke out in 1835. He was adopted by Jean Beameau, a French ship captain, who gave him an Anglicized version of his surname. Bemo traveled at sea, learned ship's carpentry, and visited many ports. He later undertook lecture tours in eastern cities to speak about his experiences. After studying in Philadelphia, he decided to work among the Seminole people removed to Indian Territory (present-day Oklahoma). In 1843 he began the work of establishing Prospect Hill day school under contract with the U.S. Indian Office and the Seminole Nation. Bemo also used his carpentry skills to contribute to the construction of a Presbyterian church school among his people. He later turned to the Baptist faith and continued to serve as a minister, leader, and educator. On September 23, 1860, Bemo baptized the Seminole leader JOHN JUMPER into that religion. (See also LOUGHRIDGE, ROBERT MCGILL; MURROW, JOSEPH SAMUEL.)

BENAVIDES, ALONSO DE *(1580–1636)* Franciscan missionary. Born on an island off El Salvador, Benavides became a Franciscan in Mexico in 1603 and 18 years later, in 1621, was appointed Father Custodian of the province of New

Mexico. He traveled extensively and visited the Apache and every pueblo in the vast region under his custodial jurisdiction as well as establishing missions throughout the province. In 1630, he completed a report, called a "memorial," for the king in which he described and located almost every Indian tribe of the province and told about the missionary work he and others were undertaking in his jurisdiction. The memorial, which brought Benavides fame, contained much erroneous information about Indians, owing to his campaign to attract more priests to the New Mexico region as well as more appropriations for the church. He exaggerated Apache population figures, suggesting that there were more than 200,000 Apache, "more than all the nations of New Spain put together." Scholars estimate Apache at 5,000 at that time. Father Benavides also suggested Pueblo peoples were eager to convert and painted the New Mexico region as a paradise. The memorial does have value for the information it contains about Indian life in colonial New Mexico. In 1630, Father Benavides traveled to Spain. He returned to New Mexico in 1633 or 1634 and later went to India.

BERDACHE A term derived from the Persian word *bardaj*, later becoming *bardaje* in Spanish and *bardache* in French, for "slave" or "kept boy." Applied to a person who adopted the dress, gender and/or behavior of the opposite sex, the term, with its limited, derogatory definitions emphasizing sexual deviance, was also applied to Native American individuals by Europeans. Berdaches, documented in more than 130 tribal cultures, generally had integral, varied roles, including those in the religious, economic, social, and sexual realms, in traditional American Indian communities. Besides bridging the gap between males and females, berdaches are said to have formed a third, alternative gender. In the area of religion, they were known to belong to religious societies; to confer special, sacred names; to participate in sacred ceremonies; to become religious leaders or to maintain other spiritual roles. With European contact, the berdache role was suppressed along with other tribal cultural and religious traditions. Examples of Native language names for berdaches include *hova* (Hopi), *kokwimu* (Keres), *Winkte* (Lakota) and *Ihamana* (Zuni). In this volume, KAUXUMA NUPIKA is also referred to as the Kootenai female berdache.

BERRY FESTIVAL *Cree* A festival described among the Sandy Lake Cree in northwestern Ontario. Its features included the singing of sacred songs, prayers that sought the help of the spirits, and a dance in a sunwise (clockwise) movement. The festival was conducted in late summer and fall when berries were available. (See also O-GIWI-MANSE-WIN.)

BERRYMAN, JEROME CAUSIN *(1810–1906)* Methodist missionary among the Kickapoo and other Native groups in present-day Kansas. He was born to Ailzey (Quisenbury) and Gerard Blackstone Berryman on February 22, 1810, in Nelson County, Kentucky. Berryman, who had seven and one-half months of formal schooling, was primarily self-educated. After receiving his license to preach in 1828, he was appointed to circuits in Missouri, where he established a mission among the Kickapoo people in 1833, taught Native children English in his home, and built a school. Berryman was appointed to the superintendency of the mission and to the principalship of the Shawnee Manual Labor School in 1840. After the deaths of his wife and two children there, he went back to Missouri in 1846 and held a number of posts in the region until his retirement in 1886. He wrote *A Circuit Rider's Frontier Experiences,* published by the Kansas State Historical Society in the 1920s. Berryman died on May 3, 1906. (See also JOHNSON, THOMAS; JOHNSON, WILLIAM.)

BI'ANKI ("Eater") *(c.1835–?)* *Kiowa* A dreamer and prophet who became known as Asa'tito'la, "The Messenger," because of his religious ways. He regularly went alone to a mountain to fast and pray for visions, generally in response to those in need of spiritual assistance. Upon his return he would bring messages from departed friends and relatives in the spirit world or knowledge of remedies to use in treating a patient. Bi'anki also invented a writing system based on the sign language of the Plains. The ethnologist James Mooney called the system, which was distinct from pictographs or English, "a well-developed germ of an alphabetic system." It was not intelligible to other tribal members, but Bi'anki taught it to his sons and was then able to correspond with them while they attended the Carlisle Indian School in Pennsylvania. They provided examples of the writing system to Mooney. Bi'anki also depicted one of his visions and explained it to the ethnologist. It incorporated the beliefs of the GHOST DANCE OF 1890 including a reunion with departed friends and relatives and a return to traditional ways. Bi'anki's efforts, and those of other former priests of the religious movement, resulted in a revival of the sacred dance among the Kiowa. A delegation of chiefs and other leaders finally convinced the government agent to approve their request to hold a Ghost Dance after dancers had been dispersed several times and threatened with punishment. The ceremony was held for four days in September 1894 on the Washita River and several thousand Indians from the Kiowa and surrounding tribes attended it.

BIARD, PIERRE *(1567 or 8–1622)* Jesuit missionary. Pierre Biard was born at Grenoble, France. In 1583, at about the age of 16, he entered the novitiate of the Society of Jesus. In 1611, he arrived in Arcadia (eastern Canada). His belief that one "who would minister to their [Indians] souls must at the same time resolve to nourish their bodies" led him to assume a medical role as well as a religious role. He presided over the recovery of one of the Micmac chief Membertou's sons who appeared to be dead, using holy relics and spoken vows. He effectively used rituals and icons and employed shamanistic healing techniques. His account about his missionary work was published at Lyon in 1616.

BIBLE TRANSLATIONS The Bible (including both the Old and New Testament) has been printed in six Indian languages north of Mexico: Massachuset, 1685; Western Cree, 1862; Eastern Arctic Inuit, 1871; Santee Dakota, 1879; Gwich'in, 1898; and Navajo, 1985. The Bible has been printed in part in at least 46 Indian languages north of Mexico. Norwegian missionaries HANS EGEDE and POVL EGEDE were the first to translate any part of the Bible into an Inuit language. Their version of the New Testament was printed into the Greenland Inuit language in part in 1744 and as a whole in 1766. The Massachuset language was the first North American Indian language into which any Bible translation was made. The latest translation is that of the complete Bible into the Navajo language, a project that began in 1944 and was finished in 1985. Over the 41 years, Wycliffe Bible and American Bible Society translators, Protestant missionaries, and Navajo translators converted the King James English version into the Navajo language. The American Bible Society, the Canadian Bible Society, and the Wycliffe Society are currently involved in a number of projects involving the translation of portions of the Scriptures into Native languages. Among the projects are those involving Carrier, Cheyenne, Choctaw, Crow, Dogrib, Havasupai, Micmac, Naskapi, Ute, and Zuni groups. Other work under way includes a new Navajo translation of Christian scriptures and a Central Yup'ik translation of the Hebrew Testament.

BIG DAY, WILLIAM (c. 1891–?) *Crow* A medicine man and peyotist who invited JOHN TREHERO, a Shoshone religious leader, to reintroduce the SUN DANCE to the Crow people in 1941. Born about 1891 in the Pryor area of the Crow reservation in Montana, Big Day had a traditional upbringing by his adoptive grandparents. As a child he was frequently ill, and his formal education ended in the fourth grade. He later worked for a time as a ranch hand and was married at the age of 19. Big Day farmed for 18 years until rheumatism prevented him from continuing. He also served as a district representative on the Crow tribal council and headed a rodeo committee at Pryor.

Baptized a Catholic at nine years of age, Big Day later became a Tipi Way adherent of peyotism. His nominal Catholicism ended when a local priest excommunicated him from the church for participating in peyote meetings. In 1938 he and his wife, Annie, attended the Shoshone Sun Dance at Fort Washakie on the Wind River Reservation in Wyoming, where they became friends with Trehero, who was one of the participants. Returning the next year, in 1939, Big Day decided to dance, and during the ceremony he had a vision. Interpreted by Trehero, it meant that he would have died if he had not participated in the Sun Dance. Big Day made a vow to dance again if his adopted son recovered from a severe illness, and he did so in 1940 at Fort Washakie following his son's recovery. When a nephew also became ill, he vowed that he would perform a Sun Dance on the Crow reservation if the child recovered. His pledge was fulfilled in 1941, and the ceremony was reintroduced among his people. Although it is not known when he died, Big Day was alive as recently as 1956 and was still a Sun Dance leader. (See also NATIVE AMERICAN CHURCH.)

BIG HEAD RELIGION A religious movement described as an offshoot of the BOLE-MARU RELIGION, which grew out of the GHOST DANCE OF 1870. The Big Head Religion began in Pomo territory and traveled northward to other California groups, including the Kato, Yuki, Wailaki, Lassik, western Wintu, and the Shasta. The regalia used in the dance was sold to another tribal group after its use. Ceremonial objects associated with the rituals included Big Head headdresses, cocoon rattles, a foot drum, and split-stick rattles. Women had a role in the dance as participants or spectators and an official watchman carried out specific duties. The Big Head religion endured within a group only for the length of time it had the regalia essential to its practice. It is sometimes confused with the Bole-Hesi, which is also referred to as Big Head. Developed after the EARTH LODGE RELIGION, its rituals were rooted in traditional Patwin and Pomo ceremonies. The approximate period of the Big Head's diffusion has been identified as 1874 to 1877. It is said to have ended after an attempt to transfer it to people from the Siletz Reservation in Oregon failed.

BIG HEADS *Iroquois* These special messengers, also called "our uncles," go from house to house and announce the beginning of the MIDWINTER, or New Year, CEREMONY of the Iroquois people (around middle to late January according to the new moon of midwinter). The name derives from the Big Heads' appearance. They wear skins, symbolic of animals taken during the fall hunt, and cornhusk masks with ropes of cornhusk braids, symbolic of the fruits of the field.

The Big Heads represent the union of the hunt and agricultural harvest and men and women's subsistence activities. The visits by the Big Heads and their message vary among the longhouses in New York and Canada.

BIG HOUSE CEREMONY *Delaware (Lenni Lenape)* A sacred ceremony known as Ga-muing or Ga'mwin among the Lenni Lenape, or Delaware, people. A version of the Unami, a tribal subdivision, included the following ritual elements. It was held in the fall of the year and was initiated by a person, usually male, who assumed its leadership responsibilities. The form the ceremony took depended upon the leader's clan affiliation. He chose three male attendants to assist him, and they in turn chose three female helpers. Preparations included notifying the people, readying the Big House or temple, and gathering wood and other essential items. The ceremony was opened by a speaker who gave thanks to the Creator and prayed for help and blessings in the year to come. The leader then recited his vision and other participants who qualified could do likewise.

The Big House ceremony lasted 12 days. During the course of the observance a person chosen as master of the hunt selected assistants to help with the ceremonial hunting. Prayers and offerings were then made to MISINGHALIKUN, the guardian of the game, asking him to let them kill deer. The deer killed during the hunt were hung in the Big House and used in each night's concluding feast. On the ninth night of the ceremony a new sacred fire, symbolizing renewal, was kindled. Two sacred drumsticks and 12 prayersticks were also brought out at this time and continued in use each night. On the 12th night women could recite their visions, and those who did so were given venison. The sacred number 12 was expressed in a number of ways, such as in sweeping on the sides of the fire and in praying. Other ritual features included the distribution of wampum to attendants, Misinghalikun's participation, and dancing. At the end of the ceremony, the deerskins were given to elderly poor people to use for making moccasins.

The Big House Ceremony was believed to benefit all of the people, to avert natural catastrophe, and to hold the members of the tribal group together. Sources indicate it ended in 1924. A number of factors made the Big House Ceremony impossible to continue, including loss of the traditional Lenape land base, population decimation through epidemics and removals, the diminishment of game animals needed for the observance, and efforts to assimilate the people. (See also DELAWARE PROPHET; ELK HAIR; PAPOUNHAN; WALAM OLUM; WANGOMEN.)

BIG MOON CEREMONY   See PEYOTE RELIGION

BIG MOUNTAIN Navajo sacred site; the most prominent feature in the heart of Black Mesa, in northwestern Arizona. The Navajo who live in and around the area consider Big Mountain sacred. There are sacred shrines on it, traditional stories about it, and frequent visits made to it for prayer, offerings, and ceremony and to collect medicinal herbs and plants used in ceremonies. Traditional Navajo believe the Creator placed them on their particular ancestral homelands and gave them the responsibility to remain on and care for the lands through prayers and offerings made at specific sacred places. Religion requires occupancy to enable an ongoing interaction between the land, people, sheep, and spirit beings. The resolution of the Navajo-Hopi land dispute, mediated through government legislation and court decisions has forced the Navajo to relocate, leaving their sacred places, springs, and plants and banishing them from their religious universe. Many have refused to leave the land, viewing it as a potentially dangerous act that might violate the stewardship and reciprocity with the HOLY PEOPLE who placed them at Big Mountain. (See also SACRED SITES.)

BIG ROAD, MARK *(fl 1950s) Lakota* An Oglala medicine man who reintroduced the SPIRIT LODGE RITUAL among the Arapaho people on the Wind River Reservation in Wyoming in 1955. Big Road, the son and grandson of medicine men, was from the Pine Ridge Reservation in South Dakota. Besides inheriting the teachings and spirits of his father and grandfather, Big Road prepared for his role by participating in vision quests and other sacred traditions of his people. He was invited to Wind River by Arapaho who had observed his work in South Dakota. The Spirit Lodge ceremony was sponsored by a couple who sought the recovery of a relative suffering from illness. Big Road, described as a man in his forties, held the Spirit Lodge, or YUWIPI, Ceremony on August 23, 1955. His helping spirits included Skadi, a white man's ghost, who had acquired fluency in the Lakota language. Big Road stayed in the Wind River area during the fall and winter. He is said to have been "very popular" among the Arapaho people who sought his assistance. Big Road's spiritual instructions prohibited him from charging them fees for his help. (See also SHAKING TENT CEREMONY.)

BILLIE, JOSIE *(c. 1887–?) Seminole* A medicine maker and assistant Baptist pastor in Florida. Shortly after birth, Billie was given a boyhood name according to the customs of his people. The name meant "go around," an allusion to an averted Seminole encounter with a military camp. He acquired the name Josie at the age of about four months among white friends his father visited at Fort Myers, Florida. Billie derived his Tiger clan affiliation from his mother and was strongly influenced by his maternal grandmother, Nancy

Osceola, as a youth. His father, a Miccosukee from the Wind clan, served as an informant and guide in 1881 during the first anthropological study of his people. As customary among Seminole boys, Billie was given an adult name when he was about 15 years old. Translated as "crazy spherical puma," it was to be his lifelong name among the Seminole. Billie's interest in medicine also began about the same time, and he acquired knowledge from various tribal doctors for approximately two years. One of them advised him to undertake a fast as preparation for receiving training to become an *ayikcomi,* or medicine maker. During four days of fasting, he and three other boys were taught sacred songs, beliefs, and methods of healing. Billie repeated the course during the next two years, then became an apprentice to one of his teachers, Tommy Doctor. Besides observing his practice, he learned herbal medicines and spiritual powers.

During his career, Billie also held a number of ceremonial positions. He served as an assistant to a medicine man who was in charge of a BUSK or GREEN CORN CEREMONY for four years before serving as his substitute for the same length of time. Billie later became affiliated with another medicine man, eventually acquiring his medicine bundle and conducting the busk associated with it for seven years. About 1943 Billie moved from his home on the Tamiami Trail to the Big Cypress Reservation after a period of trouble, including the accidental killing of a relative. Although he returned to conduct a busk the following year, the death and other factors resulted in the removal of his medicine bundle. He turned the bundle over to his brother, also an influential medicine man, and stopped attending the busk.

In 1945 Billie was converted to the Baptist faith by the Reverend STANLEY SMITH, a Creek missionary sent to Florida from Oklahoma. The following year the former medicine man enrolled in the Florida Baptist Institute for his first schooling outside his own culture. Billie was later licensed to preach by the Southern Baptists, and by 1948 he had become an assistant pastor of a church on the Big Cypress Reservation. After his conversion, he continued to serve as a doctor but not as a medicine man. The two roles, not necessarily the same in Seminole culture, involve different training and sources of power. The doctor's role involves healing while the medicine man serves as keeper of a Seminole medicine bundle among other duties. Billie was identified as an innovator who adopted a number of new ways. It is said that he introduced changes in the dress of Seminole men, initiating the practice of sewing applique strips of cloth on shirts. Billie also possessed extensive sacred knowledge, including botanical data, ceremonial songs and dances, oral traditions, and diagnostic abilities. In the early 1950s he served as an informant to the ethnologist William C. Sturtevant, who later wrote a portrait of his life.

BLACK BEAR, HARRY *(fl. 1911–1916) Lakota*   A peyotist from the Pine Ridge Reservation in South Dakota. In 1911, Black Bear and two other peyotists had requested permission from the Bureau of Indian Affairs to use peyote. Assistant Commissioner of Indian Affairs C. F. Hauke informed them that the legality of peyote was unresolved, and their request was denied. In 1916, Black Bear was charged with giving peyote buttons to Jacob Black Bear; Paul Black Bear, Jr.; John Black Cat; and James Real Bull in violation of the January 30, 1897, law against furnishing intoxicants to Indians. Indicted on May 19, Black Bear's trial occurred on September 7 and 8 in the U.S. district court in Deadwood, South Dakota, where a jury found him guilty. However, charges against Black Bear were dismissed after a "motion in arrest in judgment" from the defense attorney that the 1897 law did not apply to peyote was granted. The judge ruled the prohibition law was designed for alcoholic beverages and did not extend to peyote. (See also PEYOTE RELIGION; Subject Index for other legal cases in this volume.)

BLACK COYOTE (Wa'tan-ga'a) *(fl. 1800s) Arapaho*   Principal leader, after SITTING BULL, of the GHOST DANCE OF 1890 among the southern Arapaho. Born in the mid-1800s, Black Coyote was a religious leader, a tribal delegate to Washington, captain of the Indian police and deputy sheriff of Canadian County (present-day Oklahoma) by his forties. Deeply devout, he sought help in saving his remaining children after several had died in quick succession. During a vision he received instructions to offer 70 pieces of his skin to the sun in order for his prayers to be answered. His portrait, done by Mary Irvin Wright, indicates scars in a variety of patterns, including lines, circles, and the sacred pipe, as required by his dream.

When word of the Ghost Dance religion first reached the southern plains tribes, Black Coyote traveled from Oklahoma to relatives in Wyoming to learn more about it. Upon his return home in the spring of 1890, he began teaching the new doctrine among the southern Arapaho. He and other emissaries traveled to Nevada in August 1891 to visit WOVOKA, the originator of the religious movement. Black Coyote was convinced that the Paiute messiah showed him the spirit world through a demonstration with his eagle feather and hat. Wovoka instructed him and the other Arapaho and Cheyenne delegates to begin having larger dances, with participants from several communities, at regular intervals. Black Coyote was the ethnologist James Mooney's first informant on the Ghost Dance, enabling him to gain access to Wovoka and other leaders.

Black Coyote was described as an impressive figure, whether when riding with his wives in a coach while wearing his official uniform and medal given to him by President

William Henry Harrison or when leading the Ghost Dance. Watonga, in Canadian County, is named for him.

BLACK DANCERS *Navajo (Dineh)* Dancers who perform during the ENEMY WAY. Once a purification rite for warriors, the Enemy Way is now performed for patients whose sickness is diagnosed as a result of contact with non-Indian ghosts. On the third and last day of the ceremony, Black dancers (clowns), so called because their bodies and breechclouts are daubed with mud and charcoal, perform a Mud Dance during which the patient is dunked in a mud hole to loosen the grip of the evil causing the disease. Spectators at the event are also fair game for the clowns as well. (See also BLACKENING.)

BLACK DRINK Black drink is a tea made by boiling the leaves of the Yaupon holly in water. Southeastern Indian groups consumed it for ritual, therapeutic and social purposes. Identified as one of the sacred medicines of the Creek people, it was used in rituals such as the BUSK or GREEN CORN CEREMONY, to prepare for the deliberation and debate of council, to cement friendship and social ties, and as a cleansing, purifying emetic. The name of Osceola, the Seminole chief, is derived from *Asi Yohola,* or "black-drink singer." Other indications of the tea's importance include its daily use and its ritualized serving.

Named black drink by the British for its dark color, the beverage was called *yaupon* by Coastal North Carolina Indians, *assi-luputski* or *assi* among the Creek, and *cassina* by others. Its scientific name is *Ilex vomitoria Ait,* and its active ingredient is caffeine. After the removal to Indian Territory, the *yaupon* leaves became difficult to acquire, and the rituals associated with it were disrupted. Other "black drinks" continue to be used.

BLACK ELK (Hehaka Sapa) *(1863–1950) Lakota* Born on the Little Powder River, probably within present-day Wyoming, Black Elk is now venerated as one of the greatest holy men ever born, not only by the Lakota but by other tribal groups as well.

After John G. Neihardt, Nebraska poet laureate, interviewed Black Elk at his home in Manderson, South Dakota, on the Pine Ridge Sioux Indian reservation, the holy man's life was revealed to outsiders. In Black Elk's 18th year, he revealed the great vision he had had at nine years of age to medicine men who advised him to enact in a public demonstration the first portion of the great vision. In spring 1881 Black Elk began his career as a medicine man by performing the spectacular Horse Dance ceremony at Fort Keogh, Montana. In 1882, Black Elk successfully lamented for a vision to help him understand the powers given him in his childhood vision.

Black Elk. The renowned Lakota holy man, at Manderson, South Dakota, in 1947. *Photograph by Joseph Epes Brown. National Anthropological Archives, Smithsonian Institution.*

In 1886, Black Elk joined Buffalo Bill's Wild West Show in order to study the non-Indian way of life, and he traveled to New York and Europe. He returned to Pine Ridge in 1889 in time to witness the GHOST DANCE OF 1890 and the slaughter of Lakota at Wounded Knee in 1890. Afterward Black Elk practiced traditional healing ceremonies until 1904, when he converted to Roman Catholicism.

Baptized Nicholas Black Elk on December 6, 1904, it is believed he never practiced the Lakota religious ceremonies again and had a long career as a Catholic catechist. In 1930, 1931, and 1944, the poet John G. Neihardt visited with Black Elk, and the holy man shared his sacred teachings and old Lakota ways to save his vision for future generations. The first set of teachings, recorded in summer 1931, concerned Black Elk's great vision and the story of his life, forming a microcosm of Lakota history from the 1800s through Wounded Knee. This information was first published in 1932 in *Black Elk Speaks,* reprinted in 1961, and has since been translated into at least eight languages and is still in print. The second set of interviews, recorded in winter 1944, covered the general history of the Lakota people from creation to contact times. He gave detailed descriptions of Lakota ceremonies to Joseph Epes Brown in *The Sacred Pipe* (1947). In *The Sixth Grandfather* (1984), Raymond J. De Mallie edited the complete transcripts of Neihardt's 1931 and 1944 interviews with Black Elk. In *Black Elk's Story* (1991), Julian Rice discusses all the major Black Elk material and the various critical approaches to it. Black Elk was married twice, in 1893 and in 1906, and fathered seven children. He died on August 19, 1950.

BLACK ELK, WALLACE HOWARD (Hehake Sapa) (b. 1921)

Lakota A Lakota shaman, Black Elk was born on the Rosebud Reservation in South Dakota in 1921 and was introduced to the world of spirits at the young age of five by tribal elders. His early training was unique in that he did not have an apprenticeship with one mentor. Instead, he had eleven "grandfathers," or teachers. The first member of his family to learn English, he attributed his university-level vocabulary in that language to instruction from the spirits when he was between the ages of five and nine. He hid with his grandparents from school authorities but was tracked down and at times punished by incarceration.

Black Elk found the 1920s and 1930s difficult because of persecution against the traditional Lakota sacred ways. Practitioners who sneaked into the mountains to perform ceremonies not only had to hurry through them but had to be on guard to escape detection. After returning from four years of military service during World War II, Black Elk decided to speak out about the sacredness of Chanunpa, the SACRED PIPE, and was labeled as crazy by Christian clergymen and their followers. Sentenced to a mental hospital, he was later released after a group of observers became convinced that he was sane.

The shaman's book, *Black Elk: The Sacred Ways of a Lakota* (1990), provides a firsthand account of the life of a practicing shaman. By the time it was written, Black Elk had entered his 64th year of spiritual training and undergone more than 30 vision quests. The book includes information about the early teachings he received and his application of sacred power for the purposes of health and help. Widely traveled, Black Elk has lectured and conducted ceremonies throughout North America, Europe, and Asia, (See also BLACK ELK.)

BLACK FOX (I:no:li) (?–1895) Cherokee

A religious leader among the Eastern Band of Cherokee Indians in North Carolina. Black Fox, who was born a full-blood and did not speak English, held many leadership positions during his lifetime. He was licensed to preach by the Methodist Episcopal Church South in 1848 or 1849 and was associated with the Echota Methodist Mission on the Qualla Boundary, where he maintained registers, minutes, letters, and reports.

He later served as a sergeant in Company C, Sixty-ninth North Carolina Infantry during the Civil War. The ethnologist James Mooney referred to Black Fox as a "prominent literary character" and described him as a "councilor, keeper of the townhouse records, Sunday-school leader, conjurer, officer in the Confederate service, and Methodist preacher." A number of his Cherokee writings, including SACRED FORMULAS, were acquired from his daughter for the Bureau of American Ethnology. Black Fox, who lived to an "advanced age," died "in the ancient faith of his forefathers." Mooney also received information about the Cherokee from GAHUNI, SUYETA, and SWIMMER.

BLACK HAIRY DOG (c. 1823–c. 1883) Cheyenne

Keeper of the SACRED ARROWS who succeeded his father, STONE FOREHEAD, to the position in 1876. At the time of his father's sudden death, Black Hairy Dog was away from home. Stone Forehead was therefore prevented from cutting holy symbols on his son's skin, as successor to the keepership, and making spiritual flesh offerings as customary. This practice for new keepers then ended. Stone Forehead's widow cared for the Sacred Arrows until Black Hairy Dog returned.

Black Hairy Dog and his wife were among those who escaped when U.S. soldiers and buffalo hunters attacked Little Bull's band of Southern Cheyenne on April 23, 1875, on Sappa Creek in Kansas, while the group was en route to the territory of the northern branch of their people. Black Hairy Dog lived to assume guardianship of the Sacred Arrows. After obtaining them from his mother, he and his wife traveled to the main group of Northern Cheyenne. Pursued by soldiers, they each took two Sacred Arrows and followed different routes. Black Hairy Dog later wanted Dull Knife's band to move from its Powder River location, but Last Bull, the Kit Fox Society Chief, gave his followers an order to keep the people where they were. General Ranald Mackenzie's forces attacked the camp on November 26, 1876. The keeper saw the enemies approaching first and alerted the people. During the attack he positioned himself at a point where he could turn the tremendous power of the Sacred Arrows against the military soldiers and scouts. The keeper, his wife, and other families who survived eventually reached the Southern Cheyenne in Indian Territory. Black Hairy Dog's name also appears as "Black Hair Shepherd [Dog]."

BLACK LEGS DANCE Kiowa

A dance that continues to honor the traditions of the Black Legs Society, a warrior society established after a Kiowa victory over the Arapaho and Cheyenne in 1838.

The members of the society painted their legs black before going to battle, hence the name. The practice is believed to have originated when a war party returned home with blackened legs from a fire trap set by their enemies. Besides black leggings, symbols of the society include the Sacred Arrow, the red cape, the coup stick, and the roach headdress.

The Sacred Arrow (Pa-bon) or lance recalls the bravery of the Kiowa Poor Buffalo, one of the leaders of the Black Legs Warrior Society, who dismounted during a battle and used it to anchor himself to the ground where he remained in a stationary position and fought until he was killed. His example set a precedent and by tradition a warrior who was bound to a spot by the Sacred Arrow fought to his death, won a victory, or was released by other Kiowa warriors. The red cape of society members commemorates a brave action of Gool-ha-ee, or Young Mustang, an early leader. During an encounter with Mexican soldiers, he rode up to their commander, jerked off his cape, and killed him. The coup sticks used in the society bore feathers corresponding to the number of coups for each member. Today they correspond to military engagements of each participant, such as World War II, the Korean War, or the Vietnam War. Besides Poor Buffalo and Gool-ha-ee, early leaders of the society included Chief Black Turtle, Young Mustang, and Sitting Bear, or Satank.

The Black Legs Dance, or T'ow-kow-ghat, is performed annually in May near Anadarko, Oklahoma. It includes the performance of death songs that originated over a century ago, and sham battles and military movements. The society is also referred to as the Black Leggings Society from the stockings or leggings worn by the members during the ceremony. (See also GOURD DANCE; SOCIETIES.)

BLACK ROAD *(19th century?) Lakota* A venerated holy man among the Oglala Lakota people. As a young man, Black Road had smallpox and was sent to a solitary place by the medicine man who treated him. While he was alone, he received instructions from the Thunder Beings to establish the Sacred Bow Society. After recovering from his illness, he returned home to carry out the teachings he had received. The society he formed included sacred, ceremonial, and military functions. Those who met its strict membership requirements were highly respected. The Sacred Bow warriors stood their ground in battle until death. Officers of the society included four bow carriers, four hanger carriers, and, generally, two club bearers. A ceremony, Sacred Bow racing, was held in connection with the resignation and initiation of members. Besides his association with the society, Black Road was renowned as a healer who helped many people. He also advised and assisted the Lakota holy man BLACK ELK in carrying out the Horse Dance of his great vision. Although some of the symbols associated with Black Road are now known, the holy man kept his sacred knowledge secret.

BLACK-TAILED DEER DANCE *Blackfeet* A sacred ceremony associated with a religious society among the Piegan Blackfeet people. It is believed to have been introduced by the Kootenai and to have come from the dream of a person suffering from a serious illness. In the dream a deer appeared, took pity on the sick man, and gave him instructions that led to his recovery. The dance, generally held in the evening and lasting through the night, was sometimes held before hunting, but it could also be conducted to pray for a person who was ill. The membership consisted of both men and women who each possessed their own sacred songs. Ceremonial features included sweet-grass consecration; the performance of a dance to represent the deer; a feast around midnight; and prayers for recovery, success in hunting, or spiritual protection. Some members were described as having hypnotic powers or the ability to put a person into a trance. (See also ALL-SMOKING CEREMONY; CROW-WATER SOCIETY; DANCE FOR THE SPIRITS OF THE DEAD; STICK GAME DANCE.)

BLACKBURN, GIDEON *(1772–1832)* A Presbyterian clergyman who established a mission in the Cherokee Nation. Born on August 27, 1772, in Augusta County, Virginia, he was the son of Robert Blackburn. After his family's move to eastern Tennessee, Blackburn attended Martin Academy and prepared for the ministry under Dr. Robert Henderson. Receiving his license to preach from the Abingdon Presbytery in 1792, he began his career by holding services for soldiers he had accompanied on an Indian fighting expedition. Blackburn soon established a church called New Providence and took charge of another one in the Maryville, Tennessee, area.

In the early 1800s his interest changed from fighting Indians to converting them. Unable to obtain support for a Cherokee mission from his own presbytery, Blackburn appealed to the denomination's general assembly, which granted him $200 in 1803. With additional funds raised from other sources and the consent of President John Adams and the secretary of war, he opened a school where about 300 Cherokee students were taught rudimentary English and the principles of Christianity. Blackburn supervised the operation of the school, in addition to performing his church duties, until 1810, when ill health and limited finances forced him to resign. He then served as a college president in Tennessee, as a pastor of churches in Kentucky, and as a fund-raiser for a college in Carlinville, Illinois, which opened after his death in 1857 and was named after him. Blackburn died on August 23, 1838, in Carlinville. He was married to Grizzel Blackburn, a distant cousin, with whom he had 11 children.

BLACKENING *Navajo (Dineh)* A feature of the ENEMY WAY ceremonial. Now performed for patients whose sickness is diagnosed as a result of contact with non-Indian ghosts, it was at one time a purification rite for warriors. Black salve is applied to a patient, especially on the chin and scalp, and to faces of members of the audience. The blackening protects earth people from evil by making them invisible, especially at night, when evil is most likely to be abroad. This rite is an added precaution in connection with other ceremonials where ghost infection is suspected. (See also BLACK DANCERS.)

BLACKFEET NATION CULTURAL AND SPIRITUAL WILDERNESS PROTECTION ACT OF 1989

Legislation proposed to protect the BADGER-TWO MEDICINE area in the Lewis and Clark National Forest from drilling and other development interests. (See also PIKUNI TRADITIONALISTS ASSOCIATION.)

BLADDER FESTIVAL

Alaska Inuit An annual ceremony at the winter solstice that is like a memorial service for all game animals killed during the previous year. Celebrated from Norton Sound southward the festival is a long and complex series of purification rites, dances, song presentations, drumming, and feasts designed to ensure a successful seal hunt the following spring. The preceding year's accumulated bladders of slain seals are offered in expiation and in appeal for future success in hunting and to ensure the rebirth of the spirits of the seals, which Inuits believe are located in their bladders. The souls need conciliating because they have the power to cause hardship by diminishing the food supply.

The performance, which usually lasts five days, takes place in a community ceremonial center (*KARIGI* or *qasgiq*). The bladders of the seals, together with those of the walrus and white whales, saved from the year's hunt, are inflated, painted, and hung in the village assembly house to be honored during the festival by rituals and offerings of food and water. Ritual activities draw out the souls of seals residing in bladders hung along the wall. At the end of the festival, the bladders are taken down, deflated, removed through the smoke hole in the roof, pushed through an icehole and returned to an underwater *karigi* with the prayer that they be reborn as new animals and return the following year. They are urged to report how they have been treated during the festival, thus inspiring more animals to allow themselves to be caught by villagers. Dancers wear spirit masks and pay tribute to their helping spirits so game will continue to be plentiful.

During the festival, the men's house and residents are ritually purified by sweat baths as well as by wild celery plant smoke. On the last night, there is a village-wide distribution of gifts. In some areas, this festival is preceded by related ceremonies. One ceremony involves painting the bodies of village boys, who are led from house to house each night and offered food by women. Another involves two older men who feed a group of boys and collect from women newly made bowls filled with a berry-fish mixture. The bladder festival symbolizes renewal, so women make new clothing for everyone and the men make new dishes and create new songs. (See also CARIBOU FESTIVAL.)

BLANCHET, FRANCIS NORBERT

(1795–1883) Sulpician missionary. Born in St. Pierre, Quebec, Canada, Blanchet studied at the Sulpician seminary in Quebec and was ordained a priest in 1819. He was sent to missionary work with the Micmac Indians and Acadians in New Brunswick. After returning to Montreal in 1827 to do parish work, he was sent to Oregon Territory in about 1833. He founded a number of missions in Oregon between 1838 and 1848, was named vicar general of Oregon Territory in 1837 and first vicar apostolic in 1843, and was consecrated bishop of Oregon in

Bladder Festival. A pictographic panel from an engraved ivory drillbow depicts the conclusion of the festival when bladders, in which the souls of seals are believed to reside, are removed from the Alaskan village assembly house and pushed through an icehole, sent back underwater to be reborn as new animals the following year. This panel shows a procession of Inuit men bearing four ritual paddles and a staff of bladders around the icehole, while men stab the bladders with knives and sink them. *Smithsonian Institution, Department of Anthropology, Catalogue No. 176191.*

1845 and archbishop in 1850. Father Blanchet, who led a crusade to convert Indians to Catholicism and drive Protestants from the Northwest, was embroiled in disputes with Methodist missionaries in Oregon Territory. He fought with Secretary of the Interior Columbus Delano over the latter's assignment of Indian reservations to Protestant missionaries. The bitter Catholic-Protestant dispute led the Catholic hierarchy to create the BUREAU OF CATHOLIC INDIAN MISSIONS in Washington in 1874. Father Blanchet died in Portland, Oregon.

BLESSING WAY *Navajo (Dineh)* The Blessing Way rites hold a central position in NAVAJO CEREMONIALISM. They are the fundamental ceremonial backbone of Navajo religion and govern the entire chant way system of ceremonial cures. The rites are briefer, usually lasting two nights, and less complex than curing ceremonials. They are given any time for many reasons and benefit the entire social group. They are used to maintain harmony, for good luck, to avert misfortune, to invoke positive blessings that people need for a long and happy life, for protection, for increasing possessions, to protect livestock, to protect childbirth, to bless a new hogan, to consecrate ceremonial objects, to consecrate marriage, to install tribal officers, to protect departing and returning travelers and soldiers, to strengthen and protect a new singer, to bless possessions, to bless daily activities, and to dispel fear resulting from bad dreams. The rites are also used to renew or refresh ceremonies, singers, and their equipment. The rites are not given to cure illness, remove injury, or restore good health.

Rites include a ritual bath, prayers, songs, sometimes a sand painting of vegetable materials (pollen, meal, crushed flowers) strewn on buckskin spread on the ground, hogan consecration, breathing in the dawn, body blessing, and traditional stories. Pollen is applied to the patient, hogan, ritual object, sand painting, spectators, and everything else for consecration and sanctification. Blessing Way rites are also held at a GIRL'S PUBERTY RITE, traditional wedding ceremonies, and seed and house blessings. The Blessing Way, either in whole or in part, is added to all curing ceremonials to compensate for errors and omissions that would render the ceremonial ineffective and possibly cause illness. Navajo people say that the Blessing Way was a ceremonial held by the HOLY PEOPLE when they created people and that CHANGING WOMAN gave some of the songs. She is represented in visible form in a sand painting only in the Blessing Way.

BLOWSNAKE, SAM (Crashing Thunder) *(b. 1875) Winnebago (Ho-Chunk)* Sam Blowsnake wrote an account of his life, including his conversion to the PEYOTE RELIGION, for the anthropologist Paul Radin before 1920. He was named Big Winnebago but later became known by his English name, Sam Blowsnake.

Born in 1875, he was the fifth child of a family that later included a sister, MOUNTAIN WOLF WOMAN, whose autobiography was also recorded. His mother, Bends the Boughs, was from the Eagle clan, and his father was a member of the Thunder clan. They were later known in English as Lucy Goodvillage and Charles Blowsnake. The first published account of Blowsnake's life, *Autobiography of a Winnebago Indian,* was published in 1920. In a later, expanded publication, he is called Crashing Thunder, a pseudonym, but also the name of his oldest brother. Blowsnake wrote his autobiography in a syllabary adapted for use with the Winnebago language, and it was translated by another peyotist, OLIVER LA MERE. Cited as an example of a peyote conversion narrative, it describes Blowsnake's life and his failed attempts to fulfill his spiritual quests before becoming a peyotist. His conversion marked the beginning of changes in his life, including settling down with a wife and baby and baptism in the Peyote Religion. It also reflects the conflict between Winnebago traditionalists and adherents of the new PEYOTE RELIGION during that period. Before converting, Blowsnake was initiated into the traditional Medicine Dance, participated in Wild West shows, and was imprisoned for a time for his involvement in the killing of a Potawatomi man. Blowsnake wrote his autobiography before he was 45 years old and was still living when Nancy Oestreich Lurie recorded his sister's story in 1958.

BLUE BIRD, JAMES *(c. 1889–?) Lakota* An early, influential peyote leader among the Lakota. When Blue Bird was 14 he learned of the religious practice at a meeting led by QUANAH PARKER in Calumet, Oklahoma. From 1904 to 1907 he attended services on the Pine Ridge Reservation in South Dakota conducted by JOHN RAVE and ALBERT HENSLEY, Winnebago peyotists. After attending the Carlisle Indian Industrial School in Pennsylvania from 1907 to 1911, Blue Bird spent several years with Wild West shows. In 1916, he again attended peyote meetings led by Rave and Hensley and learned from them to be a ROADMAN of the Cross Fire peyote ritual. That year, he became an acknowledged leader of the PEYOTE RELIGION among his people. His father, an Episcopal minister, did not try to change his decision, recognizing Christian elements in the Cross Fire beliefs. Blue Bird subsequently became the organizer and director of the Native American Church of South Dakota, headquartered in Allen, and maintained the position for 50 years.

BLUE LAKE *Taos Pueblo* Sacred site of Taos religion. Blue Lake lies at 11,800 feet above sea level in the Sangre de

Cristo Mountains of northern New Mexico. According to a tribal leader, "The lake is surrounded by evergreens. We have no buildings there, no steeples. There is nothing the human hand has made. The lake is our church. The evergreen trees are our living saints . . . Blue Lake is the heart of our religion." Blue Lake has been sacred to Taos from days "far past any living memory, deep into the time of legend."

The sacred ground was seized by the federal government in 1906 and made part of Carson National Forest. As national forest land, the area was opened to recreational and commercial use by tribal members and nonmembers. Led by JUAN DE JESUS ROMERO, the Taos proved that the lake was central to Taos life and crucial to Taos religion and that denial of protected access to Blue Lake threatened the existence of the culture. On December 15, 1970, President Nixon signed into law a bill restoring Blue Lake to the Taos people. The bill granted trust title to 48,000 acres of land, 64 years after it was taken from them.

BOARD OF FOREIGN MISSIONS (BFM) OF THE PRESBYTERIAN CHURCH IN THE UNITED STATES OF AMERICA (PCUSA)

A missionary society founded in 1837, the same year a schism occurred between Old School and New School wings of Presbyterianism. Until 1869, the society served the Old Schoolers, conservative Presbyterians who had expelled their brethren and founded the BFM. At that time, the schism ended, and the organization began serving the reunited church. From 1837 to 1893, the BFM's period of service to American Indians, more than 450 missionaries served at least 19 tribes: Chickasaw, Chippewa, Choctaw, Creek, Dakota, Fox, Ioway, Kickapoo, Navajo (Dineh), Nez Perce, Omaha, Otoe, Ottawa, Sac, Seminole, Seneca, Spokane, Wea, and Winnebago (Ho-Chunk).

Missionary work among Native people by this denomination did not begin with the BFM, however. AZARIAH HORTON, the first member of the church to proselytize among American Indians, began ministering to Native people on Long Island in 1741. Other missionaries, such as DAVID BRAINERD and GIDEON BLACKBURN, also predated the society. In 1837 the Western Foreign Missionary Society, established by the Presbyterian Synod of Pittsburgh, was absorbed into the BFM.

A major objective of the BFM, according to an 1840 publication, was "to assist in making known the Gospel, for a witness unto all nations." It viewed its work with American Indians similar to that among "other heathens of a strange tongue" in worldwide foreign missions. The BFM's religious objectives were sought by "the preaching of the Gospel by the living teacher" and by "the raising up of a native ministry among the heathen." Additional work included translating and printing the Bible and other religious material, organizing churches and schools, and transforming Indian people into "civilized," self-sufficient American citizens. In 1861 the Choctaw Mission, one of the BFM's largest, consisted of "nine principal stations, two outstations, ten ordained ministers—including one Choctaw—four Choctaw licentiate preachers, twenty-nine teachers and assistants, one boys' and four girls' boarding schools, four day schools, and 'Saturday and Sunday schools.'"

Along with Catholic and other Protestant denominations, Presbyterians participated in a church-state relationship with the federal government. Under President Ulysses S. GRANT'S PEACE POLICY, for instance, the BFM nominated members from its ranks for appointments to the tribal agencies. By the 1880s, PCUSA began transferring tribes from the BFM to its Board of Home Missions. During the BFM's period of Indian work, missionaries sent nearly 14,000 letters to the denomination's New York headquarters documenting their efforts. (See Subject Index for missionaries affiliated with the board included in this volume.)

BOLE-MARU RELIGION

An outgrowth of the GHOST DANCE OF 1870. Its name comes from the Patwin word *bole* and the Pomo word *maru*. Both words are said to be associated with the dreamer-prophets who conducted the religious ceremonies as well as with the dream that was recited. One of the originators of the Bole-Maru, or Dreamer Religion, is believed to be the prophet called LAME BILL, a Hill Patwin. The religious movement spread among Patwin, Pomo, and Maidu groups, having its highest development in north-central California. The Bole-Maru leaders were dreamers whose revelations guided the direction of ceremonial activities. Ritual elements generally included performances of the Bole-Hesi Dance, the Bole or Maru Dance, and the Ball Dance. The Bole-Hesi Dance, derived from the Big Head Dance, was performed by two dancers. The Bole or Maru, also called the dress, or women's, dance, included performances by two lines of female dancers. During the Ball Dance the dancers tossed cloth balls incorporating dream patterns to their partners. For the adherents, dancing was fundamental to expressing the sacred. The religion also included the use of flagpoles, flags, cloth ceremonial dress, and a concluding feast. The Bole-Maru's teachings emphasized ethical behavior and opposed drinking, quarreling, stealing, and other vices. They also stressed belief in an afterlife and in a supreme being. Unlike some of the other religious movements stemming from the Ghost Dance, practice of the Bole-Maru form of worship continues today. The BIG HEAD RELIGION was an offshoot of the Bole-Maru religion.

BOMPAS, WILLIAM C. *(1834–1906)* An Anglican missionary known for his work in the Yukon. Born in England, Bompas traveled to Fort Simpson, British Columbia, under the auspices of the CHURCH MISSIONARY SOCIETY. He arrived at the fort on Christmas morning of 1865 and found that the Scottish-Ojibway missionary Robert McDonald, whom he was to replace, was not on his deathbed as had been reported.

Besides becoming the first bishop of Athabaska in 1874, Bompas was named bishop of Mackenzie River in 1884 and bishop of Selkirk in 1891 under new diocesan divisions. The Church Missionary Society sent him to Metlakatla in the late 1870s to try to resolve its conflict with WILLIAM DUNCAN, another mission worker, but the effort failed. After retiring in 1891, Bompas remained in the Yukon until his death. He was the author of *Diocese of Mackenzie River* (London, 1888) and *Northern Lights on the Bible* (London, 1893), based on his 25 years in the Northwest. Bompas also completed *Manual of Devotion in the Beaver Indian Dialect* (London, 1880), *A Cree Primer* (London, 1899) and *Lessons and Prayers in the Tenni or Slavi Language* (London, 1892).

BONNEY, MARY LUCINDA *(1816–1900)* A Baptist reformer whose efforts led to the formation of the Women's National Indian Association and to the establishment of missions among Native people. She was born in Hamilton, New York, to Lucinda (Wilder) and Benjamin Bonney and was educated at New York's Hamilton Academy and the Troy Female Seminary (class of 1835). In 1850, after teaching for a number of years, Bonney established the Chestnut Street Female Seminary in Philadelphia and served as its senior principal until 1888. She was active in the Philadelphia branch of the Woman's Union Missionary Society of America for Heathen Lands as well as the women's home missionary group of her church, which was interested in working with Native people. After expressing concern to reformer AMELIA STONE QUINTON about proposals to open Indian Territory (present-day Oklahoma) to white settlers, the two women began organizing popular support in 1879 on behalf of Indian causes. Bonney raised funds while Quinton organized, and their efforts resulted in the formation of the Women's National Indian Association. It advocated a number of programs, including allotment of tribal land to individuals, a home building program on reservations, and the establishment of missions. Bonney resigned as president of the association in 1884 because of other responsibilities but continued as honorary president and as a member of the executive board and missionary committee. In 1888 she married Reverend Thomas Rambaut in London and on their return home they settled in Hamilton, New York. She made annual contributions to the Women's National Indian Association until her death on July 24, 1900.

BOUCHARD, JAMES CHRYSOSTOM (Watomika, "Swift Foot") *(1823–1889) Delaware (Lenni Lenape)* The first Native American to become a Roman Catholic priest in the United States. Bouchard was born to Kistalwa, a Delaware chief, and to Monotowa, a French captive who had been brought up among the Comanche people. Kistalwa was killed by the Lakota in 1834. Influenced by Presbyterians, Bouchard joined their faith and began attending a mission school in Ohio. After converting to Catholicism in 1846, he began preparing for the Jesuit priesthood in Missouri and was ordained in 1855. Although his preference was to minister to his own people, he received orders to serve among non-Indians—as a minister to San Francisco miners. Father Bouchard also lectured on both his Native heritage and Christianity. (See also GORDON, PHILIP B.; NEGAHNQUET, ALBERT; PELOTTE, DONALD E.)

BOUDINOT, ELIAS (Galagina, "Male Deer" or "Turkey") *(c. 1802–1839) Cherokee* Cherokee spokesman and newspaper editor who promoted Christianity among his people and collaborated with the missionary SAMUEL AUSTIN WORCESTER on biblical translations. Born Galagina ("buck"), about 1802 near Rome, Georgia, his parents were Oo-watie (David Uwati) and Susanna Reese. From 1818 to 1822 he attended the Foreign Mission School in Cornwall, Connecticut, where he took the name Elias Boudinot after a school benefactor. He received additional training at Andover Seminary from 1822 to 1823 before returning home. In 1823 he and Worcester began translating the New Testament into the Cherokee language, utilizing the syllabary invented a few years earlier by Sequoyah. Boudinot was later employed as the editor of the *Cherokee Phoenix,* the first American Indian newspaper, at a salary of $300.00 per year. He edited the weekly publication from February 21, 1828, until his resignation in 1832. Boudinot also wrote the first novel in the Cherokee language, *Poor Sarah or the Indian Woman,* which was published by the United Brethren's Missionary Society in 1833. After he and several others signed an 1835 treaty, without authority, agreeing to Cherokee removal west, Boudinot was blamed for his role in the transaction. He was murdered on June 22, 1839, in Indian Territory (present-day Oklahoma), and the translations he had worked on since 1823 were cut short by his death. He married Harriet Ruggles Gold in 1826, and the couple had six children. After Gold's death in 1836, Boudinot married Delight Sargent. He was also known as Buck Watie and Stag Watie.

BOUTWELL, WILLIAM T. *(c. 1803–1890)* An early missionary who worked among the Ojibway in Minnesota Territory under the auspices of the AMERICAN BOARD OF

COMMISSIONERS FOR FOREIGN MISSIONS. A native of New Hampshire, Boutwell was educated at Dartmouth and Divinity College (Andover Theological Seminary). He was ordained in 1831 on the same day as his classmate SHERMAN HALL. Hall convinced him to join him on a mission assignment at La Pointe on Lake Superior's Madeline Island. After studying the Ojibway language at Mackinac Island, Boutwell accompanied the Indian agent Henry Rowe Schoolcraft on his 1832 expedition to the headwaters region of the Mississippi River. As a result of the tour, Boutwell changed his missionary destination from Sandy Lake to Leech Lake in Minnesota Territory. He reached Leech Lake's Pillager band in October 1833, remaining there until the fall of 1837. During that period, he initiated a program of religious instruction and other activities but was unable to convert any of the people. Instead, the Pillagers became determined that he leave their community. Boutwell offended the band members in a number of ways, including negotiating an individual land transaction outside of the customary communal ownership, aligning himself with the traders, and withholding his stockpile of food from communal use even during periods of starvation. After leaving Leech Lake, Boutwell served as a missionary at La Pointe, then settled among Euro-Americans as a farmer and preacher. Boutwell married Hester Crooks, a mixed-blood, in 1834, and she joined him at Leech Lake, where they had two children. (See also ELY, EDMUND F.)

BOW PRIESTHOOD *Zuni* Bow priests, human representatives of the WAR GODS, appointed by the chief priest, are leaders in war and protect the village. They are recruited from men who have killed an enemy. As the executive arm of the religious hierarchy, they take measures against witches and guard against impurities. They hold two ceremonies, one in March, which has to do with rainfall and crops, and one in the fall, which is a harvest festival. They appear in winter solstice ceremonies as well, at which time the sacred wooden statues of the War Gods, which figure in Bow Priest ceremonies, are carved. They have a ceremonial chamber where they keep sacred objects. (See also RAIN PRIESTHOODS.)

BOWEN V. ROY (106 S.Ct.2147) *(1986)* In this case an Alaska Native American father challenged a welfare department requirement that he provide a Social Security number for his daughter on the grounds that the practice infringed on his freedom of religion. In 1986 the U.S. Supreme Court ruled that the requirement did not violate the free exercise clause of the First Amendment, "notwithstanding belief that use of numbers would impair the child's spirit." Although the decision represented the first direct discussion of the AMERICAN INDIAN RELIGIOUS FREEDOM ACT OF 1978 by the Supreme Court, the Court indicated that the act provided guidance, not a statutory cause of action, on the issue of religious freedom. (See Subject Index for other cases regarding Native American religious freedoms included in this volume.)

BOWL (PEACH STONE) GAME *Iroquois* Ancient sacred game of chance and wagering played between two opposing sides in the longhouse. The bowl game is believed to be one of the FOUR SACRED CEREMONIES introduced to the Iroquois people by the Creator. A sacred agricultural rite when played during the SEED PLANTING CEREMONY, GREEN CORN CEREMONY, and HARVEST FESTIVAL, it is a renewal rite when played during the MIDWINTER CEREMONY. The game is also played in the home of a patient or dreamer to cure or cheer up an ailing person as well as at wakes. It was also believed that playing the game helped predict the bountifulness of certain crops or fruits. When men played against women and the men won, the pumpkin crop might be large. If the women won, the berry crop would be large.

The game is believed to be a religious act that dramatizes the struggle of fruits and crops to grow in spite of natural elements that are not always favorable. The game is also played in memory of the game played by the good brother, the Creator, against his evil brother for control of the earth during creation. Lasting from two to three days, the contest between moieties (groupings of clans) or between men and women involves shaking six peach stones, each burned black on one side, in a bowl. Scoring is based on the values given to different combinations of black and white sides turned up. At one time, it was a religious duty for each person to wager valuable possessions as the Creator had done. People bet all they had, and the game sometimes continued for days. Today, there are variations in scoring, the kind and number of counters used, kind of bets placed, and teams (either between sexes or between moieties). The Onondaga, one of the Iroquois peoples, have an elaborate bowl game that figures prominently in their Midwinter Ceremony.

BOX ELDER (Maple, Maple Tree, Dog on the Range, Dog in the Ridge, Dog Standing, and Old Brave Wolf) *(c. 1795–1892) Cheyenne* A venerated holy man, warrior and chief. Box Elder was the son of Horn or Old Horn (later called Blind Bull), a great holy man of the Suhtai band of the Cheyenne. Besides learning sacred knowledge from his father, he was also instructed by the wolves. He possessed gifts of prophecy as well as the ability to summon the spirits and communicate with them. As a warrior, he was protected in battles with the enemy by being bullet-proof. Box Elder was so renowned as a holy man that he was one of the two individuals chosen to make the shafts of the SACRED ARROWS, replacing those captured by the Pawnee in 1830. His spiritual powers were displayed in prophetic visions warning the people of approaching soldiers and a demonstration of sacred powers during Colonel Ranald MacKenzie's attack against the Cheyenne in 1876. Box Elder's blindness in old age was believed to make him even closer to the world of the spirits. Among the leadership positions he held were SUN DANCE priest, head chief of the Suhtaio, and council chief. As prophesied, Box Elder lived to an old age. He died near what is now Birney, Montana, in about 1892.

BRAINERD, DAVID *(1718–1747)* A missionary to Indians in New York, Pennsylvania, and New Jersey from 1742 to 1747. Born into the New England aristocracy on April 20, 1718, in Haddan, Connecticut, Brainerd was orphaned by 1732. He attended Yale from 1739 until 1742, when he was expelled for advocating the Great Awakening religious movement. After studying theology privately with Jedidiah Mills in 1742, he received a license to preach in Connecticut. During the same year, he also received a missionary appointment from the Scottish Society for the Propagation of Christian Knowledge. Beginning in April 1743, he ministered to Algonquians at Kaunaumeek in New York, convincing them to move to the Reverend JOHN SERGEANT'S Stockbridge, Massachusetts, missionary community. In 1744, after his ordination by the presbytery of New York, he was transferred to a Delaware River site. The following year he worked among the Delaware (Lenni Lenape) in New Jersey, at present-day Freehold, then Cranbury. His career was soon cut short by a tubercular condition, and he left the mission to his brother John. Brainerd went to Northampton, Massachusetts where his fiancée, Jerusha, one of JONATHAN EDWARDS'S daughters, nursed him during his last few months. He died on October 9, 1847, after only four years in the mission field. Impressed by Brainerd's diary, Edwards published it as *An Account of the Life of the Late Reverend Mr. David Brainerd* (1749), and it brought posthumous attention to the young missionary.

BRAY, THOMAS *(1656–1730)* An Anglican clergyman who was instrumental in forming the SOCIETY FOR PROMOTING CHRISTIAN KNOWLEDGE (SPCK), the SOCIETY FOR THE PROPAGATION OF THE GOSPEL (SPG) IN FOREIGN PARTS, and "Dr. Bray's Associates." Bray, who was born in Marton, England, graduated from All Souls College, Oxford, in 1678 and Hart Hall, Oxford University, in 1693. After serving as a curate and rector, he received an appointment in 1696 from the bishop of London to serve as commissary to Maryland. He held the position from 1696 to 1706, promoting English missionary endeavors in the colonies. While recruiting religious workers, Bray recognized the need of providing books to colonial clergymen who could not afford them. His efforts to furnish printed materials led to the establishment of libraries and to the founding, in 1699, of SPCK to support such activities throughout the colonies. Bray lived in Maryland for a brief period, beginning in 1700, visiting clergymen and working to establish the Anglican Church as the colony's religion. After his return to England, he promoted the 1701 chartering of the SPG, a society eventually providing funding and other support to Anglican efforts in America throughout the 18th century. In 1706 he became the rector of St. Botolph's Without, in Aldgate, a position he held until 1730, but continued to work on missionary causes. "Dr. Bray's Associates," formed at the end of his life, contributed to missionary efforts among blacks and Indians in the colonies and supported the chartering of the Georgia colony. The societies organized by Bray had a profound impact on American religion long after his death in 1730.

BREAD DANCE (Dakwanekawe) *Shawnee.* The Dakwanekawe, or Bread Dance, is the principal event of the ceremonial year, traditionally held in both the spring and the fall. It is believed to have been originated by OUR GRANDMOTHER, the Shawnee female deity, who is said to sometimes appear on earth to observe its performance and to participate in the singing. The ceremony customarily consists of eight dance episodes, including a women's Kokeki, or Cluster Dance, and a Wapikonekawe, or Pumpkin Dance, done by both males and females. In the spring Bread Dance, which is a prayer for crops and fertility, the women begin the dancing, and their role is dominant. In the fall, the men open the dancing, and their role as hunters is emphasized. In both observances the dancing is done by both men and women, sometimes separately and sometimes together. Twelve male hunters provide squirrels or other game while 12 female cooks prepare Shawnee corn bread. The foods are displayed until the conclusion of the ceremony when they are exchanged by the men and women. The observance ends with a Bread Dance prayer, and afterwards the people participate in secular nighttime, or stomp, dances generally lasting until dawn. (See also BUFFALO DANCE; DEATH FEAST; GREEN CORN DANCE; RIDE-IN AND WAR DANCE; RITUAL FOOTBALL GAME.)

BREATHING *Pueblo* A ritual in which a person exhales one's breath, signifying a wish, a prayer, and an expectation that the power will be magnified. A person petitioning a medicine man for a curing ritual or any society for membership utters a prayer request and blows his or her breath on a packet of cornmeal before sending it to the society head. People get power and blessings from various sacred objects by "inhaling the breath" from them.

BRÉBEUF, JEAN DE *(1593–1649)* Jesuit missionary. Brébeuf was born in lower Normandy, France. At the age of 24, he entered the Jesuit novitiate at Rouen. He was ordained in 1622 and was sent to Canada in 1625, where he worked as a missionary for 24 years. In 1626, he was sent to Huron country, where he stayed for three years. He learned the Huron language but had no success in converting the people. He returned to France and was there from 1629 until 1633, during the British occupation of Quebec, when he went back to Canada and again to Huron country. In 1634, he established a mission at Ihonatiria, a village near Toanche, but the Huron still resisted conversion. He finally converted the first adult Huron in 1637. Repeated epidemics of smallpox and influenza had reduced the Huron population and made these people angry at missionaries. After an attack on his mission in April 1640, Father Brébeuf was appointed that autumn to a mission among the Neutral Indians, but he failed to convert them. He again returned to Quebec in 1642 and two years later returned to Huron country. In 1649, in an attack on the Huron, the Iroquois captured Father Brébeuf, and he died at their hands that year near Georgian Bay, Canada.

Father Brébeuf's missions, established in the midst of two Huron clans, the Bear and Cord, enabled him to become acquainted with Huron customs and enabled him to describe their culture before a series of epidemics and wars defeated them. He mastered the Huron language and, owing to 15 years of living among them, he became an expert orthographer and compiled a dictionary and grammar of the Huron language. Father Brébeuf was canonized in 1930 by Pope Pius XI and was proclaimed patron saint of Canada by Pius XII in 1940. The history of his mission and his martyrdom were recounted by PAUL RAGUENEAU in his *Relations des Hurons.*

BRECK, JAMES LLOYD *(1818–1876)* An Episcopal clergyman who established schools and missions in Wisconsin, Minnesota, and California. He was born near Philadelphia. After studying at a Long Island academy run by the Reverend William A. Muhlenberg, Breck attended the University of Pennsylvania (class of 1838) and the General Theological Seminary in New York (class of 1841). In 1841 he volunteered for mission work in Wisconsin, where he and two other young clergymen built a house at Nashotah and began their religious efforts among the new settlers in the region. Besides conducting missionary work, Breck's goals included the establishment of a seminary and the formation of a celibate brotherhood of Episcopal clergymen. He remained at

the post for more than eight years, then resigned as the president of Nashotah and entered a new mission field in Minnesota in 1850.

Breck turned his attention to Christianizing and "civilizing" Ojibway people in the region by opening mission stations with religious, educational, and agricultural programs. He founded St. Columba mission at Gull Lake, which was later placed under the religious care of ENMEGAHBOWH, a Native clergyman, and also began a center at Leech Lake. After leaving the Indian mission field, Breck's remaining years in Minnesota were spent at Faribault, where he worked with Bishop HENRY BENJAMIN WHIPPLE and established boarding schools and the Seabury Divinity School. In 1867 he moved to California, where he again started a seminary and other schools. Breck died on March 30, 1876. He was married to Jane Maria Mills from 1855 until her death in 1862, then to Sarah Styles.

BROWN, AMELIA *(1868–1979)* *Tolowa* A traditional leader and shaman from the Smith River Rancheria in California who converted to the INDIAN SHAKER RELIGION when she was 70. After the death of her mother from childbirth complications, Brown was raised by her father. He brought her up among men, taking her into their sweat lodge, while also making certain that she learned the traditional role of Tolowa women. She became a respected smoke-doctor and herb-woman of knowledge and influence in the community. Brown joined the Shakers after testing their spiritual power against her own. While attending her first service, a concealed medicine bag she wore was detected by a Shaker woman "under power." She became a member of the group from that time on and assumed a leadership role in the church. Brown contributed to the survival of Tolowa culture through her special knowledge and lifetime work.

BRUNSON, ALFRED *(1793–1882)* Methodist missionary at Prairie du Chien, Wisconsin. Brunson was born on February 9, 1793, in Danbury, Connecticut. After serving in the War of 1812, he received his license to preach. In 1818 he organized a new circuit in Ohio and later another in Pennsylvania. Brunson began missionary work among Indians in the upper Mississippi valley in 1835. He and his family took their house from Pennsylvania to the region, an early instance of the use of prefabricated housing. In 1837 Brunson started a mission among the Santee Dakota at Kaposia, below present-day St. Paul, Minnesota. As demanded by the Santee, it was closed in 1841. Brunson served as the presiding elder of an area from Rock Island, Illinois, to the Mississippi headwaters region. He also practiced law, served in the territorial legislature, and became a chaplain during the Civil War. Brunson wrote numerous articles and a two-volume autobiography entitled *A Western Pioneer* (1872). Father Brunson, as he was called, died on August 3, 1882, at Prairie du Chien.

BUDD, HENRY (Sakacewescam, "Going Up the Hill") *(c. 1812–1875) Cree*   The first North American Indian to be ordained by the Church of England. Budd was born to a Métis mother and an unknown Indian father. In 1820 he was taken from his home at Norway House West (Manitoba) by the Reverend JOHN WEST to be educated at the Red River settlement (present-day Winnipeg). West named the boy after his former rector, the Reverend Henry Budd, a Church of England clergyman, and baptized him on July 21, 1822. By that time, the 10-year-old was able to read the New Testament and to accurately repeat the catechism. In 1922 Budd was joined at the Red River settlement by his mother and his sister, Sarah. After leaving West's CHURCH MISSIONARY SOCIETY school in 1828, Budd farmed for a time then worked for the Hudson's Bay Company. In 1836 he married Betsy Work and a year later began serving as a schoolmaster at a mission school in the Red River area. In 1840, accompanied by his wife and his mother, Budd traveled to Cumberland House near Cumberland Lake (Saskatchewan) to conduct missionary work. He remained there a short time, then relocated to W'passkwayaw, which became known as The Pas, Manitoba. Budd, who built a house from which to provide educational and missionary services, worked among Cree, Ojibway, and families of mixed ancestry. When the Reverend JAMES HUNTER arrived at the mission in 1846, Budd assisted him by serving as a catechist, interpreter, and laborer. He returned to the Red River settlement and was ordained a deacon on December 22, 1850. A few years later, in 1853, Budd's ordination to the priesthood was held at The Pas in the newly built Christ Church. Budd then spent time at Nepowewin (Nipawin, Saskatchewan) before returning to The Pas in 1854. Three years later he went back to Nepowewin, remaining there until his appointment as minister of The Pas's Devon Mission, the first Anglican mission north of Red River, in 1867. By that time, his wife and a son, Henry, who had been ordained in 1863, had died. The Native missionary, known as an eloquent preacher in the Cree language, revived the work he had started at The Pas earlier, trained teachers, and established a church government. Budd, who was called "The Praying Chief," died on April 2, 1875. The *Diary of the Reverend Henry Budd, 1870–1875* was edited by Katherine Pettipas and published in 1974.

BUFFALO CALF PIPE *Lakota*   The sacred pipe of the Lakota, given by WHITE BUFFALO CALF WOMAN, who instructed the Lakota on its meaning and care. The Buffalo Calf Pipe has played an important part in Lakota belief, from the time of its first keeper, Buffalo Standing Upright, to today. The contemporary keeper, ARVAL LOOKING HORSE, explained its history and significance in his account, "The Sacred Pipe in Modern Life," published in *Sioux Indian Religion* and information about the pipe and its keepers was also given by Lakota religious leaders, including BLACK ELK, FRANK FOOLS CROW, JOHN (FIRE) LAME DEER.

BUFFALO CEREMONY *Cheyenne*   The Buffalo Ceremony is a sacred healing ceremony of the Suhtaio, a distinct tribal group that later became a band of the Cheyenne people. Originally held for the purpose of ensuring plenty of buffalo, the ceremony is now generally pledged to cure a person suffering from illness. Its spiritual and healing powers are associated with the Buffalo People of Cheyenne belief as well as the SACRED BUFFALO HAT. The ceremony also shares renewal of life and other religious themes with the SUN DANCE. Besides priests, the participants include a man and woman who represent the buffalo bull and buffalo cow. Another person symbolizes the buffalo calf.

Ritual elements include extensive preparations to build a ceremonial or Buffalo sweat lodge. One account indicated that the construction of this sacred lodge took nearly an entire day, involving the completion of approximately 20 different operations before it was ready for use. Other elements of worship include praying with the SACRED PIPE, the preparation and making of offerings, the singing of sacred songs, and the painting of participants and objects. During the ceremony itself the participants are ritually cleansed or purified. (See also ERECT HORNS.)

BUFFALO DANCE *Hopi*   During January and the beginning of February, a period called Pamurti, social Buffalo Dances take place. They have religious overtones because the dances are believed to be effective in removing ills from a village. Males of all ages and young females of premarital status dance. Participants also include a chorus.

BUFFALO DANCE *Pueblo*   See ANIMAL DANCES

BUFFALO DANCE (Thothekawe, Pethothekawe) *Shawnee*   A ceremony conducted by the Loyal band of Shawnee, generally occurring in late August or early September. One version of its origin attributes it to the great Shawnee leader Tecumseh, who is said to have acquired it from the buffalo, his guardian spirit. Another version states that a white buffalo took a medicine man known as Daugherty to the spiritual home of the buffalo people, and they taught it to him. Because OUR GRANDMOTHER, the Shawnee female deity, did not originate it as she did other sacred ceremonies, the Buffalo Dance is conducted outside of the dance ground used for other observances. Two large kettles of corn mush, believed to be favored by buffalo, are prepared. The ritual customarily includes symbolic painting, buffalo mime, and eight sets of dances performed by both males and females either dancing together or separately. During the final Buffalo Dance segment, the dancers have a mock battle for the corn mush, which is eaten after a concluding prayer is said. Later in the evening social dances take place. (See also BREAD DANCE; DEATH FEAST; GREEN CORN DANCE; RIDE-IN AND WAR DANCE; RITUAL FOOTBALL GAME.)

BUFFALO SOCIETY *Iroquois* A private medicine society that enacts cures at the MIDWINTER CEREMONY or at private homes. Ceremonies occur at irregular intervals rather than according to the ceremonial calendar. Curing ceremonies are conducted by and for those who are or have been sick with the particular illness that the Buffalo Society cures. Its rituals include songs and a dance, and the participants eat certain foods between dances. A person who is cured by the ceremony then belongs to the society. (See also MEDICINE SOCIETIES [Iroquois].)

BULL LODGE (Buffalo Lodge) *(c. 1802–1886) Gros Ventre (Atsina)* A holy man and warrior who possessed gifts of healing and prophecy. Bull Lodge's parents were Cook Kill, or Good Kill, a Gros Ventre woman, and High Crane, or Crooked Rump, a French trader. His mother left High Crane to rejoin her people who had moved to another area, and Bull Lodge, who was brought up among the Gros Ventre, never knew his father. Entrusting his life to the sacred Chief Medicine Pipe, or the Feathered Pipe, of the Gros Ventre, he began to pray and to fast during his youth. He eventually received spiritual instructions to undertake fasts on seven different buttes in the region for specified periods of time. Each vision resulted in revelations that were to sustain him and to help his people throughout his life. Bull Lodge eventually spent 10 years as a warrior. His legendary accomplishments in battle resulted in his recognition as a war chief at the age of 40. He then began preparing to become a medicine man, declaring himself a doctor to treat his uncle, Yellow Man, who was suffering from a serious illness. Bull Lodge's powers were such that he was able to heal a range of illnesses and injuries, including gunshot wounds. After his first 19 cases, he was given the Chief Medicine Pipe of his people and held the position of chief medicine man. He was foretold of his death and was about 85 when he died. His family included a wife, four sons, and two daughters. An account of Bull Lodge's life was obtained from one of his daughters, Garter Snake (In-nietse), through a Works Progress Administration program conducted by Frederic Gone, another tribal member. It was published in 1980 as *The Seven Visions of Bull Lodge.* The holy man was also known as Buffalo Lodge.

BUREAU OF CATHOLIC INDIAN MISSIONS Created in 1874, the Catholic Indian Bureau functioned to protect and advance missionary work then threatened by President GRANT'S PEACE POLICY, issued in 1870 as a solution to many injustices that daily plagued Indian people. President Grant decided to turn Indian jurisdictions over to various church groups. These groups would in turn select agents and staff for the Indian reservations who would administer civil affairs of the agency in conjunction with mission work. Grant's policy promised to give control of each agency to the church already at work among the Indians at the time the policy was inaugurated. Although the Catholic Church claimed control of at least 38 agencies, the Indian Bureau only granted it control of eight. The church responded to this injustice and in 1874, Archbishop J. Roosevelt Bayley of Baltimore appointed General Charles Ewing Catholic Indian Commissioner in the United States and Western Territories. In 1884, the Third Plenary Council of Baltimore decreed it a permanent institution of the church. In 1894, the Bureau, superseded by a new corporation chartered in perpetuity by the archbishops of Baltimore, New York, and Philadelphia, became the Bureau of Catholic Indian Missions. The bureau still represents Indian mission business to the U.S. government today. Over the past 100 years, the bureau has obtained tribal and federal funds for mission schools, eliminated unfair discrimination against Catholic missionaries and Indians, secured the right of Catholic Indian children to adequate religious instruction, obtained title to properties used for church and school purposes on Indian reservations, and provided financial aid to the missions.

The first director of the bureau was Father John Baptist A. Brouillet (1874–1884). He secured recognition of the constitutional rights of Catholic missionaries and of Catholic Indians in the face of sectarian and political opposition and obtained for Catholic Indian schools the same assistance from the government that Protestant schools enjoyed. Monsignor J. A. Stephan (1884–1901), the bureau's second director, fought unsuccessfully against government efforts to abolish mission schools. He worked closely with KATHERINE DREXEL, who as founder of the Sisters of the Blessed Sacrament responded to his appeals for financial backing to increase the number of schools. Father William H. Ketcham (1901–21), the third director, obtained the right of Catholic pupils in government schools to attend Catholic services and to receive religious instruction from priests. He secured tribal funds for the support and education of Indian pupils in mission schools and indirect federal aid permissible under law, such as rations for children in Indian mission schools. Monsignor William Hughes (1921–35), the fourth director, worked assiduously for Indian causes and especially emphasized spiritual life and needs of Indians. He contributed enlightening articles to *Indian Sentinel* magazine published by the bureau from 1902 to 1964. Father Benjamin Tennelly (1935–76), the fifth director, was professor of theology at Catholic University in Washington, D.C. He edited the *Indian Sentinel* and wrote extensively of the Catholic Indian missions. Monsignor Paul A. Lenz (1976–   ), a former missionary in Paraguay, South America, is the sixth director of the bureau.

Today, the bureau consists of a board of directors composed of archbishops of New York, Baltimore, and Philadelphia and an executive director, secretary, and treasurer. Its office is in Washington, D.C. The bureau supports with grants one high school and 41 primary schools.

Since 1977, the bureau's board has supported the TEKAKWITHA CONFERENCE, based in Great Falls, Montana. Lay and religious conference participants now dialogue for the spiritual and social needs of the Indian community by discussing Native American liturgy, ministry, family life, catechesis, advocacy, education, and ecumenical cooperation. Two Indian bishops, DONALD E. PELOTTE and Charles Chaput, are ex-officio members of Tekakwitha Conference.

BURIAL GROUND DESECRATION   Over the years, all across the United States and Canada, there has been a systematic expropriation of Native American dead by government agents, soldiers, pothunters, and other private citizens who have taken away from graves thousands of bodies of dead Indians and thousands of associated burial goods. Native people generally believe that if one disturbs the dead or robs their graves of objects intended to secure their journeys to the afterworld, their spirits will wander.

Official U.S. federal government policy under the 1868 Surgeon General's Order to army personnel mandated the procurement of as many Indian crania as possible for the Army Medical Museum. Under that order, over 4,000 heads were taken from battlefields, prisoner-of-war camps and hospitals, and fresh Indian graves or burial scaffolds across the country. Collecting crews from newly founded museums also took Native human remains in "rip and run operations." In 1906, Congress passed the Antiquities Act, intended to protect against looting of archaeological resources located on federal lands. The act defined dead Indians as "archaeological resources" and converted these persons into federal "property." Under the act, the remains of human beings were dug up with federal permits and were subject to permanent preservation in public museums. Sev-

enty-five years later, the ARCHAEOLOGICAL RESOURCE PROTECTION ACT OF 1979 defined human remains as "archaeological resources" and converted them into "the property of the United States." If excavated under federal permits, they can be "preserved by a suitable university, museum, or other scientific or educational institution." Under these federal statutes, thousands of deceased Native Americans were dug up from their graves.

Thousands of Indian burial sites are located on federal lands managed by the Bureau of Land Management, the U.S. Forest Service, and the National Park Service. Vandals and thieves have wreaked havoc on these Indian grave sites. Countless Indian burial sites are also located on state and privately owned lands. Throughout the 20th century, looters have destroyed many of these sites. In the 1930s, a Smithsonian Institution anthropologist removed more than 300 human remains from a burial site next to the village of Kodiak Island, Alaska, despite the objections of Native residents. In the fall of 1987, 10 men leased 40 acres of farmland to dig up ceremonial objects. They disturbed more than 200 Indian grave sites searching for objects before the Kentucky State Police obtained a court order halting the digging. Tens of thousands of these ceremonial objects have ended up in private collections or the public collections of museums, state historical societies, universities, National Park Service warehouses, and curio shops.

Indian activists want the skeletal remains of their ancestors removed from museums, universities, and warehouses and returned to their descendants for proper reburial. Archaeologists and museum professionals insisted, however, that human remains were "resources," as defined by the 1906 Antiquities Act and the Archaeological Resources Protection Act, that belong in display cases, exhibits, and laboratories. Eventually, Native American organizations, museum curators, and archaeologists reached a compromise resulting in the passage of the NATIVE AMERICAN GRAVES PROTECTION AND REPATRIATION ACT signed on November 16, 1990. The law represents a major federal shift away from viewing Native American human remains as "archaeological resources" or "federal property" to viewing them as the remains of ancestors. States, too, are protecting Indian graves. Thirty-two states have passed BURIAL LEGISLATION to protect unmarked Indian graves from unnecessary disturbance. In many states, however, removing bodies or objects from Indian graves is still not a crime.

BURIAL LEGISLATION

Federal

The U.S. federal government has enacted laws to protect aboriginal remains on federal lands and Indian reservations including the Antiquities Act of 1906 and the

ARCHAEOLOGICAL RESOURCES PROTECTION ACT OF 1979, which effectively replaces the 1906 law. These laws emphasize preservation by institutions of the archaeological resources, including human remains and objects, that became federal property after recovery from federal land. The laws did not promote repatriation and reburial of aboriginal remains and grave goods. In 1989, Congress passed the NATIONAL MUSEUM OF THE AMERICAN INDIAN ACT, which focused on the inventory of Indian remains and grave goods held in the collection of the Smithsonian Institution in Washington, D.C. Tribes may request repatriation of human remains and associated grave goods affiliated with their own tribes. In 1990, the NATIVE AMERICAN GRAVES PROTECTION AND REPATRIATION ACT was passed. The law applies to collections of aboriginal materials held by federal agencies and museums receiving federal support. It does not apply to materials found on private or state property or to the Smithsonian Institution.

State

All of the states have laws that consider in some way the disposition of "prehistoric" aboriginal remains and grave goods. Some states apply criminal laws specifically against grave robbing, trespass, and vandalism or rely on their general public health and sepulchral laws. By mid-1991, 32 states (Alaska, Arkansas, California, Colorado, Connecticut, Delaware, Florida, Hawaii, Idaho, Illinois, Indiana, Iowa, Kansas, Maine, Massachusetts, Minnesota, Mississippi, Missouri, Nebraska, Nevada, New Hampshire, New Mexico, North Carolina, North Dakota, Oklahoma, Oregon, South Dakota, Tennessee, Virginia, Washington, West Virginia, and Wisconsin) implemented legislation that deals directly with reburial or repatriation of "prehistoric" aboriginal remains or grave goods. There is little consistency among the laws. Some state statutes do not apply to remains and goods found on private property except where the property owner gives express permission. Missouri and Nebraska, among others, have passed statutes that affect both state and private lands. Missouri's law, however, applies only to human remains, while Nebraska's law applies to human remains and grave goods. Nevada's law includes Indian burials located on private land dated from the middle of the 18th century until the beginning of the 20th century and applies only to artifacts taken from a burial site after October 1, 1989. (See also KANSAS UNMARKED BURIAL SITES PRESERVATION ACT; NATIVE AMERICAN HISTORICAL, CULTURAL, AND SACRED SITES ACT; UNMARKED HUMAN BURIAL SITES AND SKELETAL REMAINS PROTECTION ACT.)

BUSH DANCE *Iroquois* A ceremony whose primary purpose is to recognize the spirits connected with bushes and trees and thank them for their growth and help to people as well as to express the wish that they may continue growing. After the MIDWINTER CEREMONY, the Bush Dance is usually the first event organized by women. At the Six Nations Reserve in Canada, however, the Bush Dance, not the Midwinter Ceremony, is viewed as the first ceremony of the new ceremonial year. The moiety (tribal half) that will be the "leader" for that year presides over the dance.

BUSHY HEADS *Iroquois* This earthbound class of spirits formed a pact with people and taught them the arts of hunting and agriculture. The Bushy Heads represent people from the other side of the world where the seasons are reversed.

BUSHYHEAD, JESSE (Unaduti, Tas-the-ghe-tee-hee, Dta-ske-gi-di-hi) *(?–1844) Cherokee* The first Cherokee to be ordained as a Baptist minister. Born shortly after 1800 in the Great Smoky Mountains, Bushyhead's ancestry included John Stuart, a British agent to the Indians who had married a Cherokee woman. After attending school in Tennessee, he returned to Amohee, his hometown located on the western edge of the Great Smoky Mountains, as a devout Christian and began preaching to his people. He decided to be baptized by immersion after studying the Bible, and in 1830 a Baptist preacher from Tennessee administered the rite. Bushyhead was instrumental in converting other Cherokees to Christianity and establishing a church at Amohee.

He became a close associate of the Reverend EVAN JONES, who recommended him for an assistant missionary position with the Baptist Board of Foreign Missions in 1832. The recommendation was accepted, and Bushyhead held the post for 11 years. Following his April 1833 ordination, he served as pastor of the Amohee church while working with Evans to further missionary efforts and to translate religious works into the Cherokee language. Bushyhead also held a number of high offices among his people and served as his nation's delegate to Washington, D.C., on several occasions. In 1834 he was appointed as a justice of the Cherokee Supreme Court, and from 1838 to 1839 he and Evans were chosen to lead removal groups to Indian Territory (present-day Oklahoma) during the forced migration from their homeland known as the Trail of Tears. They reestablished their mission in the new location and continued their religious efforts.

Bushyhead served as a founder and president of the National Temperance Society among his people, traveled to New York City to address fellow Baptists at an annual meeting of the Baptist Board of Foreign Missions and completed a translation of the book of Genesis, which was published in *The Cherokee Messenger*. Although a central figure in a controversy over slavery that led to a schism between Northern and Southern Baptists, the Cherokee minister died on July 17, 1844, before the issue was resolved. The belief persisted that he was asked to resign by his missionary board over his alleged ownership of slaves, but that was not the case. According to Jones, Bushyhead had once bought one black family for the purpose of setting them free, and his wife had inherited a female slave who had also been released. Bushyhead was succeeded in his pastorate post by LEWIS DOWNING.

Bushyhead's family included his eldest son, Dennis, who served as a principal chief for two terms between 1879 and 1887. Bushyhead's Cherokee name has also been cited as Tas-the-ghe-tee-hee or Dta-ske-gi-di-hi. He has at times been erroneously identified as John Bushyhead.

BUSK *Southeast* A term derived from *puskita,* "to fast," in the Creek (Muskogee) language, Busk was generally applied to the annual religious observance, often called the GREEN CORN CEREMONY, that brought in the Creek new year. The busk has been referred to as one of the New World's "oldest unbroken ceremonial traditions." Believed to have been practiced as early as the precontact Mississippian culture, it continues as the major traditional religious observance of the Creek, Seminole, Yuchi, and other southeastern Native American groups to the present day.

Traditionally held when the green corn ripened, the ceremony served many purposes. Besides its association with agricultural growth and fertility, it was a period of renewal, thanksgiving, and amnesty. During the busk the people ritually prepared to eat the new corn, a new SACRED FIRE was kindled, transgressions committed during the previous year were forgiven, and everything was purified and renewed for the new year. Early accounts indicate that the busk was generally held from four to eight days in the town square. Today it is conducted on the "square ground" or ceremonial center of a tribal community. As earlier, ritual elements include making the sacred new fire, fasting, praying, offerings, "GOING TO WATER," medicine taking, a SCRATCHING CEREMONY, naming ceremonies, Stomp dancing, traditional ball games, and a feast of traditional corn dishes.

BUTLER, ELIZUR *(1794–?)* A physician and missionary among the Cherokee people. Butler was born in Norfolk, Connecticut, on June 11, 1974, and began working at Brainerd Mission near Chattanooga, Tennessee, under the auspices of the AMERICAN BOARD OF COMMISSIONERS FOR FOREIGN MISSIONS in the Cherokee Nation at the age of 27. After three years, he was sent to Creek Path, which later became Guntersville, Tennessee. In 1826 he was transferred to Haweis Mission near Rome, Georgia. A few years later, in 1831, he was arrested for failing to swear allegiance to the state of Georgia as required in order to obtain a license to continue working in the Cherokee Nation. Convicted and sentenced to four years at hard labor, Butler and his colleague, the Reverend SAMUEL AUSTIN WORCESTER, were imprisoned until January 14, 1833. The U.S. Supreme Court decision in their case, *Worcester v. Georgia,* which denied the state's claims of jurisdiction, remains fundamental to federal Indian law. Although the case was a legal victory for the Cherokee Nation, the law was not enforced, and Native people were forcibly removed to Indian Territory (present-day Oklahoma).

After rejoining his family at Haweis from prison, Butler returned to Brainerd Mission to escape further persecution. He was ordained on April 14, 1838 and accompanied Cherokee people to the West the following year. He later took charge of Fairfield Mission in Indian Territory, remaining in the post for 10 years until he became superintendent of the Cherokee Female Seminary. After Butler's first wife, Esther Post Butler, died at Haweis on November 21, 1829, he was remarried on August 14, 1830, to Lucy Ames.

BUTRICK, DANIEL SABIN *(1789–1851)* A Presbyterian missionary to the Cherokee people. Born in Windsor, Massachusetts, Butrick began working among the Cherokee shortly after his ordination in 1817 in Boston. He served at a number of mission stations, including Brainerd, Carmel, or Talonagy, Creek Path, Haweis, and Hightower, in the southeastern Appalachian region under the auspices of the AMERICAN BOARD OF COMMISSIONERS FOR FOREIGN MISSIONS. During the conflict of 1829 to 1833 over Georgia's law requiring whites to swear an oath of allegiance and to obtain a state license to work in the Cherokee Nation, Butrick disagreed with the position taken by SAMUEL AUSTIN WORCESTER, ELIZUR BUTLER, and other missionaries. Instead of testing the constitutionality of the requirement or signing the loyalty oath, he moved to the mission station at Candy's Creek in Tennessee and ministered to the Cherokee in Georgia as an itinerant preacher. John Thompson and Isaac Proctor, other colleagues, supported his position on the issue and also moved out of the state. Butrick viewed his role in the spiritual realm rather than the political and chose to work around the law rather than to test it. During the years 1834 to 1839, Butrick opposed plans to remove the Cherokee from their southeastern homeland to Indian Territory (present-day Oklahoma). He denounced a removal treaty obtained by Andrew Jackson through the Reverend John F. Schermerhorn in 1835, signed by a few Native leaders, which violated Cherokee law. In 1839 he arrived in Indian Territory, where he continued his work at Fairfield, Mount Zion, and Dwight mission stations until his death. Butrick contributed to the descriptions of Cherokee life collected by John Howard Payne, another early observer who investigated conditions among the Cherokee before their removal. Their manuscripts, at the Newberry Library in Chicago, include accounts of SIX CHEROKEE FESTIVALS and other aspects of the history, culture, and religion of the group.

BYHAN, GOTTLIEB *(fl. early 1800s)* A Moravian missionary affiliated with the first permanent mission in the Cherokee Nation in the Southern Appalachian states. After negotiations were held between the Cherokee National Council and Moravian representatives, the denomination was accepted "on trial." Byhan and a colleague, Abraham Steiner, traveled from Salem, North Carolina, and arrived in April 1801 to establish the mission station. The Moravians called the site Springplace. It was located in the Upper Town region of the Cherokee Nation in northwestern Georgia. The missionaries began building a cabin, farm, and other facilities. Cherokee leaders, who had accepted the missionaries to begin a boarding school, were so dissatisfied with their progress that in 1803 they gave them notice to deliver the education promised or to leave the nation. The Moravians eventually agreed to take a few boarding students, but the number of youth served remained small. Besides having a limited staff and budget, Byhan and the other missionaries did not know the Cherokee language, and the mission model they relied on was not adapted to the unique circumstances of the group.

During the removal crisis, in which the Cherokee were uprooted from their homelands and forced to move west of the Mississippi, Byhan signed a manifesto against removal with missionaries from other denominations independently of his mission board. He also refused to sign the oath of allegiance required of him and other whites in the Cherokee Nation by the state of Georgia. Byhan remained at Springplace because he believed that his federal status as a postmaster protected him from the state's new law. One of his colleagues was arrested but was released after promising to leave Georgia. Byhan, initially told by his mission board to resign the postmaster job to avoid political difficulties, was able to continue in his work at Springplace. After asking to be relieved of his missionary duties, he left the area in March 1832. Springplace Mission closed the following year.

BYINGTON, CYRUS *(1793–1868)* Pioneering Presbyterian missionary and linguist who worked among the Choctaw for nearly 50 years. Byington was born on March 11, 1793, in Stockbridge. Massachusetts, the son of Isaiah and Lucy Byington. At the age of 14, he was taken into the home of the early 19th-century scholar Joseph Wood-

bridge for instruction. Besides studying Greek and Latin, he read law with his teacher. Admitted to the bar in 1814, he practiced law in Stockbridge and Sheffield, Massachusetts, until two years later, when he began studying for a new career as a clergyman.

Byington became affiliated with the Presbyterian Church before entering Andover Theological Seminary in 1816. Graduating in 1819, he was licensed to preach and wanted to work as a missionary to the Armenians in Turkey. After receiving an appointment with the AMERICAN BOARD OF COMMISSIONERS FOR FOREIGN MISSIONS (ABCFM) in the New England area, he was asked to accompany a missionary group assigned to the Choctaw Nation in Mississippi. The group, numbering more than 20, traveled to Pittsburgh in wagons, then via a flatboat down the Ohio and Mississippi Rivers in 1820. Byington was placed in charge of the Elliot Mission, which had been established two years earlier as the first American Board mission among the Choctaw, replacing CYRUS KINGSBURY, a fellow missionary, at the post. A short time later he notified the board of his intention to remain with the Choctaw people for the rest of his life.

At Elliot Mission, Byington began studying the Choctaw language. By the end of 1822 he had started to travel to communities where no English was used, remaining for days at a time to aid his studies. He later worked with the Reverend ALFRED WRIGHT and David Folsom, a mixed-blood Choctaw leader who possessed skills in English, on a system of orthography for the Native language. In 1825 their efforts resulted in the completion of the first Choctaw-language publication, *A Spelling Book, written in the Chahta Language with an English translation,* printed in Cincinnati, Ohio. By 1827 Byington had revised the book and spent most of that year in Cincinnati, where he supervised the publication of the speller and other manuscripts while also arranging his ordination to the ministry and his marriage to Sophia Nye. The new publications assisted in the teaching of Choctaw before, or even without, English, as well as the establishment of schools in the Choctaw Nation where the Native language alone was taught and the implementation of adult-education programs. They also helped to overcome the mission's early failure at winning Choctaw converts to Christianity.

Byington, who had opposed the federal government's removal of the Choctaw from their ancestral homeland in Mississippi to Indian Territory (present-day Oklahoma), began the work of rebuilding his mission in the new location. He left Mississippi in 1834, completing his family's move the following year. After settling near Eagletown in what is now Oklahoma, Byington organized a church and worked on the Choctaw grammar and dictionary he had started earlier. From 1836 to 1844, he also prepared an annual *Choctaw*

Almanac, which cited statistics and other information about the tribe. Most of his scholarly efforts, however, focused on the translation and revision of materials for use in instruction. He supervised a female boarding school, Ianubbee, from 1844 to 1853, when he asked the ABCFM to relieve him of the responsibility. Byington began directing the Choctaw linguistic work alone after his friend and colleague Alfred Wright died in 1853.

Controversy over the issue of slavery affected Byington and other missionaries among the Choctaw. Although he shared his mission board's abolitionist views, they caused conflict with slaveholding members of the tribe. In 1856 Byington and other missionaries resigned from the American Board, and the Choctaw Mission was later sponsored by the Presbyterian Church, Old School.

Byington died in Ohio on December 31, 1868. At the time he was revising the *Grammar of the Choctaw Language* for the seventh time. Started when Byington was a young missionary in Mississippi, the book was published two years after his death. Another publication, *A Dictionary of the Choctaw Language,* was not published until 1915. Byington also completed translations of biblical works and other religious materials. His authoritative linguistic work continues to be used in the present day.

CACIQUE *Keresan and Tanoan Pueblo* A word taken from the Arawak language and used by early chroniclers to designate a priest-chief. The word was incorporated into the Spanish language and eventually imposed on the Pueblo vocabulary. In New Mexico, the term is now used by both Indians and non-Indians to designate the highest ranking priest or chief, the custodian of the spiritual and physical welfare of his people who heads the politico-religious pueblo organization.

The cacique holds office for life and has a staff as a badge of authority. He cares for the whole pueblo, acting as an intermediary between the people and the spirit world. He spends most of his time fasting, praying, and performing rituals and leads a good life so that all the spirits will bestow their blessings on Pueblo people. He sanctions all communal pueblo rituals and ceremonies. He makes yearly appointments of officers, selecting annually the two WAR CAPTAINS and assistants.

In Tanoan pueblos, each tribal moiety (half) has its own priest or cacique. The two caciques, or moiety chiefs, who serve for life and are dedicated to the spiritual and secular well being of the village, alternate their religious obligations. The summer cacique is responsible for the religious welfare of the village from the vernal to autumnal equinox, the winter cacique from the autumnal to the vernal equinox. The caciques initiate, sanction, and administer all ceremonies in which the whole village is involved as well as those associated with each moiety that include calendrically determined rites. Within the moiety, each cacique is concerned with the moiety initiations, kachina performances, and initiations

and ritual activities of the Winter and Summer Societies. The moiety chiefs alternate in appointing the nonpermanent ritual and secular officials of the pueblo, who all serve one-year terms. In Keresan pueblos, the cacique is invariably a medicine man, a spiritual, not an executive, ruler of his people. (See also TANOAN MOIETY CEREMONIAL ORGANIZATION.)

CALIFORNIA MISSION SYSTEM *(1769–1834)* Spanish Franciscan missionaries built 21 missions along the coastal trail of California composing a system whose purpose was to convert California Indians to Christianity. Members of the Hupa, Kumeyaay, Cahuilla, Pauma, Malki, Cupa, and at least 17 more tribes lived in mission captivity. For more than 200 years, however, these people have erroneously been called "Mission Indians." The missions, which stretched for more than 500 miles between San Diego and Sonoma, lasted from 1769, when Father JUNÍPERO SERRA, considered the architect of the mission system, founded the first mission San Diego de Alcala, until 1834 when the Mexican government confiscated mission lands, herds, and buildings.

A number of forces in the mission environment reduced the Indian population by more than 50 percent. The Indians' suboptimal diet predisposed them to disease. Spanish animals (cattle, sheep, horses) destroyed large numbers of Indian food-producing fields. During drought years, the Indians of southern California ate food from seeds they sowed that lay dormant in the soil for up to 20 years until the right combination of rain, sun, and fire caused them to sprout and produce. Cattle and sheep ate these emergency foods as well. Poor

Missons, South to North	Year Founded	Baptisms to 1832	Deaths to 1832	In Territory of Indian Tribe
San Diego de Alcalá	1769	6,522	4,322	Diegueño
San Luis Rey de Francia	1798	5,399	2,718	Luiseño
San Juan Capistrano	1776	4,340	3,126	Juaneño
San Gabriel Arcángel	1771	7,825	5,670	Gabrieleño
San Fernando Rey de España	1797	2,784	1,983	Fernandeño
San Buenaventura	1782	3,875	3,150	Chumash
Santa Bárbara	1786	5,556	3,936	Chumash
Santa Inéz	1804	1,348	1,227	Chumash
La Purísima Concepción	1787	3,255	2,609	Chumash
San Luis Obispo de Tolosa	1772	2,644	2,268	Chumash
San Miguel Arcángel	1797	2,471	1,868	Salinan
San Antonio de Padua	1771	4,419	3,617	Salinan
Nuestra Señora de la Soledad	1791	2,131	1,705	Costanoan
San Carlos Borromeo de Camelo	1770	3,827	2,837	Costanoan
San Juan Bautista	1797	4,016	2,854	Costanoan
Santa Cruz	1791	2,439	1,972	Costanoan
Santa Clara de Asís	1777	8,536	6,809	Costanoan
San José de Guadalupe	1797	6,673	4,800	Costanoan
San Francisco de Asís	1776	6,898	5,166	Costanoan
San Rafael Arcángel	1817	1,821	652	Coast Miwok
San Francisco Solano	1823	1,008	500	Coast Miwok
Total		87,787	63,789	

Engelhardt, Zephyrin. The Missions and Missionaries of California. *San Francisco: James H. Barry, 1908–1915.*

yields from mission fields of European-introduced crops (wheat, barley, corn), which depended on normal rainfall, could not replace emergency foods that responded to erratic rainfall. Cattle and sheep destroyed the foods that native deer, mountain sheep, antelope, and rabbits ate in drought years, reducing Indian meat sources. Eventually, Spanish animals died during the dry spells as well. Along the with destruction of Indian crops and meat sources, confinement, forced labor, punishment, the missions' overpopulation, the Indians' lack of immunity to disease, forced conversions, and the destruction of Indian identity sapped the Indians' collective strength. In 1834, 60,000 deaths were recorded, and 15,000 remaining Indians were released from the 21 missions after the missionaries were expelled.

From the beginning of missionization, Indians resisted and revolted. Uprisings took place frequently at San Diego, at missions around the San Francisco Bay area, at Santa Barbara, and at San Gabriel. The missions and their founding date are listed in the chart above.

CAMPANIUS, JOHAN *(1601–1683)* A Lutheran clergyman who ministered to Swedish colonists in Delaware and served as a missionary to neighboring Indians. Born in Stockholm on August 15, 1601, he was the son of Jonas Peter Campanius, a parish clerk. Campanius attended the Stock-

holm gymnasium, studied theology at the University of Upsala, and was ordained on July 19, 1633. He arrived at Fort Christina (now Wilmington) on February 15, 1643 and began his ministerial and missionary work.

After learning the Algonquian language of the Delaware (Lenni Lenape), Campanius started producing vocabularies and other materials. These preliminary efforts enabled him to complete a more difficult task, the translation of Luther's *Shorter Catechism.* Although it was not printed until 1696, after Campanius's death, it represents one of the earliest attempts by a European to write in a Native American language. Published in Stockholm at the expense of King Charles XI, 500 copies of the Swedish-Delaware catechism were sent to America. Campanius also recorded Native folkways, observing similarities with the ancient Hebrews. His work, which predated that of the New England missionary JOHN ELIOT by a few years, provided a foundation for William Penn and others who came after him. In 1646 he built a church at Tinicum (Tennakong), nine miles from Philadelphia. Although Campanius stayed in America for less than six years, his work earned him a reputation as the best-known minister of his denomination. After his return to Sweden in 1648, he served as the pastor of congregations at Frosthult and Hernevi until his death on September 17, 1683.

California mission system. A map shows the geographic range of missionization in California. *From* Native Americans of California and Nevada *by Jack Forbes, with permission of Natauregraph Publishers, Inc., of Happy Camp, California.*

CAMPOS, AGUSTÍN DE *(1669–1737)* Spanish Jesuit. A Jesuit from the age of 15, Campos was a protégé of Father EUSEBIO FRANCISCO KINO and ministered to Pimas nearly twice as long as his mentor. He began his ministry at San Ignacio in Pimería Alta, a vast region extending over northern Sonora and southern Arizona, in 1693 at the age of 24 and served until 1737. After Kino's death in 1711, Father Campos's missionary work kept the Pimas tied to Catholicism. He knew their language, which assisted him to baptize over 1,000 people between 1716 and 1720.

CANADIAN INDIAN ACT (Potlatch Law) *Canada* Passed in 1884 and effective January 1, 1885, this law made a person who engaged in a potlatch guilty of a misdemeanor and liable to imprisonment for a term of two to six months. The law, which emerged out of demands from Indian field agents and missionaries in direct contact with Indians of the north Pacific coast, attempted to negate the Indian past and legis-

late religious practice from 1884 to 1951. Further prohibitions of traditional dance and customs (such as the SPIRIT DANCE CEREMONIAL) were introduced in 1895, 1914, and 1933. Enforcing the law on the mainland coast of British Columbia and Vancouver Island was costly. Funds were required for building jails and paying for lawyers, court actions, and salaries for constables. The federal and provincial governments also disputed which one would enforce the law. Before the two governments reached agreement, a long campaign for repeal of the law was initiated. Although Ottawa insisted on enforcement, actual policy was lenient with potlatchers. There were a number of suspended sentences and agreements with Indians who promised to give up the custom. Indians also discovered ways to potlatch in spite of the law, surreptitiously and privately. The 1946–48 Canada Special Joint Committee of the Senate and House of Commons on the Indian Act reported a lack of success of government policy. The committee found anachronisms and contradictions in the Indian Act and recommended changes. The recommended amendment or appeal took place in the Indian Act of 1951, which removed government control excesses of culture prohibitions and of local affairs on the reserves, but by the time the government lifted its ban, serious damage had been done to potlatching rites. (See also MEMORIAL POTLATCH.)

CARIBOU FESTIVAL *Alaska Inuit* The principal ceremony of the Alaska Arctic Inuit in the inland regions, where hunting caribou is of prime importance. The rites were carried on in late winter, just before spring hunts. Each hunting group had a shaman, who called the caribou. There were taboos for the hunting group members and the community before, during and after the hunt. A temporary *KARIGI,* the place of ceremonial activity, was erected, and rituals included new clothing for men, songs, ceremonies for greeting the caribou, social festivities, and the final ceremony of thanking the caribou for their gift of sustenance to the group. (See also BLADDER FESTIVAL.)

CARDINAL DIRECTIONS See SIX DIRECTIONS

CARIGOUAN (Carigonan) *(?–c. 1634/5) Montagnais* Seventeenth-century medicine man who lived in what is now northern Quebec. Carigouan was described by the Jesuit PAUL LEJEUNE, who spent the winter of 1633–34 with him and his followers in the region south of the lower St. Lawrence. Hosted by Carigouan's brother, Mestigoit, the missionary observed the SHAKING TENT CEREMONY, feasts of the bear and other rituals. Besides observing traditional religious practices, LeJeune held conversations with Carigouan and his followers about their beliefs concerning the origin of creation, the restoration of the universe after a flood and the nature of souls, considered shadows with physical characteristics and therefore needing food, drink, and rest. Carigouan's followers included two other brothers, Pastedechouan and Sasousmat.

Although LeJeune was able to observe Carigouan's group, the medicine man was opposed to the French in general, and to LeJeune in particular. The priest in turn considered him "vile to the last degree" and tried to discredit him. Carigouan demanded presents, thwarted the Jesuit's efforts to study the Native language, and often threatened his life. LeJeune's missionary efforts were successful only when the medicine man joined his prayers at Christmas in a time of great want.

Carigouan died during the winter of 1634–35 in a fire started by one of his own people, who wanted to free himself from caring for the medicine man, by then ill. Carigouan's son was baptized by LeJeune in 1636. (See also PIGAROUICH, ETIENNE.)

CARR, JOHN H. *(c. 1812–?)* A Methodist missionary in Indian Territory (present-day Oklahoma). Born in Wilson County, Tennessee, Carr moved with his family to Arkansas in 1833 and became a minister the following year. Leaving the ministry after two years, he reentered the field about ten years later. In 1845 he joined the Indian Mission Conference, an annual conference that had been organized the year before near Tahlequah in the Cherokee Nation in present-day Oklahoma. Carr's missionary assignments in Indian Territory included six years with the Doaksville circuit in the Choctaw Nation and the superintendency of Bloomfield Academy, a school for girls that opened in the Chickasaw Nation in 1853. Under Carr's direction, the enrollment increased from 25 in 1853 to 60 by 1860. The students, generally between eight and 12 years of age, were instructed in academic subjects, domestic work, and religious topics. Carr also served as the secretary of the Indian Mission Conference from 1857 until 1866.

CASE, WILLIAM *(1780–1855)* Born in Swansea, Massachusetts, Case became known as "the father of the early Methodist Indian mission work in Upper Canada." After entering the ministry, he began his tenure in the missionary field in 1805. He worked in Upper Canada for many years, and later extended his efforts to the Mississauga, a branch of Ojibway located on the north shore of Lake Ontario. Case was appointed presiding elder of New York's Cayuga district (1810) and of Canada's eastern district (1815) before serving in the same position in the Canadian western district from 1816 to 1828. When the Upper Canada Methodists ended their

American ties, Case became general superintendent of the newly founded Upper Canada Conference.

Recognizing the effectiveness of Native religious leaders among their own people, Case carefully selected and trained a number of them for service in the mission field. Case served as a mentor to the young Ojibway minister PETER JONES but later offended him by selecting a non-Indian minister, JAMES EVANS, to retranslate materials Jones had already completed. Case's work among the Mississauga, begun in 1823, included the establishment of a chapel, school, hospital, store, cabins, and other buildings at Grape Island in the Bay of Quinte with funds raised on tours. He was joined there for a time by JOHN SUNDAY, an Ojibway missionary and chief. Case maintained his position as superintendent of Indian missions and schools when the Upper Canada Conference and the Wesleyan Methodists united in 1833, and Joseph Stinson was named general superintendent.

Case married Hetty Hubbard on May 4, 1829, and shortly before his 50th birthday became the father of a daughter. Following Hetty's death in 1831, he married Eliza Barnes, a fellow mission worker. Case was known as Keche makahdawekoonahya or "the big black-coat man" among the Ojibway. (See also CLARK, JOHN; COPWAY, GEORGE; STEINHAUER, HENRY BIRD.)

CATALDO, JOSEPH M. *(1837–1928)* Italian Jesuit missionary who worked among Indians of the Pacific Northwest for 63 years. He was born in Sicily and entered the Society of Jesus at the age of 15 years in 1852. He was ordained to the priesthood in 1862 in Belgium and sailed for America one week later. After completing his studies in California, he traveled in 1865 to Sacred Heart Mission, near Lake Coeur d'Alene, Idaho, where he studied the Kalispel language. In the winter of 1866, he began his first missionary work among the Spokane. In 1867, he introduced Catholicism to the Nez Perce people in Idaho Territory and remained with them off and on for 61 years.

The Nez Perce converts never numbered more than 300, less than 10 percent of the tribe, and Father Cataldo became frustrated by the lack of results over his lifetime. He felt he arrived too late—the Nez Perce had requested a priest as early as 1831—to offset the gains of the Presbyterian Church, which had been sanctioned earlier by the U.S. government to convert the Nez Perce. Father Cataldo enjoyed the respect of the Indians and made it a practice not to make recommendations in secular affairs. He struggled, however, with Indian agents, Presbyterians, bureaucrats in the federal government and his own order to further his missionary ends.

The occupants of Wallowa Valley, Oregon, refused to recognize the treaty by which the tribe was confined to a reservation at Lapwai, Idaho, and, under Chief Joseph,

Joseph Cataldo. Nez Perce and other tribes gathered at the March 1928 celebration of Cataldo's 91st birthday and 75th anniversary as a Jesuit priest at the old Sacred Heart mission in present-day Cataldo, Idaho. *Oregon Province Archives, Gonzaga University, Crosby Library.*

resisted, resulting in the Nez Perce War of 1877. After the war, the Nez Perce and other tribes showed little interest in Catholicism, and Father Cataldo's task was to revitalize their interest in Catholic theology. As superior of the Northwest Rocky Mountain missions from 1876 to 1892, he increased the number of Jesuits in the area threefold, increased mission stations from seven to 11 and oversaw the arrival of three orders of nuns. He established a Jesuit novitiate in Desmet, Idaho, which he considered his chief contribution; he was determined that missionary work in America should be done by American-born and -educated priests. He also founded five mission boarding schools for Indians, two preparatory schools for whites, and two colleges, one of which is Gonzaga University in Spokane, Washington, a city he helped found. In 1928, the people of Lewiston, Idaho, commemorated Father Cataldo's 75th anniversary as a Jesuit at a church he had established 60 years earlier and in March of that year the people of Spokane celebrated his 91st birthday. He died a month after the celebrations, in Oregon.

CATCH-THE-STONE CEREMONY *Lakota* A healing ceremony described as sharing similarities with the YUWIPI curing rite

and possibly derived from it. Its elements include praying, singing, and summoning spirits for assistance during the course of the meeting. The participant is given a sacred stone that is believed to provide spiritual protection. (See also EAGLE CEREMONY.)

CATCHES, PETER *(b./c. 1915–1993) Lakota* A medicine man and healer who also served as a Catholic catechist and a peyote roadman on the Pine Ridge Reservation in South Dakota. Catches, an orphan, was brought up in a Catholic mission school, and became a teacher of catechism. He eventually turned to traditional Lakota beliefs, becoming a healer and an adviser, while continuing to practice Catholicism. Instructed by a holy man in the generation before his, Catches began conducting EAGLE CEREMONY power rituals and training apprentices. He also became a SUN DANCE leader and undertook a number of responsibilities in connection with the sacred ceremony, including serving as chief dancer and instructing candidates.

According to Thomas H. Lewis, a psychiatrist and anthropologist who wrote about Catches, the medicine man started altering some of his religious practices in the 1970s.

He advised against using non-Native objects, including metal and glass, and began rejecting rides in automobiles. Living close to the natural world with few material possessions, he reached destinations distant from his home by walking. His involvement with Catholicism also changed at this time, diminishing and then ending. Lewis further noted that Catches, who had earlier rejected peyotism, began to add Half-Moon peyote ceremonies to his religious practices. The devout holy man is also known to have conducted regular fasts at BEAR BUTTE and other sacred sites, SWEAT LODGE purification rituals, Eagle curing ceremonies on a regular basis, and other traditional observances. (See also PEYOTE RELIGION.)

CATLINITE   See PIPESTONE

CELILO FALLS   An ancient place of worship and fishery for the Umatilla, Nez Perce, Yakama, and Warm Springs Indians (tribes of middle Oregon) on the Columbia River. Ceremonies took place at this sacred site, beginning with the FIRST FOOD OBSERVANCES in the spring when salmon returned, until it was flooded by construction of the Dalles Dam, completed in 1957.

CEMENTATION, OR RECONCILIATION, FESTIVAL *Cherokee*
The fifth of the six CHEROKEE FESTIVALS described by the 19th-century missionary DANIEL SABIN BUTRICK and other early observers in the Cherokee Nation before the forced removal of the tribal group from the southeastern Appalachian region to Indian Territory (present-day Oklahoma). Also called the Propitiation Festival, its purpose included removing uncleanness, and therefore the possibility of disease, as well as forming binding friendships. The Cementation, or Reconciliation, Festival was held about 10 days after the GREAT NEW MOON FEAST and took place at the capital of the Cherokee Nation. The ancient capital, Chota, or Great

Celilo Falls. Native Americans fishing around 1900 at Celilo Falls, an ancient place of worship before it was flooded by Dalles Dam in Oregon in 1957. *Oregon Historical Society, Benjamin Gifford photo, OrHi 4463.*

Echota, was located on the south side of the Little Tennessee River below Citico Creek in Tennessee. New Echota in Georgia also served as the capital for a number of years before the removal. A number of officials were appointed to help with the preparations, including seven women to serve as dance leaders, seven musicians to assist them, seven persons to clean the national heptagon or council house area, seven men to hunt game, and another seven participants to obtain seven articles to be purified. A fire maker and six assistants were also selected to make the new SACRED FIRE. These officials began fasting seven days before the observance. A dance was performed by the women the evening before the festival began. Ritual elements of the Cementation, or Reconciliation, Festival included the making of the sacred new fire with seven different types of wood, cleansing of houses by the designated seven people, the extinguishment of old fires, the securing of new fire by participants for their homes, the singing of hymns by the Jowah singer, a religious figure appointed for life, and "GOING TO WATER," or ritual cleansing in the river. The people fasted on the first and fourth days. During the festival differences or conflicts were forgotten, old clothing and other articles were discarded, and the people started anew. The ceremony in ancient times is said to have included the establishment of friendship bonds between men and between males and females from different clans. A number of local variations later occurred in the four-day observance.

CEREMONIAL LABOR (Tekipanoa) *Yaqui* The expression of a working relationship with the Christian spirits, as defined by Jesuits, involved order and rules. Its execution maintained an orderly and predictable world of the towns. Planned activities for productive purposes were applied both to the work of farming and herding for the missionaries and to ceremonial labor oriented toward Christian values and concepts. Tekipanoa was also a technique of transformation. It turned the HUYA ANIYA, the Yaqui's natural domain, into town lands.

CEREMONIAL RELAY RACE *Jicarilla Apache* The Jicarilla Apache of northwestern New Mexico hold an annual race in mid-September on San Antonio's Day. This rite, a LONG LIFE CEREMONY and part of a harvest festival, benefits the runners and other participants with longevity and health. The race is run to ensure a balanced and regular food supply for the Jicarilla, who were both hunters and food producers. The race is between the Ollero band, who represent the sun and animals, and the Llanero band, who represent the moon and plants. The race determines the relative abundance of meat or plant foods for the year, depending on the winners, or even amounts of food if no winner. The ceremonial track is laid out on a east-west course. Preparations include a preliminary race that determines the head runners, ground drawing (sacred sand paintings) in the kiva over which the runners walk absorbing the symbols and strength into their bodies and the preparation of materials for decorating the runners. Before each race, both sides dance and sing in ritual ways along the racetrack. Boys at the age of puberty are expected to participate at least once as a religious responsibility. The runners observe ritual taboos. After the race, there is feasting. See CEREMONIAL RUNNING AND GAMES.

CEREMONIAL RUNNER *Mesquakie* The ceremonial runner, called an *a'ckapawa,* was a tribal messenger who regularly ran hundreds of miles to communicate information among his own people as well as to distant groups. This highly respected position was rooted in religious belief and practice and, only individuals who were spiritually blessed and instructed could hold it. The lifelong post required strict adherence to a number of rules, including dietary restrictions, personal cleanliness, moral injunctions, and celibacy. The ceremonial runner had to willingly undertake errands no matter how difficult they were or when they occurred. Besides serving as a messenger, he also decided an issue when councilmen could not do so and announced deaths among the people. Blessed with speed, he also had the ability to control the weather and other spiritual gifts. At one time, ceremonial runners included a leader and two successors. The last remaining one, who prophesied ruinous changes for the people, was remembered in a 1920s account. His name is unknown, but in the 1860s he ran more than 400 miles from the area of Green Bay, Wisconsin, to warn Sauk people living along the Missouri River of a pending enemy attack. The ceremonial runner is believed to have been in his fifties at the time.

CEREMONIAL RUNNING AND GAMES Running plays a vital role in many Native American religions. People try to influence their fate through symbolic actions. Ritual runs or footraces are performed to hasten the growth of a crop for a good harvest, to help bring rain or snow, and to give strength to the sun in its journey. Games are played for crop growth and rain as well. Fasting, sexual abstinence, emetics, and dietary rules prepared men and women for the practical and spiritual rewards of running. The Nunivak Inuit hold a foot race during the BLADDER FESTIVAL. Running honors the dead whose spirits accompany the runners. Pueblo peoples who favor running events, kick ball, and kick-stick identify running, motion, and life force with these activities. The runners undergo transformations and become the sun on its path or rain blown by the wind. Around the solstices and equinoxes, virtually all the Pueblo peoples have ceremonial relay races associated with the movements of the sun. In February, the Tewa have a sacred ball race. A ball stuffed with seeds is kicked by men running circuits around the village. Eventually, the ball breaks open and seeds are scattered across the earth. The Jicarilla Apache hold a race in September that ensures a balanced and regular food supply. Zuni and Hopi clowns or kachinas play games or race before or between dances. There are running segments in the girl's puberty rituals of the Apache and Navajo peoples. The running feature symbolically fashions the girl's body to be as strong and upright as CHANGING WOMAN (Navajo,) or WHITE PAINTED WOMAN (Apache). Puberty running was also performed in California and up the Pacific Coast, Great Basin, and Plateau areas. (See also CEREMONIAL RELAY RACE.)

CEREMONIAL SOCIETIES *North Pacific Coast* Ceremonial societies, which each own their own dances held during winter ceremonials, exist among the Tlingit, Haida, Tsimshian, Bella Coola, Kwakiutl, Nootka, Comox, Pentlatch, Sanitch, Lkungen, Clallam, and Quileute. Membership comes through purchase by fathers, or mothers, and those who are initiated as members because they obtained guardian spirits for that particular society. Each society has distinct GUARDIAN SPIRITS, face paintings, headgear, and rattles. Only members are entitled to wear the headgear and display the face painting. The societies have initiation rituals in which the novice reaches an understanding of the qualities of the guardian spirit. (See also DANCING SOCIETIES; WINTER CEREMONIAL [North Pacific Coast and Salish].)

CEREMONIAL SPONSORSHIP *Southwest* Acquired by individuals at different stages of the life cycle, ceremonial sponsors, or parents, have ritual relationships and duties. Sponsorship makes kinship ties between unrelated people that are binding for life. Ceremonial sponsors are selected when a person becomes a member of a kachina or curing society. At Zuni, the ceremonial father is the person who cures an individual in a curing ceremonial. There are elaborate exchanges of food between the novice's family and the women of the ceremonial father's family. Hopi have sponsors for all the societies and groups to which they belong. In Apache puberty ceremonies, a lifelong relationship is established between the girl and the priest and attendant who become "mother" and "father" to her. Gifts and affection are exchanged throughout life and there are reciprocal lifelong obligations between the girl and her family and those of the sponsor. They are expected to help each other whenever the need arises. Yaqui acquire sponsors who perform duties at baptism, Catholic Church confirmation, marriage, death, and entrance into ceremonial societies.

CHANGING WOMAN *Apache* See WHITE PAINTED WOMAN

CHANGING WOMAN *Navajo (Dineh)* The principal deity called by some the "mother" of the Navajo. Child of First Man and First Woman, she was the first woman to give physical birth (after impregnation by Sun, her husband) to twin sons, Monster Slayer and Child of the Water, or Born for Water. She created Earth Surface People, whom Navajo recognize as their ancestors. Changing Woman, whose power over reproduction and birth extended to all that existed on the earth, consistently wished well to Earth Surface People. She gave the BLESSING WAY rites, the fundamental ceremony and backbone of the Navajo religion, to the Navajo.

CHANTERS FOR THE DEAD *Iroquois* A society dominated by women who hold closed meetings and who own certain songs sung at the Maple Festival and on occasions for persons troubled by dreams of departed relatives or friends. At an Ohgiwe ceremony, which relieves someone from these troubling dreams, songs are accompanied by a water drum. (See also FEAST TO THE DEAD [Iroquois]).

CHAPAYEKA   See YAQUI CEREMONIALISM

CHAPAYEKA MASKS *Yaqui* Each Chapayeka secretly makes his own sacred new mask of cowhide, goathide, or cardboard. Of great variety, the mask covers the entire head, similar to a helmet. A Chapayeka must follow rigid behavior patterns when handling and wearing the mask. They must not speak when wearing one. There are three major types of masks, including animal-like heads; odd-shaped masks that represent humans; and sharp-nosed, large-eared, sometimes horned, many-colored masks called "flower." At the end of the Waehma, all but one or two of the masks are burned because they are believed to be dangerous. The masks that are kept are saved for burial with members who die during the coming year. (See YAQUI CEREMONIALISM.)

CHAPMAN, EPAPHRAS *(c. 1793–1825)* The first Protestant missionary to the Osage people and the founder of Union Mission. After a preliminary visit to the Osage with an associate in 1819, Chapman returned to New York and assembled a delegation, including 17 adults and some children, as a mission family. They departed for their destination on the Grand River, a tributary of the Arkansas River, on April 20, 1820. After a journey of nearly 10 months, with deaths on the way, the group reached the site Chapman had selected. They then began the work of building Union Mission under the auspices of the United Foreign Mission Society of New York. Early missionary efforts were hampered by war between the Osage and the Cherokee, but eventually new stations were established and the work expanded. Chapman died on January 7, 1825, and William Vaill assumed the leadership role. Union Mission and the other early Protestant stations were closed in the 1830s by their new sponsor, the AMERICAN BOARD OF COMMISSIONERS FOR FOREIGN MISSIONS (ABCFM).

CHARCOAL (Si'k-okskitsis, "Black Wood Ashes") *(1856–1897) Blood* Blood holy man. Born in the southern Alberta homeland of his people, Charcoal was the son of the respected warrior Red Plume and his younger wife Killed Twice. As a youngster he was named Opee-o'wun, or "The Palate," but as a man he was given an honored family name, Paka'panikapi, or Lazy Young Man, and later Si-'k-okskitsis, which was translated as Charcoal. When he was 13, he was stricken with smallpox that left him scarred. Religion was important to Charcoal, and he held memberships in the prestigious Black Soldiers, Crazy Dog, Crow Carriers, Parted Hair, and Horn Societies. He also possessed the Bear Knife, the soldier's medicine pipe and the sacred objects and songs accompanying each society membership.

In 1883 Charcoal, after killing a steer belonging to a nearby rancher in order to feed his family, was apprehended and sentenced to a year in the guardhouse. Incarcerated under ball and chain, his treatment during that period was painful and severe. Upon his release, Charcoal found his wife Apinaki, or Tomorrow Woman, nearly starving, and she died in 1886. By 1891, he had married Pretty Wolverine Woman, a 26-year-old widow. Charcoal took another wife, as was customary among the Blood, in 1896. A short time later, he discovered that Pretty Wolverine Woman had been unfaithful to him and identified Pretty Wolverine Woman's cousin Medicine Pipe Stem as the other man. This discovery was a very serious matter because such a union of relatives was absolutely forbidden by tribal custom and religious memberships required an even higher standard of behavior; Charcoal later shot and killed Medicine Pipe Stem.

Charcoal's understanding of the non-Indian justice system, developed during his earlier incarceration, led him to believe that a person who murdered would automatically be hanged. Convinced that he would pay for Medicine Pipe Stem's death with his life, Charcoal wanted to arrive in the spirit world in an honorable way. According to the old ways of his people, he sought a slain enemy who would serve as his messenger to the spirits. Charcoal selected Edward McNeil, a farm instructor, as the person who would precede him to the spirit world, but his attempt on McNeil's life failed. The Blood holy man was eventually pursued by the Mounted Police in a massive manhunt but was not caught until members of his family, who had been incarcerated, co-

Charcoal. Blood holy man, in an 1897 photograph, wearing clothes provided by the photographer, Steele and Co. In March of that year he was hanged for the murder of two men, Medicine Pipe Stem and an officer of the North West Mounted Police. *Glenbow Museum, Calgary, Alberta.*

operated with the authorities to save the threatened lives of their children. Charcoal was found guilty of killing Medicine Pipe Stem and one of the officers who had pursued him and was hanged on March 16, 1897.

CHAUMONOT, PIERRE-JOSEPH-MARIE *(1611–1693)* French Jesuit missionary who ministered to Huron for 50 years. Born in France, Chaumonot became a Jesuit at the age of 21. He was sent to Canada in 1639 two years after he was ordained, and except for three years among the Onondaga in New York, 1655–58, he devoted his life to work with the Huron people. He learned the Huron language and eventually wrote a Huron grammar and dictionary of dialects. He wrote in his autobiography that "the Huron possesses no turn of phrase, no subtlely nor manner of expression that I am not acquainted with and which I have not . . . discovered." He founded the Huron mission of Notre Dame de Lorette in 1673, which eventually became a place of pilgrimage for the French. Father Chaumonot resigned in 1691, the first religious person to celebrate the golden jubilee of a priestly career at Quebec, the place where he died.

CHECOTE, SAMUEL *(c. 1819–1884) Creek* A Methodist preacher and principal chief of the Creek Nation who was born near Fort Mitchell, Alabama. In 1829 his parents moved their family to Indian Territory (present-day Oklahoma). Checote was educated in mission schools and received his license to preach from the Methodist Church in 1852. During the Civil War he joined the Confederates' First Regiment Creek Mounted Volunteers and provided military leadership as a lieutenant colonel. He commanded the regiment at the Second Battle of Big Cabin in 1864, a victory for the Confederates. After the war, he attempted to mend the division between the Northern and Southern Creek. Although he was chosen as the principal chief of his reunited people in 1867, the election was challenged by the traditionalist Northerners. Checote subsequently held the position, with the exception of four years, from 1867 to 1884. He died near Okmulgee in Indian Territory in 1884.

CHELKONA (Tcirkwena, Skipping Dance, Season Dance, Winter Rain Dance) *Tohono O'odham (Papago)* This ceremony is a blessing for rain and fertility, performed by boys and girls who carry representations of birds, clouds, rainbows, and lightning. One village performs the ceremony as a blessing for another. Performing guests are feasted and paid with gifts. Also called the Skipping Dance, Season Dance, and Winter Rain Dance.

CHEROKEE RELIGIOUS REVIVAL OF 1811 TO 1813 *(1811–1813)* A religious revival that was later named a Ghost Dance movement by the ethnologist James Mooney in 1891. According to various accounts, including one by Thomas L. McKenney, the first director of the Bureau of Indian Affairs, in 1838, the Great Spirit revealed his anger at the Cherokee for abandoning their traditional beliefs and practices and taking on the customs of the whites. The Native people were told to relinquish such non-Indian goods as clothing, plows, fiddles, and spinning wheels and to revive the ways of their ancestors. They were further told that those who failed to heed the revelation would suffer or die. A hailstorm would annihilate the whites and all their cattle, goods, and followers. Only believers who escaped to a certain location in the Great Smoky Mountains would be protected. Upon returning to their homes after the storm, they would discover the reappearance of plentiful deer and other game. The Cherokee people would then live as they had before European contact.

Evidence from various sources, as in the six messages recorded by Moravian missionaries, indicates a number of different prophecies. Some foretold an eclipse rather than a hailstorm while others predicted the destruction of the whites who were bad instead of the entire population. Still others maintained that certain adopted practices could be kept but that others would have to be discarded. Although

McKenney identified one prophet named Charley or Tsa-li, it is likely that there were several others. The only description of rituals associated with the movement was that provided by Colonel Return J. Meigs, agent to the Cherokee, on March 19, 1812. He indicated the revival of traditional religious dances, which were followed by cleansings to wash away sins and defilements. A number of factors may have precipitated the movement, including Cherokee defeat in the warfare of 1776 to 1794, the ceding of large areas of land to non-Indians, intrusions by whites into their remaining territory, internal political and class divisions, the disappearance of game, cultural change, and the occurrence of earthquakes in 1811. (See also GHOST DANCE OF 1870; GHOST DANCE OF 1890.)

CHIEF'S CONVENTION *Iroquois* Sponsored by a particular longhouse community, this is a convention in which the CODE OF HANDSOME LAKE is recited for local edification. The message to convene is delivered orally by a messenger. It is held more frequently than a SIX NATIONS MEETING and scheduled to satisfy a variety of needs, including spiritual stimulus, hearing sacred words, spiritual purging, and a show of respect to HANDSOME LAKE and the Creator. The seating is according to gender. The meeting opens with the THANKSGIVING ADDRESS and an explanation of the nature of the convention. WAMPUM is displayed during the convention. After lunch, sinners confess in public while holding wampum. Days vary according to the amount of time the PREACHER needs to finish his version of the code.

CHIHWATENHA (Chihouatenhoua, Chiohoarebra) *(1602[?]–1640) Huron* Baptized Huron Indian who early on embraced Christian spirituality. Living in Ossossane before the Jesuits arrived there, he was attracted to them from their first contacts. He made a public declaration of his faith in Christianity and was baptized as Joseph on August 16, 1637. Shortly after, he learned to read and write French. He urged other Huron to become Christians and ignored his people's rites. He defended Jesuits at great danger to himself because they were accused of being sorcerers and held responsible for the epidemics decimating the Huron people. Chihwatenha accompanied Jesuit priests on their missions to the Huron during the winter of 1640, shortly before he was murdered either by Iroquois or Huron who distrusted his association with French priests. His name is also spelled Chihouatenhoua and Chiohoarebra.

CHIMNEY ROCK This area in the Siskiyou Mountains of the Six Rivers National Forest in northwestern California, called the "high country," is crucial to California Indian religious practices. For generations, individual members, spiritual leaders, and medicine persons of the Yurok, Karok, and Tolowa tribes have traveled to the high country to communicate with the Creator, to perform rituals and to prepare for specific religious and medicinal ceremonies essential to the WORLD RENEWAL CEREMONIAL CYCLE. The high country is used to train young people in traditional religious beliefs. The area has been threatened with the proposed construction of the Gasquet-Orleans Road (G-O Road) to provide more direct transportation of logs to mills and to open a remote area to logging and other activities. The road has been planned and finished in sections and the final Chimney Rock section met with opposition from Yurok, Karok, and Tolowa peoples who also opposed earlier sections of the road. The Chimney Rock section is considered the most important region for religious activities central to the belief systems of these tribes. The decision of the district court, upheld by the U.S. Court of Appeals for the Ninth Circuit asserted that the environmental qualities of the region were fundamental to the free exercise of religion. The Supreme Court ruled in *LYNG, SECRETARY OF AGRICULTURE ET AL. V. NORTHWEST INDIAN CEMETERY PROTECTIVE ASSOCIATION ET AL.*, the "G-O Road" case, that the "freedom of religion" clause of the First Amendment does not restrict the government's management of its lands even if certain governmental actions would infringe on or destroy a religion so long as the government's purpose is secular and not specifically aimed at infringing on the religion and its action does not coerce individuals to act contrary to their religious beliefs. California intervened and protected the area by designating it a preserve.

CHINIGCHINIX RELIGION (Chingchinix, Chingichngish, Chungichnishm) *Southern California* A religion of the Gabrieliño, Luiseño, Tipai-Ipai, and other Native groups in southern California. The earliest description of its beliefs and practices was written by Father Geronimo Boscana, a Franciscan missionary, at San Juan Capistrano Mission, about 1822. He indicated that the religion centered on the teachings of Chinigchinix, variously referred to as a prophet, deity, or avenger. According to Boscana, the prophet's birthplace was identified as the Rancheria of Puba. Three sacred names, corresponding to periods of his life, were attributed to him by Native people. After death, Chinigchinix was said to have ascended to the heavenly realm, leaving no bodily traces or remains on Earth. He then watched the people from on high, sending avenging animals, and other powerful punishments to those who violated his teachings.

The Chinigchinix religion included an extensive number of sacred rituals, songs, and dances. Its principal ceremony was identified as the Pames, translated as the Ceremony of the Bird and sometimes referred to as the Eagle Ceremony. Other ritual elements associated with the Chinigchinix reli-

gion included an "Ant-Ordeal" during boys' puberty rites, an initiation rite for girls, mourning ceremonies, the use of sand paintings, a dance of thanksgiving to the prophet during an eclipse, cremation rituals at death, and *toloache* ceremonies. *Toloache* is the Spanish word for the datura plant, or jimsonweed, found growing in California. Early tribal groups used the plant, similar to how PEYOTE is used, for religious purposes, including to dream and to seek guidance. Sacred knowledge was maintained in secret, known only to qualified adherents. The religious laws were difficult, requiring obedience, endurance, and self-sacrifice.

It is theorized that the Chinigchinix religion developed just before Europeans settled in the area, a reaction to the decimation of native populations by diseases carried by early explorers. It is also viewed as the means by which Native people preserved their traditional religious system. The Chinigchinix religion was taught to other Indian groups in the region, leading to its description as an indigenous "missionary movement." Modern-day identified practitioners include adherents on the Rincon and Pauma reservations. Other spellings of Chinigchinix include Chingchinix, Chingichngish, and Chungichnishm.

CHIPS, GODFREY *(b. 1954) Lakota* A medicine man described as one of the most powerful YUWIPI men in contemporary times. A descendant of the holy man HORN CHIPS, he is believed to have inherited the great man's spiritual power and became a Yuwipi practitioner when he was only 13 years old. According to another Lakota holy man LAME DEER, Godfrey could not understand the spirits when they first spoke to him but later, with their assistance, he learned that he was to be a spokesman for them. After his family knew he was going to be a medicine man, they kept him away from school. Indian police who were after him for truancy were involved in a car accident, and he was left alone. He later received a certificate exempting him from school attendance because he was following traditional ways. Lame Deer indicates that when Godfrey became a Yuwipi practitioner, he had many of the same interests as other boys his age. Some of the differences for him included not being able to fight even if hit by another child and not going near a female having her menstrual period. Lame Deer also described how difficult it was for Godfrey, as a youngster, to tell the parents of a missing boy everything he had learned about the child's disappearance in a vision. The knowledge was such a burden that he could only tell the people where to find their son, not that he had drowned. Besides his great-grandfather, Godfrey can count a number of other Yuwipi men in his family, including James Moves Camp, Charles Chips, Sam Moves Camp Sr., Fred Ashly, Richard Moves Camp, and his father, Ellis.

CHIPS, HORN See HORN CHIPS

CHIWAT, BILLY (Chivato, Civato) *(fl. 1870–1915) Lipan Apache* One of the first peyotists in Oklahoma who, with PINERO, was a primary teacher of peyotism to Indians in that state. An account of Chiwat and Pinero exists because of their capture, in 1870, of Henry Lehmann, age 11, in Texas. Lehmann lived with them until 1879 and subsequently told of his experiences among the Lipan Apache. He indicated that he had eaten a cactus found in Mexico, which he called "hoosh" and identified as peyote. Lehmann further related that Chiwat, one of his captors, became an important tribal leader. Lehmann's account included a photograph of Chiwat, dated about 1915, showing him in a peyote tipi. Different sources confirm that peyotism was introduced to the Comanche, Kiowa, and Kiowa-Apache by Chiwat and Pinero and that they taught the Commanche leader QUANAH PARKER the peyote ceremony he used. His name is also spelled Chivato or Civato. (See also PEYOTE RELIGION; ROADMAN.)

CHONI *Yaqui* A man or woman's SACRED OBJECT, which is kept hidden and carried in a pocket. Its function is to guard its master and all of his or her belongings and to warn him or her of danger (evil spirits, wild animals). It is considered evil except as a guard for its master. Used as a tool for personal gain, it imparts no special power.

CHRISTENSEN, CHRISTIAN LINGO *(1855–1940)* A Mormon missionary who worked among the Hopi people and other Indian groups. Christensen was born to Niels Christian Christensen and Karen Nielson on April 29, 1855, in Nielstrup, Randers, Denmark. A few years later, in 1860, the family emigrated to Utah and settled in Ephraim. Christensen fought in the 1860s war waged by the Ute leader Black Hawk, against Euro-American invaders of Native lands. In 1876 he was sent to Arizona, where he later served as a missionary at Moencopi. He and his two families remained in Arizona until 1886. Christensen then moved to Moab, Utah, where he traded, interpreted, and wrote accounts of his earlier days for newspaper publication. He died in Monticello, Utah, on November 26, 1940.

CHURCH AUTHORITY See YAQUI CEREMONIALISM

CHURCH GOVERNOR See YAQUI CEREMONIALISM

CHURCH MISSIONARY SOCIETY An Anglican organization founded in 1799 to propagate Christianity in foreign lands. Initially organized for missionary work in Africa and the East, it later agreed to sponsor missionaries to Native people in Canada. The Reverend JOHN WEST received sponsorship from the Church Missionary Society in 1820 for his work in the Red River region in the Canadian Northwest. Other missionaries affiliated with the society include HENRY BUDD, WILLIAM COCKRAN, JOHN HORDEN, JAMES HUNTER, DAVID THOMAS JONES, and JAMES SETTE. (See also Subject Index for society members included in this volume.)

CIRCULAR NO. 2970 (Indian Religious Freedom and Indian Culture) A policy directive issued by John Collier, the U.S. commissioner of Indian affairs, on January 3, 1924, to superintendents of Indian agencies. It stated, in part,

> No interference with Indian religious life or ceremonial expression will hereafter be tolerated. The cultural liberty of Indians is in all respects to be considered equal to that of any non-Indian group . . . In no cases shall punishments for statutory violations or for improprieties be so administered as to constitute an interference with, or to imply a censorship over, the religious or cultural life, Indian or other.

Commissioner Collier indicated that, as of the date of the circular, some Native American people believed, incorrectly, that they still had to obtain agency permission to conduct traditional dances and ceremonies. He also noted that many American Indians further believed that their cultural practices were either opposed or banned by the government. (See also AMERICAN INDIAN RELIGIOUS FREEDOM ACT OF 1978; COURTS OF INDIAN OFFENSES.)

CITY OF BOERNE V. P. F. FLORES (No. 95–2074) *(1997)* On June 25, 1997, the U.S. Supreme Court declared that the RELIGIOUS FREEDOM RESTORATION ACT OF 1993 (RFRA) was unconstitutional. In one of the most important modern-day rulings on the sources and limits of congressional power, the Court said that Congress overstepped its power to legislate constitutional rights when it enacted a federal law designed to protect religious observances from government interference.

Writing for a 6-3 majority, Justice Anthony Kennedy said RFRA did not provide a remedy for unconstitutional acts, which would have been an appropriate act of Congress, but represented a substantive change in constitutional rights, a power he said is reserved for the judicial branch of government. The Court majority felt RFRA was not a proper exercise of Congress's § 5 enforcement power because it contradicted vital principles necessary to maintain separation of powers and the federal-state balance. It also concluded that RFRA was a considerable congressional intrusion into the states' traditional prerogatives and general authority to regulate for the health and welfare of their citizens. Justice Kennedy was joined by Chief Justice William

H. Renquist and Justices Antonin Scalia, Clarence Thomas, John Paul Stevens, and Ruth Bader Ginsburg. Justices Sandra Day O'Connor, David H. Souter, and Stephen G. Breyer dissented.

The decision stemmed from a challenge brought by a church in Boerne, Texas, after the city denied a building permit to P. F. Flores, the Catholic archbishop of San Antonio, who wanted to expand its church facilities and demolish a small, historic building. The church invoked RFRA in its lawsuit, charging the city with violating its religious rights by interfering with its expansion plans.

Although the Supreme Court decision affected freedom of religion for American Indians, it was not targeted at suppressing traditional religious expression. Peyote use for religious ceremonies remained untouched by the Court decision because that right was secured by the passage of the AMERICAN INDIAN RELIGIOUS FREEDOM ACT AMENDMENTS OF 1994 (Public Law 103–344). But attorneys from the Native American Rights Fund still were concerned that all other Indian religious practices could be affected by the Court decision.

CLAN Related lineages, the members of which claim to have a common ancestry, sometimes stretching as far back as primordial times. Clan refers to the persons of one sex of related lineages and includes the unmarried members of the opposite sex and the spouses of the married members. A matriclan consists of several sisters, their husbands, and children, and the children of their daughters, as well as their unmarried sons and brothers. A patriclan consists of several brothers, their wives, and children, the children of their sons; and unmarried daughters and sisters. Clan members, who do not necessarily reside in the same place, have strong bonds and are obligated to assist one another in times of crisis and ceremony, and on happy and sad occasions. Clan members may observe special rituals and possess traditional stories in common. Clan members are generally not allowed to marry within their own clan. The number of clans differs from tribe to tribe. The Navajo (Dineh) number over 40 clans while the Seneca count eight.

CLARK, JOHN (1797–1854) Methodist missionary who established missions in Michigan, Wisconsin, and Minnesota. Clark was born in Hartford, New York, on July 30, 1797. After converting to Methodism in 1817 and serving as an exhorter, he was licensed as a local preacher in 1819. He preached in the New York Conference, eventually meeting Indian converts of WILLIAM CASE'S mission in Canada between 1831 and 1832. In 1832 Clark volunteered to help extend Methodist efforts among Native people and built a station at Sault Ste. Marie in Michigan's Upper Peninsula to serve the Ojibway the following year. He later established the Kewawenon mission in the area as well as others in Wisconsin and Minnesota. In 1836 he was named presiding elder of the Chicago District of the Methodist organization that included Native missions at Green Bay and Oneida West. Clark later worked in Texas and New York before receiving an 1852 appointment to the Clark Street Church in Chicago. While assisting victims of a cholera epidemic, he died of the disease on July 11, 1854.

CLAY, JESSE (fl. 1912–1920) Winnebago A peyote ROADMAN who introduced the Half Moon ceremony to the Winnebago people in 1912. Clay observed the ritual while visiting in Oklahoma as a guest of a man he identified as "Arapaho Bull." This Arapaho peyotist, Jock Bull Bear, went to Clay's Nebraska home a year later and conducted Half Moon peyote meetings. After learning the ritual, Jesse Clay served as its roadman.

The Half Moon movement became the second branch of peyotism among the Winnebago after the Cross Fire ritual established earlier by JOHN RAVE. But while the Half Moon ceremony, which incorporated more Native elements, attracted followers, it did not replace Rave's version. When the Peyote Church of Christ was incorporated in Nebraska in 1921, adherents of both branches of PEYOTISM were represented as charter members. Jesse Clay served as one of the early presidents of the new church.

CLEANSING CEREMONY Tohono O'odham A general cleansing ceremony at the opening of the winter hunting season. A deer is ritually killed and cooked with corn, beans, and squash from the harvest and songs, dancing, and orations sanctify the food. At one time, the ceremony was given in each of the important Tohono O'odham ceremonial centers such as Archie and Quitovac. Today, this ceremony is performed at the Mexican village of Quitovaca (Sonora) in August, 10 days before the PRAYERSTICK FESTIVAL.

CLOUD DANCE (Corn Maiden dance) Tewa Pueblos Also called the Corn Maiden dance. Usually held in late winter or early spring before spring planting, the dance honors corn in a ritually prescribed manner. The dance is associated with agriculture, good weather, and appeals for fertility in nature. Eight women carrying colored ears of corn wear headdresses and clothes with cloud symbols to invoke the rain, dancing two at a time with a long line of male dancers. Men wear long-fringed white rain sashes. The dance equates women, corn, and clouds, all symbols for fertility.

CLOWN An important, sacred person performing activities embedded in Native American religions. Clowns have sacred functions in ceremonies and are guardians of ritual who help maintain the continuity or fertility, rain, crops, and good health. As an Apache medicine man explained, "People think that the clown is just nothing, that he is just for fun. That is not so . . . Many people who know about these things say that the clown is the most powerful." Or as a Lakota healer put it: "Fooling around, a clown is really performing a spiritual ceremony." BLACK ELK said clowns make people "feel jolly and happy at first, so that it may be easier for the power to come to them." Clowns make people observe and think about things in new ways. By causing people to laugh, they clear worry from people's minds and permit them to see higher truths. They teach by "bad" example. They mock the order of the ritual, prayers, song, holy beings, and sacred objects. They joke, satirize, and behave contrarily. They do things that are forbidden and unspeakable within a ritual framework. They create imbalance and disorder in the world in the midst of ritualized social order. Without the clown's disorder, order would not be so obvious and so justified. Clowns are also believed to cure illnesses. They have access to the same knowledge as medicine people. A Lakota medicine man said: "Being a clown, for me, came close to being a medicine man. It was in the same nature." Clowns are called different names from group to group. They are called banana ripener, crazy dancer, *HEYOKA, KOSHARE, KOYEMSHI,* blue jay, watersprinkler, and many other names.

Apache

Called "Gray One," "Long Nose" or "White Painted," the Apache clown wears a mask of rawhide, moccasins, and a breechclout, and his body is painted white with horizontal black stripes. The clown dances at the GIRL'S PUBERTY RITE and at curing ceremonials along with the MOUNTAIN SPIRITS, the four masked dancers impersonating the spirits who live in the mountain caves, imitating their movements. The clown's role at the puberty rite is that of messenger and servant of the masked dancers, carrying requests to the musicians. The clown does not talk to people during this rite for it is dangerous while impersonating a spiritual power. Apache clowns sometimes frighten children, act as disciplinarians, and police ceremonial grounds.

Pueblo

Called "delight makers," the Pueblo clowns use ridicule, pantomine, vulgarity, verbal obscenity, and uncontrolled sexuality to shatter the acceptable limits of behavior, reinforcing socially acceptable behavior by demonstrating what is unacceptable. They burlesque religious authorities, government officials, neighboring tribes, anthropologists, and other people who impact on their lives. They pick individuals, agencies, and institutions that give them the opportunity to make moral-ethical points about themselves. One order of Pueblo clowns is painted with black and white horizontal stripes from neck to ankles and wears its hair in horns or caps with horns topped by cornhusk tassels. These are called Koshare (Koshari) by the Keres people, Kosa (Kossa) by the Tewa, Koyala (Koyalah) by the Hano, Tabösh by the Jemez, Paiakyamu by the Hopi, and Newekwe by the Zuni. Another order, the mudheads, wear earth-colored globular cloth masks with knobs on them filled with seeds and sacred earth and are called KOYEMSHI (Koyenci) by the Zuni and Tachuktu by the Hopi. Some Pueblo clowns assume their roles on an occasional basis. Others belong to clowning societies like the KOSHARE, KWERANA, and GALAXY SOCIETY and attain membership after being pledged by their parents, healed by cures worked by clowns, or ritually captured. (See also HEYOKA, NAVITCU, WINDIGOKAN.)

COAL BEAR (Charcoal Bear, Black Bear) *(1827?–1896)*

Cheyenne Keeper of Esevone, the SACRED BUFFALO HAT of the Cheyenne people. Coal Bear was born sometime in the 1820s or 1830s, his birthdate variously listed as 1827, 1828, or 1836. He was the son of Half Bear, a holy man who had also served as Esevone's keeper until his death in 1869 or 1870 and was a member of the Suhtaio band. Coal Bear and his brother Wrapped Hair, both members of the Kit Fox Society of their people, were away from home at the end of their father's life. As he neared death and in Coal Bear's absence, Half Bear had taught his friend Broken Dish (also Crow White) and the man's wife, Standing Woman (also Moccasin Flap or Ho'ko), some of the sacred knowledge related to Esevone's care. After Coal Bear returned home in 1873 or 1874, he took horses and other gifts to the temporary keeper for assuming responsibility of the Hat's care after Half Bear died. As a Suhtaio and the son of Half Bear, the previous keeper, the keepership was rightfully his. When Broken Dish would not relinquish the sacred object, the military societies also made offerings to him in an effort to settle the issue peacefully. When he still refused, the Cheyenne authorities retrieved Esevone from him and restored the sacred object to Coal Bear. It was later discovered during a ceremony that one of Esevone's horns was missing and that other sacred objects had been taken from the bundle. Standing Woman had mutilated the Sacred Buffalo Hat, an act that resulted in a long period of devastating misfortune for the people. Although a new horn was made by priests to replace the missing one, Coal Bear and the rest of the people endured great sufferings. The Broken Dish family became outcasts and, as prophesied, were especially marked for misfortune.

Coal Bear served as keeper during a dark period in his people's history. Although the Cheyenne were victorious at the Battle of the Little Big Horn in 1876, other encounters with the United States military resulted in the killing of many of their people and increasing assaults on their way of life. When Cheyenne were told they had to go to Indian Territory (present-day Oklahoma) after their surrender at Fort Robinson in Nebraska, Coal Bear and his wife took the Sacred Buffalo Hat there. It is said that the keeper returned to the northern homeland of his people with the holy object in 1881. Besides sharing the suffering of the people as a whole, Coal Bear had family misfortunes. Although he was not at fault for the desecration of the Sacred Buffalo Hat, he died at an early age for a keeper. These spiritual guardians traditionally lived long, healthy lives. Coal Bear was assisted in caring for the Sacred Buffalo Hat's lodge by Coffee, a man who remained unmarried, and by his wife. Coal Bear had two wives, Glad Traveler and White Woman, and 11 children. He died in 1896 and was buried in the respectful, customary way accorded his sacred position. Coal Bear's name also appears as Charcoal Bear and, at times, Black Bear.

COCKENOE (Kukkinneau, "He Interprets") (?–1699) *Montauk* Interpreter and translator for JOHN ELIOT, the 17th-century missionary who became known as the "Apostle to the Indians." Born on Long Island in New York, Cockenoe was captured by the British during the Pequot War of 1636–37. While he was working as a servant in the household of army sergeant Richard Collicot of Dorcester, Massachusetts, Cockenoe's fluency in English became known to Eliot. The missionary arranged to have Cockenoe serve as his Algonquian language tutor. Without Cockenoe's contribution, it is unlikely that *Mamusee Wunneeta-panatamwe up-Biblum God,* known as the ELIOT BIBLE and the first complete Bible printed in America, would have been translated into the Natick dialect by Eliot. Besides this 1663 publication, Cockenoe assisted in translating other religious and educational materials for use with PRAYING INDIANS. *John Eliot's First Indian Teacher and Interpreter. Cockenoe-de-Long Island and the Story of his Career from the Early Records* by William Wallace Tooker (1896) cites a final mention of the interpreter in a deed of conveyance dated August 3, 1687.

COCKRAN, WILLIAM (1796 or 1797–1865) An Anglican missionary who began his career among Native people at the Red River Settlement (Winnipeg) in Rupert's Land (Manitoba). Of Scottish descent, Cockran was born in Chillingham, Northumberland, England. He is said to have been brought up Presbyterian, later joining the Church of England. A short time after his ordination as a deacon on December 19, 1824, and as a priest on May 29, 1825, Cockran left for the Canadian Northwest. He, his wife, Ann, and their baby son arrived at the Red River post on October 4,

1825. Cockran, the third missionary sent to the area by the CHURCH MISSIONARY SOCIETY, followed JOHN WEST and DAVID THOMAS JONES. Besides spreading the gospel, he turned to "civilization" efforts by introducing and expanding farming operations. In 1829 Cockran left Jones with the work at Upper Church and Middle Church along the Red River in the Red River Settlement and moved farther down the river. He established Lower Church (St. Andrew's) at Grand Rapids and began the same Christian agricultural settlement programs. Cockran eventually extended his efforts to the Saulteaux people under their leader Peguis. In 1836 he began building a church among them, later called St. Peter's. Although he left the Red River Settlement for Toronto in 1846, Cockran returned after a short time. In addition to continuing efforts at his earlier post, he selected a site for a new CMS mission at Portage la Prairie in present-day Manitoba among the Saulteaux. Cockran was named archdeacon in 1853. In 1857 he left Grand Rapids for Portage la Prairie, where he was assisted by his son, the Reverend Thomas Cochrane, who preferred that spelling of his name. Cochran died there on October 1, 1865.

CODE OF HANDSOME LAKE *Iroquois* The code is a narrative of the visions and travels of the prophet HANDSOME LAKE, a catalogue of sins and their punishment, a description of heaven and hell, a definition of a good way of life, and a prescription for proper ceremonies to be performed in the LONGHOUSE. The code is recited twice a year in short form by a local preacher during the first morning of the MIDWINTER CEREMONY in January and during the GREEN CORN ceremony in August. The entire code is recited by professional speakers at a SIX NATIONS MEETING in the autumn of alternate years at each longhouse (except Tonawanda, where it occurs annually, and Sour Springs, which has an irregular schedule).

At these Six Nations meetings the code (which the Iroquois call "the good word" or "the good message") is recited during four mornings before noon, followed by sermons on the text, confessions, exhortations in the afternoon and social dances in the longhouse in the evening. The Six Nations meetings ensure that the entire code is preached by an officially recognized person in each longhouse at least once every two years.

Preachers of the code begin with an account of Handsome Lake's first vision of messengers, who told him to preach against certain bad behaviors, and other incidents in the Seneca prophet's life. The preacher mentions various messages given by the Creator to four beings to communicate to Handsome Lake. These include admonitions that people should not drink alcohol, witches should confess and stop their activities, women should not practice abortion, husbands and wives should not desert each other or their children, people should help each other, and Thanksgiving ceremonies should be celebrated. Preachers also describe punishments in the afterlife. The Iroquois believe that the "good word" came from the Creator to the Four Messengers and from them to Handsome Lake, who taught it to his own grandson, Jimmy Johnson (Sosheowa), and to Owen Blacksnake.

COLLINS, MARY C. *(1846–1920)* A Congregational missionary in Dakota Territory. Collins was born in Alton, Illinois, on April 18, 1846, and later moved with her family to Keokuk, Iowa. Educated in public and private schools, she received an M.A. degree from Ripon College in Wisconsin. After teaching for three years in Keokuk, Collins went to the Oahe Mission in 1875 and began working with the Reverend THOMAS LAWRENCE RIGGS. She remained there for 10 years, serving as a teacher and social worker. In 1885 she moved to the Standing Rock Agency, where she settled near the Grand River in present-day Little Eagle, South Dakota. Collins worked there for the next 25 years as a teacher, social worker, and missionary. In 1899 she was ordained a Congregational minister, no longer having to rely on visiting clergymen to perform church services and ceremonies. After her ordination, Collins also superintended the mission field at Standing Rock. Combining simple medical treatments with preaching, her role was compared to a medicine man's by the Lakota people. Collins, who knew the leader SITTING BULL, tried to convince him to reject the GHOST DANCE OF 1890. After retiring in 1910, she returned to Keokuk, Iowa, dying there on May 25, 1920.

COLLISON, WILLIAM HENRY *(1847–1922)* An Anglican clergyman and acrhdeacon who served as a missionary among the Native people of northern British Columbia. Collison, who was born in Ireland, received his education at the Church Missionary College in Islington, England, and was ordained to the priesthood of the Church of England in 1878. Although he worked for a period at the model community established by WILLIAM DUNCAN at Metlakatla among the Tsimshian people, he did not remain there. In 1876 he began missionary efforts among the Haida at Masset on the Queen Charlotte Islands. He indicated that many Christian conversions occurred because medicine men were unable to cure the smallpox disease afflicting the people. Collison remained a missionary until the end of his life. An account of his experiences, *In the Wake of the War Canoe*, was published in 1916.

COMANCHE DANCE *Tewa Pueblos* A war dance, performed in some version by every Tewa village close to the summer solstice. The dance combines Tewa, Comanche (Plains Indian), and Spanish Catholic symbols. Tewa men have personal freedom in constructing garish costumes, elements of which are traded or purchased from Plains Indians, but the women are dressed conservatively in typical Tewa regalia. The men wear enormous feathered headdresses that never were part of Pueblo tradition and paint their bodies and faces with elaborate designs. There is often the presence of a statue of the village patron saint.

COMPERE, LEE *(1790–1871)* A Baptist missionary in the Alabama area of the Creek Nation. Compere was born to Grace Fox Compere and John Compere on November 3, 1790, at Market Harbor, England. He served as a missionary in Jamaica for two years until ill health forced him to leave. After settling in Charleston, South Carolina, he went to the Creek Nation under the auspices of the American Baptist Board of Missions in 1823. The mission station, located on the Tallapoosa River in Alabama, was called Tukabatchi at first, then Withington after a benefactor in New York. One of the Creek students at the school was JOHN DAVIS, who later became a missionary and interpreter in the West. Compere remained at the mission for six years but made few converts to Christianity. During an investigation of the killing of William McIntosh, a pro-American Creek chief and military leader, for signing a treaty relinquishing a large area of Creek land to Georgia, the missionary was treated badly by officials of that state, who demanded evidence and an oath from him concerning his knowledge of the matter. After leaving the Creek Nation, he organized the Rehoboth Church in Montgomery County, Alabama, and served as a pastor. During his years among the Creek people, he wrote a vocabulary of the Native language. Compere spent his later years in Texas, where he died on June 15, 1871.

CONDOLENCE CANE *Iroquois* A cane carved with ancient mnemonic designs preserves the memory of the eulogy chant and ROLL CALL OF THE CHIEFS and supports the performance of the CONDOLENCE CEREMONY for installing new chiefs.

CONDOLENCE CEREMONY *Iroquois* A ceremony central to the passing of authority in the Iroquois council structure; held on various Iroquois reservations in New York and Canada on the death of a ruler. The loss of a leader was a great blow, and the rites of the ceremony were devised to nullify the power of death and repair any injury done by it to the people.

The Big Condolence, one of the two kinds of ceremony, embodies the process by which clan members of the deceased chiefs are comforted and new confederacy chiefs are inducted to fill the vacated positions in the governing councils represented in the Grand Council of the Iroquois Confederacy. A small condolence elevates "the minds of the bereaved family." In the Condolence Ceremony, tribes are grouped into two sides, the bereaved and the "clearminded." The clearminded tribes are obliged to console the mourners. The ceremony is given by the "clear" moiety to the "mourning" moiety. The Older Brothers (Mohawk, Onondaga, and Seneca) condole the other side, the Younger Brothers (Oneidas, Cayuga, and Tuscarora) on the loss of one of their chiefs and the reverse when the Older Brothers lose one of theirs.

The ceremony is held in the LONGHOUSE of the mourning nation or one loaned for the occasion. It begins with the preliminary rite of greeting, "At the Wood's Edge," at a fire a short distance away. The speaker for the bereaved side greets the clearminded side. The ceremony itself begins with the recitation of the ROLL CALL OF THE CHIEFS, the first 50 men to become the sachems, or chiefs, of the Iroquois League. The condoling song, a hymn of farewell to the deceased chief follows, sung by the clearminded side. The Laws of the Confederacy are recounted, and a speaker for the clearminded side delivers the REQUICKENING ADDRESS, named for its power to restore life and lift up minds depressed by grief. After the address, the bereaved side sings a condoling song, recites the Requickening Address and returns at the end of each section one of the 15 "sympathy strings" of WAMPUM earlier passed to its side. Men who are to take the place of the deceased chiefs are presented and named and addressed on their responsibilities. A feast follows with foods appropriate for the condolence ceremony.

In late 1989, Jacob Thomas, a traditional elder and a Snipe Clan subchief from the Cayuga Nation of the Grand River Reservation in Ontario and one of the most knowledgeable about the Condolence Ceremony videotaped the speeches and songs of the ceremony. Chief Thomas resisted the idea of taping for years but eventually decided "before it gets lost, we'd better record it." There is a strict agreement about the use of the tape now stored at the Cornell University American Indian Program. The principal Iroquois ceremonies are increasingly endangered as Indian elders with oral memories learned from their own elders die with the ceremonial knowledge.

CONFESSION DANCE *Southern Okanagan* A dance believed to be a part of the PROPHET DANCE complex. It was held after unusual events in the natural environment were interpreted to signal the approaching end of the world. Both children and adults participated in the dance. They formed a circle around the leader, who began confessing his sins.

When he completed his confessions, he had each person do the same. The ceremony was held for several days and nights, then resumed at intervals until the danger was believed to have passed.

CONFESSION RITE *Iroquois* A public act that takes place in the LONGHOUSE; expected of all men, women, and children who participate in the MIDWINTER CEREMONY. Days before the ceremony begins, each person, holding a string of white WAMPUM, confesses to the Creator his or her wrongdoings since the last confession. This act purifies and cleanses the person for the performance of the sacred rites that follow during the midwinter ceremony.

COOK, CHARLES SMITH *(?–1892) Lakota* A Protestant minister and teacher. Cook, a member of the Oglala band of Lakota, graduated from Trinity College in 1881. He studied theology at the Seabury Divinity School, which was established by the Episcopal clergyman JAMES LLOYD BRECK at Faribault in Minnesota. After his ordination, Cook served as a minister and teacher on the Pine Ridge Reservation in South Dakota in the 1880s. He died there on April 15, 1892.

COOK, WASHINGTON N. *(1804–1858)* A Mormon elder who served as the president of the Mormon mission to the Creek and Cherokee people in Indian Territory (present-day Oklahoma) He was born on October 4, 1804, to Edwin and Winnifred Cook in Greenville County, Virginia. Baptized in 1843, Cook was ordained a "Seventy" (high official) the following year in Nauvoo, Illinois. In 1846 he immigrated to Utah, where he later became a founder of Palmyra. He began his mission to Indian Territory in 1855 and the following year became president of the mission. Cook died of consumption on September 4, 1858, in the Cherokee Nation. (See also DALTON, MATTHEW WILLIAM; KIMBALL, ANDREW.)

COOLIDGE, SHERMAN (Runs-On-Top) *(1862–c. 1933) Arapaho* Episcopal priest who served as a missionary on the Wind River Reservation in Wyoming. Coolidge was born to Ba-ahnoce (Turtle Woman) and Banasda (Big Heart) in 1862 near Goose Creek in Wyoming's Wind River area. Descended from Araphao headmen or chiefs, he was given the honorary name Runs-On-Top after a great-grandfather. At the age of seven, Coolidge's father was killed by Bannock enemies of their people. He also lost family members when they and other Arapaho, mistakenly believed to be a band of Lakota sought by American troops, were killed by the U.S. Cavalry. In 1870 Coolidge and his younger brother were taken captive during a Shoshone and Bannock attack against the Arapaho. The two boys were later turned over to American soldiers. They remained at Camp Brown, Wyoming, where they were cared for by the families of Army officers and renamed. Runs-On-Top was named after General William Tecumseh Sherman. In 1870 the boy was adopted by Captain and Mrs. Charles A. Coolidge, a childless couple who renamed him Sherman Coolidge.

Coolidge was baptized in the Episcopal faith at the age of nine and was educated at a number of schools. He attended Shattuck Military School in Faribault, Minnesota, where he was an outstanding student. He later began preparing for a missionary career at Seabury Divinity School, graduating in 1884. That same year he was ordained a deacon by HENRY B. WHIPPLE, the first Episcopal bishop of Minnesota. Coolidge then went to the Wind River Reservation and began his first missionary assignment. He remained there for two years, then attended Hobart College in Geneva, New York, from 1887 to 1889. Ordained to the priesthood, Coolidge returned to the Wind River Reservation to minister to the people in the area. In 1902, despite prejudices against an interracial union, he married Grace Darling Wetherbee, a white woman who had been born in Boston to an affluent family. Their wedding was performed by the Reverend JOHN ROBERTS, also an Episcopal missionary on the Wind River Reservation, who first tried to dissuade the couple from marrying. They then continued their religious and educational efforts among Native people.

In 1911 Coolidge became a founding member of the Society of American Indians, a prominent Indian rights organization. His wife authored *Teepee Neighbors* (1917), describing her experiences among the Arapaho and Shoshone at Wind River. The couple had four children, two of whom reached adulthood. A fictionalized account of their lives (*A Stone Upon His Shoulder*, by Helen Butler) was published in 1953. Sherman Coolidge died about 1933.

COPPER *North Pacific Coast* Used as a ritual entity during the winter ceremonial. Copper symbolizes the wealth of the sea and heavenly light, a commodity interchangeable with animal souls, a healing substance, and a life giver. Some believe that copper symbolizes a fusion of all forms of life. During the course of the winter rites, coppers are broken as offerings to MAN EATER.

COPWAY, GEORGE (Kah-ge-ga-gah-bowh, "Standing Firm") *(1818–1869) Mississauga (Ojibway)* Methodist missionary and author. Born in 1818 near the mouth of the Trent River in Canada, Copway was a member of the Mississauga band that lived in the Rice Lake area north of Cobourg on Lake Ontario. The Ojibway missionary PETER JONES and other Methodist missionaries eventually influenced tribal people, including Copway's parents, to convert to Christianity. Copway also converted in 1830, persuaded to do so by his mother. He attended a Methodist mission school at Rice Lake, where one of his teachers was the missionary JAMES EVANS. When the Reverend JOHN CLARK requested four Native workers to assist in the work at the Lake Superior Mission of the American Methodist Church in 1834, Copway and his cousin, ENMEGAHBOWH, were among those selected. The Ojibway left for the Lake Superior area on July 16, 1834. Copway stayed at Keweenaw Mission the first winter, then at La Pointe, where he assisted the Reverend SHERMAN HALL with biblical translations. Copway later helped Enmegahbowh and another Ojibway convert, PETER MARKSMAN, to establish a Methodist mission at Lac Courte Oreilles near present-day Hayward, Wisconsin. In the fall of 1837 Copway, Enmegahbowh, and Marksman entered the Ebenezer Manual Labor School in Illinois, under the auspices of a Methodist missionary society. Following his 1839 graduation from Ebenezer, Copway returned to Upper Canada, where he met and married a young Englishwoman, Elizabeth Howell.

Copway eventually worked at a number of other missions, including the Saugeen Mission on Lake Huron and at his home mission on the Rice Lake Reserve. In 1846, following charges of embezzlement, he was imprisoned for several weeks in Toronto and expelled by the Canadian Conference of the Wesleyan Methodist Church. He then traveled in the United States and subsequently published his autobiography, *The Life, History and Travels of Kah-ge-ga-gah-bowh (George Copway), A Young Indian Chief of the Ojebwa Nation, A Convert to the Christian Faith, and a Missionary to his People for Twelve Years; with a Sketch of the Present State of the Ojebwa Nation, in Regard to Christianity and their Future Prospects,* which became a best-seller and ran through six editions by the end of 1847. Other publications included *The Traditional History and Characteristic Sketches of the Ojibway Nation* (1850), an epic poem (1850), sketches of a European journey (1851) and a weekly newspaper entitled *Copway's American Indian* (1851). He eventually lived in poverty for several years in New York City, attempting to support his family on the income he made as a lecturer. In 1864 he and his brother David helped recruit Canadian Indians into the Union Army during the Civil War. Copway also became a healer or herbal doctor, advertising his cures in the *Detroit Free Press* in 1867. The following year he returned to Canada, going to Lake of Two Mountains, a mission in Quebec, among the Iroquois and other tribal people. Copway was baptized a Catholic there shortly before his death in 1869.

CORN (TABLITA) DANCE (Blue Corn, Green Corn, Feast and Harvest Dance) *Keresan, Tewa, Towa Pueblos* Communal ceremonies, the public portion of which is a dance given in the pueblo courtyard. The dances are open to outsiders, but photographing is prohibited. Outsiders may not view the preparation for dances taking place in the kiva. Keresan and Tewa pueblos dance and sing on their respective saint's day, the day of the saint for whom the Spanish named the village. Among eastern pueblos, the dances are given as a ceremony of the villages' major Catholic FEAST DAY, merging Native American and Catholic rites, but some of the pueblos dance on other occasions as well. The details vary from village to village, within villages and from time to time. The dances relate to germination, growth, maturation, and harvesting of crops. The term *tablita* is derived from the thin headboards of wood worn by the women. The tablitas, drums, body painting, songs, pole decoration, managing personnel, and regalia differ. One feature of the dances is the long ceremonial pole carrying a dance kilt, feathers, and medicine pouches that is waved over the dancers as a blessing throughout the ceremony. This standard also, according to Tewa scholar Alfonso Ortiz, attempts to bridge the gap between the underworld, earth, and sky. (See also COSMIC PILLAR.)

CORN EAR *Pueblo* Corn ears are sacred and have spiritual power. A perfect ear of corn is like a ceremonial leader or a mother to Pueblo peoples. It may be unadorned or dressed elaborately in feathers and jewels and placed in altars at ceremonials. These corn ears, frequently called fetishes in anthropological literature, are important SACRED OBJECTS of priests. Depending on the pueblo, most ordinary people have corn ear sacred objects that accompany them throughout life. Perfect ears of corn are used and given in name-giving rituals, initiations, and cures. (See also CORN MEAL.)

CORN GROUPS *Tewa* Southern Tewa, the Isleta and Sandia, are divided into corn groups associated with colors and directions. Parents give children to one of the five directionally oriented corn groups: white (east), black (north), yellow (west), blue (south), and all colors (above, middle, and down). The corn groups are responsible for blessing children during the first solstice ceremony after birth. They purify members, escort a curing society member to meetings, hold four-day retreats during the full moon before summer and winter solstices, and perform rituals to ensure at death the spirit reaches the afterworld where his or her group is centered.

CORN MAIDENS *Zuni* Spiritual beings who gave the gift of corn to Zuni people. There are many versions of the story about the flight of the maidens from Zuni. One story explains that after the corn maidens were harassed and insulted by the people, they fled the land. Their flight caused famine and the people sent out messengers to find them. In one account Payatamu, the culture hero who introduced corn cultivation, recovered the maidens and brought them back to the people. The maidens agreed to "give their flesh" (corn) to the people and the famine ended. The corn maidens are impersonated in the RAIN CEREMONY, a corn ceremony held every four years, in harvest rituals each fall, and in the SHALAKO CEREMONY in winter.

CORNMEAL *Pueblo* Meal, made from perfect ears of (usually white) corn, is sacred and associated with praying. The meal is held in the hand, brought to the mouth, and prayed and breathed on before it is sprinkled over sacred objects and people. Cornmeal is sprinkled as a sanctifying element over altars, prayersticks, shrines, kachina masks and other sacred objects, into springs and graves, and on corpses and killed deer. It is sprinkled to bless new houses, to delineate sacred paths, across roads to bar enemies from entering, as a road for spirits and humans to travel over, before and over kachina spirits of rain and fertility (who also carry it), and before kick stick racers. Cornmeal is rubbed on newborns and the dead. Corn-husk packets of meal accompany requests to medicine societies for a cure and to a person chosen to become one's ceremonial parent when joining a ceremonial society. In the Keres language, it is called *petana*.

CORN MOTHER *Keresan* A central figure in creation stories who is the mother of the Keres people she created. She remains beneath in an underworld and passes on information at the time of the emergence in the primeval era. She receives the dead back again when they return to her realm. She is the spirit of fertility and is represented by a corn ear. The Keres word for the Corn Mother has been variously rendered as Iariko, Iarriko, Iatik, Iatiku, and Iyatiki. (See also SACRED OBJECTS [Keresan]).

CORN SPROUTING CEREMONY *Iroquois* A food spirit supplication ceremony that takes place three to four weeks after the SEED PLANTING CEREMONY when shoots first show above ground at the end of May. The spirits are entertained so they will continue to help crops mature into a good harvest.

COSMIC PILLAR The pillar is a symbol of the cosmos, of the Supreme Creator. The pillar is perceived by many tribes to be the World Tree (which has roots in the underworld, stretches through the world of humans and animals, and has its crown in the sky world) symbolized by a sacred pole that reaches up to the Creator's abode or upholds and supports the heaven.

The cosmic pillar, or World Tree, is represented in ritual, primarily in annual festivals associated with the Supreme Being but also in shamanic rites where it is a connecting link between humans and spirits. Many tribes acknowledge the notion of a cosmic axis, a connecting link between heaven and earth that is represented by a sacred pole that is raised in the center of a ceremonial area or forms the central post of a lodge in which rites are performed. Pole climbing rites dramatize a medicine man trying to establish a direct contact with the spirit world by means of the pole. (See also CORN [TABLITA] DANCES; OMAHA SACRED POLE; SUN DANCE.)

COSO HOT SPRINGS The springs, located in southern California north of the Mohave Desert, figure in the religious history of Owens Valley Paiute-Shoshone Band of Indians and the Kern Valley Indian community as a sacred place for spiritual and physical renewal and curing. The Indians use the medicinal muds and waters of the springs and pond. Following World War II, the Department of the Navy acquired the Coso Hot Springs and surrounding lands and established the China Lake Naval Weapons Center there. Because of its use as an ammunition storage site, the navy placed certain security restrictions on its public use and access, including bathing in the springs and entry without an escort. After Congress passed the AMERICAN INDIAN RELIGIOUS FREEDOM ACT in 1978, the navy lifted certain prohibitions to allow for tribal religious use of Coso Hot Springs.

COURTS OF INDIAN OFFENSES A system of tribal courts instituted on Indian reservations in 1883 by the U.S. government. H. M. Teller, who was appointed secretary of the Interior in 1882, sought to eradicate "certain of the old heathenish dances; such as the sundance, scalp-dance, &c." and to do away with other tribal traditions and replace them with Christianity and "civilization." He worked with Hiram Price, the commissioner of Indian affairs, to formulate a plan for establishing the courts among tribal groups. On April 10, 1883, rules formulated for the courts were approved by the U.S. government. They prohibited a number of Native religious practices. As modified in 1892, offenses of the courts included:

> (a) Dances, etc.—Any Indian who shall engage in the sun dance, scalp dance, or war dance, or any other similar feast, so called, shall be deemed guilty of an offense, and upon conviction thereof shall be punished for the first offense by the withholding of his rations for not exceeding ten days or by imprisonment for not exceeding ten days; and for any subsequent offense under this clause he shall be punished by withholding his rations for not less than ten nor more than thirty days, or by imprisonment for not less than ten nor more than thirty days. (b) Plural or polygamous

marriages.—Any Indian under the supervision of a United States Indian agent who shall hereafter contract or enter into any plural or polygamous marriage shall be deemed guilty of an offense . . . . (c) Practices of medicine men.—Any Indian who shall engage in the practices of so-called medicine men, or who shall resort to any artifice or device to keep the Indians of the reservation from adopting and following civilized habits and pursuits, or shall adopt any means to prevent the attendance of children at school, or shall use any arts of a conjurer to prevent Indians from abandoning their barbarous rites and customs, shall be deemed to be guilty of an offense, and upon conviction thereof, for the first offense shall be imprisoned for not less than ten nor more than thirty days: Provided, That for any subsequent conviction for such offense the maximum term or imprisonment shall not exceed six months. (d) Destroying property of other Indians.— . . . the plea that the person convicted or the owner of the property in question was at the time a "mourner," and that thereby the taking, destroying, or injuring of the property was justified by the customs or rites of the tribe, shall not be accepted as a sufficient defense . . . . (House Executive Document no. 1, 52d Cong., 2d sess., serial 3088, pp. 28–31).

The rules also outlined such terms as duties, removal, and jurisdictions of tribal judges.

To be appointed a judge, individuals had to meet a number of requirements. Besides being "men of intelligence," they had to possess English language skills, wear "citizen's dress," and "engage in civilized pursuits." The government agents overseeing federal Indian reservations made certain the rules were enforced. By 1900 these courts existed at approximately two-thirds of the American Indian agencies. QUANAH PARKER and WOODEN LANCE served as tribal judges on the Courts of Indian Offenses in Indian Territory (present-day Oklahoma). They were eventually removed from their judgeships by Bureau of Indian Affairs officials because they violated the rule against polygamy.

COWLEY, ABRAHAM *(1816–1887)* Church of England missionary in the Canadian Northwest. Born in Fairford, England, on April 8, 1816, he was the son of Robert and Mary Cowley. He attended Farmor's Endowed School in Fairford from 1821 to 1828. Years later, in 1839, Cowley enrolled in the Church Missionary Society College in Islington, England, to prepare for mission work abroad. He was married to Arabella Sainsbury on December 26, 1840, and the couple left for the Red River Settlement in present-day Winnipeg via Montreal the following month, planning to travel to Rupert's Land with Montreal's Bishop George Jehoshaphat Mountain. In Montreal Cowley was ordained as a deacon on March 7, 1841. Finding that the bishop could not go to Rupert's Land, the Cowleys returned home. They then boarded a ship leaving for Hudson Bay. By the time they reached the Red River settlement on September 28, 1841, they had crossed the Atlantic three times in less than a year. Cowley, who had expected to assist WILLIAM COCKRAN at Red River, found he had to make other arrangements. He eventually established a mission on Little Dauphin River between Lake Manitoba and Lake St. Martin, near Saulteaux people. The mission, called Partridge Crop, later became known as Fairford (Manitoba). Cowley was ordained as a priest on July 7, 1844, by Bishop Mountain. His missionary activities included promoting agricultural efforts and livestock raising. He remained at Fairford until 1854 when he went to Indian Settlement (presently Dynevor, Manitoba) to work with Cockran. St. John's College in Winnipeg awarded Cowley an honorary D.D. in 1867. After Cockran died, Cowley succeeded him as archdeacon of Cumberland. Cowley stayed at Indian Settlement until his death on September 11, 1887, in Selkirk, Manitoba. (See also JONES, DAVID; WEST, JOHN.)

CRANBERRY DAY *Aquinnah Wampanoag* A Wampanoag festival of the harvest held on Martha's Vineyard, Massachusetts. In past times, the Wampanoag medicine man decided when cranberries were ripe, and the picking would last for days or weeks, depending on the harvest. Today, the occasion is held the second Tuesday of October and groups of adults and children (who have a holiday from school) travel to the cranberry bogs to scoop the berries.

CRAWFORD, CHARLES RENVILLE (Wakanhinape, "Appearing Sacred") *(1837–1920) Dakota* Presbyterian minister and interpreter. Born in Minnesota Territory, Crawford was the son of Akipa, a Dakota medicine man who adopted the name Joseph Akipa Renville, and Winona Crawford, also a Dakota. At the time war broke out between Santee Dakota and Euro-American settlers in Minnesota Territory in 1862, he was employed as a clerk at Yellow Medicine Agency, located near present-day Granite Falls, Minnesota. Charged by the authorities with participating in the fighting, Crawford was tried and acquitted twice by a military commission. Following a winter of detainment at Fort Snelling in Minnesota, he served as a scout for Colonel Henry H. Sibley, a military officer who fought against dissident Dakota in the region, from 1863 to 1866. Crawford, who settled on the Sisseton Reservation in present-day South Dakota, also served as an interpreter for Dakota delegations sent to negotiate treaties with the U.S. government. In 1877 he became a member of the Presbyterian Church and was licensed to preach two years later. In 1901 Crawford testified about his observations and experiences during the Dakota War of 1862 in Minnesota. By that time he had lost his fluency in English and required an interpreter. Crawford died in 1920.

CRAZY MULE *(?–1889) Cheyenne* A respected holy man and headman of the Crazy Dog Society of his people. Crazy Mule was a Northern Cheyenne of great spiritual power. He was so venerated that he was chosen together with another holy man, BOX ELDER, to assist in the work of replacing the SACRED ARROWS captured by the Pawnee in 1830. Crazy Mule was also a warrior who fought against the enemies of the Cheyenne. In 1865 and again in 1866, his bullet-proof powers were demonstrated during battles against U.S. military soldiers. After one encounter, he retrieved 27 enemy bullets from his moccasins. Not one of them had succeeded in harming him. Crazy Mule was also known to have the power to kill enemies by merely looking at them. In 1867, however, he was slightly wounded after being shot near the Big Horn River fort. For the most part, he then lived among the Southern Cheyenne in Indian Territory (present-day Oklahoma). Crazy Mule is said to have been in the tribal delegation that traveled to Washington in 1873 to negotiate an agreement with the government. The respected holy man, healer, and warrior died among the Southern Cheyenne about 1889.

CREATOR Native Americans have a belief in a Supreme Creator who is above all other spirit beings, all powers of nature, and distant from people and daily existence. As long ago as 1851, Lewis Henry Morgan, a pioneer ethnologist noted: "That the Indian, without the aid of revelation, should have arrived at a fixed belief in the existence of the Supreme Being, has ever been a matter of surprise and admiration. In the existence of the Great Spirit, an invisible but ever-present Deity, the universal red race believed. "The Creator is generally invisible, male or female, and little is known about the Creator's nature. The Creator's name varies from tribe to tribe. The Algonquians call the Creator Gitche Manitou, or Great Spirit or Creator; the Apache, Unsen, In Charge of Life or Life Giver; the Cheyenne, Maheo; the Dakota, Wakan Tanka, Great Mystery; the Hopi, Taiowa; the Keresan, Sus-sustinako, Thinking (Thought) Woman; the Maidu, Earth Initiate; the Pawnee, Tirawa; the Shoshone, Tam Apo; the Winnebago (Ho-Chunk), Earthmaker; the Zuni, Awonawilona, the Maker. In most traditional accounts, the Navajo (Dineh) Supreme Being is not named because the people believe it is an unknown power. In general, the Creator does not stay to guide the world he/she created. The Creator leaves work to the intermediaries, helpers and lesser spirits and culture heros they have created.

Creator Twins often cooperate to compete in creation. They may be brothers or sisters. In many Native American groups, it is common to tell stories about twin brothers who are culture heros. In some stories, one brother tries to create a perfect world and bring benefits to people and the other brother tries to undo and reverse the brother's work by bringing old age, disease and death. One is a positive transformer of the landscape and the founder of institutions, the other destructive.

The Seneca tell the story about the twin brothers Flint and Sprout. They are the grandchildren of the Woman Who Fell from the Sky who gave birth to a daughter who was mysteriously impregnated with twins. Sprout was born normally and is the good-minded brother; Flint was born abnormally as the evil-minded brother who burst forth from his mother's armpit, killing her. The rival twins engaged in a struggle to establish the world. Sprout, the right-handed twin did everything just as he should and told the truth. The left-handed twin, Flint, lied and was devious. Making animals from clay, Sprout created deer and Flint made mountain lions that kill deer. Sprout made berries and fruit for creatures to eat and Flint created briars, poison ivy, and poisonous plants like baneberry. Sprout made plant-eating animals that would eat up vegetation if their number was not kept down by meat-eating animals created by Flint. If meat-eating animals ate too many other animals, however, they would starve, for they would run out of meat. Thus, the twins built balance in the world.

The Navajo (Dineh) tell the story of Changing Woman, discovered and brought up by First Man and First Woman under the direction of the HOLY PEOPLE, who bore twin boys. Monster Slayer is the older, braver brother and Child Born of Water, is the younger, weaker brother. The twins set out to find their father to ask him for help in destroying monsters bothering Earth people. They learned from Spider Woman about hazards on the long and dangerous journey they were to undertake. After testing the twin brothers, the Sun recognized them as his sons, promising to help them kill the monsters. After returning from their visit to Sun, Monster Slayer set out and destroyed many of the monsters that harmed people, with the help of his younger brother. The twins allowed old age, hunger, poverty, sleep, and other monsters to live because these monsters convinced the twins they would be useful in the future.

CREATION ACCOUNTS Descriptions of world creation, the first people, and the nature of the world in which people live given in oral narratives comparable to the Bible and to sacred books of other faiths. Indian people prefer the terms *traditions, stories,* or *sacred narratives* to the term *mythology.* Indians do not think of their creation accounts as "myth," but rather they believe the events really happened and these narratives embody the world views and moral outlooks of a group. Indian creation stories refer to a distant past when animals were still humanlike and spoke with human language. The Supreme Being plays an obscure part in many of the stories, withdrawing in favor of other beings—culture heroes, twins, and tribal ancestors—who are connected to the beginning of existence. Culture heroes live in the era after the world is created but before it is inhabited by people. The hero transforms the world after creation or assists the Creator with it. There are many accounts about culture heroes, often regarded as trickster-transformers, set in a not quite so distant time when the world had assumed its present form.

Creation stories are usually recited in ritual form but not all rites involve recitals of traditional stories nor do all stories have ritual expressions. Often, a sacred aura and serious demeanor accompany the telling of the creation story. Sacred genesis accounts, often extensive, are known and told by specialists like priests or heads of clans or societies who learned the narratives from predecessors. Sacred stories sometimes are ceremonial property passed down to males of a family. There can be many versions of creation stories told by members of different families in different communities, some even contradicting one another, and storytellers have their own way of telling the creation stories. Stories are told during designated periods, usually winter, when stinging and biting animals are not out to bother the storyteller.

Most Native American accounts of creation vary according to a people's way of life, geography, climate, food eaten, other subsistence factors, and sacred history. In North America, there are endless stories regarding the creation of the world, people, animals, plants, birds, and other beings. Many tribes throughout North America (except in the Southwest, North Pacific Coast, and Arctic) began in a watery environment from which different beings bring up mud to make the earth. In the Southwest, tribes describe four or five worlds, one on top of the other, through which people climb up to eventually emerge from Mother Earth, returning there after death. In the Northwest, people descend through a hole in the sky to emerge in the present world. In some places like Southern California, the world is thought to have resulted from cohabitation between Sky/Man and Earth/Woman. "Of the Creation of mankind there are probably as many stories as there are tribes," wrote George Gibbs in 1865 in an extensive study of Northwest Indian "mythology." The following condensed accounts of world creation illustrate the diverse stories.

Arapaho

(Wyoming) In the beginning, there was only water. Man-Above, formless and invisible, told Flat Pipe, floating on the water's surface, to call on helpers to help him make a

world. Flat Pipe imagined ducks and water birds and they appeared floating around him. He told them to dive to the bottom of the water and bring him whatever they found beneath them. After the ducks failed to find anything, owing to the depth of the water, the geese tried and failed, as did the swans. Finally a turtle dove to the bottom of the water, resurfaced, and spit a small piece of earth onto Flat Pipe. The earth that Flat Pipe held grew and spread and became the world.

Cherokee

(*North Carolina*) In the beginning, all was water. The animals who lived above the rainbow were crowded and wanted more room. They wondered what was below the water, and a little water beetle offered to look. It dived to the bottom and came up with soft mud which began to grow until it became the island we call the earth. Later, it was fastened to the sky ceiling with four cords.

Diegueño

(*California*) In the beginning, when Tu-chai-pai, the Maker, made the world, the earth was the woman and the sky was the man, and the world was a pure lake covered with tules. Sky came down upon the earth. The Maker and his brother, Yo-ko-mat-is, blew and the heavens rose higher and higher above their heads until it formed a concave arch. The Maker made hills, valleys, little hollows of water, and forests and dug in the ground for mud to make the first people, the Indians.

Iroquois (Haudenosaunee)

(*New York*) In the beginning, there was no land, no people. There was a great ocean and above it air. In the air lived birds and in the ocean lived fish. Above the unpeopled world, there was Sky-World, inhabited by deities who were like people. In the middle of Sky-World there was a sacred tree with enormous roots that spread out from the floor of Sky-World. A pregnant woman who lived in Sky-World decided she wanted bark from one of the roots. She told her husband, who knew the tree was not to be mutilated by any beings in Sky-World. As he dug a hole among the roots, he broke a hole through them and his wife fell through it toward the ocean. Birds made a feathered raft to support her and broke her fall. The birds placed her on the shell of a turtle, who had agreed to rescue her. The sea creatures offered to help her and she told them to find some soil for the roots stuck between her fingers. The muskrat succeeded in diving to the bottom of the ocean and bringing from it the soil from which the earth was to grow. The woman took a tiny amount of soil and placed it on the sea turtle's back, walked in a circle the way the Sun moves in the sky and the earth began to grow. When the earth was big enough the woman planted the roots clutched between her fingers when

she fell from Sky-World and plants grew on the earth. To keep the earth growing, the woman walked as the sun goes around. When she had a daughter, the two kept walking in a circle around the earth so the earth and plants would continue to grow. (There are a number of versions of this story told throughout the Iroquois nations of the Mohawk, Onondaga, Seneca, Cayuga, Oneida.)

Navajo (Dineh)

(*Arizona, New Mexico, Utah*) The Navajo tell different versions of Navajo creation and the various underworlds. Accounts vary regarding the exact number of previous worlds or of the events or color in each. In the beginning, there was the First, or Black, World, inhabited by spirit people and HOLY PEOPLE. It was small and looked like a floating island in a sea of water mist. Creatures living in this world were thought of as Mist Beings as they had no form. They changed in later worlds to living things as we know them. Various beings disagreed and fought and the entire population emerged upward into the Second, or Blue, World through an opening. First Man and First Woman were formed in this world but not in their present shape. In the Second World, there was suffering and quarreling among the beings living there. First Man made a wand that helped carry the beings into the next world through an opening. In the Third, or Yellow, World, all the people were similar in that they had no definite form. There was a great flood and First Man attempted to save people. On his fourth attempt, he planted a female reed, which grew to the top of the sky. People crowded into the reed and climbed up into the Fourth World. In the Fourth World, First Man and First Woman formed four main sacred mountains from soil that First Man gathered from mountains in the Third World. The first fire, sweat bath, hogan, stars, Sun, Moon, seasons, harvest, and many other things were then created, as were the first human man and woman, the first Navajo. Some versions state that people went to the Place of Emergence and reached the Fifth, or present, World.

Netsilik Inuit

(*Canada*) The earth always existed, though in the earliest times, everything was in darkness. When man first appeared, he lived without sunlight and there were no animals to hunt. Nuliajuk, an orphan girl, was pushed into the sea by the people of her camp and sank to the bottom of the ocean. She became a sea spirit and created all the animals of the sea and land. There was no difference between humans and animals and all spoke the same tongue. Words had power and anything spoken could produce immediate physical effects. As soon as people wished for food, their camp was transported through air to a new place where they could obtain nourishment. When a flood destroyed the land, all animals and people died with the exception of two shamans, one of whom became pregnant. During these times, giants fought and many evil spirits went up into the air as a result of broken taboos and they made human life dangerous. The creation of the visible world took place simultaneously with the establishment of the moral order characterized by good and evil and taboos related to them.

Ojibway (Anishinabe, Chippewa)

(Michigan, Wisconsin) There are many versions of the Ojibway (Anishinabe, Chippewa) creation story. In one, Nanabozho's mother gave birth to several beings, including Nanabozho, and then died because she ignored her mother's advice to face a certain direction. Nanabozho then lived with his grandmother and sought revenge against those responsible for his mother's death. In several versions of the story, he held his brother responsible. Against the wishes of his grandmother, he did battle with brother and killed him. Nanabozho lived alone with a wolf, which drowned as it tried to kill game near water. Nanabozho transformed himself into a stump in order to get revenge for the wolf's death and attacked the underwater *manitos* (beings). Nanabozho then met an old woman in the woods from whom he learned that he only wounded, not slayed them. He killed her and disguised himself with her skin so he could travel in the water to the *manito* camp and finish killing the one(s) responsible for the death of the wolf. A flood resulted and Nanabozho climbed a tall tree to escape the water. After the water stopped, he decided to create a new earth so he told several animals to dive into the water for a piece of earth. The muskrat succeeded in collecting small pieces from which Nanabozho created a new earth large enough for all the people and animals.

Pawnee

(Oklahoma, Nebraska) In the beginning, the Power needed help, so stars, sun, moon, clouds, winds, lightning, and thunder were created. The Power told the Evening Star to order her priests to sing and shake their rattles. A great storm came up and rolled across the formless world and passed the Power, who dropped a pebble into the clouds. After the storm, the world was water. The Power sent out Black, Yellow, White, and Red stars each carrying a cedar war club. Each struck the water with the club and the waters parted and earth appeared. Again, Power told the Evening Star to order her priests to rattle and sing. Again a storm ensued. The thunders shook earth, and hills and valleys, mountains and plains were formed. Then Power created life on earth.

Tohono O'odham (Pagago)

(Arizona) In the beginning, Earthmaker made the whole earth out of a little ball of dirt. He danced on the ball and pushed it until it expanded. There was a great noise and I'itoi jumped out of the earth to help Earthmaker give the world its shape. Coyote, who was with Earthmaker from the beginning, followed Earthmaker and I'itoi everywhere while they made and shaped people of the earth.

Ute

(Colorado, Utah) In the beginning, there was nothing but blue sky, clouds, sunshine, and rain. Great He-She spirit lived in the middle of the sky and ruled above. Lonesome, he made a big hole through the heavens and looked at nothingness below. After pouring snow and rain through the hole, He-She took dirt and stone from the hole in the floor of heaven and poured it through to the void below, creating mountains, and the spirit crawled through the hole to get a better look. Because the dirt, stones, snow, and rain had formed something ugly, He-She touched the earth and trees and forests appeared. His hand created plains, grass, and small plants. He told sun to shine through the hole in the sky and as snow melted, lakes and rivers were created. These flowed east and west into great lakes, forming the oceans. He made fish, birds, and animals and left the bear in charge while He-She went back to the heavens to rest.

Winnebago (Ho-Chunk)

(Wisconsin) In the beginning, Earthmaker was alone in space. He began to cry and his falling tears formed the seas. When Earthmaker wished for something, it would come into existence. He wished for light, and light was created. He wished for the earth and the earth came into existence. But Earth was not quiet, so he made trees, but they did not quiet earth. He created the four cardinal points and four winds and placed them at four corners of the earth to act as weights holding down the island earth. But this did not quiet earth. Finally, he made four large snake beings and threw them down toward earth and they pierced through earth, quieting it.

Zuni

(New Mexico) In one of the many versions of the Zuni creation story, in the beginning, all was fog rising like steam. Awonawilona existed alone in the void. With the breath from his heart, Awonawilona created mist, then made himself into the sun. The mist thickened and fell as rain, forming the great waters of the world. Next, Awonawilona took some of his own flesh and placed it on the water, where it expanded into the shape of Mother Earth and Father Sky. These two lay together and conceived life in the four-chambered earth womb, or four underworlds, through which the first beings passed to emerge at the earth's surface.

CROSBY, THOMAS *(1840–1914)* The first Methodist missionary to Native people in British Columbia. Crosby was born on June 21, 1841, in Pickering, Yorkshire, England. He moved to Canada with his family in 1856. In response to a religious calling, Crosby left Woodstock, Canada West for British Columbia in 1862. After working initially as a laborer, he was placed in charge of an Indian school at Nanaimo on Vancouver Island the following year. Crosby, who was ordained in 1871, went to Fort Simpson (now Port Simpson) in 1874 to serve as the first full-time Methodist missionary among British Columbia's Native people. Besides working with the Tsimshian, he became instrumental in expanding Methodist missionary efforts to other groups in the region. A number of mission stations were established, including one at Kitamat among the Bella Bella people in 1876. Initially traveling by canoe along the coast and on the Skeena and Nass Rivers, Crosby later acquired a steamboat, the *Glad Tidings,* to reach distant areas. His missionary efforts included assisting in organizing native teams to preach Methodism from one village to another, encouraging Indian people to cover the cost of constructing mission buildings, and promoting agricultural fairs and other programs. Crosby wrote *David Sallosalton* (1906), about the life of a young Native preacher who died of tuberculosis; *Among the An-ko-me-nums,* or *Flathead . . .* (1907), which included the motto: "They may not want you, but they need you"; and *Up and Down the North Pacific Coast by Canoe and Mission Ship* (c. 1914). He remained in British Columbia for the duration of his career. Crosby died on January 13, 1914, in Vancouver. (See also DUNCAN, WILLIAM.)

CROSS FIRE CEREMONY   See PEYOTE RELIGION

CROW-WATER SOCIETY *Blackfeet* A religious society of the Piegan (one member of the Blackfeet Confederacy). It was founded by Iron, a Piegan man, who acquired it while living among the Crow people. Upon returning home, he ritually transferred some of his rights and powers to Curlybear, another member of the tribal group, and the society grew. Ceremonies could be held to fulfill the vow of a person seeking spiritual help for someone in ill health. Ritual elements included smoking the pipe, consecrating sacred bundles, the singing of sacred songs, dancing to pray for health and happiness, distributing gifts, and eating consecrated foods. Both men and women could belong to the Crow-Water Society, which was believed to bring prosperity to its members and to give them the power to cure the sick with their prayers. (See also ALL-SMOKING CEREMONY; BLACK-TAILED DEER DANCE; DANCE FOR THE SPIRITS OF THE DEAD; STICK GAME DANCE.)

CRY HOUSE *Cocopa, Quechan* This ceremonial structure of the Cocopa and Quechan is a place where the mourning cer-

emony, cremation rituals, and annual memorial for the dead are held. (See MOURNING CEREMONY [Cocopa].)

CUNNINGHAM, EDWARD *(1862–1920) Métis* The first Métis in Canada to be ordained a Roman Catholic priest. Cunningham, one of 11 children of John Cunningham and his wife, Rosalie L'Hirondelle, was born in Edmonton, Alberta, on July 5, 1862. His father, of Irish descent, was employed by the Hudson's Bay Company as a scout and hunter. After his father's death in 1868, his mother raised the younger children in the family alone. Cunningham began his classical studies at St. Albert, eventually attending the University of Ottawa from 1882 to 1885. He served his novitiate at Lachine in Quebec (1885–86), then continued his religious studies at St. Joseph in Ottawa (1886–88) and at Lac La Biche, Alberta (1888–90). Cunningham was ordained to the priesthood on March 19, 1890, by Monsignor Vital-Justin at St. Albert. The missions he served included Fort MacLeod, St. Albert, and Lac La Biche in Alberta, and Onion Lake in Saskatchewan. He worked among the Piegan and other groups. Father Edward Cunningham died in Edmonton, Alberta, on July 1, 1920.

CURING CEREMONIALS *Apache* Shorter ceremonials that determine the cause of illness and how to cure it begin at dusk and close by midnight. Longer ceremonials to cure or remove the illness begin at dusk and continue until dawn. Some of the latter go on for more than one night. The ritual follows a prescribed structure that includes the use of paraphernalia at certain points and chants. Pollen is an important ceremonial offering as well. The ceremonies are usually held at night for one person at a time, but the rites are also given in time of epidemics. Some ceremonies are protective and take place in the spring and summer when lightning, snakes, and venomous creatures are a danger. The ceremony involves people who care about the patient, and everyone who comes has a role. A positive atmosphere of happiness is maintained because the opposite conveys doubt and defeat.

CURING CEREMONIALS *Keresan* Communal ceremonies for purifying the entire pueblo and its inhabitants. Their purposes are to prevent sickness as well as to cure it, to purge the town of all evil influences, and to promote health and well-being of the people. A priest determines whether or not to have a ceremony and selects the medicine society that will take charge. There are curing ceremonies for individuals in society chambers. The priests look for "sickness" objects that witches have "shot" into the person. They suck out "witch-sent" objects and give medicine to the patient and relatives. A feast follows the cure. (See also MEDICINE SOCIETIES [Keresan].)

CURING SOCIETIES *Zuni* There are a number of curing or medicine societies, each specializing in curing a certain disease and whose membership is open to men and women. They heal the sick and are adjuncts in certain communal ceremonies. They are joined by women and men who have fallen ill and have been treated by members of the societies or by those who have trespassed. Anyone receiving such a treatment is required to join the society through initiation. The doctor who did the curing becomes the "ceremonial father" who acts as the patient's sponsor and prepares the sacred object for the novice. Each society has medicines and songs and initiations of new members. Members make and deposit prayersticks in shrines at solstices, deaths of members, and society meetings. The societies conduct collective ceremonies in the fall and winter, never in the agricultural seasons, which belong to the KACHINA SOCIETY or to RAIN PRIESTHOODS. Following a ceremony for rain and fertility, the societies go into retreat in their houses, during which the BEAST GODS, their patrons, spirits who are givers of medicine and long life, but also witchcraft are invoked and impersonated with masks. Individual societies hold ceremonies irregularly on occasions of initiation or curing by removing a disease object by sucking. The societies also are experts about different kinds of diseases and have rituals using altars and sacred objects. Some of the curing societies are called Newekwe (GALAXY SOCIETY), Hunters, Wood, Great Fire, Eagle Down, Ant, Little Fire, Cactus, Struck-by-Lightning, Rattlesnake, and others.

CURLY-HEADED DOCTOR (*d. 1890*) *Modoc* A noted shaman who served in a leadership role during the Modoc War of 1872–73, fought between Modoc and U.S. troops in California. During the fighting, precipitated by poor conditions arising out of tribal land losses, Curly-Headed Doctor encircled the Modoc warriors with a line or a cord painted red to protect them from the military. He told the warriors that the enemy soldiers would not be able to cross the spiritual barrier, for if they came in contact with it they would die. The shaman's oratorical powers and sacred ceremonies, along with Modoc successes against the U.S. military, contributed to his influence. In late 1872 Curly-Headed Doctor and his son-in-law, Hooker Jim, led a number of their people in a raid against a ranch to retaliate for an earlier attack by white ranchers. After killing 12 people, the dissidents fled farther south and joined Captain Jack, the Modoc leader of the war, at a natural fortification of lava beds known to the Indians as "Land of Burnt Out Fires." Captain Jack and his group provided them refuge and refused to meet the military's demand that they be turned in to the authorities. Curly-Headed Doctor and other leaders eventually surrendered to the U.S. forces. They then assisted the government in tracking down Captain Jack. After the war, the shaman and other Modoc were exiled to Indian Territory (present-day Oklahoma). Curly-Headed Doctor died there in 1890.

CUSICK, ALBERT (Sagonaquade, "He Angers Them") (*1846–?*) *Onondaga-Tuscarora* An Onondaga deacon whose contributions to ethnology in the areas of Iroquois language and culture are highly valued. Born on the Tuscarora reservation in New York on December 25, 1846, to an Onondaga mother, he was a descendant of Nicholas Cusick, a Tuscarora chief. A chief himself until he lost the position after converting to Christianity, Cusick was ordained a deacon by Bishop Frederic Huntington, the Protestant Episcopal bishop of central New York, on October 1, 1891.

CUSTALOW, OTHA THOMAS (*fl. 20th century*) *Mattaponi* A Baptist minister who served as a Mattaponi chief from 1949 to 1969. Custalow assumed the tribal leadership role among his people in Virginia after the death of his father, the preceding chief, in 1949. He was later ordained to the Baptist ministry, traveling to distant locations to hold services and revivals. When the state of Virginia leased and paved a road in the 1950s on the Mattaponi reservation in King William County, the small community drew more visitors. Custalow then opened a museum, which continues to operate in the present-day. The chief and minister was known for his showmanship and for attracting more public attention to his people. After his death, Custalow's descendants continued his leadership role among the Mattaponi.

CUSTOMS AUTHORITY See YAQUI CEREMONIALISM

D

DAILEY, TRUMAN *(fl. 1940s–1970s) Otoe* One of the most important peyote missionaries to the Navajo (Dineh) in the early 1940s, who attributed his way of conducting meetings to HUNTING HORSE, a renowned Kiowa peyotist. Elected one of the first officers of the NATIVE AMERICAN CHURCH of the United States in 1944, Dailey continued as an active member of the organization and was repeatedly chosen for various offices. Dailey's first meeting for the Navajo was conducted in 1943 at Divide Store, near Window Rock, Arizona, where he met Mike Kiyaani, who became his disciple. Dailey returned to the reservation on a regular basis for several weeks each year to conduct services. During a 10-year period when he was employed as an Indian chief at Disneyland, Dailey also conducted meetings for Navajo railroad workers in Southern California. He organized a peyote church in a hogan near Needles, California, and was in charge of services the night Jack Woody, Dan Dee Nez, and Leon B. Anderson were arrested and charged with illegal possession of narcotics. This incident led to the landmark case upholding Native American religious freedom, *PEOPLE V. WOODY.* Dailey also taught Theodore Strong, a Yakama peyotist, the Half Moon peyote ritual. With Dailey's encouragement, Strong filed articles of incorporation for the Native American Church in the state of Washington in 1977.

DAKOTA NATIVE MISSIONARY SOCIETY An organization formed in 1876 after Dakota Christians made a request to the Reverend JOHN P. WILLIAMSON for their own missionary society. Within its first decade of operation, Native people annually contributed $1,100 and supported three missionaries in their work. The Reverend DAVID GREY CLOUD served as the Dakota Native Missionary Society's first missionary.

DALTON, MATTHEW WILLIAM *(1828–1918)* A missionary who served as president of the Indian Territory (present-day Oklahoma) mission of the Church of Jesus Christ of Latter-day Saints. He was born to Mary McGovern and John Dalton on November 1, 1828, in Madrid, New York. He arrived in Ogden, Utah, on September 5, 1850, and was baptized to the Mormon faith a few months later. He began his first mission in Indian Territory in 1877 and his second in 1883. During that period he taught farming and built the mission's first house. Dalton died on March 14, 1918, in Willard, Utah. (See also COOK, WASHINGTON N.; KIMBALL, ANDREW.)

DANCE Dance is fundamental to most Indian religions. It is inseparably bound up with Native American ceremonies and is an important part of worship and ritual. Among Indians in North America, every dance has its own steps, attitudes, rhythm, song or songs with words, accompanying music, and regalia. Some dances are performed by men, others by women, and some by men and women. Some are performed by a single dancer, others by all who wish to take part. Still others are for members of certain societies. There are personal, fraternal, clan, tribal, and intertribal dances. There are dances that express gratitude and thanksgiving, mourning, patriotism, and comedy. There are dances that are social, mimic, militaristic, invocative, and offertory.

Among people from European traditions, dance has become differentiated as a "performance art" that is secular and individual-oriented in contrast to Indians, whose dances are sacred group expressions. (See list of ceremonies in the Subject Index for individual entries in this volume.)

DANCE FOR THE SPIRITS OF THE DEAD *Blackfeet* A sacred religious ceremony known to all divisions of the Blackfeet. The Dance for the Spirits of the Dead, sometimes referred to as a ghost dance, was believed to have ancient origins. Besides being attributed to a dance done by Kut-toe-yis, or Blood-clot, in the stomach of a monster, other versions of its inception exist among the people. The sacred ceremony was generally initiated when a person seeking spiritual assistance or blessings made a vow to provide it. Ritual elements included inviting the spirits of the dead to the ceremony, the singing of specific sacred songs, the symbolic painting of the dancers, the smoking of the pipe, and four periods of dancing. At the point when the spirits were invited in, they could not be called by name. (See also ALL-SMOKING CEREMONY; BLACK-TAILED DEER DANCE; CROW-WATER SOCIETY; STICK GAME DANCE.)

DANCING SOCIETIES *North Pacific Coast* Referred to as "secret societies," the members of these ritual organizations have inherited the right to impersonate spiritual beings from whom they have received power. Traditional stories account for the introduction of the dance by an ancestor who encountered a spiritual being and was instructed by that power. All those whose ancestors had an encounter with the same spiritual being from a dancing society organized in a hierarchic structure that performs the same dance. Positions in dancing societies are limited because only one person can inherit the right to represent each ancestor. Vacancies must arise before a new member can be initiated. The chief or family head, as religious leader, controls initiations and roles that initiates play. Initiations give new members the right to use family or clan crests, sacred names, songs, dances, cedar bark rings, and ritual acts. Dancing societies differ chiefly in the type of spiritual power with whom ancestors had dealings. Members of the SHAMANS' SOCIETY, THOSE-WHO-DESCEND-FROM-THE-HEAVENS, and the Nutlam perform elaborate dramatizations of ancestral encounters with respective spirit powers, displaying the gifts bestowed on the ancestors. The dancers differ from society to society. The principal performers (novices) relive the ancestral experience and become inspired (possessed by the spirit their ancestors encountered). They are abducted by the spirit who then returns them endowed with varied ceremonial prerogatives. The gifts (songs, names, masks and other regalia, and the power to perform various acts on cer-

emonial occasions) are hereditary property. (See also CEREMONIAL SOCIETIES.)

DANIEL, ANTOINE *(1601–1648)* French Jesuit missionary. Daniel was born in Dieppe, France, and entered the Jesuit novitiate in 1621 at the age of 20. He taught classes at the College of Rouen from 1623 until 1627, the time during which AMANTACHA, a Huron Indian, was baptized at Rouen. Some scholars believe that Amantacha helped influence Daniel's choice of a missionary life. Daniel arrived in Cape Breton in 1632 and was assigned to Quebec to help found a seminary for young Huron. After this failed, he returned in 1638 to missionary life, where he remained until his death in 1648 at the hands of Iroquois. Father Daniel was the first martyr of Huronia in southern Ontario, Canada. He was canonized by Pope Pius XI on June 29, 1930.

DARK DANCE (Pygmy) *Iroquois* An ancient curing ceremony, also known as Pygmy, that is an invocation to the spirits of the departed. The dance is performed at night, in darkness, in private homes, not the longhouse, at any time of the year. Members of the LITTLE PEOPLE SOCIETY who perform the ceremony sing in their own language. Performing the rite is restricted to members, those people who have benefited from the treatment of illness. A family makes the arrangements and pays for a feast that accompanies the ceremony.

DA'TEKAN ("Keeps His Name Always") *(?–c. 1883) Kiowa* A young medicine man who announced in early 1882 that he had received a vision giving him a mission to restore the buffalo among the people. He then began making medicine and took the name Pa-tepte, "buffalo-bull-coming-out," to represent his new role. He set up a sacred tipi, erecting a pole in front of it with a buffalo skin at the top, and made himself a red robe trimmed with eagle feathers. Da'tekan informed the people that if they followed his prayers and ceremonies the buffalo would return as foretold in his dream. The listeners promised to obey his instructions and rewarded him with blankets and other belongings in appreciation of his efforts. Da'tekan continued making medicine for a year, when he died without seeing his prophecies fulfilled. His efforts to restore the buffalo were depicted in an 1882 Kiowa calendar. His beliefs were revived in 1887 by the Kiowa prophet PA'-INGYA.

DAVIS, GLORIA ANN *(b. 1933) Navajo (Dineh)-Choctaw* Roman Catholic nun who was born at Fort Defiance, Arizona, on September 5, 1933. Davis entered the Order of the Blessed Sacrament in 1952 and became the first American Indian in that religious congregation. She later served as a teacher and a guidance counselor at schools in Arizona, Louisiana, and Pennsylvania, where she worked primarily with elementary children from minority backgrounds. In Arizona Davis taught at Houck, where she began broadcasting a radio program in the Navajo language and later at St. Michaels.

DAVIS, JOHN *(?–c. 1840) Creek* A missionary assistant and interpreter who coauthored biblical translations in the Creek language. Born in the southeastern homeland of his people, he was captured as a child during the War of 1812 and was brought up by a white family. After leaving Alabama for the West in 1829, he received an education at the Union Mission, located about 25 miles above the Arkansas River. He began assisting the missionaries, who considered him a valuable helper with good talents, by speaking at public meetings and serving as an interpreter. Davis coauthored, with Johnston Lykens, a Creek translation of the Gospel according to St. John, which was published by the Shawanoe Baptist Mission in Indian Territory (present-day Oklahoma) in 1835. He also contributed to the publication of two volumes of hymns in the Creek language, collaborating with the missionaries ROBERT MCGILL LOUGHRIDGE and WILLIAM SCHENCK ROBERTSON. One of his two daughters, Susan McIntosh, also assisted a missionary, ANN ELIZA WORCESTER ROBERTSON, in completing Creek translations.

DAVIS, OLA CASSADORE *(1923–) San Carlos Apache* A grandmother, traditional medicine woman, and a Western Apache traditional cultural leader who lives at the Apache San Carlos Reservation. Ola Cassadore Davis has been a tireless worker in the effort to protect the Apache people's sacred lands, ceremonies, and Dzil Nchaa Si'an, also known as MOUNT GRAHAM, a sacred mountain in the Coronado National Forest in Arizona.

Fortified by the teachings of her father, Albert Cassadore, who was a revered Apache medicine man and spiritual adviser to his people, Ola, one of 11 children, took on the task of preserving the spiritual integrity of the Apache people's traditional cultural property, Dzil Nchaa Si'an. She became chairperson of the Apache Survival Coalition, organized in 1986, to protest the construction of telescopes on the sacred mountain by the University of Arizona and its partners. Since then, Davis has visited hundreds of families on the reservation to explain the planned desecration of Mount Graham and has met with lawyers in Washington, D.C., members of other tribes, and city government officials in Rome and Florence, Italy, who opposed the telescope project.

DEACON *Six Nations Reserve, Iroquois, Canada* At Six Nations Reserve in Canada, the male and female officers who direct, arrange, and administer all longhouse activities are called deacons, whereas in the United States, the comparable officers are called FAITHKEEPERS. At the Six Nations longhouses, there are deacons who inherit the office through matrilineal descent, those who are good community workers, and those who are affiliated with hereditary chiefs as assistants. Deacons are invested at the MIDWINTER CEREMONY and GREEN CORN Festival and hold the office for life. They can be deposed, however, for unsatisfactory conduct.

DEATH FEAST *Shawnee* An annual feast held to honor the spirits of the deceased that is conducted mainly in the home rather than as a public observance, often after the GREEN CORN DANCE. As described among the Absentee Shawnee, food is prepared and served on a table in a room, and a person, selected for the role, speaks to the spirits. Besides telling them that they are fondly remembered and that the food provided has been prepared in their honor, the speaker may request that they not disturb the living. After extinguishing the lights, the room is left empty, and the feast remains on the table for a number of hours. It is believed that the spirits participate in the feast but that they eat only the spiritual part of the food. When family members return to the room, they may eat the feast, but they often find that the "spirit" and some of the food itself are gone. In some versions of the ceremony, the speaker talks to the spirits again when the family returns to the room. (See also BREAD DANCE; BUFFALO DANCE; RIDE-IN AND WAR DANCE; RITUAL FOOTBALL GAME.)

DEER DANCE *Tewa* A dance held in winter performed by young men and boys. In some Tewa villages, deer dancers are included in buffalo or game animal dances. (See also ANIMAL DANCES [Pueblo].)

DEER AND ANTELOPE CEREMONIES *Apache* The primary function of these ceremonies was to secure game animals. The deer ceremony consisted of prayers and songs to the deer the night before the hunt, instructing the animals to give up their hide and meat.

DEER DANCER (maso) *Yaqui* This dancer, along with three singers and a manager who accompanies the performance of the Pascola dancers, never appears independently and sometimes performs commercially. The Deer dancer, carrying gourd rattles, dances alone but, when beside the Pascolas, faces the crowd, like them. However, he does not interact with the audience because he dances with the seriousness of sacred devotion. The *maso* sings and dances to songs that address an ancient deer. The Deer dancer wears a deer head over a white cloth while dancing to percussion music made by rasping sticks and a water drum. The dance has symbolism that draws on Yaqui's ritual relationship to the deer and is performed as a service to the people. (See also PASCOLA DANCER.)

DEERE, PHILLIP *(c. late 1920s–1985) Creek* A medicine man and spokesman for the Muskogee, or Creek, traditionalists. Deere descended from tribal members who had resisted Euro-American domination during the Red Stick War of 1813–14, fought against removal to Indian Territory (present-day Oklahoma), and joined the leader Chitto Harjo (Crazy Snake) in his opposition to United States domination of their people. He lived on his mother's 160-acre allotment in Oklahoma, land that had been retained in the family despite federal and state efforts to break it up or change its legal status. Deere built a ceremonial fire and roundhouse at the center of the property. He and members of his family tended crops, raised cattle, and fished in the pond on their land. Deere traveled extensively in the United States and Europe to lecture on issues facing Native American people. He became associated with the American Indian Movement in the late 1960s or early 1970s, serving as a spiritual adviser for the group. In 1979 he began hosting the Youths and Elders Conference at his Creek roundhouse in an effort to bring people of different ages and backgrounds together. Deere also hosted the International Indian Treaty Council, a nongovernment organization of the United Nations. Its work includes drafting resolutions on issues of importance to native people for presentation at worldwide tribunals. Another affiliation was with the Circle of Traditional Indian Elders, an association composed of representatives of the Hopi, Lakota, Iroquois, and other groups. Deere traced his religious and political efforts back to his ancestors, viewing his work as a continuation of their struggle. He continued his ceremonies and gatherings until his death from cancer on August 16, 1985.

DEGANAWIDA (Deganawidah, Dekanawida, Dekanah-wideh) *(1500s) Huron* A prophet, statesman, and law giver who cofounded with Hiawatha the Five Nations Confederacy (the Cayuga, Mohawk, Oneida, Onondaga, and Seneca) and is a culture hero to the Iroquois peoples. Called "Heavenly Messenger," according to ancient belief, he was born among the Huron in Ontario, Canada, to a virgin mother who had been informed in a dream by a messenger from the Creator that she was to bear a son destined to plant the Tree of Peace. By performing miracles that satisfied skeptics, Deganawida and Hiawatha won many adherents to their message of peace. After convincing Atotarho, Onondaga head chief, of his message, Deganawida planted the Tree of Peace at what is now Syracuse, New York, threw war weapons under it, and founded the Iroquois Confederacy. After his work was done, he left his people. His name is also spelled Deganawidah, Dekanawida and Dekanahwideh.

DELAWARE PROPHET (Neolin) *(fl. 1760s) Delaware (Lenni Lenape)* An 18th-century prophet who was a major influence on Pontiac, the Ottawa leader, during his 1763 war against the British. Little is known about the prophet's early years, but some of his activities became known through the writings of the missionary JOHN HECKEWELDER and other early Euro-American figures. Heckewelder identified him as a "famous preacher" who, in 1762, was living in the Lake Erie area and traveling among Native people with the message he had received from the Great Spirit. He used a deerskin map he had drawn to point out the way American Indians had once lived, their land losses to the Europeans, and the path to restoring peace and prosperity. The Delaware Prophet's instructions included the relinquishment of customs adopted from the whites, a return to Native traditions and goods and abstention from the alcoholic beverages that had contributed to their diminished numbers. He told them that the Great Spirit would then assist them in their struggles against their enemies and in recovering their losses. The prophet also taught them a prayer, carved upon a prayer stick, which was to be said on a daily basis. His maps were reproduced and distributed among Indian people to serve as reminders of his spiritual teachings. The prophet's message spread to other tribal groups in the region and influenced them to unite with Pontiac against the enemy. Little more was written about the religious leader in the aftermath of Pontiac's defeat and murder. The Delaware Prophet is also referred to as Neolin, the "enlightened one." (See also KENEKUK; TENSKWATAWA; WABOKIESHIEK.)

DELORIA, PHILIP JOSEPH (Tipi Sapa, "Black Lodge") *(1854–1931) Dakota* An Episcopal priest and missionary among his people. His father, Francis Deloria, was a Yankton leader and medicine man who converted to Christianity a few years before his death in 1876. His mother, one of Francis's three wives, was from the Rosebud band of Lakota. Philip Deloria, who also became a chief, relinquished his chieftainship to become an Episcopal missionary priest. After receiving an education at the Yankton Reservation and at Shattuck Military School in Faribault, Minnesota, he served as a catechist. Deloria became a deacon of the church in 1874 and was ordained a priest in 1892. His ministry included 40 years of service on the Standing Rock Reservation, where he was instrumental in establishing St. Elizabeth's

School at Wakpala, South Dakota. Honored as one of the "Saints of the Ages" by his denomination, Reverend Deloria's statue was placed in the National Cathedral in Washington, D.C. He died in 1931. He was married to Mary Sully Bordeau, and their family included five daughters and one son, VINE DELORIA, SR.

DELORIA, VINE, SR. *(1901–1990) Dakota* A Yankton Dakota who, like his father, PHILIP JOSEPH DELORIA, became an Episcopal priest. He was born in 1901 at Wakpala, South Dakota on the Standing Rock Reservation to Philip and Mary Sully Bordeau Deloria. His education included attendance at Kearney Military Academy, where the students were noted for their courtesy and neatness. He became a cadet colonel and later recalled his experience at the academy as character-building. Following his graduation from Bard College with a B.A. degree, Deloria worked in Colorado mines and then became an Indian school adviser. He later completed General Theological Seminary and was ordained in his father's church at Wakpala. Well known among his people, Deloria spent more than 35 years ministering to them before his retirement. Named to the position of assistant secretary in the division of domestic missions, he was the first American Indian to hold a national executive post in the Episcopal Church. Before retiring in his sixties, the Reverend Deloria was named an archdeacon of the Niobrara Deaconry. A symposium speech he made in 1982 was published in 1987 as "The Establishment of Christianity Among the Sioux" in *Sioux Indian Religion* (1987). He retired to his home in Pierre, South Dakota. Deloria's children included a son, Vine Deloria, Jr., the well-known theologian, attorney, and author of *Custer Died for Your Sins* (1969), *God Is Red* (1973), and many other books.

DESMET, PIERRE JEAN *(1801–1873)* Belgian Jesuit missionary who gave a lifetime of service to Northwest Pacific and Plains Indian peoples. He was born in Belgium and arrived in America as a novice of the Society of Jesus in 1821, at the age of 20, and was ordained in 1827. Father DeSmet's first work was among the Potawatomi in Iowa from 1837 to 1839. Soon after, he was in the forefront of a commitment by the Society of Jesus to Christianize the Indians of western America. After leading exploratory parties throughout the Northwest in 1840 and 1841, he cofounded, with Father Gregory Mengarini, St. Mary's Mission, in present-day Montana, among the Flathead. It was the original Jesuit outpost among the Indians of the Pacific Northwest. He founded missions in the Columbia and Willamette Valleys as well in 1844. By 1846, he had founded a Northwest Jesuit mission network from the Rockies to the Pacific. During the 1840s and 1850s, Father DeSmet made repeated visits to the

Dakota and Lakota, winning their respect and trust because he, in turn, treated Indians with respect. He also had contacts with the Coeur d'Alene, Pend d'Oreille, Salish, Blackfeet, Crow, and more than 90 other tribes and baptized thousands. Because of his popularity among the many Plains tribes, he mediated between tribes. The U.S. government invited him to participate in seven treaty negotiations with Indians between 1851 and 1868. Father DeSmet also traveled more than 180,000 miles, crossing the Atlantic at least 16 times to garner people, supplies, and money for the missions in the United States. He informed Europeans about American Indians by writing prolifically in six languages. Father DeSmet, besides being known as one of the most effective Jesuit missionaries, is also known as a peacemaker, mediator, and valued counselor to agents of the federal government. His principal published works include *Letter and Sketches* (1843), *Oregon Missions and Travels* (1847), *Western Missions and Missionaries* (1863), and *New Indian Sketches* (1865).

DEVIL'S TOWER   See MATO TIPILA (BEAR'S LODGE)

DIAGNOSTICIAN *Navajo (Dineh)* The Navajo method of prescribing for sickness, often called divination because those who recommend treatment are prognosticians or seers. Men determine illness by gazing at the Sun, Moon, or stars; both men and women use hand-trembling. Diagnosing is a highly specialized Navajo medical practice used when the cause of disease cannot be determined by obvious symptoms. Said to be in a trance state while practicing, diagnosticians discover not only the cause of the illness but also recommend the proper form of ceremonial to be used, that is, which chant should be sung over the patient, and also recommend the practitioner who can treat the symptoms through ceremonial cure. (See also DISEASE; HAND TREMBLER; STAR GAZING.)

DICK, MIKE *(fl. 1930s) Washoe* The most powerful shaman among his people during the 1930s. He began his practice at the age of 50, following the death of his father. Dick was spiritually instructed to become a doctor and to heal patients. He kept track of the number of people he had doctored on his shaman's staff.

DIRECTIONS   See SIX DIRECTION

DISEASE Traditional Native Americans understand disease in spiritual terms. They believe body, mind, and spirit are interrelated and function together. Not only must humans, viewed as only one part of creation, and all the elements of the natural world be in balance, but people and the spirit world must also be in harmony. Disease and illness result from a lack of harmony, balance, or equilibrium between the sick person and his or her surroundings. In general, most tribes view disease as resulting from spiritual causes, including the failure to observe restrictions that regulate correct behavior, spirit possession, soul loss, witchery, and the intrusion of a foreign object, usually a small object "shot" into the victim by a witch. Bad dreams, an excess in any activity, ignorance of ceremonial law or transgressing it, and sorcery are also sources of illness. Each of these causes can create a great number of symptoms, so Indians turn to their own medical experts, such as a SHAMAN, DIAGNOSTICIAN, HAND TREMBLER, DREAMERS, or others, for diagnosis and cure that aim to restore the person's relationship with spiritual forces. They differentiate, however, between diseases with natural and spiritual causes. Childbirth complication, broken bones, accidental wounds, and other such problems are generally treated pragmatically and without ritual and ceremony.

DITCH CLEANING CEREMONIES *Pueblo* In spring the adult males of Pueblo groups traditionally turn out for the annual cleaning and repairing of irrigation ditches. The opening of community ditches is a ritual affair involving the rites of medicine societies and the deposit of prayersticks by town chiefs.

DLA'UPAC *(fl. c. 1800s) Walula* An early prophet in the Columbia Plateau region who lived near present-day Pasco, Washington. The prophet was believed to have lived before the later prophet SMOHALLA, perhaps in the early 1800s. Dla'upac was said to have been dead for five days and to have returned to life. Found singing, he told the people what he had learned in the spirit world. He prophesied the destruction of the world by fire or flood, as it had been in the past, and the return of the dead to life before the catastrophe. In addition to foretelling the future, Dla'upac told people to prepare themselves for meeting Xwampipama, the Creator.

DOCTOR CHARLEY (Tokta'mts) *(fl. c. 1880s) Modoc* An early shaman who was believed to have discovered an ailment afflicting infants and to have devised a treatment for it. He indicated that the child's heart became irritated as a result of being invisibly linked by a cord to an object in the supernatural realm. This condition was caused by a nightmare-like dream of either parent shortly after birth, when the baby was still close to the spirit world. Ritual elements used by Dr. Charley included the use of a cord grasped by those in attendance at the healing, the singing of dog and frog songs, the retrieval of the object by a spirit, disposal of the object, and a feast of water-lily seeds.

DOCTOR GEORGE *(?–c. 1930) Modoc* A noted shaman among the Modoc people whose initiation for the role is believed to have been the last such ceremony performed. It was held for five nights, as traditional, and was attended by 100 to 200 people. The ceremony included singing by the initiate, dances on the first two nights, and feasting. After completing the initiation, a person became eligible to serve as a shaman. Because illness or death could result from anyone breaking the taboos associated with the role, children in a shaman's household were considered especially at risk. Two sons and two daughters of Doctor George died, and their deaths were attributed to this cause. The shaman was known to have the ability to change the weather and was once asked to pray for rain by a cattleman in the area. After he was successful, the man paid him with food and money. Doctor George was a leader of the DREAM DANCE, a variation of the GHOST DANCE OF 1870. Attempts to suppress the movement and an effort to arrest Doctor George resulted in more secrecy on the part of the adherents. Doctor George's spirits were later said to have killed the children of an enemy. The deaths were avenged—the shaman was killed by four men, who in turn each died within a year. Doctor George's family included his wife, Sally George, who assisted at ceremonies and served as a singer, and their son, Usee George. (See also DOCTOR CHARLEY; JAKALUNUS.)

DOCTOR'S DANCE *California* Also called the doctor-making ceremony or kick dance, this initiation ceremony culminates the long and rigorous training of novice shamans, locally called Indian doctors. The ritual, held for five to 10 nights, includes the fasting, dancing, and singing of newly acquired songs by the novice and singing, kicking, praying, and smoking by the practicing shaman who assists the neophyte. The dance functions as a means by which a shaman attempts to control his or her doctor "pain," a gift from the spirit world. The "pain" is used as an ally to cure sick people. During the kick dance, tribal elders pray, dance, and make invocations to spirits. (See PAINS.)

DOMENICO *(?–1963) Luiseño* A shaman from the Rincon Reservation in California. One of eight children, Domenico (a pseudonym) was also the son of a shaman. As a youngster, he showed interest in his father's work and spent a great deal of time in solitude. Domenico also had visions at an early age. His mother was the first to acknowledge his spiritual powers, but other members of the family initially doubted him. By the time he was 18 years old, these powers were active. Domenico was able to repeat verbatim what two brothers had said about him when they returned from a distant hunting trip. He began taking patients, sharing their sufferings when he received their calls. Domenico's gifts included being able to hear and understand the spirits who appeared to him. After beginning to take patients, he became renowned for his healing abilities. Europeans, Euro-Americans, Mexicans, blacks, and Native people from other tribal groups found their way to him. His practice included healing physical ailments and assisting people experiencing emotional difficulties. He used traditional techniques and also referred patients to Western physicians when the condition warranted it. Domenico was known, for instance, to have removed all but one large gallstone from a patient. Unable to take the remaining one out, he recommended hospital surgery. Domenico did not formally charge patients, but he received contributions from those he helped. Other powers attributed to him included weather control. Although Domenico successfully healed others throughout his life, when he became ill neither his own healing abilities nor those of the hospital physicians were able to help him. As he had not trained an apprentice, he left no successor at his death.

DORSEY, JAMES OWEN *(1848–1895)* An ordained Episcopal deacon who worked as a missionary among the Ponca in Dakota Territory from 1871 to 1873. He was born in Baltimore and showed an early aptitude for linguistics, learning the Hebrew alphabet at age six. After attending Baltimore schools, Dorsey entered the Protestant Episcopal Theological Seminary in Alexandria, Virginia, in 1867 and was ordained a deacon in 1871. He acquired knowledge of the Ponca language during his period of missionary work, but ill health forced him to return to Maryland to do parish work. Dorsey began compiling a dictionary and grammar of that Native language and later, in 1878, undertook ethnological studies among the Omaha for Major John Wesley Powell of the Smithsonian Institution. He returned from his fieldwork in 1880 and prepared a major paper on Omaha sociology for publication by the newly founded Bureau of American Ethnology. He later made a number of field trips to other native groups to collect linguistic material. Dorsey's work on the Siouan language family is considered the first definitive classification. His extensive publications include *Osage Traditions, A Study of Siouan Cults, Omaha Dwellings, Furniture and Implements,* and *Siouan Sociology.* He also wrote *An Account of the War Customs of the Osages, Mourning and War Customs of the Osages, Mourning and War Customs of the Kansas,* and *Migrations of Siouan Tribes.* In addition, Dorsey completed linguistic studies and edited a Dakota dictionary and ethnography by STEPHEN RETURN RIGGS. Most of his data, still unpublished, can be found in the Smithsonian National Anthropological Archives.

DOWD, DONNY *(b. 1940s) Ojibway* A contemporary spiritual leader who was born in the late 1940s or early 1950s. Af-

ter growing up on the L'Anse Reservation in Michigan and spending part of his youth in a Catholic orphanage, Dowd eventually dropped out of high school and enlisted in the U.S. Navy. His years in the military included two tours of duty in Vietnam, where he experienced combat and the loss of friends in battle. Dowd suffered from post-traumatic stress disorder after being discharged and drifted from one job to another. He married and fathered two children, but his marriage eventually ended in divorce. For a time he lived in the Twin Cities, in Minnesota, where he participated in activities of the American Indian Movement, an activist organization that originated in Minneapolis in the late 1960s. Dowd also drifted from that involvement, turning instead to attending Native ceremonies. In the 1970s he attended a MIDEWIWIN gathering, where he and a friend were asked to help a member of the religion by praying for him outside of the ceremonial lodge. As requested, they helped the man. Dowd followed the experience by seeking out spiritual teachers. He was adopted by an Ojibway medicine man in Minnesota and began a religious apprenticeship with him and another instructor in the state. Dowd later lived in a Michigan reservation community with his new wife and family. He conducted ceremonies, including namings, funerals, sweatlodges and spring and fall observances. He also taught cultural programs at the tribal school and assisted with substance-abuse treatment efforts.

DOWNING, LEWIS (Lewie-za-wau-na-skie) *(1823–1872) Cherokee* A Baptist minister who served as chief of the Cherokee Nation from 1867 to 1872. Downing was born to Samuel and Susan Daugherty Downing in the eastern Tennessee area of the Cherokee Nation. After the removal to Indian Territory (present-day Oklahoma), his family resettled in Going Snake, one of eight districts or subdivisions established in the new location. Downing attended Baptist mission schools and was later ordained to the ministry. In 1844 he succeeded JESSE BUSHYHEAD, another Native religious leader, to the pastorate of the Flint Church, earlier called Amohee, in Indian Territory. Downing, who was regarded as a full-blood because his sole spoken and written language was Cherokee, was instrumental in the development of the traditional Ketoowah Society. He shared the abolitionist views of the missionaries EVAN JONES and JOHN BUTTRICK JONES, eventually serving in a Cherokee regiment for the Union during the Civil War. Downing, who served as a chaplain, became a lieutenant colonel. He was also selected as a delegate to Washington on behalf of the John Ross administration of the Cherokee Nation during the war. Downing later served as acting chief, then as chief with his 1867 election to the office. His administration included roles for Native leaders who had supported the Confederacy, contributing to a return to a unified government for the Cherokee Nation. Downing died on November 9, 1872, a short time after his reelection to another four-year term.

DREAM DANCE   See DRUM RELIGION

DREAM DANCE *Klamath, Modoc, Paviotso (Numu, Northern Paiute)*   The Dream Dance is described as the third phase of the GHOST DANCE OF 1870 movement on the Klamath Reservation in Oregon. It differed from the EARTH LODGE RELIGION, which preceded it, by not having a doctrine associated with a pending world catastrophe. Features identified with the Dream Dance at the reservation's Upper End included visions of the dead but not their return to earth, the belief that dreams would make a person ill if they were not acted out, the singing of dream songs and healing aspects. In contrast, the Lower End participants did not include illness and curing features. The Dream Dance was said to be closer to traditional ritualism than the Ghost Dance of 1870 or the Earth Lodge religion. After an attempt to arrest DOCTOR GEORGE, one of the leaders, participants became more secretive. The Dream Dance is believed to have been practiced for at least three years, with some features gradually becoming incorporated into the rituals of traditional religious leaders.

DREAM GUESSING RITE *Iroquois*   Held during the MIDWINTER CEREMONY and during illness, the purpose of this sacred rite is to alleviate symptoms, cure afflicted minds, guess dreams, and fulfill desires of the individual. This was a dominant ceremony at one time, and it still is among the New York Onondaga. People harassed with a persistent dream of evil or trouble relay their dreams in the form of riddles. Once the dream-riddle is guessed, people try to satisfy the riddler's desire. At some point in history, items of food replaced or acted as substitute symbols for real items. Each standard dream was represented by two or more standard symbols. At Onondaga, only medicine or spirit dreams are regarded as valid for guessing. The one who gives the correct answer makes a sacred object (miniature false face mask, lacrosse sticks) and presents it to the dreamer any time during the ceremony. The object is kept in the home of the relieved dreamer-sufferer. Dream guessing is a method of satisfying one's underlying needs to have desire fulfilled, and it permits one to help fulfill the desires of others.

DREAMERS (clairvoyants, fortune tellers) *Iroquois*   Certain men or women with spiritual powers who are called in to diagnose cases of sickness or people's dreams for a fee. They use dreams to prescribe either a ceremony or medicine to cure an ailing person.

DREAMS *Iroquois*   During sleep, an Iroquois person may experience one of two kinds of dreams that lead to ritual action. A symptomatic dream expresses the wish of a dreamer's soul. The wish, interpreted by the dreamer or by a clairvoyant man or woman, may lead to ceremonial action to help carry it out not only at the time of the dream but during the dreamer's whole life span. The community rallies around the dreamer who is fed, danced over, rubbed with ashes, sung to, given presents, and accepted as a member of a medicine society. In a visitation dream powerful beings appear in a person's dream and announce they want something done that is of importance to the entire nation. Whole rituals are said to have been revealed through these dreams, and changes in older rituals have been made on the basis of these visits through dreams. (See also DREAM GUESSING RITE.)

DREXEL, KATHERINE *(1858–1955)*   American Catholic nun. Born in Philadelphia and raised in wealth by a banker, this socialite turned instead to a life of poverty and service. Sister Drexel became a candidate in the novitiate of the Sisters of Mercy. In 1891, Sister Drexel established a new order, the Sisters of the Blessed Sacrament for Indians and Colored People, dedicated to serve African and Native Americans. She built convents and staffed schools, both catechetical and social centers, on reservations in the Southwest to extend Catholicism to Indian children. She gave thousands of dollars yearly to the BUREAU OF CATHOLIC INDIAN MISSIONS so that its projects among Native Americans could be carried on. Eventually, she built 14 boarding schools in eight different states for American Indians. After 1935, halted by a heart attack, she led a life of contemplation for two decades. Today, the Sisters of the Blessed Sacrament continue the work of Katherine Drexel as educators, nurses, home visitors, pastoral ministers, and social workers. They continue institutions such as St. Catherine Indian School in Santa Fe, New Mexico, and St. Michael Indian School in Arizona. Mother Katherine was beatified in Rome in November 1988.

DRUILLETTES, GABRIEL *(1610–1681)*   French Jesuit missionary to the Abenaki in Canada. He was born at Garat, France. He entered the novitiate of the Society of Jesus in 1629 at the age of 19 and was ordained a priest in 1641 or 1642. He sailed for Canada a year later. That year, he spent an autumn hunting season with the Montagnais in order to learn their language. He accompanied them on other winter journeys, as well as into war, and conducted the Tadoussac Mission at the junction of Saquenay and St. Lawrence Rivers during the summer. Father Druillettes then worked among the Abenaki, whose language he learned in three months. He founded a mission on the Kennebec River and demanded that Abenaki renounce liquor, live in peace with their neighbors, and give up their medicine bags, drums, and other "superstitious objects." He instructed Father Jacques Marquette in 1666 and then followed him to the West, where Druillettes had initiated a project to establish missions. He worked near Sault Ste. Marie from 1670 until 1679, returned to Quebec and died there two years later.

DRUM A drum is a sacred ritual object, regarded as alive and representing the heartbeat of a nation, the sound of the universe. The drum is used in many ceremonies and for social gatherings. Each drum is a distinct individual with a name and "voice." There are many types, including the Plains large bass drum, a hand drum with a single or double head, and a WATER DRUM. Drums may be owned by individuals or societies, clans, bands, and other tribal groups.

DRUM DANCE *Caddo* The *cah-kit-em'-bin,* or Drum Dance, is a dance that relates the origins of the Hasinai, or Caddo, people. It is always performed first in a night's cycle of dances that may conclude with the performance of a morning dance. The Drum Dance is led by men, including both singers and drummers, who circle the ceremonial grounds clockwise. Boys may join the singers in order to learn the songs, but they are not permitted to use the drum. Women and other men also participate during the course of the dance, following the lead participants. A second segment, called *wah-sha-nee'-kee,* is performed at a more rapid pace in the center of the ceremonial area. The Drum Dance traditionally incorporated 11 songs that took the people through migrations and other events in their history. Generally lasting about an hour, it reconnects the people with their ancestors and traditions. The Bear, Corn, Women's, Qvapau, and Bell are identified as other Caddo dances.

DRUM RELIGION (Dream Dance) The practice of the Drum religion, also called Dream Dance, has been described among a number of tribal groups, including the Ojibway, Menominee, Potawatomi, Kickapoo, Mesquakie, and Winnebago (Ho-Chunk). The Drum religion includes seasonal ceremonies as well as many other sacred rituals and songs. Estimates of its date of origin generally fall in the second half of the 19th century.

Tailfeather Woman, a Dakota woman, is believed to be the originator of the sacred Dance Drum and its rituals. While being pursued by United States soldiers who were fighting her people, she went into a lake and concealed herself under lily pads. During the period she was hiding, Tailfeather Woman received sacred teachings from the Great Spirit. These instructions were to be carried out and shared with other tribal groups in order to establish peace and stop the bloodshed caused by war. After the Dakota pre-

sented the first Dance Drum to the Ojibway, it was copied and passed on to other Native communities as taught in Tailfeather Woman's vision.

At the heart of the religion is the revered Dance Drum. Regarded and treated as a sacred living being, ritual care attributed to the drum includes protecting it from touching the bare ground, maintaining a light next to it at night, keeping it properly closed or covered when not in use and maintaining appropriate behavior in its presence. Drum groups or societies, generally named after drum owners, maintain the Dance Drum and its rituals. Each official, including owners, warriors, singers, drum heaters, and pipe lighters, must meet the necessary qualifications to carry out the sacred responsibilities.

According to Tailfeather Woman's vision, the Dance Drums and the sacred teachings were to be presented to other Native communities to promote brotherhood and peace. Various accounts indicate movement both within a tribe as well as to groups far from the original source in the Midwest. When a Dance Drum is ritually transferred to another tribal group, a formal presentation is made, including instructions as to its care, officials, songs, rituals, and ceremonies. Some part of the drum was often retained for use in constructing a replacement for the one given away. It is believed that all of the Dance Drums descend from the original and that a person who is a member of one drum group belongs to drum groups in other communities. Practitioners of the religion included JOHN MINK. The Drum Dance religion, sometimes mistakenly identified as the Ghost Dance, is generally described as a variation of the GRASS DANCE of the Plains by anthropologists.

DRUMKEEPER *Osage* See ACCEPTANCE OF THE DRUM CEREMONY

DUCHESNE, ROSE PHILIPPINE *(1769–1852)* French missionary. Born in France, Duchesne joined the Society of the Sacred Heart in 1804. She arrived in St. Louis in 1818 and did missionary work among children. She oversaw the founding of a dozen schools and a convent for young women of European descent. She had a lifelong desire to spread Christianity among American Indians. She first met Indians on a trip up the Mississippi River in 1818 and saw the Pawnee and Illinois camped near her convent in Florissant, Missouri. She also helped Jesuit novices with the school for Indians that they opened upon their arrival in Florissant in 1823. Finally, in 1841, at the age of 72, she lived briefly with the Potawatomi in southeastern Kansas, which she considered the high point of her life. Unable to learn the Potawatomi language and unable to teach the Indians as she had dreamed of doing, she spent a year,

1841–42, helping begin a school for Potawatomi at Sugar Creek, Kansas, near present-day Centerville. During this year she also nursed the sick, played with children, and prayed. Indeed, the Potawatomi named her, in their language, "woman-who-prays-always." She was beatified in 1940. Pope John Paul II canonized her in 1988, making her the fourth American to attain sainthood. A delegation of Potawatomi people went to Rome for the ceremony. She died at St. Charles, Missouri, where the school she had opened was recognized as the first free school west of the Mississippi River for Catholic and non-Catholic students.

DUKES, JOSEPH *(1811–1862) Choctaw* A preacher and interpreter who translated a number of religious works into the Choctaw language. Born in the Choctaw Nation in what is now Mississippi, Dukes attended an early Presbyterian mission school located at Mayhew. His academic progress was so impressive that he often interpreted for the Reverend CYRUS KINGSBURY. Dukes later worked with the Reverend CYRUS BYINGTON on a Choctaw dictionary and grammar. Following the ceding of tribal lands in the East, he eventually joined those of his people who had been removed from Mississippi to the West. By 1851 or 1852 he was preaching in Indian Territory (present-day Oklahoma) at Wheelock under the direction of the Reverend ALLEN WRIGHT and helping Wright translate the Old Testament. He later worked with Wright's successor, the Reverend John Edwards, teaching him the Choctaw language and assisting him in translating while continuing to preach. A translation of the Old Testament from Genesis to II Kings, in addition to the Psalms, has been attributed to Dukes, and it is likely that he translated portions of the New Testament as well. He also authored *The History of Joseph and His Brethren* (1831).

DUNBAR, JOHN *(1804–1857)* A Presbyterian missionary who worked among the Pawnee people under the auspices of the AMERICAN BOARD OF COMMISSIONERS FOR FOREIGN MISSIONS. Dunbar was born on March 7, 1804, in Palmer, Massachusetts. After graduating from Williams College in 1832, he attended Auburn Theological Seminary from 1832 to 1834. By the time he graduated from the seminary, he already had a mission assignment. Dunbar was ordained by the Cayuga Presbytery on May 1, 1834, in Ithaca, New York. He traveled with the Reverend SAMUEL ALLIS, JR. on a mission to the Flathead or Nez Perce people, but their plans were changed en route. They instead began working among the Pawnee in present-day Nebraska in the fall of 1834. Dunbar's wife, Esther Smith, joined him on his mission to the Pawnee after their marriage on January 12, 1837. Their missionary efforts were hampered by the devastating circumstances in which they found the people. Besides losing substantial numbers to smallpox, the Pawnee population was decimated by starvation and warfare. After a number of delays, a mission was finally established, but repeated raids by the Lakota forced it to close in 1846. Dunbar then moved to Missouri, where he farmed, taught, and served as a home missionary. In 1856 he moved near Robinson, Kansas, to be in a free state, later serving as treasurer of Brown County's board of commissioners. Dunbar and Allis both wrote accounts of Pawnee life, including "Letters Concerning the Presbyterian Mission in the Pawnee Country Near Bellevue, Nebraska, 1831–1849." The Reverend Dunbar died on November 3, 1857, in Robinson, Kansas. His son, John B. Dunbar, also wrote a series of articles on the Pawnee.

DUNCAN, WILLIAM *(1832–1918)* An Episcopal missionary among the Tsimshian at Metlakatla in British Columbia, and later in Alaska. Born near Beverley, Yorkshire, England, Duncan became a tanner's apprentice and a schoolmaster. While preparing for a teaching post in Africa at a CHURCH MISSIONARY SOCIETY training school, he was selected for an assignment among the Native people at Fort Simpson, British Columbia in 1857. Upon his arrival, he stayed at the Hudson's Bay post and began learning the Tsimshian language. He established a school where he taught English, provided religious instruction, and preached against traditional observances. After a few years, Duncan took his followers from Fort Simpson and moved them to Metlakatla, a former community site. In time he established a model Victorian village complete with its own church, houses, and police force where POTLATCH, alcohol use, and certain visitors were unwelcome. He also set up a community store and introduced a number of industries, including a salmon cannery and sawmill. The community prospered, but Duncan eventually clashed with the Church Missionary Society when it assigned a bishop, William Ridley, to Metlakatla in 1879. The conflict became a highly publicized contest over the control of the village, its property, and land. In 1882 Duncan received a letter of dismissal from the society, and five years later he relocated the majority of his followers to Alaska, where they settled on Annette Island. The missionary then began building the model village he named New Metlakatla. Under 1891 legislation, the area was set aside as a reservation for the Native people. By the end of Duncan's life, another schism had developed, this time between his Christian Mission Church and another Protestant church in the village.

EAGLE CEREMONY (Eagle Power Ceremony) *Lakota* A sacred healing ceremony with similarities in ritual to the YUWIPI ceremony. It is conducted by an Eagle Power Medicine Man or Dreamer, who derives knowledge from an older dreamer-healer and whose curing skills originate with the eagle, red hawk, or red-tailed hawk. The Eagle Ceremony is said to have differentiated from the better-known Yuwipi to recent times. It is also said to be more secret and to have fewer practitioners. PETER CATCHES, an Eagle Power Medicine Man, was identified as one of the few religious leaders who conducted such ceremonies. Also known as Eagle Power Ceremony.

EAGLE DANCE *Iroquois* This ceremonial, which includes the THANKSGIVING ADDRESS, TOBACCO INVOCATION to the spirit presiding over the society, songs, dances, speechmaking prescribed by custom, a feast, and final blessing to celebrants, has local variations. Locally, individual singers use songs that may not be part of the common repertoire of all singers. A song leader with a water drum and helpers with rattles accompany the dance. Over the years, the ceremony has undergone a change in function. At first a war and peace ceremony, it has now become a medicine dance. During the ceremony, each person is given a "ceremonial" friend. After the rite, the two treat one another as relatives, and the relationship of mutual helpfulness is lifelong.

EAGLE DANCE *Pueblo* Performed in spring, this rite is important to the ceremonial life of all the Pueblo peoples. The dance dramatizes the relationship of human beings with eagles and spiritual powers. Pueblo people who associate eagles with rain, thunder, lightning, and curing powers, honor the birds in this dance. Two young men dressed as eagles, one a male, the other a female eagle, emulate the movements of these birds in flight. Regalia varies from pueblo to pueblo, but generally the body is painted, and there is a headdress with a long, curved beak. There are great feathered wings over the shoulders and attached to the arms as well as a feathered tail attached to the belt in back. Eagle down, which represents the breath of life, is used in curing rites. The dance can be viewed by the public.

EAGLE FEATHER DISTRIBUTION *(1994)* On April 29, 1994, President Bill Clinton signed a governmental directive about the collection and distribution of sacred eagle bodies and parts used in the practice of Native American religions. The memorandum to the heads of executive departments and agencies required that Native American religious purposes have the first priority in the distribution of eagles. The president directed each agency responsible for managing federal lands to recover salvageable dead eagles found on lands under their jurisdiction and ensure that the eagles are promptly shipped to the National Eagle Repository. The memo directed that the eagle permit application be simplified and that Native American tribes, organizations, and individuals be involved in the distribution process.

EAGLE SOCIETY *Iroquois* A private medicine society of men and women whose objective is to cure its members and can-

74

didates of diseases by ritual chanting and dancing. The society members cure publicly in the longhouse at the MIDWINTER CEREMONY or in private curing rites in family homes. The ceremonies occur, therefore, at irregular intervals, unlike the calendrical rites. A person cured by the ceremony or one who has had a dream diagnosed as eagle sickness gains membership into the society. The society has special clothing and ritual equipment. A man stops the ceremonial song and dance by "striking the post" to recite war records or humorous stories or to ridicule another member. (See also MEDICINE SOCIETIES [Iroquois].)

EARTH LODGE RELIGION   The Earth Lodge religion is a later variation of the GHOST DANCE OF 1870. Named for its most prominent feature, it was advocated by the Ghost Dance leader NORELPUTUS and is believed to have been introduced among the Wintun and Hill Patwin in California in about 1871 or 1872. The Earth Lodge religion spread to the Wintu, to the Achomawi area and to the Klamath Reservation in Oregon. It also spread to the Shasta and to the Siletz and Grand Ronde Reservations, where it was called the Warm House Dance. Another area of diffusion was to the south, among the Pomo and other groups. As the religion traveled, some features were added while others were minimized or deleted. Among the beliefs associated with the religion was the imminent end of the world, the return of the dead, and the punishment of nonbelievers. It was believed that adherents would be protected from the approaching catastrophe in subterranean earth lodges, constructed for that purpose. Dreams, songs, and dances were also important elements of the religion. On the Klamath Reservation, the Earth Lodge religion was followed by the DREAM DANCE phase of the religious movement begun by the Ghost Dance.

EASTER *Pueblo*   Holy week is observed with a blend of Native religious practice and Catholicism. From Thursday until Saturday morning service, each pueblo is under restrictions. Men's weapons are surrendered until after Saturday services. On Easter Sunday people attend prayer services and after breakfast go to their respective kivas where they prepare for dances that last all day.

EASTER *Yaqui*   See WAEHMA

EASTMAN, JOHN (Mahpiyawakankida, "Sacred Cloud Worshipper") *(b. 1848) Dakota*   An ordained Presbyterian minister who was born into a prominent Santee Dakota family in March 1848 in present-day Shakopee, Minnesota. His father was Tawakanhdiota, or Many Lightnings, who became known as Jacob Eastman when he converted to Christianity in 1864. His mother was Mary Nancy Eastman

(Wakantankawin, "goddess"), the daughter of Captain Seth Eastman, an artist and military officer. John Eastman's brother, Charles Alexander Eastman, achieved prominence as a physician and author. In the aftermath of the Dakota War of 1862 in Minnesota, the family fled to Canada. During his second winter in exile, Many Lightnings was captured along with other Dakota near Winnipeg by U.S. authorities and returned to the United States, where he later served four years in an Iowa military prison. He subsequently settled in Flandreau, South Dakota, where he began farming for the first time. John Eastman attended school at the Santee Agency in Nebraska and at Beloit College in Wisconsin for a year. He lived with his father until the latter's death in 1876. Ordained the same year at Flandreau's Indian church, he immediately became its pastor. The congregation of this church had been organized in 1871 and a building was provided by the Presbyterian Mission Board in 1874. In 1878 he took charge of a government school and began teaching youth from the Santee Sioux Reservation. Active in tribal affairs, Eastman served as a delegate of his people at an annual conference in Washington, D.C., for many years. He resigned from the school in 1885 to become superintendent of the tribal group then in Flandreau. Wanting to devote more time to his ministry and farm, he retired in 1896.

EDWARDS, JONATHAN *(1703–1758)*   Congregational clergyman, author, and missionary in New England. Edwards was born on October 5, 1703, to Esther (Stoddard) Edwards and the Reverend Timothy Edwards in East Windsor, Connecticut. Edwards was educated at Yale College in New Haven, graduating in 1720, and returned to study theology from 1721 to 1722. In 1722 he accepted a ministerial position at a Presbyterian church in New York, where he remained until the following year. Edwards then became a tutor at Yale, but a lengthy illness interrupted his work in 1725. He resigned from the tutorial position in 1726 to become a ministerial colleague of his grandfather, Solomon Stoddard, at the Congregational church in Northampton, Massachusetts. He initially continued the same pastoral practices as his grandfather, who died in 1729, but introduced changes in the aftermath of the Great Awakening, a religious revival of the 1740s in New England. Edwards was dismissed from his pulpit in 1750 because of his controversial position on limiting full church membership to those who met stricter, more orthodox standards in the expression of their faith. In 1751 he began working as a missionary and minister to the Native people in Stockbridge, Massachusetts. His efforts were supported in part by the church, legislative funds, and the London SOCIETY FOR THE PROPAGATION OF THE GOSPEL IN NEW ENGLAND. Thwarting efforts by some of his colonial opponents to

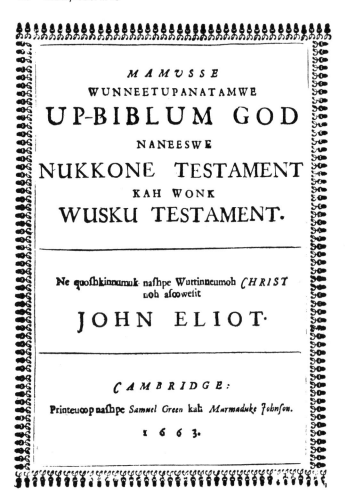

MAMUSSE
WUNNEETUPANATAMWE
UP-BIBLUM GOD
NANEESWE
NUKKONE TESTAMENT
KAH WONK
WUSKU TESTAMENT.

Ne quoſhkinnumuk naſhpe Wuttinneumoh *CHRIST*
noh aſoowelit

JOHN ELIOT·

CAMBRIDGE:
Printeuop naſhpe *Samuel Green* kah *Marmaduke Johnſon*.
1 6 6 3.

Eliot Bible. Title page from *Mamusse Wunneetupanatamwe Up-Biblum God*, John Eliot's Indian Bible of 1663. *Rare Books and Manuscripts Division, The New York Public Library, Astor, Lenox, and Tilden Foundation.*

control the funds and programs at Stockbridge, he appointed GIDEON HAWLEY as a teacher and instituted other measures. Edwards remained at the post, where he preached to the Housatonic people with the aid of an interpreter, until he was offered the presidency of the College of New Jersey at Princeton in 1757. He arrived at the school in January 1758 and died two months later on March 22, 1758. Edwards authored *A Faithful Narrative of the Surprising Work of God* (1737), *An Account of the Life of the Late Reverend Mr. David Brainerd* (1749), *The Great Christian Doctrine of Original Sin Defended* (1758), and numerous other publications. (See also BRAINERD, DAVID; KIRKLAND, SAMUEL; WHEELOCK, ELEAZAR.)

EELLS, CUSHING *(1810–1893)* Congregational missionary in Oregon Territory. Born in Blandford, Massachusetts, in 1810, Eells graduated from Williams College in 1834 and then attended East Windsor Theological Institute, which later became Hartford Seminary, in Connecticut. Following his 1837 graduation from divinity school, he accepted an invitation to do work for the AMERICAN BOARD OF COMMISSIONERS FOR FOREIGN MISSIONS in the Northwest. In the summer of 1838 he arrived at the mission station founded by MARCUS WHITMAN and NARCISSA PRENTISS WHITMAN and for the next 10 years worked at Tshimakain in northeast Washington among the Spokane Indians. Although his progress in promoting Christianity and "civilization" was slow, Eells persevered. When neighboring Cayuse people killed the Whitmans in 1847, the Spokane chief provided the missionaries at Tshimakain with a bodyguard until the danger ended. A year later, however, the mission station was abandoned because of continuing troubles with the Cayuse. Eells then farmed and taught while waiting for a new assignment from the mission board. He eventually turned down a post in Hawaii and ended his formal relationship with the missionary organization. Eells remained in the Northwest and worked as a teacher and minister among the white population. He was associated with Tualitin Academy, which became Pacific University, and served as a minister in some of the first Congregational churches in the region. He also contributed funds from his meager income to support the construction and staffing of churches. In later years Eells spent winters on the Skokomish reservation and summers working as a self-supporting missionary in the area east of the Cascades. "Father Eells" died in 1893. A Spokane primer he coauthored in 1842 was reportedly the third book printed in the Columbia River area. His son, MYRON EELLS, also became a minister to Native Americans.

EELLS, MYRON *(1843–1907)* Congregational minister in Washington Territory who was born on October 7, 1843, at Tshimakain mission, the youngest son of CUSHING EELLS and Myra Eells. An 1866 graduate of Pacific University, Eells enrolled in the Hartford Theological Seminary two years later. Following his June 15, 1871, ordination, he was appointed minister at Boise City, Idaho, by the Congregational Home Missionary Society. On January 18, 1874, he married Sarah M. Crosby, and a few months later began serving as pastor at Skokomish Agency in Washington Territory after a visit to his brother Edwin, the Indian agent. He remained there for 33 years. During that period Eells served as the pastor of Congregational churches, most of which he organized, at Skokomish, Seabeck, Dungeness, Holly, Twana, and Mt. Constance. A trustee of Pacific University and Whitman College, he also held memberships in the AMERICAN BOARD OF COMMISSIONERS FOR FOREIGN MISSIONS, the American Home Missionary Society, the Congrès International des Americanistes, the Oregon Pioneer Association, the Washington State Historical Society, and the Victoria Institute.

Eells wrote on a variety of religious, ethnological, and historical topics based on his observation of Twana, Klallam, Makah, Quinault, and other Native groups of the Puget Sound area. After almost 20 years of missionary work, he completed an unpublished compilation of six volumes entitled *The Indians of Puget Sound,* consisting of sketches, notes, and material from his published writing. Besides publishing more than 1,250 newspaper articles, he wrote such pamphlets and books as *Hymns in Chinook Jargon Language* (1878), *History of the Congregational Association of Oregon & Washington* (1881), *Ten Years at Skokomish* (1886), and *Twana, Clallam and Chemakum Indians of Washington Territory* (1886–87). A recurring theme in his writing was the culture dislocation experienced by the Native people he observed. Myron Eells died on January 4, 1907. His extensive collection of papers was bequested to Whitman College in Walla Walla, Washington.

EGEDE, HANS POVELSEN *(1686–1758)* A Lutheran minister who led a Scandinavian expedition to Greenland and established a mission settlement among the Inuit people there. Egede, who was born in Norway, prepared for the ministry between 1704 and 1705. He became interested in an early Christian Norse colony in Greenland and began seeking support for a missionary and exploration venture in the region. Egede later obtained three ships and other assistance from Danish merchants for the enterprise. He led a party of 40 people to Greenland, arriving there in 1721. Egede settled them in West Greenland at a place he named the Island of Hope, and they remained there for seven years, eventually moving to Godthaab, or Good Hope. The missionary-explorer served as the settlement's bishop and superintendent. During his 15 years in Greenland, Egede undertook exploratory journeys in the region. Inuit guides took him to Norse ruins and other areas of their territory. As a result of one expedition, a whaling station was established at Nipisat. Egede's mission station was nearly abandoned in 1733 when support was scheduled to be withdrawn, but the Moravians contributed aid. They sent missionaries Christian David, Matthew Stach, and Christian Stach from Denmark to assist in the enterprise. The Moravian denomination later carried on the principal missionary efforts in the region. In 1736 Egede returned to Denmark and established a seminary to train others for the work. He wrote *Description of Greenland* as well as several religious publications in the Native language. His son POVL EGEDE and other family members continued his efforts when he died in 1758.

EGEDE, POVL (Paul, Poul) *(?–1789)* A Lutheran missionary among the Native people in Greenland. The son of HANS POVELSEN EGEDE, Povl traveled with his parents and sib-

lings to the region in 1721. As a child there, he learned the difficult Inuit language from his playmates and other Inuit. Egede began his missionary career in 1734, and it lasted until his death 55 years later. He continued the efforts of his father, seeking support and promoting European interest in the region. Egede authored an Inuit, Danish, and Latin grammar and dictionary as well as religious publications in the Inuit language. He also maintained a journal of the Greenland work between 1721 and 1788. His cousin, Reverend Peter Egede, translated Psalms. Subsequent Lutheran and Moravian missionaries in the region contributed to the linguistic efforts started by the Egede family, and the number of Inuit religious and educational publications eventually became extensive. Povl Egede was named bishop 10 years before he died. His name also appears as Paul or Poul. See also BIBLE TRANSLATIONS.

EHNAMANI, ARTEMAS ("Walks Along") *(c. 1825–c. 1902)* *Dakota.* An early Congregational minister who was born in present-day Red Wing, Minnesota. As a youngster, Ehnamani followed the traditional pursuits of his people. After losing tribal lands along the Mississippi River, his band was removed to an area near the Minnesota River. The great privations suffered by the Dakota people later led to the 1862 outbreak of war in the region. Ehnamani, charged and convicted for his role in the conflict, was sentenced by Minnesota authorities to die. He was one of the Dakota prisoners whose sentence was commuted from death to incarceration by President Abraham Lincoln. Influenced by early missionaries to the Dakota while in prison, Ehnamani turned to Christianity and later became an ordained minister. He spent the rest of his life ministering to his people and became the first of several prominent clergymen in his family. The Reverend Ehnamani died at the age of 75 or 77. His descendant, Reverend FRANCIS FRAZIER, succeeded him to the Santee pastorate of Pilgrim Church on September 10, 1902.

ELIOT BIBLE (Indian Bible) The first complete Bible printed in America. Translated into the Algonquian language of the Massachuset by the 17th-century missionary JOHN ELIOT, it was published as *Mamusse Wunneetupanatamwe Up-Biblum God* in Cambridge, Massachusetts, in 1663. Eliot began his language studies before preaching his first sermon to the Indians in 1646 at Dorchester Mills. He was assisted in his linguistic work by Native translators, including COCKENOE and JOB NESUTAN. Eliot started his Natick translation of the Bible in 1653, and the New Testament appeared in 1661, followed by the Old Testament two years later. Published at a cost of about 1,000 pounds, most of its expense was paid by the SOCIETY FOR THE PROPAGATION OF THE GOSPEL IN NEW ENGLAND. Eliot also translated other Puritan religious and educational works into the Natick dialect for use by New England's PRAYING INDIANS. Aimed at Christianizing and "civilizing" the Indians, these works included catechisms, grammars, primers, and psalters. The Eliot Bible is considered a landmark achievement and the forerunner of biblical translations in other Native languages. (See also BIBLE TRANSLATIONS.)

ELIOT, JOHN *(1604–1690)* Pastor of the First Church in Roxbury, Massachusetts, and 17th-century missionary who became known as the "Apostle to the Indians." Born in Essex County, England, he received his B.A. degree from Jesus College, Cambridge, in 1622 and then taught in a grammar school at Little Baddow, Essex. Some time later he was asked to serve as a chaplain on a ship bound for Boston. After his November 3, 1631, arrival in New England, he eventually settled in Roxbury, where he came into contact with the Indians. Assisted by Native tutors, including COCKENOE and JOB NESUTAN, he began learning the Algonquian language of the Massachuset. Eliot preached his first sermon to the Indians at Dorchester Mills in 1646, then extended his missionary efforts to Nonantum and other settlements. By 1649 he received financial assistance for the work from the newly organized SOCIETY FOR THE PROPAGATION OF THE GOSPEL IN NEW ENGLAND. With authority from the Massachusetts General Court, Eliot began promoting the establishment of "praying towns" to bring Christian Indians under colonial rule and to segregate them from their unconverted neighbors. Beginning at Natick in 1651, the number of these New England communities eventually reached 14. Eliot also trained Native missionaries and translated Puritan religious and educational works into the Natick dialect. His *Mamusse Wunneetupanatamwe Up-Biblum God,* or the Indian Bible or *Eliot Bible,* was the first complete Bible printed in America, the New Testament appearing in 1661 and the Old Testament in 1663. Other translations, aimed at Christianizing and "civilizing" Indians, included *A Primer or Catechism in the Massachusetts Indian Language* (1654), *Up-Bookum Psalmes* (1663), and *The Indian Primer* (1669). One of his publications, *The Christian Commonwealth* (1659), was suppressed by the Massachusetts authorities in 1661 because they feared that the views expressed on an ideal commonwealth would offend the British, or home, government, and he had to retract it. With the outbreak of King Philip's War in 1675, the number of PRAYING INDIANS was drastically reduced, and much of the missionary work destroyed. Eliot died in Roxbury on May 21, 1690. He was married to Ann (or Hannah) Mumford and had six children.

ELK HAIR *(c. 1859–?)* Delaware (Lenni Lenape) A religious and political figure who is likely to have been the first peyote ROADMAN (leader) among the Eastern Delaware people in Oklahoma. In the early 1880s Elk Hair had a number of misfortunes, including the death of his wife and an illness of his own. He was eventually introduced to peyote by Johnson Bob, an Anadarko Delaware, who had learned the religious practice while among the Comanche people. After Elk Hair was cured, he became an adherent of the religion and followed the Half Moon, or Little Moon, peyote ceremony he had been taught. About 1885, while visiting the Delaware band near Anadarko, he learned of the Big Moon or Moonhead ceremony practiced by JOHN WILSON, which included Christian features. He rejected Wilson's interpretation of the PEYOTE RELIGION, believing that both peyotism and Christianity were good but that they should not be combined. At the time he was interviewed by an ethnologist, about 1929 or 1930, he had been a peyotist for 45 years. Elk Hair, who lived in Dewey, Oklahoma, was recognized not only as a peyote leader but for his leadership in traditional Delaware religious life and for his political service as a chief. (See also NATIVE AMERICAN CHURCH.)

ELY, EDMUND F. *(1809–1882)* A missionary who worked among the Ojibway people from 1833 to 1849 under the auspices of the AMERICAN BOARD OF COMMISSIONERS FOR FOREIGN MISSIONS (ABCFM). In 1828 Ely had started preparing for the Presbyterian ministry in Albany under the Reverend Edward M. Kirk, teaching music to help with expenses. He left his divinity studies in 1833, at 24, to begin an ABCFM assignment as a teacher at a Lake Superior mission station. During his tenure in the field, Ely eventually worked in Ojibway communities at Sandy Lake, Fond du Lac, Pokegama, and La Pointe. He experienced a number of difficulties, including interdenominational conflicts with Catholic missionaries, a limited number of conversions and disruptions caused by war between the Ojibway and Dakota people. His colleagues in the field included Frederick Ayer, WILLIAM T. BOUTWELL and SHERMAN HALL. After resigning from the ABCFM, Ely remained in the region until 1873, when he moved to California. He died at age 73 in Santa Rosa on August 29, 1882.

EMPLOYMENT DIVISION, DEPARTMENT OF HUMAN RESOURCES OF OREGON, ET AL. V. SMITH ET AL. (No. 88–1213) *(1990)* A legal case involving two members of the NATIVE AMERICAN CHURCH and the state of Oregon that was decided by the Supreme Court of the United States on April 17, 1990.

Respondents Alfred Smith and Galen Black were fired by the Douglas County Council on Alcohol and Drug Abuse Prevention and Treatment for using PEYOTE at religious ceremonies of their church and were denied unemployment compensation by the state of Oregon. The state supreme court held that the denial of benefits violated the First Amendment rights of free exercise of religious beliefs of the respondents. The Supreme Court of the United States vacated the judgment and sent the case back to the Oregon court for a determination on whether the sacramental use of peyote was illegal under state law. The state court, on remand, held that such use was not protected under Oregon law but concluded that the prohibition was not valid under the First Amendment's free exercise clause. When the case reached the Supreme Court, the court ruled that the possession and use of peyote by NAC members is not protected by the First Amendment. The free exercise clause permits state prohibition of sacramental peyote use and denial of unemployment compensation to individuals discharged for its use. It held that it is constitutionally *permissible* for a state to exempt the religious use of peyote from drug laws but it is not constitutionally *required*. States and the federal government do not have to create legislative exemptions to their drug law for the sacramental use of peyote. Justices Blackmun, Brennan, and Marshall dissented. Blackmun stated, in part: "I do not believe the Founders thought their dearly fought freedom from religious persecution a 'luxury,' but an essential element of liberty—and they could not have thought religious intolerance 'unavoidable.'" A new bill permitting the sacramental use of peyote in the state of Oregon was signed into law on June 24, 1991. Individuals such as Alfred Smith and Galen Black, who reportedly participated as guests in services of the PEYOTE RELIGION, would still be subject to prosecution under the act. (See also AMERICAN INDIAN RELIGIOUS FREEDOM ACT AMENDMENTS ACT OF 1994; AMERICAN INDIAN RELIGIOUS FREEDOM COALITION; *PEOPLE V. WOODY*; AMERICAN INDIAN RELIGIOUS FREEDOM ACT OF 1978; PEYOTISM; Subject Index for similar cases in this volume.)

ENDANGERED SPECIES ACT OF 1973 (16 U.S.C. 1531–1543) *(1973)*   A federal act restricting the taking of endangered and threatened species in the United States and its territorial waters and on the high seas. Its regulations also prohibit the possession or transportation of any applicable species that have been unlawfully taken. The Fish and Wildlife Service of the U.S. Department of the Interior does not allow the taking of species protected by the act for religious purposes by American Indians. An exception does allow some subsistence taking by Alaska Natives, including Indians, Aleut, or Inuit, who live in the state of Alaska. (See also AMERICAN INDIAN RELIGIOUS FREEDOM ACT OF 1978; BALD AND GOLDEN EAGLES PROTECTION ACT OF 1940; MARINE MAMMAL PROTECTION ACT; MIGRATORY BIRD TREATY ACT.)

ENEMY WAY *Navajo (Dineh)*   One of the EVIL WAY ceremonies; performed for patients who have been infected by non-Navajo (non-Dineh) ghosts.

ENMEGAHBOWH ("One Who Stands Before His People") *(c. 1810–1902) Ojibway-Ottawa*   A Methodist missionary who later became an Episcopal priest. Christianized John Johnson, Enmegahbowh was born to Ottawa parents who lived with the Rice Lake band of Ojibway, located north of Lake Ontario in Canada, and may have also had blood relatives in that nation. (Although his year of birth is generally identified as 1810, an Episcopal clergyman stated that Enmegahbowh was 36 years old when he was ordained a deacon in 1859.) As a youngster, Enmegahbowh's parents sent him to a school run by an Anglican clergyman. He attended classes with the clergyman's sons for a few months until he became homesick and ran away. He later attended a mission school established by the Methodist Episcopal Church in the Rice Lake community. Reverend JAMES EVANS convinced Enmegahbowh's parents to allow him to leave for the Methodist mission at Sault Ste. Marie to work as an interpreter.

Leaving home in 1834, never to see his parents again, Enmegahbowh spent the first few months at Sault Ste. Marie and several months at Grand Traverse on Lake Michigan and then served as an interpreter and assistant at the L'Anse mission. In the fall of 1837 he entered the Ebenezer Manual Labor School in Illinois with PETER MARKSMAN and Enmegahbowh's cousin, GEORGE COPWAY. After declining an opportunity to attend college, Enmegahbowh eventually began mission assignments in Minnesota Territory. He subsequently lived and worked among Ojibway bands at Sandy Lake, Mille Lacs, White Fish Lake, Rabbit Lake, Fond du Lac, Gull Lake, and White Earth. In the early 1840s, Enmegahbowh married a young Ojibway woman, whose parents agreed to the marriage on the condition that the couple not leave Ojibway territory. Her parents then consented to their daughter's baptism, at which she was named Charlotte. Several years later, in 1849, the Methodist Church expelled Enmegahbowh and his wife because they reportedly fought a white man who had insulted Charlotte. Enmegahbowh later began Protestant Episcopal missionary work at Gull Lake, the Ojibway leader, Hole-in-the-Day's village, where a temporary church, St. John's in the Wilderness, was eventually replaced by St. Columba mission. After his ordination as a deacon, he played a significant role in a conflict called the Hole-in-the-Day Uprising. Informants claimed that the Ojibway leader Hole-in-the-Day was planning to unite with Little Crow, a leader from the Mdewakanton band of Dakota, in an effort to drive out encroaching whites. Enmegahbowh sent warnings to Fort

Ripley, then fled from Ojibway dissidents. He traveled with his family by canoe down Gull River, and two of his children later died of exposure from the ordeal. St. Columba's was destroyed during the conflict, leaving Enmegahbowh without a church or position.

In 1863 he found temporary work accompanying an Ojibway treaty delegation to Washington, D.C., where he served as an interpreter and conducted tours. His effectiveness as a missionary was later undermined because of his connection with the unpopular treaty agreement and it took him years to regain the trust he had lost among the Ojibway. In 1868, when the Ojibway were removed by treaty from Gull Lake to the newly established White Earth Reservation in Minnesota, Enmegahbowh and about 40 of his parishioners began to reestablish St. Columba mission at White Earth. In 1867, he was ordained a priest by Bishop HENRY BENJAMIN WHIPPLE. He subsequently trained several Ojibway for ordination into the Episcopal ministry, including Fred W. Smith, who succeeded him when he retired in 1887. Enmegahbowh outlived his 12 children, most of whom died of consumption, including his son George Johnson, a gifted minister. After Charlotte died on March 30, 1895, his constant companion was a young grandson whose death the following year was a devastating loss. He died on June 12, 1902, and was buried near St. Columba mission at White Earth, Minnesota. (See also COPWAY, GEORGE; STEINHAUER, HENRY BIRD.)

EPP, JACOB B. *(1874–?)* A Mennonite missionary to the Hopi people. Born on April 6, 1874, in Koeppental, Russia, he attended elementary and high schools in Russia from 1880 to 1888 and held an assistant clerk position from 1889 to 1892. Upon his arrival in America, he continued his education in Kansas at Bethel Academy (1894–97) and Bethel Junior College (1898–1900). He also attended Union Mission Training Institute (later named the National Bible Institute) in New York from 1903 to 1905 and the Baptist Theological Seminary in Fort Worth, Texas, from 1926 to 1928. He taught in Mennonite schools and then held a teaching position at the Indian Mission School in Cantonment, Oklahoma, from 1900 to 1901. Epp began working among the Hopi in 1901 as a replacement for H. R. Voth, the pioneering Mennonite missionary who had returned to Kansas after the death of his wife. Epp stayed for two years, as planned, then left Oraibi, Arizona, in 1903 to complete medical studies in the East. During his absence from the Oraibi mission, his colleague JACOB B. FREY carried on the work. After EPP's return in 1905, he remained as a missionary until 1913. During that period his efforts included translating religious materials into the Hopi language. Epp

then held administrative, teaching, and pastor positions for the rest of his career.

ERECT HORNS (Tomsivsi) *Suhtaio* The second great culture hero, after SWEET MEDICINE, in Cheyenne belief. Erect Horns belonged to the Suhtaio, a distinct Algonquian group that had joined the Cheyenne by 1833. During a period of great famine, he made a pilgrimage to a sacred site, identified as Black Mountain, to seek spiritual assistance for the people who were suffering from starvation. At the time of his journey, the holy man was known by various names, including Standing on the Ground and Rustling Corn. Accompanied by a woman, Erect Horns traveled a great distance to reach the sacred mountain, which is believed to be located north of present-day Pipestone, Minnesota. Upon their arrival, they began receiving holy teachings from Maheo, the Creator, who was aided by Thunder and other spiritual beings. The couple were taught a great ceremony, "New Life Lodge," or "Lodge of the Generator," which later became known as the SUN DANCE. The performance of the ritual would renew the earth and bring great blessings to the people. Erect Horns was also given the SACRED BUFFALO HAT, a spiritual gift representing female power, and it became the second religious covenant, after the SACRED ARROWS, of the Cheyenne. His return home after four years of spiritual instruction was marked by the renewal of the earth, with plenty of buffalo and other game for the people to eat. When the holy man wore the Sacred Buffalo Hat, its horns stood up, and he became known as Tomsivsi, or Erect Horns. Before leaving the people, the great prophet instructed them in the sacred teachings and prophecies he had received.

ESCALANTE, FRANCISCO SILVESTRE VELEZ DE *(1745–1780)* Born in Spain, Escalante entered the Franciscan order in 1769 in Mexico City. He was a priest at Laguna Pueblo in western New Mexico for a brief period and in charge of the Mission of Our Lady of Guadalupe at Zuni Pueblo, also in western New Mexico. In 1775, the governor of New Mexico asked him to explore the country between New Mexico and California and discover a direct communication between Santa Fe and Monterey. He explored Arizona, New Mexico, Colorado, and Utah from 1775 to 1777, covering some 2,000 miles by horseback in five months. In his reports, Escalante provided information about Hopi pueblos, stated his belief that force should be used to subjugate and convert the Hopi, and recommended that a mission be established among them. In 1779, Escalante enclosed in a letter written to his superior, Fray Agustín Morfi, a summary of the Pueblo uprising against the Spanish in 1680 led by POPÉ, a Tewa medicine man from San Juan Pueblo. His account was based on sources then in the Santa Fe archives but which have been lost. He eventually was assigned to teach in Mexico.

ETTWEIN, JOHN *(1721–1802)* Moravian missionary and bishop. Born in Freudenstadt, Germany, on June 29, 1721, Ettwein worked as a shoemaker, converted to the Moravian faith, and married Johanna Maria Kymbel before arriving in America in 1754. He served as a missionary to the Delaware (Lenni Lenape) and other Native groups in the middle colonies from 1754 to 1763 and worked in North Carolina between 1763 and 1766. In 1766 he was named as an assistant to Bishop Nathanael Seidel in Bethlehem, Pennsylvania. Six years later Ettwein led a group of Native people to the Reverend DAVID ZEISBERGER's new Christian settlement in Ohio. During the American Revolution, Ettwein was arrested as a Loyalist and imprisoned for a time. He later served as a representative to the Continental Congress and Pennsylvania Assembly and he successfully negotiated the Moravian position against bearing arms. Between 1776 and 1777 Ettwein worked as a chaplain at the Continental Army hospital in Bethlehem, Pennsylvania. He became bishop of the Moravian Church of North America in 1784 and held the position until the end of his life. In 1785 he urged Congress and the Pennsylvania Assembly to establish reservations for Native converts to Christianity. He also revived the Society of United Brethren for Propagating the Gospel among the Heathens. Ettwein died on January 2, 1802, in Bethlehem, Pennsylvania. (See also GRUBE, BERNHARD ADAM; HECKEWELDER, JOHN; ZINZENDORF, NIKOLAUS.)

EVANS, JAMES *(1801–1846)* A Wesleyan Methodist missionary in Canada who invented the Cree syllabary. An English immigrant to Ontario, Evans served as a teacher in the Ojibway community of Rice Lake in the late 1820s before he was ordained. There he learned the Native language, first preaching in it in 1835. Benefiting from the linguistic work of PETER JONES, Evans was later favored by WILLIAM CASE and other Methodist missionaries for completing Ojibway translations. He expressed his intention of developing an orthography of the language to standardize the incomplete systems unique to each writer. In the late 1830s Evans was aided by George Henry, the half-brother of Peter Jones, who served as his interpreter and as the assistant missionary of the St. Clair mission. Asked to work on biblical translations, he and Henry completed an Ojibway hymnal. In 1840 Evans was appointed to superintend Methodist missionary efforts in the West. He established Rossville mission near Norway House, a post of the Hudson's Bay Company on Lake Winnepeg's northern end. Evans made the station his base and was joined there later by the Ojibway minister HENRY BIRD STEINHAUER. From there he traveled long distances, carrying

on his work and founding several other missions. He continued his linguistic efforts by mastering the Cree language, which is similar to the Ojibway. Evans first printed the Cree syllabary on a press he had made by shaping types from the sheetlead lining of tea containers with a jackknife. He was then able to teach Native people to read in their own language and to distribute religious translations. The syllabic writing system, still widely used, was later adapted for other groups. Fellow missionary JOHN MACLEAN published an account of Evans's life and work in 1890.

EVARTS, JEREMIAH *(1781–1831)* One of the founders of the AMERICAN BOARD OF COMMISSIONERS FOR FOREIGN MISSIONS (ABCFM) who was associated with the organization from its inception in 1810 until his death. Born in 1781 in Sunderland, Vermont, Evarts graduated from Yale College in 1802. He later studied law and was admitted to the Connecticut bar in 1806. Although he worked as a lawyer for over three years in New Haven, he eventually moved to Charlestown, Massachusetts, and devoted his time to missionary interests. Besides being elected a corporate member of the ABCFM in 1812, Evarts served as treasurer from 1811 to 1822 and as corresponding secretary from 1822 to 1831. In his secretarial position he handled all Congregational missions to American Indian tribes. Furthermore, most of the organization's missions to the Cherokee were founded under his leadership. He investigated the condition of Indians through correspondence and visits and became a strong opponent of removal policies that sought to relocate the Cherokee people west of the Mississippi River. His *Essays on the Present Crisis in the Condition of the American Indians,* first published in the *National Intelligencer* in 1829, criticized the state and federal governments on the issue. Evarts served as editor of the *Panoplist,* a publication of Congregationalists, from 1810 to 1821, and of the ABCFM's *Missionary Herald.* Evarts died in 1831 of consumption.

EVIL WAY *Navajo (Dineh)* These two-, three-, and five-night ceremonies are designed to exorcise Navajo (Dineh) ghosts, treat diseases traced to contact with Navajo ghosts, and combat the effects of witchcraft. Navajo believe that witnessing a death, taking the life of another human being, or visiting the remains of the Anasazi will "imbalance one's presence on earth." Rites include covering the patient with red grease or a charcoal-plant mixture and exorcistic acts that brush the patient with eagle feathers or blow ashes to get rid of the evil and sickness. These ceremonies can also be directed against ghosts of non-Navajo (non-Dineh). The ceremonies are usually performed in winter, with the exception of the Enemy Way performed during the summer for patients whose sickness is diagnosed as a result of contact with non-Indians or non-Navajo. Squaw Dance is the colloquial name for this all-night curing rite. (See also BLACK DANCERS; GHOST.)

EXALTING, OR BOUNDING, BUSH FEAST *Cherokee* The final ceremony of the SIX CHEROKEE FESTIVALS described by the 19th-century missionary DANIEL SABIN BUTRICK and other early observers of the Cherokee Nation before the forced removal of the tribal group from the southeastern Appalachian region to Indian Territory (present-day Oklahoma). The exalting, or bounding, bush feast was held during the winter after the CEMENTATION, OR RECONCILIATION, FESTIVAL. It was conducted at the capital of the Cherokee Nation. The ancient capital, Chota, or Great Echota, was located on the south side of the Little Tennessee River below Citico Creek in Tennessee. New Echota in Georgia also served as the capital for a number of years before removal. Ritual elements included the collection of tobacco from the people gathered for the feast, a march by alternating pairs of male and female participants, the use of pine or spruce boughs, dancing, a feast on the fourth night of the observance, and the making of offerings to the SACRED FIRE. This ceremony was later called a Pigeon Dance.

EXECUTIVE ORDER NO. 13007 *(1996)* On May 24, 1996, the Clinton administration issued Executive Order 13007, calling for the protection of indigenous sacred sites. The executive order, which has no enforceable power, requires each executive branch agency to accommodate access to and ceremonial use of Indian sacred sites by Indian religious practitioners and to avoid adversely affecting the physical integrity of such sacred sites.

FACES OF THE FOREST *Iroquois* Spirits who possess the power to control sickness and who instruct dreamers to carve likenesses in the form of masks. They promise that whenever anyone makes a feast, invokes their help while burning tobacco and sings curing songs, power to cure disease will be conferred on the humans who wear the masks.

FAITHKEEPER *Iroquois (New York)* An office instituted by the prophet HANDSOME LAKE; a man or woman who performs lay services essential to LONGHOUSE ceremonial ritual. Each longhouse moiety has one male and one female appointed to the position. They set the dates for the ceremonial cycle and manage, direct, and administer all longhouse functions. They also act as advisers to people, make financial decisions and supervise the longhouse burial grounds. Given ritual names during the MIDWINTER CEREMONY or GREEN CORN Festival, the faithkeepers have no special emblems, clothing, or privilege. The men act as runners and messengers, food gatherers, and waiters. The women cook, assign names, and manage the women's rituals. The faithkeepers are expected to be superior to the average worshiper morally and ethically. They are typically more religious in their attitude toward the longhouse, also. At the Six Nations Reserve in Canada, the equivalent office is called DEACON.

FALSE FACE CEREMONY *Iroquois* A ceremony held by members of the FALSE FACE SOCIETY in early spring when the ground is dry to pay respect to the FACES IN THE FOREST. The ceremony placates them with tobacco and asks that they in return disperse all diseases affecting people, livestock, and plants for the coming season and control crop-destroying winds. The ceremony combines personal curing, agricultural prophylaxis, and spirit supplication. The ceremony to dispel disease is performed at the MID WINTER CEREMONY, and GREEN CORN Festival. The ceremony also is performed to drive out witches and disease in the spring and fall and to cure illness any time of the year.

FALSE FACE MASKS See MASK

FALSE FACE SOCIETY (Society of Faces) *Iroquois* One of a number of Iroquois medicine societies with its own ritual equipment, prayers, music, membership, and methods of curing. Its tutelaries are forest spirits. The society holds a special meeting at the MIDWINTER CEREMONY for all its members and masks, and its major public performance takes place in the longhouse during this ceremony, the day varying according to the locality and longhouse. The False Faces also impersonate spirits in the GREEN CORN Festival and make spring and fall visits to the homes of longhouse members during which they purge the houses of disease through a "rite of purification." They conduct public exorcisms of disease, tornados, high winds, and witches from the entire village and conduct curing rituals in homes in response to patient dreams or the diagnosis of sickness by a clairvoyant. The society's ritual equipment consists of masks, wooden canes or staves, turtle-shell and folded bark rattles, the leader's pole with an attached small husk face, small wooden false faces, a tobacco basket, and a wooden billet for the singer. Membership includes persons cured from disease by the False Faces or persons who dream about membership in the society. Men and women belong, but women do not wear masks. Members wearing masks have special powers and can handle hot coals without being burned. They dip their hands into hot ashes and blow or rub them on a patient to cure him or her. (See also MEDICINE SOCIETIES [Iroquois].)

FAMILY CONDOLENCE RITE *Iroquois*   Rite performed when a member of a longhouse group dies. Ten days after the burial of the deceased, a condolence is given in the home or in the longhouse by members of the opposite moiety from that of the deceased to console the family of the deceased. The rite is much shorter than that of the CONDOLENCE CEREMONY of the Iroquois league, which is recited after the death of a civil chief. The speaker takes one string of WAMPUM after another as he intones a message associated with each one and passes it to the assistant.

FASTING   Fasting, voluntarily abstaining from food and drink on a total or partial basis, is a widespread religious practice among Native Americans. It may be undertaken in solitude at an isolated natural area or at a sacred site under the guidance of a qualified person. It may also be conducted as a separate religious ritual or in conjunction with another ceremony or purpose. One of the best-known religious fasts among Native American groups is the VISION QUEST. However, fasting is not limited to this purpose alone. It is undertaken by an individual or group to attain ritual purification, to seek communication from the spiritual world, to fulfill a vow or pledge, to offer a sacrifice, or to prepare for a religious role or position. It is also undertaken to seek spiritual assistance before a difficult decision or journey, to pray for peace, to seek the recovery of those who are ill, to seek solutions to serious problems, to leave the secular realm, or to restore one's harmony.

Fasts vary in duration and frequency of occurrence depending on the individual, group, or religious purpose. Ceremonial requirements, individual vows, and sacred numbers are among the factors determining the period of fasting. Ritual elements of fasts also vary. They may include guidance from a qualified instructor; the preparation of tobacco, flesh, or other offerings; the use of sacred painting; sweat lodge preparation; and praying with the SACRED PIPE. Worshipers may conclude their fasts with sweat lodge purification and interpretation of spiritual messages or teachings by a qualified person.

FATHER DANCE *Shoshone*   One account states that the Father Dance was a form of the Round Dance held at the end of the 18th and the beginning of the 19th century to ward off smallpox. Described among the Eastern Shoshone, it was sponsored by a person who had dreamed it. Assisted by two other persons, the sponsor distributed sage to each dancer. Ritual elements of the Father Dance generally included a circle with alternating male and female dancers holding sage in their hands, the sponsor in the center giving 10 prayers and 10 prayer songs for the children's health and the dancers standing still during the prayers and dancing during the singing.

The Father Dance was also called the Shuffling Dance, which was first performed by Coyote. After he taught the dance to his prey, they danced around him and shook off disease or illness. The last Shuffling Dance is believed to have occurred before World War II. It was held during a full moon in the winter months for either three or four consecutive nights. Three singers who knew the sacred songs would take turns leading the singing. The center of the circle of dancers included the singer, a fire, and a tree or pole. The dancers would conclude the dance by shaking disease away with their shawls or blankets. This dance is also sometimes called the Ghost Dance.

FAW FAW, WILLIAM (Waw-no-she) *(fl. late 1800s)* Otoe-Missouria   A prophet who started a new religious movement in the late 1800s. Believed to be influenced by the DRUM DANCE (Dream Dance) introduced to his people by the Potawatomi, Faw Faw began his new practices after experiencing a vision while he was ill. In his dream he saw two young men who gave him a spiritual message and told him that he would recover from his illness. Faw Faw initiated a ceremony, based on his vision, that included the planting of cedar trees, tobacco offerings, gift exchanges, presents for the poor, and a specific combination of design elements on clothing. It is not known when the religious movement began or ended, but it lasted from at least 1891 to 1895. Faw Faw opposed land allotment and encouraged his followers to return to Native traditions.

FEAST DAY (saint day) *Pueblo*   Religious celebrations and holiday occasions when each pueblo, except Zuni, has an "open house" for guests. Spanish missionaries assigned each village a patron saint, and a church day was set aside for veneration of this saint. This day has become a celebration combining both Catholic and Native ceremonies. On the patron saint's name day, an early morning mass is followed by a dance performed in front of the village church, a procession with the statue of the patron saint to an evergreen-covered bower in the plaza, dancing and FEASTS throughout the day, and a procession returning the saint's statue to the church.

The CORN (TABLITA) DANCE is performed at Keresan and Tewa pueblos in honor of their patron saints.

PUEBLO FEAST DAYS
New Mexico

January 23—San Ildefonso
May 1—San Felipe
June 13—Sandia
June 24—San Juan
July 14—Cochiti
July 26—Santa Ana
August 4—Santo Domingo
August 9–10—Picuris
August 12—Santa Clara
August 15—Zia
September 2—Acoma
September 4—Isleta
September 19—Laguna
September 29–30—Taos
October 4—Nambe
November 12—Jemez
November 12—Tesuque
December 12—Pojoaque

FEAST FOR THE MOURNERS *Osage* A feast conducted by the drumkeeper, dance chairman, and advisers of the I'N-LON-SCHKA CEREMONIAL DANCE when there is a death in one of the Osage tribal districts. A preliminary ritual is a purifying cedar-burning ceremony, generally conducted at dawn on the same day as the feast for the mourners. The sacred drum at the center of the four-day I'n-Lon-Schka is considered in mourning and is not released from silence until these rituals have been completed. Once they have been conducted, tribal members and relatives of the deceased are allowed to resume their planning or other activities associated with the ceremonial dance.

FEAST TO THE DEAD *Alaska Inuit and Aleut* Also called Memorial Feasts, these were public occasions held annually during which spirits of human dead were invited into the community to receive food, clothing, and gifts vicariously through their living namesakes. It was believed that souls entered the bodies of namesakes and through these living persons received the offerings. The village was cleansed in preparation for the arrival of the spirits.

A more elaborate and complex great feast to the dead was held every four to 10 years in order to free the souls of the deceased from the earth forever. It attracted hundreds within each village. For years, the nearest male relative of the dead person, assisted by relatives and friends, accumulated property and stores of food. Guests came from surrounding villages to a feast that lasted four to five days. An important feature was the distribution to the guests of great quantities of property and food in the name of the dead. The living namesakes were ritually fed and clothed from head to toe in new parkas and boots to honor and provision the souls of the human dead.

FEAST TO THE DEAD *Athabascan* See STICK DANCE

FEAST TO THE DEAD *Huron* Called the "big kettle," this common tribute to the dead was an important ritual that connected different Huron groups and cemented relations between Huron and other trading partners. Held at 10- or 12-year intervals, the bodies of individuals who did not die violent deaths were exhumed, removed from their coffins, and reburied in a common bone pit. Neighboring villages and tribes were notified about the feast so that their relatives' bones could also be reburied. A 10-day ritual, the first eight days were spent preparing the bodies for reburial and assembling participants. Each family had a feast in honor of its own dead at which presents were made to honor the dead. The presents put on display were later distributed by relatives of the deceased to friends of the family. At sunrise, the bones of the dead and grave goods were emptied into a pit lined with furs and surrounded by scaffolding accompanied by group lamenting and a final feast. Scholars report that the last Huron Feast to the Dead was held jointly with the Wyandot and Ottawa at Mackinac in 1695.

FEAST TO THE DEAD (Ohgiwe, Okiwe, Okiweh) *Iroquois* Also called "carry out the kettle," or ghost dance, this ceremony for the dead of the whole community is conducted one or two times every year by a special society of women equally represented from two moieties. The society's officers are one head woman from each moiety. The women schedule and execute the ceremonies in the spring (April) before planting begins and fall (October) after the harvest is gathered. Held all night in the longhouse, the rite includes the THANKSGIVING ADDRESS, the TOBACCO INVOCATION, the cycle of Ohgiwe songs and dances, social dancing, distribution of cloth, ribbons and candy, and the "midnight lunch," which consists of specific foods. The Ohgiwe can also be a private healing ceremony held in a private dwelling to cure ghost sickness or a renewal of former cures held briefly at the MIDWINTER CEREMONY. There are family or personal Ohgiwe ceremonies to "feed" the hungry dead, small feasts to the dead that require a speaker and a woman who cooks the foods. Since there is a belief that the dead are among the living during these rituals and that they return to their former homes to eat food, food offerings are left for them.

Feasts. A drawing by Cattaraugus Seneca artist Jesse Cornplanter, c. 1905, shows women cooking and preparing for an Iroquois longhouse feast. *New York State Library, Albany, 13801–4.*

FEASTS Ceremonial feasts, or large meals, are given as observances in themselves or in conjunction with both religious and social gatherings across Native North America. They may be held to give thanks, to celebrate a first event in a youngster's life, to observe the appearance of the first foods of the season, or to honor the memory of a deceased friend or relative. They may also be held to conclude a ceremony. Feasts for religious purposes generally require the use of specific sacred foods such as wild game, fish, berries, and corn. They are then obtained, prepared, and served according to ritual requirements. Feasts may be sponsored by an individual, family, society, community, tribal group, or other organization. They generally include offerings to the spirits, prayers of thanksgiving, and other ritual elements, depending upon the purpose. (See Subject Index for individual entries in this volume.)

FEATHER Gathered ritually from eagles and other sacred birds, feathers are required for sacred ceremonies and are attached to prayersticks, rattles, masks, and other objects used in ceremonies and curing. They are also used as offerings. They are also used alone and prayed with. The feather often serves as a bridge between the spirit world and people. Among the Pueblo feathers are believed to be the visual manifestation of breath or the representation of dripping rain. Feathers help invoke both spirits and the dead. Feathers are the essence of many rites, both private and public. (See also PRAYERSTICK.)

FEATHER DANCE This dance, conducted among numerous contemporary tribal groups, is held when an eagle feather accidentally falls to the floor or ground from a dancer's ceremonial dress. As the eagle is considered sacred, the feather is retrieved in a specific manner. The ceremonial procedure may include the singing of a special song, a request to have a veteran pick up the eagle feather, prayers by the veteran, an account of that individual's military exploits, and a dance by the veteran and/or other participants.

FEATHER DANCE *Iroquois* One of the FOUR SACRED CEREMONIES held in longhouses to please the Creator and to give thanks for benevolence throughout the past year. The Feather Dance is one of the most sacred expressions of thanksgiving in the longhouse. It is performed in ceremonies addressed to the Creator (the MIDWINTER CEREMONY and GREEN CORN CEREMONY), in ceremonies addressed to wild foods (STRAWBERRY FESTIVAL), in ceremonies addressed to cultivated foods (OUR LIFE SUPPORTER DANCES), in ceremonies addressed to celestial spirits (SUN AND MOON CEREMONY), or in ceremonies held to cure an individual. Men and women dress in regalia because it is respectful to dress for sacred rites to the Creator. Music is provided by two singers, representing each moiety, who sit facing each other on a bench and accompany the dancing with turtle-shell rattles knocked on the bench.

FEATHER DANCE (Awh-mai-goon-gah) *Kiowa* The Kiowa version of the GHOST DANCE OF 1890 known as the Awh-mai-goon-gah (Feather Dance). The Kiowa received the Ghost Dance from SITTING BULL, the Arapaho apostle, and it was subsequently reinterpreted by AFRAID-OF-BEARS, a Kiowa priest. Ritual elements specified by the Kiowa religious leader included the ordination of 10 priests, the use of a yellow cross and a cedar tree as symbols, and the gift of an eagle feather, generally worn upright during the ceremony, to practitioners. The dance itself, a circle dance, was performed according to Sitting Bull's teachings. During the Feather Dance, prayers were made to Dom-oye-alm-daw-k'hee, the Earth Creator. The federal government pressured the Kiowa to discontinue the dance, eventually withholding tribal annuities until they agreed to do so in 1916. The Feather Dance then officially ended, and the government subsequently leased the land on which it was held. Another Kiowa name for the dance is Manposo'ti-guan ("dance-with-clasped-hands").

FEATHER RELIGION (waskliki, waptashi, Feather Dance, Pom Pom Shakers, Feather "Cult") *Middle Columbia Plateau* A religious revitalization movement founded by JAKE HUNT, a Klickitat prophet, in about 1904. The Feather religion is referred to in Shahaptian as *waskliki* (spin) or *waptashi* (feather) from prominent features of its practices. Hunt, who was influenced by WASHANI beliefs

and the INDIAN SHAKER RELIGION, incorporated elements of both doctrines in his rituals. He also introduced new practices, including ritual spinning and vomiting to intitiate members into the Feather religion. These practices were believed to help initiates obtain spiritual assistance to cleanse away impurities or illnesses. In the faith, the eagle was believed to be the supreme being and its feathers to possess soul-cleansing powers. After converting to the religion, members could own eagle feathers, which were held or worn during services. Another element of the worship was the use of hand mirrors, a practice that may have derived from the prophet LISHWAILAIT, who was believed to have seen the sins of everyone when he looked into a mirror during religious services. Other features included the belief that Sunday was holy (although meetings were also held on other days) and, similar to that of the prophet SMOHALLA, Hunt's use of poles, flags, and bells. In the Feather religion, yellow was a sacred color that represented the brightness of the sun as well as the lightness of the afterworld. The drum, too, was symbolic of the earth disk, signifying a piece of land, that Hunt saw in a vision. The Feather religion also shared practices with the earlier Washani religion, including the observance of first food feasts and the use of longhouses to hold ceremonies. In common with the Indian Shakers, the Feather adherents used curing practices and rejected intoxicants. Hunt's creed was also referred to as the Waskliki, the Spinning Religion. In English other names include the Feather Dance, Pom Pom Shakers and Feather Cult. The religion is said to have declined after Hunt's death in 1914.

FEATHERED PIPE *Gros Ventre (Atsina)* One of the most sacred pipes of the Gros Ventre people. An account by Garter Snake, the daughter of the holy man BULL LODGE, indicates that the Feathered Pipe originated as a spiritual gift to First Man and First Woman. First Man, a person with two wives and two children, dreamed that he would receive something sacred. After the third such dream, he consulted elders for advice and was told to accept the gift for the good of the people. First Man stated his agreement in his fourth dream, then followed the instructions he was given. After warning the people of a coming storm, he moved his lodge outside of the camp and remained there with his older wife and one of his children. First Man subsequently received four sacred objects, including the pipe, a feathered object, an image, and a whistle. He and his wife were given the names Whistling Man and Woman-takes-the-lead and instructed in their sacred duties. Whistling Man later received other instructions in dreams concerning the Feathered Pipe, its care and its rituals. After serving as keeper for 40 years, he received spiritual guidance in ritually transferring it to a successor.

FETISH Term commonly used in anthropological literature but not common among Native Americans, who refer to important religious possessions as SACRED OBJECTS.

FIDDLER, ADAM *(1865–1959) Cree-Saulteaux* A medicine man and Methodist lay supply minister in the Sandy Lake area of northwestern Ontario. Fiddler was the grandson of PORCUPINE STANDING SIDEWAYS, the son of JACK FIDDLER, and the nephew of JOSEPH FIDDLER, shamans and leaders among the Red Sucker band of their people. Fiddler carried on the family tradition of healing patients, singing sacred songs, conducting ceremonies, and prophesying future events. He eventually became instrumental in introducing elements of Christianity to his people. After returning home from a journey to Norway House, Manitoba, with the missionary FREDERICK GEORGE STEVENS in 1901, Fiddler had a dream in which the figure of Jesus Christ appeared to him. Christ then became Fiddler's spirit guide and the shaman converted to Christianity the following year. After his conversion, Fiddler continued his traditional religious ways, including the use of the SHAKING TENT CEREMONY to seek guidance and assistance from the spirits. As the remote location of his people's homeland insulated them from the outside world, Fiddler was the only Christian presence among them for a long period of time. Consequently, he was able to interpret and modify the new teachings without the involvement or supervision of Euro-Canadian missionaries. His literacy in the Cree syllabic system devised by the Reverend JAMES EVANS enabled him to learn more of the Christian faith and to keep records of his religious activities. Fiddler eventually built three churches, the last one incorporating symbolism from the WABINO THANKSGIVING CEREMONY, a traditional religious observance. A more recent Methodist church in the area was named in his honor. Fiddler, who served in his ministerial position from 1939 to 1952, died in 1959 at the age of 94.

FIDDLER, JACK ("He Who Stands in the Southern Sky") *(c. 1820s–1907) Cree-Saulteaux* A shaman and hereditary clan leader in the upper Severn River area of present-day northwestern Ontario, the son of the shaman PORCUPINE STANDING SIDEWAYS. Hudson's Bay Company traders referred to Fiddler as Mesnawenne ("Fancy Man"), and the first reference to the name Jack Fiddler appeared in 1887; he and other family members acquired the surname because they had learned to make and play the fiddle. The Red Sucker band, known for its independence and for maintaining its traditions, had little or no contact with Euro-Canadians for a long period of time. As a shaman, Fiddler was known for his gifts of prophecy, his healing skills, and his ability to communicate with the animals that sus-

tained the people. His traditional world was shattered when he and his brother JOSEPH FIDDLER were arrested for murder in 1907. They were charged with the death of Joseph's deranged daughter-in-law, Wahsakapeequay, who was thought to have become a windigo, a feared cannibalistic being in Algonquian belief. Though the Fiddlers admitted killing the woman, they were judged in a cultural context far different from their own. According to their belief, a windigo had to be destroyed to protect the people. After the Fiddlers' arrest, they were incarcerated at Norway House, Manitoba. Fiddler later stated that he had killed 14 windigo during the course of his life. Suffering in confinement away from his own people, the elderly shaman committed suicide. Fiddler's family included five wives, at least 12 children, and many grandchildren. His son ADAM FIDDLER also served as a religious leader.

FIDDLER, JOSEPH (Pesequan) *(c. 1856–1909) Cree-Saulteaux* A shaman and leader in the upper Severn River area of present-day northwestern Ontario. Fiddler, who was also known as Chawanee or Sandy, was the son of the shaman PORCUPINE STANDING SIDEWAYS. He was a member of the Red Sucker band, a group that was untouched by Euro-Canadian contact for a long period of time and was known for adhering to tribal religious ways. His family maintained the SHAKING TENT CEREMONY, the annual WABINO THANKSGIVING CEREMONY and other sacred traditions. In June 1907 Fiddler's traditional way of life ended when he and his brother JACK FIDDLER were charged with murder. They had strangled a woman identified as Wahsakapeequay, Joseph's daughter-in-law, who had become ill and deranged. She was thought to have become a windigo, a dangerous cannibalistic being of Algonquian belief. The killing, carried out according to tribal custom, was done to end the woman's suffering and to protect the people. The Fiddlers were arrested at Caribou Lake in Ontario and taken to Norway House, Manitoba, by the Royal North West Mounted Police, who had learned of the death from a hunter. Despite testimony by the Cree missionary EDWARD PAUPANAKISS for the defense, Fiddler was found guilty of murder during a one-day trial and sentenced to be executed. The sentence was later commuted to life imprisonment. Fiddler, who was ill for most of his imprisonment, was placed in a penitentiary hospital. He dictated a letter while incarcerated, stating that killing among his people was uncommon, done only to protect the people and to relieve the suffering of those who had become extraordinarily sick and insane. He also pleaded to be sent back to his people before he died. Although appeals were made on his behalf, Fiddler's release was not authorized until September 4, 1909, three days after he had died of consumption (tuberculosis). His brother Jack, suffering in confinement, had committed suicide a few months after being imprisoned. Fiddler had two wives and five children. His nephew ADAM FIDDLER and other family members continued the family legacy of religious leadership.

FINGER (Nape, "Hand" or "Finger") *(c. 1839–?) Lakota* An Oglala Lakota holy man who instructed JAMES R. WALKER, an agency physician on the Pine Ridge Reservation in South Dakota between 1896 and 1914, on Lakota culture and religion. Finger, from the reservation's Pass Creek district, contributed information to Walker along with RED HAWK, Ringing Shield, GEORGE SWORD, THOMAS TYON, and other Oglala. Shortly before he left the reservation, the physician conducted an interview with the elderly holy man. In a meeting lasting nearly all night, Finger explained concepts important to understanding the sacred ways of his people.

FINLEY, JAMES BRADLEY *(1781–1856)* A Methodist minister in Ohio whose 50-year career included missionary work among the Wyandot people. He was born in 1781 in North Carolina. His father, who was initially a Presbyterian, then a Methodist minister, educated his son in the classics at a school he conducted in Kentucky. Finley also studied medicine but preferred hunting and the life of a frontiersman. He converted in 1801 at a revival he attended at Cane Ridge, Kentucky. It was not until 1808 that he finally joined the Methodist Church and a year after that he began traveling on a circuit. Customary to the denomination's practice, he ministered to a different circuit nearly every year. Shortly after the Wyandot mission in Ohio was placed under Methodist jurisdiction following a visit by the Reverend Moses M. Henkle in 1819, Finley was sent there. At Upper Sandusky he assisted the missionary JOHN STEWART until Stewart's death in 1823, when he set up a school and took charge of the missionary work. He continued in the work until 1827 and then held a number of other positions, including district superintendent, prison chaplain, church pastor, and conference missionary. He was also elected eight times to the general conferences of the Methodist Church, where he debated important issues, including his antislavery position. Finley's publications included *History of the Wyandott Mission* (Cincinnati, 1840), *Memorials of Prison Life* (Cincinnati, 1850), *Autobiography of Rev. James B. Finley* (Cincinnati, 1853), *Sketches of Western Methodism* (New York, 1854, 1969), and *Life Among the Indians* (Cincinnati, 1857).

FIRE DANCE *Navajo (Dineh)* Also called the Corral Dance, this curing dance is performed around a fire in a circle or "corral" of evergreen branches during the winter, the season of hibernation. The term refers to a general series of all-night dances as well as to a specific dance with which the series concludes. It is often performed on the final night of a Mountain Way ceremony. This dance, performed in public, is a popular subject with artists because it is visually spectacular.

FIRE WOLF, JOHN *(1877–1966) Cheyenne* Buffalo priest, SUN DANCE instructor, and member of the Elkhorn Society, one of the military societies of his people. Fire Wolf was born in 1877 to Yellow Woman (also named White Buffalo Calf Woman) and Chief Black Wolf. He was a Northern Cheyenne and a member of the Suhtaio, a band of the Cheyenne. Greatly respected as a priest, he was consulted about the rare opening of the SACRED BUFFALO HAT bundle in 1959. Contributions from Fire Wolf about Cheyenne religious life are included in Father PETER JOHN POWELL's books, *Sweet Medicine* and *People of the Sacred Mountain.* He shared an early account of the spiritual gift of the SACRED BUFFALO HAT and other knowledge with Powell. Fire Wolf died in 1966. (See also BUFFALO CEREMONY, ERECT HORNS.)

FIREKEEPER *Iroquois* The individual who guards the wampum that legitimizes the longhouse. The officer is chosen on the basis of trustworthiness, not clan or moiety. (See also LONGHOUSE; WAMPUM.)

FIRST CATCH CEREMONIES *Inuit* Ceremonies held for the first deer, seal, white whale, or other large game killed by a young hunter. Ritual elements include offerings and prayers to spirits, ritual cutting and honoring of individual animals (including their return to their original mediums so they can be reincarnated), distribution of the first catch to the whole community, the assistance of old men, and sometimes a feast and the distribution of gifts.

FIRST FOOD OBSERVANCES Ceremonies, feasts, dances, or other religious observances held at the first appearance, or first taking, of foods from the environment. These foods include wild game, salmon and other fish, corn, fruits, wild strawberries and other berries, roots, and wild rice. The observances, known by such names as FIRST CATCH CEREMONIES, FIRST FRUITS CEREMONIES, and FIRST SALMON RITES, are widespread among Native groups. Their ritual elements vary across tribal cultures and geographic locales. They generally include prayers, offerings, and the giving of thanks. The sacred ceremonies help avert the danger in eating unconsecrated food, ritually prepare the people to eat the rest of the crop or take, and acknowledge the food's spiritual and physical necessity to the people. Forgiveness is generally sought from the spirit of the plant or animal, indicating that the gift of food was not wantonly taken and would not be wasted. The ceremonies or feasts are deemed essential to the continuation of the food among the people.

FIRST NEW MOON OF SPRING FESTIVAL *Cherokee* One of the SIX CHEROKEE FESTIVALS described by the 19th-century missionary DANIEL SABIN BUTRICK and other early observers of the Cherokee Nation before the forced removal of the tribal group from the southeastern Appalachian states to Indian Territory (present-day Oklahoma). The First New Moon of Spring Festival was held in about March, when the grass was beginning to grow, at the capital of the Cherokee Nation. The ancient capital, Chota, or Great Echota, was located on the south side of the Little Tennessee River below Citico Creek in Tennessee. New Echota in Georgia also served as the capital for a number of years before the removal. Preparations included a meeting of the seven principal or prime counselors to determine when the new moon would appear, the performance of a Friendship Dance by selected women and the dispatching of a messenger to announce the upcoming festival. Other preliminary activities included the designation of hunters to obtain game for the feast, the dressing of a deer, and the preparation of white deer skins. Seven men were placed in charge of the festival, and seven others were selected to oversee the food preparation. On the first evening there was a performance of a Friendship Dance by the women. The following day included the ritual purification of "GOING TO WATER." On the third day the people fasted. The fourth and final day included the performance of Friendship Dances and concluding ceremonies. A short time after the First New Moon of Spring Festival, the seven counselors designated the time for a sacred night dance. Ritual elements included the performance of a religious dance, the making of a new SACRED FIRE, the extinguishment of old fires in every Cherokee home, a SCRATCHING CEREMONY, medicine taking, and the presentation of white deer skins to the festival's presiding priest.

FIRST SALMON RITES *North Pacific Coast (Northern California, Oregon, Washington), Northern Great Basin, Plateau* Many tribes along the coast of Northern California, Oregon, and Washington celebrate the first salmon catch, according to their own patterns, in the spring. These peoples believe salmon are immortal beings who voluntarily sacrifice themselves annually for the benefit of people. If the salmon is pleased with the tribe's greeting and rituals, it returns to its village under the sea and encourages other salmon to return to the tribe's fishing wates, thus ensuring a good harvest. The favor of returning can be withdrawn, so it is essential to show respect to salmon and not mistreat or kill them needlessly. The first catch of the year, taken from im-

portant fishing places, are given elaborate and ceremonious welcome and honor so the salmon beings will continue to favor the humans who fish there. The basic pattern, which has infinite variations of procedure, involves the taking of the first fish by a priest who carries it to a special altar in the presence of a group. The priest treats the first fish as an honored guest of high rank, performs rituals, including a new fire kindling followed by songs, the cooking of the fish, and sacramental tasting by each person present. After the ceremony, the fishing is open to all. The first salmon's head and bones are returned to the stream from which it was caught so it can return to its village and be reborn. Other seasonal species, such as the herring, olachen, and eel, are also honored along the northern California, Oregon, and Washington coast.

FISH, JOSEPH *(1705–1781)* A Congregational minister of the Second Church of North Stonington, Connecticut, who worked among the Pequot and the Narragansett people during the second half of his 50-year career. Fish was born in Duxbury, Massachusetts, on January 28, 1705, and was educated for the ministry at Harvard College. In 1732 he began serving as the pastor of the Second Church, a position he held until his death on May 26, 1781. During his tenure he was deeply affected by the Great Awakening religious revival, at first supporting the revival, then becoming an opponent of the Separate and Separate Baptist movement. He supplemented his parish work and income by undertaking missionary efforts among Indians, preaching to the Pequot between 1757 and 1781. Fish also served as a representative of the Company for Propagation of the Gospel in New England and as a commissioner for the Society in Scotland for Propagating Christian Knowledge. After visiting the Narragansett of Charlestown, Rhode Island, in 1765, he established a religious and educational program for them under the auspices of the New England Company. For about a decade he made monthly trips to the school, church, and homes to inspect the work. Some of his notebooks were published for the first time in 1982 as *Old Light on Separate Ways: The Narragansett Diary of Joseph Fish 1765–1776*, making available an 18th-century eyewitness account of Narragansett life. Fish was married to Rebecca Pabodie, a descendant of the Mayflower's John Alden, and they had two daughters.

FLAT PIPE *Gros Ventre (Atsina)* An ancient Sacred Pipe of the Gros Ventre people. According to belief, its first keeper, Earthmaker, floated on a raft with the Flat Pipe during a flood. After a long period of time, he encountered some birds and animals who had survived. He sent Helldiver, Turtle, Beaver, and then Muskrat diving in search of earth. Although each of the animals drowned, Earthmaker found mud on two of them. After praying and singing sacred songs over it, the bits of earth grew and grew into dry ground. The keeper eventually become lonely without other human beings and created first a man, then a woman. He remained with them for a period of time, giving them the sacred teachings of the Flat Pipe. Besides instructing them in the qualifications and responsibilities of the keeper, he taught them its ceremonies and rituals. The Flat Pipe is older than the FEATHERED PIPE of the Gros Ventre. (See also CREATION ACCOUNTS.)

FLÈCHÉ, JESSE *(fl. early 1600s)* French missionary. Born at Lantages, France, Flèché, a priest, was recruited for Acadia in 1610 because he was available and the new colony needed a priest. He has been considered the first recognized missionary to the Indians within the present boundaries of Canada. Less than a month after his arrival at Port Royal, he baptized MEMBERTOU, a Sagamo chief, and 20 or so of Membertou's relatives. By 1611, with no knowledge of the Micmac language and by working through an interpreter, he baptized more than 100 Micmac who did not understand the catechism. A 19th-century Catholic historian noted that Flèché "baptized, apparently somewhat in haste, a number of the natives, and sent an account of it to France." He was subsequently censured for his haste and for baptizing those who had virtually no instruction and were uninformed about even the rudiments of the faith.

FLEMING, JOHN *(1807–1894)* A Presbyterian minister and missionary who worked among Creek, Wea, Ojibway, and Ottawa people during his career. Born in 1807 in Mifflin County, Pennsylvania, he attended Mifflin Academy, Jefferson College (class of 1829), and Princeton Theological Seminary. Fleming was ordained as a Presbyterian minister on October 24, 1832. A short time later he began his missionary work with an assignment from the AMERICAN BOARD OF COMMISSIONERS FOR FOREIGN MISSIONS to the Creeks in present-day Oklahoma. While his bride, Margaret Scudder, opened a school, Fleming began preaching through an interpreter, JAMES PERRYMAN, and studying the Muskogee or Creek language of the people. He subsequently became the first to reduce the difficult language to writing, eventually producing a number of publications, including an elementary book of religious translations, *Short Sermon: Also Hymns, in the Muskogee or Creek Language* (Boston, 1835), *Istuti in Naktsoky, or The Child's Book* (Cherokee Press, 1835), and *The Maskokee Semahayeta, or Muskokee Teacher* (1836). His work in this area influenced the missionary ROBERT MCGILL LOUGHRIDGE, who produced later translations in the Muskogee language.

After the government closed the Creek mission, Fleming spent a year working with the Wea people in Kansas. In 1839 he served as a missionary to the Ojibway and Ottawa at Grand Traverse Bay in Michigan and began studying their languages. His missionary work ended with the death of his wife on May 21, 1839. Fleming served at pastorates in Pennsylvania for eight years and as a missionary in Illinois from 1849 to 1875. He spent his remaining years in Nebraska and died on October 27, 1894.

FLOWERS (sewam) *Yaqui* To the Yaqui, flower forms symbolize the traditional narrative that at the crucifixion of Jesus, his blood fell to earth, and was transformed into flowers. The flowers are thought to be a special weapon against evil throughout the year. They are a symbol for righteous and holy acts, for all forms of compassionate and religious expression. Flowers used in ceremonies may be real or shaped of crepe paper or confetti. In the WAEHMA, the Yaqui version of the Passion of Christ, flowers are the symbol of victory of the allies of Jesus over his enemies. Real or imitation flowers are used throughout the Waehma.

FLUTE CEREMONY *Hopi* A 16-day ceremony held in August to help mature crops and bring summer rains. The ceremony is performed in alternating years with the SNAKE-ANTELOPE CEREMONY. Conducted by the Blue and Gray Flute Societies, who begin preparations the preceding winter, the ceremony also reenacts the people's emergence from the underworld into the present, fourth world. A rite at the main village spring, considered an opening to the underworld, is followed by a procession from there to the pueblo. The Flute Societies also conduct separate ceremonies with their songs and flute music to help the sun establish the seasonal cycle. GERMINATOR (Muingwa) is their spiritual force.

FLUTE SOCIETY *Hopi* See FLUTE CEREMONY

FOLSOM, WILLIS F. *(1825–c. 1894)* *Choctaw* Methodist Episcopal missionary and interpreter. Folsom's grandmother was Aiah-ni-chich-oh-oy-oh, a Choctaw, and his grandfather was Nathaniel Folsom, a descendant of English ancestors who settled in America during the colonial period. Folsom, who was born in Mississippi, was removed with his father, McKee Folsom, and other family members to Indian Territory (present-day Oklahoma) in the early 1830s. He later attended a Choctaw Nation boarding school, Bloomfield Academy, where he converted to Christianity. Folsom was licensed to preach in about 1851 or 1852 and served as a worker and exhorter for several years before he was ordained as a deacon in 1858 and as an elder the following year. He was later placed in charge of the

Methodist Episcopal Church South at Boggy Depot in Indian Territory (present-day Oklahoma). During his career he also served as an official interpreter of the Indian Mission Conference and traveled great distances as an itinerant preacher. Although many ministers were forced to leave the mission field during the Civil War, Folsom was one of the few who remained among the people. He maintained a diary from 1856 until 1894 that detailed aspects of his approximately 50 years as a missionary. Excerpts have appeared in chronicles of Oklahoma.

FOOL'S DANCE SOCIETY *Assiniboine* According to one account, this society began after a young man received spiritual instructions concerning its purpose and rituals in a dream. He was shown the Fool's Dance and told to conduct it once a year for the good of the people. It was performed by dancers wearing head masks of various types, with slits for the eyes, and dirty, tattered garments on their bodies. The young man then introduced the society and its dance as he had promised. Membership in the Fool's Dance Society consisted of select men who were taught the sacred knowledge associated with it. Performances of the annual ceremony by the society members included prayers, songs, and dances around a buffalo. Members also conducted a ritual throwing performance with pieces of buffalo meat. During the course of the ceremony their antics included squirting blood from the buffalo at spectators, dancing with grotesque movements, and speaking in an opposite or backward manner. In addition to their powers in hunting and warfare, members were known for their healing. An account of a Fool's Dance held in 1957 indicated that it took place at the conclusion of a Sun Dance in Montana. The participants traced its origins to the culture hero, Iktomi, who gave the sacred gift to the Assiniboine during the period of their creation. This society has been compared to the WINDIGOKAN Dance of the Cree and the Plains Ojibway.

FOOLS CROW, FRANK *(c. 1891–1989) Lakota* A Teton Lakota holy man and ceremonial chief who was born in the Porcupine community of the Pine Ridge Reservation in South Dakota shortly after the Wounded Knee tragedy of 1890. The Fools Crow name came from Frank's paternal grandfather, Knife Chief, whose older son was killed by Crow Indians. Fools Crow was raised in the traditional Lakota way, his relatives protecting him from agents who would have enrolled him in school. Besides his father and grandparents, two of Fools Crow's teachers were his uncle Iron Cloud, a Lakota leader during the early reservation period, and Stirrup, a well-known holy man. At age 13, after Frank began to have strong feelings about becoming a medicine man, his father took him to Stirrup, who became his

teacher. The holy man took him on his first VISION QUEST in 1905 where Fools Crow received his spirit helpers. At that time he realized he had spiritual power but did not realize what to do with it. In 1914 Stirrup asked Frank's father to approve his choice of the young man to carry on his work as a holy man, especially as a YUWIPI leader. It was several years later, however, before Fools Crow started to use his power to heal. In November of 1913, he conducted his first KETTLE DANCE, which his grandparents taught him. A pivotal event in his life was the gift of a ceremonial pipe from Iron Cloud, who died a few days after presenting it to his nephew in 1917. From that period on, Fools Crow believed he had to heal people, and he continued to do so.

Besides learning Yuwipi and other ceremonies, he gained information and cures in other ways. He was instructed that his life as a holy man would be measured by his manner of living. Stirrup warned him that he would be expected to make sacrifices, that he would be called upon to cure people without pay, and that he could not openly argue political issues or laws with Indian people. Certain behaviors, such as drinking, womanizing, and fighting, were contrary to a true medicine man's role. Although the SUN DANCE was prohibited by the U.S. government in 1881, Fools Crow stated that it was held in secret almost every year in remote locations with small groups. When the Bureau of Indian Affairs authorized a Sun Dance at Pine Ridge in 1929, no piercing of the flesh or flesh offerings were permitted, despite pleas to include them. In 1952, Fools Crow was allowed to pierce male pledgers but first had to assume responsibility for any adverse consequences.

In 1917 Fools Crow was convinced by priests to become a Roman Catholic. He found few problems with differences between Catholicism and his traditional beliefs and practiced both. Other members of his family, notably his renowned uncle BLACK ELK, who became Catholic in 1904, also joined Christian churches. Fools Crow participated in a European tour in 1921, a Wild West show in 1927, and other traveling programs. In 1931, Fools Crow was one of the riders in what he described as "the last true and sacred Horse Dance." Fools Crow also traveled with a group publicizing western movies and appeared in a film called *War Bonnet*, which he helped to promote. Besides being a religious leader, the holy man assumed leadership of the Porcupine District of the Pine Ridge Reservation in South Dakota after his father turned the position over to him in 1925. In later years, Fools Crow continued as a religious and civil leader. During the occupation of Wounded Knee on the Pine Ridge Reservation by American Indian Movement activists in 1973, he sought peace by negotiating with federal officials and the Native American protesters to settle the armed confrontation. Fools Crow was presented with a document from government officials outlining a proposed settlement of the crisis. After it was signed by both sides, the confrontation ended. In September of 1975, Fools Crow led a large delegation of Lakota to Washington, D.C., to discuss the Fort Laramie Treaty of 1868, which established the Great Sioux Reservation, and reservation problems with government officials and President Gerald Ford. On September 5, 1975, while in Washington, Fools Crow became the first Indian holy man to lead the opening prayer for a session of the United States Senate. In the spring of 1976, fulfilling a longtime desire, he was shown the BUFFALO CALF PIPE, a rare honor, by its keeper, ARVAL LOOKING HORSE. At a vision quest in 1965 at the sacred BEAR BUTTE site, Fools Crow was told that he was to tell certain things about himself and his people to a person who would be made known to him. That person became Thomas E. Mails, who with Dallas Chief Eagle interpreting and assisting, published *Fools Crow* in 1979. Fools Crow and his wife had five children. Fools Crow died in 1989.

FOOLS CROW V. GULLET (541 F. Supp. 785 [D.S.D. 1982]) *(1982)* A 1982 First Amendment case before the Supreme Court. In this case, Lakota and Cheyenne plaintiffs, including FRANK FOOLS CROW, contended that the conduct of South Dakota's state parks department and the general public destroyed the sanctity of Native religious ceremonies at the sacred BEAR BUTTE site in the Black Hills of South Dakota and violated their right to free exercise of religion. They claimed that the defendants desecrated the ceremonial area with the construction of access roads, parking lots, and other facilities; that their use of the traditional ceremonial area was restricted while construction was in progress; that tourists were allowed to disrupt religious services by taking photographs, viewing rituals from wooden platforms constructed for that purpose by defendants, removing religious offerings, and disrupting prayers and songs; and that their religious practices were restricted at Bear Butte Lake, where they were required to camp during the period of construction. The district court ruled that the plaintiffs failed to establish any infringement of First Amendment rights and that their interests were outweighed by compelling state interests in improving access to the site, to protecting the welfare of park visitors, and to preserving the resource from further decay and erosion. It suggested that granting the petitioners' request for relief would violate the establishment clause separating the powers of church and state. Addressing the AMERICAN INDIAN RELIGIOUS FREEDOM ACT OF 1978, the court observed that "it is not clear that the Act governs the conduct of state governments or agencies" and concluded that it was "merely a statement of the policy of the federal government with respect to traditional Indian reli-

gious practices." The case was appealed to the Eighth Circuit Court of Appeals, which in 1983 affirmed the district court's decision. In November 1983, the U.S. Supreme Court denied the petition for writ of *certiorari*. (See SACRED SITES and similar legal cases included in this volume.)

FOREMAN, STEPHEN *(1807–1881) Cherokee* Presbyterian missionary. Born in Rome, Georgia, Foreman attended a mission school at Candy's Creek, near Cleveland, Tennessee, after his family moved to the area. Following the death of his father, he received assistance from Reverend SAMUEL AUSTIN WORCESTER, who helped him continue his education at New Echota, Georgia. Foreman later attended Union Theological Seminary in Virginia and Princeton Theological Seminary before receiving a license to preach from Tennessee's Union Presbytery in the 1830s. He worked as a missionary among his people during the turmoil of the removal period when the Cherokees were uprooted from their lands and forced to migrate west. Besides translating biblical works, he served as an associate editor of the *Cherokee Phoenix* and later contributed material to the *Cherokee Advocate*. In 1838 he was briefly imprisoned over the removal issue, and a short time later he helped lead one of the last groups to Indian Territory (present-day Oklahoma). After organizing the Cherokee Nation's school system in 1841, he became its first superintendent. On October 11, 1844 he was elected to the Supreme Court of the Cherokee and later served as the tribal executive councilor from 1847 to 1855. Foreman worked as a missionary in Texas during the Civil War period. Upon his return to Indian Territory, he bought the house ELIAS BOUDINOT had owned and created The Church in the Woods. He continued his religious activities there until his death in 1881.

FORMULA *California* The formulas are ancient stories recounting the manner in which something originated whose telling possessed the power to bring about a desired result. Recitations of formulas accompanied FIRST SALMON RITES, launching a new canoe, building a house, and other ritual activities. A priest, or formulist, owned these ritual formulas, which were considered property and as such were saleable and inheritable. (See also SACRED FORMULAS.)

FORTUNATE EAGLE, ADAM (Adam Nordwall) *(b.1930s) Ojibway* A pipeholder and ceremonial leader. Fortunate Eagle, a member of the Red Lake Reservation in Minnesota, attended boarding school in PIPESTONE, Minnesota, for 10 years. After graduating, he enrolled in the Haskell Institute in Lawrence, Kansas, and remained there for five years. While at Pipestone, he spent time at the sacred quarries, learning from several pipemakers in the area. Fortunate

Eagle later lived in California, where he served in a number of leadership roles. He held the chairmanship of the Council of Bay Area Indian Affairs for 10 years, taught sociology at the University of California, lectured at other institutions, and worked with prison inmates. He was also one of the leaders who participated in the takeover and occupation of Alcatraz Island in 1969 to protest the government's treatment of American Indians.

Fortunate Eagle is also a sculptor and pipemaker whose work has been exhibited in both the United States and Europe. At one time he arrived in Italy and declared it discovered in the name of Native Americans. In 1972 he became a pipeholder, a position involving ritual care and other religious responsibilities associated with the SACRED PIPE. He was acknowledged for the role by WALLACE HOWARD BLACK ELK, a contemporary Lakota medicine man, who is one of his religious teachers. Fortunate Eagle also began serving as a ceremonial leader. He indicated in a published interview that his ceremonies are limited to those he identified as intertribal, that is, they are conducted for participants from many different tribes. Fortunate Eagle is also known because of his involvement in litigation involving the use of eagle feathers. He operates the Roundhouse Gallery in Fallon, Nevada, and lives on a nearby reservation with his family.

FOUNDATION OF LIFE *Cherokee* A national ritual described among the Oklahoma Cherokee people. It is conducted as a final resort when the very survival of the Cherokee people is at stake. A number of external or internal threats may lead to its observance, including hostilities against the nation, harsh pressures from Euro-American forces, and a schism from within. At least six versions of the ritual have been identified in manuscript form in the Cherokee language.   The Foundation of Life symbolizes purification or "taking them to the water" (GOING TO WATER) of the total nation, spiritually strengthening and unifying the people against the threat. An indication of its seriousness is that it is conducted seven times in succession. The sacred ritual is performed by seven qualified participants from each of the Cherokee clans at the site and in the order determined. Elements of the Foundation of Life include tobacco offerings, the recitation of the ritual's sacred text four times by each clan representative, and the performance of a pipe ceremony held seven times with the final one occurring at dawn. In extraordinary circumstances, an individual may conduct the Foundation of Life ritual by delivering the sacred text seven times.

FOUR SACRED CEREMONIES *Iroquois* Four sacred rites addressed to the Creator given in the creation and confirmed by HANDSOME LAKE; an integral part of longhouse festivals. They are the FEATHER DANCE, the THANKSGIVING DANCE, PERSONAL CHANT, and BOWL (PEACH STONE) GAME. The sequence of performances differs among Iroquois groups in the United States and Canada. The four rites are an important part of the HANDSOME LAKE RELIGION.

FOUR SACRED PERSONS *Cheyenne* In Cheyenne belief the Four Sacred Persons guard the universe from the four directions of the southeast, southwest, northwest, and northeast. They were created by MAHEO, the Supreme Being, and they watch over, protect, and bless the people. Prayers and offerings are made to them as well as to the Sacred Powers.

FOX, MARVIN *(c. 1936–) Blood* The first treaty Indian in Canada to be ordained a Roman Catholic priest. The son of Mr. and Mrs. George Fox, Fox was born and educated on the Blood reserve near Cardston, Alberta. There he attended St. Mary's Catholic School, remembered as a student of remarkable aptitude who began his formal education without knowing English. Fox later continued his studies at St. Thomas's College in North Battleford, Saskatchewan. He was ordained to the priesthood on February 23, 1963, at St. Mary's Catholic Church, his home parish on the reserve. Several hundred members of his tribal band attended his ordination ceremony, which was conducted by the Most Reverend Francis P. Carroll, Bishop of Calgary, Alberta. Although EDWARD CUNNINGHAM became the first Métis to be ordained a Roman Catholic priest in 1890, it was not until 1963, with Fox, that the first treaty Indian in Canada attained that status. The Reverend Marvin Fox is said to have subsequently left the priesthood.

FRANCIS, JOSIAH (Hildis Hadjo, "Crazy Medicine") *(c. 1770s–1818) Creek* Renowned prophet among his people who became an influential leader during the War of 1812. Of mixed parentage, Francis was born in the 1770s to a mother who was likely of Creek descent and a white father. Little is known of his early life, but he was probably influenced by traditional tribal religious leaders. A proponent of the Native way of life who advocated war against the whites, he eventually used his spiritual powers to gain support for his cause. Besides going into trances, Francis was known to disappear under water for extended periods of time and to claim the ability to fly. He attributed his powers to a spirit who also helped him destroy enemies. Seekaboo, a prophet who traveled with Tecumseh in 1811 to seek support among the Creek and other southern tribes, was an important influence on Francis as well. Francis supported Tecumseh and attracted followers to the Shawnee leader's struggle against the white Americans. He became an active participant in the

Creek War of 1813 to 1814, opposing encroachment on tribal lands and advocating a return to traditional ways. Following the Native victory at the Battle of Burnt Corn, July 27, 1813, Francis began constructing a sacred town where only Indians would live. He asserted that Ecunchattee, or the Holy Ground, would be protected by the Great Spirit, who would surround it with a barrier and kill any whites who attempted to cross it. The two towns at the Holy Ground were eventually burned during the war. In 1815 Francis went to England for the purpose of ratifying a treaty made with the Indians by Edward Nicolls, a British military officer, who promised them an independent state as well as his country's protection and trade. Not wanting to disrupt the newly established peace policy with the United States, Britain failed to ratify the agreement. Francis remained in England for over a year, reportedly meeting with the Prince Regent before departing for home on December 30, 1816. Upon his return to Florida, he settled near St. Marks and sought to unite tribal people who had fought on opposite sides in the war. Native attacks on Euro-American settlements led to Andrew Jackson's invasion of Florida on April 7, 1818. His forces captured St. Marks and burned Francis's home and the rest of the village. Although the Creek prophet escaped, he was later captured and then asked to meet with Andrew Jackson, but the military leader refused his request. Francis and Himollemico, another native leader, were hanged on April 18, 1818, at St. Marks. The holy man was also known as Hidlis Hadjo, Hillishago, Hillishager, and Francis the Prophet. (See also MAIN POC; TENSKWATAWA.)

FRANK V. ALASKA (604 p. 2d 1068 [Alaska 1979]) (1979)

In 1975, Carlos Frank, an Athabascan, was charged with violating Alaska state law by unlawfully transporting illegally taken game. Frank's defense was that the application of the game regulation to him amounted to an abridgement of his religious freedom because the moose he had taken was for use in a funeral POTLATCH. Despite a finding that "the funeral potlatch is an integral part of the religious belief of the central Alaska Athabascan," Frank was convicted in district court, and the decision was subsequently affirmed in superior court. On appeal, the Alaska Supreme Court ruled that Frank's First Amendment rights were abridged and reversed the lower court judgments. The supreme court reasoned that although "moose itself is not sacred, it is needed for proper observance of a sacred ritual which must take place soon after death occurs." The moose meat was found to be an integral Native food, "the sacramental equivalent to the wine and wafer in Christianity." The supreme court ruled that the state had not met the burden of demonstrating a compelling interest to justify curtailing a religiously based practice. Furthermore, exemption did not vi-

olate the establishment clause separating the powers of church and state but reflected "nothing more than the governmental obligation of neutrality in the face of religious differences." (See Subject Index for additional court cases listed in this volume.)

FRAZIER, FRANCIS (*fl. late 1800s*) *Dakota* A Congregational minister who succeeded the Reverend ARTEMAS EHNAMANI to the pastorate of Pilgrim Church at Santee, Nebraska, on September 10, 1902. Before that date, Frazier ministered to Native people in the area of Naper, Nebraska, for 17 years. His children continued the family legacy of leadership and service. One of them, George Frazier, assisted him with missionary work while on a leave from medical school, and another son, FRANCIS PHILIP FRAZIER, also became a minister.

FRAZIER, FRANCIS PHILIP (*fl. early 1900s*) *Dakota* A Santee Dakota minister who was the grandson and son of Congregational missionaries. His grandfather, the Reverend ARTEMAS EHNAMANI, turned to Christianity in the aftermath of the Dakota War of 1862 in Minnesota, and his father, FRANCIS FRAZIER, continued the ministry. Frazier was educated at Santee Mission School, Yankton Academy, and Mt. Hermon Boys School. After starting college at Dartmouth, he transferred to Oberlin, where he completed his A.B. degree in 1922. He also attended Chicago Theological Seminary before beginning missionary work among the Kickapoo people in McCloud, Oklahoma. Frazier later returned to his own people, serving Lakota at Eagle Butte and Ft. Pierre. He served in the military during World War II and was eventually stationed in Germany. After the war, Reverend Frazier continued ministering to American Indian congregations. He was assisted in his work by his wife, Susie Meek Frazier, a Sac and Fox from Oklahoma.

FREEMAN, BERNARDUS (Freeman) (*fl. early 1700s*) Dutch Reformed minister who worked among the Mohawk people. Freeman (also Freerman) is believed to have been from Gilhuis in the Netherlands. He had little formal education and worked as a tailor before turning to the ministry. Freeman was ordained on March 16, 1700, as the pastor of the Albany Reformed Church in New York. When the position was later given to another minister, he went to Schenectady. He received an appointment from the governor to work among Native people and acquired proficiency in the Mohawk language. Freeman translated a number of religious works for use in instructing Native converts to Christianity. His efforts resulted in the first booklet in the Mohawk language, published in Boston in 1707. After the Society for the Propagation of the Gospel sent Reverend William Andrews to the area in 1712, Freeman worked with him and Lawrence Claesse on *The Morning and Evening Prayer, the Litany, Church Catechism, Family Prayers, and Several Chapters of the Old and New-Testament, translated into the Mahaque Indian Language* (1715). Freeman was later involved in an ecclesiastical dispute on Long Island and worked among groups of German Reformed immigrants on Staten Island and in Monmouth County, New Jersey. He also wrote three books before his death in 1741.

FREY, JACOB BENJAMIN *(1875–1957)* A Mennonite missionary to the Hopi people who was born in Greenfield Township, Kansas. After attending Greenfield District School, Frey studied at Bethel Academy in Newton, Kansas. During his last year of college he began learning the Hopi language from the Reverend H. R. Voth, who had returned from the field to teach him. Following his 1903 graduation and ordination, he left for Oraibi, Arizona, to continue the Mennonite work started by Voth and Voth's colleague JACOB B. EPP. Frey remained at Oraibi until 1905 when he began working at Moencopi, about 40 miles away. In addition to building a chapel, home, and irrigation system, he began developing an alphabet in order to translate the Bible into the Hopi language. He also completed a Hopi compilation of songs and a Bible study guide. Frey traveled to other villages where he used "heart drawings" while conducting meetings. The pictures, drawn by a young Hopi, depicted the human heart before and after salvation. He constructed a chapel at the government Indian school in Tuba City in the 1920s and was named president of the Southwest Bible and Missionary Conference in Flagstaff.

Another missionary in the field complained to the Mennonite board that Frey's teachings were false because they included a belief that the devil would ultimately be saved by God. Controversy over the unfounded complaint led the board to request Frey to resign. After his 1928 resignation, he moved to Flagstaff where he converted a former lumber camp into a grocery store and tourist business. He also taught for a time at the Oklahoma Bible Academy and continued to participate in various religious activities. In 1941 he moved to Oak Creek Canyon, Arizona and helped establish a number of Indian churches in the area.

GABLE MOUNTAIN *Yakama* A mountain sacred to the Yakama of south-central Washington and located inside the federal government's 574-square-mile Hanford nuclear reservation. A site for VISION QUESTS since ancient times, Yakama had access to traditional lands within the Hanford reservation under an 1855 treaty until the government invoked the War Powers Act of 1943 and claimed the area as a secured zone. After negotiations with the Department of Energy, on November 1, 1987, the Yakama were allowed to hold their first hour-long religious service on Gable Mountain since the government created the nuclear reservation. The Yakama Nation had to inform the Department of Energy how many people were attending the ceremony and when they were coming. The ceremony was observed by Energy Department officials.

GAGEWIN ("Everlasting Mist") *(c. 1850–1919) Ojibway* A MIDEWIWIN adherent who provided information to the ethnologist Frances Densmore about his religion's beliefs and teachings. Gagewin, a member of the White Earth Reservation in Minnesota, was the grandson of Black Hawk and the son of Mountain. He described fundamental sacred teachings to Densmore, saying, "The principal idea of the Midewiwin is that life is prolonged by right living, and by the use of herbs which were intended for this purpose by the Mide manido." His statement that practitioners were taught moderation and quietness directed Densmore's attention to "the gentle voices, the patience, and the courtesy" among religious practitioners. Gagewin also contributed information about the sacred scrolls of the Midewiwin, including their use in teaching initiates. Over 60 at the time, he served as one of Densmore's principal informants on the religion. He died on October 23, 1919. Gagewin was married to Nised Naganob.

GAHUNI *(?–c. 1857) Cherokee* A medicine man and a Methodist preacher who wrote both traditional SACRED FORMULAS and portions of Scripture in the Cherokee language. His book of writings, kept by his family after his death, was later acquired by the ethnologist James Mooney for the Bureau of American Ethnology. Although Gahuni's wife Ayasta had removed some of the pages on the advice of another shaman, eight unique formulas remained. Mooney also received information from BLACK FOX, SUYETA, and SWIMMER.

GALAXY SOCIETY (Newekwe) *Zuni* Zuni curing society of clowns who use mimicry, mummery, and burlesque to care for the sick. Their special province is curing diseases of the stomach. Membership comes after recovery from stomach ailment and initiation into the society is necessary for a permanent cure. The clowns are painted with alternating stripes of black and white and wear sloppy clothes and a tight-fitting cap painted white with cornhusk strips attached to it. Like most clowns, they have no shame, eat the inedible, burlesque both tribal and foreign elements like the kachina dancers, their Spanish neighbors, the space program, Roman Catholic rituals, and intertribal powwows. In order to startle and shock an audience, they violate all norms and cause people to laugh, releasing worries lodged in their stomachs, which cause illness in general. (See also CLOWN.)

GANDEACTENA, CATHERINE (Gandeaktena, Gandeaktewa, Gandiaktua) *(?–1673) Erie.* Baptized Erie woman. Along with her mother, she was taken to an Oneida village around 1654. In 1656 she married a Christianized Huron, and in 1668 she was baptized by Bishop Laval in Quebec. She was invited to spend the winter with Jesuit Father Pierre Raffeix, where she and a small group of newly-baptized people founded the mission of Saint François Xavier. Catherine Gandeactena's work attracted more Iroquois families to the mission. By 1673, 200 Indians, representing 22 nations, were living there. She died at the mission in 1673. Other versions of her name are spelled Gandeaktena, Gandeaktewa, and Gandiaktua.

GARRIOCH, ALFRED CAMPBELL *(1848–1934)* A Church of England missionary among the Cree and Beaver tribes in the Canadian Northwest. Born and educated at the Red River settlement (Winnipeg) in present-day Manitoba, Garrioch taught at St. John's School from 1868 to 1871. He then went into business and later into the mission field. After preliminary missionary studies at Fort Simpson, Northwest Territories, where he was ordained a deacon, he began working among the Beaver people in the Peace River area in 1876. Garrioch was later ordained a priest at Fort Vermillion, where he had founded the Unjaga mission. He served at other Canadian missions during his career, including Fort Dunvegan (1886 to 1891), Rapid City (1892 to 1895), and Portage la Prairie, until 1908. Garrioch became an authority on the Cree and Beaver languages, translating a number of religious works and compiling an English-Cree-Beaver vocabulary. Two of his publications were printed in London in 1886: *The Gospel According to St. Mark* and *Manual of Devotion in the Beaver Indian Language.* Other writings included *First Furrows: A History of the Early Settlement of the Red River Country, including that of Portage la Prairie* (1923), *The Far and Furry North: A Story of Life and Travel in the Days of the Hudson's Bay Company* (1925), *A Hatchet Mark in Duplicate* (1929), and *The Correction Line* (1923).

GEORGE, JIMMY *(?–1969) Northern Paiute (Numu, Paviotso)* A shaman who served as a healer in Nevada and California until the end of his life. George, referred to as a "singing shaman," was photographed in 1967 wearing twined bark clothing and holding some of his doctoring symbols. He also continued the traditional technology with tules, reeds found growing in marshes, by making decoys and other objects.

GEORGE, NORMAN (No'-Mun) *(?–1942) Tolowa* The first Tolowa to receive spiritual power through the Shaker faith and the organizer of the first congregation of the INDIAN SHAKER RELIGION at the Smith River Rancheria in California. He and other Tolowa began attending Shaker meetings among the Klamath in 1929, although they had witnessed the Shaker religious practices before that time while working away from home at a fish cannery. Tolowa who embraced the religion did so, in part, because the Shakers did not require them to abandon their traditional culture. After receiving power, George began organizing the Smith River congregation with help from JIMMY JACK HOPPEL and "Ery," or Ira Turner. He held meetings at his house until the construction of a church in 1930. George was the minister of the original Tolowa Shaker Church, serving the congregation with other officers, including Ellen LaFountain and AMELIA BROWN, a Nay-Dosh or Ten-Night Dance leader. The church, under Tolowa leadership since its beginning, continues as a religious influence in the present.

GERMINATOR (Muingwa) *Hopi* The spiritual deity of vegetation, crops, and germination. This male fertility spirit is also the guardian of towns and the preserver of health and is sometimes thought of as the father of humanity. The spirit is impersonated in several ceremonies—the November WUWUCHIM CEREMONY, winter solstice, and the February POWAMU CEREMONY. (See also FLUTE CEREMONY.)

GHOST The conviction among many Native Americans that there is a malignant influence associated with a dead person released at death that is capable of returning to earth as an apparition. Many groups believe that ghosts haunt burial grounds or return to earth to plague the living. Among Pueblos there is a belief that ghosts appear as owls and bring evil. Northern Paiutes offer food, beads, and other objects to the dead to get rid of the deceased person's ghost so it does not bother the living. Despite the overall fear of ghosts, some tribes feel ghosts are harmless and some even seek their protection. The Confederated Salish-Kootenai (Flathead) believe that ghosts are helpers and warn the living about an approaching danger. The Saulteaux Ojibway east of Lake Winnepeg believe ghosts are spiritual helpers who bless the living if proper offerings are made. They also believe the dead appear as personal guardian spirits, investing a person with power or skills. Western Shoshone have similar beliefs about ghosts as guardian spirits. The Navajo and other tribes in the Southwest, however, greatly fear ghosts and believe they cause ghost infection.

GHOST *Navajo (Dineh)* The conviction among the Navajo that there is a malignant influence associated with a dead person released at death and capable of return to earth as an apparition. Traditional Navajo believe that most of the dead may return as ghosts to plague the living. They take precautions to avoid delaying the journey of the spirit to the afterworld and to prevent the return of the ghost of the deceased. They obliterate footprints around the grave, dispose of the dead person's possessions, go through four days of restrictions during the journey of the spirit to the afterworld, and avoid the hogan in which the death occurred. There is little ceremony. Every part of the funeral ritual is intended to prevent or dissuade the dead person from returning to threaten relatives. A person who dies, whether in childhood or old age, releases a ghost at death, no matter how good the person was during life. The ghost of an aged person who has been respected and dies a natural death does not release a malignant influence, however. Ghosts, dark and black, appear after dark or just before death. Returning to earth in some shape, such as a coyote, owl, mouse, bird, whirlwind, human form, or dark object, they make sounds and can change their size and form. Ghosts return to earth to avenge some offense or neglect, such as improper burial of a corpse, holding back the belongings of the deceased, failure to kill a horse for the use of the deceased, or grave disturbance. Ghosts cause ghost infection. The treatment of this infection, which causes fainting, loss of consciousness, delirium, bad dreams about evil spirits, and fear at night is the EVIL WAY ceremony, for sickness caused by Navajo ghosts, or the ENEMY WAY, directed against ghosts of non-Navajo, as well as ghost medicine and the BLESSING WAY.

GHOST DANCE HAND GAME *Pawnee* A sacred ceremony that developed during the era of the GHOST DANCE OF 1890. It was based on the hand game, a traditional game of chance in many Native American cultures. The early Pawnee hand game was played by men who competed on two opposing teams of players. One individual from each team began the game, starting the play by placing his hands behind his back and concealing a special bone or die in one hand. He then brought both clenched hands forward, moving them to the rhythm of special hand game music. His opponent, sometimes distracted by the songs and motions, then guessed which hand concealed the bone before taking his turn. The score was kept with tally sticks and eventually other individuals from each side had turns playing.

The Ghost Dance Hand Game developed in accordance with the Ghost Dance movement's emphasis on restoring Native traditions. As a result of assimilationist pressures, the earlier hand game is said to have practically disappeared by 1892. Joseph Carrion, a ghost dancer who lived among the Pawnee, may have been instrumental in the hand game's evolution to a sacred ceremony. After attending an Arapaho Ghost Dance and experiencing a vision, Carrion returned home with the spiritual gift of the ceremonial game. After the Ghost Dance Hand Games started, they proliferated as a result of trance visions by other dancers. The sacred games

became an important means of expressing the Ghost Dance beliefs, especially after federal officials suppressed the dancing. In contrast to the traditional gambling game, the participants in the Ghost Dance Hand Game played for luck in life or spiritual matters rather than for winning material goods. Another departure from the earlier men's game was that both men and women could own a MEDICINE BUNDLE containing ritual objects used in connection with the religious game. Combining both traditional and Ghost Dance beliefs, the ceremony was held for four days. Each religious leader's sacred hand game was generally based on a vision and included specific ritual elements, teachings, paraphernalia, songs, and instructions. Men, women, and children participated in the ceremonies. The Ghost Dance Hand Game was studied among the Pawnee people in the early 1930s. Besides the Pawnee, other groups who held the sacred ceremony included the Arapaho, Otoe, and Wichita.

GHOST DANCE OF 1870 *(1870)* A religious movement that originated among the Northern Paiute (Numu, Paviotso) of the Walker River Reservation in Nevada and was founded by the prophet WODZIWOB. In the late 1860s he made a number of prophecies, including the resurrection of the dead and the restoration of the conditions that existed before Europeans arrived in the region. The movement arose among the Paiute people at a time of great suffering and deprivation. Besides losing their traditional landbase and means of subsistence, other calamities had occurred, including a drought, starvation, and epidemics. Elements identified with the Ghost Dance included curing and increase rites, practice of the traditional Paiute ROUND DANCE as a vehicle for the movement, and an attempt to introduce the Cry Dance, a mourning ceremony, to the Walker River people. The religious movement spread to California tribes and to the Great Basin, where local variations occurred. On the Klamath Reservation in Oregon, it developed into the EARTH LODGE RELIGION and later the DREAM DANCE. The BIG HEAD RELIGION and the BOLE-MARU RELIGION were also offshoots of the Ghost Dance. Its abrupt end after two or three years on the Walker River Reservation among its originators has been attributed to disillusionment over unfulfilled prophecies. Some of the other groups who adopted it continued to perform it. Adherents to the Ghost Dance included JOIJOI, NORELPUTUS, and FRANK SPENCER.

GHOST DANCE OF 1890 *(1890)* A messianic religious movement that began among the Northern Paiute (Numu, Paviotso) people in Nevada in the late 1880s and quickly spread to other tribal groups. It was originated by WOVOKA, a Numu prophet, who was influenced by earlier visionaries among his people. At the end of 1888 he became ill with a fever, and a short time later, on January 1, 1889, an eclipse of the sun occurred. During that period Wovoka had a visionary religious experience. He was taken to the spirit world, where he was given sacred teachings. Wovoka returned with a message of hope and peace for Indian people. He told them that the earth would be renewed, the Indian dead would return to life and misery and death would end if they followed the revelations he had received. Wovoka told the people to be good to one another, to be at peace with the whites, to be industrious and not to engage in lying, stealing, and other wrongdoing. He also told them to perform a dance for five days at a time in order to bring about the changes. As Wovoka's prophecies spread, distant tribes sent emmissaries to find out about the rumored messiah and his teachings, including, in 1889, a delegation of Plains tribal leaders such as KICKING BEAR (Lakota), PORCUPINE, SHORT BULL (Lakota), and SITTING BULL (Arapaho). The Ghost Dance eventually numbered followers among other Great Basin groups, and its practice extended from the Missouri River to the Rocky Mountains and beyond, representing a religious means of enduring the conditions under which Native people suffered during that period.

Local variations in the movement developed as tribes incorporated it into their own religious traditions, leaders added new interpretations, and practitioners learned new songs and teachings during performances of the sacred dance. Some adherents believed that whites would disappear from the country while others believed that they would remain. The dance itself was a circle dance, but performances of the dance varied. Some incorporated a center pole or tree in the dance area, sweat lodge purification, preliminary dances, dances of varied duration and other elements. "Ghost shirts," believed to be bulletproof, were adopted by the Lakota, Arapaho, and other groups and were worn during dance performances. Many dancers also experienced trances during which they visited departed friends and relatives and learned sacred knowledge. Translations of some of the tribal names of the religion include "dance in a circle" (Paiute), "dance with clasped hands" (Kiowa) and "with joined hands" (Comanche). It was also referred to as a spirit or ghost dance in many Native languages because of its association with the return of the Indian dead. Sacred Ghost Dance songs proliferated, many of them referring to the restoration of the buffalo and other game as well as to departed friends and relatives.

The Ghost Dance met with particular repression, and the government's opposition to the Ghost Dance was a continuation of its earlier suppression of other traditional religious practices. As the movement gained more and more followers, fear and hysteria escalated among whites. Military intervention was used in the Dakotas—its tragic outcome was the death of SITTING BULL (Lakota) and massacre of Lakota men, women, and children at Wounded Knee on December 29, 1890. Although the Ghost Dance is believed to have ended then, there is evidence that some tribal groups were able to continue it for a longer period of time.

Among the Kiowa, AFRAID-OF-BEARS developed an interpretation of the Ghost Dance that he called the FEATHER DANCE. Other Ghost Dance leaders included BLACK COYOTE and FRED ROBINSON. (See also GHOST DANCE OF 1870.)

GHOST INFECTION *Navajo (Dineh)*   See GHOST

GHOST KEEPING CEREMONY *Lakota*   One of the SEVEN SACRED RITES OF THE LAKOTA given to them by WHITE BUFFALO CALF WOMAN. Through this ceremony the soul of a deceased person is kept in order to purify it and to assure its return to Wakan Tanka, the Creator, when it is ritually released. Besides making certain that the soul does not have to wander about the earth, the rite serves as a reminder of death for the living. According to the holy man BLACK ELK, the first such ceremony was conducted by High Hollow Horn, the keeper of the SACRED PIPE, at the request of the father of a young boy who was greatly loved by his parents. The preparations included the making of a sacred bundle containing a lock of the child's hair, which was consecrated with sweet grass and kept in a special place in a lodge built for the purpose. Black Elk indicated that the ghost was usually kept a year, and during that time the family prepared for the day the soul was to be released, instructed by High Hollow Horn in their sacred duties. The father, who kept the ghost bundle, was required to be constantly in prayer, to maintain peaceful, harmonious relations with others, and to serve as an example to the people. He could touch neither knife nor blood and therefore could not butcher meat during this period. The mother, or another woman chosen for the sacred role, also had ritual responsibilities, including the preparation of food to be saved for the day the soul was released. The ghost bundle, taken outside in good weather, required the proper observance of prayers, and rituals at all times and for every circumstance.

As High Hollow Horn first instructed, the final ceremony includes prayers, purification, and offerings. A post ritually cut and erected in the lodge is dressed to represent the deceased. The soul is mourned by family and friends and ritually fed one last time before its release. As soon as the bundle is ritually taken out of the lodge on the final day, the soul departs for the spirit world. According to Black Elk, once the soul has been released, the bundle is not considered especially holy but may be kept as a remembrance. Other ritual elements include the distribution of goods to the poor and a concluding feast. In 1890 the Ghost Keeping rite was prohibited by the U.S. government with the requirement that all the souls kept by the Lakota be released on a specific day. In the present-day, the ghost keeping is said to last from six months to a year.

GIRL'S PUBERTY RITE   Ritual for the verge of womanhood, extensively practiced across Native North America and still observed among some tribes today. It was believed that whatever a girl did or experienced at this time would affect her entire life and that she had exceptional power over people that came near her. For this reason some tribes secluded the girls in structures set aside from the village for a few days to as long as a year. The observances differed from tribe to tribe. For the Western Apache, the occasion was one of happiness and a time for an elaborate ceremony. For the Kaska of western Canada, the occasion was one of danger. Girls were placed far from camp for a month so hunters would have no contact with them. For the Luiseño, girls rested in "hot beds" surrounded by relays of singers and dancers from other clans. Various tribes had food taboos, fasts, and numerous regulations on behavior, including the following:

Lakota

The girl's puberty rite, Išnati awiealowan, was one of the SEVEN SACRED RITES OF THE LAKOTA promised to them by WHITE BUFFALO CALF WOMAN, and the ceremony, performed after a young woman's first menstrual period, marked her transition into womanhood. She was taught the meaning of the change and the responsibilities that went with it. During the menstrual period itself the young girl was isolated in a lodge apart from the camp circle and instructed by an older woman who saw to her care. Before returning home, she underwent sweat lodge purification. According to the holy man BLACK ELK, the girl's puberty rite originated in a vision by Tatanka Hunkeshne (Slow Buffalo), who was shown how the buffalo, the relative of the people, prepared their children to live in a sacred manner. The holy man conducted the first rite for White Buffalo Cow Woman Appears, a young girl, whose father had requested it. After completing the necessary preparations, including the construction of a tipi in a sheltered location away from the camp circle, the sacred rite began. Besides purification, it included prayers, offerings and teachings before concluding with a feast and giveaway. During the rite, also known as the Buffalo Ceremony, the young girl was taught her sacred relationships as well as her duties and responsibilities to the people as a woman. She was instructed to be an example to others, to cherish all that was holy in the universe, to be merciful and generous and to be modest and fruitful. Other versions state that she was told to be as industrious as the spider, as wise as the turtle, and as cheerful as the lark.

Girl's puberty rite. A Salish girl wearing the fir boughs and goat's wool blanket that signify her adolescence. *National Museums of Canada, Ottawa.*

Navajo (Dineh)

The Navajo conducted the *kinaalda,* a four-night public ceremony, immediately or as soon as possible after a girl's first menstruation. The ceremony includes numerous elements, such as songs, prayers, taboos, purification rights, ritual dressing, ritual haircombing and tying, molding (symbolically pressing the girl's body into a woman's shape), running of races, ritual corn grinding, blessing the hogan, offering corn pollen, and painting the girl with white clay. Viewed as part of the BLESSING WAY ceremony, the *kinaalda* ushers the girl into society; invokes positive blessings on her; ensures her health, prosperity, and well-being; and protects her from potential misfortune. Like all Navajo ceremonies, the ceremony has an origin story. Believed to be an ancient ceremony, it is traced back to the first *kinaalda* of CHANGING WOMAN. The ceremony serves as an integrating and unifying force in Navajo society in general. At least 10 versions of the story of the first *kinaalda* have been published.

Western Apache

The Naihes, also called Sunrise Dance by Apache when they speak of it to non-Apache, is a four-day religious ceremony given for the Apache girls in the summer months following the girl's first menses. Preparations by the girl's family, which take several months, include selecting and preparing a ceremonial ground with various dwellings and cooking enclosures, selecting a medicine man to sing and pray for the girl, selecting a female attendant (who then be-

comes a godparent for life) to dress, paint, massage, feed, advise, and care for the girl and preparing the feast that is served to all the guests who come for the ceremony. The girl's mother, grandmother, or other close female relative makes a dress of buckskin-colored yellow, the hue of pollen, which she wears during the rite.

The girl is identified throughout the rite with WHITE PAINTED WOMAN, a prominent figure in Apache tradition who is usually credited with establishing the rite; during the ceremony and for four days after it, the girl is addressed as "White Painted Woman" and wears a dress modeled after the one worn by White Painted Woman during her stay on earth. At one point, the girl is painted with white clay, symbolic of the body paint with which the first bearer was adorned. Apaches say one objective of the ceremony is to in-

Girl's puberty rite. A girl's parents bless their daughter and her sponsor with holy pollen during this Western Apache puberty ceremony. *Photograph by Helga Teiwes. Arizona State Museum, University of Arizona.*

vest the girl with the power of White Painted Woman, which resides in the girl's body.

A singer supervises the erection of a sacred shelter, a ritual tipi that houses the girl throughout the ceremony and in which songs of the rite are chanted. The ceremonial structure for the girl's puberty rite is a symbolic representation of White Painted Woman's sacred home. It is built in a prescribed manner with four long logs (the Mescalero to the east use 12 poles). The girl's male relatives erect the main poles. The singer sprinkles each pole with pollen and prays and chants.

During the four days, there is visiting, feasting, gambling, and social dancing. In the evenings, masked dancers impersonating the mountain-dwelling spirits (*gan*) perform and drive away evil. The girl makes ritual runs to the four directions, acts intended to provide her with endurance and a long, healthy life. While lying face down, she is massaged by her sponsor to give her the form of a woman and to assure her of physical strength as an adult. Because the girl possesses special curative powers during this rite, she attends to anyone who is ill and comes to her for comfort. The girl uses ritual objects, made by her male relatives under the direction of a medicine man, including a wooden staff symbolizing longevity, with which she dances throughout the ceremony and will use years later as a walking stick; a drinking tube; scratching stick, and large buckskin, on which the girl dances. At the end of the ceremony, the girl plants a wand in the ground symbolizing her passage from girlhood to womanhood. The tipi is dismantled, guests leave, and the family remains alone at the camp for four days and nights during which the girl observes a number of ritual taboos.

In the girl's puberty ceremony of the Jicarilla Apache to the east a boy dances with the girl, and his family assists with the preparations and shares in paying the singer for the ceremony. Both the girl and boy go through rituals.

GIVEAWAY CEREMONY AND DANCE A giveaway is the ceremonial presentation of gifts to honor an individual or group. It is often held in connection with other ceremonies, such as a naming or a memorial for a deceased family member. A giveaway is also conducted to honor returning veterans, to give thanks for recovery from an accident or illness, to share blessings with others, to recognize the accomplishments of family or community members, and to express appreciation for assistance. It is often sponsored by a family whose preparations include making and/or accumulating gifts. Recipients, honored by the sponsor, receive items such as quilts, beadwork, blankets, clothing, money, household goods, and, among some groups, sometimes horses and tipis as in the past. The giveaway generally includes a person who officiates, the delivery of speeches, the presentation of gifts, the singing of honoring songs, dancing, and a feast. The giveaway, which emphasizes the values of generosity and sharing, honors both the sponsor and the recipient. See also POTLATCH.

GIVEAWAY DANCE (Gift Exchange Dance, Mahtahitowin Dance) *Cree* A ceremony held to honor Pakahk, the supernatural skeleton being of Cree belief. The Giveaway Dance, or Gift Exchange Dance, reinforces the values of generosity and sharing among the people through a formal gift exchange. Ritual elements include four nights of dancing, giving and receiving gifts, and the use of bladders filled with grease believed to be favored by Pakahk. In a variation described among the Montana Cree, a sack of lard, on which a face was painted to commemorate a deceased person, was danced with by the participants during the course of the ceremony. The Montana Cree also incorporate features of the JUMPING DANCE or Ghost Dance in their Giveaway Dance, including the use of bundles containing locks of hair from the dead. It is also called Mahtahitowin Dance.

GLUSKAP (Glooscap, Gluscap, Gluskabe) *Wabanaki (Abenaki, Maliseet, Micmac, Passamaquoddy, Penobscot)* An ancient culture hero in Wabanaki religious belief who is a prophet and protector. He is largely responsible for the landscape and its inhabitants, for innovations in the lives of people and animals that benefit life, for distributing game animals, food, fish, hares, and tobacco over the world, for protecting eagles who regulate daylight and darkness, for tempering winter, for bringing summer north, and more. It is believed that Gluskap transformed creatures of the universe into their present forms. He lives beyond the clouds but will return to save the Wabanaki if they are in dire need.

GODDEN, WILLIAM J. *(?–1914)* Episcopal medical missionary at the Everglade Cross mission on the present-day Big Cypress Seminole Reservation in Florida. Godden, an English pharmacist, was recruited for the work by Bishop WILLIAM CRANE GRAY of the Protestant Episcopal Church. After receiving instruction from a medical doctor, he took the full-time missionary position in 1905. Godden eventually served as a storekeeper at a nearby boat landing acquired by Bishop Gray, ran his small hospital and served as the sole missionary in the area. He also initiated the establishment of an instructional farm to teach cultivation methods. After his ordination as a deacon in 1912, Godden served as a minister as well as a medical missionary. He died in 1914 after nine years among the Seminole people.

"GOING TO WATER" *Southeast* A purification ritual of the Cherokee, Creek, Seminole, and other Native groups from the southeastern region. During the course of the BUSK, or GREEN CORN CEREMONY, and other ceremonies, participants are taken to a river or pond for ritual cleansing. The purposes of "going to water" include restoring spiritual harmony, washing away impurities or bad deeds, and starting anew. The ritual is conducted by a priest and is generally accompanied by fasting, praying, and other sacred elements.

GOLDEN EAGLE V. DEPUTY SHERIFF JOHNSON (493 F. 2d 1179, 1974) (1974)

A California case involving peyotist Golden Eagle, who was a passenger in an automobile stopped by the authorities on July 11, 1970, for having improper lighting. While searching the vehicle, the officers found PEYOTE. Charged with illegal possession of the substance, Golden Eagle was jailed. He told the authorities that he was a member of the NATIVE AMERICAN CHURCH, information that was confirmed by his landlady. Golden Eagle served three days in pre-trial detention before criminal charges against him were dismissed. He then filed federal charges against the arresting officer for illegally detaining him and for abuse during the period he was detained. After his case was dismissed in United States District Court, Golden Eagle filed an appeal. The United States Court of Appeals affirmed the ruling of the lower court. The court concluded that members of the Native American Church could expect the possibility of being arrested and detained while the police, in good faith, determined whether their church affiliation was valid. It contended that the police had the right to challenge anyone in possession of illegal drugs, including those claiming immunity from prosecution on the basis of religion. (See also PEYOTE RELIGION; Subject Index for related legal cases included in this volume.)

G-O ROAD CASE

See LYNG, SECRETARY OF AGRICULTURE, ET AL. V. NORTHWEST INDIAN CEMETERY PROTECTIVE ASSN. ET AL.

GOODBIRD, EDWARD (Tsakaka-sakis) (c. 1869–1938)

Hidatsa A principal informant and translator for the anthropologist Gilbert L. Wilson on traditional Hidatsa life, Goodbird also became the first member of the Fort Berthold Reservation in North Dakota to become an ordained minister. A descendant of the Hidatsa medicine man MISSOURI RIVER, he was born to Buffalo Bird Woman and Son of a Star about 1869, near the mouth of the Yellowstone. Ten days after his birth, he was named Tsakaka-sakis (Good bird) by his grandfather, the holy man SMALL ANKLE. When he was eight years old, he began attending mission school, newly introduced on the reservation. Several years later, in about 1885, pressured by government policies, his people began moving from their earth lodges in Like-a-Fishhook Village to a new location up the Missouri River. Settling in an isolated spot named Independence, they began living on allotments and farming in the way promoted by the Bureau of Indian Affairs. In 1895, Goodbird was appointed assistant farmer by the reservation agent, holding the position until the government abolished it in 1903. He then turned to Christianity and was baptized when he was 35 years old. He had previously served as an interpreter for the Congregational minister CHARLES L. HALL and other missionaries. In 1904, Goodbird became an assistant missionary in charge of the Independence station, preaching in the Hidatsa language and using Sunday school lessons for his text. He built a new chapel at Independence in 1910, a project completed with the donations and labor of his congregation. The church still stands, although it had to be moved in the 1950s when the Garrison Dam project flooded Independence and other areas of the Fort Berthold Reservation.

Goodbird's collaboration with Wilson began in 1906 and continued for 12 years. The anthropologist was adopted into Goodbird's family in about 1909 and became a member of the Hidatsa Prairie Chicken clan. As Wilson's adopted brother, Goodbird assisted him as a family member, providing detailed information, translations, and drawings. Kinship ties with Hidatsa aided Wilson's collection of tribal information and artifacts for the Museum of the American Indian and the American Museum of Natural History. Extensive work with Buffalo Bird Woman, her brother Wolf Chief, and Goodbird resulted in an unprecedented portrait of one family and their adaptation to change. Goodbird the Indian: His Story, told to Wilson and first published in 1914, is now hailed as a landmark in anthropological writing for its early use of biography to describe another culture. In 1925, Goodbird was ordained a Congregational minister at Independence. He died in 1938.

GOODEAGLE, MRS. (fl. 1890s)

Pawnee Ghost Dance visionary among the Skiri band of her people. She received a vision in which one of two eagles instructed her to hold a feast and to clothe in a certain way the Seven Eagle Brothers, an organization of men who sang the sacred songs of the GHOST DANCE OF 1890 and the GHOST DANCE HAND GAME. After Goodeagle did so, another dancer who had experienced a trance learned that Goodeagle should be called the Mother of the Seven Eagle Brothers. Other adherents included MARK RUDDER, MRS. WASHINGTON, and FRANK WHITE.

GOOKIN, DANIEL (1612–1686/7)

A Puritan and colleague of JOHN ELIOT who held a number of public offices, including that of captain of train bands and "ruler over the praying Indians." Born in England or Ireland, his parents were Mary Byrd and Daniel Gookin. At 18 young Daniel was living on his father's Virginia plantation but was granted land of his own on the James River in about 1634. While he was in London in 1639, he was issued a license to marry Mary Dolling. Two years later, accompanied by his wife and infant son, he returned to Virginia with the intention of settling on his plantation. He became a burgess, held other public offices, and was granted more land but left again in 1644. He eventually settled in Massachusetts, first at Roxbury, where he joined the First Church, then a few years later, in 1648, at Cambridge. There he served as captain of the train band, holding the post for nearly 40 years, and as a deputy to the general court. Chosen for his post with the PRAYING INDIANS in 1656 and again in 1661, Gookin preached Christianity and the English way of life. During King Philip's War he defended the Christian Indians against the colonists, an unpopular position in Massachusetts. Captain Gookin presented his views in *An Historical Account of the Doings and Sufferings of the Christian Indians of New England,* but the book was not published until 1836. Another book, *Historical Collections of the Indians in New England,* was printed in 1792. After his wife died on October 27, 1683, he married Mrs. Hannah Tyng Savage. (See also COCKENOE; MAYHEW, THOMAS; NESUTAN, JOB.)

GOOSE (Maga) *(c. 1835–1915) Lakota*   A prominent medicine man of the Teton Lakota. His specialty was the treatment of consumption. In 1911, when he and RED WEASEL provided information on the SUN DANCE to the ethnologist Frances Densmore, Goose was regarded as "the best Indian doctor on the reservation." He served as a scout in the U.S. Army between September 11, 1876, and July 10, 1882, and enlisted in the Infantry years later in 1891, serving as a corporal before his honorable discharge on April 30, 1893. During a visionary experience Goose was given sacred instructions that enabled him to heal the sick. His treatments, especially for diseases of the blood, included sweat lodge purification, dietary measures, rest and the use of the herbs he saw in his dream. Densmore describes two instances when Goose demonstrated his powers for outsiders. He successfully summoned a buffalo when a trader, who had ridiculed medicine men, requested that he do so as a test, and he located a gun that had been lost by its owner. The Teton holy man died in September, 1915.

GOOSE DANCE *Swampy Cree*   A religious ceremony whose purpose included honoring the spirits of waterfowl. The Goose Dance, or *niskisimowin,* was conducted among the Swampy Cree, a tribal group located west of James Bay and south of Hudson Bay as well as in other areas of Canada. The Swampy Cree, who speak the "n" dialect of the Cree language, are said to have held the Goose Dance in importance comparable to that of the SUN DANCE among the Plains

Cree. James Isham, an observer who wrote about his travels in the Hudson Bay region, wrote an account of the ceremony in 1793 that is believed to be the earliest written record. He identified the preparation and consumption of geese as well as singing, dancing, and prayer speeches as activities of the Goose Dance. The Reverend HENRY BUDD, the Métis Anglican priest, provided written observations of the ceremony in the 1850s. He noted that the Goose Dance was held annually in the spring and fall. Budd observed that after the people had constructed a ceremonial lodge on the first of April, the religious observance was held for twelve days. Ceremonial elements identified by other writers include the use of the first goose shot in the spring if its bones remained intact, the wearing of white duck feathers or down by the participants on their heads to symbolize the attainment of old age, and the ritual care of the bones from the waterfowl used in the ceremony. The Goose Dance is believed to have been held for the last time in the 1940s.

GORDON, PHILIP B. (Ti-Bish-Ko-Gi-Jik, "Looking into the Sky") *(1885–1948) Ojibway*   American Roman Catholic priest. Gordon was born in Gordon, Wisconsin. One of 14 children, he was educated at St. Mary's Mission School established by Franciscan missionaries on the Bad River Reservation in Odanah, Wisconsin, and at other public schools in Wisconsin. After his seminary education, he was ordained in 1913 and led his first Mass on January 6, 1914, on the Bad River Reservation. The priest subsequently attended the Catholic University of America in Washington, D.C., and served as a part-time chaplain at the Carlisle Indian School in Pennsylvania. In 1915 Father Gordon began a two-year special assignment with the BUREAU OF CATHOLIC INDIAN MISSIONS, visiting Indian schools and other agencies across the Midwest. During that period he became chairman of the advisory board of the Society of American Indians, later serving as the organization's third president. He also served as a chaplain at Haskell Institute in Kansas, where his protests against the conditions in the school led to an investigation and the subsequent dismissal of a number of employees. Gordon's activism caused him difficulties with some of his religious superiors. Although the bureau director praised his work, another official asked him to leave when his assignment expired. To his disappointment, he was sent to collect funds for an orphan home rather than to work in an Indian community. In 1918 he was finally assigned work among his own people on the Lac Courte Oreilles Reservation at Reserve, Wisconsin. He raised funds for a church after the old one burned down, assumed the work of five other Indian missions in the area and again became politically active. In 1923 he was appointed to the Committee of One Hundred, a reform group consisting of influential Americans appointed by Secretary of the Interior

Hubert Work to review federal policy toward American Indians. He worked for Indian citizenship, eventually enacted into law in 1924. The priest received an honorary doctor's degree from his alma mater the College of St. Thomas in St. Paul in 1933 and in 1942 was honored by the Indian Council Fire, an organization in Chicago. He presented the opening prayer in the House of Representatives on June 11, 1943. Gordon, for many years the only American Indian Catholic priest in the country, died in 1948. (See also BOUCHARD, JAMES CHRYSOSTOM; FOX, MARVIN; LARUSH, SISTER M. SIRILLA; NEGAHNQUET, ALBERT; PELOTTE, DONALD E.)

GOURD DANCE *Kiowa* A ceremony believed to have originated as a spiritual gift to a Kiowa warrior who had become separated from his war party. As he sought the summer encampment of his people, he heard the sound of beautiful music. He discovered that it came from a red wolf, who subsequently taught him the ceremony and told him that it was a gift for him to take back to his people. Upon his return home, he introduced the Gourd Dance, which has been maintained to the present by an influential warrior society. In 1838, according to tradition, Kiowa warriors were victorious during a great battle fought against Arapaho and Cheyenne enemies on a site with skunkberry bushes full of red berries. The Kiowa Gourd Dance Society was formed after the four-day engagement and was called T'anpeko, "skunkberry people." The skunkberries, considered a spiritual symbol, are represented by the red color on the present-day blankets of the society. Other symbols of the Kiowa Gourd Dance Society include the whip, the rope, and the bugle. Besides preserving the traditions and songs of the Gourd Dance, the society policed the annual SUN DANCE. In 1890, however, federal intervention prohibited the Kiowa from conducting the sacred ceremony. By the 1920s or 1930s the Gourd Dance traditions, too, had nearly disappeared. It was not until 1955 when Fred Tsoodle, a Kiowa, brought together former Gourd dancers to perform the dance for a special demonstration that it began to be revived. Two years later, on January 30, 1957, the Tian-paye, or Tiah-pah, Society was formally organized. It began hosting an annual Gourd Dance around the fourth of July, about the same time the Sun Dance was originally held. Features of the four-day observance include a GIVEAWAY CEREMONY, the performance of the Brush Dance, the honoring of medicine bundles and the Gourd Dance itself. The society continues to honor its origins by maintaining its ceremonial songs, rituals, and traditions. The membership, mostly male, is carefully selected and includes a drum keeper, whip man and headsmen or directors. The Gourd Dance, believed to have been diffused by the Kiowa, is also practiced among the Arapaho, Cheyenne, Comanche, Ponca, and other groups.

GRAND MEDICINE SOCIETY See MIDEWIWIN

GRANT'S PEACE POLICY (Quaker Policy) A policy established by Ulysses S. Grant when he became president of the United States in 1869; also called the Quaker Policy. The policy was named for the Indian Appropriations Act of 1869, which provided $2 million in federal funds "to enable the President to maintain peace" among the Indians. Besides seeking an end to frontier wars, the peace policy attempted to end the graft and patronage that was pervasive in the Indian service. One of the changes Grant made was the appointment of his former Civil War aide, Ely S. Parker, as commissioner of Indian Affairs. Parker, a Seneca who was the first Native American appointed to the position, helped implement the administration's new measures.

One of the elements of the Peace Policy was the congressional authorization of a Board of Indian Commissioners to oversee the Bureau of Indian Affairs. Although efforts were made to have the Board share control over the Indian department with the secretary of the interior, an advisory role was authorized. In its early years the Board of Indian Commissioners was referred to as a "church board" because its membership consisted of laymen from Protestant churches. The Episcopalian chairman, William Welsh, resigned after finding that the organization lacked any real power. Although most of the other appointees eventually resigned as well, replacements were named and the Board continued to exist until 1933.

Another component of the Peace Policy was the assignment of Indian agencies to Christian mission boards, a measure aimed at ending political appointments to Bureau of Indian Affairs posts. The church groups nominated superintendents and agents for assignments on Indian reservations and also supervised their work. The Society of Friends, or Quakers, played an important role in the new directive. The Orthodox Friends assumed control of the Central Superintendency, which included tribal groups in Kansas and Indian Territory (present-day Oklahoma). The Liberal Friends took responsibility for the Northern Superintendency, including tribes in Nebraska. The policy soon extended to other denominations that also received agency assignments across the country. Although Catholics had a long history of missionary work in Native communities, they were initially given jurisdiction in only a few agencies. Grant's federal initiative led to the expansion of missions among tribal groups, increasing the numbers of missionaries, schools, and teachers. During the period it was argued that Christianizing and educating Indians was less costly than exterminating them. The expense of maintaining troops on the frontier was greater than the amount needed to support missionaries.

Grant's Peace Policy was hampered by the fierce rivalry among the denominations for control, the political circumvention of mission boards by those seeking control of appointments to agency positions and the dissent over control being monopolized by one denomination at each agency or reservation. In 1880 the Orthodox Friends withdrew from involvement in the system. The following year the government opened reservations to missionary activity by all denominations. Henry M. Teller, appointed secretary of the Interior in 1882, ended the government's arrangement with the mission boards. However, the federal-church relationship in the Bureau of Indian Affairs continued in other ways. The churches contracted with the government to operate schools on Indian reservations, a practice that continued until 1897. Federal officials and religious groups also continued to agree that Indian people should be Christianized and "civilized."

GRASS DANCE (Omaha Dance)

The Grass Dance is identified as a modern version of the IRUSKA ceremony of the Pawnee and other tribal groups. Its name is said to derive from a bunch of grass worn at the dancer's belt. Also known as the Omaha Dance, it possesses a rich history and distinctive features. Officers of Grass Dance societies generally include a leader, caretaker of the crow-belts used in the dances, pipe keepers, whip bearers, a whistle bearer, food servers, sword bearers, drummers, heralds, singers, and servants. Besides the crow-belt or bustle, other objects associated with the dance are pipes, drums, whistles, whips, swords, and the roach, or headdress, of deer hair.

Ritual elements of the Grass Dance vary among the different groups. Some include the serving of dog meat, the scouting of the kettle in which it is cooked, the retrieval of the hot food with bare hands, and the presentation of choice pieces to honored participants. Other features cited for the Grass Dance are abstention from sexual intercourse for varying periods of time before the ceremony, warrior traditions, associations with thunder, rich song repertoires, ceremonial whipping of the participants who decline to dance, and the giving away of gifts to the poor. The Grass Dance is now frequently described as a social ceremony among many tribes by anthropologists. The Grass Dance is identified with an extensive list of tribal groups, including the Pawnee, Omaha, Lakota, Blackfeet, Gros Ventre (Atsina), Assiniboine, Crow, Ioway, Ponca, Kansa, Hidatsa, Arikara, Arapaho, Menominee, and the Ojibway.

GRASS DANCE *Shoshone*

A dance of Plains derivation that was described among the Northern Shoshone. The Grass Dance shared similarities with the NAUKIN, a ceremony held to pray for plentiful salmon, berries, and other foods.

Alternating male and female dancers formed a circle, linked fingers, and danced. Held for several days, its purpose was to pray for the grass to grow.

GRAY, ARTHUR, JR. *(fl. 1907)*

An Episcopal seminarian who organized a mission among the Monacan people of Bear Mountain, Virginia, in 1907. Gray, the son of a priest, who served as a church rector, graduated from the University of Virginia and before entering Alexandria Theological Seminary, acquired land and raised funds to establish a church and school among the Monacan. The mission had a number of deaconesses in charge of the work into the 1950s. One of them, Florence Cowan, was active on behalf of the Monacan, especially concerning school integration issues. In 1965 priests began ministering to the Monacan people at the mission established by Gray.

GRAY, WILLIAM CRANE *(1835–1919)*

Missionary bishop of the Protestant Episcopal Church who worked among the Seminole people in Florida from 1893 to 1914. Gray was born in Lambertsville, New Jersey, on September 6, 1835. After graduating from Ohio's Kenyon College in 1859, he was ordained first as a deacon and then as a priest in 1860. Gray served a ministry in the Diocese of Tennessee before beginning his service as the missionary bishop of southern Florida in 1893. The bishop took an interest in the Seminole people in his jurisdiction and began religious efforts among them. When in 1893 AMELIA STONE QUINTON of the Women's National Indian Association offered the Episcopal Church a mission her organization had purchased about 45 miles from Fort Myers two years earlier, Gray accepted it. He changed its name from Allen Place to Immokalee, and the Reverend and Mrs. Henry O. Gibbs began serving as missionaries a short time later. Bishop Gray advocated the establishment of a Seminole reservation and was instrumental in organizing the Friends of the Florida Seminoles association. His description of the Green Corn Dance is one of the earliest recorded by a Euro-American among this Native group. Gray established Christ Church at Immokalee Mission in 1896. Two years later he founded Everglade Cross mission on the present-day Big Cypress Seminole Reservation and eventually hired Dr. WILLIAM J. GODDEN as a medical missionary for the post. After Bishop Gray's retirement and the death of Dr. Godden in 1914, both Seminole missions closed. During the 21 years of missionary service, the number of Native baptisms was minimal, and there was only one confirmation, that of Billy Fewell (Hotulcahatsee). Bishop Gray died in 1919.

GREAT HOUSES *Yurok*

Big, large, or long houses that were sites of important rituals. They were used for the WORLD

RENEWAL CEREMONIAL CYCLE and child-curing Brush Dances, and important medicines for ceremonies were kept there. Each great house owned a major dance, a ritual, or a ritual prayer. Great houses owned JUMP, WHITE DEERSKIN, or Brush Dances, and ritual FORMULAS for launching a canoe used in a White Deerskin Dance.

GREAT NEW MOON FEAST *Cherokee* The fourth of the SIX CHEROKEE FESTIVALS described by the 19th-century missionary DANIEL SABIN BUTRICK and other early observers of the Cherokee Nation before the forced removal of the tribal group from the southeastern Appalachian region to Indian Territory (present-day Oklahoma). Also called the Great New Moon of Autumn and Medicine Dance, it was held at the capital after the leaves had begun to turn yellow and fall into the river waters. The ancient capital of the Cherokee Nation, Chota, or Great Echota, was located on the south side of the Little Tennessee River below Citico Creek in Tennessee. New Echota in Georgia also served as the capital for a number of years before the removal. Preparations by the principal counselors included determining when the new moon would appear, sending out hunters to secure game seven nights before the feast, selecting seven men to oversee arrangements and designating seven "honorable women" to prepare the food. The people met, and each family gave foods to the *uku,* or priest, for the feast. These included seven or more ears of corn, dried pumpkin, and samples of other food crops. On the evening before the feast the women performed the religious dance. The next day's ceremonial features included ritual purification at the river, offerings to the fire and prayers by the *uku.* The one-day ceremony concluded with a feast.

GREEN CORN *Iroquois* An important four-day ceremony held in late August when the first corn is ripe. The community gathers at the LONGHOUSE to give thanks to the Creator and all spirit forces for the ripening of crops, for making the harvest possible, and for allowing the community to witness the completion of another season of growth. Rites of the festival include naming children born since the MID-WINTER CEREMONY, the FOUR SACRED CEREMONIES addressed to the Creator, evening social dances, a women's rite, the FALSE FACE CEREMONY, and investing of the FAITHKEEPER. A CONFESSION RITE precedes the festival.

GREEN CORN CEREMONY *Oklahoma Seminole and Creek* The principal event of the ceremonial year, traditionally held over four days in late June or early July, when the first corn ripened. Now the ceremony begins Thursday afternoon and ends Sunday morning to accommodate the non-Indian work week. The ceremony is held on the "square ground," or cere-

monial center. Elements of the ritual include Stomp, Long, Ribbon, Feather, and Buffalo Dances; fasts; feasts; single pole and match ball games; building of the sacred fire; corn sacrifice; medicine taking; and the SCRATCHING CEREMONY of women, children, and men; naming ceremonies; rinsing in water ["GOING TO WATER"]; and prayer. The ceremony ends with a single pole ball game and breakfast. In the Seminole and Creek ceremonial cycle, the Green Corn Ceremony is preceded by the STOMP DANCE and followed by the STICKBALL GAME and the SOUP DANCE.

GREEN CORN DANCE   See BUSK

GREEN CORN DANCE *Shawnee* The Green Corn Dance is an observance held by the Loyal band of the Shawnee in July or August. Preparations begin with the sweeping of the Whiteoak (Oklahoma) ceremonial dance ground. The Green Corn Dance shares similarities with the principal event of the ceremonial year, the spring and fall BREAD DANCES. Vegetables and other produce, along with a kettle of corn soup, are displayed in the middle of the dance arena. As in the Bread Dance, 12 female and 12 male dancers are selected to participate. After a prayer by the priest and bundle keeper, the women begin the dancing. The six sets of dances are performed alternately by women only and men and women dancing together and include performances of the Kokeki, or Cluster, Dance, the Dove Dance, and the Pumpkin Dance. After a concluding prayer, the food on display is distributed. Social dances, considered an important part of ceremonies because they please the Creator, are held during the night. (See also BUFFALO DANCE; DEATH FEAST; OUR GRANDMOTHER; RIDE-IN AND WAR DANCE; RITUAL FOOTBALL GAME.)

GREEN CORN FEAST *Cherokee* The third of the SIX CHEROKEE FESTIVALS described by the 19th-century missionary DANIEL SABIN BUTRICK and other early observers of the Cherokee Nation before the forced removal of the tribal group from the southeastern Appalachian region to Indian Territory (present-day Oklahoma). The observance was generally held at the capital from 40 to 50 days after the Preliminary New Green Corn Feast. The ancient capital of the Cherokee Nation, Chota, or Great Echota, was located on the south side of the Little Tennessee River below Citico Creek in Tennessee. New Echota in Georgia also served as the capital for a number of years before the removal. Preparations included the summoning of the "honorable women" for a performance of a religious dance and the setting of a time for the observance. Other preliminary activities included sending out hunters to secure game, appointing festival officials and framing an arbor with green boughs in the sacred ceremonial square. On the eve of the Green Corn Feast the people gathered, and each person took a bough to carry overhead at a noon ritual on the following day. The presiding *uku,* or priest, was given a ceremonial title during the course of the ceremony. The Green Corn Feast, called "the most deeply rooted rite" of the people, by the anthropologist William Harlen Gilbert, Jr. lasted four days.

GREEN, JOE *(fl. 1930s–1950s) Northern Paiute (Numu, Paviotso)* A medicine man, Episcopal deacon, and peyotist. A member of the Pyramid Lake Reservation in Nevada, Green was well known in the 1930s as a *pohari,* or medicine man. Acquiring his power to heal during a dream, he doctored the Paiute and Washoe people who sought his help. His skill as a healer also became known outside of the area. As a devout Christian, Green regularly attended church services and served as an usher. Respected by the missionaries for his devotion and reliability, he served as a deacon and was chosen to speak at an interdenominational conference. In addition to his being a *pohari* and a Christian, Green's third religion was peyotism. In the 1950s he stated that his use of PEYOTE began 25 years earlier (in 1929), when it was introduced among his people by a visiting ROADMAN, or leader. Green indicated the value and helpfulness of all three of the religious traditions that he followed. As a *pohari,* he could not turn away people in need. He liked the Christian missionaries and hymns as well as his role in the church. Green also appreciated the curing powers of peyote and the songs and visions associated with the religion. The ministers knew him only as a devout Episcopalian. He believed that their condemnation of the PEYOTE RELIGION stemmed from not knowing anything about it, and he chose not to try to explain it to them. Green also served as a major informant on shamanism for the anthropologist, Willard Z. Park, in the 1930s. He provided information about his shamanistic powers as well as his healing methods. (See also NATIVE AMERICAN CHURCH.)

GREGORIO, JUAN *(1896–1971) Tohono O'odham (Papago)* A Tohono O'odham shaman interviewed about his people's theory of STAYING SICKNESS. He was one of the first men in his village to be educated in Anglo-American schools. He interpreted for Catholic priests, was a farm laborer for many years, and became a shaman and ritual curer for sickness concerned with war. He collaborated with a Tohono O'odham translator and linguist and a non-Indian ethnologist to provide an introduction to the study of the Piman theory of sickness. Juan Gregorio supplied information in 1967 and 1968 and consented to be listed as coauthor of a book concerning the sicknesses of his people.

GREY CLOUD, DAVID *(1840–1890) Dakota* The first missionary of the DAKOTA NATIVE MISSIONARY SOCIETY. Grey Cloud was born at Shakopee in Minnesota Territory. He was imprisoned for his role in the Dakota War of 1862, a conflict between Santee Dakotas and Euro-American forces. It was precipitated by government failures to fulfill treaty obligations and near-starvation conditions among Dakota people. While he was in prison he was converted to Christianity by Dr. THOMAS S. WILLIAMSON. Following his release, Grey Cloud served as a scout between 1866 and 1872. After receiving his license to preach in 1872, he was ordained a minister a year later and worked among his people for the rest of his life. Grey Cloud died at the Sisseton Agency in South Dakota.

GRIFFIN, VICTOR *(fl 1906–1953) Quapaw* An early PEYOTE leader who also served as a chief among his people in Oklahoma. He was at one time closely associated with JOHN WILSON, the Caddo-Delaware (Lenni Lenape) originator of the Big Moon Peyote Ceremony, and assisted him in gaining followers from the Quapaw and Seneca tribes. Griffin eventually introduced changes in Wilson's ceremony, starting on the Osage reservation, and gained recognition and adherents of his own. After Wilson died, Griffin claimed to be his successor with the right to establish peyote fireplaces or "Moons" in his name and to introduce changes in keeping with the practices of Catholicism. However, JOHN QUAPAW, another peyote leader, was identified as the individual appointed by Wilson to succeed him. Griffin, whose rite was established in 1906 or 1907, was described as a chief and "peyote priest" in a 1953 publication. (See also NATIVE AMERICAN CHURCH; PEYOTE RELIGION.)

GRUBE, BERNHARD ADAM *(1715–1808)* A Moravian missionary to the Delaware (Lenni Lenape) and Mahican. Grube was born in 1715 in Thuringen at Walschleben near Erfurt and attended school in his native community and at Jena, present-day Germany. He entered the Moravian ministry in 1740, serving small congregations in Holland and teaching at the seminary in Lindheim. In 1748 he was sent to Pennsylvania, teaching at Bethlehem for several years before volunteering for Indian mission work in Pennsylvania. In 1752, while living in a village in Pennsylvania's present-day Monroe County, he nearly lost a leg in an accident with an axe. During his recuperation he met with Indian people and studied the Delaware language. Six months later he was transferred to the Moravian mission at Shamokin. In 1753 he visited Indian villages along the Susquehanna River and later conducted a group of settlers from Bethlehem to a new tract of land in North Carolina. The following year he returned to Bethlehem, where he was married and received an assignment to go to the Moravian mission at Gnadenhutten in Ohio. On November 24, 1755, his mission station on Mahoning Creek was burned by Indians, and 11 residents were killed. Grube, accompanied by his followers, fled from the area and returned to Bethlehem, where he stayed for the next two years. In 1758 he took charge of a mission in Connecticut until 1760 when he returned to Pennsylvania and assumed the leadership of a station at Wechquetanc in Monroe County. He conducted his religious services there in Delaware and completed writings that were published by a Swiss clergyman and printer. With the outbreak of Pontiac's War in 1763, the lives of Grube and his Native followers were in danger from both Indians and whites. After boarding up the chapel and other buildings, he took his converts to Nazareth, then to Bethlehem, and finally to Philadelphia. There the danger continued with Euro-American residents, the "Paxton Boys," threatening to kill the Indians. Grube weathered the siege with help from Benjamin Franklin, who befriended him. The Moravian missionary eventually served as a pastor at Lititz in Lancaster County, a position he held from 1765 to 1785. Grube also ministered to other congregations in Pennsylvania and New Jersey for brief periods of time. When he turned 91 he walked from Bethlehem, where he spent his last years, a distance of 10 miles to spend his birthday with friends who had also worked among the Indians. (See also HECKWELDER, JOHN; POST, CHRISTIAN FREDERICK; ZEISBERGER, DAVID.)

GUARDIAN SPIRIT The concept of a guardian spirit is an ancient and nearly universal complex of beliefs and actions regarding the relations of human individuals to a special class of spirit beings that, once acquired through dreams or visions, confer specific powers, abilities, or medicine. Each of the areas of North America, except perhaps the Southwest, has certain identifiable interpretations of the guardian spirit idea. Among the Plateau peoples, all men in tribes acquired a guardian spirit. Among the Kwakiutl, people of high social rank acquired one, and among tribes in the Southeast, the California, northeast Algonquians and Inuit, the possession of guardian spirits was a prerogative of shamans. Human beings unaided by spirit power are considered weak and ineffective. With the help of powers conferred by spirit beings, humans can attain individual success in technical skills or other lines of endeavor. The names of guardian spirits are of ancient beings, many surviving in the present world as animals but some as beings neither animal nor human. Native people generally group guardian spirits in classes. The majority of spirit powers confer shaman or curing or diagnostic powers, but other spirits confer nondiagnostic, or lay, powers. Spirits whose powers fall into both shaman and lay cate-

gories are rare, but those granting two or more kinds of lay powers are numerous.

Different patterns are involved in acquiring lay and shaman powers. The guardian spirit may be sought at, or after, puberty or by mature men. There are ritual procedures involving acquisition, control, and use of spirit powers. The spirit may be inherited; purchased; or obtained by a vision induced by self-sacrifice, fasting, or purgatives; or may be received involuntarily. Many boys and girls go through a course of training and purification around puberty to prepare for a spiritual experience and to make them acceptable to spirits capable of granting help. A spirit appears to people, in human or nonhuman forms, usually in special types of vision experiences, such as a VISION QUEST, and grants shaman or lay powers.

The method by which a lay person may acquire control of and receive power from a guardian spirit generally involves training activities with an older mentor during childhood, adolescence, and early maturity; purification through fasting, bathing, and purging; a guardian spirit quest; vision encounter in the course of which the spirit confers power; suppression of the vision experience for several years; illness until the power is harnessed; and in some areas and for some groups an individually sponsored SPIRIT DANCE CEREMONIAL in winter in which the sponsor displays control of the spirit power years after the vision encounter. The first vision dance might follow a vision experience by an interval of 20 years.

A shaman acquires power from a shamanistic guardian spirit through a process of training, a spirit quest, a vision encounter in which the novice's body is possessed by the spirit, a period during which the uncontrolled possessing power abates and the possessed novice shaman obtains use of it and the direct use by the new shaman of his controlled power either in curing or victimizing. The shaman's power comes mostly from animal and bird spirits and sometimes plant spirits. Acquiring a power also often requires avoidances of certain foods. Spirits visit spots specific to certain types of power. Ritual and location of "power" spots are often treasured secrets passed from one generation to the next. Guardian spirits confer power to cure, become a great warrior or acquire wealth, or among tribes north of Puget Sound, they might bestow the right to represent some ceremonial performance representing the being. When people experience spirit power, they receive tangible evidence, a song, sacred dance, sacred dress, a MEDICINE BUNDLE, and instruction or ritual that has to be observed if they wish power to remain with them.

In some areas, people acquire characteristics of their guardian spirits and paint or tattoo themselves to resemble the spirit, decorate clothing with aspects of the spirit being, assume its name, and make a medicine bundle. Not all people are successful in seeking a guardian spirit even after numerous attempts, revealing that it is often a difficult process.

GUYART, MARIE *(1599–1672)* Ursuline nun. Marie Guyart was born at Tours, France, and had mystical experiences from her childhood on. Her parents arranged a marriage at 17 to a man who died two years later. The widow, who had a son, Claude, preferred a secluded life. On March 24, 1620, she had an important mystical experience that forever changed her and eventually brought about her vocation. In 1632, following divine commands, she entered the Ursuline novitiate at Tours, entrusting her son to her sister's care. She took her vows in 1633 and became a nun under the name of Marie de l'Incarnation. After a dream in which Canada was revealed as her destination, Mother Marie traveled to Quebec and arrived in 1639. There, she founded the Ursuline convent and became its first superior, retaining the position until her death. She set about educating French and Indian girls in the Ursuline boarding school as well as adult Indians. In her forties, she studied and mastered Indian languages, wrote French-Algonquian and French-Iroquoian dictionaries and a catechism in Huron and three in Algonquian. Marie Guyart took part in the struggles of France to establish itself in North America for more than 30 years. When she died at 72, her son was one of the principal superiors of the Benedictine order. She wrote a great deal but not all has been preserved; it is estimated that she wrote about 13,000 letters in her life, many to her son, who published some in 1681. Marie de l'Incarnation received beatification by papal decree in 1877, and the Catholic Church declared her venerable in 1911.

HABEGGER, ALFRED *(1892–?)* Mennonite missionary to the Northern Cheyenne people. Habegger was born on July 26, 1892, to Elizabeth Lehman-Habegger and David Habegger in Berne, Indiana. After graduating from Berne High School in 1912, he attended Tri-State Normal School in Angola, Indiana, for three months. Habegger later earned a bachelor's degree from Bethel College, Kansas, in 1916 and a master of arts degree from Bluffton College and Mennonite Seminary in Bluffton, Ohio, in 1917. He worked in Indiana as a teacher from 1912 to 1913 and as a principal from 1917 to 1918. In 1918 Habegger went to Busby, Montana, and began his long tenure as a missionary to the Northern Cheyenne. He returned to the East and attended Witmarsum Seminary in Bluffton, Ohio, during 1927 but resumed his missionary work in Montana some time after that. Habegger was named superintendent of the mission in 1942. He also served as president of the Big Horn County Ministerial Association from 1934 to 1935.

HAILE, BERARD *(1847–1961)* American Franciscan missionary. Born in Ohio, he entered the Franciscan Order in 1891 at the age of 17 and was ordained in 1898. Two years later, he was sent to the newly established mission at St. Michaels, Arizona, and stayed there working among Navajo (Dineh) people for more than 50 years. For 10 of those years he was in charge of the mission at Lukachukai. Father Haile devoted much of his time to studying the Navajo language and culture. Fluent in Navajo, he obtained versions of many Navajo ancient stories from his Navajo friends and published some of them on the press that he established at the

mission. He coauthored a Navajo dictionary, wrote about the Navajo language, and, as one of the first researchers to classify the Navajo chants, wrote about Navajo ceremonialism. Works include *Navajo Chantways and Ceremonials,* 1938; *Navajo Fire Dance, or Corral Dance,* 1946; and *A Stem Vocabulary of the Navaho Language, English-Navaho,* 1951. FRANK MITCHELL dictated the BLESSING WAY to Father Haile in 1930.

HAIR-CUTTING CEREMONY *Western Apache* The spring following the PUTTING ON MOCCASINS ceremony, a child has a brief hair-cutting rite. A shaman applies cattail pollen ritually to the child's cheeks and head four times and then closely crops the hair while praying for the child's long life. The Apache believe that children should undergo this ceremony at least once but ideally during four successive springs.

HAKO CEREMONY (Calumet Ceremony, pipe ceremony, pipe dance) *Pawnee* A sacred ceremony that was originally a prayer for children but also fostered friendship and peace. Much of what is known of the ceremony was recorded over a period of four years by the ethnologist Alice C. Fletcher through information provided by TAHIRUSSAWICHI, a Pawnee Ku'rahus, or holy man, from the Chawi band, beginning in 1898. Although Fletcher had observed the ceremony among the Omaha people, she was unable to obtain a complete record of it from them. After attempting to gain the information for 15 years, she succeeded among the Pawnee with the help of James Murie, a

Skidi band member, and Omaha friends. The ceremony was known by other names in the Pawnee language, but Fletcher called it the Hako because the term was used during the rituals and for ease of pronunciation. It is also known as the Calumet Ceremony.

The origin of the Hako Ceremony is unknown, but it is believed to be quite old. Father MARQUETTE described it in the 17th century among the Illinois people and wrote that one of its sacred symbols, the feathered stems, were honored among the Algonquian, Siouan, and Caddoan peoples. The ceremony was originally a prayer for children, but it also fostered intertribal friendship and peace, a dimension that may have been added at a later period. As recorded by Fletcher, its purposes among the Chawi band were to pray for children, long life, and plenty as well as to establish a bond between the two distinct groups who participated in its performance. Neither of the two groups, the Fathers and the Children, who conducted the Hako could belong to the same clan and one often came from a different tribe.

The Fathers consisted of 20 to 100 family or clan members of the man, called the Father, who initiated a performance of the ceremony. His group included the priest in charge of a shrine sacred to rain, two doctors with a knowledge of healing plants and singers. The Father also chose a Ku'rahus, a man venerated for his sacred knowledge, to be in charge of the Hako from start to finish who in turn selected an assistant and an apprentice to participate. The objects sacred to the ceremony were ritually prepared only under the guidance of a Ku'rahus. The Children consisted of the relatives of a leader called the Son, who was chosen by the Father to receive his group. The Father was generally a chief or a prominent member of the tribe, and the Son was his equal.

Each of the leaders and their followers had specific ritual obligations to fulfill. The Hako was an intricate, detailed series of observances, including nearly 100 songs, that had to be performed in the proper sequence. Fletcher's account indicates two segments, the preparation and the ceremony, with several divisions and 20 rituals. Four other rituals could also be added, including comforting the child, prayer to avert storms, prayer for the gift of children, and changing a man's name. The first three rituals were held in the Father's lodge before his group started a journey to the Children. The five-day ceremony included ritual purification, prayers, smoking, consecration, songs, exchanges, anointing, painting, male and female representations, processions, thanksgiving, feasts, dancing, and blessings. The Hako, also described as an adoption ceremony, was not associated with agriculture, hunting, war, or tribal festivals. The Ku'rahus who served as Fletcher's informant commented: "We take up the Hako in the spring when the birds are mating, or in the summer when the birds are nesting and caring for their young, or in the fall when the birds are flocking, but not in the winter when all things are asleep. With the Hako we are praying for the gift of life, of strength, of plenty, and of peace, so we must pray when life is stirring everywhere."

Today the Hako is called the pipe ceremony or Pipe Dance among the Pawnee people. Hako has also been identified as the Wichita word for pipe.

HALF-MOON CEREMONY   See PEYOTE REGION

HALL, CHARLES L. *(?–1940)* Congregational minister on the Fort Berthold reservation in North Dakota from 1876 until his death in 1940. Initially a New York architect, Hall became a missionary under the auspices of the AMERICAN BOARD OF COMMISSIONERS FOR FOREIGN MISSIONS and received training from the families of STEPHEN RETURN RIGGS and THOMAS S. WILLIAMSON. Upon arrival at Like-a-Fishhook Village at Fort Berthold, Hall could speak the Dakota language and introduced a song that began "Ho-Washte." He then became known as Ho-Washte, or "Good Voice," among the Arikara, Hidatsa, and Mandan on the reservation. Until Hall learned the languages of these tribes, he used hymns, sermons, and Bible readings translated into Dakota by Riggs, Williamson, and other missionaries. Since the entire Bible was never translated into Arikara, Hidatsa, or Mandan, Dakota Bibles continued to be used. By 1883, Hall was able to correspond in the Hidatsa language and later supervised the translation of religious pamphlets into that language as well as Mandan and Arikara. EDWARD GOODBIRD, Hidatsa translator for the missionary, became his assistant in 1904. The Reverend and Mrs. Hall had no converts to Christianity for 11 years because they required that Native people stop practicing their own traditions. One of their first converts was Poor Wolf, an elder, who found such demands as giving up Indian songs and medicine bags a difficult sacrifice. Hall's second wife, Susan Webb, was also a missionary. She started her work in Santee, Nebraska, at the Dakota mission of ALFRED LONGLEY RIGGS. Besides their goal of converting Indians to Christianity, they sought to "civilize" them as well. One way was by setting up cottages, or boardinghouses, overseen by matrons, where children were taught assimilationist ways of life along with academic and vocational training. Fort Berthold Congregationalists were still called Ho-Washte in the 1980s.

HALL, SHERMAN *(1800–1879)* A Congregational missionary to the Ojibway at La Pointe on Lake Superior's Madeline Island. Born in Weathersfield, Vermont, in 1800, he attended Phillips Academy, Dartmouth College (class of 1828) and Andover Theological Seminary (class of 1831). In

1831 he was ordained by the Reverend Lyman Beecher, married Betsey Parker, and left for the La Pointe assignment with his wife and another missionary, WILLIAM T. BOUTWELL. Hall established a mission at the fur-trading post, the first at the site since the early Jesuits, under the auspices of the AMERICAN BOARD OF COMMISSIONERS FOR FOREIGN MISSIONS. He devoted his efforts to learning the Ojibway language and building a program of Christianization and education. In charge of one of the largest mission stations in North America, he held an influential position that enabled him to secure government support for the schools he established in the region. Between 1833 and 1856 he either translated or supervised translations of religious and educational materials into the Ojibway language. These included textbooks, hymns, and biblical materials. His New Testament translation, completed with the assistance of Henry Blatchford, a native interpreter, was published in three editions during his lifetime. Hall remained at La Pointe until 1852, when the government offered him the superintendency of an experimental manual labor school to be established at another Ojibway settlement. He resigned from the position a short time later, in November 1854, after the ABCFM decided against helping support a mission there. Hall then settled on a farm he had purchased in Sauk Rapids, Minnesota, and became the minister of a Congregational church there. He also served as a judge of probate and superintendent of schools before his death on September 1, 1879.

HAMATSA DANCE *North Pacific Coast* The dance performed by the Hamatsa, the prestigious figure of the SHAMANS' SOCIETY who impersonates the MAN EATER spirit. The initiation of a Hamatsa dancer, the son of a chief who inherited the right to the performance, involves four days of ritual purification and the initiate's disappearance from the village (said to be kidnapped by spirits that inspire him to perform macabre acts) where he receives instructions about the society's rites. While the initiate is absent, the ceremonial house is prepared, and some masked dancing and other social activities take place. The initiate returns, possessed by the spirit's macabre desires. Spectators are menaced, and property destroyed. The Hamatsa manifests spirit possession by doing acts no person would do of his own volition. Comic interludes contrast with solemn parts of the ritual. He sings, dances, and does other ritual acts that finally pacify the Hamatsa dancer. Lengthy purification rites follow as well as taboos on the initiate, some for up to four years. Dancers in this society are arranged into two groups, the sparrows and the seals, with roles in the WINTER CEREMONIAL. The youth being initiated into the Hamatsa society attains powers to communicate with animals and the rights and privileges of impersonating the animal in ceremonial dances. The Hamatsa is accompanied by a retinue representing spirits that dwell with the man eater.

HAMBLIN, JACOB *(1819–1886)* A frontiersman and missionary ordained "Apostle to the Lamanites" by Brigham Young, president of the Church of Jesus Christ of Latter-day Saints. He was born to Daphne Haynes and Isaiah Hamblin on April 2, 1819, in Salem, Ohio. After converting to the Mormon faith, Hamblin was baptized on March 3, 1842, in Wisconsin and went to Nauvoo, Illinois, the same year. He traveled to Utah with other family members in the spring of 1850 and arrived in Salt Lake City several months later. A few years after settling in the Tooele valley, Hamblin and other Mormons (including IRA HATCH) were sent to establish mission stations among the Paiute in southern Utah. He sought peace as Indians fought against the invasion of their lands. In 1858 he began leading short-term missionary expeditions to the Hopi in northern Arizona. He also established a number of frontier settlements in Utah, Arizona, Nevada, and California. As a pioneering missionary, Hamblin sought the cooperation of Native people in reinforcing Mormon influence in the area. He was ordained "Apostle to the Lamanites" on December 15, 1876. Two years later he moved to Arizona and settled in Amity. He remained there until 1882, when he resettled in Pleasanton, New Mexico. Hamblin died there on August 31, 1886. His family included four wives and 24 children.

HANBLECEYA *("crying for a vision")* *Lakota* One of the SEVEN SACRED RITES OF THE LAKOTA people. Believed to exist before the gift of the Sacred Pipe, the rite is undertaken in solitude by a single individual who is prepared and guided by a holy person. The sacred rite is conducted for many reasons. Besides seeking spiritual guidance, a person may pray for peace in the world, for assistance before a difficult decision or undertaking, for healing of a relative or friend suffering from illness, for understanding a vision or a dream, or for the safe return of loved ones from a journey. It may also be done to give thanks for any number of gifts or blessings. According to the account given by the holy man, BLACK ELK, one of the most important reasons it was conducted was to help a person recognize his oneness with all other beings in the universe.

The first VISION QUEST generally starts at adolescence, but it can be repeated. An individual wishing to undertake the rite takes a filled pipe to a holy man and asks him to serve as his guide. If agreement is reached, preparations begin. The petitioner decides on the number of days, generally up to four, for the vision quest and starts to receive instructions. After a sweat lodge purification ceremony is conducted, the person is left in solitude at a ritually prepared pit on a hill or mountaintop. Wearing only a breechcloth and moccasins, he carries a blanket or robe and a sealed pipe. During the vision quest he is not permitted to drink or eat. Constantly praying in a spirit of humility, he conducts himself as instructed by his holy teacher. During his solitude he is to be observant and alert for spiritual messages. His faith may be tested, and he is cautioned to continue praying with the pipe. At the end of the vision quest, his helpers return for him and take him to a sweat lodge. During the concluding purification ceremony, he reveals all that happened to him, and it is later interpreted for him by the holy man. According to Black Elk, females could also conduct a vision quest after undergoing purification, their rites were held in a different location, and other women assisted the petitioner.

HAND TREMBLER ("motion-in-the-hand") *Navajo* Using a form of diagnosing, or divining, this person's function is to determine the cause of a person's illness, to prescribe ritual treatment, and to select the right practitioner. A member of the patient's immediate family selects the hand trembler, who can be a man or a woman, and offers a fee. The trembler uses pollen, songs, and prayer offerings of turquoise and shells and invokes particular spirits to locate lost persons or property, stolen goods, or water. As soon as he or she sings, his or her hands and arms begin to shake violently. The way in which the hand moves as it shakes provides insight into the information sought. Hand tremblers acquire their ability suddenly. It cannot be inherited, nor can it be learned. If a trembler successfully diagnoses a patient, he or she consults a medicine man who knows prayers and songs to be used. The chosen trembler is thought to be possessed by a powerful spirit. (See also DIAGNOSTICIAN.)

HANDSOME LAKE (Skaniadariio) *(1735–1815) Seneca* Allegany Seneca prophet who founded a religion. Born in the Seneca village of Conawagas on the Genesee River, Handsome Lake witnessed the devastation of the Iroquois Confederacy. After the American Revolution, Iroquois were damaged by factionalism, illness, and land cessions. Before his first vision, he drank considerably and suffered from depression and bitterness. He sang sacred songs to the dead, properly sung only at the FEAST TO THE DEAD, while drunk after the death of his daughter. On June 15, 1799, during the STRAWBERRY FESTIVAL, while Handsome Lake was ill, he had his first vision. Three messengers told him to preach the message against alcohol, witchcraft, love magic (the use of love potions), and abortion as well as to tell people guilty of these things to admit their wrongdoing, repent, and never sin again. Because Handsome Lake was still too weak to speak publicly, his half-brother Chief Cornplanter told the people

of the visions. On August 7 after dreaming about the fourth messenger and falling into a trance, he had a second vision of a sky journey. Led by a guide, Handsome Lake visited heaven and hell and was told about the moral plan of the cosmos. His third vision, on February 5, 1800, concerned the Great Spirit's worries about the condition of the Iroquois.

Handsome Lake's first gospel contained several themes—forecasts of world destruction, a definition of sin, a refusal to believe in and follow the "good word" that Handsome Lake revealed and a prescription for salvation that included belief in practices recommended by Handsome Lake. These practices included: confession and a promise by witches, purveyors of love magic, and abortionists to cease sinning; strict temperance; performance of correct ritual; and adherence to the ancient calendar of ceremonies devoted to the Creator. He singled out four rites in particular—the THANKSGIVING DANCE, FEATHER DANCE, PERSONAL CHANT, and BOWL (PEACH STONE) GAME. He proposed several major ritual changes, such as the disbanding of medicine societies, but met with resistance. He introduced confession as a major sacrament, similar to the practice of requiring confession of a suspected witch. He proposed but failed to eliminate the anniversary mourning ceremony.

Handsome Lake preached a second gospel after 1803 in which he emphasized temperance, peace, keeping land instead of selling it, acculturation and domestic morality. His preaching, called the "good word," or *gaiwiio,* was effective, and a renaissance occurred on many Iroquois reservations between 1799 and 1815. Thus, before his death, Handsome Lake was able to see spiritual reformation among his people, but the political strife that plagued his career continued after his death. After a generation of disorder and the proselytizing by Christian missionaries, disciples of Handsome Lake revived his words and organized them into a new religion, the Code of Handsome Lake. His grandson, Jimmy Johnson (Sosheowa), developed a version of the code in the 1840s at Tonawanda that has become the standard by which other speakers' versions are judged. With the help of Blacksnake, Handsome Lake's nephew and disciple, the HANDSOME LAKE RELIGION, or Longhouse Religion, combined elements of Iroquois and Christian beliefs.

Handsome Lake believed, however, that he was picked to revive traditional religious observances of the Iroquois, not to create a new religion. After his death, a CONDOLENCE CEREMONY was performed because Handsome Lake was an important leader.

HANDSOME LAKE RELIGION (Longhouse Religion) *Iroquois* This religion, practiced on Iroquois reservations in the United States and Canada, is an amalgamation of ancient

Handsome Lake. A drawing by Cattaraugus Seneca artist Jesse Cornplanter, c. 1905, shows Allegany Seneca prophet Handsome Lake preaching in a longhouse while holding a wampum belt. *New York State Library, Albany, 12845–29.*

tradition, elements borrowed from Christianity, and innovations of HANDSOME LAKE, a Seneca prophet. The headquarters of the religion of Handsome Lake is on the New York Seneca Reservation at Tonawanda, where the wampum strings of Handsome Lake are kept. The heart of the religion is the "good word" (*gaiwiio*) or CODE OF HANDSOME LAKE. Men who know the Code of Handsome Lake are called upon to preach it. Every longhouse has three or four preachers, each of whom knows a slightly different version of the code, varying according to the identity of the preacher from whom he learned it, but the substance is the same. Every fall, in September or October, delegates from each of the 10 longhouses meet at Tonawanda to arrange that fall's itinerary of SIX NATIONS MEETINGS when the code is recited. This repeats the time during autumn when messengers were sent from Handsome Lake's headquarters to recite his *gaiwiio* to the 10 autonomous longhouses. Some of the preachers are officially authorized to preach at other longhouses during the Six Nations Meetings, but some preach only before their own congregations.

HANO CEREMONIALISM *Tewa* A Tewa-speaking pueblo on the Hopi First Mesa in Arizona, Hano observes ceremonial activities that are overseen by a religious hierarchy headed by a village chief. The ceremonial structure is like that of Hopi, although Hano has its own ceremonial calendar. Ceremonies are distributed in such a way that each clan

"owns" or controls at least one ceremony. (See also HOPI CEREMONIALISM; PUEBLO CEREMONIALISM; TEWA CEREMONIALISM; ZUNI CEREMONIALISM.)

HARE, WILLIAM HOBART *(1838–1909)* Bishop of the Protestant Episcopal Church who became known as the "Apostle to the Sioux." Hare was born in Princeton, New Jersey. He attended the Academy of the Protestant Episcopal Church in Philadelphia, where his father served as headmaster from 1846 to 1857, and the University of Pennsylvania, where he was admitted as a sophomore in 1855. After withdrawing in his junior year, he began studying for the ministry at the Episcopal Divinity School while teaching at St. Mark's Academy in Philadelphia. Hare was admitted to the deaconate on June 19, 1859, and then served as an assistant to Dr. M. A. DeWolfe Howe at St. Luke's Church. In 1861 he took charge of St. Paul's Church in Philadelphia and married Howe's daughter, Mary Amory Howe, on October 30th of the same year. Ordained to the priesthood on May 25, 1862, Hare went to the Minnesota diocese the following year, hoping the change would benefit his wife's health. There he observed the conditions among Native people during the aftermath of the Dakota War of 1862, which was fought between Santee Dakota and Euro-American forces. The conflict was precipitated by a number of factors, including a drastic reduction of the tribal land base, corruption and fraud in the distribution of goods promised by the government in treaties, and conditions of hunger and poverty. The war resulted in deaths on both sides, the displacement of Dakota from their homes, the incarceration of captives, and the hanging of 38 Dakota men at Mankato, Minnesota Territory, on December 26, 1862, the country's largest mass execution. Hare returned to Philadelphia in 1864, where his pastoral work included managing St. Luke's parish during his father-in-law's absence and assuming a rectorship at the Church of the Ascension. His wife died during the same period, on January 7, 1866.

Hare's missionary career began in 1871 with his appointment as secretary of the Foreign Committee of the Board of Missions. Elected bishop of the missionary jurisdiction of Niobrara in present-day South Dakota in 1872, he began ministering to the Sioux. His nearly 37 years of mission work included supporting the advancement of "civilizing" influences among them. Highly regarded by government officials and policy reformers, Bishop Hare founded five boarding schools and expanded missionary work in the region. In 1883 he became bishop of South Dakota after the House of Bishops changed the boundaries of his jurisdiction and replaced Niobrara with the more up-to-date state name in his title. Moving from the Yankton agency to Sioux Falls, he founded All Saints School for girls and served whites as well as Indians until his death. In 1891 and 1892 the House of Bishops sent him to oversee its missions in Japan and China. A short time later, in 1893, he led an effort to reform South Dakota's divorce laws. After a trip abroad in 1896, Hare's health continued to deteriorate. He died on October 23, 1909.

HARVEST DANCE *Pueblo* An agricultural dance performed by men and women in August or September to offer thanks for the summer's bounty. After several hours of dancing, villagers toss food and hundreds of items to singers, dancers, and observers in appreciation of the performance and the harvest.

HARVEST FESTIVAL *Iroquois* A four-day ceremony held in summer to honor cultivated foods and at which the OUR LIFE SUPPORTER DANCES are performed. The people thank the Creator and spirit forces for permitting Iroquois people to have a full harvest. Regalia is worn by men and women befitting a dance addressed to the Creator.

HARVEST (THANKSGIVING) FESTIVAL FOR CROPS *Zuni* An annual ceremony held after the gathering of crops. This ceremony of the Zuni War Society, or BOW PRIESTHOOD, involves dancing by alternating groups of girls, warriors (dancing in the plaza and indoors), and burlesque dancers, characteristic of a war ceremonial. At the end of the dance, the dancers throw baskets of food to the crowd.

HASCALL, JOHN *(1941–) Ojibway* A contemporary medicine man and Catholic priest. A member of the Crane clan, Father Hascall conducts "healing Masses" among Native people. He combines traditional beliefs, including the use of the SACRED PIPE, with Roman Catholic theology. His blending of these religious traditions is said to have met with support from coworkers and superiors in the church. In 1986 Father Hascall became president of the TEKAKWITHA CONFERENCE. (See also NATIONAL ASSOCIATION OF NATIVE RELIGIOUS.)

HASKELL, THALES HASTINGS *(1834–1909)* A Mormon missionary who was born in North New Salem, Massachusetts, on February 21, 1834. Thales went to Utah with members of the Church of Jesus Christ of Latter-day Saints in search of his father who had traveled to California. He remained in Salt Lake City, where he worked as a tradesman and became a member of the Mormon faith on February 21, 1852. During his career Haskell worked with JACOB HAMBLIN and was a member of most of Hamblin's mission expeditions to the Hopi people. His first wife, Marian Woodberry, was killed by an adopted Indian boy who accidentally shot her. Haskell worked for a long period of time as a missionary in Arizona and in the San Juan area of Utah even though the church released him from missionary responsibilities. He learned a number of Native languages, a valuable skill during his peacemaking efforts. A pioneer of Bluff, Utah, he became a postmaster after moving to Manassa, Colorado, in 1886. Haskell died there on July 13, 1909. His family included his wife, Margaret J. Edwards, and their seven children.

HATCH, IRA *(1835–?)* A Mormon missionary who was born to Ira Stearns Hatch and Wealthy Bradford Hatch on August 5, 1835, in Saratoga, New York. In 1849 he and his family moved to Bountiful, Utah, settling 10 miles from Salt Lake City. When he was 20 years old, Hatch was called to missionary work by Brigham Young, president of the Church of Jesus Christ of Latter-day Saints. Hatch worked among Native groups in Utah, Colorado, New Mexico, and Arizona. During the course of his missionary career, he learned 13 American Indian dialects, becoming particularly proficient in the Navajo language. Hatch married Sarah Spaneshank, the daughter of a Paiute woman and a Navajo chief, and they had four children. Hatch worked with another pioneering missionary, JACOB HAMBLIN, for a large part of his life.

HATCH V. GOERKE (502 F. 2d 1189 [10th Cir. 1974]) *(1974)* This 1974 case involved a challenge to a school's regulation on student hair length. In this case the students' parents claimed that the code violated their right to bring up their children in accordance with the values of their own religion and culture. The federal court ruled against the plaintiffs, refusing to become involved in the operation of state-run public schools. (See also *NEW RIDER V. BOARD OF EDUCATION; TETERUD V. GILLMAN; UNITED STATES EX REL. GOINGS V. AARON;* and Subject Index for other legal cases included in this volume.)

HAVEN, JENS *(1724–1796)* Moravian missionary who founded missions in Labrador among the Inuit people. Haven was born in Wust, Jutland, Denmark, on June 23, 1724, into a Lutheran family. After completing an apprenticeship to a joiner, he was accepted into the Moravian settlement at Herrnhut, Saxony, Germany, in 1748 and stayed there for a decade. In 1758 he began foreign mission work among the Inuit in Greenland, spending four years at the new Lichtenfels station. After obtaining permission from his denomination to go to Labrador in 1764, he traveled on an exploratory expedition to the Strait of Belle Isle. Based on his reports, the Moravians decided to establish a mission in the region. Unable to obtain land grants from the authorities until 1769, Haven spent time in the interim at placements in the Netherlands. In 1770 he again left for Labrador, where he and two other Moravian missionaries selected a site in the Nuneingoak area. Haven later returned to London to make final preparations for the new station. In 1771 a group of 14 Moravians, led by Christoph Brasen, established the Nain mission at the selected Nuneingoak site. Haven remained in Labrador until 1784. During that period he undertook exploratory expeditions in the region, built and led a mission station at Okak from 1776 to 1781, and worked to establish another station at Hoffenthal (Hopedale). In 1784 he returned to Herrnhut, where he eventually became blind. Haven died on April 16, 1796. He was married to Mary (Butterworth), and they had two sons. (See also KOHLMEISTER, BENJAMIN GOTTLIEB.)

HAWLEY, GIDEON *(1727–1807)* An English missionary who ministered to the Indians for more than 50 years during the colonial period. He graduated from Yale in 1749 and was licensed as a preacher a year later. Hawley's missionary career started in 1752 at Stockbridge, Massachusetts, under the auspices of the SOCIETY FOR THE PROPAGATION OF THE GOSPEL in NEW ENGLAND among the Indians. He served as a schoolmaster, teaching Iroquois students from distant communities. A short time later, disputes among the colonial authorities at Stockbridge led him to accept an offer to establish a mission among the Six Nations Iroquois. In 1754 he was ordained for the work in Boston, then left for his post near what is now Windsor, New York. In addition to attempting to convert and "civilize" the Native people, Hawley served as an interpreter and participated in councils. His work was eventually disrupted by the French and Indian War, and in 1756 he left for Boston, where he accepted a commission as chaplain to a regiment. Illness intervened, and he was later sent on a temporary mission to the Mashpee Indians of Cape Cod. Hawley secured a permanent appointment, and he remained at Cape Cod from April 8, 1758 until his death on October 3, 1807. (See also APES(S), WILLIAM; SERGEANT, JOHN.)

HAYDEN, BRIDGET *(1815–1890)* Irish nun. Born in Ireland, Hayden became a nun with the order of the Sisters of Loretto of Kentucky in 1842. Later, she answered the call of Father Schoenmakers, founder of the Osage Mission on the Neosho River in Kansas. She arrived at the mission in 1847 and established a school to educate Indian girls. After the Osage Mission closed, she chartered St. Ann's Academy, a boarding school for Indian and white girls in 1870. She was in charge of the school until she died.

HEADMEN *Iroquois* The leader of each side, or moiety, in each Iroquois tribe. There are two groups, one composed of women, the other of men, each of which has a leader referred to as "head," a permanent office to which men and women are elected within certain clans. Headmen are invested with the office at the GREEN CORN ceremony or the MIDWINTER CEREMONY. They observe the stars and ripening of fruits. They call meetings of the faithkeepers to set dates for the festivals. They appoint persons to perform tasks such as singing, dancing, preaching, managing evening social dances, serving food, carrying messages, and arranging lodging for visitors. (See also IROQUOIS CEREMONIALISM.)

HECKEWELDER, JOHN *(1743–1823)* A Moravian missionary to the Delaware (Lenni Lenape) and other Indians in Pennsylvania and Ohio. He was born in Bedford, England. In 1754 his family moved to America and settled in the Moravian community of Bethlehem, Pennsylvania. After attending school for three years, Heckewelder was sent to assist in the operation of a farm near Nazareth, Pennsylvania. In 1759 he wanted to do Indian mission work with DAVID ZEISBERGER and CHRISTIAN FREDERICK POST in the Ohio Territory but was indentured to a Bethlehem cedar cooper instead. He served as a messenger to Native communities on occasion from 1763 to 1771 and during that period, studied their language, traditions and history.

It was not until 1771 that he began regular mission work by becoming an assistant to Zeisberger, serving communities of Moravian Christian Delaware at various Ohio locations. In 1780 Heckewelder married Sarah Ohneberg in the first wedding of a white couple in Ohio. Heckewelder often accompanied Indian groups on their travels to protect them from frontiersmen. In 1781 he and a party of converts were taken prisoner by a company of British and their Indian allies and charged with being spies for the Americans. Although summoned to Detroit for arraignment before the post commandant on two occasions, Heckewelder was eventually allowed to return to Ohio. During his absence from missionary work, whites massacred 96 Christian Indians at Gnadenhutten, a Moravian settlement. In 1786 he retired from active mission work and moved to Bethlehem, where he continued to serve his church. During this period Heckewelder was called upon to assist the new United States government through his knowledge of Indian life and language. In 1792 he accompanied a treaty commission to Vincennes, Indiana, and the following year provided the same service for a similar delegation. In 1801 he returned to Gnadenhutten to administer the settlement, which by then consisted of the descendants of the mission's earlier converts. Upon his return to Bethlehem in 1810, he began to record some of his knowledge of Indian life and eventually completed a number of valuable ethnological publications, including information on the "famous preacher," the DELAWARE PROPHET. "Account of the History, Manners, and Customs of the Indian Nations, Who Once Inhabited Pennsylvania and the Neighboring States" was published in *The Transactions of the Historical & Literary Committee of the American Philosophical Society* (1819). Other publications include *A Narrative of the Mission of the United Brethren among the Delaware and the Mohegan Indians from its Commencement in the Year 1740 to the Close of the Year 1808* (1820) and *Names which the Lenni Lenape or Delaware Indians Gave to the Rivers, Streams, and Localities within the States of Pennsylvania, New Jersey, Maryland, and Virginia, with their Significations* (1872). (See also GRUBE, BERNHARD ADAM.)

HE'DEWACHI CEREMONY *Omaha* A ceremony believed to be older than the OMAHA SACRED POLE and said to be associated with the cultivation of corn. It took place during the summer and in later years at the end of the ANOINTING THE SACRED POLE CEREMONY. The He'dewachi was maintained and conducted by hereditary keepers, who oversaw each detail of the observance. The ceremony, led by the two Sacred Tribal Pipes, included three days of preparatory rituals, then a dance and festival on the fourth day. The central object in the ceremony was a pole ritually cut from a cottonwood or willow tree. The pole was painted with alternating bands of black and red to represent a number of symbolic meanings, including night and day. It also represented a man as well as a tree and signified life-giving forces in the universe and the

unity of the people. Seven types of wood were considered sacred to the ceremony, including the cottonwood, birch, box elder, ironwood, ash, and both hard and soft willow. Charcoal used as black paint came from the elder; the pipe stem was made of ash; rattles were made with seeds from the ironwood; and wands given to the people were willow. The He'dewachi ceremony, described as a "festival of joy" by the ethnologists Alice C. Fletcher and Francis La Flesche, was participated in by men, women, and children.

HENNEPIN, LOUIS *(c. 1640–1701)* Born in Belgium, Hennepin became a Recollet friar and traveled to Canada as a missionary in 1675. In 1678, La Salle obtained the services of Hennepin as chaplain for his shipbuilders at Fort Frontenac on Lake Ontario. In 1679, he accompanied Rene-Robert Cavelier de La Salle on his new ship on an expedition through the Great Lakes to Illinois country. In 1680, La Salle sent a party that included Hennepin to explore the upper Mississippi. Hennepin's account, *Description de la Louisiane* (1683), described his adventures and claimed credit for considerable exploration. During an exploratory trip in Minnesota, Hennepin was captured by the Sioux and he was eventually rescued by Duluth. During his captivity, Hennepin traveled over much of Minnesota and "discovered" and named St. Anthony's Falls, at the site of present-day Minneapolis. Duluth took Hennepin to Canada where in 1682 he returned to France and published his first book. About 1690, he was expelled from France for unknown reasons. He returned to Belgium, where he published books dealing with his North American travels. *Nouvelle Decouverte* (1697) appeared in English in 1698 as *A New Discovery*. In it, he claimed to have discovered the Mississippi River and appropriated without credit what Membré, his fellow missionary, had written.

HENSLEY, ALBERT *(c. 1875–?)* *Winnebago* Peyote ROADMAN and missionary among the Winnebago and other tribal groups. According to a brief account of his early life, written for an Indian school superintendent in 1916, Hensley's mother died when he was a baby, and his paternal grandmother took care of him until her death when he was five years old. He then lived with various families until he was seven, at which time he went to live in his father's home. Anthropologist Alice C. Fletcher arranged for him to attend the Carlisle Indian School in Pennsylvania after he agreed to run away from his father, who was opposed to schooling. He arrived in Carlisle on December 22, 1888, and stayed until June 15, 1895. After JOHN RAVE, Hensley was one of the most active Winnebago peyote leaders. There is general agreement that the two of them established the Big Moon, or Cross Fire, ritual among the Dakota and Ojibway. Like the peyotist QUANAH PARKER, Hensley was both a political and religious leader. He wrote a number of letters to the Bureau of Indian Affairs on a wide range of issues, including a strong defense of the PEYOTE RELIGION. In 1921, when the Winnebago of Nebraska became the first tribe to incorporate a peyote church outside the state of Oklahoma, Hensley was a charter member. The Peyote Church of Christ, amended in 1922 to the NATIVE AMERICAN CHURCH of Winnebago, Nebraska, included both Cross Fire and Half Moon adherents in its membership.

HESI CEREMONY *Maidu, Patwin, Wintu* A sacred ritual of the KUKSU RELIGION, whose rituals symbolize rebirth to ensure plentiful harvests and to secure health and general prosperity of the people. The ceremony took place in a dance house in late September–early October and May and lasted four days and nights. It included a variety of dances, with extremely elaborate regalia, clowning, individual singing, and long ritual orations conducted by a shaman who, during a trance, visited the abode of the dead, where he received instructions for the ceremony. During Hesi, the shaman put on a sacred cloak and became Moki, a messenger from the keeper of the abode of the dead. He delivered a long speech, which was a message from Moki, instructing people about proper conduct. Moki also mediated to the keeper of the abode of the dead the needs of people during the ritual orations. The Hesi society not only celebrated the usual seasonal events like first fruits rites, but also conducted a cycle of dances to animal spirits.

HEYOKA *Lakota* The sacred clown or contrary in Lakota culture whose spiritual powers came from the *wakinyan*, or thunder beings, in the west. A person who dreamed of thunder or lightning or their associated symbols (such as a horse, swallow, frog, or dragonfly) was obligated to act out the vision in a ceremony known as the Heyoka kaga ("clown making"). Failure to comply meant punishment by death from the thunder beings. The *heyoka* behaved in opposite or contrary ways and performed antics that made the people laugh. The holy man JOHN (FIRE) LAME DEER describes the clown as "an upside-down, backward-forward, yes-and-no man." Examples of *heyoka* behavior include dressing warmly in hot weather, wearing few or no clothes in the winter, crying rather than laughing, and speaking rapidly, slowly, or backwards. The *heyoka* possessed great spiritual powers, and his antics were considered holy. (See also CLOWN; HEYOKA CEREMONY.)

HEYOKA CEREMONY (Heyoka kaga, "Clownmaker" ceremony) *Lakota* A ceremony performed by the *HEYOKA*, those who had dreamed of thunder beings. Until the vision was publicly reenacted before the people as required, the in-

dividual feared thunder and lightning. During the ceremony the *heyoka's* backward or opposite antics brought great laughter. According to the Lakota holy man JOHN (FIRE) LAME DEER, being a sacred clown "brings . . . honor, but also shame. It gives you power, but you have to pay for it." During the ceremony the KETTLE DANCE was performed, which included the singing of holy songs and the ritual preparation of a boiling pot of dog meat. During the course of the performance, the *heyokas* danced around the scalding kettle and plunged their bare hands into it to retrieve the head and other morsels of the spiritual food. Their frolics included splashing one another and exclaiming over the coldness of the pot and its contents.

HIACOOMES *(c. 1610–1690) Pokanoket* A Native preacher said to have been the first of the New England PRAYING INDIANS to convert to Christianity. Hiacoomes lived at Great Harbor, now Edgartown, on Martha's Vineyard, where the younger THOMAS MAYHEW, a Congregational clergyman, had settled with a few English families in 1642. A member of the Pokanoket tribe, he was estimated to be in his thirties when he converted. His 1643 conversion, the first for Mayhew, occurred three years before JOHN ELIOT, the noted English minister, began his missionary work on the mainland. Under Mayhew's instruction, Hiacoomes learned to read English and studied the Bible. Serving at first as the clergyman's interpreter and helper, he soon began doing his own missionary work. Impressed that he and his family had survived epidemics in 1643 and 1645, Indians became more willing to listen to Christian teachings. Hiacoomes began preaching in 1645, reportedly becoming an effective missionary. By 1651 he and Mayhew ministered to two Indian congregations and the number of converts had reached nearly 200. Hiacoomes preached twice each Sunday, after consulting Mayhew for advice on his sermons. Continuing the missionary work alone after Mayhew's death in 1657, he became pastor of a Native church established on Martha's Vineyard in 1670 after the elder Thomas Mayhew declined the position. Hiacoomes and John Tackanash, another praying Indian, were ordained as pastor and teacher on August 22, 1670, by John Eliot and John Cotton, also a New England minister. The Native pastor in turn ordained a successor before his death in 1690. A son, John Hiacoomes, became a preacher and schoolmaster at Assawampsit, or Middleborough, in 1698.

HIERARCHIC RITUALS AND SPEECHES *Iroquois* See THANKSGIVING ADDRESS

HILL, CORNELIUS *(?–1907) Oneida* Chief of the Bear Clan and the first Oneida to become an ordained Episcopal priest.

Hill was educated at Nashotah House seminary in Wisconsin. He was taken there by the school's founders, JAMES LLOYD BRECK and William Adams, when he was 12 years old. Hill later began serving as a chief of his people at a young age, eventually serving in the leadership role for many years. In the 1860s he led the opposition against allotment, the breaking up of tribally owned land into individual units for distribution among tribal members, on the Oneida reservation in Wisconsin. The struggle continued for many years, resulting in allotment in the 1890s and disastrous land losses for the Oneida. Hill also served as an interpreter and organist at the Episcopal Church in Oneida, Wisconsin, for a long period of time. He was ordained a deacon on June 27, 1885, and to the priesthood in 1903. The esteemed Oneida leader died a few years later, in 1907.

HILL, EMILY *(1911–1988) Shoshone* A medicine woman from the Wind River Reservation in Wyoming. Hill's father died when she was a young child. Her mother remarried, and the family eventually included nine children. Hill began attending the reservation boarding school at the age of six and continued her education until she was about 18. During that period she was first exposed to English and other non-Indian teachings, with students punished for speaking the Shoshone language. Following her school years, Hill married and had three children. Hill's traditional healing practices included her belief in dreams and prayers as well as the sacred knowledge she had acquired from an elderly woman who served as her teacher. She used both Native and Western medicine to help heal people. Hill maintained her faith in the Naraya, or Ghost Dance, religion, which was practiced at Wind River well into the 20th century. When the dances were no longer held, she and her sister continued singing the sacred songs. Hill was also an adherent of the SUN DANCE religion, joining the women singers at the ceremonies until her health declined. As a respected elder, she spoke out at tribal council meetings. Hill and four other Shoshone women singers collaborated with the author Judith Vander on a book called *Songprints* (1988). It includes information about Hill's life and her extensive repertoire of Shoshone music, much of it learned from her mother. Emily Hill entered a nursing home in 1986 and died on January 14, 1988. Other adherents to the Ghost Dance on the Wind River Reservation included TUBY ROBERTS, NADZAIP ROGERS, WILLIAM WASHINGTON and WHITE COLT.

HINMAN, SAMUEL D. *(?–1890)* An Episcopal missionary among the Dakota people. A native of Connecticut, Hinman prepared for the ministry at Seabury Divinity School in Faribault, Minnesota. After his ordination as a deacon on September 20, 1860, Hinman went to the Red-

wood Agency (or Lower Sioux Agency) in Minnesota Territory. He was accompanied by EMILY J. WEST, another missionary, who assisted him in establishing a mission and school. The work ended when the Dakota War of 1862 broke out between Santee Dakota and Euro-American forces, sending Hinman and others fleeing to Fort Ridgely. After working among the Dakota at Fort Snelling for a winter, Hinman relocated with the Native people sent to the Crow Creek Reservation in South Dakota in 1863. Hinman was eventually assigned to the Santee Reservation in Nebraska. His work included building a church and school, training native catechists, and working on translations. After an 1870 tornado destroyed the mission, he began the work of rebuilding. The Reverend Hinman served as archdeacon of the Nebraska and Dakota Indian work until 1873. When the Niobrara missionary jurisdiction was established in 1872, the Reverend WILLIAM HOBART HARE was named bishop. Conflicts with Bishop Hare led to Hinman's removal for misconduct in 1878. In 1886 he went to the Birch Coulee mission in present-day Morton, Minnesota, where he married Mary Myrick, his second wife, of mixed-blood. His suspension ended in 1887. Hinman died on March 24, 1890.

HOAG, ENOCH *(c. 1856–?) Caddo* Peyote ROADMAN who was also a prominent Ghost Dance leader. He served as assistant to peyote leader JOHN WILSON for a time, then developed a variation of Wilson's Big Moon Peyote ceremony. In 1896, he became tribal chief, a position he held for 30 years. At the time he became chief, it is likely that he was at least 40 years old since the Caddo reportedly considered anyone under that age as too young for the office. For a number of years before 1896, Hoag served as an apprentice to his predecessor, Chief Whitebread. (See also NATIVE AMERICAN CHURCH; PEYOTE RELIGION.)

HOGAN *Navajo (Dineh)* The traditional Navajo (Dineh) family dwelling, which is itself a sacred place. The hogan is a microcosm of the Navajo homeland. The posts represent the four sacred mountains. A traditional hogan is constructed according to instructions prescribed by TALKING GOD, one of the HOLY PEOPLE, found in the Navajo creation story. Sections of the hogan correspond to the structures of the universe. For example, the earthen floor represents Mother Earth, and the round roof symbolizes Father Sky. The doorway faces east since the Sun's rays and songs and prayers began in the east. Once a hogan is built, a fire is started in the fireplace or stove located at the hogan's center. This is the heart of the home. The hogan is then blessed in a ceremony prescribed in the creation story. Navajo recognize two main hogan types: the forked stick (male) hogan named for its cone-like shape with three poles jutting from the pointed top and the (female) stacked log hogan usually with six or more sides. Male hogans are used only for ceremonial events, whether for one, five, or nine nights. They are sanctified with a BLESSING WAY ceremony. Today, families keep a log hogan for ceremonies. Female hogans are used for all other activities.

HOLINESS RITE *Apache* A complex four-night curing ceremony designed to relieve bear or snake sickness. Initiated and sponsored by the patients and their families, the ceremony, a LONG LIFE CEREMONY, takes place whenever the need arises. Its origin and justification are found in the ancient stories, and it has existed "from the beginning." Representatives of the sick person approach a recognized practitioner with ceremonial gifts, requesting the ceremony, which is performed for more than one and up to 12 patients at a time. The patients are subject to elaborate treatments that are intended to frighten away the bear and snake, both believed to be evil powers. Two sacred structures, a corral and a ceremonial tipi, are built. The ceremony involves singing, bear impersonation, public dancing, ground drawings with sand, feasts, drinking liquid medicine, and, on the fourth night, the appearance of spirit impersonators and sacred clowns who are permitted to do things others are forbidden to do during a ceremony. Dietary and behavioral restrictions are placed on the patient and impersonators. On the fifth day, there is a ritual procession with sprinkling of corn meal on sacred objects, ceremonial racing, and the tipi is dismantled.

HOLY DANCE *Eastern Dakota* The Holy Dance, or Wakan wacipi, is described as a former ceremony practiced among the Mdewakanton, Wahpeton, Wahpekute, Yanktonai, and other eastern Dakota people. The Wakan Society and its ceremonies are said to correspond to the MIDEWIWIN lodge of neighboring Ojibway and other tribal groups. One source indicated that the Holy Dance was generally held two or three times a year in each village. Religious elements included initiating candidates for membership, ritual "shooting" of shells into the bodies of participants, dancing, and feasting. The Holy Dance is also referred to as the Dakota MIDEWIWIN, Medicine Dance, or the Wakan Dance. (See also RED FISH; WAKAN FEAST.)

HOLY DANCE (MORRISON), ROBERT *(?–1972) Lakota* Herbalist and healer. Holy Dance, a Brulé, was a member of the Rosebud Reservation in South Dakota. About six months after having a vision in which he was told to look at the natural world around him and to help those who approached him for help, he treated his first patient. He eventually became known for his healing powers among both Native and non-Native people in the area. Besides his extensive knowledge of botanical remedies and Lakota traditions, Holy Dance also became known for his beautifully crafted flutes and pipes. A presentation he made at the 26th Annual Plains Anthropological Conference in 1968 was later published as "The Seven Pipes of the Dakota Sioux" in the *Plains Anthropologist.* Other information about his life and work was recorded by T. H. Lewis, a psychiatrist and medical anthropologist. After his wife's death in the late 1960s, Holy Dance's health began to deteriorate. After refusing to have surgery on his eyes, he left his wheelchair and returned to such former activities as horseback riding. Holy Dance also continued to make prophecies and foretold his own death. He died in the winter of 1972, as he had said he would.

HOLY PEOPLE *Navajo (Dineh)* Among the deities referred to as Holy People are the Sun, Earth, Moon, Sky, CHANGING WOMAN, TALKING GOD, Hero Twins (Born-for-Water and Monster Slayer), Thunders, Winds, and Failed-to-Speak People. The Holy People have the power to aid or harm people on earth. During certain ceremonies, they may be persuaded or coerced into aiding in the restoration of a person who has become ill through contact with them. They are unpredictable and not always well disposed toward Earth Surface People, ordinary human beings whom they created and who were ancestors of the Navajo (Dineh), but they may be on people's side on a particular occasion. The Holy People are powerful and mysterious and belong to the sacred world. They travel on sunbeams, rainbows, and lightning and live in an underworld. (See also SANDPAINTING; YEI.)

HOLY WAY CEREMONIES *Navajo (Dineh)* These two-, five-, or nine-night ceremonies are used to treat illnesses whose cause is attributed to the Holy People. One type of Holy Way ceremony is directed against the attack of the angry spirit, and the other restores and maintains peaceful conditions. The emphasis in one is on driving out evil caused by being struck by lightning, snakebite, bear maulings, and similar occurrences, and, in the other, on attracting good and summoning Holy People. The Holy Way chant rituals are intended to render the patient immune to further attack. They are meant to cure the effects of breaking ceremonial restrictions, sexual excess, incest, or other sexual irregularities. A typical Holy Way chant consists of about 12 ceremonies, sets of acts and certain procedures, especially singing. There is a consecration of the HOGAN, unraveling of woolen strings, notification to humans and spirit beings of procedures within the hogan, sweats and emetics, offerings, bathing, SANDPAINTING, figure painting and token tying, eating mush, all-night singing, medicines, and dawn ceremonies. Objects from the singer's equipment are applied to the patient's body from the feet upward to the top of the head. During the ceremonial and for four days after, numerous restrictions on behavior are observed. In carrying out any Holy Way ceremony, there is always a particular causative factor in mind, and this affects the details of the ceremonial. The person arranging the ceremony requests a combination of rites. (See also NIGHT WAY.)

HOLY WIND *Navajo (Dineh)* A spiritual being that gives life, thought, speech, movement, and behavior to all living things and serves as the means of communication between all elements of the living world. The Holy Wind exists all around and within the individual, entering and departing through respiratory organs and the body's surface. It is conceived of as a single phenomenon, although it has various appearances, sizes, effects, and directions of rotation in different situations. It directs the movements of the body and leaves the body at death, going to the afterworld.

HOMALDO *(fl late 19th c.) Wintu* A Bole-Maru dreamer and prophet. Homaldo was a member of the rancheria (a small reservation) of Dachimchini in California. He became known as Jo or Mexican Jo after returning from Mexico, where he had learned the Spanish language. Influenced by the EARTH LODGE RELIGION of the religious leader NORELPUTUS, he prophesied that the Indian dead would return to life and that the end of the world was approaching. These beliefs gave way to the BOLE-MARU RELIGION, an outgrowth of the GHOST DANCE OF 1870. Homaldo contributed to the Bole-Maru's development and took its teachings to neighboring rancherias. He has been described as the first Bole-Maru dreamer among the Wintun. In contrast to LAME BILL'S doctrinal contributions to the religion, Homaldo was remembered more for his demonstrations of miracles.

HOME DANCE *Hopi* See NIMAN KACHINA CEREMONY

HOPI CEREMONIALISM *Hopi* Hopi ceremonies form a complex that symbolizes the traditional Hopi worldview. They depict a series of related ancient episodes, the annual rendering of which is believed necessary for the harmonious operation of the universe. Hopi believe if people do not carry out ceremonial obligations faithfully, the sun may not turn back from its winter "house"; rain may not fall; and plants, animals, and human beings may not be fertile. Hopi believe people must participate by performing certain rites at prescribed times in certain ways, and they must also participate with their emotions and thoughts by prayer. Hopi believe they are interrelated in a web of obligations that must func-

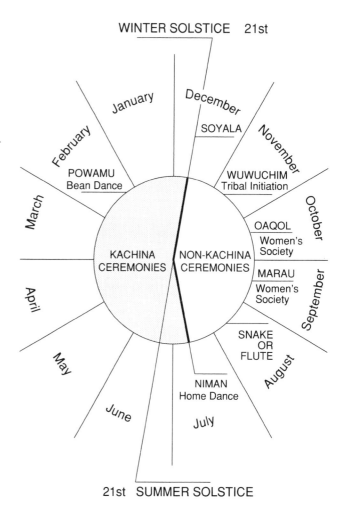

Hopi ceremonial calendar. A generalized schema shows names and time periods of Hopi ceremonies. There are variations in the cycle from mesa to mesa and village to village.

tion harmoniously for the perpetuation of all. Ceremonies are performed to initiate Hopi men into their religious duties, to carry out the necessary functions, to turn the sun back toward the Hopi country, to purify the villages, to renew the world and to ready the fields and children for fertility, growth, and fruition.

Hopi divide the year into halves. Day and night, summer and winter alternate in the upper and lower worlds. Seasons are reversed above and below. People live in the upper world from birth to death, return to the lower world at death, and are reborn. The year is also divided between rites performed by masked kachina dancers who impersonate the KACHINA spirits and ceremonies in which the kachinas do not appear. Around winter solstice, depending on the village and calendar, kachinas are thought to return to Hopi villages, and in mid-July, after summer solstice, they disappear or "go home" to the underworld. The ritual cycle requires reciprocity. Prayer offerings that "feed" spirits make obligatory requirements on them to reciprocate with rains so the crops will grow.

The Hopi calendar is almost identical for major villages, where ceremonies are organized, despite minor variations in the kachina cycle and other rituals from mesa to mesa. The entire course of the Hopi way of life unfolds every year in an annual cycle of religious ceremonies. The year may begin with WUWUCHIM, which enacts the emergence of people to the new world, the first fire and germination of life. SOYAL follows next, marking the winter solstice and the time when the people's dwelling place was erected on Earth and the Sun redirected on its course to give warmth to germinated life, and the first kachinas arrive to consecrate growth. The POWAMU CEREMONY follows when plant life appears, children are initiated into the Kachina and Powamu Societies, and the agricultural season, with the first kachina ceremony, starts. Some villages, however, begin with Soyal and still others with Powamu. These are followed by the summer ceremonies, NIMAN KACHINA, FLUTE, or the SNAKE-ANTELOPE ceremony. The annual cycle ends in the fall with ceremonies symbolizing maturity and fruition performed by women's societies, in a sequence that differs from village to village—LAKON, MARAW, and OWAQALT—and must end by Wuwuchim.

Every ceremony is an orchestrated unit combining movement, singing, drumming, impersonating, and painting to express the Hopi worldview. Each ceremony is owned or controlled by a single clan or by several. The ceremony is usually "given" to a clan before the emergence from the underworld by one or another of the spirits. A lineage within the clan is in charge of the ceremonial equipment and furnishes the chief official. Each ceremony is performed in a KIVA constructed by one or several clans. In the "parade" of ceremonies, representing the ceremonial year of the Hopi, each ceremony is under the direction of a certain clan. (See Subject Index for entries related to Hopi ceremonialism included in this volume.)

HOPI DANCES *Hopi* Hopi dances are divided into two categories, sacred and secular. The sacred dances include all KACHINA DANCES, the SNAKE-ANTELOPE CEREMONY dance, and the women's societies' dances, while secular dances include the butterfly, buffalo, eagle, and others. The Hopi believe that dances and the accompanying songs are powerful instruments and that their proper use ensures rain for crops, fertility, and prosperity for Hopi and all people on earth. (See also HOPI CEREMONIALISM.)

HOPPEL, JIMMY JACK (Jimmy Jack) *(1884–1969) Yurok* An Indian Shaker minister who introduced the religion among the Yurok at Requa, California. In 1919 he left his home in the town of Klamath, near Requa, after having family conflicts. He became a Shaker in 1926, resolving to change his life and to return home to preach among his own people. At Requa he began his mission, traveling from house to house to introduce the religion. Although conversions came slowly, Jimmy Jack eventually had enough followers to justify building a church. It was completed on his land near Klamath in the spring of 1927. Shakers from as far away as Mud Bay in Washington state attended its Easter Sunday dedication. The Shaker minister had relatives among the Tolowa and influenced members of that group who traveled to Requa to learn about the religion from him. He is also called Jimmy Jack. (See also INDIAN SHAKER RELIGION.)

HORDEN, JOHN *(1828–1893)* An Anglican missionary to the Cree people of Moose Factory on James Bay in Ontario. Horden was born in Exeter, England where he was later educated at St. John's School. After serving in a trade apprenticeship, he became affiliated with the CHURCH MISSIONARY SOCIETY in 1850. The following year he was sent to Moose Factory and remained there for the rest of his life. In 1872 he became the first Anglican bishop of Moosonee in Ontario. Besides baptizing many Native people, he translated biblical works into the Cree language. In this endeavor he convinced other Anglican workers of the value of using the syllabic system devised by the missionary JAMES EVANS. One of his workers was Thomas Vincent, a mixed-blood, who was noted for his missionary work in the area. Horden spent 42 years at Moose Factory and died there on January 12, 1893. He was married to Elizabeth Oke in 1851.

HORN CHIPS (Ptehe Woptuh 'a, Chips, Tahunska) *(1836–1916) Lakota* One of the most renowned holy men among the Lakota people. Horn Chips was a member of Chief Lip's Wajajes, a band of Brulé who joined another band, the Oglala, 1854. Known as the medicine man of the famous Lakota leader Crazy Horse, most of the details of his life remain a mystery. One account indicates that he lost his family when he was young and then lived with his grandmother. Laughed at by other children, he decided to end his life. On his way to an isolated area to kill himself, he heard a voice. It told him not to commit the deed, that he would achieve greatness. As instructed, he then went on a vision quest where he received a message from the spirit world.

Another account describes Horn Chips as a *HEYOKA* who helped Black Horse, a man who had sought him out after dreaming of thunder. Horn Chips supervised Black Horse's vision quest, then later interpreted his vision to mean that he was also to become a *heyoka*. The YUWIPI curing ritual, although believed to be older than the holy man, can also be traced to Horn Chips.

Various accounts describe the holy man as a friend, mentor or adopted relative of Crazy Horse. A descendant of Horn Chips indicates that the two, who were destined to be great men, lived in the same household for a period of time with Crazy Horse's uncle and that the uncle conducted a ceremony to make them brothers. The medicine man later provided spiritual guidance and assistance to the leader, protecting him by making him bulletproof.

Besides the gift of prophecy, the powers attributed to Horn Chips included the ability to change the weather, to find lost objects, and to locate missing people. At one time the holy man was reportedly tested by the Pine Ridge Agency superintendent who ordered a demonstration in a lighted room. The police chief wrapped and tied Horn Chips up himself and those present observed the appearance of flashing lights. After they disappeared, the holy man was untied.

Horn Chips continued his sacred ways until his death in 1916. He not only trained Black Horse and other apprentices but continued his legacy through his family. Several accounts note that the Moves Camp and Chips families, his relatives, continue to dominate Yuwipi practice at Wanblee and other areas of the Pine Ridge reservation in South Dakota. Horn Chips is also known as Chips or Tahunska (His Leggings).

The holy man JOHN LAME DEER stated: "Without him, maybe our religion would have died out. During the darkest years he kept his vision alive, worked it for the good of the people. . . . If he hadn't taught us, there would be no medicine men left among us now." (See also CHIPS, GODFREY.)

HORNFOLD See BOX ELDER

HORSEMAN SOCIETY See YAQUI CEREMONIALISM

HORTON, AZARIAH *(c. 1715–1777)* A minister and the first member of the Presbyterian Church to proselytize among American Indian tribes. Horton graduated from Yale in 1735 and was ordained by the New York Presbytery in 1740. The following year he began missionary work with the Native people living on the eastern end of Long Island. His mission included the establishment of a church at Poosepatrick, south of Brookhaven, and another at Shinnecock, west of Southampton. He also became the pastor in South Hanover, New Jersey, after the congregation's separation from Hanover in 1748. Horton's pastorate in the community known for a period as Battle Hill and then Madison ended in November, 1776. He died on March 2, 1777 at the age of 62.

HOUSE BLESSING RITE *Navajo (Dineh)* The blessing of a new home, a ceremony in itself, is part of the general BLESSING WAY rite. It involves laying new oak sprigs in the HOGAN walls at the cardinal directions, sprinkling the places with cornmeal, saying appropriate prayers, and singing required songs.

HUBBARD, JEREMIAH *(1837–1915)* A Quaker who served as a missionary to Wyandot (Huron), Seneca, Ottawa, Modoc, and other Native groups in Indian Territory (present-day Oklahoma). He was born on April 7, 1837, to Joseph and Matilda Hubbard in Henry County, Indiana. After attending Indiana schools, he served as a teacher in Indiana, Missouri, Kansas, and Indian Territory for more than 20 years. In the winter of 1879–80 he left teaching to begin missionary work. A short time later Hubbard received a request from the executive committee of Friends on Indian Affairs to work with the people of Quapaw Agency in Indian Territory on a part-time basis. Hubbard, known as "Uncle Jerry," continued his native ministry until he retired in 1913. His autobiography, *Forty Years Among the Indians,* was published in 1913, two years before his death, in Miami, Oklahoma. Hubbard and his wife, Mary G. Sheward Hubbard, had 10 children.

HUNKA CEREMONY *Lakota* One of the SEVEN SACRED RITES OF THE LAKOTA foretold by WHITE BUFFALO CALF WOMAN. Translated as the making of relatives, its purpose was to establish a binding relationship among fellow human beings. According to an account by BLACK ELK, the Lakota holy man Matohoshila (Bear Boy) received the ceremony in a vision. In his vision, Matohoshila saw a patch of corn, which he later saw while traveling away from home. Not knowing who it belonged to, the holy man picked it and took it back to his people just as the vision foretold. Messengers of the Arikara, an enemy of the Lakota, subsequently arrived with gifts to ask for the return of their sacred plant. Matohoshila, understanding the meaning of the vision, told his people that the exchange would fulfill one of the seven sacred rites, establishing an enduring friendship and peace with the Arikara that would be an example to other nations.

After setting up a sacred tipi as the Lakota holy man instructed, the Arikara visitors selected a man to represent their entire nation, and he was later offered the pipe by Matohoshila, who represented the Lakota Nation. Preparations were then made for the rite according to the holy man's instructions. During the Hunka ceremony, which lasted for several days, ritual activities were carried out by both the Lakota and the Arikara. They included prayers, songs, purification, and offerings. During part of the ceremony, the Arikara were instructed to pretend to scout for the enemy, the Lakota. As they performed, they sang songs and waved cornstalks symbolizing the movement of the corn when the Great Spirit's breath was upon it. After "capturing" Matohoshila and other participants, the Arikara exchanged gifts with the Lakota, then led a procession. Five Lakota "captives," including a woman and two small children, who represented their entire nation, were led to the sacred lodge. There they were hidden behind buffalo robes and painted with symbolic red and blue colors. When they emerged, they had undergone a sacred transformation representing their new relationship and obligations. The ceremony concluded with prayers, offerings, and a feast.

Other accounts of the Hunka indicate that it was performed in early times but that it later took on particular ritual form. A Lakota winter count, a pictographic record or calendar noting "they sang over each other with horsetails," referring to the wands waved during the ceremony, corresponds to the year 1805. The relationships created during the ritual were strong, sacred bonds. Two people could become brothers, sisters, brother and sister, father and child, or mother and child. A Hunka helped his or her kin as needed, sometimes at great sacrifice. According to Black Elk, the sacred rite established peace within an individual, between two people, and between two nations.

HUNT, JAKE (Titcam Nashat, Earth Thunderer) *(c. 1860s–c. 1910–1914) Klickitat* Founder of the Waptashi, or FEATHER RELIGION. Hunt was born during the 1860s in the Klickitat community of Husum, Washington, on the White Salmon River's east bank. He was raised in the WASHANI RELIGION, following the teachings of SMOHALLA, but was later influenced by the INDIAN SHAKER RELIGION through a leader named Wasco Jim, who conducted a healing ceremony for Hunt's ill son. He failed to cure the boy but succeeded in converting a number of Husum residents. Hunt was also influenced by a vision told to him by Wasco Jim in which the Shaker healer was instructed to wear buckskin trousers and to use feathers in his religious services. Hunt converted to the Shaker faith after he was informed that his wife, Minnie Coon, who became ill soon after their son, could not be healed unless he joined that religion. Despite efforts to save her, Minnie died a month after her son's death. Hunt then turned against the Shakers and withdrew from the group.

Hunt's religious beliefs were also formed by a vision his niece had during his son's funeral. She saw LISHWAILAIT, the Klickitat prophet, standing in the center of a circular disk of light, which symbolized an area of land. He was dressed in traditional clothing, wore two eagle feathers in his hair, and carried a small drum and drumstick.

After Minnie Coon died, Hunt had the same vision, and it led to his establishment of the Waptashi faith. Hunt's vision instructed him to stop grieving for his wife and son, to make a hand drum to use in religious services, and to gain converts in seven lands. He erected a longhouse in his home

community, took a new name, Titcam Nashat, and began preaching. He was joined in his efforts by four of his sisters who helped him establish the Waptashi religion.

The new faith incorporated features of both Washani and Shaker practices. Hunt continued to follow FIRST FOOD OBSERVANCES and other traditional practices, but he added the Shaker prohibition against alcohol use and aspects of the Shaker curing or healing rituals. Unlike the Washani faith of Lishwailait, Hunt was the only person who could receive spiritual power from the Creator. At his ceremonies, held on Sundays, he expanded the use of eagle feathers, and converts either held them or wore them in their hair. Another feature expanded by the Waptashi prophet was the use of mirrors representing the disk of his vision. Hunt also established an initiation rite that included the spinning of initiates, during which they saw images of ancestors, and ritualized vomiting to cleanse themselves of sin.

After establishing the Waptashi religion among Husum's Klickitat, Hunt began seeking converts in other areas. He succeeded in gaining followers among the Wishram band up the Columbia River at Spearfish, where he built a longhouse and remarried. He eventually converted among the Rock Creek band, still farther up the river, then traveled to other communities. After failing to cure a dying young man on the Umatilla Reservation in Oregon, Hunt was retaliated against by the Bureau of Indian Affairs agent there. The agent, who opposed traditional religious practices, ordered that Hunt's hair be cut and his sacred objects destroyed. He also ordered the holy man to choose between incarceration or banishment from the Umatilla Reservation. The trip, Hunt's longest, took place between 1905 and 1907 and ended with his return to Husum. Hunt died sometime between 1910 and 1914 at Spearfish, and the Waptashi faith reportedly declined with his passing.

HUNTER, JAMES *(1817–1881)* An Anglican missionary who worked among the Cree at The Pas, on the Saskatchewan River, and later in the Canadian Northwest. Hunter, who was born in England, began his Indian mission efforts in 1844 under the auspices of the CHURCH MISSIONARY SOCIETY and remained at The Pas for about 10 years. He and his wife completed a number of biblical translations and other materials. Before going to the Yukon, Hunter was placed in charge of St. Andrew's Church at the Red River Settlement and was appointed archdeacon of Cumberland. In 1858 he traveled to the Canadian Northwest and initiated Church of England missionary efforts, to the resentment of Oblate clergymen, in the Mackenzie River region. After returning to England in 1864, Hunter held the vicar position at St. Matthew's Church at Bayswater in London until his death in 1881. His treatise, *A Lecture on the*

Grammatical Construction of the Cree Language, was published in London in 1875.

HUNTER'S ASSOCIATION *Keresan Pueblos* Headed by a priest, this organization of men helped hunters secure game. It is in charge of the Buffalo Dance, in which bison, deer, and antelope are impersonated. Membership in the group is voluntary, and only those who have been duly initiated (in four-day rites) may possess the knowledge. They have a ceremonial house in which rituals are performed and paraphernalia is kept. Before communal hunts, the society performed rituals that gave hunters power over their prey.

HUNTING CEREMONIALS *Inuit* These ceremonies, like the BLADDER FESTIVAL, honor an animal that is hunted and provides nourishment. They involve elaborate contrivances rigged up to be moved by strings, ceremonial paddles, and portrayals of hunting scenes and of animal behavior, often with the use of masks, followed by the distribution of goods. (See also CARIBOU FESTIVAL.)

HUNTING DANCE *Seminole* A dance described among the Cow Creek Seminole in Florida; also called Snake Dance. Performed during the full moon in September or October, its purposes included praying for good hunting and protection from snake bites for the hunters. A 1946 account indicated that the ceremony was held for nearly a week and included one night of hunting. Three Seminole men conducted the ceremony, assisted by two boys who served as "deer tail bearers." Both males and females attended the Hunting Dance. Its ritual elements included ball games, snake dances, hunting, and a concluding feast of game and other foods.

HUNTING HORSE (Old Man Horse) *(c. 1846–1953) Kiowa* Renowned ROADMAN comparable in stature to other influential peyote leaders such as QUANAH PARKER, JOHN RAVE, and JOHNATHAN KOSHIWAY. Hunting Horse, who lived to be 107, was baptized a Methodist in 1900. He and his son Cecil Horse were both active as peyotists and as members of the Methodist Church. Hunting Horse is known to have conducted a peyote ceremony attended by I-See-O, the early Kiowa peyotist and military scout, and visiting military officers from Fort Sill, Oklahoma, in 1923. DELOS KNOWLES LONEWOLF served as the interpreter of the event, which was recorded in a newspaper account. Hunting Horse, also a former military scout, was buried with military honors when he died in 1953. His name also appears as Old Man Horse.

HUNTING RITUALS *Montagnais-Naskapi* The Montagnais-Naskapi believe that animals have a spiritual existence similar to people. This belief leads to a number of practices linked to every phase of hunting. Each hunter bears the responsibility to propitiate the spirits of killed animals through rituals because animal spirits may revenge themselves and harm the hunter. The hunter who is ignorant or who willfully disregards proper rituals to appease the animal spirits may cause the disappearance of game or may bring famine, starvation, illness, or death to himself. A complex relationship must be observed between the hunter's soul and the spirit of animals he hunts. The hunter feels he is in constant debt to animals for the sacrifice of their lives on his behalf. This sacrifice must be acknowledged by observing proper behavior toward animal spirits through observance of the dictates of the soul and toward the body of the animal itself. The bear in particular is subject to complex ceremonies directed at appeasing its spirit. After it is killed, there are complicated procedures for disposing of flesh, skin, fur, and bones, as well as special dances and food taboos. (See BEAR CEREMONIALISM.)

HUNUNWE *(?–c. 1890s) Waiem* A Washani religious leader. Hununwe, a member of the Waiem tribe, later lived on the Umatilla Reservation in Oregon. She was brought up in the WASHANI RELIGION, practicing it from childhood. After experiencing a temporary death that lasted about four days, she returned to life. Hununwe got out of her coffin and began teaching what she had learned in the spirit world. Besides telling the people that the country was created for Native Americans, she told them to follow the precepts of the Washani religion. Hununwe prophesied that she would return permanently to the spirit world in four years. She served as a Washani leader at Cayuse until her prophecy came true. Hununwe was said to have allowed only traditional buckskin clothing, rather than cloth clothes, at her longhouse services. She was married to Nukshai, a Walla Walla, who assumed the religious leadership after her death. Hununwe was described as "one of the best preachers anywhere around" by a Waiem man who remembered her.

HURLBURT, THOMAS *(1808–1873)* Methodist missionary and linguist. Hurlburt was born to Hannah (Mosier) Hurlburt and Heman Hurlburt in Augusta, Upper Canada on March 3, 1808. Although he evidently received a good education, little is known about his schooling. His 45-year career as a missionary began in 1828 with a position at Muncey in Middlesex County. He was sent to the Saugeen band near Lake Huron in 1834 and was ordained a year later. Other Canadian placements eventually included St. Clair, Lake Superior, Alderville, Rice Lake, Norway House, Garden River, and Manitoulin Island missions. In 1837 he was sent to the St. Clair mission, where he began assisting the Reverend JAMES EVANS in the development of a Cree orthography. He also continued this work at the Lake Superior mission, which became known as Pic River. He mastered several Native dialects, and it was said that he was the only Methodist worker in the country who could preach to Indian people without the aid of an interpreter. In 1861 he began producing a monthly journal in Ojibway and English called *Petaubun* ("Peep of Day") at the Sarnia mission station in Ontario. With the exception of five years of ministerial work among non-Indians, Hurlburt's career included service in nearly every Methodist Native mission of the day in Canada. He also worked for seven years, from 1844 to 1851, at missions in Missouri and neighboring territory in the United States. Hurlburt was named as chairman of the Hudson Bay District in 1854, traveling to Norway House to begin the duties of the new post. His writings included *Evidences of the Glories of the One Divine Intelligence as Seen in His Works* (Toronto, 1867) and "A Memoir on the Inflections of the Chippewa Tongue" in the fourth volume of *Historical and Statistical Information Respecting the History, Conditions and Prospects of the Indian Tribes of the United States; collected and prepared under the direction of the Bureau of Indian Affairs per Act of Congress of March 3d, 1847* (Philadelphia, 1851–1857), edited by Henry R. Schoolcraft. He also translated a number of religious works into Cree and Ojibway. Hurlburt worked mainly at St. Clair and Manitoulin Island missions at the end of his life. He died on April 14, 1873.

HUSK FACE SOCIETY *Iroquois* One of a number of Iroquois medicine societies with its own ritual equipment, prayers, music, membership, and methods of curing for a specific illness. The societies represent agricultural spirits from the other side of earth who are the tutelaries of the society. Membership, for both men and women, comes through dream or cure. The society makes public performances in the longhouse at the MIDWINTER CEREMONY when they dispel disease. They appear as heralds for the False Faces during spring and autumn visitations of houses in the United States and Canada and act as door openers and police in the longhouse during the FALSE FACE CEREMONY. During the year, they participate in private feasts held to treat some person who has had a particular dream involving them, or they treat an uncured sickness. Ritual equipment includes masks made of cornhusks, hoes, and wooden shovels (and cornbread paddles at Six Nations Reserve). The Husk Face Society members have special powers to cure when they wear masks. They can handle hot coals without being burned, and they blow ashes on patients to cure them. They speak no language other than puffing. (See also MASKS [husk face mask]; MEDICINE SOCIETIES [Iroquois].)

HUYA ANIYA *Yaqui* The natural domain of the Yaquis before the Jesuits arrived. The realm of timeless events, where the YOANIA manifests itself, the source of all things (food and everyday objects), as well as the source of special powers of dance and song. After the Jesuits came and urged the building of towns, the *huya aniya* became a specialized part of a larger whole rather than the whole itself. It became the other world, the world surrounding the towns, structured places where everything contrasted sharply with all that was outside the towns. The power of the *huya aniya* came to individuals on an unsolicited, unexpected, and uncontrolled basis. An inhabitant of the *huya aniya* might appear to a Yaqui in a dream or vision. Yaqui believed that the dwellers of the *huya aniya*, the sources of the power there, were immortal, as were certain ancestral people who also lived in the *huya aniya*. These immortal beings who give the *huya aniya* its special qualities make their power available for human use when they choose. Yaqui make no material representations of these spirits.

INDIAN INMATES OF NEBRASKA PENITENTIARY V. GRAMMER (649 F. Supp. 1374 [D. Neb. 1986]) *(1986)* In this 1986 case, Indian inmates in Nebraska charged that the prison warden's refusal to allow them to use peyote in religious services violated their First Amendment rights and the AMERICAN INDIAN RELIGIOUS FREEDOM ACT OF 1978. Although the central role of peyote in the NATIVE AMERICAN CHURCH, supported by that act, was recognized, the court ruled that the prison's security needs superseded the First Amendment right to use peyote during Native American Church services. (See also PEYOTE RELIGION; Subject Index for related cases included in this volume.)

INDIAN SHAKER RELIGION A Native religion founded by JOHN SLOCUM (Squ-sacht-un), Squaxin, at Mud Bay, near Olympia, Washington. In 1881, Slocum became ill, apparently died, and subsequently returned to life with a divine mission to fulfill among Indian people. About a year later, following the construction of a church and the start of his religious work, he again fell ill. His subsequent recovery was attributed to the uncontrollable trembling experienced by his wife, MARY SLOCUM, as she approached his sickbed. The "shaking" was interpreted as a manifestation of divine power and became an important part of Shaker services. With this episode, interest in Slocum's message grew, and the new practice became known as the Indian Shaker Religion. The movement spread to tribes from California to British Columbia, acquiring unique local interpretations throughout the region. Blending Native and Christian beliefs, the Indian Shakers used crucifixes, candles, bells, and pictures in their churches. At first they rejected the Bible, accepting instead John Slocum's message as a direct revelation of the will of God. Opposition to the religion was manifested by the Indian agent Edwin Eells, who informed practitioners that two conflicting religions on the reservation would not be tolerated and that they were to accept the Christian missionary's guidance or not hold religious meetings. Assisted by attorney James Wickersham, the Shakers held a charter meeting on June 6, 1892, in public defiance of Eells to affirm their freedom to worship. Although white and Indian opponents disrupted this gathering, Wickersham issued official-looking documents to intimidate them from creating other disturbances. Subsequently, the Indian Shaker religion won its right to practice and has had Indian adherents through the present. Besides John Slocum, other religious leaders of the faith included AMELIA BROWN, NORMAN GEORGE and JIMMY JACK HOPPEL.

INFANTRY See YAQUI CEREMONIALISM

INITIATION CEREMONY *Cocopa* Boys and girls nearing marriage age were initiated in a combined ceremony as part of a big harvest fiesta or in connection with Keruk, the MOURNING CEREMONY. During the four-day ceremony, the boys' nasal septum was pierced and the girls' chin was tattooed. The ceremony was followed by 12 days of restrictions and ceremonies to ensure ritual purity to the initiates.

INITIATION CEREMONIES *Pueblo* Children from five to 12 years old are initiated into kivas, moieties, kachinas, and other tribal societies, which introduce them to full participation in ceremonial pueblo life and make them recognized members of the pueblo. Gravely ill children and adults may be dedicated to and initiated into societies once they are cured. Rituals of initiation may include choosing a ceremonial parent or sponsor, fasting from salt and meat, headwashing, naming, hunting in a sacred way, purification, retreats, ceremonial whipping with yucca switches, depositing prayersticks, present-giving by the family of the initiate, and observing taboos. During some initiations, initiates are treated as infants because they will be "reborn" through the ceremony, and in others, novices are brought into contact with fearful beings with which the society is associated. The initiate is frightened so he will no longer be afraid. The initiate receives ritual objects associated with membership, along with the right or duty to dance, cure, hunt, go on pilgrimages, or fight in special ways. Initiations may occur every four years when there are enough novices, or they may be performed at regular annual ceremonies as well. Initiations set up new family relationships between the family of the novice and the family of the initiate's sponsor or godparent.

I'N-LON-SCHKA *Osage* A religious ceremonial dance that the Osage received from the Ponca and the Kaw, or Kansa, tribal groups in the mid-1880s. It came to the Osage people after their removal from Kansas to Indian Territory in present-day Oklahoma and helped to sustain them during that period of great stress and upheaval. The I'n-Lon-Schka, which took the place of religious traditions practiced earlier in Kansas, has now survived for over a century. I'n-Lon-Schka, meaning "playground of the eldest son," honors an eldest son of the Osage people but also serves many other purposes. It is related to the Omaha GRASS DANCE, sharing a number of similar features. After receiving the ceremony from the Ponca and the Kaw, the people made it distinctively Osage.

The four-day I'n-Lon-Schka is held three weekends in June at three Osage communities in Oklahoma. It starts on Thursday afternoon and is held in large dance arbors at each site. At the center of I'n-Lon-Schka is a sacred drum, which is cared for and protected by an eldest son who is the Drumkeeper. It is treated with great respect and children are taught appropriate behavior in its presence. Each village owns its own drum, which remains in the community and is not allowed to be removed. Besides the Drumkeeper, other positions associated with the I'n-Lon-Schka include the chairman of the Dance Committee, committeemen, advisers, tail dancers (those selected for the honor of dancing a solo at the end of a song),

whipmen (officials bearing ceremonial whips to drive the dancers), water boys, head cook and assistant cooks, drum warmer, singers, and the town crier, who holds an honorary life appointment to call the dances and fulfill other duties. Because preparations for the ceremony occur throughout the year, I'n-Lon-Schka's influence extends beyond the June performances. Variations occur in each Osage community's ceremony, but ritual elements generally include a preliminary cedar-burning ceremony, opening prayers, the singing of 160–200 separate songs during the four days, dancing by the participants, feasts, and ceremonial giveaways. Other ceremonies associated with the I'n-Lon-Schka are the PASSING OF THE DRUM CEREMONY, ACCEPTANCE OF THE DRUM CEREMONY, and INTRODUCTION TO THE DANCE CEREMONY.

The I'n-Lon-Schka originated out of a warrior tradition, later including veterans of the United States armed services and other participants. After World War II, women were admitted to the dance area. Besides dancing on the outer edge of the arena, they are involved in many other aspects of the ceremony. The people follow the rules and regulations established by an Osage council in the 1880s, handed down by oral tradition. The I'n-Lon-Schka is maintained as a sacred religious ceremony and is never commercialized.

INTRODUCTION TO THE DANCE CEREMONY *Osage* In this ceremony an Osage male is introduced to the dance during breaks in the four-day I'N-LON-SCHKA observance. A boy or man of any age is eligible for the initiation but is required to know his clan affiliation and Osage name. He is generally presented by his parents and grandparents to the I'n-Lon-Schka dance chairman. Ceremonial features include tying a roach, a headdress associated with the earlier IRUSKA of the Pawnee, on the participant's head. The roach is now made with deer hair and other materials and an eagle feather is attached to its center. The feather is said to represent men and the red hair of the deer tail symbolizes fire. Another feature of the Introduction to the Dance Ceremony is the presentation of a giveaway by the family. After the gift-giving is concluded, the boy or man is taken to the appropriate area of dancers in the arena. He is then considered officially connected to the I'n-Lon-Schka Ceremonial Dance.

INUA *Inuit, Aleut* See PERSON

INUPIAT COMMUNITY V. UNITED STATES (746 F. 2d 570 [9th Cir. 1984], cert. denied, 474 U.S. 820 [1985]) *(1985)* In a series of legal actions in 1984, the Inupiat community in Alaska sought to protect its indigenous land base. It sued the United States, the secretary of the interior, the state of Alaska, and a number of oil companies for violating its rights in the Arctic slope area by drilling for oil. It also attempted to recover damages for trespass in their territory for the period prior to the passage of the Alaska Native Claims Settlement Act of 1971. The Inupiat community claimed that the United States had breached its trust responsibility by not protecting the Arctic slope area against development. In its challenge of the 1979 Beaufort Sea lease-sale on environmental grounds, the Inupiat community's religious claim was also addressed. The court concluded that the federal government's actions did not create a serious obstacle to the community's free exercise of religion. It further found that the government's interest in developing the area outweighed the alleged claim of religious interference. (See Subject Index for additional court cases dealing with religious freedoms.)

IROQUOIS CALENDRICAL CEREMONIES *Iroquois* Primarily held in the LONGHOUSE, these are ancient and public ceremonies for the community as a whole. The purpose is to give thanks to the Creator for the continued natural blessings of good weather, crops, and wild foods. Most of these ceremonies are related to subsistence activities, such as harvesting and hunting. There are around 17 calendar ceremonies spread over the year in a more or less fixed order and held at approximately the same time each year. Because each longhouse community is independent and manages its own affairs without reference to what other longhouses do, the number of ceremonies included in each longhouse ceremonial calendar varies, and the sequence of rites within ceremonies varies from longhouse to longhouse. Also, when the rite occurs, it may vary in details of execution from longhouse to longhouse. The typical cycle begins with the MIDWINTER CEREMONY, a New Year's ceremony, and is followed by the BUSH DANCE, the MAPLE FESTIVAL, SEED PLANTING CEREMONY, SUN AND MOON CEREMONY, After Planting Ceremony, STRAWBERRY FESTIVAL, RASPBERRY CEREMONY, BLACKBERRY CEREMONY, BEAN CEREMONY, THUNDER DANCE, LITTLE CORN CEREMONY, GREEN CORN, OUR LIFE SUPPORTER DANCES, HARVEST FESTIVAL, and End of Summer Ceremony. These ceremonies predate the traditions of the HANDSOME LAKE RELIGION and are performed substantially the same way as they were in precontact times. (See also IROQUOIS CEREMONIALISM; LONGHOUSE RELIGION.)

IROQUOIS CEREMONIALISM *Iroquois* The Iroquois ceremonies are concerned with rituals of thanksgiving and hope and rituals of fear and mourning. The ceremonial year is divided into two periods, one under male control, the other under female control. The winter ceremonies are sponsored by the men, and the women are sponsors during the summer

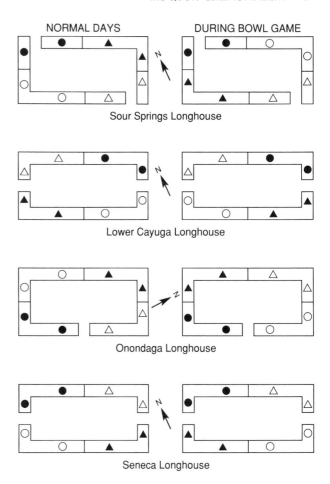

Iroquois ceremonial moiety. This diagram shows the seating during the Midwinter Ceremony at the four longhouses on the Six Nations Reserve, according to moiety affiliation and gender. Triangles symbolize men, circles, women; solid symbolizes the moiety that includes the Wolf Clan, open, the moiety that includes the Deer Clan. The four longhouses differ among themselves in assigning clans to moieties and in the labels for the moieties. *Reprinted by permission of the Smithsonian Institution Press from Handbook of North American Indians: Northeast (vol. 15), edited by Bruce G. Trigger. Smithsonian Institution 1979. p. 459, fig. 11.*

ceremonies. At the conclusion of the BOWL GAME on the last day of the MIDWINTER CEREMONY, the chiefs formally transfer the duties of the presiding officers to the women, who take full charge of subsequent rites in the longhouse until the conclusion of the GREEN CORN ceremony in August at the maturity of corn. At that time, the women turn official duties back to the chiefs.

There has been a great deal of tribal and local political autonomy, owing in part to the great distances that separate Iroquois villages. There were no national or confederate religious gatherings until after 1800, with the advent of the HANDSOME LAKE RELIGION. Therefore, although the same ceremonies are shared by the longhouses, local groups in

New York and Canada time their ceremonies differently. Midwinter begins at different times on the various Iroquois reservations. Summer dances depend on weather and ripening of crops and thus begin at different times in New York and Canada.

The tribe itself is divided into two ceremonial halves. Each moiety is complementary to the other, and all action between the two groups is reciprocal. For certain ceremonies, longhouses are spatially organized into halves, or moieties. Each moiety considers half of the longhouse, with its stove, door, and seating as its own. The CONDOLENCE CEREMONY, ceremonial dances and games, and preparation of ceremonial foods and other ritual events also employ this duality. On each side there are two groups, one composed of males, the other of females. Each group has a leader, referred to as "head," a permanent office to which he or she is elected. Ritual leadership is vested in one of the moieties on each ceremonial occasion. At the Sour Springs longhouse in Canada, leadership changes for each occasion, but at the Onondaga and Seneca longhouses in New York, one moiety holds leadership for an entire year.

Ceremonialism involves the use of Iroquois languages for public announcements, speeches and prayer, reciprocity in behavior between sexes and moieties, feasts of special foods appropriate to the occasion, song and dance, burning of Indian tobacco, the THANKSGIVING ADDRESS, which opens and closes almost every ritual occasion, interpreting dreams and acting out what they require, confession of sins, and special ritual paraphernalia. (See also IROQUOIS CALENDRICAL CEREMONIES; LONGHOUSE RELIGION; MEDICINE SOCIETIES [Iroquois].)

IRUSKA *Pawnee* A society whose members had the ability "to extinguish the life in the fire" or overcome other medicine powers. The original membership consisted of doctors or medicine men who were the leaders of various Pawnee societies. As doctors, their healing powers included the treatment of burns. According to one account, Crow-feather, a member of the society, was given the Iruska Dance. Unlike other members, he was not a medicine man. Crow-feather, who never participated in ceremonies, was known to wander the hills alone. One time, while he was out, he noticed smoke rising in the distance. Approaching it, he observed strangers roasting corn around a fire. Besides handling the hot corn, they sang songs and manipulated the fire with their hands. Before long, Crow-feather was invited to participate. The mysterious people told him that they were saddened by his cries and decided to give him a new dance. He was instructed to call it *iruska*, meaning the "fire inside of all things," and to take part in a difficult ceremony before being given the sacred teachings. Its ritual elements included sing-

ing, dancing toward a kettle of water on a fire, and a mock attack on an enemy. During the ceremony, the mysterious strangers swung hot corn husks at Crow-feather. After he ignored the burns and other attempts to scare him away, the participants placed him over the fire. Crow-feather at first screamed from the pain but eventually failed to feel it. The ceremony concluded with singing, four charges and retreats of the dancers toward the fire, the transformation of the participants into birds or animals, and the departure of all but one participant. He told Crow-feather to go home with four husks of burned corn and to return the following day for an explanation of the ceremony.

Upon returning, Crow-feather participated in another ceremony and was given a headdress, a dance belt or bustle, and additional teachings. After concluding a series of meetings with his instructor, Crow-feather gave him gifts and thanks. Crow-feather then introduced the Iruska and its teachings to qualified participants among his people. He built a sweat lodge, then invited eight medicine men to determine if they understood the fire. The four individuals who survived the test became singers for the ceremonies to be held. Preparations included avoiding contact with women for 30 days, daily bathing in the creek, the singing of songs 40 times, and the announcement of the upcoming dance. After a specified time, the ceremony was held. Ritual elements included smoke offerings, the initiation of candidates, and dancing through the singing of 40 songs. After bathing the following morning, the participants were painted, and a smoking ceremony was conducted. Other features included a mock attack on the fire by the dancers, the retrieval of meat with bare hands from a boiling kettle, and the whipping of participants with corn husks that had been dipped into the hot liquid. When the dancing concluded, Crow-feather taught the members to make Iruska headdresses and bustles, explaining their symbolic meanings. Another meaning of the term *iruska* or *irushka* is said to refer to the headdresses worn by the participants.

Names for this ceremony attributed to other tribal groups include Hethushka (Omaha), Helocka (Iowa), Helucka (Kansa), and Heyoka (Lakota). (See also KETTLE DANCE.).

IRVIN, SAMUEL M. *(1812–1887)* A missionary who established a Presbyterian mission among the Iowa, Sac, and Fox peoples in present-day Kansas. A native of Pennsylvania, Irvin began working among these groups in 1837, the year they were removed from their lands in what is now Missouri. Working under the auspices of the AMERICAN BOARD OF COMMISSIONERS FOR FOREIGN MISSIONS (ABCFM), Irvin's first nine years among the Native people were spent primarily in their homes instructing them. In 1843 he received a printing press from New York, one of the first in the region.

Irvin and his colleague, the Reverend William Hamilton, produced a number of Indian-language publications, including an elementary book, a children's catechism, a hymnal and an Iowa grammar. In 1845 the ABCFM began constructing a new mission building, which eventually housed a boarding school. Progress at the school was slow, and the enrollment remained low. In 1854 Irvin indicated that most of the children enrolled were orphans and that they included Blackfeet, Iowa, Sac, Fox, Sioux, and Pawnee students. He and his wife remained at the mission until it closed in about 1863. Irvin then devoted his efforts to Highland University, which was established in the same area. He died in 1887.

ITIWANA *Zuni* A ceremonial name for Zuni pueblo, meaning both "middle place" and "middle time." The dual nature of the term reflects the Zuni belief that the center of space is also the center of time. Zuni is thought to be the middle of the cosmos, around which all activity takes place, and ceremonies are held at the "middle times" of the year, about December 22, the winter solstice, and June 22, the summer solstice. During a 20-day period designated as *itiwana,* during the winter and summer solstice months, ceremonies go on in which all ceremonial societies come together that perform in turn the rest of the year. (See ZUNI CEREMONIALISM.)

J

JACK AND CHARLIE V. R. ([1985] 4 C.N.L.R.) *(1985)* A legal case involving the practice of Native religion considered by the Supreme Court of Canada in 1985. Anderson Jack and George Louie Charlie, members of the Tsartlip band who lived on the Tsartlip Indian Reserve in Saanich, British Columbia, were charged with hunting and killing a deer out of season in violation of the Wildlife Act (R.S.B.C. 1979, c. 433). The appellants testified that they had committed the deed to help their relative, Elizabeth Jack, obtain raw deer meat for a burning ceremony on behalf of the spirit of her great-grandfather. Extensive evidence presented in the case indicated that the religious practice was carried out among the Coast Salish people who believe that spirits of the deceased linger near where they once lived and that their needs, including hunger, must be addressed by the living. It further indicated that the traditional ceremony was genuine and that the accused were sincere in their beliefs. Counsel for Jack and Charlie contended that the Wildlife Act interfered with the freedom of religion of their clients and that it should be held inapplicable to them. Among the points discussed in the case was whether defrosted or stored deer meat, as a trial judge suggested, would have been suitable for the burning ceremony. The appellants contended that the use of such meat would be sacrilegious. The Supreme Court of Canada ruled against Jack and Charlie on October 31, 1985. The Court held that the Wildlife Act neither prohibited the burning ceremony nor interfered with the appellants' freedom of religion. Other important Canadian religious freedom cases include *BEARSHIRT V. THE QUEEN* and *REGINA V. MACHEKEQUONABE.*

JACKSON, HENRY *(fl. mid-19th century) Achomawi* Leader of the EARTH LODGE RELIGION on the Klamath Reservation in Oregon. An Achomawi or Atsugewi from the Pit River area of California, Jackson was captured and enslaved by Modoc people. After a treaty was negotiated, he remained among the Klamath, Modoc, and Paviotso (Numu, Northern Paiute) people on the reservation established by the agreement. Following the Modoc War of 1872–73, he and a fellow tribesman, PIT-RIVER CHARLEY, returned to California on a visit. They participated in ceremonies of the Earth Lodge Religion, a variation of the GHOST DANCE OF 1870, then in practice there. After attending dances at Falls City and Alturas, Jackson and Pit-River Charley returned to Oregon. In 1874 they began introducing the Earth Lodge beliefs at Yainax, located in the area known as the "Upper End" on the Klamath Reservation. Jackson remained there when Pit-River Charley left for the reservation's "Lower End." The movement then gained adherents in both areas. Jackson was said to communicate with the dead during trances and revealed teachings to his followers. He also led the dancing and singing at the ceremonies.

JACKSON, SHELDON *(1834–1909)* A Presbyterian clergyman whose missionary assignments started in Indian Territory (present-day Oklahoma) and culminated in Alaska. Born on May 18, 1834 in Minaville, New York, Jackson graduated from Union College in 1855 and Princeton Theological Seminary in 1858. His first assignment was at a school among the Choctaws in Indian Territory, but he only remained there from 1858 to 1859 because he suffered malaria attacks that forced him to seek a new location. During the 1860s Jackson served as a minister at two Minnesota churches, first in La Crescent and then in Rochester, which provided a base for missionary work over an extensive region. From 1869 to 1882 he was the superintendent for the Presbyterian Board of Home Missions in Montana, Wyoming, Utah, Colorado, New Mexico, and Arizona. In that capacity he helped organize seven presbyteries and three synods, after having established most of the churches in them. As pioneering editor from 1872 to 1882 of the publication that became the *Presbyterian Home Missionary,* Jackson was able to focus attention on the needs of frontier mission work. Jackson first visited Alaska in 1877, when he went there to see about starting missions. He later helped supervise both cultural and religious activities in the region and established a mission school and anthropological museum at Sitka. He worked with agents of other denominations to divide the mission field in the territory. From 1884 to 1909 he served as superintendent of the Presbyterian Board of Home Missions in Alaska and as editor of *North Star* between 1887 and 1897. In 1885 he became the first general agent for education in Alaska, traveling widely to implement elementary instruction throughout the region until his 1906 resignation from the position. Besides his work with churches and schools, Jackson sponsored the importation of reindeer from Siberia in 1891 to benefit Native subsistence. He died on May 2, 1909, in Asheville, North Carolina.

JACOBS, PETER (Pahtahsega, "He Who Comes Shining" or "One Who Makes the World Brighter") *(c. 1807–1890) Mississauga (Ojibway)* Methodist missionary. Born near Rice Lake north of Lake Ontario in Upper Canada, Pahtahsega's parents and other close relatives died when he was a young child, and he grew up poor and lonely. After seeking an education at Belleville, near the Bay of Quinte, about 1825, he received financial help for his school expenses from benefactors. He was called Peter Jacobs after the sound of his Ojibway name and was influenced to embrace Christianity by Reverend WILLIAM CASE and later by Reverend PETER JONES, a native missionary. Jacobs also attended the Credit Mission school. He eventually led prayers and served as an interpreter to the missionaries in their efforts to convert the Mississauga. In 1829 he received additional training under the auspices of the Dorcas Missionary Society. After maintaining a store in the early 1830s, he returned to missionary work in 1836. He later traveled with the Reverend JAMES EVANS to initiate Methodist efforts in the Lake Superior region. Besides founding stations, they established a number of religious and educational programs. Jacobs assisted Evans at Rossville near Norway House (Manitoba) and Fort Alexander (Manitoba) before leaving for England in 1842 to be ordained. Upon returning home, Jacobs

worked at Fort Frances on Lac La Pluie (Rainy Lake) until 1850 and later worked in other Ojibway reserves in Upper Canada. Jacobs was dropped from the Methodist conference in 1858, reportedly for raising funds in the United States without the sanction of his church. Although Jacobs may have reconverted in 1867, his later years were marked by alcoholism and poverty. Besides assisting other missionaries with translations, he wrote *Journal of the Reverend Peter Jacobs, Indian Wesleyan Missionary . . .* (Toronto, 1853). He died on September 4, 1890, at the Rama Reserve, near Orillia, Ontario. Jacobs had a daughter with his first wife, Mary, a member of the Credit band, who died in 1828. He was remarried in 1831 to Elizabeth Anderson, and they had five children. Two of his sons became missionaries of the Church of England. One of them, also named Peter Jacobs, worked with FREDERICK AUGUSTUS O'MEARA on Ojibway-language publications.

JAKALUNUS *(fl. late 1700s–early 1800s) Modoc* Famous shaman whose spiritual powers were legendary among his people. His spirits were said to give him extraordinary ability and protection. Besides fighting against tribal enemies on his behalf, they sent a warning whenever anything unusual occurred. One way they did this was to make one of the sacred objects in his home move around: according to one account, Jackalunus used his porcupine hairbrush at noon to determine if visitors were on the way. He also owned a pipe that lit up by itself once he had added tobacco. Although Jakalunus advised against it, a Klamath doctor insisted on making a trade for the pipe. The pipe did not remain with the new owner because the spirits returned it to the Modoc shaman's home. It is believed that Jakalunus remained alive for a time even after being shot with arrows by Klamath enemies.

JOGUES, ISAAC *(1607–1646)* French Jesuit missionary. Born in Orleans, France, he studied as a novice in the Society of Jesus from 1624 until 1636 when he was ordained a priest. That same year, he went to Quebec. He lived among the Huron for five years learning their language. The next five years he spent exploring the regions as far west as Sault Ste. Marie, where he introduced Catholicism. Captured by the Mohawk in 1642, he was permitted to live. While captive, he was able to baptize more than 60 children. In 1643, a Dutch missionary, JOHANNES MEGAPOLENSIS, helped free him. After several months of recovery in France, Father Jogues returned to Canada. He served as an ambassador for the French government during 1645, trying to secure peace with the Mohawk. After a treaty was signed in 1646, Father JEROME LALEMANT, superior of Jesuits in Quebec, decided to send Father Jogues to Iroquois country in order to maintain peaceful relations with Native people and to establish a

Catholic mission. Again captured by Mohawk, he was charged with bringing disease to Native people and he was killed in 1646 by members of the Mohawk Bear Clan who resented Jogues's interference in the tribe's civil and religious affairs. He was beatified in 1925 and canonized in 1930 by Pope Pius XI.

JOHNSON, JOHN See ENMEGAHBOWH

JOHNSON, THOMAS (1802–1865) Methodist missionary among the Shawnee and other Native groups in present-day Kansas. Johnson was born in Nelson County, Virginia, on July 11, 1802. After being admitted to the Missouri Annual Conference in 1826, he was sent to open a mission among the Shawnee in 1830. His brother, WILLIAM JOHNSON, was sent to the Kaw located on the Kansas River at the same time. Thomas learned the Shawnee language and expanded the mission work. Eventually, his efforts extended to 13 tribes, including the Delaware (Lenni Lenape), Kansas, Kickapoo, Peoria, Shawnee, and Wea. By 1838 Johnson sought funds from the general missionary society of his denomination and the federal government to build a school and dormitories to accommodate the increased numbers. He was successful, and brick buildings were constructed to house the Shawnee Manual Labor School and other missionary enterprises. In 1841 Johnson left the mission because of ill health but returned six years later to superintend the Shawnee work. After the removal of Native people from Kansas to Indian Territory (present-day Oklahoma), the school and mission declined, then closed. Johnson helped form the first Kansas territorial government, serving as president of the senate. He also continued to work with the declining population of Native people in the territory. He died of a bullet wound on January 2, 1865. Friends believed that his death was a consequence of his pro-Union Civil War stance.

JOHNSON, WILLIAM (1805–1842) A Methodist missionary who was sent in 1830 to establish the first Christian mission among the Kaw people. Born in Nelson County, Virginia, on February 2, 1805, Johnson immigrated to Missouri with his father in 1825. He was licensed to preach a short time later, appointed to the district of New Madrid in 1829. The following year he was named missionary to the Kaw, at a location about 10 miles from present-day Topeka, Kansas. His efforts there were interrupted when he was placed in charge of the Delaware (Lenni Lenape) mission in 1832 and was later placed among the Shawnee people. Johnson returned to the Kaw mission in 1835 and resumed his work. By then a log house and other out-buildings had been established for the work. He and his wife learned the Native language, finding it helpful in implementing their programs.

Johnson's second assignment to the Kaw lasted more than seven years. On April 6, 1842, he traveled to the Shawnee mission on business and died there a short time later. His brother THOMAS JOHNSON also worked among the Kaw.

JOIJOI (fl. 1870s) Mono Chief of the North Fork Mono and proselytizer of the GHOST DANCE OF 1870. Joijoi may have started practicing the new religion sometime early in 1871, after a Paiute missionary had visited his people in south-central California. He eventually traveled to Nevada to learn more about the Ghost Dance from a Paiute leader named Moman. Once the faith had been introduced among the North Fork Mono, Joijoi traveled, or sent emissaries, to groups farther south to preach the doctrine. He became influential in diffusing the new religion in the area. Joijoi sponsored the first Ghost Dance in his territory at a site called Saganiu in about May 1871. Many tribal groups were represented, including the Yokuts, Holkuma, Woponuch, and Western Mono. The first gathering included preaching of the new beliefs by Joijoi and another leader, the use of a pole in the center of the ceremonial space, face painting, alternating male and female dancers, and six nights of dancing. After the Saganiu dance, other dances were held in the region about once a month, but by 1875 they were no longer conducted.

JONES, DANIEL W. (1830–1915) Mormon missionary who worked among the Ute people and served as president of a mission in Mexico from 1876 to 1877. Jones was born to Wylie Jones and Margaret S. (Cloyd) Jones on August 6, 1830, in Boonslick, Missouri. After serving in the Mexican War, he traveled to Utah, where he was baptized in 1851. Jones later contributed to a Spanish-language translation of the Book of Mormon and wrote *Forty Years Among the Indians*. He died on April 29, 1915, in Mesa City, Arizona.

JONES, DAVID THOMAS (c. 1796–1844) Church of England missionary at the Red River settlement in present-day Winnipeg, Manitoba. It is likely that Jones, who was brought up farming, was born in Wales. After attending Lampeter Seminary there for two years, he was accepted as a candidate for mission work by the CHURCH MISSIONARY SOCIETY in 1820. He was ordained a deacon in December 1822 and became a priest in April 1823. By June 1, 1823, he was on his way to his new post and was writing entries in his journal. Jones succeeded JOHN WEST, the pioneering missionary, in his duties at Red River, the first Protestant mission established in the Canadian Northwest. Soon after his arrival, he met Peguis, a Saulteaux chief, and requested that Peguis send Indian boys to be educated. In 1824 Jones built Middle Church (St. Paul's) several miles from the original mission and later started a day school there. The following year, in response to his request for another worker, the Church Missionary Society sent WILLIAM COCKRAN to the area. In 1828 Jones went to England on a leave. When he returned, he was accompanied by his bride, Mary (Lloyd). In 1832 Jones proposed the establishment of a boarding school at Upper Church. Sometime after it was built, it was named the Red River Academy. Cockran was critical of Jones and his social ties with Hudson's Bay Company officials, and a rift developed between the two missionaries. Mary Jones, who assisted in the work of the mission, died on October 14, 1836. Devastated by her death, Jones decided to leave the area. He left for England with his children in 1838. Jones served as a curate, professor, and rector before his death on October 26, 1844, in Llangoedmor, Wales.

JONES, EVAN *(1788–1872)* A Baptist missionary who began his work among the Cherokee people in 1821 and remained with them until he died. Born in Brecknockshire, Wales, on May 14, 1788, Jones lived in England until immigrating to America in 1821. He and his family settled near Philadelphia, where they joined a Baptist church. Jones volunteered to help establish the Valley Towns Mission in eastern Tennessee under the auspices of the Baptist Foreign Mission Board. He and his family joined their pastor, the Reverend Thomas Roberts, in the work. Jones was ordained to the ministry on August 21, 1824, and became superintendent of the mission the following year. Among the difficulties he encountered were language barriers, budgetary constraints, and competition from Cherokee *adonisgi,* or medicine men, and Methodist missionaries.

He later faced more serious problems. In 1833 he was placed on trial for murder in a case involving the deaths of his sister-in-law and her newborn baby during childbirth. Although he and his wife were acquitted, rumors about the scandal persisted. An opponent of the policy of removal of Native Americans from their homeland, Jones was expelled from the Cherokee Nation by the federal government in August 1836 for his role in the resistance. He was later appointed by John Ross, the principal chief, to help lead a contingent of Cherokee people to Indian Territory (present-day Oklahoma). Jones was federally expelled from the Cherokee Nation a second time in 1839.

The expulsion order was not rescinded by the federal government until March 29, 1841. Jones then began rebuilding his missionary efforts around full-blood tribal members, as he had in the east. He edited the Baptist journal, *The Cherokee Messenger,* the first periodical to be published in Indian Territory. He also continued his work on biblical translations. After his northern mission board ordered the Baptist workers among the Cherokee to expel slaveholders from church membership, Jones and his son, the Reverend JOHN BUTTRICK

JONES, became actively opposed to slavery. They were instrumental in organizing the Ketoowah Society, a secret antislavery society that appeared in the 1850s, to counter the Knights of the Golden Circle, a proslavery group among the Cherokee people. In the furor over the slavery issue, John B. Jones was ordered to leave the Cherokee Nation by the federal agent, Robert J. Cowart, for supporting abolitionism.

Evan Jones remained among the Cherokee until shortly after the Civil War broke out, then left for Lawrence, Kansas. He continued his efforts there, supporting the Union struggle. In 1863 Jones was appointed to represent the Cherokee Nation in Washington, D.C. by assisting Chief John Ross and other members of the tribal delegation in their negotiations with the federal government. Two years later, on November 7, 1865, he and his family were granted citizenship by the Cherokee National Council. Jones retired from mission work in 1870. He died on August 17, 1872, and was buried at Tahlequah in present-day Oklahoma. Evan Jones was married to Elizabeth Lanigan in 1808. She imigrated to America with him and assisted in his missionary efforts at Valley Towns. After her death on February 5, 1831, Jones married Pauline (or Paulina) Cunningham.

JONES, FLORENCE (Pui-lu-li-met, "Eastern Flower-Woman") *(b. 1909) Wintu.* Doctor of ancient healing practices of the Wintu people. Baptized a Methodist, during her childhood she had encounters with tribal animal spirits. At 17 she experienced her first trance, after which older Wintu shamans cared for her and established her as a shaman in her own right. During her trances, her spirit helpers (the spirits of animals, souls of departed relatives, spiritual forces residing in sacred places, and so forth) appeared after being summoned through appropriate rituals.

She diagnosed illnesses with the diagnostic powers of spirit helpers acting through her hands during a healing seance. She also sucked "PAINS" from patients, predicted locations of lost objects or lost souls, and administered traditional herbal medicines to patients of her own and neighboring tribes. In January 1987 Florence Jones retired from most of her doctoring duties and confined her practice to doctoring among her people. She oversaw the education of several young Wintuns in healing practices. She held public ceremonies at Mount Shasta around Easter and mid-August each year. When not in use, Florence Jones's doctoring paraphernalia, always treated with great respect, was hidden. On August 13, 1995, Florence Jones retired from doctoring during a ceremony that took place on Wintun sacred grounds.

JONES, JOHN BUTTRICK *(1824–1876)* A northern Baptist missionary in the Cherokee Nation from 1855 to 1874. His parents, Elizabeth (Lanigan) and EVAN JONES, began working with the Cherokee at Valley Towns mission in eastern Tennessee in 1821. Jones spent his childhood there, becoming as fluent in the Cherokee language as the Native people were. He attended an academy in Sylvia, Arkansas, and Madison University in Hamilton, New York. Jones graduated from Rochester Theological Seminary in June 1855 and was ordained a month later. He then went to Indian Territory (present-day Oklahoma), where he resumed missionary work with his father. His efforts included working on translations, traveling on preaching tours, supervising churches, and training Indian ministers. Jones and his father also played a leading role in the establishment of the traditional Keetoowah Society, a secret organization formed in the 1850s. Its activities included countering pro-slavery forces in the Cherokee Nation. In 1860 the federal agent expelled Jones from the Cherokee Nation because of his abolitionist activities. Fearing mob action against him if the authorities removed him to Arkansas, he left in secret for Alton, Illinois.

Jones hoped to continue his Cherokee translations in exile, but his mission board would not support the work. He eventually traveled to East Rodman, New York, where he served as a pastor of two churches in the area. After receiving a commission as chaplain of the Third Indian Home Guard Regiment in 1862, he worked with Cherokee refugees of the Civil War. Between 1863 and 1865 he ministered to the sick, held services, and taught freedmen. After resigning his military chaplaincy in May 1865, Jones sought support for Cherokee reconstruction. After working temporarily as a federal pension agent, he received an appointment to Indian Territory under the auspices of the Baptist Home Mission Board. Headquartered in the Cherokee Nation, he began the work of rebuilding after the war. Jones also undertook work for the Cherokee Council, including translating treaties and preparing bilingual textbooks. He became a citizen of the Cherokee Nation when its National Council passed an act granting citizenship to him, his father, and their families on November 7, 1865.

In 1870 he was appointed federal agent under GRANT'S PEACE POLICY, holding the position until 1874. During that period he opposed efforts to put the Cherokee Nation under territorial government, tried to resolve court jurisdictional problems, and attempted to protect tribal boundaries and resources from intruders. Jones died on June 13, 1876.

JONES, PETER (Kahkewaquonaby, "Sacred Feathers")

(1802–1856) Mississauga (Ojibway) A Canadian Ojibway leader and Methodist missionary. Kahkewaquonaby was born on January 1, 1802, in Burlington Heights, above Lake Ontario, to a Mississauga mother, Tuhbenahneequay, and a Welsh father, Augustus Jones. He grew up among his mother's people in their community on the northwestern

Peter Jones (Kahkewaquonaby). Portrait of the 19th-century Mississauga missionary, April 1832. This is one of at least two paintings done by Matilda Jones, an English portrait artist, at her studio in London. *Victoria University Library, Toronto.*

shore of Lake Ontario. At the age of 14, he went to live with his father and Mohawk stepmother at Grand River near present-day Paris, Ontario, and remained with them for seven years. During that period Kahkewaquonaby worked on the family farm, attended school, and became known as Peter Jones. In 1823 Jones converted to Christianity at a revival meeting presided over by the Methodist missionary WILLIAM CASE. A short time later, he began a career devoted to spreading Christianity among the Ojibway and other tribal groups, serving as interpreter, translator, and missionary. The Credit River Mississauga, his mother's people, appointed Jones as chief after the incumbent, John Cameron, died in 1828. As a leader, he struggled to retain tribal lands and to establish model Christian communities and schools.

During the course of his career, Jones made three trips to Britain. The first, in 1831, was a fund-raising tour for the Upper Canadian Methodists of London, Bristol, Birmingham, and other English communities. He preached more than 60 sermons and made numerous speeches on North American Indians. He also had an audience with royalty and met his bride-to-be, Eliza Field, whom he married in New York City on September 8, 1833. On a subsequent trip, in October 1837, Jones went to England as an official representative of the Credit River Mississauga to present a petition to Queen Victoria seeking title deeds for the Mississauga reserves in Canada. As the tribal group had already surrendered large territories to the English Crown, it sought to secure the remaining lands from the threat of removal or dispossession. His third trip, in 1845, was undertaken to raise funds for a residential school and an accompanying model farm. On August 4, 1845, he was photographed in Edinburgh, Scotland, and the calotypes taken became identified as the oldest surviving photograph of a Native North American.

Jones translated hymns, scriptures, and other religious materials into the Ojibway language. His linguistic work benefitted other missionaries, including JAMES EVANS and THOMAS HURLBURT, who eventually competed against him for translation assignments from their superiors. Jones wrote *A Collection of Chippeway and English Hymns for the Use of the Native Indians,* an 1840 publication that was reprinted numerous times and in use as recently as 1969. After his death in 1856, two books based on his notes and diaries were published: *Life and Journals of Kah-ke-wa-quo-na-by* (1860) and *History of the Ojebway Indians: With Especial Reference to Their Christianity* (1861). Relatives of Jones, including George Henry and DAVID SAWYER, also served as missionaries and translators. The Ojibway missionary died on June 29, 1856. (See also COPWAY, GEORGE; JACOBS, PETER; STEINHAUER, HENRY BIRD; and SUNDAY, JOHN.)

JOURNEYCAKE, CHARLES (Neshapanacumin) *(1817–1894) Delaware (Lenni Lenape)* A principal chief and a Baptist minister. He was born on the Upper Sandusky in Ohio on December 16, 1817, to Sally Williams Journeycake and Solomon Journeycake. His mother, who served as an interpreter for Methodist missionaries among the nearby Wyandot, converted to Christianity in 1827. The following year the Delaware were removed from their homeland and began the long journey to Kansas. Journeycake was baptized there in 1833, becoming the first Delaware west of the Mississippi River to be converted to Christianity. A short time later he began preaching, and in 1841, when the Delaware and Mohegan Baptist Mission Church was organized, he became one of its charter members. Journeycake served as an assistant missionary for several years and preached to Native people in a number of languages, including Delaware, Shawnee, Wyandot, Seneca, and Ottawa. In 1854 tribal leaders sent him to Washington, D.C., to conduct business on behalf of their people, and the following year he was selected as chief of the Wolf clan.

Although he was chosen as principal chief by the Delaware in 1861, the United States government recognized another leader in the position. Journeycake later helped negotiate a new homeland in Indian Territory (present-day Oklahoma) for the Delaware after Euro-American settlers pressured them to leave Kansas. The tribal group moved to their new location in 1867 and began the work of rebuilding. Journeycake, recognized by the federal government as the principal chief by then, continued in the leadership role. Following the dedication of a new church, he was ordained on September 23, 1872, and served as the pastor until the end of his life. He died on January 3, 1894, and was buried near Alluwe, Oklahoma. Besides his work as chief and minister, Journeycake translated religious tracts and a hymn book. He married Jane Socia, a Delaware woman, in 1837, and they had 14 children.

JUMP DANCE *Northwest California (Hupa, Karok Yurok)* Ritual dance promoting tribal unity and community solidarity in a public dance held during the WORLD RENEWAL CEREMONIAL CYCLE. Men march in a line from their village to a sacred spot renewed and cleansed by a priest. Here they dance and, at certain places in each song, leap. The performers wear dentalium shell necklaces and red woodpecker scalp headbands and carry decorated cylinder-shaped dance baskets all made especially for public display. Much of the regalia, regarded as treasures, must be borrowed from tribal members and assembled for the dancers. Men prepare for the dancing and singing, women prepare food for the community, and spiritual leaders prepare the dance grounds, emphasizing community cooperation.

JUMPER, JOHN *(c. 1822–1896) Seminole* A principal chief and Baptist minister. Born in Florida about 1822 or 1823, Jumper was descended from influential leaders among his people, including Micanopy and Jim Jumper, who served as chiefs before him. He participated in treaty councils in Florida and eventually became one of the first of his people to immigrate to Indian Territory (present-day Oklahoma). In 1848 Jumper was a member of a delegation that advised Comanche leaders to make peace with the whites. He also returned to Florida in an effort to convince the rest of his people to immigrate to the West. Jumper, who favored the education offered by missionaries, requested that the BOARD OF FOREIGN MISSIONS of the Presbyterian Church establish schools among the Seminole. Although he joined the Presbyterian Church in 1857, he later became a Baptist. During the Civil War he supported the Confederacy and served as a major of the First Seminole Mounted Volunteers in 1861. He later held the rank of lieutenant colonel and served as acting colonel. Jumper was ordained a Baptist

minister in 1865 and retired from political office in 1877. He devoted his efforts to his church near Sasakwa until the end of his life. Chief Jumper died on September 21, 1896.

JUMPIN' DANCE *Confederated Salish-Kootenai (Flathead)* A dance generally identified as a wintertime observance that began on January 1 and lasted for four nights. Its purposes included praying for the health, continuity, and prosperity of the people. One account indicates that participants incorporated a jumping movement during the course of the dance. The Jumpin' Dance was conducted in a circle and in a clockwise direction. Ritual elements included the singing of a song and the delivery of a prayer by each participant at intervals in the observance.

JUMPING DANCE *Cree* A sacred ceremony, also referred to as a Ghost Dance, conducted among the Montana Cree to communicate with the spirits of the dead. A description written after the turn of the century indicated the following features: an annual observance held in the spring or fall where families would bring bundles including locks of hair taken from a deceased person, the holding up of the bundles by the participants in the first round of dancing, the contin-

uation of the dance after the bundles had been hung at the rear of the ceremonial lodge, and a concluding feast contributed to by families who had brought bundles. It also noted that the bundles became larger as skin or cloth pieces were added to the wrapping on a yearly basis, and other locks of hair were added as deaths occurred. A more recent description emphasized that spirits return to tell people about the afterlife and to warn them to follow the Creator's teachings during the ceremony and that the observance was sometimes made with a feast by itself, without a dance. Some of its features are also incorporated with the GIVEAWAY DANCE.

JUNE MEETING *Long Island, New York* A post-1790 Christian adaptation of an ancient practice honoring New York's Long Island American Indian ancestors. On the Poosepatuck Reservation, where it is held annually during the second weekend of June, the observance is also called the Feast of the Dead, as well as the Feast of the Moon of Flowers or the Feast of the Strawberry Moon. Elements associated with the Poosepatuck's June Meeting include Christian and indigenous features, such as prayer and the serving of traditional foods. The spiritual gathering is also observed on the Shinnecock Reservation, where it is held on the first Sunday in June.

Jump Dance. Northwest California Native American men publicly display their necklaces, red woodpecker scalp headbands, and dance baskets during an 1896 jump dance. *Photograph by A. W. Ericson. Humboldt State University.*

K

KACHINA (cachina, kacina, katcina, katchina, katsina katzina.) *Pueblo* A Hopi term, now a general term, by which similar spirits among Pueblo peoples have come to be called by the outside world. Keresan Pueblo themselves call these spirits *shiwana;* Zuni call them *koko;* and Tewa people call them *okhua.* They are powerful spirits of the dead in the form of plants, birds, animals, and humans whose function is to bring rain, ensuring crops and the continuity of life. Kachinas were said to live at the SAN FRANCISCO PEAKS (Hopi), Wenima (Keresan), lakes, and springs during part of the year, and to have come to pueblos in person to dance and sing for people and to bring rain. They stopped coming years ago, however, and now invest their impersonators with their spirits. Masked male dancers who have been ritually initiated therefore, become kachinas after suitable preparation, losing their personal identities and becoming imbued with the spirit of the beneficent beings they represent, possessing the power of the real kachinas. Kachinas are depicted visually through masks, paint, and regalia.

Kachinas possess power that human beings do not. The kachinas bring rain and affect fertility, curing, and growth. Though they are not worshiped, they require veneration and respect from human beings or they will not respond. Ritualized dancing, ceremonial behavior, the presentation of ritual objects, and "a good heart" compel kachinas to reciprocate with the desired benefits. Improper behavior on the part of humans may cause kachinas to withhold rain, producing misfortune. Kachinas visit various villages at certain times of the year and dance publicly. The number for each group varies from a few in eastern pueblos to an enor-

mous number in the western pueblos. Among Zuni and Keresan Pueblo, the kachina season lasts the entire year, while the Hopi kachina season lasts half the year, from winter solstice to summer solstice. Hopi believe that people who conform to ceremonial laws and the Creator's pattern become kachinas when they die. Tewa people believe that those who devote their lives to religious activities join kachinas after death. Hopi view them as friends, although not all are benevolent; they fear the ogre kachinas who punish the offenders of ceremonial laws. Besides masked dancers, some kachinas are represented by dolls.

Hopi

Hopi recognize more than 250 kachinas, or spirits, each with its own appearance and behavior. They are difficult to classify because they differ from mesa to mesa, village to village, clan to clan. Certain kachinas have a name that is based on their appearance, the name of a bird or mammal, a name for sounds it utters, or a name that does not translate. Kachinas can be male or female, can represent a quality, other Indian groups, animals, or plants. Old kachinas can disappear and new ones can be introduced. Certain kachinas always appear in the same roles. They are believed to be ancient and generally beneficent beings, although there are demons among them who threaten children. There are about 30 official, or chief, kachinas (Mong, Mongwi) that take principal parts in the major nine-day ceremonies conducted the first half of the year. They dance individually rather than in groups. The Masau'u (GERMINATOR) kachina represents the spirit of the earth and does not live in mountains like other kachinas. He may visit the Hopi any time of the year, the only kachina who appears outside the normal kachina season. He comes after the NIMAN KACHINA CEREMONY, when other kachinas have departed, and dances in a planting and harvesting rite. Mastop Kachina appears during SOYAL and represents a male power of human fertility alone. His name signifies a gray fly that carries the germ cells of humanity. The Soyal kachina, a chief kachina, is the first kachina to appear during the year. He appears the day following the WUWUCHIM CEREMONY and announces Soyal. The Soyoko Kachinas, with fearsome appearances, are disciplinary ogres whose role is to guard and enforce the social/ceremonial laws of the pueblo by exercising positive and negative sanctions. Parents warn children that these ogres will come and eat them if they do not behave. There are other different kinds of runner kachinas (Wawarus) that challenge men to races and female kachinas (Kachin-manas) impersonated by men. Single or paired kachinas appear in the kachina parade at the POWAMU CEREMONY and in mixed dances of spring and early summer. Companies of 15 to 30 kachinas may appear in one-day ceremonies that have no fixed dates.

Zuni

Zuni spirits of the dead include several orders of spirit beings, such as deities, past heroes, ancestral dead, and numerous spiritual allies. They pass overhead hidden behind clouds to bring lifegiving rain to Zuni or approach the pueblo in the form of ducks. Besides bringing rain, kachinas may have special attributes to bring an increase in crops or livestock, bring game, ripen corn, and produce other plants. Most kachinas live in their own village, KOLHU/WALA-WA, which lies under water. They require the permission of PAUTIWA, the kachina chief, to sing and dance for Zuni people, and he directs all the kachina activities from the spirits' village. When Zunis need a kachina or dance group to come, they send prayersticks four days or more in advance to Kolhu/wala-wa, and Pautiwa decides who is to visit, sing, dance, and bring gifts. Other kachinas who are not under Pautiwa's control live in other kachina villages, like SHIPAPOLINA, east of Zuni, and at other locations scattered about. Some Zuni kachinas include LONG HORN (Sayatasha), the rain priest of the north who brings long life to people and is only impersonated in the Shalako ceremony; six Shalakos whose impersonators are appointed and make their sole appearance in late fall in the Shalako ceremony Shulawitsa, the Fire God, whose impersonator appears twice a year during Shalako and at summer solstice when he leads kiva groups on a pilgrimage to the sacred lake in the west. Ancestral kachinas belong to particular clans and only men from that clan may impersonate them. (See also KOKO; MASKS [kachina; *shiwana*].)

KACHINA CEREMONIES *Pueblo* The KACHINA ceremony begins with a retreat by the leaders of the priesthood to the KIVA, lasting one to four days in the eastern pueblos and up to 16 days in western pueblos. During this time, private rites are held that culminate in a public performance by kachina members who have been initiated. During these ceremonies women feed the kachina dancers and priests. Public performances take the form of a slow procession along a fixed course with a leader in the center. Clowns also participate in kachina ceremonies.

KACHINA DANCES *Pueblo* Today, in order to obtain the rain-making power of the kachinas who stopped coming to the pueblos long ago, men impersonate them in dances by wearing masks, sacred clothing, and body paint in traditional designs. They carry sacred objects like rattles, evergreen branches, bows and arrows, and staffs. When people do this, they believe they lose their personal identity and become the spirit of the kachina they are impersonating. Some kachina dances occur at fixed times of the year, others take place at times specified by leaders who control and manage the rites. There are individually sponsored kachina dances as well. Kachina dances have both private and public aspects; private rituals take place in KIVAS prior to public ceremonies held in village plazas. In Rio Grande Keresan pueblos, the masked dances are closely guarded against view by non-Indians. Male dancers wear kilts woven of cotton and embroidered with colored yarn and a sash with a woven design. Female dancers wear black dresses, shoulder blankets, woven belts, and white buckskin boots.

Hopi

Masked Hopi men impersonate kachina spirits in ceremonies held in village kivas and plazas from winter solstice to mid-July, the first half of the year. During this period, there are major dance ceremonies, including the SOYAL, winter solstice ceremony, in December; Pamuya, night dances, in January; POWAMU, the Bean Dance, in February; the Water Serpent Ceremony in February or March; and the NIMAN KACHINA CEREMONY, Home Dance, in July. Niman is the last appearance of kachinas before they return to their homes in the SAN FRANCISCO PEAKS. (During the second half of the year, from July to December, no masked dances take place.) Many of the dances are held in kivas where only the initiated witness them. During the first half of the Hopi year, late spring, there are also one-day ceremonies in village plazas. The kachinas dance in long lines in which all the dancers may wear the same mask and dress, or they may dress differently, representing a variety of kachina spirits in mixed kachina dances. Dances start at dawn with the arrival of kachinas in the plaza led by a priest. New songs may be composed for each dance, the number of songs determining how many times the kachinas will come into the plaza to dance during the day. These songs express the desire for rain, good crops, fertility, and growth. The dancers usually bring gifts for the children on their first entrance.

Zuni

The Kachina Society has membership divided into six groups, each associated with one of the six kivas at Zuni Pueblo. The kiva groups each have a dance, or kiva, director, who decides the type of dance and dates for dances. Zuni dances are organized in a calendrical series based on dance presentations by successive kiva groups that perform in a ceremonial order. Each of the six kiva groups is required to dance at least three times annually. Kachina winter dances take place a few weeks after the winter solstice. During a period of five to six weeks, each of the six kivas presents a masked dance, with the other five kivas sending dancers. Kachina summer dances take place in plazas after the summer solstice and each kiva presents a dance. Each of the kachina groups from the six kivas dance after the SHALAKO festivities in early December before the solstice. (See also MASKS [Kachina].)

KACHINA DOLLS *Hopi, Zuni* Small carved figures with likenesses of the masked impersonators of KACHINA spirits who appear in ceremonies. Parents give them as ceremonial gifts to children, not as toys, but rather as educational objects that are meant to be treasured and studied so that young Hopi and Zuni learn to know what different kachinas look like. The dolls, which are usually given to girls by kachina dancers during a kachina ceremony, are taken home and hung on walls or house rafters so they may be constantly seen by children. Men carve dried roots of cottonwood trees, coat them with kaolin and paint them either with natural substances or commercial paints to resemble the masked and dressed impersonators. They attach features and realistic decorations. Hopi craftspeople now make the largest number of dolls for the tourist trade, and Zuni make them in smaller numbers, but many of these do not represent authentic kachinas. Zuni resist reproducing anything of a sacred nature, have restricted outsiders from reproducing ceremonial activities and ritual objects for decades, and have sanctioned their own people against this behavior.

KACHINA SOCIETY *Pueblo* Kachina ceremonial organizations differ from pueblo to pueblo. In general, however, Kachina Society members function as impersonators of the KACHINA rainmaking spirits in masked dances that are performed to induce rain to come and irrigate the fields and crops. The kachina societies are open to men and, at some pueblos, to women. Membership is for life after an initiation rite formalizing membership is conducted by a society in charge of the kachina dance group being joined. Initiation rites differ from pueblo to pueblo. After they are admitted to the organization, men are given a mask to wear whenever they dance. In Keresan pueblos, medicine associations and CLOWN organizations control and manage the kachina organization and activities, and the CACIQUE and his assistants have leadership roles in kachina ceremonies. At Zuni, a kachina chief directs the Kachina Society. At some pueblos, the kachina organization is identified with a KIVA organization. Affiliation is voluntary at some pueblos and obligatory for boys and girls at others. Kachina organizations are tribal-wide in western pueblos and are joined by children at ages six to 10 at Hopi, Hano, Acoma, and Laguna pueblos but usually restricted to males at Zuni pueblo. Zuni girls are rarely initiated into kachina organizations. At Acoma, girls are initiated into kachina organizations, but they do not wear masks. In all groups, the number of kachina dancers varies with the number of men in a particular kiva with which the organization is associated.

KACHINA SOCIETY INITIATION *Hopi* Initiation into a KACHINA SOCIETY begins the religious life of all Hopi boys and girls. Every Hopi child between six and 10 must be initiated into either the Powamu or Kachina Society, each of which has different rites of initiation. Initiations are usually held every four years during the annual POWAMU ceremony in February. The child's parents and a ceremonial parent (selected to sponsor each child who then acquires a new set of relationships via the ceremonial parent's clan) choose the society. Ceremonial procedures vary from Hopi village to village. Kachina initiations mark the introduction of a child to a new status in the tribe. To make the change in ritual status, a child is given a new name that is used ceremonially. Each child then has the privilege of returning to the underworld at death.

Tewa

Boys between 12 and 14 years of age are inducted into the Summer or Winter kachina organizations in a rite that makes boys men. The novices receive religious instruction and rituals that must never be revealed are introduced to them.

Zuni

At Zuni, every boy between ages five and eight is initiated into one of six KIVA groups, therefore becoming a member of the Kachina Society, whose membership is divided into six groups, each associated with a kiva. A male relative from the father's household who sponsors the boy and becomes a ceremonial father decides which kiva group the boy joins.

KANEEDA (Kaneta, John Wickliffe) *(fl. 1800s) Cherokee* Baptist missionary who was converted to Christianity by the Reverend EVAN JONES. Formerly a Cherokee *adonisgi*, or priest, Kaneeda was baptized in 1829 and served as exhorter until 1830. At that time he was elected as a deacon, licensed to preach, and christened John Wickliffe. He became an assistant of the Baptist mission board in 1830 and was ordained on April 18, 1833. Active in the struggle against the forced removal of his nation from their Native lands west to Indian Territory, Kaneeda served on the Cherokee Council with JESSE BUSHYHEAD and other leaders. After the fight was lost, he helped minister to the people rounded up by the military and awaiting departure to the West. During the removal he provided assistance to detachment leaders Jesse Bushyhead and Evan Jones and served in the role of assistant manager. Kaneeda later served as minister at Delaware Town Church in the Cherokee Nation West from 1847 to 1857. His name also appears as Kaneta.

KANSAS UNMARKED BURIAL SITES PRESERVATION ACT
(Kansas House Bill 2144) *(1989)* A bill signed into law on April 24, 1989, by the governor of Kansas, Michael Hayden, that bans the unregulated public display of human remains and protects unmarked graves from unnecessary disturbance. Supporters of the bill included the Pawnee and six other American Indian tribes concerned about protection of Native burial grounds in the state. The legislation stemmed from a Kansas incident involving the public display of skeletal remains from an Indian cemetery on privately owned land that had been dug up and exhibited as a tourist attraction. Caddoan descendants of the decedents sought assistance from the Native American Rights Fund, an organization that specializes in protecting Indian rights, in ending the grave desecration in the state. The law, which went into effect on January 1, 1990, applies to human remains and interment goods on both public and private land.

Provisions of the bill make it illegal to willfully destroy any unmarked burial ground, to possess or display human remains or goods, to engage in commerce with the remains, or to discard any such materials. Penalties for violating the law call for fines as high as $100,000 and the awarding of damages, attorney's fees, and other relief to any person with a kinship, cultural, tribal, or scientific interest in preserving a burial site and its associated remains. Overseeing the act is the Unmarked Burial Sites Preservation Review Board, which includes representation from Kansas tribal groups, a historian, an archaeologist and a physical anthropologist. The board's responsibilities include maintaining a confidential register of the state's unmarked burial sites and administering the issuance of one-year permits for scientific or educational purposes. The legislation also contains provisions for the reburial or disposition of remains. The measure was enacted with overwhelming support from both houses of the state legislature.

(See also UNMARKED HUMAN BURIAL SITES AND SKELETAL REMAINS PROTECTION ACT.)

KARIGI *(qasgiq, kashim, qaggi, qashe) Inupiat Inuit*
Also called *qasgiq* by Yupik speakers, *kashim* by people in southern Alaska and Russian speakers, *qaggi* in coastal Canada, and *qashe* in Greenland. This is an oversized community ceremonial center used for village ceremonies and festivals. The most noticeable structure in an Inuit community, in Alaska it developed into a men's club or dance house, at times the communal residence and workplace of men and boys, where they eat, sleep, make gear for hunting, take sweat baths, tell stories, play games, smoke pipes, and instruct male children. On ceremonial occasions, such as the FEAST TO THE DEAD and the BLADDER FESTIVAL, the community gathers at the *karigi*. It is a nexus between the secular and sacred worlds; passage by celebrants through the house entrance tunnels, doorways, and smoke holes symbolizes the passage between worlds and between different states of being. The *karigi* smoke hole serves as a passage permitting movement and communication between the world of the hunter and the hunted, between the world of the living and the dead.

KAUXUMA NUPIKA ("Gone to the Spirits"; Bundosh, Bowdash, Manlike Woman) *c. 1790–1837) Kootenai*
Kauxuma Nupika is variously described as a courier, guide, prophetess, warrior, and mediator. She was born in the Lower Kootenai area of the Northwest Coast. A childhood name attributed to her was *ququnok patke* or "one standing (lodge) pole woman." By 1808 she had married an explorer named Boisverd, who had traveled with David Thompson, trader-explorer, across the Rocky Mountains. Thompson later requested that she be sent back to her family. Upon returning home after being away for over a year, the young woman reportedly told people that she had been transformed into a male while among the whites. Calling herself Kauxuma nupika, she was said to claim spiritual powers and to begin adopting male clothing and roles, in the manner of a BERDACHE. She eventually took successive wives and participated in war parties. On one excursion her brother discovered that she had not been changed into a man as she had claimed, and he refused to use the new name she adopted, Qanqon kamek klaula ("Sitting-in-the-water-Grizzly"). The Kootenai woman and her spouse served as couriers, eventually guiding Alexander Ross and other traders on their travels along the Columbia River. During the journey she delivered prophecies to various Indian groups, predicting a devastating epidemic. After this message of impending disease nearly resulted in her death at the hands of some of the people, she later revealed other predictions. These included foretelling the arrival of whites who would give the

Indians gifts of all sorts of goods and implements. She then received rich presents of horses and goods in tribal communities. Upon returning home, Kauxuma Nupika settled among her people. Accounts from the oral tradition indicate that she became a shaman with healing powers. Kauxuma Nupika was killed by Blackfeet warriors in 1837 while mediating peace between them and a group of Flathead. One account of her death indicates that her spiritual powers made her difficult to kill. She was shot several times, then stabbed, but her wounds kept healing by themselves. After a portion of her heart was cut off, she died. It is said that no animals bothered her dead body. She was also called Bundosh, Bowdash, and Manlike Woman.

KEEPER The caretaker or guardian of a sacred object or objects. As custodian, a keeper's role includes the performance of the rituals, ceremonies, and caretaking associated with the article(s) in his or her keeping. Qualifications, selection, duties, length of service, compensation, succession, and other aspects of the role are determined within tribal cultures. (See Subject Index for specific entries listed in this volume.)

KEEPERS OF THE TREASURES A cultural council of American Indians, Alaska Natives, and Native Hawaiians that works to preserve, affirm, and celebrate Native cultures through efforts centered on maintaining Native languages and cultures. A national organization founded in 1991, Keepers of the Treasures also works to protect and conserve places that hold historic and sacred significance to indigenous peoples. In fulfilling this mission, it provides technical assistance and identifies potential funding sources. In addition, the group provides information on legislative and regulatory issues affecting activities associated with the preservation of cultural heritage.

Keepers of the Treasures, which has offices in Santa Fe, New Mexico, publishes a quarterly newsletter and hosts an annual conference. The conference brings together repatriation specialists, tribal elders, and other members of constituent tribal groups to discuss issues critical to the preservation of cultural heritage.

KENEKUK (Kenekuk, "Putting the Foot Upon a Fallen Object" or "Putting His Foot Down," the Kickapoo Prophet, Pakaka, Pah-kah-kah") *(c. 1790–1852) Kickapoo* A prophet and leading chief of the Vermilion band of Kickapoo, who were located along the Wabash River and in Illinois before their removal to Kansas. Little is known of Kenekuk's early years, but he had reportedly been cast out by his people for murdering an uncle while under the influence of alcohol. He then traveled to various settlements in Indiana and Illinois until he was taken in by a Catholic priest who instructed him in Christianity and "civilization." Kenekuk became determined to make amends for his earlier misdeeds by teaching his people and they welcomed him back. By his mid-twenties he had become the leader of a group of peaceful, religious followers. To ensure his people's survival, he helped them to adjust to the changes brought about by contact with Euro-American society. Kenekuk urged his followers to live in peace with their neighbors, to refrain from drinking, and to retain their land. He explained his religious doctrine to a military officer in St. Louis in 1827, providing a diagram illustrating the teachings he had received from the Great Spirit. Kenekuk had strict injunctions against drinking, quarreling, stealing, warfare, and other vices. The explorer and artist George Catlin, who visited Kenekuk in 1831, painted his portrait and listened to him preach. He also witnessed the sobriety and peaceable manner of his followers.

Kenekuk was able to resist Euro-American efforts to dispossess his people of their traditional lands until 1832. At that time, pressures, including federal policies aimed at relocating Native Americans away from their homelands to make way for white settlement, could not be overcome. In 1832 Kenekuk signed his only land cession, the Treaty of Castor Hill, which ceded Kickapoo lands in Illinois and created a reservation in Kansas. Kenekuk then led about 400 people, including more than 100 converts he had gained among the neighboring Potawatomi, to an area near Fort Leavenworth, where he again put into practice the beliefs that had earlier helped to protect the Vermilion band. He was able to maintain traditional customs among his people while outwardly incorporating features of Christianity. Despite urging his followers to burn their medicine bags and to have men rather than women farm the land, other tribal traditions were maintained. Kenekuk's adherents refused to learn English, continued performing Native songs and dances, and enforced tribal menstrual taboos. The prophet also sold his followers prayersticks, small wooden boards on which Algonquian symbols were carved, for their use in reciting prayers. These practices were condemned by missionaries who attempted without success to convert Kenekuk and his band to Christianity. Consistent with his efforts to retain Kickapoo territory, Kenekuk opposed plans that would have divided tribal land into individual allotments.

Kenekuk's religious beliefs are variously attributed to inspiration from Christian missionaries or the teachings of the DELAWARE PROPHET and the Shawnee prophet TENSKWATAWA. His tenets helped his people survive a period of great upheaval. Considered God's messenger, the prophet inspired a loyal following of pious adherents. After Kenekuk's death in 1852, the band survived by continuing to live by his teachings. There are many variants of Kenekuk's name, which also appears as Pakaka and Pah-kah-kah.

KERESAN PRIESTHOODS Priests are divided into categories on the basis of function and membership. There are managing priesthoods whose members impersonate the Koshare and Kwerana (sacred clowns), direct public rituals, cure, and have seasonal activities. There are curing priesthoods that allow women as auxiliary members and treat internal diseases caused by witchcraft and priesthoods with male members only that treat external, or skin, diseases caused by angry animals. There are slaying priesthoods with male members who either killed an enemy and joined the Warriors or killed a cougar, bear, or eagle to qualify as Hunters. Recently, the Hunters have assumed many of the older military rituals. During the solar rites in February and November, the various priesthoods cooperate. (See also KOSHARE; KWERANA SOCIETY.)

KERESAN PUEBLOS The Keresan-speaking pueblos include those located in the Rio Grande Valley—the Zia, Santa Ana, San Felipe, Santo Domingo, and Cochiti—and those located in western New Mexico—Acoma and Laguna. (See also TEWA PUEBLOS; TIWA PUEBLOS; TOWA PUEBLOS.)

KETTLE DANCE (Cehohomni wacipi, "dance around the kettle dance") *Lakota* One of the oldest Lakota dances, it is associated with both the HEYOKA CEREMONY and the YUWIPI ceremony. The HEYOKA, or sacred clown, re-enacts his visions of the thunder gods at a Heyoka ceremony. Besides making the people laugh with backward, or contrary, antics, the sacred clowns perform a Kettle Dance around a boiling pot of ritually prepared dog meat. After saluting the kettle, they thrust their bare hands into the scalding hot pot to retrieve the head and other pieces of meat. Their antics include splashing one another and commenting on the coldness of the pot and its contents. The Kettle Dance, performed to honor the thunder-beings, concludes with a feast. During the Yuwipi curing ceremony it is believed that the Kettle Dance is performed by the spirits of the thunder-beings and that they can be seen in the darkened room by the medicine man. The ritual preparations and sacred songs are performed for these spirits who arrive during the course of the curing rite to help the Yuwipi man. Besides saluting the kettle, the Heyoka spirits retrieve meat and frolic around just as the humans do in their performance. The dance concludes with a dog feast. The Kettle Dance is also associated with the GRASS DANCE and secular performances were held in various settings.

KICKING BEAR (Mato Anahtaka) *(c. 1846–1904) Lakota* Apostle of the GHOST DANCE OF 1890 among the Lakota. Born in about 1846, he became a warrior who fought at the battles of the Rosebud, Little Bighorn, and Slim Buttes in 1876 and 1877. Kicking Bear, the nephew of the renowned leader SITTING BULL, served as a band chief among his wife's Minneconjou people and settled on the Cheyenne River Reservation in Dakota Territory. After hearing of the new faith promulgated by the prophet WOVOKA, Lakota leaders selected a delegation in 1889 to travel to Nevada to learn about the Northern Paiute religious leader's teachings firsthand. Kicking Bear, chosen as the emissary from Cheyenne River, left for Nevada with his brother-in-law SHORT BULL and other delegates. They met with Wovoka, who told them of the world to come where the earth would be replenished and the Indian dead would return to life.

Combining the teachings of Wovoka with observations of the Ghost Dance among the Arapaho, Kicking Bear became a leader of the new faith among his people. Under his leadership and that of Short Bull, the Ghost Dancers wore ghost shirts that were believed to protect them from enemy bullets. Although pressured to stop practicing the religion by agency authorities, including an incarceration on the Pine Ridge Reservation in South Dakota for refusing to disclose the purpose of his visit to Nevada, Kicking Bear continued to lead the sacred dance. The Ghost Dance was quickly targeted for repression by agents and missionaries, who had already banned the SUN DANCE and other traditional religious practices under the authority of the COURTS OF INDIAN OFFENSES. On October 9, 1890, Kicking Bear introduced the new dance on the Standing Rock Reservation in the Dakotas at the invitation of his uncle Sitting Bull. Fearing Kicking Bear's spiritual power, Indian policemen sent by the agent to arrest him failed to carry out the order. With the arrival of federal troops later in the year to stop the dancing, Kicking Bear and other adherents fled to the Stronghold, an area in the Badlands of South Dakota.

Events surrounding the Ghost Dance among the Lakota escalated in December 1890. Sitting Bull's arrest was ordered by James McLaughlin, the government agent at Standing Rock who feared the leader's influence and resistance to assimilationist policies. Sitting Bull was murdered on December 15, 1890, when fighting broke out between his followers and the tribal policemen sent to carry out McLaughlin's order. The Minneconjou leader Big Foot of Cheyenne River, who feared for the safety of his people, led more than 300 followers to seek protection from the Lakota leader Red Cloud at Pine Ridge. Big Foot's band was intercepted by the military and taken to Wounded Knee Creek. After a gun reportedly discharged, the troops opened fire and killed Lakota men, women, and children on December 29, 1890. Big Foot and the other victims were later buried together in a common grave at the site. Kicking Bear and other Ghost Dancers surrendered to General Nelson A. Miles in January 1891.

Incarcerated at Fort Sheridan in Illinois until spring, Kicking Bear and other Ghost Dance participants were released to Buffalo Bill Cody for two years to travel abroad with his Wild West show. One of their stops was Washington, D.C., where a model of Kicking Bear's body was made by Smithsonian Institution representatives and photographs were taken. The Ghost Dance leader returned home in November 1892, later moving his family to a remote area along Wounded Knee Creek that became Manderson, South Dakota. Kicking Bear died in 1904 at the age of 58.

KICKSTICK RACE *Keresan Pueblo* A ritual race to "call the *shiwana*" (rainmakers). Runners dressed alike but divided into two teams run toward the west, kicking their respective kicksticks. While some runners gather cottonwood boughs, the other team members kick the kickstick around the turning point and start back toward the pueblo. After circling the plaza four times, the runners cross the finish line, separate and go to their respective KIVAS. (See also CEREMONIAL RUNNING AND GAMES.)

KIMBALL, ANDREW *(1858–?)* A missionary who served as president of the Indian Territory mission of the Church of Jesus Christ of Latter-day Saints. He was born to Ann A. Gheen and Heber C. Kimball on September 6, 1858, in Salt Lake City, Utah. Kimball was baptized in 1866, two years before his father died. He attended school until he was about 16 years old, then worked at railroading, ranching, and other jobs to support his mother and sisters. He was ordained a deacon in 1878, an elder in 1880, and a "seventy" in 1884. On January 28, 1885, Kimball began his mission in Indian Territory (present-day Oklahoma), where he worked among the Cherokee people. After he was joined by other elders, they extended their efforts to the Choctaw and Creek Nations. Kimball was placed in charge of the mission and remained in the position until 1897. During the period of his presidency, the number of Mormon elders in Indian Territory increased from one to 61, and the region covered expanded to five states. He was later active in numerous religious and civic positions, including service in the Arizona legislature.

KINGSBURY, CYRUS *(1786–1870)* A Congregational missionary to the Cherokee and the Choctaw people. Born in New England, Kingsbury was educated at Brown University (class of 1812) and Andover Theological Seminary (class of 1815). After his 1815 ordination as a Congregational minister, he began working for the AMERICAN BOARD OF COMMISSIONERS FOR FOREIGN MISSIONS (ABCFM). He visited southern Indian groups, then advised the board to start missions in the region. In 1816 he obtained approval

from the Cherokee Council to start the work and obtained a site a short time later. Kingsbury and two other missionaries arrived in the area in January 1817 and founded the first ABCFM Indian mission station, Brainerd, near Chattanooga, Tennessee. Two months later they began a school and developed an educational plan similar to the one established earlier by Moravian missionaries. Kingsbury remained at Brainerd until 1818 when the ABCFM sent him to establish new mission stations among the Choctaw. He was instrumental in obtaining government support for similar endeavors through the passage of a bill establishing a "civilization fund," or support for education, passed by Congress in March 1819 (3 US Stat. 516–517). Kingsbury's work among the Choctaw people lasted until the end of his life. He established a system of mission stations and schools in their southeastern homeland, then resettled with them in Indian Territory (present-day Oklahoma) during the removal period of the 1830s. Wanting to continue working with the Choctaw, Kingsbury and his colleague, CYRUS BYINGTON, resisted pressures from abolitionists on the board and attempted to remain neutral during the furor over slaveholding. After the ABCFM ended its sponsorship of missions to the southeastern tribes in 1859, he obtained support from the Old School Presbyterians and later from a Southern Presbyterian agency.

KINO, EUSEBIO FRANCISCO *(1645–1711)* Italian Jesuit missionary. Born of Italian parents at Segno in the Tyrol of present-day Austria, he was educated by German Jesuits at Trent, Hall, Innsbruck, and Ingolstadt. He entered the Society of Jesus in 1665 and was ordered to proceed to Cádiz, Spain, although he longed to work in China. He later went to Mexico and arrived in Mexico City in 1681. Kino struggled to reopen and maintain missions in Baja California but failed. In 1687, he was sent to missionize Pima (Akimel O'odham) in Sonora and Arizona and became the chief missionary to the Pima in northern Mexico and southern Arizona (Pimeria Alta). He founded the mission of Delores at the Upper Pima village of Cosari in 1687. Kino hoped to save baptized Indians from involuntary servitude and fought silver mine and ranch operators who tried to exploit Indians. After establishing the first chapel in Pimeria Alta in 1688, he began a series of journeys that extended over a period of 24 years to parts of Pimeria as far as the Gila and Colorado Rivers. These journeys brought him renown as an explorer, cartographer, historian, and missionary. From 1687 to 1711, he founded more than 24 missions in what is now Sonora, Mexico, and two in Arizona located near present-day Tucson (San Gabriel and San Xavier). He also directed the construction of 14 mission complexes, for which Indians were free to work and were not held in bondage or lashed. He did not seek to destroy Native culture but tried to convert Indians to Christianity through patient teaching. Due to him, Catholic ritual took root in Piman culture. In time, he trained Pima to fight Apache who resisted the Spanish. He introduced Western thought to Pima and Yuman settlements scattered over 50,000 square miles. He established ranches, with herds of livestock, orchards, and vineyards and constructed irrigation systems to water them. He introduced European foodstuffs, especially wheat, and developed a stable Piman economy, believing that a comfortable material life was as essential as a spiritual one. Father Kino learned several Indian languages and translated Christian doctrine and prayers into all of them. He composed vocabularies and grammars. Finally, he was a propagandist and promoter who tried to convince the Spanish authorities that Indians were eager to become Christians. His misrepresentations of the Pima served his purpose of luring more missionaries to Pimeria Alta. His *Historical Memoir of Pimeria Alta: A Contemporary Account of the Beginnings of California, Sonora, and Arizona,* was published in 1708.

KIRBY, ALBERT *(1875–?)* An elder of the Church of Jesus Christ of Latter-day Saints who served as a missionary in Indian Territory (present-day Oklahoma) from 1898 to 1900. During that period Kirby maintained a daily journal of his experiences from the time he left his home in Hyde Park, Utah, until his period of service ended. He and his fellow missionary, James M. Anderson, visited both Indians and non-Indians and relied on their hospitality for food and lodging. Kirby's journal indicated that he walked more than 4,000 miles, visited more than 4,500 families and saw eight conversions to his faith.

KIRBY, WILLIAM WEST *(c. 1826–1907)* An Anglican missionary who worked among Cree, Chipewyan, Kutchin, and other groups in Manitoba and the Northwest Territories for 26 years. Archdeacon JAMES HUNTER first journeyed to the Mackenzie region for the Anglicans in 1858 to explore the possibility of establishing missions there. Based on his favorable report, Kirby left for the region from his post on the Red River the following year. Assisted by Hudson's Bay Company officials, he established a church and school. He also studied the Native language. In 1861 or 1862 he traveled to the Yukon, where he preached to the Kutchin and conducted language studies before returning to Fort Simpson on the Mackenzie River. Kirby left the region in 1869 for York Factory on Hudson Bay and remained there until he retired from mission work in 1878. He translated a number of religious works, including the New Testament, prayer books, and hymns into the Chipewyan language. Kirby also completed a hymnal in the Cree language. In 1876 he was named the first archdeacon of the diocese of Moosonee (Ontario). After leaving York Factory in 1879, he took a parish assignment in New Jersey. He died on September 7, 1907 at the age of 81.

KIRKLAND, SAMUEL *(1741–1808)* Congregational missionary to the Iroquois who was a protégé of ELEAZAR WHEELOCK. The son of a minister, Kirkland was born on November 20, 1741, in Norwich, Connecticut. He prepared for college and missionary work at Wheelock's school in Lebanon, Connecticut, where his Indian classmates included Joseph Brant, who would later become a well-known ally of the British, and other Mohawk. In 1762 he entered the College of New Jersey, now Princeton, as a sophomore and graduated in 1765, having started his first mission to the Indians the year before. Kirkland later wrote of his journey to Canadasaga (now Geneva, New York), the main village of the Seneca, his adoption into the chief sachem's family and other experiences.

Besides becoming acquainted with people from the Seneca Nation, he studied their language and began missionary work. Following his 1766 ordination in Lebanon, Kirkland returned to New York, where he began permanent work among the Oneidas. He lived in their principal village at Canowaroghare (Oneida Castle) and conducted missionary activities in the area until the end of his life. Following a disagreement and break with Wheelock in 1770, he began working under the auspices of the Boston Board of Commissioners for the London Company for the Propagation of the Gospel in New England and Parts Adjacent in America. Kirkland was instrumental in keeping the Six Nations out of the Shawnee war with the Virginians in 1774–75.

Initially counseling Iroquois neutrality during the American Revolution, he later aided the American side by enlisting Oneida and Tuscarora support. During the war he directed Oneida scouts, served as a chaplain, and provided other services. His contribution was formally recognized by Congress as well as Connecticut, Massachusetts, and New York legislatures. After the war, he returned to Canowaroghare and began rebuilding the church and mission. He assisted at the 1784 Treaty of Fort Stanwix, which was negotiated between Congress and Iroquois tribal groups over territorial boundaries and other issues. Kirkland later received over 4,000 acres of land near Utica from the Iroquois and New York State in recognition of his services.

Elected to the American Academy of Arts and Sciences in 1791, Kirkland presented a census of the Six Nations. In 1792 General Henry Knox, secretary of war, requested that he travel among the Iroquois, counseling them against joining the Ohio Indians in warfare against the government.

Successful in that effort, Kirkland turned his attention to his plan for a school. He obtained a charter for Hamilton Oneida Academy in January 1793 and contributed land and money for the coeducation of Indian and white boys. Although it initially educated Indians, the academy was reorganized in 1812 as Hamilton College and primarily served whites. Kirkland continued his missionary work among the Oneida until shortly before his death on February 28, 1808.

KIVA *Pueblo* Sacred ceremonial chambers characteristic of ancient and contemporary Pueblo villages. Used mostly by men, they are circular or rectangular, may be below ground, partly underground or aboveground and are either detached or adjacent to private houses. They symbolize a womb of Mother Earth from which people are born and the underworld from which they first emerged. Each kiva has a small hole in the floor, an earth navel called a *sipapu,* which symbolically denotes the umbilical cord leading from Mother Earth and the path of the people's emergence from the underworld. The ladder through the roof represents the reed up which people climbed during the emergence into the world above. Often a wooden stairway leads to the kiva roof, where people descend into the interior by ladder.

These tribal, communal buildings, with fire pits and altars, are used for a number of purposes. When ceremonies are held there, men and women dance groups use them for dressing, preparing for dances, resting, and rehearsing songs between performances. Men use kivas to discuss governing the pueblos, to decide when to plant crops or plan rituals, to build altars, to train the young, and to pray. At Hopi in Arizona kivas are thought of as "belonging" to a particular clan or clans, although kiva membership is not primarily by clan. Each village clan and religious society has its own kiva, so the number varies from village to village. At Old Oraibi in Arizona it is believed there are 13 kivas. KERESAN PUEBLOS along the Rio Grande in New Mexico have two kivas where affiliation is along kin lines or residence lines. Kiva memberships can be shifted, unlike clan affiliations, with permission from kiva heads. TANOAN PUEBLOS in New Mexico appear to have one communal kiva and one or more associated with dual divisions of the society. The Tanoan Pueblo of Taos, New Mexico and the Zuni Pueblo have six kivas, one for each of the four cardinal directions and the nadir and zenith. Kivas are off limits to tourists and should not be photographed or trespassed.

KLAH, HOSTEEN *(1867–1937) Navajo (Dineh)* Noted medicine man, singer, sand painter, and weaver. Klah's great-grandfather Narbona, born about 1766, was a great war chief of the Navajo. His mother had made the Long Walk in 1864, when the Navajo were starved off their land by an expedition led by Kit Carson and forced to leave their homeland for Bosque Redondo, or Fort Sumner, 300 miles away. While he lived with his relatives, Klah learned ceremonies from his uncle, an Apache medicine man. Later, apprenticed to other medicine men, he studied for 24 years before holding his first NIGHT WAY CEREMONY (Yeibichai). In the fall of 1917, when 49 years old, he held a nine-day Yeibichai—letter perfect in chant, symbolism, and ritual—that established him as a great medicine man. Klah knew at least the Hail Way, Chiricahua, Wind Way, and Mountain Way ceremonies.

Over many years, Klah was a major informant for a number of scholars, including Gladys Reichard, Mary Cabot Wheelwright, whom he permitted to record many of his songs, and Franc Johnson Newcomb, who recorded sandpaintings taken from Klah's ceremonies. Klah mastered weaving and executed sand painting designs used in healing ceremonies into woven tapestries, now housed in the WHEELWRIGHT MUSEUM in Santa Fe, New Mexico (formerly the Museum of Navajo Ceremonial Art). Klah's understudy, Beaal Begay, died unexpectedly in 1931, and since Klah never trained another youth, many sacred Navajo prayers and rituals were lost with his death, which was noted around the world. He recorded some ancient stories, rituals, and sandpaintings, however, so some of his knowledge would remain with the Navajo after his death. Klah also preserved Navajo ceremonial knowledge for outsiders as well.

KLIEWER, HENRY J. *(1871–1943)* A Mennonite missionary among the Cheyenne and Arapaho in Indian Territory (present-day Oklahoma). Born on April 9, 1871, in Berdjitsceff, Russia, Kliewer attended public school in Harvey County, Kansas, before studying at Halstead Seminary from 1890 to 1893. He held teaching positions at the Cantonment Mennonite Mission School in Indian Territory (1893–95), at a district school in Manitoba, Canada (1895–96), and at schools in Kansas (1896–98). Kliewer served as a missionary to the Cheyenne and Arapaho people for nearly 40 years, working at Hammon from 1898 to 1928 and at Thomas from 1929 to 1936.

KOHLMEISTER, BENJAMIN GOTTLIEB *(1756–1844)* Moravian missionary in Labrador among the Inuit people. He was born in Reisen (Rydzna, Poland) on February 6, 1756, the son of a baker. Following his father's death, Kohlmeister served an apprenticeship in Warsaw to learn cabinetmaking and eventually came in contact with a Moravian congregation. Kohlmeister became a member of the religious settlement at Herrnhut, Saxony, and later went to another community in Christiansfeld, Denmark. In 1790 he began missionary work in Labrador at Okak, one of the Moravian stations in the region. During his 12 years there he supervised the school, learned Inuktitut, oversaw trade with the Native people and served as a doctor. In 1802 he was sent to Hopedale, another Labrador mission station. A year later he was instrumental in sparking a religious awakening, or revival, that soon included all three Moravian stations (Okak, Hopedale, and Nain). On leave in Europe in 1806, Kohlmeister explored with his mission board the possibility of expanding his work in Labrador. In 1811 he left Okak on an expedition to the Inuit of the Ungava Bay region with a fellow missionary and 15 Native people. Although reports were favorable for the establishment of a new mission, the proposal was canceled. In 1818 Kohlmeister was named superintendent of Labrador missions and began working at Nain, the headquarters. He remained in the region for six more years before returning to Europe. He lived at Herrnhut and Neusalz (Poland) until his death on June 4, 1844. Kohlmeister and another missionary, George Knoch, wrote *Journal of a Voyage from Okkak, on the Coast of Labrador, to Ungara Bay . . . (London, 1814)*. Kohlmeister's religious works included a translation of the Gospel of John into Inuktitut. He was married to Anna Elizabeth Reimann in Labrador, and they had four children. (See also HAVEN, JENS.)

KOKO *Zuni*   The Zuni term for the ancestral spirits that bring rain (and fertility) when they appear as clouds. They come from mountains or from Kachina Village at the bottom of the sacred lake near Zuni. This area is also the home of the dead who in life were initiated into the Kachina Society. The term also refers to masked dancers who impersonate the spirits in ritual dances and to the masks worn by men when impersonating the spirits. When people imitate the clothing and dances of the *kokos*, they are animated by the spirits. (See also KACHINA [Zuni].)

KOLHU/WALA-WA (Kohlu/wala:wa, Ko/lhu/wa/a la:wa, Kothluwala'wa)   A sacred site of Zuni Pueblo, New Mexico that dates back to ancient times. The site is composed of about 10,000 acres, with two small mountains, a lake, springs, caves, minerals, and shrines located outside the pueblo boundaries in northeast Arizona. Called Zuni Heaven and Kachina Village by non-Indians, this site is the place of Zuni origin, home of their dead, and the basis of their religious life. When the United States established a reservation for Zuni in 1877, it did not include Kolhu/walawa or most of the also-sacred trail leading to it. The site was parceled in a checkerboard pattern with sections owned by federal, state, and private interests. It was returned to the Pueblo in 1984 in legislation approved by Congress and signed into law by President Reagan. After lengthy negotiations between the pueblo and its attorneys,

private owners (ranchers who use the area for grazing), the Bureau of Land Management, the state of Arizona, and Apache County, Arizona, Senator Barry Goldwater introduced legislation that instructed the Interior Department to obtain permission from local landowners for Zuni to cross the land. In 1990, a U.S. district judge permitted Zuni to cross 18 to 20 miles of an Apache County ranch for a four-day, 100-mile round-trip journey from the Zuni reservation in western New Mexico to Kolhu/wala in eastern Arizona every four years just after summer solstice. The federal government and tribe filed suit against the landowner asking that the pilgrims be given an easement. The tribe has continually used a portion of the rancher's land, who has owned it since the 1940s, every four years since 1924 and hundreds of years prior to that. Easement allows no more than 60 pilgrims on foot or horseback to follow a 50-foot-wide path across the property every four years. (See SACRED SITES for additional sites included in this volume.)

KONTI *Yaqui*   A dramatic ritual of the Yaqui 20th-century religious calendar in Sonoran (Mexican) towns. Every Sunday morning a procession of civil, military, and church-based groups move out of the church and perform devotions of prayer and song before each of four crosses in a cemetery surrounding the church. When the religious and secular organizations visit these "four corners" weekly, it symbolizes the circuit of the traditional territory of the angels and prophets at the time the boundary was defined and made sacred in the timeless past. Efforts to revive the Konti ceremonial in Arizona Yaqui settlements have yet to succeed. The Konti is also a ritual referred to as a "surrounding" that symbolizes taking possession. For example, the Yaqui Customs Authority, a ceremonial organization, employs it frequently when it takes possession of the household whose members are hosts at a Lenten fiesta, and the Infantry uses it when it takes over a cross during Lent. (See also YAQUI CEREMONIALISM.)

KONTI VO'O *Yaqui*   A Yaqui term, literally translated as "way," that refers to the stations of the cross. During the WAEHMA season (the Yaqui version of the passion of Christ), a pathway along the outer margin of the plaza is lined with 13 crosses of mesquite wood. The first cross, or station, is directly opposite the doorway of the church. Each station consists of a single cross, except the 11th, which represents Calvary and consists of three crosses. In different Yaqui towns, the crosses vary in size and construction.

KOOTENAI FALLS   On the Kootenai River in northwest Montana, falls sacred to the Kootenai Indians of Montana, Idaho, and British Columbia. The falls represents the center of the world to the Kootenai and is their most sacred place, where individuals commune with spirit forces that provide direction to the tribe. Tribal members embark on vision quests at the falls, fasting and praying for a vision. The falls are openings to spiritual forces that communicate the "destiny" for the people. Against the wishes of the Kootenai, the Bureau of Indian Affairs, representing seven Montana-Idaho rural electric cooperatives, tried to get a dam and hydroelectric power plant approved for Kootenai Falls. The tribe wrote in an affidavit filed with the Federal Energy Regulatory Commission that

> the area of Kootenai Falls is the pivot, axis, and foundation of tribal existence in political, social, and spiritual terms. Vision questing is the means by which the powers of that sacred center became accessible to the tribe in the form of messages, medicine, inspiration, and energy . . . The entire religious life of the tribe depends on members who have received visions.

The Federal Energy Regulatory Commission staff filed a 400-page recommendation urging the commissioners to turn down the power companies' request for a license. Montana's natural resource department also opposed the dam. On June 25, 1987, the commission issued a unanimous decision denying the construction license, a nine-year battle to protect the falls from development. (See SACRED SITES for related cases included in this volume.)

KOOTENAI FEMALE BERDACHE See KAUXUMA NUPIKA

KOSHARE (Kushali) *Keresan* One of the CLOWN societies among the Keresan pueblo peoples, it is composed of men, with a few women, who serve for life. This society has a headman, special ceremonial house, regalia and ceremonial ritual objects. The society alternates ceremonial control annually with the KWERANA SOCIETY. The society is mainly concerned with fertility of animals and plants and with crop growth rather than curing. The society supervises many ceremonies, and its members function as clowns and perform social control and policing functions.

The members of the society impersonate the original Koshare who have an eternal home in the East near sunrise. Ordinary people in the pueblos can represent them if they are properly initiated, clothed, and equipped. When they impersonate Koshare spirits, it is as if the real Koshare were present because the spirit and power of the original Koshare are with the impersonators. People may join the society of their own volition, by vow after a cure from a serious illness, or by trespass (walking in a sacred area by design or accident). The body of the Koshare clown is painted with white clay, with black horizontal stripes around the torso, arms and legs, black rings around the eyes and mouth, and hair smeared with white clay paint and tied up in two "horns" with corn husks. The clown wears a breechclout, no foot coverings, and carries deer-hoof rattles. Also spelled Kushali.

KOSHIWAY, JOHNATHAN *(1886–1971) Sac and Fox* Proselytizer and ROADMAN who was the principal teacher of the PEYOTE RELIGION to the Ioway, Kickapoo, and Sac and Fox in Kansas. Described as "the Grand Old Man of peyote," he worked for more than 40 years influencing the development of his religion. Born on the Sac and Fox Reservation in Kansas in 1886, he attended the Chilocco Indian School in Oklahoma and Haskell Institute in his home state. His first experience using peyote, in 1903, occurred on the Otoe reservation where he married an Otoe woman. Interested in religion, Koshiway was reported to have taken Bible classes, to have been associated for a time with Jehovah's Witnesses and the Reorganized Church of Jesus Christ of Latter-day Saints, and to have become a Presbyterian minister and a shaman. Before 1910, he learned the Otoe peyote ceremony of Charles Whitehorn and later took it to Kansas. In 1914, while living on the Otoe reservation with his wife's people, Koshiway initiated the founding of the First Born Church of Christ, which was the second peyote church to be organized and the first to be legally incorporated. He subsequently influenced the spread of peyotism among the Winnebago (Ho-chunk), Omaha, Menominee, Navajo (Dineh), and, through the NATIVE AMERICAN CHURCH, other tribal groups. In his later years, he lived on the Navajo reservation, where he died in 1971 at the age of 85.

KOTIAKAN (Cota'aqan, Coteea'kun) ("Brood of Young Ducks Scattering in Alarm") *(?–c. 1890) Yakama (Yakima)* Yakama dreamer-prophet who was a supporter and assistant of SMOHALLA, the 19th-century Washani religious leader from the Wanapam tribe of the Pacific Northwest. Kotiakan may have been related to Smohalla, but in any case, they shared close tribal and religious ties. Kotiakan lived among a Yakama band at Pa'kiut Village on the Yakima River near present-day Parker, Washington. According to one informant, he at one time gambled and was considered a bad man until the WASHANI RELIGION changed his life. Believed by some to be the originator of the creed followed by Smohalla, Kotiakan was at least instrumental in formulating its beliefs and rituals. Although both leaders incorporated aspects of Christianity into the religion, their emphasis was upon adherence to traditional culture and livelihood. They believed that by reviving the teachings of their ancestors and by participating in the WASHAT DANCE, they could resist the encroachments of white civilization. They also believed that their ancestors would be returned to life and that whites would be driven from the earth.

According to the ethnologist James Mooney, Kotiakan was gentler than Smohalla and "more disposed to meet civilization half-way." Despite his moderation, the Yakima dreamer-prophet was arrested and incarcerated in 1885, primarily because of his religious leadership. Indian agent R. H. Milroy viewed leaders such as Kotiakan as a barrier to "civilizing" and Christianizing Native people and had him arrested, ostensibly for not sending his children to school. He was handcuffed, leg-ironed, given little food or water, and uncuffed only when ordered to saw wood. During Kotiakan's incarceration, many of his followers fled to Smohalla's community at Priest Rapids in present-day Yakima County, Washington. After several weeks of confinement, Kotiakan escaped on March 19, 1885. He died about 1890 and was succeeded by Tiana'ni ("Many Wounds"), his stepson, who died about two years later. Sha'awe (or Shaw-wawa Kootiacan), a younger son of Kotiakan, then assumed the chieftainship while the religious leadership went to a man known as Billy John. Also known as Cota'aqan or Coteea'kun.

KOYEMSHI (mudheads) *Zuni* One group of Zuni sacred Kachina clowns thought to be spirits of divine origin. Ten men serve as Koyemshi impersonators and are appointed at the new year to serve for a full year, participating in retreats and ceremonies. Each of the 10 has an individual personality reflected in his name and mask. Popularly called mudheads, they wear earth-colored globular cotton masks with knobs on them filled with cotton wool and seeds, the rings around their eyes, and mouths varying in shape. The masks and bodies are colored pink with sacred lake kachina clay. Around their necks they wear a packet of seeds of corn. The Koyemshis appear at the beginning of the SHALAKO CEREMONY in late November, making rounds in pairs of all newly built or renovated Shalako houses while they sing and tell jokes about people of the village, play games, and chase the giant Shalakos. They retire to houses especially for the mudheads for the ceremony, perform house blessing rites, and pray. Before departing, the mudheads visit each household in the village and bless people with long life. At the end of the ceremony in December, they are paid for their year-long efforts by gifts contributed by every household. With humorous antics and reversed behavior,

Koyemshi. Zuni mudhead clowns, by an anonymous Zuni artist. Koyemshi are one group of Zuni sacred clowns that participate in ceremonies and retreats. *Courtesy of the School of American Research, Santa Fe, New Mexico.*

they overturn the sacred patterns and commonsense notions of everyday life. They correspond to the Hopi Tachuktus. (See also CLOWNS.)

KUKSU RELIGION *Cahto, Coast Miwok, Costanoan, Esselen, Konkow, Maidu, Nisenan, Patwin, Pomo, Salinan, Wintu, Yuki* A religious system with a set of rites performed only by those who, usually as boys, have been initiated and instructed in long and formal sessions by the Kuksu Society. The society has ceremonial dances in a large, circular, earth-covered dance house in which spirits are impersonated by society members wearing "big-head" headdresses of radiating feathered sticks. The impersonators petition the spirits for renewal of the world and the continuation of environmental abundance. During the ceremony, society members instruct initiates between the ages of eight and 16 in sacred knowledge. It is believed that the initiation makes the boys healthy, long-lived, and strong. The cycle of Kuksu dances are believed to bring rain, nourish the earth, and produce good crops. The complete cycle of ceremonies in which dances represented different spirits varies from group to group and village to village, but they share certain features, including the special dance house, ceremonial director, spirit impersonators, dance regalia, and log foot drum. Initiated participants enact a journey that serves as a metaphor for death and rebirth.

KUSHUWE, JACK *(fl. late 19th–early 20th c.) Ioway* A peyote ROADMAN (leader) who also served as a Presbyterian minister. About 1899 Kushuwe enrolled in the Chilocco Indian boarding school in Oklahoma, where he remained until he ran away at the age of 18. Upon returning home, he was sent to another school and earned a reputation through his leadership in Bible classes and in Y.M.C.A. work. He later became a Presbyterian minister and raised a family. After one of his daughters was stricken with a serious illness, he took her to a number of doctors and specialists, but they were unable to help her. Kushuwe also tried to cure her by conducting peyote meetings, incorporating features of his Christian beliefs, but his daughter remained seriously ill. It was not until he went to the Kiowa reservation and was assisted by peyotists that his daughter recovered. Kushuwe was told that peyote had not helped him in his own services because he had departed from the original rules of the religion by mixing Christianity and PEYOTE RELIGION. He then continued to run meetings but changed them to be consistent with earlier teachings.

KWERANA SOCIETY (Kurena, Kwiraina, Kwirana, Kwirena, Quirana) *Keresan* One of the CLOWN societies among the Keresan pueblo peoples; composed mainly of men, with a few associated women, who serve for life. It alternates ceremonial duties annually with the KOSHARE clown society. This society has a headman, special ceremonial house, and ritual objects and is concerned with fertility of the fields and crop growth. It takes charge of some ceremonies and has its own retreats. Men may join the society of their own volition, by vow after a cure from a serious illness, or by trespass, walking in a sacred area by design or accident. The Kwerana's face is striped orange and black, and his body is divided in half vertically with the right side orange and the left side white; hair is done up on top of the head in a single bunch. The society conducts a dance at harvest time.

L

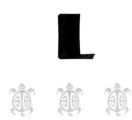

LACOMBE, ALBERT (Man of Good Heart) *(1827–1916)*
One of the first Roman Catholic missionaries sent to the Canadian Northwest. Lacombe was born in Quebec and educated at L'Assomption College. He joined the Oblate Order and was ordained a priest in 1849. He spent his life in service to Indians, working among the Blackfeet and Cree in particular. He wrote a dictionary and grammar of the Cree language as well as other books in Cree and Blackfeet. In 1861 he founded Saint Albert mission for Cree-Métis; in 1865 he founded Saint Paul des Cris; and in 1895 he founded Saint Paul de Métis. He acted as a diplomat for the Canadian government, negotiating treaties with Athabascan bands and negotiating with Plains Indian leaders. Among some tribal people, he was also called "Man of Good Heart."

LACROSSE *Iroquois* A ceremonial game, part of the THUNDER DANCE that appeals to the Seven Thunders to continue their service to people. The players undergo a ritual purification, an emetic, before the game begins. The game involves two teams that try to get a hard ball (a little smaller than a baseball) into the opposition's net. Each man carries a stick with a small net on the end with which he throws or carries a ball. Wagers were often taken on the outcome of matches between tribes. After the game, there is singing and dancing followed by the longhouse ritual of giving thanks to the spirits above the earth. Tobacco and food are distributed to the players. This ceremonial game has developed into a popular modern sport.

LAFITAU, JOSEPH FRANÇOIS *(1681–1746)* Canadian missionary to the Mohawk. Born in France, Lafitau entered the Jesuit order and was ordained as a priest in 1711. Soon after, he was sent to the Caughnawaga Mohawk village in Quebec, where he remained from 1712 to 1717. He learned the language, and he described Iroquois culture in works published in Paris in 1724. Using his own observations to throw light on earlier cultures, he tried to compare American Indian cultures to ancient Greeks and prehistoric tribes of Europe. He tried to show Iroquois and Huron with their complex cultures were remarkably like the ancient Greeks. He has been called the founder of "scientific ethnology."

LAKON SOCIETY (Basket Dance) *Hopi* A women's society whose ceremony is performed in October. The public ceremony involves four Lakon maidens each carrying corn of a different color. They perform within a circle of women who dance with woven food baskets. After the dance, women toss the baskets to spectators and to men and boys of the pueblo. The society members possess the power to heal skin troubles through the use of certain plants. Also spelled Lakone. The ceremony is also called the Basket Dance. (See also MARAW SOCIETY; OWAQLT SOCIETY.)

LALEMANT, JEROME *(1593–1673)* French Jesuit missionary. Born in Paris, France, he entered the Jesuit novitiate in Paris in 1610 at the age of 17. After years of study and teaching, he went to Canada in 1638. He was named superior of the Huron mission the year of his arrival. In 1645, he began his appointment as superior of Jesuits in Canada with his residence at Quebec. His first period of office, 1645–1650, covered the time when ISAAC JOGUES, ANTOINE DANIEL, JEAN DE BREBEUF, his nephew Gabriel Lalemant, and three other missionaries were killed during the Iroquois attack on Huronia (southern Ontario) and the Huron mission Lalemant had organized and administered was destroyed. After returning from France, he was again superior of Jesuits from 1659 to 1665 and supervised the resettlement of Huron displaced by war with the Iroquois. Father Lalemant's writings in the *Relations des Jesuites de la Nouvelle-France* from 1639 to 1644 describe Huron life. He died in Quebec.

LA MERE, OLIVER (*fl. early 20th c.*) *Winnebago (Nebraska)* An early peyote leader among his people. La Mere was one of the Winnebago peyotists who sought official permission to obtain peyote for religious use. W. E. Johnson, a special officer of the Bureau of Indian Affairs from 1906 to 1911, had halted shipments. La Mere had been apprehended in Sioux City, Iowa, for possession of peyote and his supply ordered destroyed. The commissioner of Indian affairs requested the names of the adult practitioners among the Nebraska Winnebago and granted permission for members to each use a limited, specified number of peyote buttons per week. The federal policy was inconsistent and did not extend to allowing shipments of peyote to the adherents. Although the peyotists in Winnebago, Nebraska, sought baptism and membership in the local church at one time, the clergyman would not accept them. In 1921 they formed the Peyote Church of Christ, and Oliver La Mere served as one of its early presidents. (See also PEYOTE RELIGION.)

LAME BILL (Munkas, Budkas, Bulkas, Katao, Itinash) (?–*c. 1900*) *Hill Patwin* A dreamer and prophet identified as one of the originators of the BOLE-MARU RELIGION, an outgrowth of the GHOST DANCE OF 1870. Lame Bill, a member of the small reservation of Lolsel in California, was an innovator who combined elements from traditional ceremonies and new ideas to create the Bole-Maru religion. Although identified as an initial supporter of the EARTH LODGE RELIGION beliefs associated with the Ghost Dance of 1870, he only continued them for a short time. Dances used in his Bole-Maru services included the Toto, or Blanket, Dance with both male and female participants, the Bole Hesi, which he originated from the sacred HESI CEREMONY, and the Bole Dance performed by men as well as by women in costume carrying tule whisks. Lame Bill also established the use of a flag or flagpole in front of the dance house to indicate when ceremonies were taking place. He took his teachings to the Pomo and Hill Patwin, and they eventually spread to other groups in the region. Lame Bill's influence

has been described as widespread and the religion he originated has persisted to the present. Other names for Lame Bill include Budkas, Bulkas, Katao, and Hinash.

LAME DEER, JOHN (FIRE) (Tahca Ushte) (*c. 1900–1976*) *Lakota* A prominent holy man. Lame Deer, a Lakota, was born after the turn of the century in a log cabin between the Rosebud and Pine Ridge Reservations in South Dakota. His mother was Sally Red Blanket and his father was Wawi-Yohi-Ya (Let-Them-Have-Enough), who became known as Silas Fire. Lame Deer spent a lot of time with his grandparents, having as strong a relationship with them as he did with his parents. The family lived in a remote area, far from the influences of the outside world. It was not until Lame Deer was about five years old that he first saw a white man. After the Bureau of Indian Affairs notified his family to send him to school, however, pressures on his traditional way of life began. For eight years Lame Deer attended a government day school, where the third grade was the highest level taught, on the Rosebud Reservation. When he was 14 years old, he was told by the authorities that he had to attend boarding school. Although he attended for a time, he was constantly in trouble with school officials, who sought to change his cultural ways.

When Lame Deer was 16, he went to a hilltop pit for his first HANBLECEYA or VISION QUEST. Alone for four days and four nights, he saw before him his great-grandfather, Tahca Ushte (Lame Deer), the Minneconjou chief who had been shot and killed in a battle with General "Bear Coat" Miles. Lame Deer then understood that he was to take his great-grandfather's name. His vision also told him that he would become a medicine man who would teach others. In time, the instructions he received were fulfilled. Lame Deer eventually became a medicine man with the help of Lakota holy men, including Chest, Thunderhawk, and Good Lance. He went through many experiences before fully realizing his visionary teachings. He was a rodeo clown named Alice Jitterbug, a bootlegger, a tribal policeman, a soldier, a potato picker, a sheepherder, a square dance caller, a jail prisoner, and a sign painter. He stated in his autobiography: "A medicine man shouldn't be a saint. He should experience and feel all the ups and downs, the despair and joy, the magic and the reality, the courage and the fear of his people."

Lame Deer also tried other religions, including several Christian denominations and the NATIVE AMERICAN CHURCH. His final preference was for the traditional beliefs of his people: "I have my hands full just clinging to our old Sioux ways—singing the ancient songs correctly, conducting a sweat-lodge ceremony as it should be, making our old beliefs as pure, as clear and true as I possibly can, making them stay alive, saving them from extinction. This is a big enough task for an old man." Besides healing with herbs and conducting YUWIPI and other sacred ceremonies, Lame Deer's vision foretold that he would teach 24 medicine men. At the time he told his life story to Richard Erdoes, who coauthored his autobiography, *Lame Deer: Seeker of Visions* (1972), he had taught 18 medicine men. Lame Deer died in 1976.

LANCASTER, BEN (Chief Gray Horse) *(c. 1880–1953)* *Washoe* Peyote ROADMAN and missionary. Born about 1880 near Mountain House, Nevada, Lancaster was introduced to PEYOTE RELIGION among the Southern Cheyenne in 1921 when he was employed as a farmhand near Clinton, Oklahoma. He also traveled around the country selling "Chief Gray Horse's Indian Herbs" for about 10 years. Lancaster introduced peyotism among the Washoe in 1936 and served as a missionary to neighboring tribal groups. His peyote meetings were patterned after the Tipi Way of the Kiowa, Comanche, and other tribes, with some exceptions, including a more prominent role for women and an unfixed order of songs. He was also known as Chief Gray Horse.

LAROCHE DAILLON, JOSEPH DE *(?–1656)* French Recollet missionary. Born in Paris, he arrived in Quebec in 1625. In 1626 he went to the land of the Neutral Indians in southwestern Ontario, where he spent months studying their language and catechizing them. His unpublished account, dated 1627, constitutes the first study of the customs of the Neutrals and one of the earliest descriptions of the Huron peninsula. He returned to France, where he died.

LARUSH, SISTER M. SIRILLA (Way-johnie-ma-son, "Busy Body") *(1892–1976)* *Ojibway* A Roman Catholic nun who served the St. Francis Solanus Church on the Lac Courte Oreilles Reservation in Reserve, Wisconsin, her birthplace, for some 30 years. She was born in 1892 and named Fabiola, later shortened to Lola. She attended a local mission school and Hayward Indian School before entering a Milwaukee convent in 1908. She returned to Lac Courte Oreilles in 1925, after years in Milwaukee and Nebraska, as Sister M. Sirilla and requested permission from her order to work there. The original Catholic church at Reserve had burned down in 1921, and the rest of the mission had deteriorated. She began the work of restoring and rebuilding the mission, enlisting the help of area residents with her colleague Fr. PHILIP B. GORDON. Years later, in 1962, she left the reservation, eventually working at missions in Chicago and in Mississippi. Sister M. Sirilla died in 1976 and was buried at Lac Courte Oreilles.

LAWYER, ARCHIE B. *(?–1893)* *Nez Perce* A Presbyterian missionary who worked among the Nez Perce people. He

was the son of Chief Hallalhotsoot ("the talker") and the grandson of Twisted Hair, the leader who welcomed the explorers Lewis and Clark to his Nez Perce homeland. Hallalhotsoot became known for his oratory and for supporting treaty-making with the United States government. He was opposed by Chief Joseph (the elder), who refused to agree to further Nez Perce land cessions in 1863. Archie Lawyer was one of the first students of SUSAN LAW MCBETH, an early Presbyterian missionary who trained a number of Native ministers. Lawyer opposed Chief Joseph (the son of Joseph the elder), TOOLHULHULSOTE, and other leaders, who represented the antitreaty faction of their people and resisted confinement on a reservation and the loss of their homeland during the Nez Perce War of 1877. In the aftermath of the conflict, Lawyer served as a missionary to the tribal resisters who had survived the war and had been removed to Indian Territory (present-day Oklahoma). Ordained in 1881, Lawyer reported a total of 120 members in his church by 1883, the largest membership then organized in the Synod of Kansas. Two years later Lawyer was back in Idaho working as a missionary at Lapwai agency among the Nez Perce. In 1890 he opposed ROBERT WILLIAMS, a fellow minister, for his total condemnation of tribal cultural practices. The conflict led to a split and to Lawyer's formation of the Second Presbyterian Church of Kamiah. Lawyer also became an opponent of the ethnologist Alice Fletcher, who was sent by the government to parcel Nez Perce lands into individual allotments, and of McBeth and her sister, who favored Williams in the dispute.

LeCARON, JOSEPH *(c. 1586–1632)* French Recollet missionary. Born near Paris, he was brought to New France in North America by Samuel de Champlain in 1615. On August 12, 1615 he celebrated the first mass in Huron country. He founded the first mission in Huron country and twice stayed with the Montagnais tribe. He wrote an unpublished relation (narrative about his missionary work) that was a study of the customs of Indians of New France as well as an analysis of the "obstacles" in the way of their conversion. He returned to France in 1629 when New France became an English possession, thereby putting an end to his missionary work. He wrote dictionaries of the Huron, Algonquian, and Montagnais languages, but none exist today.

LeCLERCQ, CHRISTIEN *(1641–after 1700)* French Recollet missionary. Born in France, he departed for Canada in 1675 and was assigned to a post at Perce on the Gaspé coast from 1675 to 1686. Father LeClerq ministered to the Micmac, studied and learned their language and customs and developed a system of ideographs, or figurative letters, for recording their language. This writing serves as a basis for present-day Micmac writing. He also created a dictionary. He published a volume, the *Nouvelle relation,* a source of information about the history of Canada and documentation about the Micmac of Gaspé Peninsula. The volume has both been devalued for its "mediocre details about the life and the everyday customs of the tribe" and praised for offering a fine "picture of the family life of the Indians." Father LeClercq died sometime after 1700.

LEE, GEORGE P. (Ashkii Hoyani, "Boy Who Is Well Behaved and Good") *(b. 1943) Navajo (Dineh)* The first American Indian to become a general authority of the Church of Jesus Christ of Latter-day Saints. He was born in 1943 in Towaoc, Colorado, to Mae K. Lee (Asdzaa Lichii) of the Bitter Water clan and to a medicine man, Pete Lee (Hastiin Jaaneez Yee Biye), of the Under the Flat-Roofed House People clan. One of 17 siblings, Lee was called Ashkii Yazhi, Little Boy, until he was given a sacred name, Ashkii Hoyani (Boy Who Is Well Behaved and Good). He attended a government boarding school at Shiprock, New Mexico, for two years after a Mormon trader, assisting the Bureau of Indian Affairs, helped him enroll. Because a religious preference, other than the Native American traditional faith, had to be indicated on the application, Lee's mother told the trader to write in the name of his religion. After completing the second grade at Shiprock, Lee attended school in Aztec, New Mexico, where he was promoted to the fifth grade. When he was 12, he became a member in one of the first children's groups to participate in an official Indian foster placement program sponsored by the Church of Jesus Christ of Latter-day Saints. He was transported to Orem, Utah, where he lived with the Glen and Joan Harker family.

Lee remained in their home for seven years, returning to his Navajo family during summer vacations, until he graduated from Orem High School in 1962. He excelled in school, achieving many honors, and became a devout Mormon who later served as a missionary on the Navajo reservation. He attended Brigham Young University, where he earned a bachelor's degree and a doctorate in educational administration, and Utah State University, where he completed a master's program. In Arizona Lee taught at the Rough Rock Demonstration School and later served as president of the College of Ganado. He received many honors, including a fellowship from the U.S. Office of Education for the 1970–1971 academic year, a Ford Foundation Fellowship Award and the Spencer W. Kimball Lamanite Leadership Award. His autobiography, *Silent Courage,* was published in 1987.

Lee's achievements culminated in his 1975 appointment as a full-time member of the First Quorum of the Seventy, a general authority, by president Spencer W. Kimball of the Church of Jesus Christ of Latter-day Saints. The position in the high council meant that he would work with the president, the Quorum of the Twelve Apostles, and other high leaders in administering the affairs of the church.

On September 1, 1989, however, Mormon leaders announced that Lee had been excommunicated for "apostasy and other conduct unbecoming a member of the church." His excommunication was the first of a general authority to occur in 46 years. According to Lee, the action stemmed from his disagreement with the other church leaders over the role of American Indians in the religion and from other charges he had presented in a 23-page letter to Ezra Taft Benson, the 90-year-old church president, and the 12-member quorum.

LEE, JASON *(1803–1845)* Methodist missionary. Lee was born in Stanstead, Quebec, near the border of Vermont in 1803. Three years after converting to Methodism at the age of 23, Lee attended a religious academy at Wilbraham, Massachusetts. He was licensed to preach in 1830 and served as a minister in Stanstead for two years. In 1832 he was ordained a deacon and later an elder by the New England Conference of the Methodist Episcopal Church.

Lee's work with Native Americans began in 1833 after the missionary society of his church selected him to head a mission to the Salish-Kootenai. Lee set out for the Pacific Northwest with his nephew, the Reverend Daniel Lee, and lay assistants. Although the project was abandoned, the missionaries located a station in the Willamette Valley near what is now Salem, Oregon. A short time later, the settlement was established. In 1837 another missionary group, including the missionary ELIJAH WHITE, arrived, and the Methodist work began expanding to Fort Nisqually, The Dalles, Clatsop Plains, and Oregon City. The following year Lee returned to the East, where he sought prospective colonists, support for his mission work and territorial status for Oregon. A group of 50 people, known as the "great reinforcement" was organized to supplement his efforts. The reinforcements led by Lee, arrived at the mouth of the Columbia River on May 20, 1840, to carry out the missionary's plans.

Lee eventually viewed the effort to convert Indians to Christianity as futile and turned his attention to temporal concerns. Besides helping to organize the territorial government, he concentrated on Americanizing the region. He also founded several schools, including the Oregon Institute, which was later renamed Willamette University. In 1844, while traveling East, Lee learned that he had been dismissed from his post by the mission board of his church, which charged him with neglecting his missionary duties while promoting Euro-American settlement and other interests in the region. Although he was later exonerated of the blame, he was not reinstated, and the mission stations were closed in 1845. Lee never returned to the Pacific Northwest. He died on March 12, 1845, in Stanstead, Quebec. In 1906 his remains were moved to Salem, Oregon, and reinterred.

LEJEUNE, PAUL *(1591–1664)* French Jesuit missionary. Born in France, he entered the Jesuit novitiate in 1613 at the age of 22. In 1632, he was appointed superior general of the mission in Canada, a position he held until 1639. He mastered the language of Montagnais Indians and devised a program to settle them in a village that established him as the founder of the Jesuit missions in Canada. LeJeune, who equated civilization and Christianity with village life, developed a plan for a Montagnais village called St. Joseph de Sillery. In his *Relation* of 1634, he spelled out his plan for conversion and cultural change. From 1639 to 1649, he was a missionary at Quebec, Sillery, Tadoussac, Trois Rivières, and Montreal. LeJeune returned to Paris in 1649 after Iroquois destroyed the Huron mission, becoming procurator of the Canadian mission until 1662. He was the first and most prolific editor of the *Relations des Jesuites de la Nouvelle-France,* a huge body of literature published between 1632 and 1673 in France, a significant source of information about Indians and the personalities and work of missionaries. The first 11 relations are the work of LeJeune. Of the 41 volumes, 15 are entirely LeJeune's, and he contributed to all the others until 1662. He died in Paris. (See also NEGABANAT, NOEL.)

LEMOYNE, SIMON *(1604–1665)* French Jesuit missionary. Born in France, he entered the Jesuit novitiate in 1622 at the age of 18. He went to Quebec in 1638 and ministered to the Huron until 1649. He learned the Huron language and spoke it fluently. He was also known as an ambassador of peace to the Iroquois. He made six trips between 1654 and 1662 into Iroquois country to work for the release of French captives. He died in Quebec. The American Jesuit-run LeMoyne College, located at Syracuse, New York, honors Father LeMoyne's memory.

LIFE WAY CEREMONY *Navajo (Dineh)* Ceremonies for injuries resulting from accidents, sprains, strains, fractures, bruises, swelling, cuts, and burns. The ceremony, performed any time of the year, can last from two to 16 nights. It is characterized by the use of a life medicine administered in a turtle shell. (See also NAVAJO CURING CEREMONIES.)

LIGHTNING CEREMONY *White Mountain Apache* A ceremony for the community in the spring and summer when lightning occurs frequently. The ceremony protects everyone within the area from this danger and is also performed to cause rain and ensure good crops. It is held as well for the community when some evil influence is thought to be at work. The men who conduct this ceremony acquire the songs, ceremonial prayers, and knowledge through personal religious experience with spiritual power. Men who conduct this ceremony are spoken of as holy and are considered invested with spiritual power of a high quality.

LILLEY, JOHN *(fl. mid-19th century)* Presbyterian missionary who worked among the Seminole people in Indian Territory (present-day Oklahoma). JOHN BEMO, a Seminole who had been adopted by a French ship captain, had spoken to a group that included Lilley at a church in Philadelphia about the problems his people faced with their forced removal to territories in the West. Bemo accompanied Lilley and his family to Indian Territory in 1848. Upon their arrival, they began building a mission at Oak Ridge in the Creek Nation at a location selected by the Reverend ROBERT MCGILL LOUGHRIDGE for the first Seminole church school. At a meeting attended by the Seminole chief Micanopy, who had given the missionaries permission to open the school, and the Seminole war chief Cowakogee (Wild Cat), the Lilleys were disheartened by Cowakogee's criticisms of the slow pace of the construction work and the fact that teaching had not begun. Eventually the educational work started, and Lilley, his wife, and Bemo served as teachers. In 1855 Lilley and his wife returned to the East to seek medical treatment for the trachoma that afflicted both of them. Although they reopened the Oak Ridge mission in 1856, the work was later disrupted by the Civil War. After the war John Lilley went back to Indian Territory, building a Seminole mission in 1866. Lilley's wife, Mary Anne, was an important partner in the missionary efforts and wrote an unpublished autobiography describing her family's work among the Seminole people.

LIMPY, JOSEPHINE HEAD SWIFT (Stands by the Fire) *(1900–1980) Cheyenne* Keeper of Esevone, the SACRED BUFFALO HAT of the Cheyenne people. Limpy was the descendant of previous keepers, including her grandfather COAL BEAR and her father, Head Swift, and had learned the holy ways of the Sacred Buffalo Hat and keeper's position in her family. After her father died in 1952, the Cheyenne authorities offered the keepership to a man named John Teeth. When he turned it down, the Sacred Buffalo Hat was placed in Limpy's keeping. Her guardianship, which was to be temporary, lasted until 1958. She was noted for the great care and devotion with which she carried out the daily duties of caring for Esevone. In 1969 the Sacred Buffalo Hat was again placed in Limpy's care after James Black Wolf's tenure as keeper ended. She continued in the position until 1973 when she requested that a new person be selected. Limpy, who died in 1980, was succeeded by JOE LITTLE COYOTE.

LINSCHEID, GUSTAV A. *(1875–1942)* A Mennonite missionary to the Cheyenne people. Born in Austria in 1875, Linscheid was educated at Bethel College in Newton, Kansas. After holding administrative positions at the Cantonment Mennonite Mission School in Oklahoma from 1895 to 1898, he served as a missionary at Arapaho, Oklahoma, between 1900 and 1904. In 1904 he and his wife went to Busby, Montana, where they were placed in charge of the mission station among the Northern Cheyenne. Linscheid remained there until 1920, then returned to Oklahoma to work with the tribe's Southern people. He served as secretary-treasurer of the Conference of Indian Missionary Workers of Oklahoma from 1923 to 1927. In 1930 he became the editor of *The Cheyenne and Arapaho Messenger.*

LISHWAILAIT ("Smoking") *(1820s–c. 1890s) Klickitat* A prophet of the WASHANI RELIGION. Lishwailait lived near Husum, Washington, in the area of the White Salmon River. When his mother died, after mourning her for five days, Lishwailait saw her appear. She told him not to grieve for her or others who had died. She also told him about the relationship between Native people and the earth, and Lishwailait began to preach his vision within a year. He told his followers that foods supplied by the earth in natural cycles would nourish them and help them multiply. He also taught other religious concepts, such as the meaning of the drum. Lishwailait, who was a contemporary of Washani prophet SMOHALLA, was said to have practiced his beliefs from the time he was 21 until his death at the age of 86. Like Smohalla, he had a flag and a sacred messenger bird. He also owned a symbolic buckskin shirt with red, white, and blue stars, which he wore at Sunday observances. His spiritual powers included the ability to know when people had done something evil. Lishwailait was said to demonstrate the appearance of a colored object in the palm of each hand. One was gold and one silver, to which he said Native people would become enslaved. Considered one of the great religious leaders of The Dalles area during the mid-19th century, Lishwailait's influence lasted long after he died. Lishwailait and JAKE HUNT, the founder of the FEATHER RELIGION, also lived in the same community and were believed to be related. He was also called Lishwahlite.

LITTLE ANGELS (Angel Guard) *Yaqui* See WAEHMA

LITTLE CORN CEREMONY *Iroquois.* Also called small green corn or corn testing ceremony, this rite is scheduled at the time when corn is not yet ripe. The purpose is to encourage food spirits to continue their duties in the final ripening stage. (See also GREEN CORN.)

LITTLE COYOTE, JOE (Night Fighter or Night Killer) *(b. 1940s) Cheyenne* Keeper of Esevone, the SACRED BUFFALO HAT of the Cheyenne people, chief and leader in the Kit Fox Society, one of the military societies of his people. Little Coyote was a descendant of warriors and priests. His great-grandfather was White Frog, or Fringe, a member of the Suhtaio band of the Cheyenne, who had fought against the enemies of his people and who had served as a priest in the MASSAUM CEREMONY and the SUN DANCE. His great-grandmother, also a Suhtai, was the niece of COAL BEAR, a 19th-century holy man who had served as the Keeper of Esevone. Little Coyote's grandfather, Henry Little Coyote, also held the keepership of the Sacred Buffalo Hat, serving in that capacity between 1959 and 1965. His wife, Brenda Bear Chum Little Coyote, was likewise the descendant of a Keeper of Esevone. Her great-grandfather, Black Bird, held the sacred position during the 1920s and 1930s.

The selection of Joe Little Coyote as Keeper of Esevone was made by the Northern Cheyenne military societies and approved by the Council Chiefs in the spring of 1973. A short time later the new keeper, who had succeeded JOSEPHINE HEAD SWIFT LIMPY, decided to seek permission to take the Sacred Buffalo Hat to NOAHA-VOSE (Bear Butte), for renewing ceremonies. After approval was granted for the serious undertaking, extensive preparations began. The return represented the first time the Sacred Buffalo Hat had been taken to the sacred site since the 1870s.

After becoming the keeper, Little Coyote was permitted to continue his association with the Northern Cheyenne Research and Human Development Association, an organization dedicated to the preservation and revitalization of tribal ways. As the association's first executive director, he was instrumental in its development. During his brief tenure as keeper (1973–74) he sought spiritual help for his people from modern-day threats, including strip-mining, to preserve their traditional sacred ways. The Harvard-educated Little Coyote also became an oil and gas administrator among the Northern Cheyenne.

LITTLE PEOPLE Tiny beings or creatures known to Native groups across North America. They are known to inhabit particular land or water areas. In some groups they are characterized as speaking the Native language, wearing hide garments, and possessing playful natures. Others believe them to be invisible to all or most people and to be capable of harming and/or helping human beings. Some descriptions also refer to their sacred knowledge and healing abilities. The

Native names of the Little People vary from group to group. Among the Yavapai, the Little People are thought to be about three feet tall, with round heads, and to live in certain mountains. They are represented in the Mountain Spirit dance ritual. Other examples include Iyaganaske (Chickasaw), M-me-m-mege'-soo (Cree) and YEHASURI (Catawba). An example of a sacred society involving Little People is found among the Iroquois. (See also POOR COYOTE; ROCK BABY.)

LITTLE PEOPLE SOCIETY *Iroquois* This society performs the rites, including the DARK DANCE, that are preeminently the religion of the "Little Folks," or Pygmies, whose good-will is sought by all Indians and who are believed to be next to humans in importance and very powerful beings. They demand proper attention, or they will inflict punishment on those who neglect them. Meetings are called at any time for the purpose of appeasing the spirits of certain sacred objects that have become impotent or are called by members who are troubled by certain signs and sounds. Nonmembers gain membership by requesting the services of the society.

LITTLE RITE *Apache* This daytime celebration is an abridged version of the full Apache puberty ritual and celebration. Family and friends gather for a feast and a token ceremony in which the celebrant might wear ceremonial dress and run in the ritual manner. The girl, singer, women, men, and children are marked with pollen and presents are distributed. (See also GIRL'S PUBERTY RITE.)

LITTLE WATER SOCIETY *Iroquois* A strictly private medicine curing society with no public ceremony, dances, or paraphernalia. The principal ceremonies are meetings held three or four times a year to renew the strength of the society's medicine by singing a series of songs. There are a large number of injunctions concerning society members who are custodians of the sacred medicine, the patient, and the medicine itself. Anyone but menstruating women may, on payment of sacred tobacco, attend rites to renew the strength of Little Water Medicine. Of all the medicine, Little Water is depicted as the strongest and most dangerous. Members of this society are people who have been cured by the medicine or who have had a dream involving the ceremony. (See also MEDICINE SOCIETIES [Iroquois].)

LOBERT *(fl. 1870s) Klamath* Shaman whose DREAM DANCE was said to be the first held on the Lower End of the Klamath Reservation in Oregon. After his dream, Lobert built an earth lodge with a center pole that extended through the roof's smoke-hole. His spiritual instructions included sacred songs, a dance, and particular face painting. Lobert

dreamed that the adherents who successfully climbed the center pole to the roof of the ceremonial earth lodge would go to heaven. The Dream Dance, a later variation of the GHOST DANCE OF 1870, is said to have ended in 1878 in Lobert's area of the reservation.

LOFTY WANDERER *Yavapai* The grandson of Old Lady White Stone, who planted all healing herbs, this spirit cleared the world of all monsters. He received special powers from his fathers, Sun and Cloud, after searching for them. He made his aged grandmother young again with lightning. Before leaving the world, he taught all beings their right ways and then sent different groups of humans to different places throughout the world with the Yavapai alone remaining at the center of the world. Lofty Wanderer could bring the dead back to life and taught people the right song for every purpose. Yavapais appeal to Lofty Wanderer for help in ritual and individual prayer.

LONE BEAR, SAM *(1879–1937) Lakota* A peyote ROADMAN among the Lakota and other tribal groups. Lone Bear, a member of the Oglala band of his people, was born to Alice Plenty Brothers and Oliver Lone Bear and lived on Lone Bear Creek in South Dakota. He attended the Carlisle Indian Industrial School in Pennsylvania from February 1892 until July 1897. Two years later, in 1899, he joined Buffalo Bill Cody's Wild West Show and, in 1902, accompanied it to Europe, where it toured until 1906. Lone Bear, an early peyote missionary to the Lakota, traveled extensively in the West. He introduced the Cross Fire peyote ceremony to a number of tribes, including the Ute in Colorado and Utah. His success as a religious leader was marred by troubles with the law, leading to his incarceration at McNeal Island Federal Prison in Steilacoom, Washington, for nearly two years in the 1930s on charges of taking an underage girl across state lines for immoral purposes. Lone Bear was married to Ella Sirawap, a Ute, and later to Mamie Charley of Fallon, Nevada, and had several children. He returned to the Pine Ridge Reservation in South Dakota sometime after his release from prison and became ill a short time later. JAMES BLUEBIRD and other peyotists conducted a Cross Fire ceremony for Lone Bear before his death at the age of 58. During Lone Bear's lifetime, he assumed the names Peter Phelps, Sam Loganberry, Chief S. C. Bird, Leo Coyote, and Leo Okio, among others, to avoid arrest. (See also NATIVE AMERICAN CHURCH; PEYOTE RELIGION.)

LONEWOLF, DELOS KNOWLES *(1870–1945) Kiowa* One of the first Kiowa licensed to preach by the Methodist Church. He was born during the summer of 1870 near present-day Gotebo, Oklahoma. After the death of his father,

Saudle-kon-geah (Black Turtle), he was adopted by his uncle, Chief Lone Wolf, and acquired his name. Lonewolf began his education at the age of 14 at the Kiowa School near Anadarko, Oklahoma, where he was named Delos Knowles after a teacher. He later attended the Chilocco Indian School for some years, then enrolled in the Carlisle Indian Industrial School in Carlisle, Pennsylvania, from which he graduated in 1896. As a student, Lonewolf achieved fame as a fullback on the Carlisle football team and was active in Christian religious activities. He also attended Metzger College in Carlisle, Pennsylvania. During his years at Carlisle he often went to Washington, D.C., where he served as an interpreter to Chief Lone Wolf. Upon returning home, he farmed the land and served his people in a leadership role. Lonewolf was licensed to preach in 1923 and was active in churches of the western district of the Indian Mission Conference. He was married to Ida Wassee, with whom he had six children, and then to Bessie McKenzie. Lonewolf died on March 15, 1945.

LONG, SAM (c. 1912–) *Shoshone* A peyote ROADMAN. Long moved to Lee, Nevada, when the Te-Moak Indian Reservation was established in the 1930s for landless Shoshone from Elko and Ruby Valley. Long attended his first peyote meeting, a Tipi Way ceremony, in Ibapah, Utah, in 1934 and regularly attended Cross Fire peyote ceremonies until 1937. By that time, he had learned to be a roadman and began to conduct Cross Fire meetings in Ruby Valley. These meetings were attended by his father, John Long, an early peyotist, and other relatives. Like JOHN WILSON (Caddo), Long attributed variations in his ceremonies to divine revelation. He included the use of a staff patterned after one given to his father by SAM LONE BEAR, revered by this small group of peyotists, in Ibapah, Utah, in 1929; an altar cloth embroidered with a blue silk heart on which the Chief Peyote rested; and the reversal of the ceremonial direction from clockwise to counterclockwise. Long did not use the midnight water ritual, a tobacco ceremony, a sand altar, a fire or cedar-incensing, but he did keep the sacred number four. In his ritual, a "gravy" was made by grinding and mixing peyote with water. Each time after using the peyote, participants could drink from the freshwater available to them. Omer C. Stewart, an authority on the PEYOTE RELIGION, questioned whether Long's innovations would survive because of the small size and isolation of these peyotists. (See also NATIVE AMERICAN CHURCH.)

LONG, WILL WEST (Wili' westi') (1875–1947) *Cherokee* A ceremonial leader who made valuable contributions to scholarly studies of Cherokee culture and language over a 60-year period. He was born on the Qualla Reservation in North Carolina to Sally Terrapin and John Long, a Baptist preacher. As a child he was trained in Cherokee culture by his traditionalist mother and maternal uncle. At the age of 16 he went to Old Trinity College in Randolph County, North Carolina. After several months he ran away, later returning and staying for about a year. Besides learning English at the school, Long was taught the syllabary invented by Sequoyah by an older Cherokee classmate. Following his return to the reservation, he came to the attention of the ethnologist James Mooney, who began his study of the culture there in 1887. Long became Mooney's scribe, copying sacred formulas and other materials for him and serving as an interpreter. Long began attending Hampton Institute in Hampton, Virginia, in 1895, remaining there until 1900. He later went to New England to continue his education and worked in Conway, Amherst, North Amherst, and Boston. He returned home permanently shortly before his mother died in 1904.

Long then resumed his studies of Cherokee culture, working to preserve the traditional knowledge of his people. Besides learning from family and clan relatives, he eventually sought knowledge in the larger tribal community. One of his teachers was a cousin, Charley Lawson, who taught him to carve ceremonial Booger masks and to sing traditional songs. His relationship with Mooney continued until the ethnologist's death, and Long also worked with many other prominent scholars during his lifetime, including Leonard Bloom, William H. Gilbert, Mark R. Harrington, Frank G. Speck, and John Witthoft. Under Long's guidance and leadership, members of the Big Cove community reenacted Cherokee ceremonies in order that they could be recorded and preserved. He also worked with Speck on translating SACRED FORMULAS and other data written in the Sequoyan syllabary by Cherokee priests. Active in community life, he served on the Cherokee Council for 30 years. At the end of his life he had several works in progress. Besides his efforts with Speck, he was writing a dictionary with George Myers Stephens and was engaged in an ethnobotany study with John Witthoft. In addition to his cultural studies, Long was a farmer. Will West Long died on March 14, 1947. (See also SWIMMER.)

LONG HORN (Sayatasha) *Zuni* The human counterpart of spirit rainmakers, who is rain priest of the north, heads the RAIN PRIESTHOODS, and is keeper of the Zuni ceremonial calendar. He establishes the date for the winter SHALAKO ceremony, supervises all activities preceding the appearance of the Shalakos, and appears the afternoon of the first day. He performs prayers and other rites at sacred shrines and then retires to the home built for him, where he performs house blessing rites and prays into the next day. The projection of the right side of the mask accounts for Long Horn's name and symbolizes long life for the people.

LONG LIFE CEREMONY *Apache* One of several Apache ceremonies that have their origin in ancient stories rather than in personal encounters with spiritual powers. A person who is not required to have a direct encounter with spiritual powers may be taught by elders. Long life ceremonies include the GIRL'S PUBERTY RITE, a CEREMONIAL RELAY RACE, and the HOLINESS RITE, a four-day curing rite.

LONGHOUSE *Iroquois* The structure that is the focus of traditional Iroquois social, political, and religious life. Contemporary buildings are modern counterparts of ancient long bark lodges. Modern longhouses are not residences but rather centers for many kinds of public activities, both secular and sacred. They are long and rectangular with a fireplace or stove (modern equivalents of hearths in bark lodges) at or near each end. People sit on rows of benches, possibly tiered, that line both long walls or on additional benches along the short walls. There is an open, central area for the drummer's bench, dances, and other ritual activities. During many ritual events, the benches are placed in the center of the floor running lengthwise and the assembly dances around the central benches and between the two stoves.

Men, women, and children occupy seats according to gender or moiety depending on the ceremonial occasion. The stoves are named, depending on the gender or moiety sitting at the ends. For example, they may be called the women's or men's stove or the Wolf (moiety) or Deer stove. Seating during the MIDWINTER CEREMONY differs from seating during the summer ceremonies, the FOUR SACRED CEREMONIES of the Creator and social dances. When the participants are grouped into "sides," or moieties, the stoves or "fires," identify and symbolize the moieties. Each moiety considers that half of the longhouse in which its stove is located as its own territory. Most longhouses have two doors, east and west, each associated with a moiety on certain occasions. On other ceremonial occasions, the west door is associated with the women and the east door is associated with the men, an invisible line separates male and female halves of the longhouse, and men and women enter separately and sit apart.

Each longhouse is legitimized by owning a LONGHOUSE WAMPUM, comparable to a charter of each congregation. The term *longhouse,* in a religious sense, includes the ceremonial building itself, the general congregation of the followers of the HANDSOME LAKE RELIGION, and a specific organization that arranges the annual calendar of services. The congregation is a ceremonial and jurisdictional entity conducting its own rites for its own congregation, bound only by general Iroquois patterns and institutions. The content and philosophy are the same at various longhouses, but the details of execution vary. Two HEADMEN and two headwomen, a woman and man from each moiety, set the times for ceremonies. A longhouse is symbolized by a fire that is burning. When a longhouse is discontinued, it is said "A fire is out." All "fires" are equal except Tonawanda, which is considered the "head fire."

There are longhouses in New York at Coldspring, on the Allegany Seneca Reservation; at Newtown on the Cattaraugus Seneca Reservation; at Tonawanda, on the Tonawanda Seneca Reservation; at Onondaga, on the Onondaga Reservation; and at Saint Regis, on the Mohawk Reservation. There is a longhouse among the Seneca-Cayuga in Oklahoma. In Canada, there are longhouses at Onondaga, Sour Springs, Seneca, and Lower Cayuga (all located on the Six Nations Reserve), one on the Oneida Reserve in Ontario, and one on the Kanawake (Kahnawake) Reserve in Quebec. (See also IROQUOIS CALENDRICAL CEREMONIES; IROQUOIS CEREMONIALISM; LONGHOUSE RELIGION.)

LONGHOUSE RELIGION *Iroquois* This religion emphasizes thankfulness to the Creator for what has been provided in the course of seasonal changes. It involves returning thanks to the Creator and expressing gratitude for the existence of various terrestrial and celestial beings (spirit forces) in the world, as well as those in people's dreams or visions, and those in traditional stories. The Iroquois acknowledge, honor, and please spirit forces (whose goodwill is necessary and who appreciate being listened to) through ceremonials. On occasion, people's dreams indicate what spirit beings desire. In return, it is believed that the spirit forces will continue their duties for the benefit of people.

Each spirit force is recognized and celebrated at a calendrical ceremony and has a traditional set of rites (dances, songs, speeches) appropriate to it. The food associated with the spirits being honored is served at a feast at the end of the ceremony. There is a close connection between the Longhouse religion of calendrical ceremonies and the HANDSOME LAKE RELIGION, which emphasizes the performance of these ancient longhouse annual ceremonies devoted to the Creator. HANDSOME LAKE, the prophet, considered these an important part of the behavior he required of his followers. Short versions of the CODE OF HANDSOME LAKE are also preached at major calendrical ceremonies. (See also IROQUOIS CALENDRICAL CEREMONIES, IROQUOIS CEREMONIALISM.)

LONGHOUSE RELIGION See WASHANI RELIGION; WASHAT DANCE (RELIGION)

LONGHOUSE WAMPUM *Iroquois* The strand of shell beads that legitimizes each LONGHOUSE, similar to the charter of a congregation. The composition of wampum strands varies from longhouse to longhouse. The wampum is displayed during the recitation of the CODE OF HANDSOME LAKE, during the CONFESSION RITE, and occasionally at important conventions when there is a wampum reading for revivalistic purposes.

LOOKING HORSE, ARVAL (Sunka wakan wicasa, "Horse Man") *(b. 1954) Lakota* Hereditary keeper of the BUFFALO CALF PIPE (Ptehincala hu cannunpa), "the most sacred possession of the Lakota people and the very soul of their religious life." The son of Stanley and Celia Looking Horse, Arval is from the Cheyenne River Reservation in South Dakota and is a Minneconjou through his father. He states that he is the 19th hereditary keeper from his family.

Selected for the position in 1966 when he was 12 years old, Looking Horse stated: "Just before a keeper of the Sacred Pipe dies, he has a vision of who to give the Pipe to. It is always given to a blood relative, either a man or a woman." In his case, the previous keeper was his grandmother, Lucy Looking Horse, who taught him how to carry on the responsibility. According to the Lakota holy man JOHN (FIRE) LAME DEER, the Looking Horses are descendants of the Elk Head clan, traditional pipe keepers.

The Sacred Pipe is kept in the Green Grass community of the Cheyenne River Reservation in South Dakota, where it is ritually cared for and protected. Looking Horse's first Sacred Calf Pipe ceremony as keeper occurred in 1974 at a SUN DANCE in Green Grass. In 1980, following instructions from the spirits, the pipe was put away for seven years to avoid disrespect and to give the people time for reflection. Looking Horse recounts the oral tradition of the pipe from the WHITE BUFFALO CALF WOMAN and its first keeper, Buffalo Standing Upright, to the present in "The Sacred Pipe in Modern Life," published in *Sioux Indian Religion* (1987). His name also appears as "Orval."

LOOKOUT, FRED *(1865–1949) Osage* A political and religious leader who served as principal chief of the Osage Nation for 26 years. Born near present-day Independence, Kansas, in 1865, Lookout was reared by his paternal grandmother following the death of his mother when he was an infant. He grew to adulthood in Kansas and Indian Territory, eventually recalling buffalo hunts with his father, a leader among his clan and band. Lookout attended the Carlisle Indian Industrial School in Pennsylvania a short time after it opened in 1879. He returned home several years later, sometime before his father died in 1884. Lookout married Julia Pryor (Mo-se-che-he), a Bear clan member, and engaged in farming near Pawhuska, Oklahoma, the Osage capital.

In 1908, Lookout was elected assistant principal chief of the Osage Tribal Council, which was established as an eight-person governing body under a 1906 allotment act. Several years later, in 1914, he was appointed principal chief by Secretary of the Interior W.L. Fisher. Following the death of his eldest child, he and his wife mourned according to Osage custom, including distributing all their possessions to others before leaving their home to travel around the reservation.

On his return home, Lookout joined the PEYOTE RELIGION, becoming a ROADMAN and presiding over religious services in the newly introduced faith among the Osage. He continued to serve as a political leader, winning elections as principal chief in 1924, 1926, and 1928 and eventually winning five consecutive four-year terms beginning in 1930. Lookout died on August 28, 1949, at Pawhuska.

LOUGHRIDGE, ROBERT McGILL *(1809–1900)* A Presbyterian missionary among the Creek people. Loughridge was born in Laurensville, South Carolina, in 1809 but spent his childhood in Alabama. He was taught by the Reverend John H. Gray, attended Mesopotamia Academy, and graduated from Ohio's Miami University in 1837. After a year at Princeton Theological Seminary, he returned to Alabama upon his father's death. Loughridge remained in the area, where he taught and continued his theology studies. He was licensed to preach on April 9, 1841, ordained on October 15, 1842, and then left Alabama with his bride to work among the Creek.

He established a school at Coweta in Indian Territory (present-day Oklahoma) and began teaching in June 1843. The Creek Council and the Presbyterian board agreed to jointly support the school in 1847 along with one that opened later, in 1850, at Tullahassee. Loughridge's mission flourished, with 12 missionaries working in 1855, and by 1861 many Creek had attended school, two churches had been established, and two Native ministers had been trained. Loughridge produced a number of publications in the Muskogee dialect, including *Muskokee Hymns*, based on the work of JOHN FLEMING, in 1845 and *Translation of the Introduction to the Shorter Catechism* in the following year. Loughridge, who was expelled by the Creek during the Civil War, began working as a minister at various locations in Texas until 1880.

Although activity at his mission resumed in 1866, Loughridge did not return until 1881. He took charge of the Tullahassee school from 1883 to 1885 in a new building provided by the Creek Council at Wealaka. Loughridge then preached among the native people and worked on his

English and Muskokee Dictionary, published with a collaborator, David M. Hodge, 1890. After ending his work among the Creek at the age of 79, he ministered to churches in Oklahoma and Texas until a few years before his death.

LOWRY, HENRY H. *(?–1935) Lumbee* The first presbyter of the Lumbee Methodist Conference. The conference was organized in 1900 after Lowry led a group of his people away from the established Methodist organization to establish a Native conference dedicated to the goal of Lumbee self-determination. Following these actions, Lowry and his followers were expelled from the Methodist Episcopal Church in 1902 and warned against baptizing members or conducting marriage ceremonies. The newly established organization was named the Holiness Methodist Church of the Lumbee River Annual Conference, generally known as the Lumbee Methodist Conference. Lowry's nine children, who pioneered in various professions among the Lumbee people, included two medical doctors, a pharmacist, educators, and a minister who completed a divinity degree. By 1974 the Lumbee Conference included seven churches. After Lowry died in 1935, he was succeeded by other family members. (See also MOORE, WILLIAM LUTHER.)

LULS *(fl. c. 1870s) Umatilla* Umatilla prophet. Luls was influenced by the teachings of the WASHANI religious leader SMOHALLA. He was believed to have died and returned to life. Luls received sacred teachings in the spirit world, later revealing some of them to his followers. Besides showing them a dance he had seen performed, he instructed them to live in kindness. His spiritual powers increased to such an extent that he was able to tell the thoughts of those who attended his dances. In contrast to Smohalla's practice of using seven drummers, Luls had four. Luls chose seven girls for a role in the dance. Wearing white deerskin dresses, they circled the ceremonial lodge while the other people danced. He also used a symbolic heart on a string, but not the flags characteristic of Smohalla's rites, in his religious practice. Before he died, Luls was sorrowful because the traditional sacred ways were disappearing.

LYNG, SECRETARY OF AGRICULTURE, ET AL. V. NORTHWEST INDIAN CEMETERY PROTECTIVE ASS'N. ET AL. *(No. 86-103) (1988)* A 1988 Supreme Court case involving a sacred site in northern California. At issue was a U.S. Forest Service plan to construct a paved road and to allow timber harvesting in an area of the Six Rivers National Forest near the sacred CHIMNEY ROCK site. A number of Native American individuals and groups, including the Yurok, Karok, and Tolowa, challenged the land use proposal as a violation of their rights under the free exercise clause of the First Amendment on the grounds that it would irreparably damage the natural setting essential to their religious practice. On April 19, 1988, the Supreme Court ruled against the respondents' free exercise claim. The Court held that the U.S. Contitution did not provide a principle that could uphold their legal claims "even assuming that the Government's actions here will virtually destroy the Indians' ability to practice their religion." It further held that the AMERICAN INDIAN RELIGIOUS FREEDOM ACT OF 1978 did "not create any enforceable legal right" authorizing a permanent injunction against the paved road and timber harvesting, though it also ruled that the government's right to use its own lands should not "discourage it from accommodating religious practices" such as those of the respondents. Justices Brennan, Marshall, and Blackmun dissented. Brennan stated, in part, "I find it difficult . . . to imagine conduct more insensitive to religious needs than the Government's determination to build a marginally useful road in the face of uncontradicted evidence that the road will render the practice of respondents' religion impossible." This litigation is generally referred to as the "G-O Road" case. The decision prevents people who practice Indian religions from challenging government land management decisions even when those decisions impair or destroy the ability to practice their religion. (See also SACRED SITES for similar legal cases included in this volume.)

McBETH, KATE See SUSAN LAW McBETH

McBETH, SUSAN LAW *(1830–1893)* Presbyterian missionary among the Choctaw in Indian Territory and, for 20 years, among the Nez Perce in Idaho. She was born in 1830 in Doune, Scotland. After emigrating in 1832, her family eventually settled in Wellsville, Ohio. After her father died when she was 17, McBeth contributed to the family's support by working as a milliner in Wellsville. She graduated from Steubenville Female Seminary in 1854, then taught at the Wellsville Institute, Fairfield Female Seminary in Iowa and the State University of Iowa in Fairfield. In 1858 the BOARD OF FOREIGN MISSIONS OF THE PRESBYTERIAN CHURCH invited her to apply for work with the Choctaw, and she began work at the Goodwater Mission in Indian Territory teaching Indian girls from age six to 18. After the Civil War forced the suspension of the mission, McBeth returned to Fairfield University. She became one of the first female agents of the United States Christian Commission in 1863 and assisted the Protestant relief organization in ministering to the sick and wounded, including three years at Jefferson Barracks in St. Louis. During the war years she also wrote tracts for soldiers, published as *Seeds Scattered Broadcast* in 1869. In 1866, after the war, she helped establish a home for females who were newcomers to the city of St. Louis and working for substandard wages. She returned to Wellsville in 1873 when her mother became ill. While there, Susan suffered a stroke, reportedly caused by the sudden death of Eben Law, her cousin and fiancé. Al-

though partly paralyzed, she accepted an opportunity to work with the Nez Perce after the death of her mother.

McBeth taught at Lapwai Agency from 1873 to 1874 as a government employee. She then went to Kamiah, about 40 miles from Lapwai, to take over the work of HENRY HARMON SPALDING in training Indian men for the ministry. In addition to her aim of Christianizing the Nez Perce, McBeth sought to replace tribalism with assimilationist teachings and to do away with polygamy and other Native customs. She also worked on a dictionary of the Nez Perce language, which went uncompleted to the Smithsonian Institution after her death. During the government's war with Chief Joseph and his followers in the spring of 1877, McBeth left the reservation until the fall of that year, when she returned to Lapwai under the auspices of the Presbyterian Board of Foreign Missions. Shortly after her sister, Kate McBeth (1833–1915), joined her at Lapwai in 1879, they went to Kamiah, where Susan resumed her work of training Native ministers and Kate set up a school for women. Although prompted by health reasons to move to Mount Idaho in 1885, her students followed her there, and she continued her school. When the ethnologist Alice C. Fletcher was appointed by the federal government to direct the division of tribally held Nez Perce land into individual allotments under the provisions of the Dawes Severalty Act of 1887, her efforts were supported by the McBeth sisters. Susan McBeth, who became known as "little mother" to the Nez Perce, died in 1893 at Mount Idaho and was buried near the Kamiah Mission Church. The Indian ministers she trained included James Hayes, ARCHIE B. LAWYER, Enoch Pond, Mark

Williams, and ROBERT WILLIAMS. After Susan died, Kate continued the work until her own death 22 years later.

McCOY, ISAAC (1784–1846)
A Baptist missionary and Indian agent. He was born near Uniontown, Pennsylvania, to William McCoy, a clergyman, and his wife. When his family moved to Kentucky in about 1790, McCoy attended public schools there. In 1803 he married Christiana Polke, with whom he had 13 children, and the following year they moved to Vincennes, Indiana, where he was licensed to preach by the Baptist Church. A short time later he was ordained as pastor of the Maria Creek church, a post he held for eight years. Appointed missionary to the Indians in 1817, by the following year McCoy was preaching among the Wea in Indiana. In 1820 he organized a school for children from neighboring tribes, but it closed two years later. McCoy also established missions among the Potawatomi and Ottawa in Michigan Territory.

Because white encroachment forced the relocation of his missions more than once, McCoy became convinced that the establishment of a permanent territory for tribal people would be the only way to protect their welfare. He believed that, removed from the harmful influences of Euro-American settlers, the Indians could gradually become accustomed to Christianity and "civilization." McCoy began promoting a plan that included the removal of tribal people west of the Mississippi River and the establishment of an Indian state. In 1827 his ideas on the issue were published in *Remarks on the Practicability of Indian Reform*. Two years later he received an appointment to a commission that worked on removing the Ottawa and Miami tribal groups to the West. In 1830 McCoy was appointed to serve as an Indian agent and government surveyor by John C. Calhoun, President Andrew Jackson's secretary of war. McCoy assisted in selecting and surveying lands in present-day Kansas and Oklahoma and helped remove Indians to their new locations. Despite his efforts at removal, McCoy's plan for an Indian state was never realized.

McCoy's other publications include several editions of the *Annual Register of Indian Affairs within the Indian Territory* (1835–38) and a *History of Baptist Indian Missions: Embracing Remarks on the Former and Present Condition of the Aboriginal Tribes; Their Settlement within the Indian Territory, and Their Future Prospects* (1840). In 1842 he founded the AMERICAN INDIAN MISSION ASSOCIATION, serving as its first corresponding secretary and general agent. The earliest Baptist missionary in the central region of the country, McCoy worked nearly 30 years among Native Americans. He died in Louisville, Kentucky on June 21, 1846. (See also MEEKER, JOTHAM).

McDOUGALL, GEORGE MILLWARD (1821–1876)
Methodist missionary. Born in Kingston, Upper Canada, McDougall was raised on a farm near Barrie. After commanding lake schooners, he entered the ministry in 1849 and was sent to the Sault Ste. Marie area to establish the Garden River mission. After his 1854 ordination, he served as a missionary at the Rama Indian Reserve from 1857 to 1860, then went northwest to the Norway House station in Manitoba. While superintending the Methodist district of Saskatchewan, McDougall recommended the establishment of Victoria Mission in present-day Pakan, Alberta, during a visit to the area in 1862. His son, JOHN MCDOUGALL, HENRY BIRD STEINHAUER, and THOMAS WOOLSEY carried out the move. Victoria Mission became the base of operations for the McDougalls until the 1870s when the headquarters were moved to present-day Edmonton. It attracted a number of new settlers to the region and became a stop on the journey from Fort Garry (present-day Winnipeg) and Fort Edmonton (Edmonton, Alberta). In 1868 he convinced the Methodist conference to send him additional workers, including four ministers and two missionary teachers. As European contact altered the traditional way of life for Native people, intertribal conflicts escalated, and raids were carried out against encroaching settlements. McDougall and his son organized a rally to promote peace among the Cree and Blackfeet on the plains. In 1873 he opened a new mission at present-day Morley in an effort to establish order and eventually acquired large land holdings in the region. Two years later he was named a commissioner to the Saulteaux and Swampy Cree to begin preparing them to negotiate a treaty. He was still working at this task when he perished during a snowstorm. John McDougall and JOHN MACLEAN both wrote biographies of his life.

McDOUGALL, JOHN (1842–1917)
A Methodist missionary who was born in Owen Sound, Canada West, and spent his childhood at the Indian missions conducted by his father, the Reverend GEORGE MILLWARD MCDOUGALL. Besides attending mission schools and Victoria College in Cobourg, McDougall learned from assisting his father on assignments to the Northwest. In 1860 McDougall, together with HENRY BIRD STEINHAUER and THOMAS WOOLSEY, established Victoria Mission at present-day Pakan, Alberta. The following year George McDougall moved the Methodist mission headquarters there. John was later ordained to the Methodist ministry in 1872 at the denomination's first conference west of Lake Superior.

After George McDougall died in 1876, John assumed the task of preparing the Saulteaux Swampy Cree for negotiating treaties. Although McDougall shared his father's emphasis on Christianizing and "civilizing" Native people, he sometimes demonstrated some of the Indian influences he had acquired. While serving as a delegate to a Winnipeg conference, he camped out rather than staying in city accommodations with his fellow ministers. In 1912 when he helped organize the first Calgary Stampede rodeo, he succeeded in displeasing his peers by arranging to have a group of Native people appear in traditional dress. During the North West Rebellion, a resistance movement led by the Métis leader Louis Riel against the government, he assisted the Alberta Field Force by making advance contacts to Indian communities. In later years he was named Indian commissioner for the three provinces in the Far West.

Considered an authority on the Cree language, McDougall, with the Reverend E. B. Glass, produced *Primer and Language Lessons* and revised the Cree *Hymn Book,* both published in 1908. From 1899 to 1902 he served on an interdenominational committee working on a revised translation of the Bible from Swampy Cree for use by the Plains Cree, and this work was also published in 1908. Besides his linguistic publications, McDougall completed a number of books about his experiences in the West: *Forest, Lake and Prairie: Twenty Years of Frontier Life in Western Canada, 1842–62* (Toronto, 1895); *Saddle, Sled, and Snowshoe: Pioneering on the Saskatchewan in the Sixties* (Toronto, 1896); *Pathfinding on Plain and Prairie: Stirring Scenes of Life in the Canadian North-west* (Toronto, 1898); *In the days of the Red River Rebellion: life and adventure in the far west of Canada (1862–1872)* (1903); and *On Western Trails in the Early Seventies* (1911). He also wrote a biography of his father: *George Millward McDougall: The Pioneer, Patriot and Missionary* (Toronto, 1888). The missionary JOHN MACLEAN wrote an account of John McDougall's life and work, *McDougall of Alberta* (1927).

MACLEAN, JOHN *(1851–1928)* Methodist missionary who worked among the Blood in Canada. MacLean was born in Kilmarnock, Scotland, and traveled to Canada West in 1873. Educated at Victoria College and Illinois Wesleyan University, he was ordained to the Methodist ministry in 1880 and sent to the Blood Indian Reserve the same year. He did missionary work among the Blood until 1889 and later authored a number of publications, including *The Indians: Their Manners and Customs* (Toronto, 1889 and 1907) and *Canadian Savage Folk: The Native Tribes of Canada* (Toronto, 1896). He wrote accounts of his fellow missionaries—JAMES EVANS, in *James Evans: Inventor of the Syllabic System of the Cree Language* (Toronto, 1890), and JOHN MCDOUGALL, in *McDougall of Alberta: A Life of Rev. John McDougall, D.D., Pathfinder of Empire and Prophet of the Plains* (1927). MacLean also completed works for young readers, including a portrait of the Native missionary HENRY

BIRD STEINHAUER, *Henry B. Steinhauer: His Work among the Cree Indians of the Western Plains of Canada* (n.d.); *The Hero of the Saskatchewan: Life among the Ojibway and Cree Indians* (Barrie, Ont., 1891); and *Vanguards of Canada* (1918), a book about missionaries. A work of fiction, *The Warden of the Plains, and other Stories of Life in the Canadian West,* was published in Toronto in 1896.

McLEOD, DICKSON C. *(1802–1840)* Methodist missionary who worked among the Cherokee people in the Southeast from 1828 to 1832. Born in North Carolina, McLeod was admitted to preach by his denomination in 1823. He and other Methodist missionaries in the field opposed the forced removal of the Cherokee people to Indian Territory (present-day Oklahoma), a position not endorsed by their mission board in Tennessee. McLeod was eventually taken into custody by Georgia authorities after he inquired about his colleague, JAMES JENKINS TROTT, who had been arrested a second time on July 6, 1831, for violations stemming from a new law requiring whites in the Cherokee Nation to swear to an oath of allegiance to the state of Georgia. After protesting the treatment of Trott and the other men arrested, including ELIZUR BUTLER and SAMUEL AUSTIN WORCESTER, he was forced to join them on a 110-mile march to Camp Gilmer for incarceration. Four days after their arrival, McLeod was released because he lived in an area of the Cherokee Nation located in Tennessee.

McMURRAY, WILLIAM *(1810–1894)* Anglican clergyman whose career included missionary work among the Ojibway people in the area of Sault Ste. Marie. Soon after his birth near Portadown, Ireland, he was taken to Canada. Educated in Toronto, he received his D.D. and D.C.L. at Trinity College. He began his missionary work in 1832 and subsequently established a station at Garden River near Sault Ste. Marie. He was ordained to the priesthood of the Church of England in 1833. During the same year he married Charlotte Johnston (Ogenebugakwa, "Wild Rose"), the mixed-blood daughter of John Johnston from Sault Ste. Marie. In 1840 McMurray began serving as rector of Ancaster. Years later, in 1875, he was named archdeacon of Niagara. McMurray died on May 19, 1894, and was succeeded at Sault Ste. Marie by FREDERICK AUGUSTUS O'MEARA. His second wife was Amelia Baxter. With his first wife, McMurray had three sons and a daughter.

MAHEO *Cheyenne* Creator of the universe in Cheyenne belief. He gave SWEET MEDICINE (the prophet), the SACRED ARROWS and a code of laws at NOAHA-VOSE, or BEAR BUTTE, for the Cheyenne people. He also gave the SACRED BUFFALO HAT to ERECT HORNS, the Suhtai culture hero, on another sacred mountain. The dead live in peace near Maheo in Seana, the place of the dead. The word for the Creator has various spellings in Cheyenne and other interpretations in English. (See also FOUR SACRED PERSONS; MASSAUM CEREMONY.)

MAIN POC ("Crippled Hand," "Lame Hand," "Left Hand," "Withered Hand," Wenebeset, Wapakee) *(c. Mid-1760s–1816) Potawatomi* A shaman who was a WABENO, or "firehandler," and an influential leader in the period before the War of 1812. Although Main Poc's place and date of birth are unknown, he may have been born in southern Michigan in the mid-1760s. His name derives from his being born without a thumb or fingers on his left hand, a deformity he regarded as a special sign from the Creator. He claimed that he had been given spiritual powers to compensate for his crippled hand, including the ability to protect himself and others from enemy bullets.

Like his father, Main Poc became a Potawatomi war chief. Besides opposing the Americans and raiding their settlements, he led war parties of Potawatomi, Kickapoo, Sac and Fox, and other allies against Osage and other tribal enemies. Main Poc journeyed to Greenville, Ohio, to meet the Shawnee prophet TENSKWATAWA in 1807, conferring with him for nearly two months. He evidently accepted some of the prophet's teachings but rejected others. He agreed with Tenskwatawa's denunciation of the Americans but refused to give up intoxicating beverages or intertribal warfare. After leaving Greenville, he passed through Fort Wayne, where the Indian agent William Wells tried to turn him against Tenskwatawa and into an ally of the United States.

In 1808 Wells took the Potawatomi Wabeno to Washington, D.C., hoping to convince him to make peace with the Osage and support the Americans. Main Poc met with President Thomas Jefferson, informing him that he planned to continue his intertribal warfare. In 1810 the Potawatomi leader was wounded during a fight with Osage hunters. Claiming that he had taken a bullet aimed at his wife, Main Poc assured his followers that he had not lost his protective spiritual power. The following year his wounds healed, and he continued to influence tribal allies against the Americans. In an 1812 skirmish he was again wounded, this time with a bullet to the neck. After the British and Indian defeat at the Battle of the Thames in 1813, Main Poc went to northern Indiana, where he tried to rally opposition to the Americans. Learning that the British had made peace, he settled near Manistee on Lake Michigan, where he died in 1816. There are numerous variations and translations of his name, including "Lame Hand," "Left Hand," and "Withered Hand." The Potawatomi shaman was also known as Wenebeset ("Crafty One") and Wapakee.

MAN EATER *North Pacific Coast* Called Man Eater at the Mouth of the River, Cannibal-at-North-End-of-World or Baxbakualanuxsiwae in Kwakiutl, this spirit located at the north end of the world, a place of darkness, disease, and death, is believed to inhabit and take over certain persons, replacing or supplementing their normal faculties at special ceremonial times. The appetite of the spirit being expresses itself in bizarre cravings that are fulfilled in order to pacify the being. This man eater spirit, the dominant one in the winter ceremonials of the North Pacific Coast peoples, is impersonated among the Kwakiutl people in the HAMATSA DANCE by one of the highest-ranking chiefs or his sons.

MANITOHKAN A religious image or effigy described among the Cree people; also known as Manto Kan. Manito is translated as Great Spirit or Supreme Being while Kan is variously interpreted into English as "imitation of," "representation of," or "came from." Great spiritual power was attributed to the Manitohkan, and people made offerings and said prayers to it. Only qualified individuals made the figure, which was generally made from a log of quaking aspen, dressed in clothing, placed in an upright or seated position, and sometimes secretly situated in an isolated area. One account states that individuals could pick up a gift from the offerings around it and leave another gift or tobacco in return. Another account, although stating that the tradition was practiced until about 1940 among the Montana Cree, indicates that it might have persisted after that time.

MAPLE FESTIVAL *Iroquois* A festival held when sap begins to flow in maple trees, usually around the second week of February. On the festival morning, families return thanks to maple trees for sap runs and ask for their continuation. They burn tobacco as an invocation to the spirits. There is a FEATHER DANCE, the passing of sap, a feast, and social dances. In the evening, people sing songs of the CHANTERS FOR THE DEAD, a society that owns certain songs sung at the Maple Festival.

MARAW SOCIETY (Marau, Marawu, Mamzrau) *Hopi* A women's rain-making and curing society whose ceremony is performed in September or October. In its public appearance, Maraw members dance and sing all day in the plaza and throw ritual objects and food to bystanders. Maraw members have the power to cure rheumatic fever with certain plants. Throughout the last four days of their ceremony, the women make fun of men belonging to the Wuchim Society just as the men taunt Maraw women during their own WUWUCHIM CEREMONY, which follows soon after. This society has a maskless kachina dance. During the initiation of new members every four years, the Maraw may perform the

Palhik'mana dance, with the women wearing towering head-dresses, or a Howenai scalp dance borrowed from the Rio Grande pueblos and converted by Hopi women to a harvest dance. (See also LAKON SOCIETY; OWAQLT SOCIETY.)

MARINE MAMMAL PROTECTION ACT (16 U.S.C. 1371[a], 1372[a]) *(1972)* A federal act passed in 1972 with implications for the expression of Native American religions. The Fish and Wildlife Service of the U.S. Department of the Interior issued regulations restricting the taking, possessing, and transporting of marine mammals in accordance with the law. Protected mammals include dugongs, manatees, polar bears, sea otters, and walruses. An exemption exists for Alaskan Natives, including Indians, Aleut, and Inuit, "to take non-depleted species in the non-wasteful manner for subsistence purposes." The scope of this provision was litigated in *People of Togiak v. United States.* Another exemption applies to mammals taken before December 21, 1972. (See also AMERICAN INDIAN RELIGIOUS FREEDOM ACT OF 1978; EAGLE PROTECTION ACT; ENDANGERED SPECIES ACT; MIGRATORY BIRD TREATY ACT.)

MARKSMAN, PETER (Kah-goo-dah-ah-qua, "Marksman" or "The Man that Shoots Straight," Ma-dwa-qwun-a-yaush, Ringing Feather) *(c. 1815–1892)* Ojibway Methodist Episcopal Church missionary and interpreter. Marksman, a member of the Catfish clan, was born in the Fond du Lac area near the west end of Lake Superior. His mother, Wa-me-te-goo-zhe-qua, was a mixed-blood Ojibway woman from that locale. His father, Ah-zhah-we-gwun, was the son and grandson of hereditary chiefs from Mackinac Island. Marksman, whose twin brother died at birth, was the youngest of seven children. In keeping with traditional beliefs about the spirituality and specialness of twins, his parents carefully tended his upbringing. They dedicated him at an early age to the MIDEWIWIN religion, and he was ordained or initiated into it while still a boy.

Marksman first heard Christianity preached in 1830 at Sault Ste. Marie by a Baptist missionary. He was later greatly influenced by Canadian Native Methodists such as JOHN SUNDAY, PETER JONES, John Kahbeege, and John Taunchy. In 1833 Marksman overcame the opposition of his parents and accompanied Kahbeege on a mission to Mackinac Island. He received instructions from the missionary while they traveled together. On his return to Sault Ste. Marie, Marksman was baptized by the Reverend Peter Jones on June 16, 1833. He then served as a missionary under the Reverend JOHN CLARK. In 1837 Marksman was sent to Ebenezer Seminary in Illinois with two other Ojibway, GEORGE COPWAY and John Johnson (ENMEGAHBOWH), and remained there for two years. He then returned to missionary work on a full-time basis. During his long career his placements included Flint, L'Anse, Kewawenon, Sault Ste. Marie, Saginaw, and Bay Mills in Michigan. Although Marksman fell from the Methodist ranks at least twice, he was reinstated both times. Besides ministerial work, he served as an interpreter, teacher, and surveyor.

Marksman was married in 1844 to Hannah Morien, who assisted him in his missionary work. He died on May 28, 1892, at Kewawenon mission. His biography was later written by the Reverend JOHN H. PITEZEL. Another Ojibway name for the native missionary was Ma-dwa-gwun-a-yaush, or Ringing Feather.

MARQUETTE, JACQUES *(1637–1675)* French Jesuit missionary to Canada. Born in France, Marquette entered the Jesuit novitiate in 1654. In 1665 he was assigned to go to Canada and arrived in 1666 in Quebec, where he studied Montagnais and other Indian languages with GABRIEL DRUILLETTES. By 1673, he was fluent in six languages. He learned the dialects sufficiently for him to start missionary work among the Algonquian tribes dwelling around Lake Superior. In 1669 he moved to Chequamegon Bay, the western end of Lake Superior, which he abandoned in 1671 because of fear of Sioux attacks. He moved Ottawa and Huron to Mackinac Island, where he built Saint Ignace. In 1673 he got permission to go with Louis Jolliet to explore the territory southwest of his station. During the journey, Marquette and Jolliet established contacts with Illinois, Missouri, Potawatomi, Quapaw, and other peoples. On his return voyage, Marquette reestablished contact with the Illinois and founded a mission at Kaskaskia village in 1675. He preached among them but died soon after. Scholars debate whether Marquette authored *Recit,* about the 1673 expedition, and whether he was ever ordained a priest. Although he has been commemorated by monuments, and a university, railroad, river, cities, and avenues bear his name, some scholars maintain his place has been exaggerated in history.

MASAU'U (Masao, Masaw) *Hopi* The Hopi spirit, pictured as a skeleton, in charge of the underworld and the earth's surface, as well as death, fire, fertility, creation, darkness, and war. As ruler of the underworld, Masau'u is the spirit of death. He stands at the entrance to the underworld mediating between the living and the dead. He has power to cause the metamorphosis of nature and takes many forms. He is the deity responsible for teaching Hopi about using fire and who is blind by day and unable to face the sun, walking out only at night as befits a spirit of the underworld and darkness. He is sometimes impersonated without a mask in the fall, spring, and summer ceremonies.

MASHUNKASHAY, BEN *(c. 1879–?) Osage* The first drumkeeper of the Osage I'n-Lon-Schka ceremonial dance drum at Pawhuska, Oklahoma. Mashunkashay was chosen for the role at the age of five. Mashunkashay's grandson later served in the role from 1972 to 1976. The drumkeeper is an eldest son, considered a special blessing, whose duty is to care for the drum belonging to his community and to perform numerous duties associated with the I'N-LON-SCHKA CEREMONIAL DANCE of his people. (See also ACCEPTANCE OF THE DRUM CEREMONY; PASSING OF THE DRUM CEREMONY.)

MASK Masking is a feature of many Indian religions throughout North America of pre-European origin. This tradition disturbed many missionaries, who interpreted masking as idol worship. Masks are believed to be alive, representing beings that exist in the spirit world. As ceremonial aids, they are as powerful as the beings they represent. Masks are sacred objects that are made according to strict tribal procedures. A large number of Indian ceremonies involve masking. Participants wear masks to venerate tribal ancestors, call on spirit helpers, impersonate spirits, transform their identity, and assume a changed personality. Masks may also represent healing spirits and are used to treat the ill. Sometimes priests wear the masks, sometimes other participants do, and sometimes every participant wears one. Examples of masks from various tribes follow.

Aleut and Inuit

Masks are symbolic manifestations of spirits that people represent in dancing festivals or that shamans represent in curing and other activities. The person wearing a mask aims to appropriate the spirit it represents and to honor the spirit temporarily personified. Ordinary people and shamans wear masks during ceremonies honoring important food animals, such as the bear, caribou, seal, and whale. Masks depicting the animal's spirit or "person" are worn in the BLADDER FESTIVAL, general hunting festivals, and the MESSENGER FEAST. Most masks are used for a single dancing festival after which they are burned or buried in the ground.

Shamans use masks for curing, for consultation with spirits at times of crisis, on visits to the land of the dead, and for prognostication. Masks carved by shamans are designed to influence spirits of animals important to subsistence or to represent the shamans' spirit aids. Shamans determine their masks' physical shape either from a vision or from tradition, delegating carvers to make them or making their own. Ordinary people carve their own spirit masks.

There is an astonishing variation in Inuit masks. Made of spruce or cottonwood driftwood, they differ in size, paint styles, ornamentation, facial features, and the use of human and animal appendages. Variations are so great that

Inuit mask. This mask represents a *tunerak,* a being that controls the supply of game. *Dover Publications Pictorial Archive Series.*

placing the location of a mask is sometimes impossible. In general, masks south of the Bering Strait are extremely diverse in style and form. They represent humans (either with realistic features or abstract), objects, plants, and celestial beings. Masks representing spirit aids may have animal or bird heads represented on half the mask and a human head represented on the other half. Another mask form has an animal head with a small human head somewhere on it. Some masks are hinged, with outer representations of an animal or bird and an inner portion revealed by pulling a cord. There are also masks representing entire animals, animal heads, or complete bodies with moveable limbs and masks with diverse appendages.

Iroquois

Among the Iroquois people, masks portray spirit forces that affect their welfare and are themselves entities animated by the forces they portray. The wearer of a mask behaves as if he were the spiritual being whom he impersonates. Made either of wood or braided corn husks, these images are believed to possess power to help people when respectfully used. The power comes from the world of spirits who dwell in forests, under water, in the air or ground, and in darkness. Three orders of medicine societies use masks in public or private rituals—the FALSE FACE SOCIETY, the HUSK FACE SOCIETY, and the Mystic Animal Society.

False Face Masks that represent forest spirits are carved from the soft wood of live trees by men. They are carved by members of the False Face Society and are modeled on dreams revealing the appearance of a guardian spirit. The features are carved on a living tree and then cut free while a prayer is addressed and tobacco burned to the evolving mask and spirit forces it represents. The wooden false faces include many forms of masks. Iroquois believe that the false face masks are powerful and must be treated with respect, or the power they represent can be turned against those who do not observe rules regarding their care. The masks are anointed at times with sunflower oil, offered tobacco, and addressed as "grandfather." Periodically they are fed, talked to, and sung to. Features common to the masks are red or black paint or both; large staring eyes made of copper or brass pieces, pierced for pupils; large, frequently bent noses; contorted mouths; long, flowing hair; and arched brows. The mouths are the most variable feature and are often the basis of classification systems. The masks are used in ceremonies and in curing rituals to frighten away malevolent spirits and purify the sick. Iroquois recognize two main classes of false faces: the common faces and doorkeepers, or doctors.

Common False Face Masks These masks, one of the main classes of false face masks, represent common faces, spirits who live in forests and in the wind. Traditional mouths (which have their origin in traditional narratives) include a crooked mouth, smiling straight lips, hanging mouth, a whistling mouth, spoon mouth blower, modified distended mouth, straight distended mouth, and a bi-funnelate blower. (Spoon lips are rare in Canada.) Common faces enter a house, crawl and jump-hop, dance, and cure by blowing ashes on a patient. When not in use, certain rituals must be done to the masks. Common false face masks include beggar masks, new masks that debut as beggars at the MIDWINTER CEREMONY or appear first with the common faces in their rituals. After the beggar masks are worn in many performances or the STIRRING ASHES RITE or are borrowed and owned by several people and have accumulated several bags of tobacco offerings for their services, they graduate into the class of great doctor masks.

Doorkeeper, or Doctor, Masks These masks, one of the main kinds of false face masks, represent spirits who inhabited the rim of the earth. Doorkeeper masks have long hair, are painted red or black, and portray the pain the spirit endured when a mountain struck his face and broke his nose. Doorkeepers dance erect, in contrast with common faces, the other spirits impersonated by the False Face Society. The masks are used in curing rites.

Husk Face Mask Made of braided or twined corn husks, the husk face masks represent agricultural spirits. When members of the Husk Face Society wear the masks, they have special powers and can handle hot coals without being burned. (Because of the tousled halo of husked ends, the husk faces are also called BUSHY HEADS.) Made by women and worn by men, the masks frequently portray females and symbolize fertility. There are two sizes, one that covers a man's face and varies considerably in shape, and a miniature version. Husk face masks are depicted as either old or young, male or female, as are the beings whom they represent in the rites. All the masks are provided with little tobacco bags on the foreheads.

North Pacific Coast Peoples

Carved for performances of dances, these masks represent individuals or particular categories of people, such as ancestors or guardian spirits. They are worn generally in the winter and at night. North Pacific Coast peoples wear masks during a potlatch and at postfuneral ceremonies. Face masks are worn at feasts given by chiefs, in ceremonies performed by shamans and in the winter ceremonies that reenact ancient stories. Of the many types of mask, some have animal or human faces with mechanical parts that move eyes, eyelids, jaws, and lips. Elaborate bird masks open to reveal inner forms. Some masks are non-naturalistic. The variations in North Pacific Coast masks help define tribal origin. Masks of the Kwakiutl and Nootka are massive compared to those of the Tsimshian, Haida, and Tlingit peoples, which are simpler. Masks are made of wood and feathers, twigs, cedar bark, hair, metal,

Northwest Pacific Coast mask. This Bella Bella dancing mask from British Columbia is shaped like a bird's head, with a movable lower jaw. *Dover Publications Pictorial Archive Series.*

shell, cloth, or fur. Masks usually have facial painting that represents crest designs or shamanic spirit helpers.

Pueblo

Pueblo KACHINA masks have a sacredness and power of their own. They are treated with reverence and are periodically fed with cornmeal and other sacred substances. When wearing a kachina mask, a man is transformed from a human into something greater. It is believed that the spirit whom the mask represents dwells within the dancer. When the mask is removed, the man loses that power. Masks may be individually owned, as among the Zuni, or kept and cared for by clans, as among the Hopi, or kept by KIVA chiefs, as among the Acoma. Pueblo Indians dislike the use of masks as art objects. Beyond this general set of beliefs, there is a great elaboration and diversity among the Pueblo peoples.

Hopi Among Hopi, certain kachina spirits belong to certain clans and the right to wear and keep a mask representing these spirits is inherited. The clan kachina masks are kept in households by clan heads or chiefs of a particular maternal family and its lineage. The mask must be fed ceremonially and addressed by the proper names. The guardian of the mask must know prayers and songs connected with it. The masks may be made of leather, skin, basketry, cloth, or gourds and decorated on the back, top, or sides with feathers. Masks are painted with symbols and have accessories attached to them like ears and noses. They are sacred when painted. The masks may have one or two horns, headdresses (including tablitas), and different kinds of mouths. The color on masks is symbolic and indicates the direction from which kachinas come, for example, yellow indicating north to northeast. Ruffs made of skin and branches hide the space between the mask and body. Among the different types of masks, some are cylindrical cases, or helmets, made of two pieces of rawhide stretched together. Some are circular made by stretching cloth over a yucca sifter basket. Some are face masks made of leather and show the wearer's hair. Some are half-masks that cover the upper half of the face with the lower half hidden by a beard or feathers. A spherical mask made from felt may be stretched over a rounded post.

Zuni To the Zuni people, masks portray spirits and are entities animated by the spirits they portray. There are more than 100 types of masks, each with a name portraying a particular spirit. Made of leather or sheepskin, molded in every size, these types include half-masks, complete face masks, or helmet masks that encircle the head. Masks may have realistic symbols or stylized geometric symbols and feathers.

There are two categories of mask types. The first is made up of the ancient and unchanging chief or priest kachina masks that represent high-ranking kachina spirits and that have been constructed under spiritual tutelage. They reside in clan houses where they are fed ceremonially by a clanswoman, whose duty is inherited from maternal ancestors. The improper handling of these masks, which are tribal property, by the impersonator and family can bring death and disaster. Only a priest may wear a priestly kachina mask in ceremonies. The other category of masks are individually owned property. They are treated as a man's personal sacred object, assuring him of status among kachinas after death. These masks appear in rain dances and performances of Zuni's six kivas and are buried at the kachina village after an individual's death. (See also CHAPAYEKA MASKS; MASQUETTES; MISINGHALIKUN MOUNTAIN SPIRIT DANCERS; PASCOLA DANCER; YEIBICHAI MASK.)

MASON, SOPHIA THOMAS *(1822–1861) Cree* A translator who assisted her husband, WILLIAM MASON, with his missionary work and linguistic efforts. She was born at the Red River settlement in Canada on November 15, 1822. Sophia's mother was a Native woman and her father, Dr. Thomas Thomas, was a chief factor of the Hudson's Bay Company and governor of the Northern Department. After her father's death in 1828, Sophia lived in the homes of the Reverend DAVID THOMAS JONES and the Reverend WILLIAM COCKRAN. She was educated at the Red River Academy, where she was offered a governess position in 1843. She instead married the Reverend William Mason and accompanied him to the Rossville mission north of Lake Winnipeg in Canada. Fluent in the Cree language she learned as a child from her mother, Mrs. Mason assisted with translations. She also worked in the mission day school, visited Native people in their homes and tended her growing family. In 1858 the Masons went to England to oversee a translation of the New Testament. After arriving in England, Mrs. Mason began suffering from pleurisy. Despite illness and the birth of her ninth baby, she continued her Cree biblical work. After the New Testament translation was completed in 1859, the Masons began working on the Old Testament. Sophia's husband wrote that her knowledge of the language was invaluable and that she worked night and day on a final translation. Sophia Mason died on October 10, 1861, in London, England. By then the last of the Old Testament translations had just been printed.

MASON, WILLIAM *(fl. 19th century)* Wesleyan Methodist missionary who later became a member of the Church of England. Mason was sent to Lac la Pluie (now Rainy Lake) in Canada under the auspices of the Wesleyan Missionary Society of England about 1840, where he was assisted by HENRY BIRD STEINHAUER, who served as his interpreter. In 1843 Mason married SOPHIA THOMAS (MASON), an educated mixed-blood, at the Red River settlement in Canada. A short time later, the couple left for the Rossville mission tnat was located north of Lake Winnipeg. It was superintended by the Reverend JAMES EVANS who had created a Cree syllabary. After Evans died, Mason continued the linguistic work Evans had started. Mason was assisted by his wife, who had learned the Cree language from her mother. The couple remained at the Rossville mission until the Methodists discontinued it in 1854. Mason then joined the Anglican Church and lived at York Factory for four years. He and his wife later traveled to England to oversee the publication of the New Testament in the Cree syllabary. After its 1859 completion, they worked on a translation of the Old Testament. Although only William Mason's name was on the work, his Native former colleagues John Sinclair and Steinhauer contributed to it. The final translations were most likely done by Sophia Mason. The missionary couple had nine children.

MASQUERADE FESTIVAL (Kelek) *Alaska Inuit*   Following the BLADDER FESTIVAL, the *kelek* involved singing songs of supplication to the spirits of game, accompanied by masked dance performances directed by a shaman that recreated his past spiritual encounters, to elicit their participation in the future. Powerful masks representing spirits of game animals and the shaman's spirit helpers are created especially for the dramatic performance. The shaman directs the construction of the masks, through which the spirits are revealed, drawing on shamanic visions.

MASQUETTES *Iroquois*   Miniature wooden or corn husk masks that are kept as talismans, or personal sacred objects, to commemorate a dream that led to a cure. They are sometimes hung on the hair of larger masks and "ride along" in traveling rites. The masquettes are also kept to protect the health of the owners. During the days of the DREAM GUESSING RITE held during MIDWINTER CEREMONY, masquettes are presented to a dreamer by the person who guesses correctly the contents of the dream and has the obligation to make the dreamer a protective object. Owning a masquette entails an obligation to renew a ceremony and social relationships with the dream guesser. (See MASK.)

MASSAUM CEREMONY *Cheyenne*   An ancient holy ceremony of the Tsistsistas (Cheyenne) that is variously referred to as a contrary, animal or earth-giving ritual. The name *Massaum* comes from the Cheyenne word, *massa'ne,* meaning "crazy" and is said to derive from the participation of members of the Hohnuhkuh Society, a sacred contrary society, and their performance of extraordinary healing and other feats. The Massaum was brought to the Cheyenne by the great prophet SWEET MEDICINE, who first performed it

at NOAHA-VOSE, the sacred BEAR BUTTE. Tsistsistas bands gathered for the Massaum's annual performance each summer to renew its sacred covenant. The ceremony, which ritually reenacted the creation of the universe, took five days to complete. Ritual elements included the construction of sacred lodges, sweat lodge purification, the symbolic representation of all animal species, ritual or ceremonial hunting, the teaching of hunting rules, and the representation of night and day. The religious activities performed each day were accompanied by sacred songs, ritual smoking, symbolic painting, consecration, and prayer. The participants included a pledger, priests, and assistants. Sources indicate that the Massaum Ceremony was last performed among the Northern Cheyenne in 1911 and among the Southern Cheyenne in 1927. Confinement to reservations, government and missionary opposition to the observance, and the Euro-American destruction of buffalo and other animals essential to its performance are among the reasons the complex Massaum Ceremony could not be continued. SAND CRANE, the Keeper of the SACRED BUFFALO HAT, was one of the priests who helped conduct the 1911 ceremony in Montana.

MAT FAAR TIIGUNDRA (Canyon Mine) *Havasupai*   The place where the Havasupai originated, Mat Faar Tiigundra, is an indispensable part of the Havasupai religion and the site where individuals and the earth are renewed each year. The site is now located on government land in Kaibab National Forest in Arizona. When the Forest Service issued a permit to open a uranium mine at Mat Faar Tiigundra, the Havasupai took legal action, claiming that the mine at Mat Faar Tiigundra and Wii'i gdwiisa (Red Butte), the navel of the Havasupai mother, would endanger the sacred sites and the Havasupai people and religion as well. The Havasupai argued that the Forest Service's decision violated their First Amendment right to freely exercise their religion because "if the uranium mine is sunk, the sacred resting and meeting place of the Life Spirit . . . and the Spiritual Grandmother will be destroyed, the annual renewal of the Earth will not occur, and the Sacred Mother will die." The U.S. district court decided against the Havasupai claim in April 1990. (See SACRED SITES for related entries in this volume.)

MATACHIN DANCE *Pueblo*   Performed in some version by Pueblo throughout New Mexico, scholars debate the origin and hidden meanings of this dance. One theory holds that the dance was taught to the Indians by early Franciscan missionaries. Male dancers, matachins, dressed in black pants and vests, wear miters with long colorful ribbons hanging down the back and cover their faces with fringe and scarves. One young girl, called a *malinche,* dressed in white or tan, dances between two lines of matachins. Other performers include a male soloist, a young boy impersonating a bull, and two clowns ("grandfathers") who wear masks. The bull is ritually killed and revived by the clowns. The music is European in character. Ceremonial clothing differs from pueblo to pueblo and incorporates Indian and European characteristics.

MATACHIN DANCE *Yaqui* See YAQUI CEREMONIALISM

MATHIAS, BAPTISTE *(1876–?) Kootenai* Flathead Lake Kutenai historian and SUN DANCE chief. Mathias was born in 1876 and lived near Elmo, Montana. He maintained a pictographic history of the Kootenai people that was started by his father in the 19th century. The traditional record, kept on a "buckstring calendar," began in 1826. Mathias transferred it to paper in 1910 and continued to add new entries. He was interviewed by the writer Carling Malouf in December 1950 about his extensive knowledge of Kootenai history. Mathias, with his son as interpreter, gave an account of historic events recorded in the calendar. He related the succession of Kootenai chiefs, indicating that they were chosen for their spiritual powers and warrior reputations in the early days. He also discussed land settlements, tribal wars, and other information. Malouf identified Mathias as "the last of the Sun Dance Chiefs" among his people.

MATO TIPILA (Bear's Lodge, Devil's Tower) A sheer rock tower that rises more than 1,200 feet above the trees and plains in the northeast corner of Wyoming, the formation known as Mato Tipila (Bear's Lodge) or Devil's Tower is sacred to at least 23 tribes, including the Lakota, Nakota, Dakota, Arapaho, Cheyenne, Chippewa, Crow, Kiowa, and Shoshone, who have practiced their religious and cultural ceremonies there for centuries. Native people have made pilgrimages to Mato Tipila to pray and take part in sweat lodge rites, vision quests, and prayer offerings. A SUN DANCE has been held there annually since 1984.

The explosion of interest in rock climbing has led to an increase in the number of registered climbers at Devil's Tower. The volcanic monolith has become one of the premier rock-climbing sites on the American continent. Using new technology, including the use of battery-operated power drills to insert bolts into the tower, rock climbers from around the world have climbed the mountain and disrupted ceremonies that are conducted every year in June.

The National Park Service (NPS) tried to limit disruptive activities at the Devil's Tower National Monument, designated as America's first national monument by President Theodore Roosevelt in 1906, that it determined placed a burden on such worship and to protect the cultural resources of those lands. The plan called for a voluntary cessation of rock climbing in the month of June so that tribal worship could be conducted in a peaceful setting not disrupted by rock climbers and/or tourists. The NPS implemented the voluntary climbing ban in 1995 after nearly two years of consulting with American Indians, rock climbers, environmentalists, and others. It did so to balance the competing interests of Indians and rock climbers and to encourage tolerance and respect for Indian religious practices. To promote compliance with the ban, the NPS posted a sign at the base of the tower asking visitors to stay on the trail (and away from Indians conducting ceremonies at off-trail locations) and developed a cross-cultural education program that offers information to visitors about the historical and cultural significance of the tower to American Indians. Most rock climbers have shown respect for the Indian religious practitioners and have supported the program.

The NPS was sued by commercial climbing guide companies contending that NPS actions unconstitutionally violated the Establishment Clause of the First Amendment and Equal Protection component of the Fifth Amendment. On April 3, 1998, Judge William F. Downes of the U.S. District Court in Wyoming ruled that the NPS's climbing management plan at Devil's Tower National Monument was constitutional. In his ruling, Judge Downes stated that: ". . . the voluntary climbing ban is a policy that has been carefully crafted to balance the competing needs of individuals using Devil's Tower National Monument while, at the same time, obeying the edicts of the Constitution." Judge Downes upheld all aspects of the NPS's program stating that, "While the purposes behind the voluntary climbing ban are directly related to Native American religious practices . . . the purposes underlying the ban are really to remove barriers to religious worship occasioned by public ownership of the Tower. This is in the nature of accommodation, not promotion, and consequently is a legitimate secular purpose . . . The government is merely enabling Native Americans to worship in a more peaceful setting." The rock climbers, represented by the Mountain States Legal Foundation, have appealed the District Court's ruling to the Tenth Circuit Court of Appeals.

MAYHEW, EXPERIENCE *(1673–1758)* A Congregational missionary and fourth-generation member of his family to preach among New England Indians. He was the son of John and Elizabeth Mayhew, the grandson of THOMAS MAYHEW (2) and the great-grandson of THOMAS MAYHEW (1), the first governor of Martha's Vineyard. Born at Chilmark, Massachusetts, he learned the language of the local Indians as a child and later studied other dialects. Mayhew began preaching to Native people in 1693 and a short time later was asked to teach in the English church at Tisbury on Martha's Vineyard. From then until his death, he worked for the SOCIETY

FOR THE PROPAGATION OF THE GOSPEL IN NEW ENGLAND. In 1709 his translation of portions of the Bible in the Massachuset language was published as *Massachusee Psalter*, which was viewed by J. H. Turnbull as second only to the ELIOT BIBLE in importance. In 1713, at the request of the New England Company, he visited Indians on the mainland. After preaching to the Pequot through an interpreter, he traveled to the Mohegan but found that most of them were away hunting. Without an audience for a sermon, Mayhew left a letter to be translated to the hunters on their return home. On his way back to Martha's Vineyard, he stopped among the Narragansett and met with Ninnicraft, the head sachem, who refused to let him preach to his people because of his objections to the behavior of Christians. A second tour for the company a year later was also a failure. In 1720 Mayhew was awarded an honorary degree by Harvard College. He completed other writings, including *Indian Converts* in 1727 and *Grace Defended* in 1744. (See also COCKENOE; ELIOT, JOHN; GOOKIN, DANIEL; HIACOOMES; NESUTAN, JOB; PRAYING INDIANS.)

MAYHEW, THOMAS (1) *(1593–1682)* First governor of Martha's Vineyard and missionary to the Indians. Born in England to Matthew and Alice Barter Mayhew in 1593, he became a merchant in Southampton. Before 1632 he immigrated to New England, where he oversaw the enterprises of Matthew Cradock, a London merchant. Admitted as a freeman to the Massachusetts Bay Colony on May 14, 1634, Mayhew engaged in various mercantile enterprises and acted as Cradock's agent until the relationship ended in about 1637. In 1641 he purchased patents to Martha's Vineyard, Nantucket, and the Elizabeth Islands. About a year later his son THOMAS MAYHEW (2), a Congregational clergyman, settled on Martha's Vineyard and began preaching to the Massachuset Indians, converting HIACOOMES to Christianity in 1643. When his son died at sea in 1657, Mayhew continued the missionary work himself. With his knowledge of the Native language, he was successful in converting a number of Indians, not only to Christianity, but also to the English way of life. Despite his magisterial duties and advanced age, Mayhew sometimes walked great distances to conduct services among the Indians. Between 1664 and 1667 he was assisted in his efforts by the New England minister John Cotton. After the first Native church was established in 1670, Mayhew's age, health, and magisterial duties forced him to decline the pastorate, and an Indian was appointed instead. During King Philip's War, which was fought between English colonists and New England tribal groups from 1675 to 1676, the Christian Indians of the Vineyard remained loyal to the English, and a Native guard was formed to protect the settlement. Mayhew died on March 25, 1682, the first of five generations of his family to become missionaries to the Indians. His great-grandson, EXPERIENCE MAYHEW, continued the family's missionary work. (See also COCKENOE; ELIOT, JOHN; GOOKIN, DANIEL; NESUTAN, JOB; PRAYING INDIANS.)

MAYHEW, THOMAS (2) *(c. 1621–1657)* Congregational clergyman who was the first English missionary to the Indians of New England. Born in England, he was the only son of THOMAS MAYHEW (1), the first governor of Martha's Vineyard. He was the leader and pastor of a settlement of colonists in present-day Edgartown, and he began missionary work among the Indians in the area, acquiring proficiency in the Native language. His first conversion was that of HIACOOMES in 1643, three years before JOHN ELIOT began his own Indian missionary work on the mainland. Although he encountered early resistance from Native people, the number of converts steadily increased. He opened a school in 1652 that was quickly filled with Indian children "apt to learn, and more and more" to come. Mayhew also collaborated with John Eliot on Indian tracts published in London, including *The Glorious Progress of the Gospel* and *Tears of Repentance*. For many years he paid the costs of the mission with his own funds. Shortly before his death, however, the SOCIETY FOR THE PROPAGATION OF THE GOSPEL IN NEW ENGLAND became a patron of his work as well as that of Eliot. Accompanied by an Indian convert, Mayhew set sail for England in 1657 to promote support for his missionary efforts and to attend to family business matters, but the ship was lost at sea. He was married to Jane Paine, the daughter of Thomas and Jane Paine. Their three sons succeeded him in civic and religious positions on Martha's Vineyard. (See also COCKENOE; GOOKIN, DANIEL; NESUTAN, JOB; PRAYING INDIANS.)

MAZAKUTEMANI, PAUL ("He Who Shoots as He Walks") *(c. 1806–1885) Dakota* An early convert to Christianity in Minnesota Territory, Mazakutemani helped the missionary STEPHEN RETURN RIGGS organize the Hazelwood Republic, a separate band of Dakota who had adopted Euro-American farming, Christianity, and other aspects of "civilization." Mazakutemani's mother, a member of the Wahpeton band, became known as Old Eve. His father was a Mdewakanton from Kaposia, near present-day St. Paul. Other members of Mazakutemani's family included his brother Cloud Man, a subchief and the great-grandfather of the missionary JOHN EASTMAN, and his cousin Little Crow, who led Dakota forces against Euro-American opponents in the Dakota War of 1862. In 1835 Mazakutemani was one of the first students at the Lac qui Parle mission school of the Congregational minister THOMAS S. WILLIAMSON. Besides studying Christian teachings and "civilized" ways, he learned to write in the Dakota language. Mazakutemani was among those who signed the Treaty of Traverse des Sioux in 1851, an agreement with the U.S. government that resulted in the loss of most of the Mississippi Valley homeland of the Santee Dakota.

Mazakutemani and other Dakota people who had been influenced by the missionaries at Lac qui Parle joined Reverend Riggs at the new mission he had developed near Hazelwood Creek in Minnesota Territory in 1854. They began building individual farms and formed a republic that the government agent recognized as a "civilized" band in 1856. The bylaws of Hazelwood Republic called for the relinquishment of a number of tribal customs and the adoption of Euro-American dress and ways. Mazakutemani served as the group's first president. Riggs eventually attempted to obtain citizenship for the members of Hazelwood Republic but was turned down by territorial authorities.

During the Dakota War of 1862, generally called the Sioux Uprising of 1862, Mazakutemani served as a spokesman and proponent of peace. A number of factors had contributed to the war, including the diminished land base of the Dakota people, the failure of the government to honor treaty commitments, assaults on the Dakota way of life, and conditions of hunger and illness in tribal communities. Mazakutemani, a member of the antiwar faction, helped form the Friendly Soldiers' Lodge with Cloud Man and other Santee to work toward peace. He served as a spokesman at many Dakota council meetings, urging measures that included the release of captive women and children. He later served as a scout for Colonel Henry H. Sibley, the Army officer who led military campaigns against Dakota forces during the period. In 1867 Mazakutemani was awarded $500 for his services during the war. About 1880 he wrote a narrative in the Dakota language about the conflict, translated by Reverend Riggs for the Minnesota Historical Society. Mazakutemani continued as an active civic and religious leader until the end of his life. He died on the Sisseton Reservation in South Dakota on January 6, 1885. Another translation of Mazakutemani's name is "walks shooting iron" and he was also known as Little Paul.

MEDEULIN *Malecite* An individual who was born to be a medicine person or one who acquired this power in later life. These people could cure the sick, injure enemies, transform into various animals, and walk in hard ground, sinking into it as if it were snow or mud.

MEDICINE BAG A small buckskin pouch filled with various sacred "power" or medicine objects. The bag is concealed in the clothing or suspended from cords worn around the neck or waist. Medicine men and women use their medicine bags containing sacred items in doctoring the sick. Apache people also have personal medicine objects, such as arrowheads, feathers, bird and animal parts, shells, fossils, rock crystals, and carvings from lightning-struck trees. Traditional Indians believe that, when properly used, their medicine objects give them spiritual power in certain areas. There are medicines for influencing every undertaking in life, for controlling sickness and death, and for invoking mysterious powers of the universe. (See also MEDICINE BUNDLE.)

MEDICINE BUNDLE A wrapped sacred object or collection of objects. It may be owned by an individual, family, society, clan, band, community, or an entire tribal group. Specific origin stories, beliefs, powers, rituals, songs, responsibilities, and/or taboos are generally associated with each one. Medicine bundle practices vary from tribe to tribe. Among the Blackfeet, for example, at least 13 different categories of these sacred bundles have been identified. Each category in turn is extensive. The objects in a medicine bundle are sometimes seen in a dream or vision or acquired through inheritance and/or purchase. Guardianship, ownership, and the performance of the sacred rituals associated with each bundle is entrusted to a qualified individual or individuals. Bundles have great powers that benefit people. They may have the power to cure, to make the wearer clairvoyant, to call game animals, or to assure success in hunting or war. If mistreated, they are believed to have power to cause great harm. Bundles are considered to be alive and must be treated with respect and cared for by those who possess the proper qualifications. They are rarely publicly displayed. (See also KEEPER; MEDICINE BAG; MEDICINE BUNDLE [Navajo]; WATERBUSTER (MIDIPADI) CLAN BUNDLE.)

MEDICINE BUNDLE *(jish)* *Navajo (Dineh)* An assemblage of sacred objects kept in small pouches or bags and used by Navajo (Dineh) ceremonialists to perform traditional curative or preventive religious ceremonies. The term *jish* applies to the medicine bundle as well as to all of its contents. A Navajo *jish* is considered to be alive, a source and repository of sacred power that can attract good or drive off evil. It must be approached, handled, and used in acceptable ways, or misfortune will result. The contents of the *jish* have symbolic meanings, ceremonial use, and ancient prototypes. The powers that dwell in and emanate from individual pieces of the total assemblage of ritual equipment are affected by factors such as the age of the equipment and the completeness of the collection of objects, as well as by successful demonstration of their power by previous owners. Individual *jish* components can also be acquired as a loan or gift, through purchase or trade, collected in a natural setting, or inherited near the end of an apprenticeship with a teacher, who makes up the medicine bundle for the student. The newly qualified singer and ceremonial equipment are blessed in a ceremony. There are numerous rites concerned with protecting and using the sacred equipment. *Jish* are individually owned, and the singers or relatives have the right to decide their fate, passing them on as gifts or trading or selling them to Navajo or non-Navajo. Upon the singer's death, his bundle may be burned with him or may be inherited by his or his sister's children. *Jish* may be abandoned or retired, and in some cases they may fall into non-Indian hands, including museums and private collectors.

MEDICINE ELK, JAMES (Blind Wolf) *(1907–1974) Cheyenne* Keeper of the SACRED ARROWS. Medicine Elk, a Northern Cheyenne, was born to Mary Bird Bear and Medicine Elk. In his youth he participated in the sacred MASSAUM CEREMONY, which was later identified as the last one held among the Southern Cheyenne in Oklahoma. Medicine Elk married among this branch of his people, becoming a Sacred Arrow Lodge priest. When the Cheyenne authorities had difficulties finding a new keeper, Medicine Elk told them that he would assume the position until a permanent replacement was named. He was concerned that the Sacred Arrows not go to a museum, as rumored, and wanted to make certain they were taken care of in their rightful place among his people. Medicine Elk held the sacred position from 1962 to 1971. During that period, he fulfilled a vow to pray at NOAHA-VOSE (BEAR BUTTE) His successor as keeper of the Sacred Arrows was EDWARD RED HAT.

MEDICINE MAN/WOMAN An English term applied to many Native American religious leaders and healers beginning in the 17th century and continuing until the present time. In every tribe, these religious specialists have various names depending on whether they work with herbs or specialize in certain ceremonies. In non-Native languages, they have been called priests, medicine men or women, caciques, singers, shamans, and herbalists. Each tribe has its own name for these religious practitioners responsible for sacred knowledge and practices, which are mostly stored in their memories. Much of this knowledge is secret, the property of religious leaders, and considered too dangerous for others to come into contact with. Medicine men and women are ritually prepared and empowered to use the knowledge.

The role of the medicine man and woman varies from group to group. In general, however, there is usually some spiritual indication, such as a childhood vision, that signals a person is predisposed to becoming a medicine person. Others become medicine people by heritage, by a "calling" from the spirits, or by voluntary pursuit of the powers. This is fol-

Julie Plenty Wolf. A medicine woman participating in the 1966 Sun Dance at Pine Ridge Reservation in South Dakota. *With permission of Paul B. Steinmetz, S.J.*

lowed by spiritual and physical training with established holy people, training that is essential for a medicine man or woman to attain full power. The training incorporates intellectual, ritual, and gymnastic elements. The training may include a VISION QUEST, which may suggest an apprenticeship of learning ritual and curing techniques. Medicine men and women lead ceremonies, rites, and dances, conduct prayers, preside over life-cycle events, find objects lost in time and space, and instruct potential medicine people.

Because some Indian people assign the cause of some diseases to spiritual forces, a number of these medicine people are regarded as possessing the spiritual powers enabling them to diagnose and cure disease. They are compensated for their services. Among the Navajo (Dineh), singers, curers, diagnosticians, or herbalists are knowledgeable about ceremonials and disease. Practitioners, who may be women, have special ritual equipment, and they select certain SANDPAINTINGS or plant medicines according to the actual disease or causal factors considered relevant, or the patient or family may request such a selection. They know the methods of petitioning the great forces of earth and sky on behalf of those ill in body or in spirit.

A single practitioner, who must know at least one complete chant, can usually learn only a few major chants in his lifetime, as it requires years and a prodigious memory to learn exactly the origin histories of the Navajo and hundreds of long prayers and songs and to know about plant medicines, symbolism, dry paintings, and ritual acts of particular ceremonies. No special visionary or mystical gift is necessary to become a good singer or herbalist, and he or she must serve an apprenticeship with an instructor for several years, making financial and personal sacrifices to get training. They are paid for conducting the ceremony, the fee varying with reputation, time spent, distance traveled, and rarity of the ceremonial knowledge. (See also CACIQUE; DIAGNOSTICIAN; SHAMAN; the Subject Index for individual entries.)

MEDICINE MEN'S ASSOCIATION *Navajo (Dineh)*   An association of Navajo ceremonial practitioners organized in the late 1970s for the first time in Navajo history. These practitioners, who formerly operated as individuals, formed a political organization because ceremonial paraphernalia were being burned by churches on a certain part of the reservation. In 1979, the association incorporated into a nonprofit corporation and created by-laws to further its purpose of preserving Navajo healing ceremonies and practices and to ensure that Navajo culture not be lost. The association has been working to reclaim MEDICINE BUNDLES, or *jish,* from museums, to bring Native healing ceremonies to inmates of New Mexico State Penitentiary in Santa Fe, to recruit and establish training programs for medicine men of the future, and to have employee health insurance plans cover Native healing ceremonies.

MEDICINE SOCIETIES *Iroquois*   These medicine societies function as trustees of rituals for the benefit of the community. They include the BEAR SOCIETY, BUFFALO SOCIETY, EAGLE SOCIETY, FALSE FACES SOCIETY, HUSK FACES SOCIETY, LITTLE WATER SOCIETY, OTTER SOCIETY, LITTLE PEOPLE SOCIETY, and the Society of Mystic Animals. They act as intermediaries between spirit tutelaries and an individual who needs their help. Each society honors different animal spirits and calls on the power of its tutelary to cure disease, chase witches, and divert natural catastrophes (such as drought). Society members invoke the spirits in their rituals. Restricted medicine societies limit their membership, and their major curing rites are conducted in private sessions in the homes of sick people. Unrestricted societies are open to persons who wish to further curing by joining with per-

formers. One who needs the society's cures becomes a member by having the society perform its rituals on one's behalf. Membership also comes through having a dream.

Each society owns a distinct set of songs and other rituals that are addressed to a particular set of spirits associated with that society and each has an origin story that recounts the origin of its most important rites. The paraphernalia, procedures, and methods of effecting cures are also particular to each group. All but the Otter Society have music associated with the rites. The societies observe a general pattern of rites beginning with the THANKSGIVING ADDRESS, a TOBACCO INVOCATION burned in honor of spirits, the program of songs and dances of the particular society, a blessing on those participating, and a feast of soup that is distributed and eaten at home.

MEDICINE SOCIETIES *Keresan*   Medicine associations have important religious functions in these pueblos. Most Keresan pueblos have two or more curing or medicine societies that have other functions as well. They deal with sickness due to spiritual causes. They employ sacred objects, medicines, and other ritual objects to cure. Women may belong to the societies, but they do not cure. Membership may be voluntary, compulsory through being "trapped" (a ritual capture after entering on purpose or by accident a sacred area defined by the society while it performs a ceremony), or undertaken by vow during an illness and recovery. Each society has a chamber in which initiations take place, solstice ceremonies performed, and retreats held. Each society has a headman, and members wear prescribed attire. Members prepare for and invoke spirit forces through prayers, songs, and offerings. The ritual and symbolic acts of medicine society curing rites also deal with the forces of witchcraft. Medicine societies also assist at KACHINA DANCES and initiations.

MEDICINE SOCIETIES *Tewa*   See TANOAN MOIETY CEREMONIAL ASSOCIATIONS

MEDICINE WHEEL   A Native American spiritual site in north-central Wyoming used by a number of North American Indian tribes. Located atop 10,000-foot-high Medicine Mountain is a circle, approximately 80 feet in diameter constructed of mountain rock and boulders. Estimates of the wheel's origination date range from 10,000 B.C. to A.D. 1450. The U.S. Forest Service has plans to develop the Medicine Wheel site that will enhance tourist visitation and use of the site as well as cut timber from the spiritual mountain. Tribes have requested that certain days before and after summer solstice be considered as "high" spiritual days for certain ceremonies. The Forest Service response is that tribes conduct prayers on sacred days after 9:00 P.M.

and finish by 6:00 A.M. each day. Tribes wish to enlarge the historic protection area beyond the diameter of the wheel. Indians propose that tribal members have exclusive use of the site for ceremonial purposes for 12 days at each solstice and equinox. Indians want no disturbance of the natural habitat within a two-and-a-half-mile radius and want protection of sacred and medicinal plants, arrowheads, trails, and sites. A coalition opposes Forest Service development plans that include a visitor center and access road. On September 28, 1996, seven parties signed a Historic Preservation Plan: the Big Horn National Forest, the Advisory Council on Historic Preservation, the Wyoming State Historic Preservation Office, Big Horn County Commissioners, the Federal Aviation Administration, the Medicine Wheel Coalition for Sacred Places, and the Medicine Wheel Alliance. The latter two groups, both with predominantly Native American boards, have been working actively since 1988 for the preservation of Medicine Mountain from timber harvesting, mining, and tourism.

The agreement stipulates that 20,000 acres (most of Medicine Mountain) will be marked as an "area of consultation." No mineral withdrawal, no timbering, no tourist development will take place without consultation with the signatory parties. Any Forest Service proposals for the area must be agreed to by the seven signatory parties to the agreement. Traditional Native uses supersede all other uses. In addition, 24 days annually will be set aside, during which enrolled Native tribal members will have exclusive use of the area. If requested, provision will be made for short ceremonies at the Medicine Wheel during the regular season. Wyoming Sawmills has appealed the plan because it opposes the closing of a road that has been used for commercial logging purposes. (See also SACRED SITES.)

MEDICINES *Kawaiisu* In Kawaiisu belief four principal medicines were originally given to the people. These included jimsonweed, tobacco, nettle, and red ants. (See also ROCK BABY.)

MEEKER, JOTHAM *(1804–1855)* Baptist missionary and printer who worked among the Potawatomi, Ottawa, Ojibway, and Shawnee during his 30-year career. Meeker was born in Ohio's Hamilton County on November 8, 1804, and later learned the printing trade in Cincinnati. He became a missionary in 1825, serving as a teacher and minister to the Potawatomi, the Ottawa, and then the Ojibway at missions in present-day Michigan. In 1832, after mastering the related languages of the three groups, he began experimenting with developing an orthography using English characters. A year later he was sent to the newly created Indian Territory and began working at the new Shawnee mission near what is now Kansas City, Kansas. Meeker completed the first printing in the territory in 1834, publishing a hymn in the Shawnee language on March 8, then a primer written in Delaware on March 21. He eventually printed approximately 65 works in 10 Native languages, using his system of orthography, as well as in English. In 1837 he moved to a mission among the Ottawa in the territory near present-day Ottawa, Kansas, where he remained until the end of his life. After moving the printing equipment to his mission in 1849, he produced a bilingual code of the Ottawa tribal laws and a few other publications before his death on January 12, 1855. (See also MCCOY, ISAAC.)

MEGAPOLENSIS, JOHANNES *(1603–1670)* Reformed Dutch clergyman whose ministerial work in New Amsterdam (now New York) included the Mohawk. Named Jan van Mekelenburg, he was born to Catholic parents in Keodyck, Holland, and raised in their religion. When he was about 23, he joined the Reformed faith and later wrote that he was "thrust out" from his family because of his conversion. Megapolensis served as a minister in Holland from 1634 to 1642, then bound himself to Kiliaen van Rensselaer for six years to minister to the Dutch colony at Rensselaerswyck (now Albany, New York). He left Holland with his wife, Machtelt, and four children on June 14, 1642, and arrived in New Amsterdam on August 4. Shortly after preaching his first sermon in van Rensselaer's storehouse, he began establishing relations with the Mohawk who annually traded at Fort Orange. He learned their language and became one of the earliest missionaries to visit their communities. Because of his good relations with the Mohawk, Megapolensis was able to barter with them for the 1642 release of ISAAC JOGUES, a Jesuit they had captured. The Reformed minister criticized Catholic missionaries for baptizing Native people who did not understand what baptism meant and who looked upon it as harmful magic. His refusal to conduct baptisms himself may have contributed to his friendly relations with the Indians. When his six years of service to van Rensselaer expired, he arranged to return to Europe in 1649, but Governor Peter Stuyvesant and others persuaded him to serve as a minister in New Amsterdam. He accepted the offer and served in the position for the rest of his life. In addition to his religious work, Megapolensis also became involved in politics. In 1664 he and his son Samuel were among those who helped convince Peter Stuyvesant, the governor of the New Netherland colony in present-day New York and New Jersey, to surrender Dutch control of the area to the British. A short time later, Megapolensis swore allegiance to the king of England and continued his church work under the protectorate of the new regime. His publications included several tracts and *A Short Account of the Mohawk Indians,* which was first published in Holland in 1644.

MEMBERTOU *(?–1611) Micmac* Chief of a Micmac band and a shaman who prophesied about hunting or war. He attended the sick, blew on them, danced, and predicted recovery or death. He was the first Micmac sagamore (chief) to be baptized, without preparation, by JESSE FLÈCHÉ in Canada on June 24, 1610. He received the name of Henri, the King. Membertou renounced shamanism, refused to practice polygamy, and before dying asked to be buried with the French, although he initially wished to be buried with his ancestors.

MEMORIAL FEAST *Inuit* See FEAST TO THE DEAD (Alaska Inuit and Aleut)

MEMORIAL POTLATCH *Bella Coola, Haida, Kwakiutl, Tlingit, Tsimshian* A ceremonial cycle of rituals to mourn the death of a chief and pass on his title and privileges to a descendant. The cycle could take several years to complete. The memorial potlatch has been called by one scholar the "central ceremonial system of the entire sociocultural order." The rites emphasized the balanced reciprocity between members of two moieties, the bereaved clan acting as hosts and the other as guests. When a chief died, there were traditionally eight days of mourning, in which all members of the tribe took part. The bereaved clan was comforted by the opposite side, who after four days, cremated the corpse and put the ashes in a lineage grave house or box. Formalized wailing, mourning songs, and lamenting took place at the funeral. The mourning period ended with a feast, clan member songs in memory of the dead relative, condolence speeches, and gift giving to members of the moiety opposite from that of the deceased. Gift giving benefited and honored the dead while raising or maintaining the prestige of the descendents who bore his name. About a year after death, the remains of the dead person were placed in a newly erected grave house or MORTUARY POLE. The services were performed by the mourners' opposites, for which they were publicly thanked, feasted, and remunerated at a final potlatch that completed the mortuary rites.

The memorial potlatch varied with the rank, status, and wealth of the deceased and matrilineage. Only the wealthy gave great potlatches, with help from clanmates. Sponsored by the *matrikin,* it was planned months ahead to accumulate the necessary property and food. It required the building or rebuilding of a new house, which was "danced together" by the host and clanmates before the guests were entertained. It stood as a memorial to all the dead of the clan. The potlatch rites included wearing ceremonial clothing decorated with lineage and clan crests; performing ancestral songs and dances; recounting ancestral stories; exchanging words of condolence for words of gratitude between guests and hosts; bestowing names (titles) of the deceased (as well as ceremonial regalia) on the immediate successors and other close *matrikin;* feasting; and the distribution of food and gifts by the hosts to the guests for rendering services, for coming to console the new chief, and for witnessing and accepting the announcement of the name-title transfer to the new chief. The condolence speeches delivered by guests at the funeral and memorial potlatch to which the hosts responded with their speeches of gratitude attempted to diminish the impact of death as well as create the image of harmonious relations between moieties. Guests also thanked their hosts for their generosity with songs and dances. The dead were believed to be present during the ceremony, so food, water, and clothing were offered, through burning, to all dead members of the matrilineage group. The dead were made tangible at the potlatch through masked impersonation or symbols (sacred lineage regalia). The potlatch marked the final act of separation between the deceased person and the living and signaled the end of mourning observed by the matrilineal kin of the deceased who sponsored the potlatch. After the potlatch, the dead were no longer supposed to be mourned. (See also POTLATCH.)

MESCAL BEAN CEREMONY An ancient religious practice that once flourished among a number of Central and Southern Plains Indian groups. Believed to have originated before European contact, it has been theorized that the ceremony was the forerunner of peyotism. The mescal bean (*Sophora secundiflora*), considered a sacred medicine, was used in various ways during rituals. The ceremony had names and features unique to each tribal group with the practice. It is sometimes called the Deer Dance, Red Medicine Society, Whistle Dance, and Wichita Dance.

MESSENGER FEAST (Inviting In) *Alaska Inuit* A ceremony lasting four days to a few weeks that appeals to the spirit guardians of the performers who wear masks representing them. The ceremony is celebrated from the Kuskokwim River north to Point Barrow. Taking place in January, the feast derives its name from the fact that the host community sends messengers to a guest community with an invitation to the event. The messengers take sticks with a pictorial or mnemonic record of what the hosts want to receive as gifts. The ceremony involves singing, humorous and ceremonial dances, shamanic trances, honoring of creator beings and game animals, offerings to spirits, mask burning, and feasting. The hosts perform masked dances, and the guests likewise perform in the village assembly house. In these dances, people re-create their past spiritual encounters and hope for aid in the future. Elaborate masks reveal shamanic spirit helpers and the spirits of various natural resources. Through song and dance, shamans instruct carvers about making the masks. Children are initiated into adult roles at this time, and youths wear special masks while learning dances. The primary purpose of the event is to exchange gifts, with mutual hosting between villages and considerable rivalry as to the quality and quantity of gifts given during the Messenger Feast. The feast is an important social event, bringing renewal, rebirth, and reaffirmation of social values as well as redistribution of wealth within and between villages.

METHVIN, JOHN JASPER *(1846–1941)* Methodist minister and educator; one of the major mission figures of the Anadarko area of Indian Territory (present-day Oklahoma) from 1887 until his retirement in 1908. He was born December 17, 1846, to John and Mourning Glover Methvin near Jefferson, Georgia. He was educated in Georgia rural schools and at Auburn and Talmadge Institutes until his schooling was interrupted in 1862, when he joined the Confederate army. He later studied law and was admitted to the Georgia bar before turning to religion. The Methodist Episcopal Church, South, licensed Methvin to preach in 1870 and ordained him as a local deacon in 1874. He worked as an educator through the 1870s. Methvin became president of Gainesville College in 1880, and from 1883 to 1885 he served as president of Butler Female College, also in Georgia. In 1885 he accepted the superintendency of New Hope Seminary, a Methodist school for Choctaw girls, in Indian Territory, and was also ordained an elder. The following year the Methodist relationship with the school ended and Methvin was appointed superintendent of Seminole Academy. When that school also passed out of Methodist hands, he was appointed to initiate missionary efforts in the West and chose Anadarko, an Indian Agency with 10 or 12 tribes as his base. Methvin's work there focused upon the Apache, Comanche, and especially the Kiowa. His ministry included establishing a church, "camp work" (evangelizing American Indians in their homes) and founding a school that opened in 1890, constructed with Methodist mission funds on land Methvin had obtained from the government. In 1890 the Women's Board of Missions assumed responsibility for the school and in 1894 named it Methvin Institute in honor of its founder and supervisor. A year before Methvin's 1908 retirement, the school closed. He later wrote a history of Anadarko and reminiscences for publication in *The Chronicles of Oklahoma.*

MEXICAN V. CIRCLE BEAR (370 N.W. 2d 737 [S.D. 1985]) *(1985)* In this case the Supreme Court of South Dakota granted recognition to a tribal court order of March 20, 1985, on the disposition of a dead body according to tribal custom. The court concluded that although tribal traditions differed from state law on burial customs, it was not reason enough to deny a tribal order based on that custom from taking effect. (See also AMERICAN INDIAN RELIGIOUS FREEDOM ACT OF 1978; Subject Index for other cases in this volume.)

MEXISTET (Large Lad) *Palouse* A dreamer-prophet who adhered to the WASHANI RELIGION and traveled among the Nez Perce people with his religious teachings. Mexistet followed two earlier Palouse prophets: SOMILPILP (a contemporary of SMOHALLA) and Husiskeut.

MIDEWIWIN *Ojibway* The religious society of the Ojibway and related tribal groups whose primary purpose was to prolong life. Basil Johnston, a Canadian Ojibway author, defines the term as a contraction of *mino* ("good") and *daewaewin* ("hearted"), also meaning "the sound" or "sounding" from the drums used "to summon the spirit of well-being." One version of its origin states that the Midewiwin was a sacred gift sent by Gitche Manitou, the Creator, to help the people during a time of hardship and suffering. The society, also called Mide, combined moral teachings and codes of conduct with a knowledge of plants and herbs to heal and to prolong life. After a lengthy, costly period of instruction by a recognized Midewinini, or Mide priest, candidates were formally initiated into the society's membership of four or more degrees or orders. Preparations for initiation included instruction in origin traditions, ritual procedures, herbs and medicines, prayers and songs, and moral teachings. Attainment of each degree brought with it corresponding responsibilities, knowledge, and entitlements, such as the right to conduct certain ceremonies or to use particular sacred objects. In some communities ceremonies were held annually or semiannually, in the spring or fall, and lasted for several days, depending upon the number of initiates. One of the essential ceremonial features was a ritual "shooting," which caused a candidate to fall down as though dead. The initiate's revival symbolized spiritual renewal and power, the ending of one way of life and the beginning of another. The sacred scrolls of birch bark containing writings and illustrations preserved the sacred history and knowledge and served as mnemonic aids for the individuals qualified to use and to interpret them. Membership in the society was generally attained as a result of seeking treatment during an illness, after a dream, or through an apprenticeship to the Mide priesthood. The Midewiwin promoted health and life not only by healing but by its dedication to a moral code of conduct.

Early Euro-American references to Midewiwin practices among the Ojibway include those of two North West Company traders, who wrote accounts of their 1804 observations.

Fuller descriptions of the religious complex began to appear later in the 19th century. These accounts generally ascribe a postcontact date of origin to the Midewiwin. The religion is said to have spread from the Ojibway to a number of other tribal groups, including the Eastern Dakota, Fox, Ioway, Menominee, Omaha, Ponca, Potawatomi, and Winnebago (Ho-Chunk). Written accounts indicate that the Midewiwin began to decline at the end of the 19th century because of a number of factors, including the dispersion of Ojibway bands, missionary and government persecution, the cost of initiation and instruction, and the reduced numbers of qualified priests and successors. Although generally described by outsiders as a religion in decline, the Midewiwin continues in some locations to the present day.

Other names include Grand Medicine Society, Medicine Lodge Society, and Mide Society. (See also GAGEWIN; MINK, JOHN; MIS-QUONA-QUEB; REDSKY, JAMES, SR.; REFLECTING MAN, JOHN; WABENO.)

MIDWINTER CEREMONY *Iroquois* Also called the New Year's Ceremony, this nine-day ceremony to close the old year and begin the new is the most important of the IROQUOIS CALENDRICAL CEREMONIES and the most important LONGHOUSE event of the year. It is timed in accord with stars or luminary observations, whereas crop maturity determines the other festivals. The prophet HANDSOME LAKE observed Midwinter should begin five days after the first January new moon following the Christian New Year. (Formerly, the ceremony was held five days after the first new moon following the zenith of Pleiades.) Today, several longhouses follow Handsome Lake's plan, but the ceremonial may nevertheless begin on different dates at various longhouses.

The ceremony falls into two parts. The first, concerned with curing, dream fulfillment, renewal, and personal well-being, and the second, concerned with the four sacred rituals and food spirit observations, result from the fusion of Handsome Lake's teachings and the agricultural calendar. People express their gratitude to the Creator, and they use appropriate observances to thank the spirit forces who fulfilled their duty the previous year. The CONFESSION RITE takes place before Midwinter begins. The Midwinter is heralded by two messengers ("our uncles" or "BIG HEADS") who visit each house and announce the event. The "uncles," each representing a moiety, make a circuit of the houses, announce the New Year, and conduct STIRRING ASHES RITES in the stove of each home. There is a series of DREAM GUESSING RITES in which a song, dance, or game may be performed to renew a dream. The FOUR SACRED CEREMONIES are performed in the morning because they are the rites in honor of the Creator and "morning belongs to the Creator." The order of the four rituals differs from longhouse to longhouse.

The Midwinter Ceremony also involves the giving, receiving, and burning of tobacco. Collections of tobacco and a TOBACCO INVOCATION are made at different points in the ceremony. There are series of dances, differing in various longhouses, honoring corn, beans, and squash—the three sisters. Curing rituals are performed by the medicine societies, if requested through dreams, on behalf of those who are ill or on the anniversaries of those who have been cured. The FALSE FACE SOCIETY performs. There are rites for naming children born since GREEN CORN six months earlier and there are afternoon games of SNOW-SNAKE, LACROSSE, and tug-of-war and evening social dancing and feasts. The Midwinter Ceremony represents almost every aspect of longhouse activity, including the teachings of Handsome Lake, and compresses into a few days many important rites of the Iroquois. (See also IROQUOIS CEREMONIALISM.)

MIGRATORY BIRD TREATY ACT (16 U.S.C. 703–712) *(1916)* A federal act of 1916 restricting the taking, possessing, and transporting of migratory birds or their parts. These restrictions affect Native people who use the birds or their parts for religious purposes. Unlike the BALD AND GOLDEN EAGLE PROTECTION ACT, the Migratory Bird Treaty Act has no provisions authorizing permits to use the birds or their parts in religion. Subject to restrictions, some authorized hunting of designated migratory birds is allowed. As in the Eagle Protection Act, there is an exemption for items lawfully acquired before the date of the legislation. Treaties with Canada, Japan, and the Soviet Union allow the taking of some species, within restrictions, by Inuit and Indians for subsistence purposes. (See also AMERICAN INDIAN RELIGIOUS FREEDOM ACT OF 1978; ENDANGERED SPECIES ACT; MARINE MAMMAL PROTECTION ACT.)

MIGUELITO *(1865–1936) Navajo (Dineh)* A Navajo (Dineh) chanter who was the authority on the Male Shooting and Bead Chants that he had learned from teachers. Although Navajo teachings hold that sand- paintings should not be made permanent, Miguelito was persuaded by non-Indian friends to reproduce patterns of SANDPAINTINGS in permanent mediums, although he was disturbed about breaking taboos. Gladys Reichard lived and studied with Miguelito and published *Navajo Medicine Man* in 1939. In it are the explanations of the Bead and Shooting Chant traditional stories and sandpaintings as told to Reichard by Miguelito.

MILITARY SOCIETY See YAQUI CEREMONIALISM

MINK, JOHN (Zhonii'a Giishig, "Sky Money") *(c. 1850–1943) Ojibway* A MIDEWIWIN priest and a DRUM RELIGION leader who lived into his nineties among his people on the Lac Courte Oreilles Reservation in Wisconsin. He was given the name Zhonii'a Giishig by his maternal grandfather, a speaker of the people. Fasting many times as a youngster, he received spiritual power to heal and learned many sacred songs and medicines. Two years after his first wife died in childbirth, Mink remarried, and during this period he began learning about the religion of his people from Ojibway elders. Toward the end of his life, he provided information about his religious practices to the anthropologists Joseph B. Casagrande and Robert Ritzenthaler. Casagrande wrote an account of the Midewiwin priest's life, "John Mink Ojibwa Informant," and it was published in *In the Company of Man: Twenty Portraits of Anthropological Informants* in 1960. By the time the anthropologists knew him, Mink had outlived four wives and many children, who had died while young, and lived alone. His knowledge of traditional Ojibway ways was considered unsurpassed and included an extensive repertoire of stories, songs, medicines, and ceremonies. His grandson JAMES MUSTACHE was also a prominent Ojibway spiritual leader.

MISINGHALIKUN *Delaware (Lenni Lenape)* A sacred mask being of the Lenni Lenape, or Delaware, people whose origin and practice varied among the different tribal divisions. The Unami defined Misinghalikun as "living mask" or "living solid face." For them, its spiritual purpose included serving as guardian of the animals, a role it received from the Creator. Misinghalikun was embodied in a wooden mask, half red and half black which was ritually cared for by a keeper. He appeared in bearskin clothing and could sometimes be seen riding on a buck, herding deer. Among the Unami, Misinghalikun had a spring ceremony and also participated in the BIG HOUSE CEREMONY.

MIS-QUONA-QUEB (Red Cloud) *(fl. late 1700s to the early 1800s) Ojibway* A legendary war leader in the Lake of the Woods region of Canada who became a chief only when he had passed several spiritual tests. The story of his life was written by JAMES REDSKY SR., a MIDEWIWIN priest, who learned it through the oral tradition. According to Redsky, Mis-quona-queb was born in the area of Buffalo Bay and Northwest Angle in Ontario to Si-Si-Bas and Pegum-we-we. While fasting in solitude as a young man, he acquired a spiritual protector who taught him sacred powers and mysteries. Mis-quona-queb's powerful medicine, legendary among the people sustained him when he led war parties against the Dakota. He became the chief of the Lake of the Woods Ojibway after demonstrating his ability with the SHAKING TENT CEREMONY, proving his healing powers and dreaming a name for a new baby. Mis-quona-queb also joined the

Midewiwin religion and continued to lead his people until he died at the age of 86.

MISSOURI RIVER *(fl. mid-19th century) Hidatsa* A medicine man who helped lead his people upriver to Like-a-Fishhook village in about 1845 after their former villages at the mouth of the Knife River in present-day North Dakota were struck by smallpox. Keeper of the tribe's sacred Midipadi, or WATERBUSTER CLAN BUNDLE, Missouri River used it for guidance in planning the layout of a new village when the people stopped at a hooklike bend in the Missouri. His descendants, Buffalo Bird Woman, Wolf Chief, and EDWARD GOODBIRD, described Missouri River's role in planning Mua-iduskupe-hises (Like-a Fishhook) in firsthand accounts of their lives provided to the anthropologist Gilbert L. Wilson. Before Missouri River's death, the Midipadi bundle was transferred to the next keeper, SMALL ANKLE.

MISTAPEO *Montagnais-Naskapi* The "great soul" of a man, the force that provides guidance through life. The soul reveals itself in dreams, and people who try to interpret their meanings can obtain closer contact with their souls. The latter dictates, for example, the proper ritual practices to be observed in hunting game animals successfully. The inner life of the Montagnais-Naskapi was dominated by the self-study of dreams.

MITCHELL, FRANK *(1881–1967) Navajo (Dineh)* A prominent singer of the BLESSING WAY, the backbone of Navajo ceremonials. Born at Wheatfields, Arizona, Mitchell was among the first Navajo to attend the government-established school at Fort Defiance before the turn of the century. He was known to his people as Big School Boy. Besides his career as a singer, he was active in public service as a headman, one of the first members of the Navajo tribal council, as a chapter officer, and as a judge in the COURTS OF INDIAN OFFENSES. Mitchell shared with over a dozen scholars the structure of the Blessing Way rite—the details of procedure in performing it, its uses, and how to renew the MEDICINE BUNDLE. He dictated the traditional narrative of the Blessing Way to Father BERARD HAILE in 1930. From 1957 on, he worked with David P. McAllester and permitted a film and sound track record of the Blessing Way to be made. In 1963, Charlotte Frisbie joined the project and studied with Mitchell the puberty ceremony, also filmed, corn grinding songs, and types of Blessing Way songs. In 1963, Mitchell recorded his life history in a 12-hour narrative. Until Mitchell's death in 1967, he and Frisbee worked on a Mitchell genealogy, details about his life, and recordings of additional Blessing Way songs and prayers. The Mitchell family worked with the editors after Frank's death. Baptized a Catholic during his school days and again two years before he died, his funeral took place at the Franciscan mission in Chinle, Arizona.

Copies of the ceremonial materials recorded by Frank Mitchell and tapes of his life story are at the University of New Mexico, Wesleyan University, and the Library of Congress. Their use is restricted by the family.

MODESTO, RUBY (Nesha, "Woman of Mystery") *(1913–1980) Cahuilla.* Medicine woman. Born on the Martinez Reservation to a Serrano mother from the Morongo Reservation and a Desert Cahuilla father from the Coachella Valley in California, Modesto grew up learning the traditional ways of her father's people and did not speak English or attend school until after she was 10 years old. A member of the Dog clan, she inherited shamanistic teachings and traditions through clan relatives. Family members who were *puls,* or shamans, included her father, grandfather, great-grandfather, and a number of uncles. At about the age of 10, Modesto received her dream helper, Ahswit, the eagle, but she did not become a shaman until later in life. As a youngster she dreamed to such a high level, the 13th, that she required the help of an uncle, a shaman, to end the coma-like state she had been in for several days. Although Modesto's mother took her to the Moravian church on the reservation and she followed Christianity for a long time, she eventually chose to be a *pul* rather than pursue Christianity. As a medicine woman, she specialized in healing individuals possessed by demons. Respected for her knowledge of Desert Cahuilla culture and traditions, Modesto taught the Native language on the reservation and was a guest lecturer at colleges in the area. She also served as an informant to anthropologists, coauthoring an article in the *Journal of California Anthropology* (1977) and a book, *Not for Innocent Ears: Spiritual Traditions of a Desert Cahuilla Medicine Woman* (1980), which includes her autobiography. Modesto lived on the Martinez Reservation with her husband, David, and their family until her death on April 7, 1980.

MOIETY One-half, or side, of a tribal group. (See also IROQUOIS CEREMONIALISM.)

MO-KEEN, LOKI *(c. 1830–1934)* A Mexican who was captured as a small child by the Kiowa. Mo-Keen was "given" to the TAI-MAY, or sacred symbol, of the SUN DANCE. By having a captive carry out prescribed rituals, punishment was avoided for the tribe if taboos were inadvertently broken. His special duties included unwrapping the holy object for ceremonial exposure. Mo-keen, who shared the Kiowa faith in the Tai-may, lived to be more than 100 years old. He died in 1934. (See also BLACK LEGS DANCE; GOURD DANCE.)

Ruby Modesto. Desert Cahuilla medicine woman. *Photograph by Guy Mount, Sweetlight Books, Sedona, Arizona.*

MOLAWIA *Zuni* A ceremony held at the end of each year, in December, after the *KOKOS,* or spirits, depart and just before the winter solstice. Ten young Zuni girls, representing the sacred CORN MAIDENS, participate in footraces. The ceremony enacts the departure and return of the Corn Maidens and demonstrates respect for their crop.

MON 'HIN THIN GE *(c. 1800–c. late 1880s) Omaha* The last keeper of the Omaha's Tent of War, which lodged an ancient cedar tree and other venerated objects. In 1884 Mon 'hin thin ge turned over the contents of the Tent to ethnologists Alice Fletcher and Francis La Flesche for placement in the Peabody Museum at Harvard University. Changed conditions among the Omaha people brought about by contact with the dominant Euro-American society had caused knowledge of the ceremonies connected with the Tent of War to nearly die out. With advancing age, the hereditary keeper feared his increasing feebleness would cause an accident with the sacred objects and that the Omaha would suffer punishment as a result. Because of these factors, he agreed to relinquish the articles in his keeping, telling Fletcher and La Flesche:

These sacred articles have been in the keeping of my family for many generations; no one knows how long. My sons have chosen a path different from that of their fathers. I had thought to have these articles buried with me; but if you will place them where they will be safe and where my children can look on them when they wish to think of the past and of the way their fathers walked, I give them into your keeping. Should there come a time when I might crave to see once more these things that have been with my fathers, I would like to be permitted to do so. I know that the members of my family are willing that I should do this thing and no others have a right to question my action. There are men in the tribe who will say hard things of me because of this act but I think it best to do as I am doing. (*The Omaha Tribe,* 453–454)

In 1888 the contents of another Sacred Tent, which included the OMAHA SACRED POLE, were turned over to the Peabody Museum by their keeper, SHU'DENACI. Fletcher and La Flesche wrote about these holy men and the sacred objects entrusted to their care in *The Omaha Tribe,* which was published by the Bureau of American Ethnology in 1911. In 1989, the sacred pole was returned to the Omaha tribe. Other objects have also been returned by the Peabody Museum.

MONOHA *Yaqui*   The dance master of the matachin dancers who leads and who is ordinarily the best of all the dancers. There may be several Monohas, although only one serves in the leader capacity during any one dance. See also YAQUI CEREMONIALISM.

MOON SPIRIT *Alaska Inuit*   An important male spirit in the heavens who controls all animals and has the power to regulate fertility among women. Shamans journey in altered states beyond ordinary boundaries of experience to the moon in search of spiritual aid and to plead for game.

MOORE, WILLIAM LUTHER *(?–1931) Lumbee*   Methodist preacher who founded a number of churches in Robeson County, North Carolina. After his colleague and friend, HENRY H. LOWRY, organized a separate conference of Methodism among the Lumbee people, Moore remained with the original organization and contributed to its growth and development. It became known as the "White Conference" because of its association with the national church. An important figure in Lumbee history, Moore served as both a religious and educational leader. He was respected in the community not only for his pioneering leadership but for his service to the poor. His family also contributed leaders to other professional fields among the Lumbee people. By the 1970s the North Carolina Conference of the United Methodist Church included 1,800 Lumbee members and 10 churches.

MORGAN, JACOB (Casimera) *(1879–1950) Navajo (Dineh)*   Morgan, the first Navajo (Dineh) to be ordained as a Methodist minister, also served his people as tribal chairman between 1938 and 1942. He was a full-blood and a member of a traditionalist family from New Mexico. Morgan converted to Christianity while attending an off-reservation boarding school in Grand Junction, Colorado. In 1898 he enrolled at Hampton Institute in Hampton, Virginia, and remained there through his graduation in 1900 and for postgraduate work between 1901 and 1903. Morgan then returned to the Southwest and began teaching music and carpentry in a Bureau of Indian Affairs school. He also engaged in religious activities, including work on translating the Bible into the Navajo language. Morgan became a delegate to the tribal council in 1923, representing the Shiprock District of the reservation. He was known as a progressive for his advocacy of acculturation and his opposition to the maintenance of many traditional elements of Navajo culture and religion. During the 1930s he opposed the Wheeler-Howard Act, which included provisions aimed at organizing tribal lands in severalty. After becoming the chairman of the nation's largest tribal group in 1938, Morgan sought a more active role for the council in addressing Navajo issues and needs. During his administration he fought against the PEYOTE RELIGION on the reservation, signing a resolution adopted by the tribal council against the practice on June 3, 1940. Morgan's leadership also included service as the American Indian Federation's first vice-chairman. In recent times his people honored him as a "pathfinder," recognizing his role in developing the San Juan County area, among other contributions.

MORSE, JEDIDIAH *(1761–1826)*   A Congregational clergyman who served as secretary of the Society for the Propagation of the Gospel among the Indians and completed a report commissioned by the government on the condition of Native people. He was born in Woodstock, Connecticut, in 1761. He graduated from Yale College in 1783 and received his license to preach two years later. He then taught in Norwich, Connecticut, before returning to Yale as a tutor in June 1786. Morse was ordained on November 9 of that year and worked in Georgia a few months before beginning a 30-year ministerial career at the First Congregational Church in Charleston, Massachusetts. He was a Calvinist whose strong support of orthodoxy involved him in religious controversy throughout his ministry. To combat the progress of liberal theological views, he undertook a number of activities. He edited the *Panoplist* from 1805 to 1810; he opposed the candidate chosen as Hollis Professor of Divinity at Harvard; in 1808 he became one of the founders of Andover Theological Seminary; and he assisted in founding Boston's

Park Street Church. Besides his work on behalf of orthodoxy, Morse also helped found the New England Tract Society in 1814 and the American Bible Society in 1816. From 1811 to 1819 he served on the prudential committee of the AMERICAN BOARD OF COMMISSIONERS FOR FOREIGN MISSIONS. Morse's interest in American Indians, manifested during his ministry, continued after he left Charleston in 1819. He completed his work on Indian affairs for the secretary of war and published his report in 1822. Besides this activity, Morse spent his remaining years in New Haven writing and sometimes preaching. He is best known as the "Father of American Geography" for his extensive and popular writing on the subject. Morse died June 9, 1826.

MORTUARY CYCLE *North Pacific Coast*   The cycle consists of the funeral and several memorial feasts culminating in a MEMORIAL POTLATCH held a year or more after an individual's death in which the deceased is honored and those who worked at the funeral are rewarded by the maternal relatives of the deceased.

MORTUARY OBSERVANCES   Mortuary practices of Native Americans differed substantially across North America, but generally each group prepared the body for the afterworld. Traditionally bodies may be ritually prepared for burial. In some tribes, faces are painted. In others, clan members put moccasins on the feet of the dead relative. In pueblos, cloud masks of cotton cover the face, and cornmeal is rubbed on the body. In some tribes the names of the dead are usually not used. Some groups burn property for the dead at the time of the funeral and at annual burnings to supply the ghosts of the dead with clothing, food, and property in the afterworld. In many tribes, people believe that properly performed burial practices ensure some protection against ghosts who might return to this world to bother the living. Traditionally the method of burial was in graves, pits, holes in the ground, stone graves, mounds, cabins, houses lodges, wigwams, or caves. Bodies were mummified, and the remains placed in the earth, in caves, mounds, boxes, and scaffolds. Bodies are deposited in urns or buried on the surface of the ground, covered with earth, bark, rocks, or snow or exposed, as well as placed in the hollows of trees or logs. Bodies were cremated with bones and ashes placed in pits in the ground or in boxes placed in scaffolds or trees. Bodies were buried aerially in boxes, scaffolds, or trees and in canoes. Today, many Native Americans observe Christian burial customs because of laws prohibiting traditional practices.

MORTUARY POLE *North Pacific Coast*   A pole set up alongside or near the grave of a deceased chief. After cremation, the ashes of a deceased chief were placed in a temporary container. A year or more later, the ashes were redeposited into a new box that was placed inside a new or rebuilt grave house or mortuary pole that could contain the remains of one or at most two or three persons. The box containing the chief's remains might be placed in a niche in back of the pole or might be supported in a fork at the top. Mortuary and memorial poles were reserved for aristocracy. (See also MEMORIAL POTLATCH.)

MOSQUITO DANCE *Natchez, Cherokee*   The Mosquito Dance, believed to be of Natchez origin, is performed by women to awaken the men who have grown sleepy or fallen asleep after long nights of participating in ceremonial activities. Using straight pins, formerly thorns or sticks, they jab the sleepers awake during the dance. The Mosquito Dance is performed in northeastern Oklahoma at a Cherokee ceremonial ground to carry out its original purpose and to ensure its survival.

MOUNT ADAMS *Yakima (Yakama)*   Sacred mountain in Washington State. In 1897, 121,000 acres of the Yakima Reservation were included in the Gifford Pinchot National Forest or sold off 10 years later because of a surveying mistake. In the 1930s, after the original treaty map was discovered, the Yakima began steps to regain the land. In 1968, the Indian Claims Commission ruled that the disputed acres belonged to the Yakima. Of the original 121,000 acres, 100,000 had gone into private (98,000) or tribal (2,000) ownership. President Nixon restored 21,000 acres and Mount Adams to the Yakima, transferring control from the Department of Agriculture to the Department of the Interior, under an executive order signed on May 20, 1972. This action ended a nearly 40-year-old dispute between the Yakima and the federal government over the ownership of Mount Adams. President Nixon said he returned the land to right a wrong the U.S. government had committed. (See also SACRED SITES.)

MOUNT GRAHAM *Apache*   A sacred Apache mountain located in the Coronado National Forest, adjacent to the San Carlos Apache Reservation in southeastern Arizona. Mount Graham (Dzil Nchaa Si An, as it is known to Apache in eastern Arizona) is sacred to the San Carlos Apache Indians as well as to the Zuni Pueblo in New Mexico. Considered by Apache traditionalists to be "the chief of all mountains" and the central source of spiritual guidance, the mountain is the sacred home of their *gan,* called MOUNTAIN SPIRITS, or "crown dancers" in English, who taught the early Apache their songs and dances and taught them to gather healing herbs and water. They appear in different spiritual ceremonies and are critical in the processes of spiritual healing. Mount Graham is home to several natural springs, stones, minerals, and several species of plants and animals used in traditional spiritual ceremonies. It is also home to eagles, whose feathers are gathered and used for spiritual purposes and ceremonies. The mountain is a location of a number of Apache burials, including those who lost their lives in battles against enemies of the people. There are many religious shrines, both Apache and Zuni, on the peaks of Mount Graham dating back more than a 1,000 years. It is the place where ritual specialists go to pray and dream.

Mount Graham, encompassing more life zones and vegetative communities than any other mountain in North America, offers a rich variety of landscapes, of animal and insect species, including some—notably the red squirrel—found nowhere else in the world. Additionally, the mountain offers a wonderful view of the heavens.

The Apache have long accommodated recreational uses of the mountain but considered commercial and scientific ventures antithetical to the mountain's spirituality. In 1870s, following the massacre of Apache in Arivaipa Canyon, the U.S. Forest Service (USFS) took over Mount Graham, although the mountain and surrounding lands had been reserved for the San Carlos Apache through treaty. Since then, Mount Graham's sanctity has been disturbed. In 1890, the mountain was opened to lumber companies. At the time of this encroachment on Mount Graham, the Apache did not protest because they could have been imprisoned and/or shot for leaving the reservation. Forty years later, in 1930, a 30-mile highway wound around the mountain, opening it to commercial exploitation.

In the late 1980s, Mount Graham faced its greatest challenge when the University of Arizona (UA) and its partners—the Max Planck Institute for Radioastronomy in Bonn, Germany, and the Arcetri Observatory in Florence, Italy, as well as the Vatican in Rome—proposed to build seven giant telescopes on the Mount Graham summit at a cost of $200 million. Of 280 U.S. sites considered, the university contended this one alone offered both accessibility and outstanding visibility.

In 1987, the U.S. Forest Service rejected a proposal to build seven telescopes on Mount Graham's twin peaks. The UA issued a counterproposal to build three scopes on Emerald Peak, the most environmentally and spiritually sensitive peak, with additional land reserved for the other four planned scopes. Senators John McCain (R-Ariz.) and Dennis Deconcini (R-Ariz.) attached a rider to the 1988 Arizona-Idaho Conservation Act designating Emerald Peak as an astrophysical reserve exempt from the environmental assessment processes dictated by the National Environmental Policy Act, the National Forest Management Act, and the Endangered Species Act. The rider passed without hearings or testimony, eliminating court challenges to the telescope

on the basis of environmental law. At the time, Congress was not informed about the importance of Mount Graham to the Apache people, according to a subsequent report of the General Accounting Office, watchdog of Congress. The rider allowed the UA to circumvent the normal approval process by the U.S. Forest Service and the U.S. Fish and Wildlife Service. The act, signed by President Reagan, ordered the secretary of agriculture to issue a special-use permit for the construction of three telescopes before environmental reviews were completed. In October of 1989, the UA ordered the cutting of 1,000 trees in an old-growth forest on Mount Graham to build a road.

On July 10, 1990, the San Carlos Apache Tribal Council passed its first (unanimous) resolution opposing the telescope project as "a display of profound disrespect for a cherished feature of our original homeland as well as a serious violation of our traditional beliefs." On October 2, the UA, Vatican, and the Max Planck Institute ordered the removal of more trees for the project, but tree cutting was suspended because of winter snows. In June 1991, the San Carlos Apache Tribal Council sent letters opposing the telescope project, signed by every council member, to the German, Italian, and Vatican collaborators. (More letters were sent to the German parliament in August 1992, the Vatican in October 1992, and to the Italian parliament in October of 1994). Also in June, the Apache Survival Coalition, organized in 1990 to defend Mount Graham, filed a lawsuit against the USFS about legal violations that took place on the mountain.

On March 8, 1992, Father George Coyne, Vatican observatory director, issued a formal statement that Mount Graham was not holy because the Apache did not have title to the mountain, written records, burial grounds, or seasonal dwellings that would prove its sacredness. Coyne also argued the Apache were being manipulated by environmentalists. He issued another statement on May 25 that Apache beliefs were "a kind of religiosity to which I cannot subscribe and which must be suppressed with all the force we can muster."

In March of 1993, portions of a Booz-Allen (a consulting firm hired by UA to draft a report on the Mount Graham project) study that justified selection of Mount Graham for a telescope project, for years withheld by the UA, were ordered released, thanks to the persistence of Dr. Robin Silver of the Maricopa Audubon Society who filed for the report's release under the Freedom of Information Act. The study revealed a "divide and conquer strategy toward the Apaches that was intended to destroy their traditional beliefs." The study also admitted the UA relied on bad data when selecting Emerald Peak for the largest telescope—in a wind tunnel that has the state's highest rainfall and cloud cover blocking the heavens 50 percent of the time. The UA wanted a new site, Peak 10,298 (its elevation), one-half mile west of its current site.

In December 1993, despite the fact that the UA moved the site for the largest telescope outside the area that Congress exempted from environmental laws, USFS ruled that no further tests were needed. On December 7, 1993, at 5:00 AM, the USFS cut 250 spruce and fir trees near the summit to make room for the telescope, clear-cutting first and refusing to wait for the imminent decision of the 1991 Apache lawsuit to stop construction of the observatory on appeal in the Ninth Circuit Court in San Francisco. (In April of 1994, the court rejected the Apache Survival Coalition's claims in opposing the telescope project). Clear-cutting, approved by Manuel Pacheco, UA president, prevented opponents from filing an injunction against clear-cutting. Two days later, the head of the U.S. Fish and Wildlife Service, whose mission is to oversee endangered species, stated her agency may have erred in approving the site for the largest of the telescopes on Mount Graham. On December 14, 1993, OLA CASSADORE DAVIS, chairperson of the Apache Survival Coalition, issued a news release drawing a parallel between the Pearl Harbor attack and the university's December 7th attack on the sacred mountain.

In January 1994, the University of Toronto joined 20 other institutions (Harvard University, Ohio State University, among others) in formally withdrawing its support of the telescope project.

On July 28, 1995, Federal Judge Alfredo Marquez ruled the University of Arizona could not cut any more trees at the site of the third and only unbuilt telescope called the Large Binocular Telescope) in the observatory complex until further environmental studies were done.

In October 1995, the UA wanted to construct a third telescope on Mt. Graham without first carrying out the environmental and cultural studies required by law. It enlisted the services of Arizona representative Jim Kolbe, who placed a rider on the House Appropriation Bill to exempt the telescope project from federal laws that call for environmental and cultural studies. No hearings were held. In November, Kolbe's bill passed both houses of Congress exempting the UA from performing various cultural and environmental studies before building the scope. In late December 1995, President Bill Clinton vetoed the Interior Appropriations bill containing Kolbe's Mt. Graham provision. But in April 1996, the president signed the federal bill, including the Kolbe rider, which allows the UA to build telescopes on Mount Graham without making studies. Four months later, he asked Congress to repeal the Mount Graham rider. The President's Advisory Council on Historic Preservation, an executive agency, declared that the entire observatory project violated the National Historic Preservation Act because it harms Apache culture and religious life.

On August 30, 1997, Wendsler Nosie, former San Carlos Apache tribal council member, was arrested by University of Arizona police officers after praying on Mount Graham. Nosie, charged with trespassing, the first Apache to be cited, walked on a road that the UA claimed was its own. Acquitted of state criminal trespass charges five months later, Graham County judge Linda Norton recognized "an Apache's right to go to Mount Graham when called by God to pray or collect herbs."

MOUNT SHASTA   A mountain sacred to the Hupa, Karuk, Modoc, Pit River, Shasta, Wintu, and other Native peoples. Historically, these tribes have participated in ceremonies on Mount Shasta, located in northeastern California. Some tribes see the mountain, which is featured in many creation stories, as the home of their Creator. The Wintu continue to conduct their ceremonies in designated places on the mountain. The Shasta and Pit River people go to the mountain for spiritual training, healing, or for gathering medicines. Although tribes have differing traditional beliefs about the mountain, they all agree that one should not travel above the tree line unless for a specific reason and with special preparation.

In 1957, the Shasta Ski Bowl was constructed on the mountain's south slope, an area lying within the jurisdiction of the U.S. Forest Service, which manages the entire mountain area except for the State Wilderness Area. In 1978, the Ski Bowl closed because avalanche and "white out" conditions made it impossible to see. In 1985, a new ski resort was proposed at the abandoned ski area. U.S. Forest Service officials were in favor of reviving the ski area, but lawsuits in 1991 by local tribes, the Sierra Club, and the Save Mount Shasta organization, and the struggle to save their sacred sites on and around Mount Shasta by individuals such as Wintu elder FLORENCE JONES, stopped the development.

After a court-mandated Forest Service environmental study documented that Mount Shasta was a major spiritual and medicine mountain of central cultural significance, not only in ancient times, but continuing to the present, in March 1994, the Keeper of the National Register of Historic Places recommended that the area from 4,000 feet to the summit of the mountain be eligible for historic preservation. Such a designation would mandate a policy of preservation, limit the use of natural resources and commercial development, and allocate funds to implement a management program. Under pressure from private property groups, on November 18, 1994, the keeper made the decision to reduce the boundary of the Mount Shasta Historic District to the area above 8,000 feet and Panther Meadows, a sacred site on the mountain.

The revised decision, which shrunk the Historic District from 150,000 acres to 19,000 acres, was based on the argu-

Mountain Spirit Dancers. A painting by Allan Houser, an Apache artist, depicts Apache dancers who impersonate mountain spirits (*gan*) in ceremonies to promote the welfare and happiness of girls who have reached puberty or to prevent epidemics, ward off evil, or cure certain illnesses. *Denver Art Museum.*

ment that the original integrity of the mountain had been altered due to logging and therefore lacked "historic integrity." This decision would allow the lower level of Mount Shasta to be developed and/or logged. Pressure by ski interests forced the Forest Service to open up a review. In February 1998, the Shasta-Trinity National Forest announced it was recommending that the permit for construction of a ski resort on Mount Shasta be revoked. In an unprecedented action, the U.S. Forest Service revoked the permit, invoking the National Historic Preservation Act. This was the first time that a major federal government project or sponsored project was stopped because of its adverse impact on Native American cultural property. (See also NATIONAL HISTORIC PRESERVATION ACT AMENDMENTS OF 1992; SACRED SITES.)

MOUNTAIN SPIRITS (gan) *Apache* These spirits play a crucial role in the religion of Western and Eastern Apache of Arizona and New Mexico. They guard sacred places, guard Apache against sickness and danger, and are the custodians of wildlife. They resided on earth long ago but departed in search

of eternal life. They now live in certain mountains and in places below the ground, and they travel and live in clouds and water as well. Masked MOUNTAIN SPIRIT DANCERS impersonate the *gan* at numerous ceremonies, including the elaborate GIRL'S PUBERTY RITE, curing ceremonials, and ceremonies for staving off evil-like epidemics. The Apache call these masked dancers *gan*. Mountain spirits are similar to YEIS of the Navajo and KACHINAS of the Pueblo.

MOUNTAIN SPIRIT DANCERS *Apache* Called Crown Dancers by non-Apache, these dancers act under the supervision of a shaman who "makes" or prepares them for performances. A shaman acquires the right to perform the Mountain Spirit Dance ritual by sleeping near a holy place and having a vision in which the *gan* (mountain spirit) teaches him the ceremony he may imitate.

The dancer's upper torso is painted with symbolic designs, and he wears a mask (called PAINTED ON, a term referring to anything with symbolic designs) surmounted by an upright thin wooden headdress called "horns" painted with symbols as well. The mask, made by the sha-man, consists of a hood to cover the dancer's head, gath-ered at the neck by a drawstring. The mask is made of cotton-cloth, buckskin or, more recently, canvas. Two tiny holes are cut for the eyes and sometimes one for the mouth. The masks display a symbol that indicates the dancer's clan; the style varies among Apache groups. The dancers put the masks on after following prescribed ritu-als, and they are later stored in caves.

The Mountain Spirit headdress is an enormous, upright headpiece, resembling a candelabra balanced on top of the dancer's head. It is made of slats of wood, soaked in water, and heated until they can be fashioned into curved prongs. The lower end of the headdress is secured to the top of the cloth hood. The "horns" recall the mountain spirits, who protect game animals. The styles of headdresses differ from group to group. The Western Apache headdress has a U-shaped bow frame that is placed over the head, with slats attached to the frame. The Chiricahua version consists of a horizontal bar to which vertical slats are tied with thongs. At each end of the supports, two or four short lengths of wood ("earrings") are hung by thongs and strike against one an-other like soft chimes. The headpiece of the Mescalero is shaped like an *E* turned on its side, with the short bars pro-jecting upward from the frame. All of the carved and painted headdresses are guarded with care and revered.

Each mountain spirit dancer carries a painted wooden wand in each hand. Usually a group of four masked dancers and a CLOWN impersonate the *gan* for the public good, to prevent epidemics, to ward off evil, or to diagnose and cure certain illnesses. A "black one," who is very dangerous, may appear in some ceremonies to stave off epidemics. A youth must be 18 or older before being allowed to impersonate the *gan*. On March 29, 1965, the Mescalero Apache performed the Mountain Spirit Dance at the White House.

MOUNTAIN SPIRIT HEADDRESS See MOUNTAIN SPIRIT
DANCERS

MOUNTAIN SPIRIT MASK See MOUNTAIN SPIRIT DANCERS

MOUNTAIN WOLF WOMAN (Xehaciwinga, "To Make a Home in a Bluff or a Mountain, as the Wolf Does") *(1884–1960) Winnebago (Ho-Chunk)* A Winnebago woman whose account of her life, including her conversion to the PEYOTE RELIGION, was recorded by her niece by adoption, Nancy Oestreich Lurie, in 1958. Mountain Wolf Woman was born in April 1884 at her grandfather's home at East Fork River in Wisconsin. A member of her father's Thunder clan, she was later given a holy Wolf clan name by an elderly woman who cured her when she was very sick. Mountain Wolf Woman at-

Mountain Wolf Woman. A Winnebago (Ho-Chunk) woman whose account of her life, including her conversion to the Peyote Religion, was recorded by her niece by adoption in 1958. *Photograph by Nancy Oestreich Lurie.*

tended a government school for Indians in Tomah, Wiscon-sin, then later enrolled in a Lutheran mission school at Wittenberg, also in Wisconsin. She was taken out of school to participate in a marriage arranged by her brothers against her wishes. Angry at the arrangement, she vowed that her children would choose their own spouses. Mountain Wolf Woman eventually left her husband, taking their two children with her. She later married Bad Soldier, a member of the Bear or Soldier clan, and they remained together until his death in 1936.

Mountain Wolf Woman eventually participated in three religious traditions: the medicine lodge, Christianity, and peyotism. She and her second husband were introduced to the Peyote Religion in Nebraska. After using peyote me-dicinally to ease the pain of childbirth, Mountain Wolf Woman saw its benefits and became an adherent. She ob-served both the Half-Moon and Cross Fire versions of the peyote ceremony among her people and personally experi-enced a vision in which she became an angel and saw Christ. Mountain Wolf Woman also used peyote with Lakota people in Martin, South Dakota, where she was adopted by a family who had lost a daughter. A practitioner until the end of her life, she financed a meeting in 1958 to commemorate the 50th anniversary of peyote's introduction into Wisconsin. True to the Winnebago belief that certain elders could foretell their own deaths, Mountain Wolf Woman prophesied hers. She died on November 9, 1960, a short time before her story was published as *Mountain Wolf Woman: Sister of Crashing Thunder.* Her family included 11 children, three of whom had died, at least 38 grandchildren, and nine great-grandchildren. She was the sister of SAM BLOWSNAKE, also a peyotist.

MOURNING ANNIVERSARY CEREMONY *Maidu, Niseman* An annual mourning ceremony in honor of the dead practiced by tribes of the Sierra Nevada in California. Among the Maidu, the ceremony is held in early autumn, often on a cemetery site or near it (burning ground). The mourners go to the overseers of the burning grounds and apply for a string of beads that permit them to mourn at that particular ground, wearing the string as a necklace. The rite takes place around a central fire, surrounded by a circular brush wall, and includes burning of large amounts of property and food, accompanied by wailing, crying, and singing in honor of the dead. A director gives orations, followed by a celebration. After the ceremony, there is gambling, games, and feasting. Recipients of strings of beads are entitled to burn (or "cry") for a period of five years, after which the string is burned.

MOURNING CEREMONY (Karuk, Keruk, Chekap) *Cocopa* A ceremony to ensure that the deceased will not remain or return to bother the living. These annual memorial ceremonies are held for relatives who died during a span of years preceding the rituals. People send their relatives gifts, food, and offerings through these memorial services and make farewells to ensure that relatives are never mentioned or mourned again and to avoid illness or evil that dead relatives might visit on the living. Usually held in winter, the Keruk lasts six days (formerly eight), while the Chekap is between one and four days. Appointed leaders take charge of notifying people, preparing the ceremonial mourning structure ("cry house"), and delivering the ritual speeches (a narrative about the first death house constructed by the Creator) required before its construction. Families of the deceased, with help from relatives, sponsor the ceremonies and gather the supplies. There are dietary restrictions, ritual wailing, singing, dancing, bathing for purification, game playing, races, and food and money distributions to persons attending the ceremony. The ceremonial effigy (called a *mishkwa*) of the most important person being commemorated was at one time burned along with mourning garments and the "cry" structure to provide a haven for the dead in the next life. More often today, the belongings of the deceased are sold or given away.

MOURNING CEREMONY *Diegueño* An anniversary mourning ceremony conducted one year after a person's death. A description of a mourning ceremony held in the 1960s included a wake, or *valoria,* a sing, and a Christian mass. Its dual purpose was to end the mourning period and to dismiss the departed. By providing offerings and rituals, it was believed that the spirit would be pleased and leave the living alone. Generally sponsored by an individual or family and held on a weekend, preparations included notifying singers and guests, hanging cloth on meetinghouse walls, placing an altar with offerings and a photograph of the deceased in the ceremonial building, and cooking food. A wake held from sundown to midnight incorporated Christian prayers, candle-lighting, Spanish hymns, and expressions of mourning. Mourners were also served an evening meal in the meetinghouse. The sing, which started at midnight, was conducted by one or more traditional singers and included dancing. The dancers were initially showered with coins by the sponsoring family of the mourning ceremony. These were later picked up and distributed to mourners who were not relatives. A Catholic requiem mass was conducted in the local church the next morning, followed by services at the grave. Offerings, including new cloth, assembled at the gravesite were later given to strangers present. The mourning ceremony concluded with lunch, sometimes the distribution of cigarettes, and socializing.

MOURNING CEREMONY *Havasupai* A commemorative occasion (repeating cremation) at which mourners weep; dance; sing; harangue the crowd; and burn clothing, food, and baskets.

MOURNING OBSERVANCES *Inuit* A rigid system of taboos and obligations controls Inuit during mourning. The customs are observed to forestall the evil powers of ghosts and to show esteem for the departed. After a death, there are taboos regarding the securing and consumption of food. People make offerings of food either at the grave or at festivals for the dead because it is believed that the soul persists after death and retains its human needs and desires. There is a taboo against hunting during mourning, and against working with sharp knives (to avoid cutting or injuring the ghost that may be present for several days). Mourning observances may be held for three, four, or five days, depending on the length of time that the soul is believed to stay in the body after death. Some Inuit believe the soul leaves the body immediately; others believe it stays with the body for up to four or five days. Almost without exception, Inuit continue to deposit offerings, food, clothing, or implements for the dead at graves. The FEAST TO THE DEAD and other festivals to express deference and placate the departed occur months or years after the funeral.

Inuit people also believe that all animals possess souls and that slain animals must be properly treated, lest their souls return to the other world bearing a grudge that discourages other animals from being caught, retaliation that amounts to the punishment of a food shortage. The Inuit show respect to the souls of animals, believing that animals do not object to being killed as long as hunters treat them respectfully. There is a formal system of observances and taboos that Inuit believe must be obeyed in order for animals to allow themselves to be killed. Each animal has its own set of taboos and restrictions. For example, most Inuit groups give sea mammals a drink of water after they are killed. They observe other practices regarding dead animals, such as keeping products of land and sea separate, and others that are analagous to mourning customs for dead relatives. They offer food and weapons to slain animals, similar to grave deposits left for ghosts of dead persons. These acts are intended to provide for the souls of animals after they have been killed. (See also BLADDER FESTIVAL; CARIBOU FESTIVAL.)

MOYAONE *Piscataway*   Sacred site associated with ancient Piscataway burial grounds, located in present-day Maryland near Washington, D.C. Reported as the Piscataway Chiefdom's capital town by Captain John Smith in 1608, Moyaone has also been the site of annual vigils for the Piscataway Feast of the Dead ceremony in modern times. Moyaone, which was once slated for development into a sludge pit, survived in part because of its proximity to Mount Vernon. In 1961, Congress created Piscataway National Park "to preserve for the benefit of present and future generations the historic and scenic values . . . of lands which provide the principal overview from the Mount Vernon estate." Piscataway chief Turkey Tayac also contributed, placing 20 acres of land in trust with the National Park Service for the park's creation, in an effort to protect the site from development. A verbal agreement between Chief Tayac and Department of the Interior secretary Stewart Udall reportedly mandated both Piscataway access to the site and burial place for Tayac on the land he contributed. However, Piscataway tribal members had to engage in a series of political struggles to have the promises honored. In 1976, when Chief Tayac became ill with leukemia, he contacted the Department of the Interior to make certain his rights to burial at Moyaone were intact. To his distress, he was told by Interior officials that such an agreement was nonexistent. Tayac, armed with evidence and support, sought that the burial arrangement be upheld. Representative Gladys Noon Spellman introduced a bill to Congress to allow any Piscataway chief to be buried at the site, but the measure failed. In November 1979, another bill,

introduced by Senator Paul Sarbanes, passed and permitted the Piscataway to bury Chief Tayac, who had died a year earlier, at Moyaone. However, the Piscataway continue to have difficulty with both the National Park Service and the Alice Ferguson Foundation, which is composed of white landowners near the vicinity of the site, in gaining access for tribal religious purposes.

MUDHEADS   See KOYEMSHI

MUHTE *Yaqui*   A personal ritual that is an important accompaniment to all devotions at the permanent church altar and the temporary PAHKO (feast-day) altars. The basic elements of the ritual are prayers, genuflexion, and the sign of the cross.

MURDOCK, ANN HARDING (Sun Tama) *(?–1969) Matinnecock*   A charismatic leader among the Matinnecock, an Algonquian group on New York's Long Island, during the 1950s. Murdock's vision of leading the tribe out of obscurity contributed to the revitalization of the group, which in 1958 became reactivated as the Matinnecock Indian Tribe. It is believed that Murdock's guardian spirit was Tackapusha, a colonial-era sachem. Murdock died in 1969 and a few years later, by 1975, four religious ceremonies had been revived among the descendants of the historic Matinnecock. Revitalized with the assistance of Wallace Pyawasit, a Menominee religious leader, they include Nunnowa ("Indian Thanksgiving"), a midwinter ceremony, and naming and pipe ceremonies.

MURROW, JOSEPH SAMUEL *(1835–1929)*   Pioneering Baptist missionary in Indian Territory (present-day Oklahoma). He was born in Jefferson County, Georgia, on June 7, 1835, to Mary Badger Murrow and John Murrow. After attending rural schools for 15 years, he enrolled in Springfield Academy and taught for a short time. Murrow was licensed to preach in 1855 and entered Mercer University the following year. After his ordination in 1857, he became a missionary in Indian Territory under the auspices of the Rehoboth Baptist Association of Georgia. Murrow worked among several different tribal groups, including the Creek and Seminole. During the Civil War he was assigned to a Confederate refugee camp consisting primarily of women, children, and elderly men from the Five Civilized Tribes. After the war, he taught for a time, then returned to missionary work. Besides founding the community of Atoka, he eventually organized more than 75 Baptist churches in Indian Territory. He also trained and ordained many Native pastors. He was instrumental in the establishment of Atoka Baptist Academy, the Murrow Indian Orphan Home, and Indian University in Bacone, Oklahoma, which later became Bacone College. Murrow's journalism efforts included the Atoka newspaper, the *Indian Missionary,* and the *Indian Orphan.* He became nationally known as the "Father of Freemasonry in Oklahoma" for his contributions to the order. Murrow received doctor of divinity degrees from Indian University (1889) and Mercer University (1923). He died on September 8, 1929 at the age of 94. After the death of his first wife, Murrow married Clara Burns, and the couple had four children.

MUSTACHE, JAMES (Opwagon, "Pipe") *(b. 1904–c. 1990s) Ojibway* A traditional spiritual leader among the Ojibway of the Lac Courte Oreilles Reservation in Wisconsin. Mustache was born on November 18, 1904, in a wigwam and was named Oma scuj (Elk) by Opwagon, a medicine man. Raised by his grandparents, who spoke only the Ojibway language, he was taught the religious and cultural traditions of his people. His grandmother, Iikwezens (Little Girl), was a midwife and his grandfather, Zhonii'a Giishing (Money Sky), was a MIDEWIWIN priest who was also known as JOHN MINK. Called "Little Pipe" by family members after the person who had named him, the young man also became known as Bimiibatod Omascuj, or "Running Elk," because

he was constantly in motion. About 1911 he started attending the Catholic mission school in Reserve, Wisconsin, but was withdrawn by his grandparents after a short period because of efforts to convert him. He was then sent to Wisconsin's Hayward Indian school, where he completed the eighth grade. He ended his schooling at the Tomah Indian school, also in the state, after attending for about two years. In 1921 Mustache enlisted in the military and served four years at Fort Snelling in Minnesota. He later worked in the Civilian Conservation Corps with an assignment on the Lac du Flambeau Reservation. While living there he met and married the daughter of a religious leader, Rising Sun, and they had a son, also named James. Mustache conducted traditional ceremonies, including namings, weddings, and funerals. He was a leader at tribal and intertribal gatherings, such as the annual Honor the Earth celebration. A member of the Lac Courte Oreilles tribal court, he officiated at its first marriage. He served as a delegate to the National Congress of American Indians and represented his people in a variety of settings. His efforts to preserve Ojibway traditions included the use of computer technology to program Native language instruction. An honored spiritual leader and elder, his legacy continues through his life and work.

NACHI *Hopi* A standard (a stick or sticks with feathers attached) or decorated pole. Planted on a KIVA where all can see it, the *nachi* signals spirits and people that a sacred and private ceremony is going on and that none but members may enter the kiva. It is raised at sunrise and taken down at sunset.

NAKAIDOKLINI (Noche-del-Klinne, "Freckled Mexican"?) *(?–1881) Apache* A prophet among the White Mountain band of Apache on the San Carlos Reservation in Arizona who became known in 1881 when he introduced a new dance believed to have the power to return life to the dead. During its performance he stood at the center of the participants, who were arranged as spokes in a wheel facing him, and blessed them with sacred pollen. In June 1881 he announced that he would return two chiefs to life after he had received gifts of horses and blankets. His followers complied, and he held the dance near his home until August. Colonel E. A. Carr, the commander at Fort Apache, received a report that Nakaidoklini had told his followers that the deceased chiefs would not return to life because of the white presence in the area. The government agent then ordered that the medicine man be arrested, killed, or both. After efforts to lure him to the agency failed, Colonel Carr took 85 troops and 23 scouts to his village on August 30, 1881. Although Nakaidoklini submitted to the arrest, a conflict later broke out. A number of people were killed, including the medicine man.

NAME-SOUL *Inuit* One of the three souls that Inuit distinguish. The name-soul abides in a person's name and possesses abstract traits of the person to whom it refers. It persists after the person's death through the custom of naming children after relatives who have recently died. The infant embodies the dead person's soul and completes the reincarnation process. In some regions, Inuit were more casual about bestowing names. Babies might be named after the most recently deceased person or, in other regions, the name of any deceased person would do. In some places, name bestowal was an occasion for ceremony. (See also SOUL [Inuit].)

NAMING PRACTICES Traditionally, Indian people gave their children everyday or ritual names in naming ceremonies. Some people like the Tewa gave babies their first names at birth, selecting them from natural phenomena appropriate to the season. This first name became the name by which the child was known in the village in everyday conversation. The Lenni Lenape, or Delaware, Indians named a child at three or four years, when the parents were sure the Creator intended the child to remain in their care. The Hopi Pueblo people initiated boys and girls between the ages of six and 10 into kachina organizations and gave them ceremonial names to indicate their change in ritual status. Among the North Pacific Coast peoples, middle-aged people between 45 and 60 received names that made them bona fide members of lineages. Until then, they were considered only relatives of lineage members.

Traditionally, girls in certain tribes received new names at first menstruation. Boys received new names after initiation into religious societies or after successful hunts or war expeditions. Boys, and girls to some degree, received sacred names after FASTING or a VISION QUEST. In some cases, a young man could not assume a hereditary name of his father until he achieved a certain status or the community approved of the new name. Some names were derived from dreams.

Children were often given several names. The Navajo first provided a kinship name that identifies a person's relationship to other family members. Such names translated into terms such as one's "maternal nephew who is the middle son of one's youngest sister" or "one's mother's father's brother." Navajo nicknamed their children and also provided a Euro-American name used in school or non-Navajo situations. They also gave people "holy" or "war" names that are part of one's personal power. Navajo consider it impolite to use these names in a person's presence because names that have power are worn out by overuse.

The Delaware, like the Navajo and other tribal groups, also had a private, sacred name known only to the person, the family, and the Creator. These names were not disclosed beyond the family to protect their sanctity and purpose.

Traditionally, the Dakota/Lakota received several names over a lifetime. The birth name showed the order of birth into a family, such as first-born daughter or last-born son. Later, a medicine person gave to the child an honor name that referred to great deeds of the child's ancestor. Children also received nicknames and a deed name given after a person accomplished some act of extraordinary bravery. According to Ella Deloria, Dakota anthropologist, "In Dakota, you do not say . . . 'What is your name' but, 'In what manner do they say of you?' That means 'According to what deed are you known?' The deed of an ancestor was memorialized in a phrase applied to a descendant of his. Such a one was really an engraved memorial tablet walking around."

In many tribes children were named after distinguished tribal relatives, elders, or ancestors in hopes the child later would live up to the attributes of the former. Some men acquired a dozen or more names in a lifetime by performing a succession of distinctive deeds.

In many tribes, young men carried on the name of an esteemed warrior who had died. After the death of such a warrior, at the prescribed time, his relatives gathered and chose the man to bear the name.

Naming ceremonies are still conducted. (See also O-GIWI-MANSE-WIN.)

NAME-TAKING CEREMONIES *North Pacific Coast* Among some North Pacific Coast peoples, middle-aged persons between 45 and 60 years were not considered bona fide members of lineages but rather descendants or relatives of members until they received a name in a ceremony. Names determine the lineage's internal organization of status and role. When an incumbent of a high status name died, senior members of lineages met to select a successor, the nearest matrilineal relative of the deceased. A name was formally assumed by giving a feast (witnessed by lineages of opposite moieties). Name-taking was a way of recruiting new members into a senior group.

NAPESHNEE, JOSEPH (Napeshneeduta, Nape Shneedoota, "Red Man Who Flees Not") *c. 1800–*1870)

Dakota The first full-blood Dakota male to convert to Christianity later served as a ruling elder in the Presbyterian Church. A member of the Mdewakanton band, Napeshnee included among his relatives some of the principal chiefs of his people and the trader Joseph Renville, who was married to his mother's sister. Napeshnee's age was estimated at around 40 when he was baptized at Lac qui Parle, Minnesota, on February 21, 1840, and given the name Joseph. His wife, who died within a few years, joined the church at the same time, and four children, three by former wives, were baptized. Following the death of his wife, he chose to marry Pretty Rainbow, an orphan who had been raised by her grandmother, an early convert. Although he paid a purchase price according to the customs of his people, the young woman would not stay with him, perhaps because of their age difference, and repeatedly ran away. Failing to convince her to return, Napeshnee eventually married a Christian woman nearer his age who remained with him until she died. They moved to the Dakota leader Little Crow's village, a few miles from Fort Snelling, on the Mississippi River, where other relatives lived and where the game was more plentiful. Napeshnee became ill there, but his people refused to help him unless he returned to traditional beliefs and customs. Refusing to do so, his family suffered without food and aid until a visiting acquaintance helped them.

Following his move to a newly established Dakota reservation in Minnesota, Napeshnee became the leading farmer among the Mdewakanton band of his people. During the Dakota War of 1862 he befriended white residents in the area, and in the spring of the following year he was hired as a government scout, a position he held for several years. When that employment ended, Napeshnee returned to Lac qui Parle. Beginning to suffer the infirmities of old age, he was unable to build a house for his family, and they had to live in a tent. Napeshnee supported them without government assistance by gardening, hunting, and fishing. Greatly respected by both Indians and whites, he served as a ruling elder in the Presbyterian Church for close to 10 years. Napeshnee died in July 1870 at Lac qui Parle, one observer estimating his age at more than 90. The Reverend THOMAS S. WILLIAMSON wrote an account of his life, "Napeshneedoota: The First

Male Dakota Convert to Christianity," which was published in *Minnesota Historical Collections* in 1880. His name also appears as Nape Shneedoota.

NATIONAL ASSOCIATION OF NATIVE RELIGIONS (NANR)

An organization established in 1971 for American Indian religious leaders in the Roman Catholic Church. It was founded by Brother Lorenzo Martin and Sister GLORIA DAVIS. By the late 1980s its membership included more than 100 native deacons, priests, and other religious leaders, and it was coordinated by Sister Genevieve Cuny, a Dakota Catholic.

NATIONAL HISTORIC PRESERVATION ACT AMENDMENTS OF 1992 (16 U.S. Code470) *(1992)* The National Historic Preservation Act (NHPA) was amended to require federal agencies to consult with tribes about the effects their actions may have on traditional religious places. The NHPA has been used to seek protection for sacred places, but the 1992 amendments explicitly made such sites eligible for the National Register of Historic Places.

Section 106 of the law provides a tool for preserving Native American sacred sites. A procedural law, it mandates a full consultation with traditional practitioners and extensive documentation and analysis of natural places considered to be traditional cultural properties. Criteria for registry exclude identifiable material traces of use or regular visitation, but a nominated property would need to have explicitly defined spatial boundaries, play a role in ongoing traditions, and be linked to the history of a group or of a personage significant to that group.

NATIONAL MUSEUM OF THE AMERICAN INDIAN ACT

Legislation that includes provisions for the repatriation to American Indian tribes and to Native Hawaiians, upon request, of Native human remains collected by the Smithsonian Institution. Under the act, signed into law on November 28, 1989, by President George Bush, the museum must inventory the human remains in its collection and identify their origins to the extent possible. It must then notify the appropriate tribal groups of its findings and return skeletal remains when the evidence indicates that they are connected with a specific tribe and that tribe requests the return. The legislation also applies to funerary offerings associated with a particular remain or burial site but it does not address return of cultural items. The number of American Indian human remains in the Smithsonian collection has been estimated at 18,000. In spring 1991, the Natural History Museum of the Smithsonian Institution agreed to return more than 700 human remains and associated burial goods to the Larsen Bay Tribal Council of Kodiak Island,

Alaska. The remains and artifacts were removed in the 1930s from a burial site adjacent to an ancient Native village on Larsen Bay, taken to Washington, D.C., and put into storage. (See Subject Index for additional entries on legislation included in this volume.)

NATIONAL NATIVE AMERICAN PRISONERS RIGHTS ADVOCACY COALITION   Formed in June 1995 in Boulder, Colorado, the National Native American Prisoners Rights Advocacy Coalition (NNAPRAC) consists of Indian nations, organizations, and concerned activists who are working within the U.S. prison systems. Members of the coalition include the Native American Rights Fund, the National Congress of American Indians, the International Indian Treaty Council, Navajo Nation Corrections Project, Oglala and Rosebud Sioux Tribes, and the Native American Church of North America. The primary purpose of the coalition is to seek increased protection for the free exercise of religion and culture by Native American prisoners in the corrections setting, which has been identified as a pressing criminal justice, rehabilitation, and human rights issue, all of paramount importance to Indian nations. The coalition uses two approaches, legislation and negotiation, to protect religious rights of imprisoned Indians.

For many years, one major problem of Native Americans who are incarcerated has been the denial of their right to practice traditional Native American religions in federal and state prisons. This long-standing criminal justice problem was documented in congressional hearings as early as 1978 during the passage of the AMERICAN INDIAN RELIGIOUS FREEDOM ACT OF 1978 (AIRFA). The problem was also documented in oversight hearings on the free exercise of religion of Native Americans by the Senate Committee on Indian Affairs and the U.S. House Subcommittee on Native American Affairs in 1992 and 1993.

The NNAPRAC wants increased federal protection for the free exercise of religion because it is an essential component in the correctional rehabilitation of Native offenders and the cultural/spiritual well-being of reservation communities of returning offenders released or paroled from prison. Native spiritual practices are important for the spiritual healing of the Native prisoners and have proven to be successful in the rehabilitation of the mind, body, and spirit. Until 1978, countless ceremonial practices were banned and outlawed and religious structures and articles destroyed in an effort to assimilate Native peoples into the dominant society.

In 1978 Congress passed AIRFA intending to protect the rights of American Indians to practice their traditional religions. Imprisoned Native people, however, have had no legal protection under AIRFA. Many have been denied access to spiritual leaders, despite the fact that other prisoners are consistently provided access to priests, ministers, rabbis, and other religious leaders. Sweat lodges; eagle feathers; long hair worn in a traditional fashion; headbands; medicine bags; possession of sage, cedar, and tobacco; and other practices necessary for Native spiritual expression have been banned as "security risks" by one prison after another. Traditional spiritual practices benefit Native prisoners to an extent that no other type of prison-sponsored program has before. Native prisoners who participate in sweats and other ceremonies benefit through rehabilitative changes, reductions in alcoholism and antisocial behavior, decreased recidivism, and improved self-esteem and dignity.

Some prison officials, however, engage in coercive or destructive tactics to either discourage Native American prisoners from practicing their spiritual traditions or punish them for asserting their constitutional right to its free exercise. Lawsuits and complaints against state departments of correction have been filed in Arizona, California, Indiana, Minnesota, Missouri, Nevada, New York, Oregon, Pennsylvania, Texas, Washington, and Wisconsin.

The passage of the RELIGIOUS FREEDOM RESTORATION ACT OF 1993 (RFRA), supported by a broad coalition of religious groups, provided some protections for Native religious practices in prisons. Some prisons even formed "RFRA committees" to deal with prisoners' requests for religious accommodation. Requiring prisons to demonstrate how a religious practice was a security risk, rather than allowing them merely to assert this, did provide some imprisoned Natives greater religious freedom for a time. But in June 1997, the U.S. Supreme Court struck down RFRA as unconstitutional, a decision that adversely affected the religious and spiritual practices of all Native American prisoners in the U.S. prison system. Some prisons, which had been adhering to the law, responded immediately, clamping down on Native prisoners. The NATIVE AMERICAN CULTURAL PROTECTION AND FREE EXERCISE OF RELIGION ACT OF 1994 would have protected Native American spiritual practices in prison "to the same extent as prisoners of other religious faiths," but no action was taken on the bill because of issues regarding sacred sites.

As of 1999, no federal law protected the right of Native American prisoners to practice their traditional religions. NNAPRAC, which has suggested legislation at the state level instead, has been seeking increased federal protection for the free exercise of religion.

NATIVE AMERICAN CHURCH   A church established in Oklahoma in 1918 by adherents of the PEYOTE RELIGION, which is centered on the sacramental use of PEYOTE, a small, spineless cactus that grows principally in present-day Mexico

and the state of Texas. The peyote religion has ancient roots among indigenous groups in the Rio Grande valley, where the plant grows. The peyotists sought to protect their religion from attack by organizing along the lines of mainstream churches in the dominant society. There are two primary ceremonies associated with peyotism: the Half-Moon ceremony, which derives its name from the shape of the altar used, and is also called the Tipi Way, the QUANAH PARKER Way, the Comanche Way or the Kiowa Way; and the Big Moon ceremony, introduced by JOHN WILSON, a Caddo ROADMAN or leader, which became known as the Moonhead and Cross Fire.

The Native American Church is not the earliest peyote church. In 1914 the first church of peyotism on record was referred to in a United States court hearing as the Peyote Society or Union Church Society. Little is known about this religious organization, and it is likely that it was not legally incorporated. The second peyote church, also organized in 1914, was called the First Born Church of Christ. It was initiated by JOHNATHAN KOSHIWAY, Sac and Fox roadman, for Otoe peyotists in Oklahoma. Legally incorporated, the articles of incorporation for the First Born Church of Christ were drafted with assistance from attorney Henry S. Johnston of Perry, Oklahoma. The charter named Charley Whitehorn as the deacon, or first officer, as well as 10 directors, one of whom was Koshiway. In the organization's statement of purpose, Christianity was emphasized, tobacco prohibited from its services, and peyote was not mentioned. Furthermore, the First Born Church of Christ did not attempt to include peyotists beyond the Otoe tribe. In contrast, the Native American Church sought statewide representation and openly acknowledged the use of peyote. The incorporation of the Native American Church in 1918 established one central church with branch churches subject to its jurisdiction. The first officers were Frank Eagle (Ponca), president; Mack Haag (Cheyenne), vice president; George Pipestem (Otoe), secretary; and Louis McDonald (Ponca), treasurer.

The purpose of the Native American Church was set forth in articles of incorporation signed on October 10, 1918:

> to foster and promote the religious belief of the several tribes of Indians in the State of Oklahoma, in the Christian religion with the practice of the Peyote Sacrament as commonly understood and used among the adherents of this religion in the several tribes of Indians in the State of Oklahoma, and to teach the Christian religion with morality, sobriety, industry, kindly charity and right living and to cultivate a spirit of self-respect and brotherly union among the members of the Native Race of Indians, including therein the various Indian tribes in the State of Oklahoma.

The establishment of the Native American Church in 1918 was soon followed by the organization of peyote churches in other states. In 1921 the Winnebago of Nebraska became the first tribal group to incorporate a church of peyotism outside the state of Oklahoma. Known as the Peyote Church of Christ, it was incorporated in Thurston County, Nebraska, and its charter signed by 38 people. ALBERT HENSLEY and JESSE CLAY were among the signers of the charter, which had representation from adherents of both Cross Fire and Half Moon peyotism. Early presidents of the Peyote Church of Christ included OLIVER LA MERE and Jesse Clay. A 1922 amendment to the charter changed the name to the Native American Church of Winnebago, Nebraska. Other peyote churches were also organized among tribal groups in South Dakota, Montana, Idaho, Wisconsin, Iowa, Utah, and New Mexico.

The 1918 Oklahoma charter establishing the Native American Church was amended in 1944, resulting in a new name, the Native American Church of the United States. The first officers of the national organization were Mack Haag (Southern Cheyenne), Alfred Wilson (Southern Cheyenne), Joe Kaulity (Kiowa), TRUMAN DAILEY (Otoe), and FRANK TAKES GUN (Crow). Following a decision by Oklahoma peyotists to return to the name "Native American Church," the Native American Church of the United States obtained a separate charter in 1950. Five years later, the national organization changed its name to the Native American Church of North America in order to include Canadian peyotists.

In 1954 Canadian peyotists had incorporated themselves into the Native American Church of Canada in Red Pheasant, Saskatchewan, Canada. Two years later, Native adherents invited a team of medical specialists to participate in an all-night peyote ceremony near Fort Battleford, Saskatchewan. Fearing that the government would prohibit them from importing peyote from Texas, the peyotists hoped that firsthand observation by independent experts would help dispel misconceptions about their religion. As reported in newspaper accounts, the specialists concurred that Native religious use of peyote was not harmful and agreed that the ceremony they had attended was both beautiful and unusual. Canadian peyotists had been identified among the Blood, Cree, Ojibway, and Assiniboine tribal groups as early as the 1930s. One source also reported peyotists in Manitoba, Alberta, and Saskatchewan after the 1950s period.

In 1958 peyotists incorporated the Native American Church in California and Nevada. In 1966 the Native American Church of Navajoland was formed by Navajo peyotists in southern Arizona; their organization remains independent of the Native American Church of North America. (In contrast, Navajo peyotists from the Four Corners area are affiliated with the international church.) Consisting of the largest Navajo group of peyotists, the Native American Church of Navajoland sought incorporation from the state of Arizona in 1970 and 1971 but was refused because of opposition to the use of peyote. In 1973 it was incorporated by the state of New Mexico. Other small, independent peyote groups exist among the Navajo. One of them is the Northern Native American Church Association, which was organized by Raymond Tso of Shiprock, New Mexico, and included a few dozen followers by the early 1970s.

Recent sources indicate that the Native American Church is incorporated in 17 states. Membership figures, difficult to determine, have been estimated at anywhere from 100,000 to 250,000 members. It is a minority religion even among Native Americans, with many tribal groups having no Peyote Way adherents. There has been a great deal written about the religion, in part because of the controversy over the use of peyote and the efforts to suppress it. Besides adhering to its ethical code, which includes brotherly love, care of family, self-reliance, and the avoidance of alcohol, the Native American Church, since its inception, has fought for the First Amendment rights of its members. (See Subject Index for the legal cases involving peyote use included in this volume.)

NATIVE AMERICAN CHURCH OF NEW YORK V. UNITED STATES (468 F. Supp. 1247 S.D.N.Y., 1979)

(1979) In this case, the Native American Church of New York claimed that federal statutes prohibiting psychedelic drugs were discriminatory. The church, founded by Alan Birnbaum in 1976 and consisting of a predominantly white membership, is not affiliated with traditional American Indian peyote religious organizations. The Native American Church of New York claimed that federal practices allowing only American Indians the religious use of drugs was a violation of its First Amendment rights. The church sought to be allowed the sacramental use of psychedelic drugs it viewed as deities. The court denied the Native American Church of New York its request that LSD, psilocybin, mescaline, and marijuana be exempt from legal prosecution. The court ruled that dangerous drugs could be restricted, even when used for religious purposes. It further ruled that the Native American Church of New York had the same legal protections as American Indians for access to the exemption to federal drug laws for the religious use of peyote. The church, however, would have to prove that it was a legitimate religious organization where peyote was used as a sacrament and regarded as a deity. (See also NATIVE AMERICAN CHURCH; PEYOTE RELIGION; and Subject Index for related legal cases included in this volume.)

NATIVE AMERICAN CHURCH V. NAVAJO TRIBAL COUNCIL (272 F. 2d. 131, 134–35, 10th C. [1959])

(1959) A case in which the NATIVE AMERICAN CHURCH challenged the Navajo tribal council's ordinance prohibiting possession, use, or sale of peyote on the Navajo Reservation, claiming that it violated the freedom of religion provision of the First Amendment. Following an April 14, 1958, raid on a Native American Church service at Shiprock, New Mexico, peyotists Shorty Duncan, William F. Tsosie, and Frank Hanna Jr. were arrested and subsequently found guilty and sentenced with fine and jail penalties by Joe Duncan, judge of the Navajo tribal court. Following a dismissal of their complaints by the U.S. district court of New Mexico, a notice of appeal was filed by the Native American Church to the U.S. Court of Appeals. In denying the appeal, the court found that no provision in the U.S. Constitution made the First Amendment applicable to Indian nations nor was there any law of Congress doing so. (See also PEYOTE RELIGION; Subject Index for other legal cases involving peyote use included in this volume.)

NATIVE AMERICAN CULTURAL PROTECTION AND FREE EXERCISE OF RELIGION ACT OF 1994 *(1994)* This act, developed specifically to recognize the cultural importance of Native American sacred places, failed to pass in the 103rd Congress. Provisions regarding sacred sites were a sticking point for the administration and for various senators and representatives from states with development and extraction industries.

In Title I of the act, "Protection of Native American Sacred Sites," essential points are made about the privacy of Native American religious and ceremonial practices:

> 11) many Native American traditional cultural practices, including religious and ceremonial practices, require a measure of privacy and isolation; and certain cultural ceremonies and activities cannot be performed if non-participants can observe the practices or ceremonies or activities, even from a distance, and in some situations the lack of privacy or isolation inhibits, infringes upon, interferes with, or precludes certain Native American traditional cultural practices, including traditional religious practices; (12) some Indian tribes, such as the Pueblo of New Mexico, as well as some aspects of Native Hawaiian cultures, have traditional cultural and religious tenets that prohibit disclosure of information concerning their sacred sites and their traditional beliefs and practices, mandate secrecy, and impose internal sanctions to enforce those prohibitions, making it impossible for them to identify the manner in which any particular governmental activity would have an adverse impact on their traditional cultures or impose a burden on the free exercise of their religions;

> (13) lack of sensitivity to, or understanding of, Native American traditional cultures, including Native American religions, has resulted in the absence of a coherent policy for the protection of Native American sites, and the failure to consider the impact of federal activities upon Native American sites.

NATIVE AMERICAN GRAVES PROTECTION AND REPATRIATION ACT Signed into law by President George Bush on November 16, 1990, this landmark act will help protect Indian gravesites from looting and require the repatriation to tribes of culturally identifiable remains, funerary objects, sacred objects, and objects of cultural patrimony taken from federal or tribal lands if certain legal criteria are met. The law does not apply to burial remains found on state or private property. The act gives tribes a new set of legal procedures to use in reclaiming artifacts of religious or ceremonial significance from museums with federal support. The law obliges museums to make an inventory of their human remains and grave goods and notify appropriate tribes of their holdings. Cultural objects stolen from tribes must be returned when asked for as well. The bill was supported by most tribes, the American Association of Museums (AAM), and the Society for American Archaeology (SAA). The American Association of Museums had opposed the legislation until the measure was amended to address museums' concerns about "raids" on their collections. The law limits the kind of objects legally subject to claim and requires Indian claimants to meet strict legal tests before they can repossess objects. Proponents of the bill hope the legislation will not only return important cultural items to tribes but also foster improved relationships between tribes and Indian people on one hand and museums and the scientific community on the other. (See also BURIAL GROUND DESECRATION.)

NATIVE AMERICAN HISTORICAL, CULTURAL AND SACRED SITES ACT The Native American Historical, Cultural and Sacred Sites Act, passed by the state of California in 1976, includes a provision for identifying and cataloging sites sacred to Native Americans. Another provision calls for forms of state action to assist them in obtaining and maintaining access to these sites on both private and public lands. It also provided for the establishment of the Native American Heritage Commission, with Native representation, to oversee the act's implementation. The act also influenced the deliberations for the American Indian Religious Freedom Act, passed two years later. (See also AIRFA and Subject Index for additional entries on legislation included in this volume.)

NAVAJO CEREMONIALISM *Navajo (Dineh)* Navajo ceremonialism is a highly complex system of curing

ceremonials, divination rites, prayer ceremonies, and other rites established by the HOLY PEOPLE, or Navajo deities.

The aim of Navajo ceremonies is to restore harmony in the universe once it has been disturbed. The Navajo embrace the view that the universe is an orderly all-inclusive, unitary system of interrelated elements with a place and function for everything, from the tiniest insect to the largest mountain, from thunder and lightning to people. The principle of reciprocity governs people's relations with the other elements, the order and rules, by which people live, given by the Holy People.

The universe contains evil as well as good. Humans, for example, despite their goodness while alive, contain an evil component that becomes a dangerous GHOST after death that can hurt the living if not controlled. If the normal order, harmony and balance among elements in the universe itself are disturbed, evil ensues. Improper contact with inherently dangerous powers like ghosts of the dead, certain animals or lightning, breaking taboos related to spiritual powers, or excesses in gambling can lead to rupture of the natural harmony. Illness results, and ritual cures are required to set things right.

Navajo ceremonies are filled with symbolism, expressed in songs, prayers, stories, music, ritual objects, and SANDPAINTINGS. The Holy People are attracted to the ceremony by the offerings and prayers. If they judge the performance to be correct and complete, they are compelled by the ethics of reciprocity to set things right, cure the patient, and restore harmony in the universe. There are no priesthoods or religious societies in traditional Navajo practice. The ceremonies are held when needed and are not tied to a fixed ceremonial calendar, except for a few seasonal restrictions.

Curing ceremonials deal with the causes of disease rather than the disease itself. In general, four groups of causes predominate: infection from animals, from natural phenomena, from ceremonies themselves, and from evil spirits. Infection from an animal, especially a bear, deer, coyote, porcupine, snake, or eagle may result from being injured by it, hunting or trapping it, killing it, eating it, mishandling it, dreaming about it, or even just seeing it under certain circumstances. Infection from natural phenomena includes injury by lightning or whirlwinds, seeing or eating the flesh of animals killed by them, being near where they strike, or having anything to do with objects affected by them.

A ghost, the spirit of the dead, is especially dangerous, and almost any disease may result from any sort of contact with the dead or with their possessions, from dreaming about them or from improper burial. Navajo distinguish between the spirits of dead Navajo and dead non-Natives. Infections also result from contact with enemies and through WITCHCRAFT. Ceremonies may infect a person by improper behavior during a ceremony, transgressing restrictions imposed on the patient, or neglecting to do proper rituals.

A Navajo DIAGNOSTICIAN or practitioner is employed to discover the cause of illness and recommend a ceremony. In general, the patient and family decide on the ceremonial after the diagnosis. Most ceremonials to cure disease are conducted by trained specialists called singers or chanters. Individual chanters may be expert in from one to six ceremonies. A patient with more than one ailment may require more than one ceremony to be cured. Certain ceremonies cure one but not other ailments. The ceremony may last from one to nine nights. Navajo reckon the length of their ceremonies by the number of nights involved, so there are one-, two-, three-, five-, and up to nine-night ceremonies.

The ceremonies are grouped based on their similarities in ritual pattern, traditional associations, and causal factors against which the cure is directed. HOLY WAY CEREMONIES, which compose the largest groups, are employed when illness is traced to offenses against various spirits and Holy People. EVIL WAY chants are used for curing sickness caused by ghosts, either native or foreign. LIFE WAY CEREMONIES are employed in cases of bodily injury. BLESSING WAY chants are added, in whole or in part, to curing ceremonies to compensate for errors or omissions. Wyman and Kluckhohn, in their work, *Navajo Classification of Their Song Ceremonials,* list 58 distinct ceremonies.

The ceremonies are held in the hogan of the sponsor who institutes the ceremony and assumes the principal responsibility for paying for it. Ceremonial restrictions apply to the patient and singer/curer. Ritual acts are carried out in a fixed order, prescribed by a traditional origin story that sets forth the ritual elements. There is a particular ceremonial order involved in the application of substances to parts of the body (bath suds representing cleansing, meal, pollen, chant lotion, consecrated sand, or other objects). Special objects and materials are disposed either to the north or east.

In ceremonies in which sandpainting plays a role, the cause of illness being treated is attributed to impaired relationships with specific life-giving forces in the Navajo cosmos. These forces are associated with certain Holy People whose powers have become directed against the life forces of the ailing person. Rites are enacted to appease the Holy People and persuade them to remove their life-threatening influence.

Many discrete elements are fitted into each ceremony, including the use of ritual equipment like medicine bundles, masks to impersonate the deities, rattles, bullroarers, vessels for medicine (herbal, mineral, animal), minerals for sandpaintings, corn and plant pollens, precious stones, shell, digging sticks, arrows, whistles, flints, feather brushes, and chant tokens. Each ceremony may include activities like songs, dances, body painting, prayer, sweating, the use of emetics and ceremonial suds baths, vigils, the telling of traditional stories, hogan consecration and prayerstick-making. These same elements are used over and over again in different combinations in different ceremonies.

(See also Subject Index for additional entries on Navajo ceremonialism included in this volume.)

NAVITCU *Tohono O'odham* The ceremonial clown that wears a white buckskin mask, a kilt, and a topknot of turkey feathers appears at the PRAYERSTICK FESTIVAL, entering from the north. He has healing power and has taught people to request favors by giving him cornmeal, which he never refuses. At the festival, these clowns carry on antics among people. They also give performances at the planting, harvesting, and rainmaking ceremonies. (See also SAGUARO FESTIVAL.)

NECK, MEDICINE (Or Mitchell) *Potawatomi* Peyotist. Medicine Neck was arrested in 1914 for introducing peyote on the Menominee Reservation in Wisconsin and brought to trial in Milwaukee's U.S. district court for violating an 1897 federal law prohibiting the introduction of intoxicants on Indian reservations. The judge ruled that the law prohibited alcoholic beverages but did not apply to peyote; therefore, Medicine Neck was found not guilty. (See also PEYOTE RELIGION; Subject Index for additional peyote cases included in this volume.)

NEELY, RICHARD (Neeley) *(1802–1828)* One of the first Methodist missionaries to the Cherokee people. Born in North Carolina, Neely moved to Rutherford County, Tennessee, during his childhood. He converted to Methodism in 1819 and was licensed to preach in 1821. In 1822 Richard Riley, a mixed-blood member of the Cherokee Nation, invited him to his home to preach. Neely subsequently convinced the Tennessee Conference of the Methodist Episcopal Church to support work among the Cherokee beginning in 1824. The number of converts increased from 33 the first year to 400 in 1827. Both he and his colleague, JAMES JENKINS TROTT, married mixed-blood women and started families in the Cherokee Nation. Neely's life was cut short by tuberculosis, and he died in 1828. His last name was also spelled Neeley.

NEGABANAT, NÖEL *(c. 1600–1666) Montagnais* One of the Montagnais chiefs, Negabanat and his followers settled near the Jesuits at Sillery, near Quebec. He was baptized December 8, 1638, and took the name of Nöel in honor of Nöel Brûart de Sillery. After convincing the Abenaki to ask for a missionary, Negabanat went among them with Father GABRIEL DRUILLETTES in 1651. He later followed Druillettes to Boston and Plymouth to try to persuade

Penacook, Mahican, and others to join the French against the British during the French and Indian wars. The French honored him, giving him a place of distinction at ceremonies. He met with the missionary PAUL LeJEUNE in 1638 and decided to settle his family at St. Joseph de Sillery, a village designed by Jesuits for Montagnais in order to remold their lifestyle and religious practices.

NEGAHNQUET, ALBERT *(1874–1944) Potawatomi* One of the first full-blood American Indians to be ordained a Roman Catholic priest. Born in 1874 near St. Mary's Mission in Topeka, Kansas, Negahnquet later moved to the Potawatomi Reservation in Indian Territory (present-day Oklahoma) with his family. Educated in the Catholic school run by Benedictine monks at Sacred Heart Mission, he progressed rapidly in his studies and was befriended by his teachers. He subsequently enrolled in the College of the Propaganda Fide in Rome, where he was ordained to the priesthood in 1903. He then returned to the United States and began working among Indians, first in Oklahoma and then in Minnesota. For reasons unclear, he was laicized in 1941. There is evidence this might have been related to problems of cultural conflict and racism within the church. (See also BOUCHARD, JAMES CHRYSOSTOM; GORDON, PHILIP B.; PELOTTE, DONALD E.)

NESUTAN, JOB *(?–1675) Praying Indian* One of the PRAYING INDIANS who assisted the English missionary JOHN ELIOT in translating the Scriptures into the Natick dialect of the Massachuset. DANIEL GOOKIN, who recounted the missionary experience among the Indians, wrote that "he was a very good linguist in the English tongue and was Mr. Eliot's assistant and interpreter in his translations of the Bible, and other books of the Indian language." Eliot himself referred to Nesutan on October 21, 1650, as follows: "I have one already who can write, so that I can read his writing well, and with some pains and teaching, [he] can read mine." Gookin recorded his death: "In this expedition [July 1675] one of our principal soldiers of the praying Indians was slain, a valiant and stout man named Job Nesutan." (See also COCKENOE; HIACOOMES; MAYHEW, THOMAS.)

NEUFELD, HENRY T. *(1888–1968)* A Mennonite missionary who worked among the Cheyenne people from 1912 to 1927. Neufeld was born on October 16, 1888, near Inman, Kansas. After attending Bethel College, he married Helena Toews on August 12, 1912, and began his mission to the Cheyenne the same year. He eventually worked with both the Southern and Northern branches of the tribe. Neufeld was later associated with the Oklahoma Bible College in Meno, Oklahoma, and founded the Bethel Mennonite Church in Enid. He died in Denver City, Texas, on July 19, 1968.

NEW FIRE CEREMONY *Hopi* The first significant ritual of the WUWUCHIM CEREMONY. Two Horn priests kindle a new fire with flint and native cotton that is kept going with coal. The new fire represents cosmic power directed from the Sun to MASAU'U deity of the nadir, death, and the underworld, who then projects its warmth to Earth and people. The ritual kindling of the fire takes place at dawn before the Sun comes up. Brands from the new fire are carried to light fires in other kivas.

NEW FIRE CEREMONY *Zuni* An important part of the winter SOLSTICE CEREMONIES around which are grouped rites of exorcism and fertility and taboos. The ceremony suggests that by rekindling the hearth fires and the Sun's fire, all life may begin to warm again.

NEW RIDER V. BOARD OF EDUCATION (480 F.2d 693 [10th Cir. 1973]. cert. denied 414 U.S. 1097, 94 S.Ct. 733, 38 L.Ed. 2d 556 [1973]) *(1973)* This case, heard by the Tenth Circuit Court of Appeals, concerned three Pawnee junior high school students who had been placed on suspension for failing to comply with a public school's regulation on hair length. The regulation, which prevented male students from wearing their hair in braids, was challenged by the Oklahoma students and their parents. They filed suit, claiming that the school had violated their freedom of religion as well as other rights protected by the First and Fourteenth Amendments of the U.S. Constitution. The Tenth Circuit Court of Appeals affirmed the lower court's dismissal of the case on the grounds that no significant constitutional claims were involved. *New Rider v. Board of Education* was denied certiorari by the United States Supreme Court, with Justices William O. Douglas and Thurgood Marshall dissenting. Justice Douglas challenged the premise made by the Tenth Circuit Court of Appeals that hairstyle cannot be a form of constitutionally protected expression, finding the attempt to impose uniformity on the Pawnee petitioners repugnant and the issues raised in the case "far from trivial." (See also *HATCH V. GOERKE; TETERUD V. GILLMAN; UNITED STATES EX REL. GOINGS V. AARON;* Subject Index, for related legal cases included in this volume.)

NIELSEN, NIELS LAURIDS *(1863–1941)* A Danish Lutheran missionary who worked among the Cherokee of Oklahoma. He was born in Vorgod Parish, West Jutland, Denmark, on March 22, 1863, one of five children of Knud Nielsen, a schoolteacher, and his wife. After attending the training school of the Danish Mission Society in Copenhagen, he left for America and arrived in Menominee, Michigan, in 1888. He worked at a sawmill until he enrolled in the Trinity Lu-

theran Theological Seminary in Blair, Nebraska. In 1892 he went to Tahlequah, where he began studying the Sequoyan syllabary, and later that year he opened a school at Pumpkin Springs among the Cherokee people. Nielsen, who was ordained in 1894, eventually opened other mission stations and schools. After the Moravians closed their New Springplace mission near Oaks in 1898, he moved the Lutheran mission's headquarters there. Nielsen worked at the post until 1924, when he accepted a ministerial position in Audubon, Iowa. He died on February 9, 1941.

NIGHT WAY CEREMONY (Yeibichai) *Navajo (Dineh)* Nine-night Holy Way ceremonial. The Night Way is conducted by a chanter for the cure of a patient only after the first killing frost in fall and before the first thunderstorm in spring. Ceremonial rites include singing, dancing, pollen blessings, pressing of prayer bundles to the head and body of the patient, drinking herbal infusions, face painting, SANDPAINTINGs, masking, sweat baths, offerings, and intervals of prayer chants. One of the types of ceremonies most often seen by visitors, Night Way ceremonials are either "inside" affairs that do not conclude with a public exhibition or they are public affairs in which various groups of dancers appear. The patient decides what should be performed in public. The ceremony takes place in a hogan and participants include the singer and assistants, the patient, relatives, friends, and the HOLY PEOPLE. During the Night Way, there are also initiations of boys and girls into the Navajo (Dineh) tribe that make them recognized members as well as full participants in the community's ceremonial life. On all nights there is dancing, and on the final night masked dancers (the *YEI*) who impersonate the *yei* spirits appear.

NIMAN KACHINA CEREMONY *Hopi* The 16-day ceremony held in July, also called the Home Dance, that sends the KACHINA spirits back to their homes. At the summer solstice, the kachinas begin their ceremonial departure to the San Francisco Peaks. Their work is done in the upper world so they return to the lower world, where it is winter solstice. The Niman is performed by different kivas in rotation each year. Rituals include prayerstick making, a pilgrimage for spruce whose branches and twigs are worn by all the kachinas, mask painting, ritual planting of spruce trees in the plaza, and cornmeal sprinkling of dancers. The dancers appear at sunrise, midmorning, and afternoon and distribute gifts to children. Shortly before sunset, the kachinas dance a farewell dance and file out of the plaza. This ceremony includes the sacrifice of eagles, which are "sent home" with the kachinas. The feathers of the eagles are used to construct prayersticks for future ceremonies.

NISBET, JAMES *(1823–1874)* The first Presbyterian missionary to Indian people in the Canadian Northwest. Nisbet, the son of a shipbuilder, was born on September 8, 1823, at Hutchisontown, Glasgow, Scotland. His family immigrated to Canada West in 1844, settling at Oakville on the shore of Lake Ontario. In Canada Nisbet worked for a time at carpentry, a trade he had learned through an apprenticeship in Glasgow, before completing four years of theology studies at Knox College in Toronto. He graduated from the college in 1849 and was ordained to the ministry the following year. Nisbet then served as a pastor at Oakville and as a missionary to other townships in the area.

In 1862 Nisbet was sent to the Red River area of present-day Winnipeg by the Foreign Mission Committee of the Canada Presbyterian Church. His assignment was to assist another missionary, the Reverend John Black, and to explore the possibility of establishing a mission among Native people in the Hudson's Bay Company region. Nisbet recommended a number of sites to the Foreign Mission Committee, but the board did not approve the expenditure of funds to open a new mission for several years. In 1866, after finally obtaining support from the committee, he began working among the Cree at a site he named Prince Albert (Saskatchewan). The Cree people opposed Nisbet's efforts because they feared a mission settlement would attract Euro-Canadian settlers who would take their land and buffalo. Nisbet, who overcame the opposition with the assistance of an interpreter, eventually built a farm and a school. By 1872, a representative of the Foreign Mission Committee recommended that Nisbet close the mission's farming operation and spend more time itinerating among distant tribal bands. The missionary agreed to the changes but died a short time later on September 20, 1874, at Kildonan, Manitoba. Nisbet was married to Mary MacBeth in 1864, and they had four children.

NOAHA-VOSE (Nowah'wus) *Cheyenne* The most sacred site of the Cheyenne people. Noaha-vose is the mountain where SWEET MEDICINE, the prophet, received great teachings from MAHEO, the Creator. Sweet Medicine returned from the holy place with the SACRED ARROWS, a code of laws, and other spiritual gifts and teachings for the people. Known in English as BEAR BUTTE, it is part of the Black Hills in South Dakota. Another spelling is Nowah'wus, a Tsistsistas word defined as "where people are taught."

NORELPUTUS *(?–c. 1902) Yana-Wintu* Chief of the Northern Yana and leader of the GHOST DANCE OF 1870. He was born to a Wintu mother and a Northern Yana father. His knowledge of the Ghost Dance came through the Achomawi, a tribal group in California. After embracing the beliefs of the religious movement, Norelputus advocated the construction of subterranean earth lodges to protect adherents from the prophesied end of the world. This doctrinal change was introduced to the Wintun and Hill Patwin of California in 1871 or 1872. Although Norelputus traveled with his message in these areas, more distant communities learned of it from other sources. This variation of the Ghost Dance became known as the EARTH LODGE RELIGION. Norelputus was also identified as a BOLE-MARU RELIGION leader. He reportedly died about 1902 among the Wintu at Baird. His name also appears as Nelelputa.

NUAKIN (Nuakkinna, ta-nu'in) *Shoshone* A dance described among the Lemhi Shoshone people. It was held in the spring in supplication for plentiful salmon, berries, and other foods. Alternating male and female participants formed a circle, linked fingers, and danced in a clockwise movement. The Nuakin (also Nuakkinna or ta-nu'in) was conducted over several days and ended with a feast. In the early 1900s it was already described as a dance practiced in former times.

OAKCHIAH *(c. 1810–1849) Choctaw* Licensed preacher and ordained deacon in the Mississippi Conference of the Methodist Episcopal Church. Oakchiah was born about 1810 in the Choctaw Nation (present-day Mississippi). Although he was named William Winans at his baptism, he was a full-blood who was called Oakchiah all of his life. As an early convert, he encountered ridicule and threats from tribal members, including his own father, for adopting Christianity and becoming a preacher. After he was licensed to preach and admitted to the Mississippi Conference, Oakchiah itinerated for two or three years then was ordained a deacon. During the 1830s period of the government's removal of Choctaw and other tribal groups from their southeastern homelands to Indian Territory (present-day Oklahoma), Oakchiah requested the conference to grant him a placement in the new location. After the removal, he is said to have lost some of the zeal that had characterized his earlier religious life in Mississippi. In 1843 he was readmitted to itineracy and assigned to the Puckchenubbee circuit in the southern part of the Choctaw Nation in Indian Territory. Upon returning from a church conference, Oakchiah became ill and died at Fort Smith, Arkansas, on November 2, 1849.

OAKERHATER, DAVID PENDLETON (Okuhhatuh, "Making Medicine" or "Sun Dancer") *(1844–1931) Cheyenne* Cheyenne warrior, artist, and Episcopal missionary. Making Medicine, as he was called, served as an officer of the Bowstring Soldier Society of his people and fought against Osage, Ute, Otoe, and other enemies. He was among the Southern Plains warriors taken hostage by the U.S. military in 1875 during the Red River War. While incarcerated at Fort Marion in St. Augustine, Florida, he came under the "civilizing" influences of Richard Henry Pratt, the military officer who guarded the prisoners. Upon his release, he became a protégé of the Reverend John Bartlett Wicks, an Episcopal clergyman of Paris Hill, New York. Wicks trained him and Zotom, another former hostage, to become missionaries upon their return to Indian Territory. Making Medicine arrived at the Wicks home for schooling about May 20, 1878, and his educational expenses were paid by Mrs. George Pendleton. He was baptized on October 6, 1878, as David Pendleton and was confirmed a short time later. Oakerhater was ordained an Episcopal deacon in Syracuse, New York, on June 7, 1881, becoming "the church's first Indian clergyman." He then returned to Indian Territory and assisted in establishing the Cheyenne Agency's Episcopal mission. Oakerhater served at the Whirlwind Mission of the Holy Family near Watonga, Oklahoma, and continued ministering to the people for 50 years. He died on August 31, 1931. In 1985 David Pendleton Oakerhater's memory was honored by the addition of his name to the Episcopal Church's calendar of saints.

OCCOM, SAMSON ("On the Other Side") *(1723–1792) Mohegan* Mohegan clergyman from New London, Connecticut, who was the first Indian student of the Reverend ELEAZAR WHEELOCK, founder of Moor's Charity School for Indians and Dartmouth College. Occom studied at

Wheelock's private school in Lebanon, Connecticut, for nearly five years, improving his self-taught knowledge of English, Latin, Greek, and Hebrew. Prevented by poor health from attending college, he taught in New London, Connecticut, in 1748, then became a teacher and preacher to the Montauk Indians of Long Island from about 1749 to 1764. Licensed as a Presbyterian minister by clergymen in Connecticut, Occom was ordained in 1759 by the Suffolk presbytery of Long Island. From 1766 to 1767 he traveled to England and Scotland with the Reverend Nathaniel Whitaker to raise funds for Wheelock's Indian school. The first Indian known to preach in those countries, Occom succeeded in raising more than £12,000, which freed Wheelock from dependence on missionary societies and enabled him to found Dartmouth College in Hanover, New Hampshire. Wheelock's departure from the "Indian business" was one of the main causes of a break in relations between the two men. Occom stated: "your having so many White Scholars and so few or no Indian Scholars, gives me great Discouragement." He continued to live in New England, teaching and preaching among Native groups from 1768 to 1784, but is said to have turned more and more to excessive drinking. After the Revolutionary War he was instrumental in resettling remnants of New England tribes, who became known as the Brotherton Indians, in Oneida County, New York. He served as their minister from 1784 until his death in 1792 at New Stockbridge, New York. He married Mary Fowler (also known as Mary Montauk, in 1749), with whom he had 10 children.

OFFERINGS A contribution, sacrifice, or presentation that is an act of religious worship. Offerings are designed to please, placate, and invoke the spirits so they in turn promote individual and community welfare. Practitioners make offerings when they pray for food, freedom from illness, good weather, rain, good crops, success in hunting, fishing, and war, and the preservation of home and the family. Songs, dances, feasts, and ceremonies are given as offerings to please spirit beings. Offerings may include, depending on belief, PRAYERSTICKS, prayer feathers, eagle down, foods like corn meal and pollen, prayer meal (corn meal mixed with ground white shells and turquoise), and miniature implements, such as bows and arrows. Native people burn sweetgrass, sage, birch bark, cedar, and tobacco as offerings to spirits. People also make offerings to SACRED OBJECTS, like MEDICINE BUNDLES, ancestors, and KACHINAS. Offerings are used in many ceremonies. (Offerings accompany ceremonial requests to make sacred objects or to request assistance from a holy man or woman.) Offerings may be left on rocks and shrines and at natural sites.

O-GIWI-MANSE-WIN *Cree* A ceremony for an O-giwi-manse (guardian or godfather) described among the Sandy Lake Cree in northwestern Ontario. The participants include children and adults who have been named by the O-giwi-manse. Held at least once a year, the ceremony generally lasts for several hours. After the O-giwi-manse or elder prays with his pipe, a cup of sacred water is circulated, and each participant drinks from it. In this way the necessity of water to life is acknowledged and symbolized. A plate of food is then circulated that contains a sampling from the feast to follow. The O-giwi-manse speaks to the participants he has named, sharing wisdom he has acquired during his life. The ceremony concludes with a feast of such foods as bannock, meat, fish, and berries.

OKIPA *Mandan* The major four-day religious ceremony of the Mandan people of the Upper Missouri region; Okipa, also spelled O-kee-pa, has been translated as "to look alike." The name is said to derive from the idea that bull dancers, participants in the ceremony, should be the same size and dress alike. The Okipa was conducted annually to pray for plentiful buffalo, to avert a repetition of a catastrophic deluge, and to obtain other spiritual blessings. The artist George Catlin observed the ceremony in 1832, five years before smallpox drastically decimated the Native population. He wrote and illustrated a description of the Okipa as an eyewitness, providing the first such account of a complex Plains Indian ceremony. Beginning in 1832, Catlin published three descriptions of the Okipa over a 35-year period. His account, subjected to criticism by the explorer and author Henry Rowe Schoolcraft and the superintendent of Indian affairs in St. Louis David D. Mitchell, is now considered a classic in ethnology. After Catlin's visit to the Mandan in 1832, the explorer and naturalist Prince Maximilian zu Wied-Neuwied and the Swiss artist Karl Bodmer spent time visiting the region the following year. These Europeans also depicted the Okipa ceremony from descriptions they received during that period.

Conducted when the willow leaves were fully grown, the sacred observance reenacted the earth's creation and the history of the Mandan people. It was pledged by a man who met essential qualifications, including having had a vision of buffalo singing songs of the Okipa ceremony. Ritual elements described by Catlin included a celebration of the "subsiding of the waters" that ended the deluge in Mandan history; the performance of bull dances each day to pray for the return of the buffalo to sustain the people; the abstention by about 50 young male candidates from eating, drinking, or sleeping for four days as part of their preparation for becoming warriors; flesh offerings by the young men; the performance of a ritual called Feast of the Buffalos; and the use of the sacred number "four" throughout the religious observance. The complex ceremony was opened by the Mandan deity, Lone Man, who symbolically defeated Foolish One, a figure who performed clown antics. The Okipa also included dancers who symbolized night and day and reenacted other aspects of creation. The ceremony, conducted in an ancient dialect, concluded with a sweat lodge ceremony.

Archaeological evidence suggests that the Okipa was performed hundreds of years before Catlin witnessed it in 1832. Sources indicate that the ceremony was prohibited by the military officer placed in charge of the Fort Berthold Reservation in North Dakota and that it was last held in 1889 or 1890. A centennial edition of George Catlin's *O-kee-pa: A Religious Ceremony and Other Customs of the Mandan* (1867) was published by Yale University Press in 1967.

OLMSTED, JARED *(1811–1843)* Missionary among the Choctaw people in Indian Territory. Born on August 19, 1811, in Norwalk, Connecticut, and educated at the Courtland Academy in New York, Olmsted was sent to the Choctaw Nation in present-day Oklahoma by the AMERICAN BOARD OF COMMISSIONERS FOR FOREIGN MISSIONS about 1836. He established a home and school for boys near Fort Towson during the seven years he and his wife, Julie, worked there. The school, named Norwalk after his birthplace, continued to operate following his death on September 19, 1843.

OMAHA SACRED POLE *Omaha* Known as the "Venerable Man," the Sacred Pole symbolizes the unity of the Omaha tribe and its governing authority. One account of the pole's origin states that while a council discussing ways of keeping the people together and safe from extinction was in progress, the son of one of the leaders left on a hunt. Returning home at night, the young hunter became lost in the forest. While stopping to rest and to look at the stars to get his bearing, he saw a light in the distance. He approached it and found that it came from a tree that was completely aglow. Mystified, he observed that the light neither gave off heat nor consumed the tree. He continued to observe it, finding that it resumed its usual appearance during the day but at night again began to glow. When the young man reached home, he told his father and together they returned to the area. Seeing for himself the mysterious tree his son had described, the older man also observed four animal paths leading to it. After telling tribal leaders of the discovery, they agreed that it was a spiritual gift that would help unify the people and the governing council, the Seven Chiefs. The tree was then ceremonially cut down and taken home.

From its origins, the Sacred Pole was central to the Omaha people. It was kept in its own Sacred Tent and treated with reverence at all times. Special prayers, songs, and rituals associated with the pole were conducted by the people. A two-part ceremony, ANOINTING THE SACRED POLE, was held annually during the summer, although it may have been held twice a year at an early time. During the ceremony, both males and females participated in the rites, and each had specific duties. The pole stood for the tribal governing authority and the man's role as defender and provider of the home. It also stood for the women's role as mother of the Omaha people, and during her portion of the rites she prayed for continuity and plenty. The ceremony commemorated the pole's origin among the Omaha people and gave thanksgiving for the spiritual gift of the buffalo. If errors occurred, a ceremony of contrition was required.

The Sacred Pole and the holy objects associated with it were cared for by a hereditary keeper whose duties included conducting the appropriate rituals, prayers, and songs. When the people traveled on buffalo hunts or for other purposes, the pole was carried on the keeper's back. After the traditional ways were disrupted by white encroachment and the decimation of the buffalo, the Omaha keepers were faced with difficult decisions regarding the sacred objects in their care. In 1888 Francis La Flesche persuaded SHU'DENACI (Yellow Smoke), the keeper, to turn the Sacred Pole and its belongings over to him and to another ethnologist, Alice C. Fletcher, for transfer to Harvard's Peabody Museum for safekeeping. Over a century later, in the summer of 1989, the Sacred Pole was returned to the Omaha tribe following a year of negotiations with the museum. The Sacred Pole is made of cottonwood and rests upon another piece of wood, the *zhi'be* or "leg," at a 45° angle. With a scalp tied to the top or "head," the pole symbolizes a man. (See also MON'HIN THIN GE.)

O'MEARA, FREDERICK AUGUSTUS *(1814–1888)* Anglican clergyman who served as a missionary among the Ojibway people. O'Meara was born in Wexford, Ireland, and attended Trinity College in Dublin, from which he graduated in 1837. After taking holy orders at the Church of Ireland, he was sent on a mission to Canada in 1838. He succeeded WILLIAM MCMURRAY as a missionary at Sault Ste. Marie, where he also ministered to the Native people at nearby Garden River. O'Meara initiated Christianization and educational efforts and studied the Ojibway language during the two-year period he spent there. In 1841 he was sent to Manitoulin Island, traveling to Sault Ste. Marie, Garden River, and other stations in the region. Besides building a school at Manitoulin Island, he translated the Book of Common Prayer (1846), the New Testament (1854) and other religious works into the Ojibway language. He was later assisted by the Native minister PETER JACOBS. Their joint translations included the Pentateuch and a *Hymn Book for* *the Use of Ojibway Indian Congregations.* O'Meara remained at Manitoulin Island for more than 18 years, leaving in 1859 to take a position at Georgetown, Canada West. He later taught Ojibway to Jabez W. Sims, who succeeded Peter Jacobs at the mission post. In 1877 O'Meara became one of the founders of a divinity school in Toronto. He died on December 17, 1888, at Port Hope, Ontario. He was married to Margaret Johnston Dallas, with whom he had five children.

ONASAKENRAT, JOSEPH (Onesakenarat, Joseph Akwirente, Chief Joseph, and "White Feather", Sose, Le Cygne) *(1845–1881) Mohawk* Iroquois chief and Methodist missionary. The son of Lazare Akwirente, Onasakenrat was born on September 4, 1845, near the Sulpician mission of Lac-des-Deux-Montagnes (Oka, Quebec) and raised in the Roman Catholic faith. The mission, established in 1721, was located on land granted to the Sulpicians in 1718 by King Louis XV for resettling Algonquian and Iroquois converts. The Native people and the Catholic priests eventually fought over the land's ownership in a conflict that was to last for many years. Onasakenrat, an excellent student, was viewed by the Sulpicians as a young man who could be groomed to become a Native proponent of their missionary point of view. At the age of 15 he was sent to the Sulpicians' Petit Seminaire de Montréal and remained at the college for three years.

After returning to Oka, Onasakenrat served as secretary to the Sulpicians. A few years later, on July 25, 1868, he was elected principal chief by the Iroquois. The 22-year-old leader soon protested against the Sulpicians, criticizing their control of the Oka missionary settlement and accusing them of being responsible for the poverty of the Native people. The conflict resulted in the majority of the Iroquois in the community renouncing Catholicism and joining the Wesleyan Methodist Church. Onasakenrat then continued his opposition to the Sulpicians. On February 18, 1869, he challenged the priests on their control of wood-cutting rights by cutting down an elm tree without permission. A few days later he and 40 supporters marched to the residence of the Sulpicians and warned them against remaining at Oka, an action that prompted the priests to obtain a warrant of arrest. Onasakenrat was arrested with two other Iroquois chiefs on March 4, 1869, and was jailed for several weeks. He later petitioned the federal government on the land issue but the Sulpician claim to ownership was affirmed.

When the Sulpician church burned down on July 15, 1877, Onasakenrat, his father, and other Native people were arrested and charged with arson. Released on bail, Onasakenrat served as an interpreter for the Methodist missionary at Oka. By 1880 his translations from the French to the Iroquois included the Gospels and a hymnal.

After his ordination to the ministry by the Montreal Conference of the Methodist Church of Canada in 1880, he received an assignment to serve as missionary to the Iroquois communities of Caughnawaga and St. Regis. Onasakenrat then became a proponent of peace, urging his people to accept Sulpician resettlement offers, but thereby lost support. He died at Oka on February 7, 1881, the same year the arson case against him was dismissed. After his death, Onasakenrat's policy of peace was voted out and only a small number of Oka's Iroquois agreed to relocate to Ontario lands bought for them by the Sulpicians. In 1910 the Sulpician title to the land at Oka was upheld by the Supreme Court of Canada. Onasakenrat was also known as Sose and Le Cygne.

ONE HORN SOCIETY (Kwan) *Hopi* The members of this society are charged with the duty of conducting the spirits of the dead to the Hopi graveyard. Kwan men who impersonate MASAU'U, the spirit of the dead, wear their dress in reverse of customary order to symbolize the dead as the opposite of the living. The Kwan chief installs the village chief. During the WUWUCHIM CEREMONY a One Horn closes the roads leading into the village by drawing cornmeal lines across each. The One Horn priest reopens a road by cutting the cornmeal line with a sacred object.

ONEIDA INDIAN NATION OF NEW YORK V. CLARK (593 F. Supp. 257 [1984]) *(1984)* Suit filed by the Oneida Nation against the secretary of the interior. The dispute arose over irregularities in the tribal election in which the Bureau of Indian Affairs failed to grant an extension in the deadline to accommodate a person's religious duties. The court held that neither the First Amendment nor the AMERICAN INDIAN RELIGIOUS FREEDOM ACT OF 1978 (AIRFA) were violated by the denial of the deadline extension. It also ruled that AIRFA protected only the Native American religious rights secured by the First Amendment and did not constitute a separate cause of action. The litigation has been described as "the earliest non-land case" invoking the American Indian Religious Freedom Act.

OOKAH DANCE *Cherokee* A sacred ceremony described by the 19th-century missionary DANIEL SABIN BUTRICK and other early observers of the Cherokee Nation before the forced removal of the tribal group from the southeastern Appalachian region to Indian Territory (present-day Oklahoma). Held every seven years, the Ookah Dance was conducted at the capital town of the Cherokee Nation. The ancient capital, Chota, or Great Echota, was located on the south side of the Little Tennessee River below Citico Creek in Tennessee. New Echota in Georgia also served as the capital

for a number of years before removal. The Uku, or priest, was titled Ookah and conducted a dance of thanksgiving at the four-day observance. Other officials included seven counselors, messengers to notify the people, men to direct the feast, women to oversee the cooking, and honored attendants to assist the Uku. Participants were not allowed to touch unsanctified objects, and the heptagon, or council house area, was purified if a transgression occurred. Ceremonial elements included ritual bathing of the Ookah as well as sacred dance and consecration rituals. The observance was also marked by fasting, a vigil of silence, and other sacred activities. (See also SIX CHEROKEE FESTIVALS.)

OSUNKHIRHINE, PIERRE PAUL (Pierre-Paul Masta, Wzokhilain) *(fl. 1830–1849) Abenaki.* An Abenaki missionary of St. Francis, near Pierreville, Quebec, who was noted for his translations of religious works. Educated at Moor's Charity School established by ELEAZAR WHEELOCK in Hanover, New Hampshire, Osunkhirhine became an adherent of the Congregational faith. In 1829 or 1830 he returned to St. Francis as a government teacher and began introducing Protestantism among his people. Osunkhirhine encountered opposition from Joseph-Marie Bellenger, the local Catholic missionary, and after several years, the Abenaki religious leader lost his government position. He then obtained support from the AMERICAN BOARD OF COMMISSIONERS FOR FOREIGN MISSIONS for his work. Osunkhirhine, who was ordained by the Presbyterians in 1836, organized a Congregational church in 1838. He translated religious materials, including the Gospel of Mark, into the Abenaki language. They were published from 1830 to 1844. Osunkhirhine is also identified as Pierre-Paul Masta and Wzokhilain.

O'TOOLE *(fl. 1870s) Klamath* A dreamer who carried the message of the GHOST DANCE OF 1870 to the Lower End of the Klamath Reservation in Oregon. O'Toole helped organize a dance attended by 40 or 50 families at Williamson River Flat. Given sacred songs and teachings in a dream, he was also instructed to conduct a ritual. O'Toole built an earth lodge and taught the religious ceremony to those who participated. It is said that he saw returned dead people among those in attendance. (See also DREAM DANCE, EARTH LODGE RELIGION.)

OTTER SOCIETY *Iroquois* A society of women with a distinctive water sprinkling rite. Members spray water at ceremonies by dipping a corn husk splasher in buckets of medicine water and shaking them at people. The members of this society are organized to give thanks to water animals and to retain their favor. They appease the otters and other

water animals who are supposed to exercise influence over health, fortunes, and destinies of people. The Otter Society has no songs or dances. Members cure by going to a spring and conducting a ceremony, after which they enter a sick person's house and sprinkle the patient with the spring water. This society is especially active during the MIDWINTER CEREMONY. (See also MEDICINE SOCIETIES [Iroquois].)

OUR GRANDMOTHER, THE CREATOR (Papoothkwe, Shikalapikshi, Libikapo'shi) *Shawnee.* The female deity of the Shawnee people who gave them a code of laws and most of their principal religious ceremonies. According to one account of Our Grandmother's place in creation, she received spiritual assistance in creating human beings after being the sole survivor of a great flood. Kokomthena, as she is called in the Shawnee language, is believed to be weaving a basket or net called a *shkimota* that, if completed, will signal the end of the world. At the end those who maintain the traditions and laws will be taken into the *shkimota* but those who are bad will not. It is also believed that Kokomthena sometimes appears on earth to observe the performance of Shawnee religious ceremonies. At times an extra voice, attributed to her, can be heard joining the singing. Other names for Our Grandmother include Papoothkwe, Shikalapikshi and Lithikapo'shi. (See also BREAD DANCE; BUFFALO DANCE; DEATH FEAST; GREEN CORN DANCE; RIDE-IN AND WAR DANCE; RITUAL FOOTBALL GAME.)

OUR LIFE SUPPORTER (OUR SUSTENANCE) DANCES *Iroquois* Food spirit ceremony following the GREEN CORN ceremony that includes the Feather Dance and a series of women's dances, differing in various longhouses, honoring corn, beans, and squash. The purpose of the dance is to entertain the food spirits and to thank them.

OWAQLT SOCIETY (Owaqol) *Hopi* A women's society whose rites relate to fertility and whose ceremony is performed any time between the Maraw and WUWUCHIM ceremonies, usually in late October. The society's altar, kiva rituals, and public dance differ little from those of the MARAW SOCIETY. The women throw baskets instead of food to bystanders. (See also LAKON SOCIETY.)

OWL, W. DAVID *(1893–c. 1981) Cherokee* Baptist minister whose pastorate among the Seneca on the Cattaraugus Reservation in New York State lasted for more than 35 years. Born in 1893 in Cherokee, North Carolina, he attended school on the reservation and continued his education at the Hampton Institute in Virginia. Besides completing the school's blacksmithing trade course in 1913, he earned an academic diploma in 1915. He then entered the Young Men's

Christian Association College in Springfield, Massachusetts, where he studied physical education and rural sociology. He was awarded a degree in 1918. Following military service in the army, he taught in a private Episcopal mission school in North Carolina, then accepted an assignment from the Presbyterian Church among the Pima (Akimel O'odham) Indians at Sacaton, Arizona. His work there led to an appointment as director of physical education at Haskell Institute in Lawrence, Kansas, where he met his future wife, Janie Crow, a Seneca from Oklahoma. After marrying in June 1923, the couple moved to New York, where David at-tended the Rochester-Colgate Divinity School until his graduation in 1927. He then started his full-time ministry on the Cattaraugus Reservation in New York. Besides his work at the Pleasant Valley Baptist Church, Owl served churches of other denominations in the area. Honors received by the minister during his long career included the Golden Arrow Award for work among American Indians, from the Indian Council Fire in Chicago, and a special tribute by the Grand Lodge of the Iroquois Temperance Society and the state of New York in 1969. The Reverend Owl, who retired in 1960, died about 1981.

P

PACHAVU *Hopi* Held once every four years or more at the end of the POWAMU CEREMONY, this observance is performed when adult men have been initiated into Wuchim the preceding year. Bean maidens carry large plaques of bean sprouts and beans molded from cornmeal and march to the singing of chief *(mong)* kachinas. The Warrior Mother kachina appears, accompanied by other kachinas, and joins with the Bean maiden procession that moves into the plaza for a final grand assembly of a host of kachinas. (See also WUWUCHIM CEREMONY.)

PAHKO (Fiesta) *Yaqui* In YAQUI CEREMONIALISM, a Pahko is an important part of maintaining the Yaqui religious system, linking together two parts of the Yaqui universe, the Christian world of church and town and the HUYA ANIYA, the traditional Yaqui spiritual realm. It also integrates into a single functioning social unit the church and the household. A Pahko is hosted by a particular household for church groups and is carried out on the occasion of a child's funeral, a death anniversary, the leave taking of the spirits of the dead in November, a Lenten *pasada,* a hosting of the Matachin Dance, the annual SAINT'S DAY FIESTA, and a wedding. Townspeople witness that a household has fulfilled its religious obligations by hosting a Pahko.

All but the annual patron saint's day is celebrated at a private household ceremony given by a married couple or at least two sponsors, male and female, called Pahkome. The church groups and PASCOLA DANCERS are invited to the household, which has been ritually transformed into a church, with the household cross serving as a temporary al-

tar. The household *ramada* (arbor) built for the occasion is divided into two parts, with the church officiants carrying out rituals on one side and the Pascolas carrying out rituals on the other side. The Pahko involves dances, prayers, Pascola clowning, and sermonizing. The church groups, Pascolas, and relatives of the Pahkome eat together as groups and do not mingle.

PAHO See PRAYERSTICK

PA'-IÑGYA ("In the Middle") *(fl. 1887–1894) Kiowa* Prophet. In 1887, Pa'-iñgya revived the prophecy of the medicine man DA'TEKAN that the buffalo would return to the people, and laid claim to Da'tekan's spiritual powers. Pa'-iñgya asserted that the whites had caused the buffalo to disappear and would eventually be destroyed. Claiming to be invulnerable and able to kill possible offenders with a glance, he began a series of ritual observances with help from 10 assistants he had selected. Announcing the time for the buffalo to return and the whites to be destroyed, he instructed his followers to gather near his headquarters on the reservation's Elk Creek in present-day Oklahoma. He further announced that after four days the reservation agency, the schools, the whites, and Indian nonbelievers would be destroyed by a great whirlwind and fire. In addition, soldiers who might pursue the adherents would be destroyed by a glance, and their bullets would not harm them. Kiowa followers abandoned home and school and went to Elk Creek, where they waited for the prophecy to come true. When it did not,

Pa'-iñgya explained that some of his instructions had been violated by the people and that the return of the buffalo was postponed. When news of an Indian messiah reached the Kiowa in 1890, the medicine man saw it as the fulfillment of his prophecy. In 1894 he assisted in reviving the GHOST DANCE OF 1890 on the Washita River.

PAINS *Hupa, Karok, Maidu, Shasta, Tolowa, Yorok* Considered to be actual, physical objects, sent by an offended spirit, that cause disease. Evil people also shoot pains into bodies, producing illness that requires removal by a doctor/shaman. Traditional California healers, called doctors, extract "pains" by sucking them out while in a trance. Among peoples like the Hupa and Yurok in northwest California, the power of doctors/shamans rests on maintaining "pains," received in a dream from spirits in their own bodies. After the dream, there is a long and rigorous course of training provided by older, experienced shamans that accustoms novices to the presence of "pains" and leads to the shaman's control over them. This arduous period of instruction includes praying, fasting, dancing, singing, purifying, hiking, abstaining from sex, and social isolation. A public dance terminates the training and announces the doctors' readiness to heal the sick. Pains come in pairs to doctors as well as to the people they make ill.

PAINTED ON *Apache* A term for any object bearing ceremonial designs—SANDPAINTINGS, hoops and staffs, buckskin objects, *gan* masks, and so forth. "Painted on" are holy and prayed to because they are personifications of spiritual power. Only certain ceremonies include the right to make "painted on." Eventually these objects must be disposed of in some cave or rock crevice, with appropriate prayers and under the instructions of the shaman who directed their making. Some "painted on" are made for use in a single ceremony and must be put away shortly afterward; others are made for an individual and may be kept as long as his power lasts. (See also MOUNTAIN SPIRIT DANCERS.)

PALMER, MARCUS *(1795–?)* A missionary-physician to the Cherokee people in Indian Territory (present-day Oklahoma) who worked under the auspices of the AMERICAN BOARD OF COMMISSIONERS FOR FOREIGN MISSIONS. From Greenwich, Connecticut, Palmer arrived at Union Mission in Indian Territory on February 18, 1821, and later worked at Harmony Mission for several years. He married Clarissa Johnson, who had traveled west with the same group of missionaries, on August 24, 1824. After receiving a restricted license to preach in 1825, Palmer was later ordained in 1830. He served as the supervisor of Mulberry Mission in Arkansas, which was moved in 1829 to Sallisaw Creek in Indian Territory and renamed Fairfield Mission. Besides supervising religious and educational work, Palmer provided medical services to the Cherokee people. After his first wife died of consumption in 1835, he married Jerusha Johnson. An 1838 report by the American Board indicated that the Palmers were still in charge of Fairfield Mission.

PALOU, FRANCISCO *(1723–1789)* Spanish Franciscan missionary. Born in Spain, he was a student of JUNÍPERO SERRA in Palma and was ordained into the Franciscan order in 1749. He came to Mexico with Serra in 1749. Beginning in 1769, the two explored Upper California and founded several missions. He wrote about the Spanish missionaries and California Indians and has been called the "Father of California History." (See also CALIFORNIA MISSION SYSTEM.)

PAPOUNHAN (Papoonan) *(?–1775) Munsee* The leader of a Munsee nativist movement who sought to restore tribal traditions that had been lost, or nearly lost, as a result of European contact. Following the death of his father, Papounhan mourned in the woods alone for five days. During that period he received a revelation from the Creator and then returned home to put his religious teachings into practice. As a result of the French and Indian War, Papounhan and his band moved from Lackawanna, where he had preached around 1752 to 1756, to an area north of Tioga in Pennsylvania. In 1758 the tribal band relocated again to Wyalusing along the Susquehanna River. Described as strictly adhering to the ancient ways of their forefathers, Papounhan and his followers were non-Christian and had no interest in adopting European ways. Called "Quaker Indians," they did not believe in war, did not drink, and lived on the Susquehanna in an orderly town with well-constructed houses and plenty of corn. They believed that good could be found in the revelations of other groups and and willingly listened to the Quakers and Moravians in the area. After hearing teachings from those groups, the Munsee eventually decided, in 1763, to replace Papounhan with a Christian missionary. A Moravian, DAVID ZEISBERGER, subsequently filled the post, established Friedenshuetten mission, and baptized Munsee tribal members, including Papounhan. Papounhan later devoted his efforts to Christianity in the area of the Muskingum River between 1772 and 1775. Papounhan's name also appears as Papoonan. Other prophets among the tribal group included the DELAWARE PROPHET and WANGOMEN.

PARKER, QUANAH (Kwaina, "Fragrant") *(c. 1845–1911) Comanche* The influential principal chief who was also one of the most important ROADMEN, or leaders, in the early PEYOTE RELIGION in Indian Territory (present-day Oklahoma). Born about 1845, Parker's father was Peta

Nocone (Noconi, "Wanderer"), chief of the Comanche's Kwahadi (Quahada) division. His mother, Cynthia Ann Parker, was a white woman who had been captured at about 12 years of age during an 1835 raid on a Navasota River settlement in Texas and later became Nocone's wife. Following his mother's recapture in 1860 and his father's death a short time later, Quanah was left without parents in his teens. Rising to leadership as a successful warrior, his influence grew after his people were confined to a reservation in Indian Territory. In earlier times leadership in the tribe was decentralized, with each of the numerous autonomous Comanche bands having its own leader. Confinement to a limited area of land and the government's fostering of a centralized tribal government with a single, or few, leaders changed the tribal political organization. Taking the surname of his mother, who had died soon after her recapture, Parker quickly adapted to the assimilationist ways promoted by government agents and Christian missionaries. He promoted the development of schools, churches, and other institutions among his people. By leasing tribal lands he became a successful businessman who built a large house and ranch. Despite adoption of a "civilized" lifestyle, he maintained a number of Native traditions, including polygamy, and was influential in the development and diffusion of the Peyote Religion in Indian Territory.

Parker's involvement with peyote is believed to have started about 1885, after peyotists successfully used it to treat him for a wound or ailment. As a respected and influential chief, he contributed to the spread of peyotism by attracting followers to his beliefs, by defending Native use of peyote against powerful opponents, and by being an apostle of a particular ceremonial form. As a roadman, he adhered to the Half Moon peyote ceremony taught to him by Lipan Apaches BILLY CHIWAT and PINERO. This ceremony, with its half-moon-shaped altar, also became known as the Comanche Way, the Kiowa Way and the Quanah Parker Way. (Parker did not adopt the Big Moon variation introduced by JOHN WILSON, the Caddo roadman who lived in the same vicinity.) Parker was awarded one of three judgeships on the COURTS OF INDIAN OFFENSES after the tribal court system was organized at the consolidated Kiowa, Comanche, and Wichita Agency in 1886. His appointment was approved by federal officials although he practiced peyotism and maintained other traditions that the government had established the tribal courts to help eradicate. Parker remained a judge until 1898, when he was dismissed, not for practicing the Peyote Religion, but for polygamy. He was later among a group of known peyotists employed by the Bureau of Indian Affairs at Anadarko in Indian Territory.

Besides defending peyote use behind the scenes, Parker fought openly as well. He and other peyotists testified before the Oklahoma Constitutional Convention in 1907 and successfully defended their right to the religious use of peyote. When a special officer of the Bureau of Indian Affairs burned a peyote crop in Texas in an effort to eradicate peyotism, the Comanche leader used his political influence to obtain a large amount of peyote in Mexico for his own use and that of other peyotists. Other tribes, in addition to the Comanche, who were influenced by Parker's peyotism included the Arapaho, Caddo, Delaware (Lenni Lenape), Otoe, Pawnee, and Ponca. Parker is also said to have taken the Red Bean Ceremony (MESCAL BEAN CEREMONY) and the peyote religion to the Potawatomi in Kansas, about 1908.

Parker made numerous trips to Washington, D.C., participated in Theodore Roosevelt's inaugural events, hosted influential leaders at his home, and had a town in Texas named Quanah in his honor. The Comanche chief and roadman died near Cache, Oklahoma, in 1911.

PASCO SAM (Weonoumpt, "Going Along Singing") *(?–c. 1920s) Wanapam* Medicine man who helped spread the sacred teachings of SMOHALLA, the prophet, among the Palouse people. Born at White Bluffs, he was known as Weonoumpt to the Native people in the area located below the Priest Rapids of the Columbia River at Priest Rapids. Pasco Sam became a top range worker among the stockmen who employed him in southeastern Washington. As an elder, he lived on the Colville Reservation in Washington and led WASHAT DANCES. Pasco Sam died sometime in the 1920s and was buried in Nespelem, Washington.

PASCOLA DANCER *Yaqui* A performer at each of the important devotions of the Christian calendar, integrating the *HUYA ANIYA*, the Yaqui realm of timeless events, and the Christian world of the towns—bringing together the ritual experience of the two kinds of spiritual power. In Yaqui ceremonialism, this mutual participation of Pascola dancer and church-based ritual involves the interaction of two opposing conceptions of the universe within a common framework of religious expression.

The Pascola dancers are not part of either the church or town authority but are household-based, yet their participation is essential for fulfillment of the goals of the church organization. The Pascolas dance at Pahkos, or fiestas, at the request of the Pahkome, hosts of the fiesta. They are considered auxiliaries of the Pahkome and hosts to the church group. A fiesta is not possible unless one Pascola and his accompanying musicians open and close it.

The Pascola Dance is directed toward a human audience rather than a spiritual patron. The dancers face the

Pascola dancer. A masked Yaqui Pascola dancer in 1955, dancing to the music of flute and drum during San Ignacio fiesta. *Photograph by G. Iacono. Arizona State Museum, University of Arizona.*

the Pascola mask is not feared. The masked part of the ceremony is accompanied by the music of drum and whistle, the unmasked part to that of the Mexican harp and violin.

Because every fiesta must begin with a Pascola and musicians, the Pascolas provide an element of continuity in the Yaqui ceremonial year.

PASSING OF THE DRUM CEREMONY *Osage* A ceremony conducted after a drumkeeper has decided to pass or transfer the sacred drum associated with the I'N-LON-SCHKA CEREMONIAL DANCE to a new drumkeeper. Variations exist in the three Osage communities on the procedure they follow for filling the position. Generally, the new drumkeeper has to meet certain criteria, including being a qualified eldest son. When the individual chosen for the honor and responsibility agrees to accept the role, an announcement is made, and the transfer takes place. An ACCEPTANCE OF THE DRUM CEREMONY is held the following June during the four-day I'n-Lon-Schka Ceremonial Dance. (See also BEN MASHUNKASHAY.)

PATHESKE (Long Nose) *(fl. 1850s) Winnebago (Ho-Chunk)* A prophet who introduced a new dance, which he called the Friendship Dance, about 1852 or 1853. After ritually fasting for several days, Patheske indicated that he was taken to the other world, where he saw a group of spirits performing the dance. He then taught the Friendship Dance to the people, as instructed, and told them that it was to be held at intervals for a period of one year. At the end of that time, the people were to go on a war expedition against their hereditary enemy, the Dakota. He designated a young man named Saraminuka to serve as the expedition's leader. After the people performed the dance until spring as they had been instructed, Patheske announced a new revelation and canceled the war plan. Denouncing him as an impostor, his followers then abandoned the Friendship Dance. A short time later Saraminuka was killed in an accident, and his death was viewed as spiritual retribution for not carrying out his role in Patheske's prophecy. The prophet died a few years later while serving as a tribal delegate to Washington, D.C.

PAUPANAKISS, EDWARD *(1840–1911) Cree* Methodist missionary. Born at Norway House, Manitoba, Paupanakiss was a full-blood Cree whose father was a shaman. His Christian influences included education under Reverend JAMES EVANS and employment by the Hudson's Bay Company during his youth. After converting to Christianity in 1873, Paupanakiss held a religious leadership position at the Nelson House Mission from 1874 to 1880. He also served as a local preacher before becoming ordained about 1889. After his ordination, he continued to work in the Indian mission

audience, not the altar set up on the other side of the *ramada* (arbor). In their initial ritual the leader or manager of the Pascolas, who is not himself a dancer, takes the dancers to the house yard cross to say the necessary prayers before the night of dancing and clowning.

The Pascola Dance is an individual rather than a group performance, and each Pascola has an individual style that includes different uses of arms, body postures, and personally conceived dance steps. The dancers learn skills through direct solicitation of the "little animals" in the *huya aniya*, particularly the goat. The opening ritual includes prayers to the little animals, and the Pascolas clown, dance, and tell stories, involving members of the audience in their antics and providing relief from the religious ceremonies.

The Pascola Dance itself alternates between a masked and an unmasked performance. The Pascola's mask is generally an adult male face carved in relief out of cottonwood, although it may also represent dogs, coyotes, or goats, with considerable variation. The mask, which barely covers the face, is painted dull black and has a long beard of white horsehair. Designs are applied to the masks by painting, incising, or inlaying objects into the wood. Unlike the masks of the Yaqui CHAPAYEKA, which are considered dangerous, field. When he was sent to Oxford House to work with FREDERICK GEORGE STEVENS and others, he served a number of Algonquian groups in the area. By 1907, when he testified at the trial of the shaman JOSEPH FIDDLER, Paupanakiss had served as a local preacher for eight years and as a missionary for 18 years. He died on July 26, 1911, at Norway House.

PAUTIWA *Zuni* The KACHINA chief of the spirit village of KOLHU/WALA-WA. He is considered benovolent and kind. He controls the ceremonial calendar, and no kachina can visit the Zuni Pueblo unless Pautiwa approves and sends it. He presides over the spirit village and receives the spirits of the dead. He appoints important kachinas, sanctions their impersonations, and approves of ceremonies. Human beings appeal to him when they are in trouble or need help. He travels in the shape of a duck. His grandfather is Kiaklo, who acts as his speaker every four years when initiations of young boys are announced, and he visits the pueblos to ensure that boys are initiated into kachina cults. Pautiwa's visits, or his impersonation by kachina members, is limited to three appearances each year, at the solstices and at the MOLAWIA ceremony of the CORN MAIDENS.

PEACH DANCE *Havasupai* An annual harvest festival held at Havasupai, Arizona, in late August or early September to give thanks to the Creator for crops and to petition for continued protection and care. The rituals involve dancing, feasting, horse racing, trading, and visiting.

PECK, EDMUND JAMES *(1850–1924)* Anglican missionary who worked among the Inuit people of Hudson Bay and completed extensive linguistic work. Peck was born on April 15, 1850, in Rusholme near Manchester, England. After serving more than 10 years in the British navy, he enrolled in an institute of the CHURCH MISSIONARY SOCIETY in 1875. The following year he began the work that was to last most of his life. After devising a syllabary for the Inuit language, he began translating religious works. In addition to his devotional materials, he wrote *Eskimo grammar* (Ottawa, 1919), which was later reprinted in 1931 and revised in 1954. Another book, *The Eskimo, our brethren of the Arctic,* was published in 1922. Peck died on September 10, 1924, in Toronto.

PEKWIN *Zuni* A most revered and most holy man in Zuni; the human counterpart and deputy of the Zuni spirit Kiaklo. (Kiaklo received all of the Zuni people's stories during a visit to the Council of the Gods, which resides under the Lake of the Dead.) He holds responsibility for the welfare of the community and coordinates the annual calendar of the Zuni ceremonial system. He is the Sun Priest, spokesman for the

sun, or deputy to the sun father and announces the winter and summer solstice ceremonies that honor the sun. He prepares and deposits prayersticks in shrines at sacred Corn Mountain and in the fields as offerings to the sun and deceased sun priests while observing food fasts and continency. He is the chief of other priests, installs new priests, and as supreme head of the Zuni Pueblo presides over the council of priests who have political authority over the Zuni Pueblo. He is supposed to know and be able to recite all of the stories of Zuni creation. When the office of Sun Priest is vacant, another chief presides.

PELOTTE, DONALD E. *(b. 1945) Abenaki* The first American Indian Catholic bishop in the United States. Born in Maine, Pelotte's mother is French Canadian and his father is Abenaki. When he was 14 years old, he entered the seminary. He was educated at Fordham University, where he earned a Ph.D. in theology. In 1986 Pelotte became coadjutor bishop of the Gallup diocese, which comprises more than 55,000 square miles in northeastern Arizona and northwestern New Mexico. Bishop Pelotte's consecration on May 6, 1986, elevated him to the highest position held by an American Indian in the Catholic hierarchy. His investiture included Apache and Zuni dances, Mass, gifts of pottery and sacred corn, and Indian prayers chanted to drums. (See also BOUCHARD, JAMES CHRYSOSTOM; GORDON, PHILIP B.; NEGAHNQUET, ALBERT.)

PEOPLE V. FOSTER ALPHONSE RED ELK (Criminal Number 17157, Second Appellate District, California Court of Appeals, 1970) *(1970)* In this California case Red Elk, a Lakota, was arrested on an automobile theft charge and was found to possess PEYOTE. He was convicted on both auto theft and narcotics possession charges. Red Elk appealed his drug conviction as well as the conditions of a three-year sentence of probation. The sentencing terms required that he not possess or use narcotics and that he stay away from drug users or dealers. Red Elk, who stated that he was a member of the NATIVE AMERICAN CHURCH, testified that the probation conditions prohibited him from freely practicing his religion and from associating with other peyotists. The California Court of Appeals upheld his conviction but ruled that the terms of his probation were illegal. The court reaffirmed that legitimate practitioners of the PEYOTE RELIGION could use peyote but concluded that Red Elk was not a bona fide member of the Native American Church. The court held that he could not legally use the substance until such time as he became a legitimate practitioner of the faith. The probation conditions were found to be illegal because they violated the defendant's First Amendment rights and his potential pursuit of religious expression. (See Subject Index for related legal cases included in this volume.)

PEOPLE V. WOODY (61 Cal.2d 716, 40 Cal.Rptr.69, 394 P.2d 813)

A landmark California Supreme Court case concerning the use of PEYOTE. Navajo peyotists JACK WOODY, Leon B. Anderson, and Dan Dee Nez were arrested on April 28, 1962, during a NATIVE AMERICAN CHURCH service conducted by ROADMAN TRUMAN DAILEY in a hogan near Needles, California. The defendants were convicted of violating section 11500 of the Health and Safety Code, which prohibited unauthorized possession of peyote. The case was then appealed to the district court of appeals in Los Angeles, where the conviction was upheld. A further appeal to the California Supreme Court was made by the peyotists, who contended that the sacramental use of peyote was essential to their religious faith. They further contended that their right to freely exercise their religion had been violated. The prosecution argued that compelling state interests necessitated an abridgement of the First Amendment rights of the defendants and sought to convince the court that peyote use resulted in harmful consequences. The California Supreme Court reversed the convictions and acquitted the defendants. The court held that any compelling state interests were outweighed by the First Amendment rights of the peyotists. It further held that peyote use presented "only slight danger" to the state and to its enforcement of laws. In reversing the judgment of the lower courts, Justice J. Tobriner wrote: "We preserve a greater value than an ancient tradition when we protect the rights of the Indians who honestly practiced an old religion in using peyote one night at a meeting in a desert hogan near Needles, California." Banning the use of peyote by the defendants, he stated, would take away "the theological heart of Peyotism." (See also PEYOTE RELIGION; Subject Index for related legal cases included in this volume.)

PERRYMAN, JAMES (Pahos Harjo) (?–c. 1882) Creek

A Baptist minister and interpreter. One of the eight children of Benjamin Perryman (Steek-cha-ko-me-co), a prominent Creek town chief in Alabama. Perryman family members arrived in Indian Territory in 1828 and settled in an area that later became Wagoner County, Oklahoma. James was educated in mission schools and served as an interpreter to JOHN FLEMING, the Presbyterian missionary who worked among his people. He helped translate two of the first books written in the Creek language. Perryman later assisted ANN ELIZA WORCESTER ROBERTSON in translating the Bible, contributing to Ephesians, Titus, James, and most of the book of Acts. He also aided in the completion of a Creek hymn book. Initially a Presbyterian, he eventually became a Baptist and served as a minister of that faith for 30 years. During the Civil War Perryman served on the side of the Confederacy. He died about 1882 at Coweta. His nephews JOSEPH MOSES PERRYMAN and THOMAS WARD PERRYMAN also served as ministers.

PERRYMAN, JOSEPH MOSES (1883–?) Creek

A minister who served two denominations, Presbyterian and Baptist. Born in 1833, he was the grandson of Benjamin Perryman, a Creek town chief and the son of Moses Perryman. After attending school at Coweta Mission in Indian Territory (present-day Oklahoma) until 1853, he studied for the Presbyterian ministry for three years and received his license to preach in 1860. During the Civil War he served the Confederacy in Company H, First Creek Regiment of Mounted Volunteers, attaining the rank of first lieutenant. After the war ended, he was ordained a Presbyterian minister at Wapanucka in the Chickasaw Nation in present-day Oklahoma. Besides forming the North Fork Presbyterian Church, he took charge of the mission school under the auspices of the South Presbyterian Synod. Perryman ended his Presbyterian affiliation about 1878 and a short time later was ordained to the Baptist ministry. His uncle JAMES PERRYMAN and his cousin THOMAS WARD PERRYMAN were also ministers.

PERRYMAN, THOMAS WARD (1839–1903) Creek

A Presbyterian minister, translator, and political leader who was born to Hattie and Lewis Perryman at Big Springtown in Indian Territory (present-day Oklahoma) on July 24, 1839. He enrolled in the Tullahassee Mission school when it opened on March 1, 1850, and remained there until 1858. When the Civil War broke out, he enlisted in Company H of the First Creek Regiment of Mounted Volunteers on August 9, 1861, and fought for the Confederacy. He later reversed sides, joining the Union army on December 7, 1862, as part of Company 1, First Regiment, Indian Home Guards, of the Kansas Infantry. After his honorable discharge on May 31, 1865, Perryman returned home and went into business with his brothers. About 1872 he enrolled in religious studies under the Reverend WILLIAM SCHENCK ROBERTSON for a three-year period. During that time he assisted the missionary's wife, ANN ELIZA WORCESTER ROBERTSON, in her Creek translation work, completing Genesis and the book of Psalms. Perryman was licensed as a minister in 1875 and ordained the following year by the Kansas Presbytery. He was then placed in charge of the Creek Nation's western district. Perryman was also active in the political life of his people. He began serving the first of several terms in the Creek House of Warriors in 1868, as a district attorney in 1871, and as a presiding officer of the House of Kings in 1891 and 1896.

Although he ran for principal chief in 1895, he was defeated. Perryman died on February 11, 1903, in Kansas City. After his first wife died, he married Eva L. Brown, a mission school teacher who assisted in his religious work. Perryman's uncle JAMES PERRYMAN and his cousin JOSEPH PERRYMAN were also ministers.

PERSON *Inuit, Aleut* Called *inua* in the northern Inuit language and *yua* in the Bering Sea language, a "person" is a distinct order of spirit beings. Inuit and Aleut of Alaska unlike the Inuit of central and eastern regions believe that places, objects, animals, and nonhuman creatures have "persons" distinct from souls. "Persons" are spiritual projections of the idea of each type. For example, the "person" of a walrus is not the "person" of an individual walrus but that of the band or species. The animal "person," which has a perpetual existence, controls the activities of all members of the species. It is also referred to as "owner" or "generic spirit" or the guardian spirit of a species. (See also SOUL [Inuit].)

PERSONAL CHANT *Iroquois* One of the ancient FOUR SACRED CEREMONIES given by the Creator, in which a man or pair of men express thanksgiving. The chanter, who has his own set of songs, which are to some extent property of his family and clan, progresses across a room, alternating between walking and singing, standing and praying. The chant is composed of individual thanksgiving for one's wife, family, or life of a friend. The ceremony was formerly a warrior's boasting song or the last song sung by a warrior before death. The prophet HANDSOME LAKE, who permitted no warlike demonstrations to invade the longhouse, transformed the chant into an expression of thanksgiving. Men sing personal chants during the MIDWINTER CEREMONY, GREEN CORN, SUN AND MOON CEREMONY, and the HARVEST FESTIVAL. Women also sing personal chants at some planting ceremonies.

PETTER, BERTHA ELISE KINSINGER *(1872–?)* Mennonite missionary to the Cheyenne people. Born in Trenton, Ohio, Petter was also educated in Ohio, attending elementary school in Trenton, the National Normal University in Ada, and Wittenberg College in Springfield, where she earned a bachelor's degree in 1896. In 1910 she also completed her master's degree. Kinsinger taught in the Mennonite mission school in Cantonment, Indian Territory (present-day Oklahoma), from 1896 to 1900 before serving as a gospel worker in mission camps and assisting RODOLPHE CHARLES PETTER in his Cheyenne linguistic work from 1900 to 1911. After her marriage to Petter in 1911 in Cantonment, she continued to serve as his assistant. Besides her other missionary duties, she contributed to the completion of his Chey-

enne publications by helping with researching, proofreading, and related tasks. After Rodolphe Petter's death in 1947, Bertha remained in the parsonage next to the church renamed in his honor and was still living there in 1959. It is uncertain when she died.

PETTER, RODOLPHE CHARLES *(1865–1947)* Mennonite missionary and linguist among the Cheyenne people. Born on February 19, 1865, at Vevey on Lake Geneva, Switzerland, Petter attended the Basel Missionsschule from 1883 to 1889. During the course of his military training, he met Samuel Gerber, a Mennonite, and visited the Jura Mountain members of the Mennonite religion who told him of mission work among American Indians. He arrived in New York with his wife, Marie Gerber, in 1890 to begin mission work under auspices of the General Conference Mennonite Church. After spending a year at Oberlin College in Ohio, the couple left for Cantonment, Indian Territory (present-day Oklahoma), to begin their work among the Southern Cheyenne. Upon their arrival in 1891, they began learning the Native language. Petter later amazed members of the tribe's northern division with his fluency in the language during an 1899 visit, and they named him "Cheyenne Talker." Following the death of his wife, Marie, in 1910, he married BERTHA ELISE KINSINGER (PETTER), another Mennonite missionary, on November 28, 1911. In 1916, after 25 years among the Southern Cheyenne, the Petters moved to Montana, where they began working with the Northern Cheyenne. An authority on the Cheyenne language, Petter devised a writing system and completed a number of publications, including *English-Cheyenne Dictionary* (1915), *Cheyenne Grammar* (1952), and *Reminiscences of the Past Years in Mission Service Among the Cheyenne* (n.d.). He also translated the entire New Testament, portions of the Old Testament, *Pilgrim's Progress*, and a hymnal. His mission reports appeared mainly in *The Mennonite*. Petter's death on January 6, 1947, ended more than 55 years of missionary work among the Cheyenne people. The Lame Deer Mennonite Mission Church on the reservation in Montana was renamed the Petter Memorial Mennonite Church in his honor. The Rodolphe Petter Collection is housed at Bethel College in Kansas.

PEYOTE A species of small, spineless cactus found in a limited growth area, principally in present-day Mexico and the state of Texas. Its name comes from *peyotl*, a Nahuatl word meaning "caterpillar," describing the down-like center of the peyote "button." Classified as *Lophophora williamsii* since 1894, peyote has a long history of usage among indigenous people in the growth area of the plant (and beyond), for religious and medicinal purposes. The exposed top of the plant, the portion harvested, is cut off and dried into buttons. The remaining roots eventually produce more buttons. Peyote, which possesses psychedelic properties, contains a number of alkaloids, including anhalamine, anhalonine, anhalonidine, lophophorine, mescaline, and peyotine. It has often been incorrectly identified as mescal, perhaps because it grows in similar areas and has other physical similarities.

Peyote is the sacrament of the NATIVE AMERICAN CHURCH and is essential to the practice of the PEYOTE RELIGION. As a sacred plant of divine origin, it is believed to possess great healing and teaching powers. Its use, circumscribed by the tenets and practices of the Peyote Religion, occurs in a ritual or ceremonial context. Tribal names for peyote include *wokwi* or *wokowi* (said to refer to cacti in Comanche), *walena* (the Taos word for medicine) and *seni* or *se-nay* (the Kiowa name meaning prickly fruit). The peyote, generally chewed or made into tea, tastes bitter and is known to produce nausea or vomiting in those who are unaccustomed to it. Contrary to popular belief, it is neither harmful nor habit-forming. A large, special peyote button, selected for placement on the altar during a religious service, is known as the Chief Peyote or Father Peyote. Peyote use, of pre-Columbian origin among Native people, was first recorded at the time of the Spanish conquest of Mexico. Condemned by Catholic missionaries, peyote was banned in 1620 by an edict of the Spanish Inquisition. Peyotism opposition has continued since that time, despite evidence of its ancient religious origins and practices, expert medical testimony attesting to its non-harmful effects, and First Amendment protection of freedom of religion.

PEYOTE AND PENTAGON RULE Native American U.S. soldiers will be allowed to use PEYOTE, the sacrament of the NATIVE AMERICAN CHURCH, in religious ceremonies under a draft rule issued on April 27, 1997, by the Pentagon. The rule would make Pentagon policy consistent with the AMERICAN INDIAN RELIGIOUS FREEDOM ACT AMENDMENTS OF 1994 *(P. L. 103–344, 108 Stat. 3125)* signed on October 6, 1994, by President Bill Clinton that protects Native Americans' right to use peyote in their religious services.

Under the military guidelines, drawn up by Captain Mel Ferguson of the navy and executive director of the Armed Forces Chaplain's Board, peyote use is restricted to enrolled tribal members who are also members of the Native American Church. The draft rule would bar the use or possession of peyote on military vehicles, aircraft, and ships, but it would allow the use and possession on military bases with the consent of the commanding officer. The celebrant must stop using peyote at least 24 hours before returning to active duty. The rule would apply to more than 9,200 members of the armed services, 5 percent of whom belong to the Native American Church, which has about 250,000 members. Peyote is a holy medicine that provides spiritual insight and peace of mind.

Soldiers will have to notify their commanding officers of their plans to participate in religious rites in which peyote will be ingested. They also have to notify their superiors after returning from such ceremonies because of concerns that worshipers will be "impaired" by the effects of the medicine. Peyote "buttons" contain mescaline that stays in the body for about 12 hours.

Soldiers fear informing their superiors about their religious practices will damage their military careers. Native soldiers have reported being threatened with punishment and disqualification from high-risk jobs and discouraged from enlistment for acknowledging their membership in the Native American Church.

PEYOTE RELIGION A religion with pre-Columbian origins that is centered around the sacramental use of PEYOTE, a small spineless cactus found growing principally in the Rio Grande valley in present-day Mexico and the state of Texas. The indigenous people in the growth area of the plant are believed to have begun using *peyotl,* as it was called in the Nahuatl language, for religious and other purposes as long as 10,000 years ago. It is likely that peyote was used then, as in more recent times, to heal, to pray, to prophesy, to locate lost articles, and to seek spiritual aid. By the time the Spaniards arrived in Mexico, peyotism already had a long history of existence and was known to tribal groups far beyond the region where the plant grows. Peyote use was first recorded by the Franciscan missionary Bernardino de Sahagun, who described it among the Chichimec tribal group in Mexico in the 1500s. He noted that the Chichimec, who called the plant peiotl, believed that its powers included protecting them from danger. Other descriptions began to appear, including those condemning its use. In 1620, during the Spanish Inquisition, an edict was issued banning peyotism as an act of superstition. The Inquisitors decreed that repercussions would result for anyone who disobeyed the decree just as they would for those suspected of heresy in the judgment of the Catholic Church. Hearings involving court cases prosecuted under the edict were held in 45 Spanish settlements or towns over the next 265 years.

In the United States peyotism is believed to have originated with tribal groups in or near the growth area of peyote at the start of the 19th century. These included the Carrizo, the Lipan Apache, the Mescalero Apache, the Tonkawa, and the Caddo. The evidence seems to favor the Carrizo, a Coahuiltecan group, who originally lived in the growth area and were likely to have used peyote before the Spanish arrived. A 1649 account documented Carrizo peyotism, indicating that it included an all-night ceremony with drumming and singing. It is believed that peyotism was diffused by the Carrizo to the Lipan Apache and Tonkawa, who in turn took it to the Kiowa, Kiowa-Apache, Comanche, and other tribes in Indian Territory or present-day Oklahoma. BILLY CHIWAT and PINERO, Lipan Apache who are identified as the earliest peyotists in Indian Territory, conducted peyote ceremonies for QUANAH PARKER, the Comanche chief who became a peyote ROADMAN, or leader, and other tribal people.

One Kiowa version of the Peyote Religion's origin indicates that a long time ago a young pregnant woman was traveling far from home on a food-gathering expedition. Unable to keep up with the other people in her party, she became separated from them. The woman, exhausted and afraid, gave birth to her child alone, without the comfort and assistance she would have received from family and friends. In her weakened, helpless state she received spiritual help. The woman was directed to the peyote plant and instructed to eat some of it. Her strength miraculously returned and she was able to travel. With the guidance of the plant's spirit, she found her people. The woman then instructed them in the songs, prayers, and rituals of the sacred plant. The people continued to sing and pray with peyote, receiving visionary inspiration and other blessings from it. The young woman who brought the sacred gift became venerated in religious services as the Peyote Woman.

There are two primary ceremonies in the Peyote Religion: the Half-Moon and the Big Moon. The Half-Moon (also called the Tipi Way, the Quanah Parker Way, the Comanche Way or the Kiowa Way) is named for the crescent-shaped altar on which the Chief Peyote rests. This ceremony is generally described as older and more traditional than the Big Moon variation (which also became known as the Moonhead and Cross Fire) introduced by JOHN WILSON, the Caddo roadman. First described in Indian Territory by the ethnologist James Mooney in 1891, the Half-Moon Ceremony is believed to have originated among Native people in the peyote growth area. According to Omer C. Stewart, an authority on the Peyote Religion, Mooney's descriptions reveal a ceremony different from that conducted in Mexico but with basic similarities, a ceremony with Christian influences but so different that Christians attempted to eradicate it, and a ceremony that has continued to be conducted in essentially the same way to the present.

The Big Moon peyote ceremony, the second primary ceremony, was originated by John Wilson, who introduced it some time after 1800 in Indian Territory. Wilson attributed his ritual to divine revelation. It is also likely that he was influenced by Half-Moon peyotism, since the two ceremonies share basic similarities. The main difference introduced by

Wilson was a larger, horseshoe-shaped altar, rather than the crescent-shaped one. The ceremony, reflecting Wilson's exposure to Catholicism and other religions, was characterized by its incorporation of biblical and Christian influences. In contrast, the Half-Moon Ceremony had more frequent references to traditional elements, including origin stories of peyote, the use of tobacco, and concepts such as the Great Spirit and Mother Earth.

The differences between the Half-Moon and Big Moon Ceremonies were often a matter of degree, since both incorporated aspects of Indian culture and Christianity. The two ceremonies shared many commonalities. Both emphasized the divine role of peyote and its power to teach and heal; both opposed the use of liquor and believed that peyote destroyed the taste for it; and in both, peyote was taken to concentrate and to learn, not for visions. Wilson reportedly held Big Moon Ceremonies, not only for the Caddo, but also for the Delaware (Lenni Lenape), Osage, Quapaw, and Wichita. Ethnologists identified the Winnebago (Ho-Chunk), Kickapoo, Omaha, and Potawatomi as patterning their peyote ceremonies after Wilson's.

In time, Wilson's Big Moon Ceremony developed into the Cross Fire ritual, which shared similar features. The adherents of both ceremonies included preaching, prophecy, baptism, and other similarities and limited or prohibited tobacco use. Other shared features of the Big Moon and Cross Fire were more elaborate altars, ashes formed into ceremonial designs, the construction of permanent churches and altars, and, in some areas, peyote cemeteries. According to Stewart, since about 1900 the Cross Fire had become an alternate form of peyotism among the Ojibway, Menominee, Sioux, Shoshone, Ute, Gosiute, and, later, the Navajo (Dineh). Peyotists often attended both Half-Moon and Big Moon peyote ceremonies when they had the opportunity. Although following a particular way and aware of the differences, they often enjoyed one another's services.

The all-night peyote service, usually called a meeting, generally takes place on Saturday. Among the participants are the roadman, the leader; the chief drummer, who provides drum accompaniment to the sacred songs; and the cedarman, who places cedar in the fire to consecrate ritual objects. Ceremonial objects include a staff, rattle, whistle, drum, and a feather fan. A large, special button of peyote, selected as the Chief Peyote, is placed on the altar. Other peyote buttons are also present to be used by the participants during the course of the ceremony. Ceremonial elements, with some variations, generally include the consecration of the drum and other objects in cedar smoke, the distribution of tobacco for ritual smoking in those ceremonies where it is included, the passing and use of peyote, the singing of an opening song, the circulating of the staff, fan, drum, and rattle to each participant, who sings four songs with them before giving them to the next person, and the continuation of singing until midnight. It also includes the Midnight Water Call, when the fireman brings a pail of water into the ceremony for cedar smoke consecration. After offering some of the water to Mother Earth, the participants pass it around to drink. Following the Midnight Water Call, there is a brief recess, which is a period of quiet before the ceremony resumes.

The meeting continues with singing, the taking of peyote, participant prayers, and perhaps a healing ceremony. At sunrise the Dawn Song, a special sacred song, is sung by the roadman. The Peyote Woman, often the wife of a participant, brings in the water for blessing, and it is then circulated among the worshipers to drink. A ceremonial breakfast follows at which corn, meat, fruit, and water are served. The ceremony may conclude with a talk by the roadman or a Bible reading, if it is a Cross Fire ritual. The final song, the Quitting Song, is then sung.

In 1918 the NATIVE AMERICAN CHURCH was organized by adherents of the Peyote Religion who sought to protect their religious practices from attack by anti-peyotist adversaries. Peyotism opposition has been manifested at the federal, state, and local levels. Peyotists have been involved in extensive litigation to fight for the right to practice their religion. Some legal cases, including *PEOPLE V. WOODY* and *STATE OF ARIZONA V. MARY ATTAKAI,* have been favorable to peyotists. Others, including the United States Supreme Court's 1990 decision in *EMPLOYMENT DIVISION, DEPARTMENT OF HUMAN RESOURCES OF OREGON, ET AL. V. SMITH ET AL.,* have not. (See Subject Index for other legal cases involving peyote use included in this volume.)

PEYOTE WAY CHURCH OF GOD, INC. V. SMITH (556 F.Supp. 632 [1983]) *(1983)* A U.S. District Court case heard in Dallas, Texas, when Immanuel Paradeahtan Trujillo filed suit to test the constitutionality of federal and Texas state narcotics laws that allow the use of PEYOTE by members of the NATIVE AMERICAN CHURCH. The Texas statute prohibits the exemption to its drug laws for use of peyote by church members with less than one-quarter degree of Indian blood. Trujillo's newly established Peyote Way Church of God, which sought the religious use of peyote for Native Americans of less than 25 percent Indian blood and non-Indians, also included adherence to Mormon dietary laws in its practices. The church claimed that the state's law violated its free exercise and equal protection rights under the First and Fourteenth Amendments. The district court ruled against the Peyote Way Church of God, while upholding the constitutionality of the religious ex-

emption. It held that the United States had a special fiduciary responsibility to American Indians and had a duty to preserve Native American religion and culture. The court indicated that Congress recognized this duty in the AMERICAN INDIAN RELIGIOUS FREEDOM ACT OF 1978. It stated that the federal and Texas exemptions acknowledged the necessity of peyote to the survival of a Native American religion. (See also PEYOTE RELIGION; Subject Index, for related legal cases included in this volume.)

PEYOTISM OPPOSITION Efforts to suppress the indigenous use of PEYOTE, a small, spineless cactus that grows primarily in the Rio Grande valley, can be traced back to the early Spaniards in the New World. With the Spanish conquest of Mexico and the earliest written accounts of peyotism, the Catholic authorities began their attempts to eradicate the practice. Viewing peyote use as evil and fearing its spread, missionaries preached against it. In 1620 during the Spanish Inquisition, an edict was issued banning peyotism as an act of superstition. The Inquisitors warned that those who disobeyed the decree would suffer the same punishment as those suspected of heresy. Hearings involving court cases prosecuted under the edict were held in 45 Spanish settlements or towns over the next 265 years.

Just as the Spanish conquest had brought powerful opposition against peyotism centuries earlier in Mexico, Christian missionaries and Indian agents of the federal government began opposing the religious practice in the United States at the end of the 19th century. First noting peyote use among tribal groups in Indian Territory (present-day Oklahoma), the authorities began efforts to eradicate it. Peyotism, along with other indigenous religious and cultural practices, was viewed as heathen superstition that had to be rooted out and replaced by Christianity and "civilization." Peyotists became subject to raids, arrest, and incarceration. By 1918, followers of the PEYOTE RELIGION had organized the NATIVE AMERICAN CHURCH in an effort to protect their religious beliefs and practices. Efforts to suppress peyote have been manifested at the federal, state, and local levels through directives, legislation, and litigation.

Federal Opposition

On June 6, 1888, E. E. White, the Indian agent overseeing the Kiowa, Comanche, and Wichita agency in Indian Territory, or present-day Oklahoma, originated an order that stated:

> Wherefore all Indians on this Reservation are hereby forbidden to eat any of said [mescal] beans, or to drink any decoction or fermentation thereof, or liquor distilled therefrom, or to sell or give to any Indian or have in his possession, any of these beans. Any Indian convicted of

Delegation of peyotists. The delegation that appeared with the medical committee before the Oklahoma Constitutional Convention to decide the legality of peyote in the state in 1907. They are, front row, left to right: Tennyson Berry (Kiowa-Apache); Codsy (Kiowa); Chief Apache John (Kiowa-Apache); Otto Wells (Comanche); Chief Quanah Parker (Comanche); Chief Apheatone (Kiowa); Little Bird (Cheyenne); Young Calf (Cheyenne); second row, right to left: Ned Brace (Kiowa); Joseph Blackbear (Cheyenne); and on the end, Leonard Tyler (Cheyenne). *Fort Sill Museum, Oklahoma.*

violating this order will be punished by the cutting of his annuity goods and rations according to the aggravation of the case.

The order was eventually adopted by the federal government as a general policy on Indian reservations. Two years after E. E. White's directive, Bureau of Indian Affairs Commissioner Thomas J. Morgan wrote:

> The Court of Indian Offenses at your agency shall consider the use, sale, exchange, gift, or introduction of the mescal bean as a misdemeanor punishable under Section 9 [on intoxicants] of the Rules governing the Court of Indian Offenses.

The COURTS OF INDIAN OFFENSES, established in 1883, prohibited a number of tribal customs including the performance of "old heathenish dances," plural marriages, practices of medicine men, property destruction associated with death and burial customs, and the use of intoxicants. Agents assigned to reservations and/or judges serving on the tribal courts enforced the regulations on Indian reservations.

A federal law making it an offense "to furnish any article whatsoever under any name, label, or brand which produces intoxication to any Indian ward of the Government" was passed in 1897 (Act of January 30, 1897, 29 Stat. 506). Some officials believed that the law applied, not only to alcohol, but to peyote as well. Court cases testing this application included the arrests of peyotists MEDICINE NECK (Potawatomi) in Wisconsin (1914), WILLIAM RED NEST (Lakota) in South Dakota (1915), and HARRY BLACK BEAR (Lakota) also from South Dakota (1916). The federal statute was found not to apply to peyote. Nonetheless, peyotists continued to be harassed under the 1897 law or through orders from Indian agents. Raids, arrests, confiscation of property, fines, and jail terms continued for adherents of the peyote religion.

In 1912 the board of commissioners, appointed to oversee the Bureau of Indian Affairs, began to lobby for a federal law banning peyote. The first federal bills were introduced by South Dakota representative Harry L. Gandy and Kansas senator W. W. Thompson. The Gandy bill, proposed in 1916, sought to prohibit "traffic in peyote, including its sale to Indians, introduction into the Country, importation and transportation." Thompson's anti-peyote bill (S. 3526), introduced during the same period, was blocked in the Senate and later replaced by another bill. After the Gandy bill's defeat in 1916, it was resubmitted in 1917. Following hearings on peyotism in 1918, the efforts to enact a law to prohibit peyote culminated in an anti-peyote bill, passed by the House of Representatives but defeated in the Senate. In 1923, after other defeats, anti-peyotists succeeded in adding an amendment to an Indian appropriation bill for $25,000 to suppress "traffic in intoxicating liquors and deleterious drugs, including peyote, among Indians."

Although federal anti-peyote bills continued to be introduced for a number of years, it was not until 1937 that another one had much impact. At that time, New Mexico's senator Dennis Chavez, influenced by anti-peyotists Mabel Dodge Luhan and Judge Henry A. Kiker, submitted Senate bill 1399 "to prohibit the interstate transportation of anhalonium, commonly known as peyote." After a full hearing on the measure, it was defeated. In 1963, Florida representative Dante B. Fascell attempted to add peyote to the law regulating the sale of marijuana; however, the proposal failed. Peyotists continue to be arrested under other federal drug laws, including the Drug Abuse Control Act of 1965, the Federal Food, Drug, and Cosmetic Act of 1965, and the Controlled Substance Act of 1970, although they allow peyote use in bona fide religious ceremonies of the Native American Church. A 1979 report on the AMERICAN INDIAN RELIGIOUS FREEDOM ACT OF 1978 noted that some federal officials, unaware of the exemptions, confiscated peyote from religious practitioners.

State and Territorial Opposition

The first statute to prohibit the use of peyote was effected in Indian Territory in 1899 through the efforts of A. E. Woodson, the federal agent of the Cheyenne and Arapaho agency in Darlington. It states:

Section 2652—That it shall be unlawful for any person to introduce on any Indian reservation or Indian allotment situated within this Territory or to have in possession, barter, sell, give, or otherwise dispose of, any "Mescal Bean," or the produce of any such drug, to any allotted Indian in this Territory . . . Any person who shall violate the

provisions of this Act in this Territory, shall be deemed guilty of a misdemeanor, and, upon conviction, thereof, shall be fined in a sum not less than twenty-five dollars, nor more than two hundred dollars, be confined in the county jail for not more than six months, or be assessed both such fine and imprisonment in the discretion of the court. (Oklahoma, *Session Laws,* 1899, pp. 122–23).

After a raid on a peyote ceremony and the arrest of peyotists in 1907, the law was tested in court. The peyotists involved were sentenced to a fine and incarceration by a probate judge. After an appeal to Oklahoma's district court in Kingfisher County, the case was dismissed because the peyotists had used peyote, not mescal, and the two substances were not the same. Another case, also in 1907, was dismissed for the same reason a short time later. That same year, an attempt was made to amend the 1899 statute to forbid the use of peyote, but the proposed legislation was defeated.

Elsewhere, anti-peyote legislation resulted from the efforts of Bureau of Indian Affairs officials to ban peyotism. In Kansas, for instance, the superintendent of the Prairie Potawatomi agency, worked for the enactment of a state law banning peyote use and arrested a number of peyotists as soon as it was passed in 1919. According to Omer C. Stewart, the author of *Peyote Religion* (1987), by the beginning of 1924, 26 peyotists had served jail terms in that state. Other states in which anti-peyote laws were passed included Utah, Colorado, and Nevada (1917); Arizona, Montana, North Dakota, and South Dakota (1923); Iowa (1925); New Mexico and Wyoming (1929); and Idaho (1933). A recent source indicates that all of these states, except Idaho, North Dakota, and Utah, later amended their anti-peyote laws to allow for bona fide religious use by the Native American Church. Other states that passed anti-peyote laws included California (1959), New York (1965), and Texas (1967). The California and New York laws are said to have been aimed at non-Indian drug abusers and to have had little effect on Native Americans. The Native American Church of North America successfully lobbied to have Texas, where pilgrimages are made to obtain peyote, amend its law. The exemption to the Texas Narcotics Law of 1969 states:

The provisions of this Act relating to the possession and distribution of peyote shall not apply to the use of peyote by members of the Native American Church in bona fide religious ceremonies of the church. However, persons who supply the substance to the church are required to register and maintain appropriate records of receipts and disbursements in accordance with rules promulgated by the director. The exemption granted to members of the Native American Church under this section does not apply to a member with less than 25 percent Indian blood.

Compliance with the terms of the exemption proved to be difficult for the Native American Church, peyote suppliers, and state officials because of the record-keeping requirements and the stipulation that peyote church membership information be provided.

Tribal Opposition

Navajo (Dineh) Although peyotism began in one area of the large Navajo Reservation of the Southwest before 1920, it escaped the notice of tribal officialdom over the next 20 years. In 1940, however, in response to pressure from anti-peyotist Mabel Dodge Luhan, an influential New Yorker who had married a Taos Indian, Antonio Luhan, New Mexico's Senator Dennis Chavez requested an investigation of peyotism on the reservation in 1940. The investigation culminated in the Navajo tribal council's passage of an anti-peyote ordinance on June 3, 1940. One of the objections to peyote use was that it was not a traditional Navajo religious practice. The ordinance amended the Navajo's Code of Tribal Offenses to read:

> Any person who shall introduce into the Navajo country, sell, or use or have in possession within said Navajo country, the bean known as peyote shall be deemed guilty of an offense against the Navajo Tribe, and upon conviction there of shall be sentenced to labor for a period not to exceed nine months, or a fine of $100.00 or both.

Adopted by a vote of 52 to one (peyotists HOLA TSO was the only councilman who dissented) and signed by tribal chairman JACOB C. MORGAN, the ordinance was subsequently approved by officials of the Department of the Interior. Despite periodic petitions by Navajo peyotists to have the tribal council amend the ordinance to allow the use of peyote for religious purposes, it continued in effect until 1967. At that time, the Navajo tribal council formally accepted the U.S. Constitution's Bill of Rights. In light of First Amendment protection of the freedom of religion, the ordinance was reconsidered, and after nearly two days of debate, it was amended by a vote of 29 to 26. The amendment permitted the use of peyote in connection with the religious practices of the Native American Church.

Taos Pueblo Modern peyotism at Taos Pueblo is said to have begun about 1896 and was quickly followed by opposition from the Catholic Church, Bureau of Indian Affairs officials, and non-peyotist tribal leaders. In 1917, Domencion Cordova, governor of the pueblo, ordered a raid of a peyote meeting conducted by Geronimo ("Star Road") Gomez. Peyote fans, a drum, a gourd rattle, and other objects were confiscated, and a fine was levied against Gomez. In another instance, peyotists had their kiva memberships taken away as punishment. Although the number of peyotists was small, the issue was divisive at Taos.

The controversy over peyote at Taos continued in the 1930s. Objects confiscated years earlier had not been returned to peyotists but had been transferred to other officials with each new administration at the pueblo. Although the peyotists offered to pay a fine to obtain their property back in 1931, the issue was not resolved. In 1934 the opposition to peyotism became more intense with the election at Taos of Geronimo Gomez as lieutenant governor and Telesfor Romero, another peyotist, as council member. Besides openly holding a peyote meeting, Gomez and Romero returned confiscated objects to their owners. Mabel Dodge Luhan, who lived at the pueblo and opposed peyotism, reported these events to Commissioner John Collier. As a result, the peyotists were removed from office and the lieutenant governor jailed. After additional arrests and more dissension at Taos, Collier influenced the tribal leaders to allow peyotists to hold meetings at the pueblo under certain conditions, including refraining from proselytizing. Luhan and other anti-peyotists continued to lobby against peyote. She and her attorney influenced Senator Dennis Chavez of New Mexico to submit federal anti-peyote legislation. In 1937 Chavez introduced Senate Bill 1399, which would have prohibited the interstate transportation of peyote, but it was defeated. (See also Subject Index for legal cases related to peyote use included in this volume.)

PICOFA CEREMONY *Chickasaw* A three-day ceremony conducted by the Aliktce, or healer, to treat an ill patient. Members of the patient's clan participated on the third day. They performed the turkey, duck, bear, buffalo, snake, and other dances around the SACRED FIRE to pray for the patient's recovery. The ceremony, also described as a healing fast, was concluded at dawn. Following a declaration by the Aliktce that the patient had been healed, the clan participants held a feast.

PIERCE, WILLIAM HENRY *(1856–?) Tsimshian* Methodist preacher who served as a missionary to Native people on the northwest coast of British Columbia. Pierce, who was born to a Tsimshian mother and to a Scots father, grew up among his mother's people. He later recalled the dissension caused in the community by the arrival of Christian missionaries. Sent to school by his grandfather, he was ordered home by the Tsimshian chief. After converting to Methodism, Pierce served as an interpreter and began his career as a missionary. In 1910 he wrote *From Potlatch to Pulpit, Being the Autobiography of the Rev. William Henry Pierce, Native Missionary to the Indian Tribes of the Northwest Coast of British Columbia,* which was later edited by the Reverend J. P. Hicks, with biographical information included for the years 1910–1933, and published in 1933. The account includes autobiographical information as well as a description of the POTLATCH and other tribal traditions.

PIERSON, ABRAHAM *(1609–1678)* Congregational missionary to the Native people of Long Island and the first pastor at Southampton, Long Island; Branford, Connecticut; and Newark, New Jersey. Born in Yorkshire, England, Pierson graduated from Trinity College, Cambridge, and was ordained a deacon at the Collegiate Church at Southwell, Nottingham, in 1632. In 1640 he went to Massachusetts, where he was admitted to the church in Boston and ordained at Lynn. At the end of that year, he moved to Southampton and established a church. Seven years later, he settled in Branford, where he served as pastor for about 20 years and engaged in missionary work with neighboring Indian people. Pierson translated a catechism into the Quiripi dialect under the auspices of the SOCIETY FOR THE PROPAGATION OF THE GOSPEL IN NEW ENGLAND. Entitled *Some Helps for the Indians Shewing Them How to Improve their Natural Reason, to Know the True God, and the True Christian Religion,* it was published in England in 1659. In 1667 Pierson moved to Newark, where he served as pastor, assisted by his son Abraham for nine years, until his death on August 9, 1678. (See also PRAYING INDIANS.)

PIGAROUICH, ETIENNE *(fl. mid-17th century) Montagnais* Shaman who converted to Catholicism in 1639. As a medicine man, Pigarouich followed traditional practices, including interpreting dreams, healing the sick, holding the SHAKING TENT CEREMONY, and singing dream songs to pray for success in hunting, and he achieved spiritual power by fasting in isolation for five days and five nights. He discussed his beliefs with the Jesuits, who condemned "all his knaveries." In 1637 Father PAUL LEJEUNE challenged the shaking tent ceremony, wagering that either Pigarouich himself, or Satan, caused the tent to shake and not *khichikouekhi,* "those who make the light," as believed. The shaman responded by going hunting rather than accepting the missionary's challenge. Upon his return, LeJeune continued to ridicule and defy him. Pigarouich, said to have burned his sacred objects around 1637, was converted and baptized in 1639. When he married a second time, after his wife and children had died in an epidemic, he had a Christian marriage ceremony. In 1643 Pigarouich was at Sillery, where he brought others to prayer and was said to be an eloquent speaker.

After being attacked among his own people at Trois-Rivières, perhaps for converting, Pigarouich went to Quebec, where he was said to have fallen into wicked ways. During the winter of 1643–44 he returned to his traditional religious practices several times and was exiled for a period

by the French and some of his own people. Pigarouich eventually sought forgiveness from Father JEAN DE BRÉBEUF but was refused. Another priest, Father Buteux in Montreal, heard his confession and later wrote "what he will do is known to God alone, as He alone knows whether he is truly contrite." Pigarouich caused the Jesuits concern both as a shaman and as a convert because they knew his influence could either help or hinder their efforts to Christianize the Native people. The priests made no reference to him after 1644. (See also CARIGOUAN.)

PIKUNI TRADITIONALISTS ASSOCIATION An association formed by seven Blackfeet spiritual leaders in Montana in 1986 to preserve Native traditions and sacred sites. Its priorities include efforts to protect the BADGER-TWO MEDICINE area in the Lewis and Clark National Forest from drilling operations and other development interests. These threats to the land prompted the Pikuni Traditionalists Association to formulate the BLACKFEET NATION CULTURAL AND SPIRITUAL WILDERNESS PROTECTION ACT OF 1989, which proposes federal safeguards for maintaining the natural, undisturbed quality of the area. It also seeks adherence to the Blackfeet rights to the area under an 1896 agreement. The protection of Badger-Two Medicine and other sacred sanctuaries is viewed as essential to the continuation of traditional religious practices.

PINAPUYUSET *(fl. c. mid-19th century) Umatilla* Pinapuyuset, identified as the last of the WASHANI leaders among his people to die, was primarily a dreamer of sacred songs. He was a contemporary of the dreamer prophets LULS and SMOHALLA.

PINERO *(1861–?) Lipan Apache* An early peyote ROADMAN who, along with BILLY CHIWAT spread peyotism to Indians in Indian Territory (present-day Oklahoma). In 1870 Chiwat and Pinero captured Henry Lehmann, aged 11, in Texas. Lehmann lived with them until 1879 and subsequently told of his experiences among the Lipan Apache. He indicated that he had eaten a cactus found in Mexico that he called "hoosh" and identified as peyote. Pinero provided his own account of his beliefs in the *American Indian YMCA Bulletin* (November 1918):

> I am a Lipan Apache. I live five miles northeast of Indiahoma, Oklahoma, on my allotment. I am 57 years old. I knew about peyote before any of these Indians in Oklahoma country knew about it. I first ate peyote in Mexico. My great-grandfather was the first (Lipan Apache) to make use of it in Mexico; it was brought among the Indians here years after. It was used as a medicine at first, and no woman or young people ate it as they do now. It is called mescal-peyote in Mexico; here in Oklahoma it is called peyote.

Different sources confirm that peyotism was introduced to the Comanche, Kiowa, and Kiowa-Apache by Chiwat and Pinero and that they taught QUANAH PARKER the peyote ceremony he used. (See also NATIVE AMERICAN CHURCH.)

PIPESTONE   Pipestone is a soft red stone that is sacred to the Dakota and other Native groups. Used in making the SACRED PIPE, pipe bowls, and other objects, the principal source of the stone is at a quarry in Pipestone, Minnesota. One account of the origin of the stone states that during a great flood members of various tribal groups went into highland areas in an effort to escape the rising water. Unable to survive the deluge, all but one person perished, and the bodies of those who had died, from many tribal groups, turned to stone. The young woman who managed to escape later gave birth to twins, beginning the repopulation of the land. The sacred site became a neutral territory where the stone could be quarried in peace. Archaeological evidence indicates a long history of Native American use of the pipestone quarry. The area first came to the attention of Euro-Americans in the 19th century, primarily through the work of the artist George Catlin. Although not the first non-Indian visitor, Catlin publicized his visit in the 1830s through his paintings and writings. He also took samples of the stone, later called "catlinite" by Euro-Americans, to Boston for chemical analysis. The pipestone quarry's long history of occupancy saw numerous changes in jurisdiction. In 1851 the Sisseton, Wahpeton, Mdewakanton, and Wahpekute bands of Dakota lost the site as well as other lands in Minnesota Territory in treaties at Traverse des Sioux and Mendota. In an 1858 treaty the Yankton people relinquished millions of acres of land but retained unrestricted use of the quarry. Two years later a Minnesota survey created a reserve around the site, an action that did not deter homesteaders from encroaching on the land. In 1891 Congress authorized the construction of a government boarding school in the area, a decision challenged by the Yankton people. After a 1926 ruling by the United States Supreme Court, the tribal band later received monetary compensation for land taken for the school. The federal government then held title to the site, and the Yankton people retained rights to its use. Other developments included the formation of the Pipestone National Park Association, later renamed the Pipestone Shrine Association, in 1932. Its members sought federal protection for the site and enough land for a park. In 1937 the Pipestone National Monument was created by an act of Congress. Native pipe makers continue to mine the sacred stone from the quarry on a permit basis.

PIT-RIVER CHARLEY (*fl. 1870s*) *Achomawi* A leader of the EARTH LODGE RELIGION on the Klamath Reservation in Oregon. An Achomawi or Atsugewi from the Pit River area of California, Pit-River Charley had been captured and enslaved by Klamath and Modoc people before the treaty period of the groups. After the treaty was negotiated, he remained on the Klamath Reservation.

Following the Modoc War of 1872–73, he returned to California with HENRY JACKSON, another former captive. During the visit they participated in Earth Lodge religious ceremonies. After attending dances at Falls City and Alturas, Pit-River Charley returned to Oregon. He introduced the Earth Lodge teachings in the area of the Klamath Reservation known as the Lower End in 1874. Under his leadership three ceremonial dance houses were constructed there. He was said to communicate with the dead during trances, revealing his teachings in ceremonies that included sacred singing and dancing. The Earth Lodge religion shared similarities with the GHOST DANCE RELIGION OF 1870 but also incorporated local traditional elements.

PITEZEL, JOHN H. (*1814–1906*) Methodist missionary among the Ojibway at Sault Ste. Marie in Michigan's Upper Peninsula. Pitezel was born in Frederick County, Maryland, on April 18, 1814, and later, at the age of nine, moved to Ohio with his family. He received his license to preach in April 1834, enrolled in Norwalk Seminary for one year, and began an assignment on the Lima Circuit in Ohio in 1835. After serving on the Lower Sandusky and Tecumseh circuits, he began his appointment at Sault Ste. Marie in 1843. Pitezel was named superintendent of the Indian Mission District of the Michigan Conference, holding the position from 1848 to 1852. He later wrote *Lights and Shades of Missionary Life* (1857), describing his efforts among the Ojibway people in the region. Pitezel also wrote a biographical account of one of his Native converts, PETER MARKSMAN, entitled *Life of Reverend Peter Marksman, an Ojibway Missionary* (1901). After serving at other placements in Michigan, he retired. In 1870 he received another appointment but returned to retirement after one year. Pitezel died on May 4, 1906.

PIXLEY, BENTON (*fl. 1820s*) A 19th-century Presbyterian missionary who worked among the Osage people at Harmony Mission in Missouri and Neosho Mission in present-day Kansas. Pixley, a college graduate, was a Greek and Latin scholar. When Harmony Mission was established in 1821 under the auspices of the UNITED FOREIGN MISSIONARY SOCIETY, missionaries, including Pixley, traveled from the East to begin the work. Pixley remained at Harmony Mission until 1824, when he was sent to establish Mission Neosho, the first mission in present-day Kansas, under the auspices of the same missionary society. The following year the Osage relinquished their Missouri lands under the terms of a treaty and removed to the Neosho County area. Accompanied by his wife and two children, Pixley began the work of constructing a home and providing school and church services. The following year Daniel B. Bright, a farming instructor, and Cornelia Pelham, a teacher, arrived to supplement the missionary efforts of the family. Daily instructions were provided to Osage children for two months each year. The Reverend Pixley studied the Osage language by accompanying the people on hunts and spending time in their homes, but Mission Neosho was short-lived, closing in 1829, having failed to convert the Osage to Christianity or to an alien way of life. After he closed the mission, Pixley moved to Independence, Missouri, where he served as the first Presbyterian minister in that community.

PLENTY WOLF, GEORGE (c. 1901–1977) *Lakota* An Oglala YUWIPI man and SUN DANCE leader from the Pine Ridge Reservation of South Dakota who was trained by the famous holy man HORN CHIPS. Plenty Wolf sought the medicine man's assistance after a fall from a horse at age 28 left him partially deaf and suffering from injuries. Horn Chips took him on a VISION QUEST to fast and to pray for four days and four nights. The spiritual instruction he received at that time was the beginning of his long years of service as a sacred man among his people. At later vision quests he continued to gain knowledge that guided his life. Besides conducting Yuwipi and other sacred ceremonies, Plenty Wolf trained other medicine men. His guidance of a young man through the sweat lodge, a vision quest, and a Yuwipi ceremony was recorded by anthropologist William K. Powers in his book, *Yuwipi: Vision and Experience in Oglala Ritual.* Plenty Wolf was also a practicing Catholic who served as a catechist in his early years. In 1971, when Powers last saw him, the holy man had suffered a number of misfortunes. His wife and helper, Julie, had died, he had lost important ritual objects, and the afflictions of age and ill health had taken their toll. Shortly thereafter, Plenty Wolf became ill and died following a beating by a group of youngsters. His life had been hard, as had been foretold in his first vision. Plenty Wolf died on January 22, 1977, at the age of 76.

PO HA GUM *Paiute* Religious leader and healer, either male or female, who received spiritual powers through dreams. The Po ha gum's healing practices included the use of eagle feathers, herbal medicines, and sacred songs and dances. The healer also received spiritual assistance during a trance state and was then able to prescribe curative measures for a patient.

POINT, NICHOLAS (1799–1868) French Jesuit missionary. Born in France, Point joined the Society of Jesus in 1819 and

took his vows in 1827. In 1835, he was sent to the United States to assist Jesuits in Kentucky. There, he joined the faculty of St. Mary's until he was chosen to go to Louisiana and assume responsibility for establishing a Jesuit college in 1837. Removed in 1840, he reported to St. Louis and was sent to Westport, Missouri, the staging area for wagon trains going west. In 1841, he assisted Father PIERRE JEAN DESMET in founding the first Catholic mission in the Northwest among Salish and Kootenai (Flathead) peoples in the Bitter Valley. He founded the first mission among Coeur d'Alene of northern Idaho in 1842 and initiated the first mission activity among Blackfeet in 1846. In less than nine months as the first priest among the Piegan Blackfeet, Point baptized more than 650, nearly all children, translated ordinary prayers into an Indian language and instructed men, women, and children in Christian doctrines. Appointed official diarist of the missionary party by DeSmet, Point chronicled the history of mission work and the effects of Christian teachings on Indians and described Indian life and customs. He made observations regarding the functions of medicine in Indian life and hunting practices. Although he received no formal art training, he was the first to depict scenes from Indian life of the Rocky Mountain region, graphic representations of Indians he knew and of their customs. After six years among Indians of the Rocky Mountains, he left the region in 1847 at his own request and went to Canada. In Canada, he established a mission to the Ottawa on Grand Manitoulin Island, retired from active work, and died in Quebec.

POLLEN A sacred substance used in prayer and rituals, symbolizing life and renewal. It may come from cattail, corn, oak, pine, pinon, sunflower, or tule. Used as a ceremonial offering, pollen sanctifies objects, dancing grounds, trails, and Sandpaintings over which it is sprinkled. Pollen is also often sprinkled on the head or put in mouths. It is similar in ritual use and symbolism to CORN MEAL. Navajo believe that the body becomes holy when one travels over a trail sprinkled with pollen.

POM POM Pom Pom (bum bum) is Chinook jargon for, or equivalent to, WASHAT or WASHANI. It refers to the tambourine used in the religious practice and has also been defined as "drums beating like hearts." The term has further been applied to FEATHER RELIGION adherents, who have been called Pom Pom Shakers.

POND, SAMUEL W. AND GIDEON (*Samuel—1808–1891; Gideon–1810–1878*) Samuel Pond was a Congregational missionary who became known for his linguistic work among the Dakota people in Minnesota Territory. Born in 1808, he received a brief elementary education, then was apprenticed to a clothier and later taught school. Assisted by his brother, Gideon, Pond began his study of Dakota linguistics and culture in 1834. He left his hometown of Washington, Connecticut, for St. Louis in 1833, two years after he had joined the Congregational Church. To recover from cholera contracted on his journey, he went to Galena, Ohio, where he was joined by Gideon. From there, they went to Fort Snelling in Minnesota. The post commander convinced the brothers to work with the Dakota leader Little Crow's band of Mdewakanton Dakota at Kaposia, nine miles from the fort. After a short time, they accepted a proposal from Laurence Taliaferro, the government agent for the Dakota, to settle in the village of another Dakota leader, Cloud Man, on the shore of Lake Calhoun, now part of Minneapolis, to teach farming and "civilization" to the Mdewakanton living there. Believing that a knowledge of the Native language would assist them in their missionary efforts, they began an intensive study of Dakota. In the summer of 1836, prompted by conflicts with a fellow missionary, Samuel Pond returned to Connecticut to upgrade his qualifications and was ordained a Congregational minister the following spring. Upon his return to Minnesota, he resumed his linguistic work. In 1839 the Ponds began to tutor STEPHEN RETURN RIGGS, who later published the first Dakota dictionary under his name in 1852.

The two brothers found their difficult linguistic work disrupted by changes occurring in the Dakota community. Conflicts with Ojibway, assimilationist policies, and government treaties altered traditional communities. When new reservations were established in the western part of Minnesota Territory under the terms of an 1851 treaty, the Ponds decided against moving with the Dakota. They stayed in eastern Minnesota, founding and serving churches in white communities, Samuel at Shakopee until his 1866 retirement and Gideon at Bloomington until his death in 1878. During Samuel's retirement years his writings included two studies, an ethnography entitled *The Dakota or Sioux in Minnesota As They Were in 1834* and a reminiscence later published in *Minnesota History* as "Two Missionaries in the Sioux Country." The latter is critical of Stephen Riggs, whose Dakota dictionary and grammar included a significant amount of material from the Ponds and THOMAS S. WILLIAMSON. Although the publication states that the information was "Collected by the members of the Dakota Mission" and identifies Riggs as the editor, the issue of authorship became controversial. The dictionary and grammar were started and developed by the Ponds, with material from other contributors, including Riggs and Williamson.

PONZIGLIONE, PAUL M. *(1818–1900)* Italian Jesuit missionary. Born in Italy to an aristocratic Italian family, he went into the Jesuit order in 1839 at the age of 21. He was ordained a priest in 1848. He went to the United States and was assigned in 1851 to the Osage Mission in southeastern Kansas, founded by the Dutch Jesuit priest Father John Schoenmakers. He learned the Osage language and wrote articles and a prayer book in Osage. He worked among the Osage people until 1870, when the Osage were forced to move to Indian Territory (present-day Oklahoma). He made visits to them every year before he departed for Milwaukee in 1889. As a tribute to his work, the Osage contributed toward the expense of building St. Francis Church at St. Pauls, Kansas (formerly the Osage Mission). Father Ponziglione established 60 missions over Kansas as well as in Missouri and Indian Territory.

POOR COYOTE *(?–c. 1920s) Cree* A medicine man whose spiritual assistance from the LITTLE PEOPLE of Cree belief greatly enhanced his healing abilities. He often encountered these beings in the vicinity of his home on the Rocky Boy Reservation in Montana. Known as M-me-m-mege'-soo, the Little People were known to be about two and a half feet in height, wear hide garments, speak Cree, and possess healing powers. Poor Coyote once noticed them playing with broken marbles discarded by children who had visited him. He later bought new marbles and left them as an offering. When he returned to the area, he found that the marbles had disappeared. He also discovered a doorway in the bank of a creek. Upon entering, he saw tiny possessions belonging to the Little People. Poor Coyote later realized that these beings had enhanced the power of the medicine he had carried with him. Their spiritual gift assisted him in many ways. He was able to tell whether those who approached him were honorable, to better help those who were ill, and to foretell future events. Poor Coyote's stature as a great medicine man grew among his people.

POOR MAN, MERCY *(b. c. 1922) Lakota* A licensed minister of the Christian Life Fellowship Church on the Rosebud Reservation in South Dakota. The church, which is relatively new, consists of fundamentalist Assembly of God adherents and sponsors a home for troubled children. Poor Man, who lives on the Rosebud Reservation in Mission, South Dakota, attended a Catholic mission school as a child. In a 1984 interview, later published in *Sioux Indian Religion* (1987), she described her upbringing as non-traditionalist and counted both Episcopalians and Catholics in her family. She and her husband, John, a devout Christian who served as a warden in the Episcopal Church, had eight children. In the early years of their marriage, the couple could not afford their own home. During that period, at a point she described as her poorest, she decided to pray. After kneeling and praying with her children beside her, Poor Man stated that she had a spiritual experience that helped free her from bad habits and strengthened her Christianity. She returned to school in her 40s, completed a degree in education, and became a teacher. In the Christian Life Fellowship Church she serves as an assistant minister and teaches Sunday school classes. The congregation is small and includes about 30 members. Although the membership is predominantly Indian, the church would like to include more non-Indian members. She stated that the services include Scripture readings, prayers for healing, a lot of singing, testimonials from people in the audience, and a concluding meal. According to Poor Man, there is no attempt to convert people from other faiths. She stated that her church welcomes all who attend but would also like to reach those having problems. Poor Man, who prays in the Lakota language when Native speakers are present, is a licensed minister but considers herself a sister rather than a reverend.

POPÉ *(?–1690) Tewa* A medicine man from San Juan Pueblo. Popé is the person generally credited as being the leader of the Pueblo Rebellion fought against the Spanish on August 10, 1680. Other Pueblo leaders who joined as well included Jaca of Taos, Catiti of Santo Domingo and Tupatu of Picuris. The Spanish seized and punished Popé at least three times for his loyalty to traditional spiritual beliefs, for holding ceremonies, and for refusing to convert to Christianity. In 1675, he was one of a large group of medicine men taken to a Santa Fe prison and charged with witchcraft. After release from prison, Popé hid at Taos Pueblo and organized the all-pueblo uprising that ousted the missionaries. Every effort was made to keep the Spanish from learning about the revolt. Women were not permitted to know, and Popé put his brother-in-law to death on suspicion of treachery. News leaked out, and Popé and the others struck on August 10, three days earlier than the intended date. In the first few days, about 400 Spanish men, women, and children were killed, including 21 priests. Approximately 250 Indians were killed. The Spanish retreated down the Rio Grande to El Paso. After the revolt, the pueblos were free to practice their traditional culture and religion. Popé ordered baptized Indians washed with yucca suds, Spanish language and baptismal names forbidden, and other Christian objects of Spanish culture destroyed. He ordered death for those who opposed him. Because of his demands, he was deposed and although reelected in 1688, the alliance he helped build dissolved by the time of his death in 1690.

PORCUPINE (Hishkowits) *(c. 1847–1929) Arikara/Lakota* Ghost Dance priest among the Northern Cheyenne people. Born about 1847 to a Lakota woman and to an Arikara fa-

ther, White Weed, Porcupine married a Cheyenne woman and lived most of his life among the Northern Cheyenne. He served as a warrior who became known, along with Red Wolf, for devising and implementing a plan to derail a Union Pacific Railroad train in 1867. Porcupine was later among the Cheyenne who followed the Cheyenne leaders Morning Star and Little Wolf from Indian Territory (present-day Oklahoma) to their northern homeland in Montana. The long journey that began in the fall of 1878 was a terrible ordeal for the band members, with soldiers and civilians in relentless pursuit. Although Porcupine was among the Cheyenne survivors, he was one of those charged with the murder of frontiersmen. He was eventually released for insufficient evidence. Porcupine became a leader of the GHOST DANCE OF 1890 after journeying to Nevada in November 1889 to visit WOVOKA, the Paiute prophet. Upon his return, he gave a thorough account of his findings over a five-day period in council. Porcupine was arrested at the turn of the century for his Ghost Dance practices and sentenced to hard labor at Fort Keogh, Montana. He was incarcerated until March 28, 1901. Porcupine also served as a council chief among the Cheyenne.

PORCUPINE STANDING SIDEWAYS (Pemicheka) *(c. 1771–1891) Cree-Saulteaux* Shaman and clan leader. Porcupine Standing Sideways's origin is shrouded in mystery. It is believed that he first appeared among members of the Sucker clan somewhere in the Severn River area of present-day northwestern Ontario before 1823. He was then a young man and was first seen standing on top of a lodge. When approached by the startled villagers, Porcupine Standing Sideways told them his name and revealed that he had lived before and was again returning. His name appeared in Hudson's Bay Company records in 1823 along with those of other Native people from Sandy Lake. Because Porcupine Standing Sideways lived during the period before outsiders intruded on his people's way of life, he followed traditional customs without interference. As a leader of the Sucker clan, he utilized his legendary spiritual powers to protect the people. Porcupine Standing Sideways had five children, including three sons who died tragic deaths. One of them, Peter Flett, was killed after it was believed that he had turned into a *windigo,* a feared cannibalistic being. The other two, JACK FIDDLER and JOSEPH FIDDLER, were shamans who were charged with murdering a woman said to be possessed in the same way. The death of Porcupine Standing Sideways was recorded in a post journal in 1891. He was 120 years old.

POSHAYANKI *Zuni* Head of the BEAST GODS who instituted the medicine societies and patron of the medicine societies, as well as a culture hero to the Zuni people. He lives in a sacred place, Shipapolina.

POST, CHRISTIAN FREDERICK *(c. 1710–1785)* Moravian missionary who worked among the Mahican, Delaware (Lenni Lenape), and other tribal groups. Born in Conitz, East Prussia, Post was trained as a cabinetmaker before traveling to America in 1742. Influenced by the philosophy of Count NIKOLAUS LUDVIG ZINZENDORF he attempted to unite various German groups around Bethlehem, Pennsylvania, into one church. In 1743 he traveled to New York with Christopher Pyrlaeus and other Moravian missionaries to work with Native converts near Poughkeepsie. Post married Rachel, a Wampanoag, the same year and was making progress at the mission when war intervened. He and the other Moravian missionaries, under suspicion by the white settlers, were arrested and ordered to leave the state. Post and DAVID ZEISBERGER were then sent by the Moravians to work among the Iroquois but again faced arrest and were later imprisoned for nearly two months. Two years after Rachel died in 1747, Post married a Delaware Christian named Agnes and they lived in the Wyoming valley region. In 1758 Post served as an envoy at the request of Pennsylvania's governor and council in an effort to persuade Tedyuskung and other Indian leaders to become allies of the British against the French. He reported to the governor and then went to Ohio to start a settlement for Native converts but soon left to extend missionary efforts in other parts of the region. After leaving the Moravian missionary service in 1762, he eventually went to Nicaragua, where he worked among the Mosquito Indians. Post retired in 1784 at Germantown, Pennsylvania, where he died in 1785. Post's journals were published in Charles Thompson's *Causes of the Alienation of the Delaware and Shawanese Indians from the British Interests* (London, 1759; Philadelphia, 1867). (See also GRUBE, BERNHARD ADAM; HECKEWELDER, JOHN.)

POSTIYU *(fl. 19th century) Chitimacha* Reportedly one of the last medicine men among his people. He lived in a Native community at Plaquemine Bayou in Louisiana. Postiyu was remembered as a storyteller, a singer of corn harvest and other songs, and a person who was loved by children. He was also known to parch corn to make his own *sofki*, a traditional food, and to possess the ability to make horses win or lose races.

POTLATCH *North Pacific Coast* Derived from the Chinook word meaning "to give away," this event combines feasting and the formal distribution of gifts (or transfer of wealth) according to a person's rank among an audience serving as witnesses to this public event. The feasting and gift giving are

Potlatch gathering. A group of Tlingit in ceremonial regalia in front of Chief Shake's house in Wrangel, Alaska, in 1885. *Photograph by G. T. Emmons. Courtesy of the Royal British Columbia Museum, Victoria, British Columbia.*

necessary after displays of ceremonial rites, including the name-givings, which include puberty rites when a girl assumes a new adult name and status, marriage, death, headstone raising, house building, totem pole raising, investiture of an heir, elevation of a young person to a new position, the "sale" of a COPPER, WINTER CEREMONIALS, oil feasts, and displays of spiritual properties. Property is distributed to demonstrate a man's ability to uphold his status. Potlatch forms vary from tribe to tribe, from small-scale affairs to lavish ones. Goods given away at potlatches are always returned later when the original recipient holds a potlatch of his own. Potlatching as an economic exchange strengthens tribal solidarity. There is a religious character to this exchange as well as a socioeconomic one. At potlatches, chiefs impersonate spirits, whose names they bear, whose dances they dance, and who possess them. Once extensive in duration, today's potlatches are primarily incorporated into a single day or evening of feasting, singing, and distribution of gifts.

The CANADIAN INDIAN ACT of Parliament made it a criminal offense to hold a potlatch. Government agents broke up any distribution of goods and confiscated ceremonial goods. People held potlatches in secret, but when the government lifted its ban in 1951, serious damage had been done to potlatching rites. (See also GIVEAWAY CEREMONY, DANCE, MEMORIAL POTLATCH.)

POTLATCH LAW   See CANADIAN INDIAN ACT

POWAMU CEREMONY (Bean Dance) *Hopi*   The ceremony, lasting 16 days in February, has two purposes. Children are initiated into and exposed to the religious instruction of the KACHINA SOCIETY and the rites prepare the Hopi world for planting and the growth of another season. The Powamu and Kachina Societies are the principal ones that participate in the ceremony. On the 16th day, there is a public ceremony at which the kachinas bring and give away mature bean sprouts to the people. There is a procession of many different kinds of kachinas, who dance in the plaza (PACHAVU CEREMONY). In this ceremony, the fearsome-looking Soyoko kachinas come and discipline the children of the village. On the 16th day every four years or so, young children are initiated into the Kachina or Powamu Societies.

POWELL, PETER JOHN (Ho-honaa-ve-ahta-nehe, "Stone Forehead") *(b. 1928) Adopted Cheyenne*   An Episcopal priest and historian of the Cheyenne people. Powell grew up in Philadelphia, where his father served as a parish priest and army chaplain. In 1941, at the age of 13, he interviewed an elderly Lakota man on the Crow Creek Reservation in South Dakota while visiting reservations with his family. During his high school years, he assisted in recataloging the Plains

Indian collection at the University of Pennsylvania Museum. After studying philosophy at Ripon College, he attended seminary at Nashotah House in Wisconsin. Ordained in 1953, he was assigned to St. Timothy's parish in Chicago. Powell began working with urban Indians, many of whom had arrived in the city under a relocation program sponsored by the Bureau of Indian Affairs. He founded St. Augustine's Indian Center in the early 1960s, and it grew into the largest Native case-work agency in the country. In contrast to early missionaries, Powell identified his role as helping Native people preserve their cultural traditions rather than proselytizing or converting them. After obtaining the approval of Cheyenne leaders to record the history of their people, Powell began researching and writing while maintaining his other duties. In 1969 he completed *Sweet Medicine*, a two-volume work that documented Cheyenne sacred ways and the life of the Cheyenne prophet SWEET MEDICINE. He continued the account in *People of the Sacred Mountain*, which won an American Book Award for history in 1982. Besides his adoption into both Northern and Southern Cheyenne families, Powell has also been adopted by Lakota and Crow people. The Cheyenne named him Stone Forehead after one of the most revered keepers in their history. Granted unprecedented participation in sacred ceremonies, Powell also began serving as one of the Northern Cheyenne chiefs in 1962. In 1973 he became a research associate at the Newberry Library in Chicago. Powell's family includes his wife, Virginia, their four children, and many relatives by adoption.

POWER CONCEPTS   Native people believe that power or energy exists in all objects, animals, people, and spirits in the universe. The Algonquians call it *manito;* the Siouan tribes call it *wakanda;* the Iroquois call it *orenda;* the Chinook call it *tamanous;* the Salish call it *sulia.* Although there are differences in the significance of the terms, the fundamental notion of all of them is that a power inherent in the objects of nature is more potent than the natural powers of people. (See also APACHE POWER CONCEPTS.)

PRAYER DANCE *Ojibway*   A dance that combined traditional and Christian elements. Introduced by Joseph Abita Gekek, a member of the Pembina band, in 1882, the Prayer Dance included the use of a drum blessed by a member of the Benedictine order and a Native dance form. Gekek's dance helped gain Catholic converts among the Red Lake band until the Benedictine priest saw it performed some time after its development. Angry that participants were wearing rosary beads, he destroyed the drum. As a result, a number of the Ojibway people became opposed to the mission.

PRAYERSTICK *Pueblo* Prayers to bring rain or for good health are often accompanied by offerings called prayersticks, used extensively by the Pueblo of Arizona and New Mexico. They are sticks to which feathers, shells, and other items are attached. They differ in length, shape, and the painting and carving executed on them and have different kinds of feathers and objects attached to them, according to the pueblo in which they are made and the spirit to whom they are dedicated. Prayersticks are made ceremonially and often consecrated with sacred cornmeal, tobacco smoke, and other rites. After prayers have been breathed into them, they are deposited in shrines, springs, fields, or riverbanks or under shrubs and trees, sunk in irrigation ditches, carried long distances to mountains, or put under floors, in rafters, in caves, or on altars where spirits may see them and honor the petitions that accompany them. Prayersticks for family offerings are made on the occasion of ceremonies and are deposited by authorized people. Individuals also make prayerstick offerings.

The preparation and planting of prayersticks is a principal feature of Zuni worship and ritual. Thousands are made annually. Zunis offer prayersticks to the dead throughout the year—after a family death, at the SHALAKO ceremony, and at solstices, when women dedicate them to the moon and men to the sun. Kachina impersonators plant prayersticks dedicated to the spirits they impersonate; society members plant prayersticks at solstices and throughout the year dedicated to deceased members and to their patrons. The prayersticks are made at home or in ceremonies. People ritually prepare themselves before and after making them. The stick indicates to whom it is offered. Feathers convey breath prayers to the spirits, and it is believed that the breath of prayer combines with the breath of spirits to whom they are offered to form clouds behind which rainmakers work.

Hopi call their prayersticks *paho*. Navajo (Dineh) and Apache prayersticks are similar to those of the Pueblo. Havasupai place prayersticks in the ground at the source of a spring.

PRAYERSTICK FESTIVAL (Vigita, Vikita) *Tohono O'odham (Papago)* A sacred ceremony held in August in the villages from the southern part of the reservation. The ceremony's purpose is to "keep the world in order" as well as bring rain for the crops. At places that mark where the Tohono O'odham people first settled, they hold sacred PRAYERSTICK festivals to get rain and other blessings. Ritual participants include a feast leader, head ceremonial clown called a NAVITCU, 30 or more village clowns, a head cornmeal sprinkler, corn dancers, singers, and musicians. In each village, people build a temporary brush enclosure in which prayersticks and other sacred objects are made and newly composed songs learned. Images are made to illustrate the words of the songs and later carried through the village by groups of men wearing gourd masks. During the ceremony, clowns with healing powers circle among people. The ceremony ends with a distribution of prayersticks to all people.

PRAYING DANCE See PROPHET DANCE

PRAYING INDIANS American Indians of various tribes who were converted to Christianity by early missionaries, including the 17th-century New England minister JOHN ELIOT who organized "praying towns," or settlements, for Native converts. After delivering his first sermon to the Indians at Dorchester Mills in Massachusetts in 1646, Eliot became proficient in the Algonquian language with the assistance of Native translators COCKENOE and JOB NESUTAN. Intent on Christianizing and "civilizing" the Indians, the New England minister gradually increased the number of Indian converts. Eliot, DANIEL GOOKIN, the THOMAS MAYHEW family, and other missionaries urged the Indians to adopt the English way of life in settlements under colonial authority.

The first praying town, Natick, was established in Massachusetts by Eliot in 1651, and by 1675 the number of these settlements had grown to fourteen. The earliest towns included Hassanamesit, Magunkaquog, Nashobah, Okommakamesit, Punkapog, and Wamesit in Massachusetts. Others, found primarily in the Nipmuc region of Connecticut, included Chabanakongkomun, Manchaug, Manexit, Wacuntug, Pakachoog, Quantisset, and Wabaquasset. About 1,100 praying Indians lived in these settlements while others could be found around Plymouth, on Cape Cod, and among the Mohegan. The New England missionaries hoped to separate the "praying Indians" from their unconverted neighbors, to curtail their mobility and to bring them under colonial control. The praying towns were small, the largest having about 30 adult males. Most of them suffered from English encroachment on the land, ineffective management by colonial overseers, and opposition from Native people who were against Christianization and colonization. The entire population of Christian Indians in southern New England has been estimated at 2,500 at the outbreak of King Philip's War in 1675, when Wampanoag and other tribal groups fought against the English settlers and the praying Indians. Among their ranks were Native missionaries and teachers who used the ELIOT BIBLE and other Algonquian translations in their work.

During King Philip's War, the praying Indians were under attack from both sides. The English suspected them of allying with the enemy while the opposing Indians viewed them as traitors. Some offered their help to the English, while others abandoned the towns to fight on the Indian side. The population of these towns was greatly reduced by the war, from approximately 1,100 to about 300, and the mission work nearly obliterated. By 1682, only four of the praying towns remained.

PREACHER *Iroquois* The modern term for those people qualified and officially recognized by a committee of chiefs to recite the CODE OF HANDSOME LAKE.

PRELIMINARY GREEN CORN FEAST *Cherokee* The second of SIX CHEROKEE FESTIVALS described by the 19th-century missionary DANIEL SABIN BUTRICK and other early observers of the Cherokee Nation before the forced removal of the tribal group from the southeastern Appalachian region to Indian Territory (present-day Oklahoma). The Preliminary Green Corn Feast was held at the capital in midsummer when the corn ripened. The ancient capital of the Cherokee Nation, Chota, or Great Echota, was located on the south side of the Little Tennessee River below Citico Creek in Tennessee. New Echota in Georgia also served as the capital for a number of years before removal. At the proper time a messenger was sent to pick seven ears of corn for the principal, or prime, counselors and to announce the time of the feast to the people. Six days of hunting ensued for the hunters while the seven counselors fasted for the same period of time. On the sixth day, the people assembled for the evening's ritual activities. They carried with them fresh corn, and the hunters contributed fresh meat. An all-night vigil and religious dance was then conducted. Ritual elements on the seventh day included delivering seven ears of corn to the *uku*, or priest, the making of a new fire from the bark of seven trees and offerings of tobacco and corn to the fire. When the feast ended, the *uku* and the seven counselors fasted for an additional seven days. The people then gathered for a one-day fast, concluding the Preliminary Green Corn Feast. One Cherokee name of the religious observance translates as "roasting ear's time."

PREPARATION OF OFFERING CLOTHS *Lakota* A ceremony performed when an offering is made to the Sacred Calf Pipe (also Ptehincala hu cannunpa, the BUFFALO CALF PIPE), the holiest possession of the Lakota people. A description of a 1964 ritual indicated that it was conducted by a YUWIPI leader named Joe Thin Elk, a descendant of the Sacred Calf Pipe's keepers. Thin Elk, then 76 years old, had made annual pilgrimages within the state of South Dakota from his home in Mission to the Cheyenne River Reservation, where the Sacred Calf Pipe is kept. He had walked the distance of about 150 miles each year until his advanced age prevented him from doing so. The Sacred Calf Pipe, which is kept in a bundle and rarely exposed, draws Lakota religious practitioners and other visitors who wish to pray in its presence. It is ritu-

ally cared for and protected by its hereditary keeper. A trip to the Sacred Calf Pipe was not made in connection with the described ceremony. Ritual elements included prayers by Thin Elk with his pipe, sweetgrass consecration, tobacco offerings to the four directions and to the earth and sky, and the ritual preparation of red, black, yellow, white, green, and blue offering cloths. After completing the ceremony, Thin Elk indicated to the participants that he would go alone to the hills in the middle of the night and again pray over the offerings. (See also LOOKING HORSE, ARVAL; SACRED PIPE).

PRETTY-SHIELD *(c. 1857–?) Crow* Crow medicine woman. Pretty-shield told her life story to author Frank Linderman through an interpreter and with the use of sign language sometime before 1932. About 74 years of age when she was interviewed, her account of the female side of Native life was among the first recorded. Pretty-shield recalled the traditional lifeways of her people before European contact and the disappearance of the buffalo. She spoke about many Crow customs, including those related to childhood, courtship, marriage, and childbirth.

Born near the Missouri River, Pretty-shield was named, as was customary among her people, on the fourth day of life. Her name, Pretty-shield, came from her paternal grandfather and was associated with a medicine shield that he owned. She became a "Wise one," or medicine woman, in part through the spiritual assistance she received in a vision while mourning the death of a baby daughter. After

Pretty-shield. A medicine woman of the Crow, in a 1931 photograph. *Permission for use granted by the heirs of Frank Bird Linderman, Sarah J. Hatfield, personal representative of heirs.*

assuming the role, Pretty-shield, like her grandfather, possessed the right to name children. A member of a respected family, her clan, the Sore-lips, was also prominent and produced many Crow leaders, including Chief Plenty-coups. During her childhood she spent nearly as much time with her aunt, a River Crow, as with her mother. When she was 13 years old, Pretty-shield was promised as a wife to Goes-ahead by her father. Before her marriage, at 16, she adopted a baby girl whose parents had been killed. Pretty-shield and two of her sisters were eventually married to Goes-ahead, each one maintaining a lodge, but she was the only one to bear him children. Before turning 17, she became ill with smallpox, the disease that later killed her father and many other Indian people. Pretty-shield was spared through the efforts of a medicine man, Sharp-shin, who healed her. She eventually had five children and many grandchildren.

Her story was published in 1932 as *Red Mother* and later as *Pretty-shield: Medicine Woman of the Crows*. It includes an account of her medicine dream, or vision, and her subsequent spiritual help from ants. She outlived all but one of her children and raised two families of grandchildren. Her husband, Goes-ahead, and her uncle, Half-yellow-face, were both scouts for Custer and survived the Battle of the Little Bighorn. Pretty-shield's memory of their account of the historic confrontation is included in the book. When Linderman interviewed her, she was raising grandchildren and trying to cope with the changes introduced among her people.

PRIBER, JOHANN GOTTLIEB (Pryber; Preber) *(fl. 1734–1744)* An early missionary to the Cherokee, known as Christian Priber. Little is known of his early life, but he was said to have come from a Saxon (German) family and to have had a good education. An army officer and a skilled linguist, he reportedly had subversive ideas that caused him to flee to England. He immigrated to South Carolina about 1734 and settled among the Cherokee two years later. Headquartered at Tellico in Tennessee, Priber attempted to organize an ideal Christian republic among the southern tribes. He mastered the Cherokee language, adopted Native dress and warned the Indians against European encroachment. He also worked at developing a confederation of tribes and advocated that Indians trade with Europeans only until reaching independence. Priber's activities aroused suspicions among the English colonists, who were convinced that he was a French agent or Jesuit. In 1739, when South Carolina authorities were sent to arrest him, Priber was protected by the Cherokee. However, he was captured in 1743 and incarcerated as a political prisoner at Fort Frederica in Georgia. He died a few years later in the prison. Priber's surname is also spelled Pryber or Preber.

PRICE, PETE *(c. 1868–1951) Navajo (Dineh)* Prominent singer of the BLESSING WAY, the backbone of NAVAJO CEREMONIALISM. Born near Ft. Defiance, Arizona, Price desired as a youth to become a medicine man, which led to his study with a singer. Eventually, Price learned the Blessing Way, ENEMY WAY, and portions of other ceremonials. He headed a group that met Albert I, king of the Belgians, in 1919 when the monarch and his family visited Gallup, New Mexico. He gave the king a Navajo rug and received in turn a gold medal "about as big as a flapjack" according to trader Charlie Newcomb. Price performed dances in Europe and President Herbert Hoover presented him with an American flag upon his return. During the 1930s, Price acted as an informant to Richard Van Valkenburgh, Indian Service anthropologist, and Williard Williams, a University of New Mexico professor researching Navajo religious beliefs and sacred sites. In May 1938, Price performed a HOUSE BLESSING rite, normally used to dedicate Native dwellings rather than public buildings, for the new Ft. Defiance Indian Hospital. Each room in the hospital was blessed with white cornmeal. Just before his death, Price was baptized a Catholic, and he died at the hospital he had blessed 14 years earlier.

PRIVACY OF NATIVE AMERICAN RELIGIOUS AND CEREMONIAL PRACTICES See NATIVE AMERICAN CULTURAL PROTECTION AND FREE EXERCISE OF RELIGION ACT OF 1994.

PROPHET DANCE (Dream Dance, Ghost Dance, Praying Dance, Religious Dance) *Columbia Plateau region of the Northwest coast* Prophet Dance is the name coined by the anthropologist Leslie Spier for a religious movement found among Native groups of the Plateau area of the Northwest. He believed that it was present in the region at least as early as the beginning of the 19th century. Spier also argued that the Prophet Dance was the source of later religious movements, including the WASHAT DANCE (RELIGION), the religion of the prophet SMOHALLA, the GHOST DANCE OF 1870 and GHOST DANCE OF 1890, the FEATHER RELIGION, and possibly the INDIAN SHAKER RELIGION. It was characterized by the emergence of a dreamer, or prophet, who had generally received sacred knowledge during a temporary death experience or vision. This religious leader often pointed to events in nature, including earthquakes, falling stars, and the appearance of falling volcanic ash, as signs of the approaching end of the world. According to the doctrine, the world would then be renewed, and the people would be reunited with those who had died. A number of prophets also foretold the arrival of Europeans to the region and the ways in which that event would affect Native life. Ritual elements of the religious movement generally included the performance of a circle dance, with different forms depending upon the group, over a period of several days. In some tribal groups, sins were confessed by the leader and each participant. In others a "marriage or touching dance," was held, involving the selection of spouses by touch during its performance. Many of the dreamers or prophets also proselytized, taking their religious teachings to other tribal groups. Others attracted distant followers who had heard of their spiritual powers. Besides dancing and praying, the people were instructed to live righteously and to follow the religious teachings and traditions of their people.

There is disagreement among scholars about the origin of the Prophet Dance. Some scholars agree with Spier and believe that it was a precontact movement and the source of both Ghost Dances. Others argue that it developed as a Native reaction to population decimation and other aspects of European contact. The Prophet Dance is known by many names, including the Dream Dance, Ghost Dance, Praying Dance and Religious Dance.

PUBLIC APPROPRIATION AND COMMERCIAL EXPLOITATION OF NATIVE AMERICAN CULTURAL, RELIGIOUS, AND INTELLECTUAL PROPERTY BY OUTSIDERS

The public appropriation and commercial exploitation of cultural and intellectual property by individuals and groups who act in the name of American Indians without the proper credentials or authority to do so. Such practices, rooted in colonization, are pervasive and take a number of forms, including bogus shamans who offer pseudo-religious workshops or sweat lodge and pipe ceremonies as well as VISON QUESTs to non-Indians for a fee; the creation of ersatz tribal groups, such as the "Bear Tribe" or "Smoki," initiating members and performing "borrowed" rituals; the tribally unauthorized use of American Indian sacred music to sell CDs or concerts; the tribally unauthorized production, use, or sale of tribal religious images and/or ritual objects (pipes, turtle shell rattles, medicine pouches, tobacco ties, prayer feathers, and so on); and the appropriation of American Indian identities, names, and credentials by outsiders who then pose as legitimate tribal spokespersons or religious practitioners. These offensive practices are condemned by bona-fide tribal nations as cultural exploitation, detrimental and dangerous to the survival and well-being of their people.

Among the many Indian nations, organizations, and individuals condemning the appropriation and exploitation of American Indian religious practices are recognized traditional spiritual leaders and elders of the Lakota people. Lakota spirituality in particular has become a fad to many non-Indians, whose naïveté has been exploited by pseudo-medicine men and women who make a profitable living performing sacred Lakota rites. In excerpts from a 1993 "Declaration of War Against Exploiters of Lakota Spirituality," passed unanimously by an international gathering of 500 representatives of U.S. and Canadian Lakota, Dakota, and Nakota Nations, they spell out their objection:

Whereas for too long we have suffered the unspeakable indignity of having our most precious Lakota ceremonies and spiritual practices desecrated, mocked, and abused by non-Indian 'wannabes,' hucksters, cultists, commercial profiteers, and self-styled 'New Age shamans' and their followers; and

Whereas our precious Sacred Pipe is being desecrated through the sale of pipestone pipes at flea markets, powwows, and "New Age" retail stores; and

Whereas pseudo-religious corporations have been formed to charge money for admission into phony "sweatlodges" and "vision quest" programs; and

Whereas sacrilegious "sundances" for non-Indians are being conducted by charlatans and cult leaders who promote abominable and obscene imitations of our sacred Lakota sundance rites; . . .

We urge traditional people, tribal leaders, and governing councils of all other Indian nations, to join us in calling for an immediate end to this rampant exploitation of our respective American Indian sacred traditions by issuing statements denouncing such abuse; for it is not the Lakota, Dakota, and Nakota people alone whose spiritual practices are being systematically violated by non-Indians.

The Hopi have also issued statements concerning property rights, such as the following excerpt from the Internet home page of the Hopi Cultural Preservation Office:

Through the decades the intellectual property rights of Hopi have been violated for the benefit of many other, non-Hopi people that has proven to be detrimental. Exploitation comes in many forms. For example, numerous stories told to strangers have been published in books without the storytellers' permission. After non-Hopis saw ceremonial dances, tape recorded copies of music were sold to outside sources. Clothing items of ceremonial dancers have been photographed without the dancers' permission and sold. Choreography from ceremonial dances has been copied and performed in non-sacred settings. Even the pictures of the ceremonies have been included in books without written permission. Designs from skilled Hopi potters have been duplicated by non-Hopis. Katsina dolls have also been duplicated from Hopi dancers seen at Hopi. Although the Hopi believe the ceremonies are intended for the benefit of all people, they also believe benefits only result when ceremonies are properly performed and protected.

All of these actions are breaches of Hopi intellectual property rights, used by non-Hopi for personal and commercial benefit without Hopi permission.

Those who appropriate aspects of indigenous cultures for their own purposes often dupe others, who then become part of the problem for Native people. Abusing private cultural and religious practices desecrates their sacredness, disrespects tribal sovereignty, and indeed, endangers the people.

PUCK HYAH TOOT ("Hungry Birds Circling to Land to Feed" or "Birds Feeding in a Flock," Johnny Buck)

(1878–1965?) Wanapam. A leading prophet in the Priest Rapids area of the Columbia River in Washington State. Known as Squamiethla in his youth, he later received an adult name, Puck Hyah Toot, from his father, Watastahicht (Standing Dancing), after recovering from smallpox. His mother, Tsalamukht, was from Chamna, a village near the mouth of the Yakima River. When his parents left the area for Idaho, Puck Hyah Toot stayed with the prophet SMOHALLA, his uncle and teacher. Besides curing him of smallpox, the famous teacher trained him for 12 years in the

Puck Hyah Toot. A first-roots feast conducted in the 1960s by Puck Hyah Toot, the nephew of the religious leader Smohalla. The menu included newly dug roots and other traditional foods, such as berries, venison, salmon, and black eels. The feast took place before the Washat Dance. *Courtesy of Robert H. Ruby.*

WASHANI RELIGION and its sacred WASHAT DANCE (RELIGION). He and Smohalla's son, Yo-Yonan (YOYOUNI), both became priests after learning the teachings. With Yo-Yonan's death in 1917, Puck Hyah Toot remained alone to carry on the sacred ways. After a year of mourning, he married his cousin's widow, Wallulami. Years later he told the writer Click Relander about Smohalla and his teachings in order that they not be forgotten. Although referred to as the "Last Prophet of the Wanapums," Puck Hyah Toot was succeeded by his son and grandson. The prophet was also known as Johnny Buck.

PUEBLO CEREMONIALISM

The annual cycle of Pueblo ceremonies, integrated into the social organization, reflecting seasonal changes and the subsistence activities associated with each season. The ceremonies are primarily for bringing rain, an abundance of crops, animals, or children, or the cure of a disease. Conducted by organized priesthoods, religious societies, or other groups, they are carried out in an annual round according to a religious calendar keyed to seasons, except for ritual performances associated with the Catholic calendar that have exact dates. With their action, dance, and music, these ceremonies are communal public prayers that focus on group rather than individual concerns. Activities frequently center on group harmony and community health. Every song, gesture, action, article of clothing, and ritual object has a symbolic meaning. Frequent symbols in Pueblo ceremonies are corn, seeds, clouds, kivas, sacred mountains, underworlds, altars, lightning, plazas, water, pole standards, witches, kachinas, bear, deer, sun, moon, stars, and birds. Village rituals are held in plazas and kivas. A large number of rites are common to Pueblo ceremonials in general, including offerings of meal or pollen, the use of prayersticks, the preparation of food, beads, and implements, BREATHING rites, smoking, ritual narratives, exorcising with ashes or cedar bark, hair washing, fasting, and abstention from intercourse. Ceremonial knowledge can be used for good or evil. Witches use ceremonial knowledge for personal benefit, not for the good of all. (See also Subject Index for Pueblo ceremonies covered in this volume.)

PUEBLO SPIRITS

The principal spirits include the creator of life, a guardian of the lifeways, or "roads" of people, an earth mother, a destroyer-divinity of death, a serpent controlling all water, one who "owns" game animals, and an embodiment of corn. The Pueblo priests orchestrate the interaction of spirits with the community through a series of complex ceremonies that occur throughout the year, including KACHINA DANCES, initiations, observances for the dead, solstice ceremonies, hunting, and other activities. The names of spirits and their importance vary from pueblo to pueblo. In all the pueblos except Hopi, the generative force of earth is female. At Hopi, that function belongs to GERMINATOR, a male spirit.

PURIFICATION RITES These rites, which vary from group to group, empty the body of all poisons and excesses through bathing or washing heads, sweatbaths, emetics (herbal drinks that induce vomiting), smoking, smudging (blowing smoke of cedar, sage, or sweetgrass on the body), waving ashes, brushing, fumigation by burning pinyon gum and cedar, and ceremonial whipping. Spiritual purification may involve ritual abstention from certain foods and sexual intercourse, especially when preparing for a ceremony.

PUTTING ON MOCCASINS (First Moccasin Ceremony)
Apache A ceremony that celebrates a baby's first steps takes place after the child is at least seven months old and before the child is two years old. A practitioner conducts the ceremony, whose purpose is to keep the child healthy and strong. Held at the new moon, children wear newly made outfits and don their first moccasins. There are prayers, ritual songs, dances, games, blessings with pollen, a present giveaway, and feasting.

Q

QUAPAW, JOHN *(?–1928) Quapaw* Early peyote ROADMAN and political leader among his people in Indian Territory (present-day Oklahoma). JOHN WILSON, the Caddo-Delaware (Lenni Lenape) originator of the Big Moon peyote ceremony, appointed Quapaw as his successor. Quapaw's duties included performing wedding ceremonies, officiating at peyote organization affairs and making special invocations during services for the ill. In 1924, when he was elderly and serving as an assistant chief, he was afflicted with a serious illness. Although he was an adherent of the PEYOTE RELIGION who had doctored many people, he sought treatment for himself from other sources, including both medical and herb doctors. When they were unable to help him, he turned to WILLIE THOMAS, a visiting Delaware leader, who conducted a peyote meeting for him. Quapaw then recovered and used the experience to reaffirm his belief in peyotism, emphasizing that he should not have gone back on his religious faith during that period. After the incumbent chief died, Quapaw assumed the position and held it until his own death in 1928. (See also GRIFFIN, VICTOR.)

QUINNEY, JOHN *(fl. 18th century) Mohegan or Stockbridge* Interpreter for the Reverend JOHN SERGEANT, 18th-century missionary to the Housatonic Indians in Massachusetts. Quinney assisted the minister in translating and printing religious works, including the assembly's catechism, which was printed in Stockbridge, Massachusetts, in 1795. Although details of his life are unknown, some of his descendants became prominent. His son, Joseph Quinney (also Quanaukaunt and Quinequaun), served as the town constable of Stockbridge and

in 1777 succeeded Solomon Unhaunnauwaunutt as chief of the Mohegan. Another Quinney, also named Joseph, became a deacon of New York's Stockbridge Church in 1817 and the following year helped lead his people in their emigration from that state to the West.

QUINTON, AMELIA STONE *(1833–1926)* Organizer of the Women's National Indian Association who established a large number of missions among Native groups. Born in 1833 in Jamesville, New York, she grew up in nearby Homer influenced by the religious faith of her grandfather, who had served as a Baptist deacon. She attended Homer's Cortland Academy, then became a "preceptress" in a school near Syracuse. After teaching for a year at a Georgia seminary, she married the Reverend James Franklin Swanson from that state. Quinton returned north after he died and taught for a year at the Chestnut Street Female Seminary in Philadelphia before moving to New York City to do volunteer work. An early member of the Woman's Christian Temperance Union, she became an organizer for the group locally and at the state level. She also married her second husband, the Reverend Richard L. Quinton, and they settled in Philadelphia. Quinton's involvement in Indian rights began in 1879 through the influence of her friend MARY LUCINDA BONNEY. Concerned about ongoing pressures to open Indian Territory (present-day Oklahoma) to white settlers, the two women began a petition drive on behalf of honoring treaty obligations. They later formed a committee that grew into the Women's National Indian Association, one of the first Indian reform organizations in the country. Through

Quinton's organizing efforts, the association had more than 80 branches in 28 states and territories by 1886. She initially served as secretary and president. Quinton advocated a new government policy of Assimilation, emphasizing the allotment of tribally owned lands to Indian individuals, and wrote a petition on the issue that was presented in the U.S. Senate in 1882. She organized, traveled, and delivered speeches to secure popular support for the cause until 1887, when the Dawes Severalty Act, which broke up tribal lands into individual holdings or allotments, was passed. She then turned her attention to other Indian reform issues and continued to foster the growth of the association. Besides promoting compulsory education and liquor prohibition, she sought civil service status for Bureau of Indian Affairs personnel. The association's missionary efforts were the "crowning joy" of Quinton's work and led to the establishment of 50 Indian missions, which were eventually turned over to different denominations. The influential group supported the government ban on Native dances and customs, including polygamy. In 1901 the organization became the National Indian Association and in about 1904 moved its headquarters to New York. After declining reelection as president because of declining health, Quinton continued to chair the association's missionary department. She worked for several years in California on behalf of landless Indians and on other issues. Upon her return east by 1910, Quinton lived in Ridgefield Park, New Jersey, where she later died at the age of 93.

RABBIT HUNTS *Pueblo* Rabbit drives are held before, during or after ceremonies, notably in eastern pueblos and at Hopi Pueblo, particularly in connection with the WUWUCHIM CEREMONY. The organization of the hunt, the hunt fire, the ritual treatment of rabbits killed, and the assignment of game have ceremonial aspects. The War Captains, or hunters, distribute the rabbits. At Hopi, the kachina impersonators distribute the rabbits during Wuwuchim.

RAGUENEAU, PAUL *(1608–1680)* French Jesuit missionary. Born in Paris, he entered the Paris novitiate in 1628 and arrived in Quebec in 1636. He went to Huron country the next year. In 1645, he became superior of the Huron mission until 1650. He wrote the *Relations des Hurons* for 1646, 1647, 1648, and 1649, which recount the destruction of the mission and the martyrdom of Fathers JEAN DE BRÉBEUF and Gabriel Lalemant. The *Relation* for 1650 describes the abandonment of Huronia after it was attacked by Iroquois and the emigration and resettlement of Huron under the protection of a Quebec fort. Ragueneau recognized that the uncompromising attitude of early missionaries was not appropriate. He supervised the exodus to Quebec of remnants of the Huron Nation. In 1650, he was named superior of Jesuits in Canada until 1653. In 1662, he left for France in order to plead for sending troops to Canada to fight the Iroquois, and he never returned to Canada. In Paris, he became a representative of the Jesuit missions in Canada.

RAIN CEREMONIAL (Thlahewe) *Zuni* A sacred dance enacted every four years in August when corn is a foot high. The ceremony is supposed to reproduce a ceremony held at the time of the third appearance of the CORN MAIDENS. Women assume the leading parts in this ceremony.

RAIN HOUSE (smoking house, round house, *vahki*) *Tohono O'odham (Papago)* Also called a "smoking house," "round house," or *vahki*, this ceremonial structure using the brush-and-mud-covered form of construction is a storage place for jars with fermenting saguaro cactus pulp used during the Tohono O'odham SAGUARO FESTIVAL during the summer. The rain house is a place of private rituals involving the making of sacred cactus wine, singing, and dancing. The rain house is accompanied by a *ramada* (arbor) called a *watto.*

RAIN PRIESTHOODS (Ashiwanni) *Zuni* Priesthoods whose duty is to fast and pray for rain. Membership is open to men and women who are associated with the matrilineal household groups of a specific clan or children of that clan. Six of the rain priesthoods are paramount and are associated with the six directions. The rain priest of the north, LONG HORN, heads the priesthood. Other rain priests each maintain a ceremonial room, sacred objects and altars. The power of priests resides in their sacred objects, called *ettowe,* one for each priesthood, that represent the *uwanammi,* the rain beings. These are the most sacred objects among the Zuni people. When not in use, they rest in a special chamber in the house of the maternal lineage. The priesthoods have important roles in summer when they go into retreats to pray for rain for four to eight days each consecutively from summer solstice into September, the critical period for rain. The priesthoods also have winter retreats. Other societies' provinces are curing and hunting. (See also BOW PRIESTHOOD; CURING SOCIETIES.)

RAINBOW NATURAL BRIDGE *Navajo (Dineh), Paiute, Pueblo* A traditional sacred site in Utah. Rainbow Bridge holds a position of central importance in the religion of some Navajo people living in that area. For generations, Navajo singers have performed ceremonies near the huge sandstone arch, and water from a nearby spring has been used for other ceremonies. Navajo believe that if humans alter the earth in that area of the bridge, their prayers will not be heard by spirits and their ceremonies will be ineffective to prevent evil and disease. Completion of Glen Canyon Dam on the Colorado River and creation of Lake Powell in Arizona in 1963 was said to have drowned some of the Navajo spirits and denied them access to a prayer spot sacred to them. The National Park Service, which manages Rainbow Bridge (designated a National Monument in 1910), provides boat trips to the arch. Tourists desecrate the sacred site with noise, litter, and defacement of the bridge itself and because of the flooding and presence of tourists, the Navajo no longer hold ceremonies in the area of the bridge. The Navajo filed a suit in 1977 to prevent the penetration of Rainbow Natural Bridge's opening by the rising of Lake Powell. The Navajo claimed the bridge, located in Bridge Canyon near Navajo Mountain in Utah, to be "of the highest [religious] importance . . . occupying a position of profound significance and veneration by the Navajo people . . . The desecration of Rainbow Bridge, a sacred object and symbol, will cause the applicants and Navajo people much suffering, anguish, and humiliation." Alteration of the site, it was claimed, made therapeutic ceremonies ineffective. In addition to the Navajo, some San Juan Paiute and Pueblo people still consider Rainbow Bridge to be a sacred place. In 1980, the Tenth Circuit Court ruled against the Navajo plaintiffs in *BADONI V. HIGGINSON.*

RALE, SEBASTIEN (Rasle; Rasles) *(1657–1724)* French Jesuit missionary. Born in France, he joined the Society of Jesus in 1675 at the age of 18. He was ordained at Lyon and arrived at Quebec in 1689. He was first sent to the Abenaki mission near Quebec. There he mastered the Eastern Abenaki language and its pronunciation in five months and began his French-Eastern Abenaki dictionary, which eventually consisted of 7,500 distinct Abenaki words. About 1693, he was sent to Illinois country, which gave him an

opportunity to learn Ottawa, Huron, and Illinois languages. In 1694, he founded the Eastern Abenaki mission at Norridgewock on the Kennebec River in Maine, which he served for the next 30 years until his death. Father Rale supported the pro-French factions that opposed English claims to Abenaki territory, and he tried to halt the intrusion of Protestant ministers into Abenaki country. He was killed during the destruction of his mission by English troops in 1724. The dictionary to which Rale devoted nearly 30 years of study is preserved at Harvard University. It was published in 1833. His name is also spelled Rasle and Rasles.

RAND, SILAS TERTIUS *(1810–1889)* Baptist missionary among the Micmac of the Maritime Provinces. Born in Cornwallis, Nova Scotia, he was educated at a Baptist seminary. After entering the ministry in 1834, he served in a number of pastorates and then became a full-time missionary to the Micmac in 1849 under the sponsorship of his denomination. A short time later he organized the nondenominational Micmac Missionary Society, which was in effect until 1865, and became independent of his Baptist sponsors. He devoted his efforts to teaching among the Micmac people and studying their language and culture. Rand made few converts among the Roman Catholic Indians and soon turned to educational endeavors but was unable to obtain enough support to open a school. He succeeded in calling attention to the sufferings of the Micmac and completing significant language and folklore studies. Rand translated major portions of the Bible and compiled a grammar (Halifax, 1875) and dictionary (Halifax, 1888). He also wrote *A Short Statement of Facts Relating to the History, Manners, Customs, Language, and Literature of the Micmac Tribe of Indians in Nova Scotia and P.E. Island* (Halifax, 1850) and *Legends of the Micmacs* (New York, 1894). Rand continued his Micmac work until his death in 1889.

RASPBERRY CEREMONY *Iroquois* A food spirit ceremony designed to give thanks for the recurrence of the raspberry season and to supplicate food spirits to continue their work. It is scheduled when raspberries ripen.

RATTLE A device or object that produces rhythmic percussive sound; generally used for both religious and secular purposes by most tribes except some Inuit. It is used in rituals, religious feasts, and shamanistic performances. Rattles are made of animal hoofs, bird beaks, shell pods, tortoise and turtle shells, gourds, cowhorn, bark, and rawhide sewn together. Filled with seeds, pebbles, corn kernels, or other materials, depending on the sound desired, they are sometimes fastened to belts or made into necklaces or anklets so as to make sounds when the wearer moves. On the Northwest Coast, shamans use oval wooden rattles with carvings that represent spirit helpers. Rattles are objects of great respect and are essential in ceremonies.

RAVE, JOHN *(c. 1855–1917) Winnebago* The first peyote ROADMAN among his people. A Winnebago from Nebraska, Rave was a descendant of the Bear clan. He went to Oklahoma in the late 1800s, either in 1889 or from 1893 to 1894, where he tried taking peyote for the first time. Although his initial experience was frightening, he later become convinced of its holiness. Soon after his conversion, he introduced the religion among the Winnebago people. His ceremony, similar to the Big Moon variation initiated by the peyote leader JOHN WILSON, became known as the John Rave Cross Fire ritual. Its features included Christian symbols, baptism of initiates, and public confession. Rave attributed his recovery from a serious illness and changes in his life to the healing power of peyote. Because he introduced peyotism to the Winnebago people and had the earliest followers among them, his ritual was sometimes referred to as "old man fire." Rave died in 1917 after he had been committed to an insane asylum. Although he may have been afflicted with senility, opponents of peyotism used his condition to denounce its practice.

RED FISH *(?–1928) Dakota* Yanktonai chief and medicine man who was a leader of the Wakan wacipi (HOLY DANCE, also called Dakota MIDEWIWIN) among his people. Red Fish was noted for the spiritual powers he manifested during ceremonies of the sacred society. He was known to take a plum tree branch into the ceremonial lodge and place it in the earth, then to begin singing and dancing around it. Blossoms and leaves would first appear, followed by small plums. After they had grown and ripened during the period of a few minutes, Red Fish would pick them and toss them to other people present. Besides leading the WAKAN FEAST, the holy man was known to attend the ceremonies conducted by other tribal groups. Toward the end of his life he gave his medicine bundle to Major A. B. Welch of Mandan, North Dakota. Others had sought segments of it earlier, but he would not relinquish his sacred objects until he knew he was near the end of his life.

RED HAT, EDWARD (Holy Standard or Fan Man) *(1898–1982) Cheyenne* Keeper of the SACRED ARROWS of the Cheyenne people. Red Hat, a Southern Cheyenne, was born in 1898. His mother was Walks in the Middle and his father was Red Hat. In 1971 he was named to the holiest position among the Cheyenne, the keeper of the Sacred Arrows. Red Hat was highly respected for his knowledge of the religious ways of his people. His family had the authority to make the Blue Sky, a sacred object that symbolized the heavens in the Sacred Arrows renewing ceremonies. During his tenure as keeper, Red Hat approved the efforts of the Northern Cheyenne Research and Human Development Association on behalf of reviving and preserving the traditions of his people. He also fasted and prayed on NOAHA-VOSE, the sacred BEAR BUTTE, and conducted his duties as keeper. From 1971 until his death on February 24, 1982, Red Hat instructed the author Karl H. Schlesier on Cheyenne sacred ways.

RED HAWK (Cetan Luta) *(c. 1829–?) Lakota* Nineteenth-century Oglala shaman. He was an informant to JAMES R. WALKER, an agency physician who recorded information about Lakota religion and culture on the Pine Ridge Reservation in South Dakota between 1896 and 1914. Red Hawk described himself as a holy man who knew Bear medicine and other sacred knowledge, including language, ceremonies, and songs. He was also a warrior who had found his medicine to be good during war and who had earned the right to wear the split eagle feather. Red Hawk stated that he had been given wisdom by his Hunka Ate, or adopted father, a wise man who was listened to by the people. In 1913 he was photographed in New York by Joseph Kossuth Dixon. From the White Clay district of Pine Ridge, Red Hawk, GEORGE SWORD, FINGER, and THOMAS TYON were among the Oglala who instructed Walker.

RED NEST, WILLIAM *Lakota* Peyotist from the Pine Ridge Reservation in South Dakota. He was indicted on September 11, 1915, by a South Dakota grand jury "Under the Act of January 30, 1897, for selling and giving intoxicants to Indians." Several years earlier, in 1911, Red Nest, HARRY BLACK BEAR, and Charles Red Bear had received written denial of their request for permission to use peyote from assistant commissioner of Indian affairs, C. F. Hauke. Red Nest, identified in 1916 by Bureau of Indian Affairs Superintendent John R. Brennan as one of five Oglala peyote leaders, formed the idea of a Cross Fire peyote cemetery and donated land for it. In 1917 the case against him was dismissed by the U.S. attorney. (See also PEYOTE RELIGION; Subject Index for other cases involving peyote use included in this volume.)

RED WEASEL (Itun'kasan-luta) *(c. 1831–?) Lakota* Red Weasel was regarded as "the highest authority" on the SUN DANCE among the Teton or western division of his people when the ethnologist Frances Densmore interviewed him and the medicine man GOOSE in 1911. He began his religious training at an early age after being selected as a successor to his uncle, Wi'ihan'bla (Dreamer-of-the-Sun). His instructions included preparing to undertake the "highest office" of the sacred Sun Dance. He eventually served as an intercessor four times, offering prayers taught to him by his uncle. The last time he assumed the role was at the 1881 ceremony, believed by some to be the final Sun Dance conducted by the Teton division of his people. When he was interviewed by Densmore, he was approximately 80 years old and had traveled over 40 miles in a wagon for the meeting at Standing Rock agency in North Dakota. The esteem for him was such that many elders stated, "We have fine weather because Red Weasel is with us."

REDSKY, JAMES, SR. (Eshkwaykeezhik, "Last sky") (1899–?) *Ojibway* Mide priest. Born on October 31, 1899, at Rice Bay in the Lake of the Woods region of Canada, Redsky began studying the intricate MIDEWIWIN religion at the age of 12 under his uncle, Baldhead Redsky, who was a leading holy man in the area. After attending a school established by the Presbyterian Board of Missions, he served in the 52nd Canadian Light Infantry Regiment during World War I. Upon returning to the Shoal Lake Reserve, he resumed his religious studies and made a living from the land or through employment as a carpenter and as a guide. After completing a lengthy, costly apprenticeship in the Midewiwin religion, Redsky was given all of his uncle's SACRED SCROLLS. With the changes introduced among his people through Euro-Canadian contact, the number of traditional practitioners dwindled. As an elder and without a religious successor, Redsky decided that his Midewiwin knowledge should be preserved. He interpreted the scrolls for Selwyn Dewdney, who published the information in *Sacred Scrolls of the Southern Ojibway* (1975). The scrolls were then sold to the Glenbow Foundation in Alberta. Redsky was ordained an elder of the Presbyterian Church in 1960 and later wrote *Great Leader of the Ojibway: Mis-quona-queb* (1972), a biography of the legendary MIS-QUONA-QUEB.

REFLECTING MAN, JOHN (?–1956) *Plains Ojibway* Well-known MIDEWIWIN priest and ritualist on the Turtle Mountain Reservation in North Dakota. Reflecting Man often danced in the leadership role of the masked WINDIGOKAN "hunter" at ceremonies. The hunchbacked "hunter" figure of the sacred contrary society carried a crooked bow and arrows and was said to hunt snakes. Reflecting Man was also a noted healer. As a Nanandawi, or bone sucking healer, he removed illness-causing foreign objects from his patients. He was also known to possess a curing rite that came from the buffalo. His extensive knowledge of traditions was further manifested in flute-making and his repertoire of songs. Reflecting Man is said to have continued holding the sacred Midewiwin ceremonies until the end of his life.

REGINA V. MACHEKEQUONABE 28 O.R. 309 (1897) A case heard by the Ontario Divisional Court on February 8, 1897, to determine whether an Indian prisoner was properly convicted of manslaughter at his trial on December 3, 1896, at Rat Portage. The evidence presented at the previous trial indicated that he had shot and killed another Indian man, believing that he was a *windigo,* a cannibalistic being who could assume human form. After a *windigo* had been reported in the area, the community had taken measures to protect itself by posting pairs of guards or sentries, including Machekequonabe, to maintain a watch. While on duty, he and another person saw what they believed to be the *windigo* in the distance. They chased the figure, and Machekequonabe shot at it after their challenges went unanswered. The individual turned out to be his foster father, who died soon after the incident. Machekequonabe's counsel argued that the following of a religious belief would be an excuse in common law, that the Indian people concerned believed in the *windigo* and that there was no intent to harm or to kill another human being. The court upheld the Rat Portage jury's verdict of manslaughter. Other important Canadian cases involving religious freedoms include *BEARSHIRT V. THE QUEEN* and *JACK AND CHARLIE V. R.*

REINERT V. HAAS (585 F. Sup. 477 [1984]) (1984) In this case, Indian inmates in Iowa argued in district court that prison regulations prohibiting the wearing of headbands interfered with their exercise of religious rights. The headband as a symbol of the sacred circle was found by the court to be analogous to a Christian cross or medal. The right of the Indian inmates to wear headbands was upheld, the court reasoning that the public's interest was best served by protecting the constitutional rights of all its members. (See also Subject Index for other cases involving the religious freedoms of Native Americans included in this volume.)

RELIGIOUS FREEDOM RESTORATION ACT OF 1993 An act to protect the free exercise of religion, the Religious Freedom Restoration Act (RFRA) was signed by President Bill Clinton on November 16, 1993. The act, the product of the work of the AMERICAN INDIAN RELIGIOUS FREEDOM COALITION, passed unanimously in the House of Representatives, received three no-votes in the Senate, and was endorsed by the president.

The law was passed by Congress in direct response to the Supreme Court's 1990 ruling in *EMPLOYMENT DIVISION, DEPARTMENT OF HUMAN RESOURCES OF OREGON, ET AL. V. SMITH ET AL.* that religious groups cannot ordinarily exempt themselves from generally worded laws. The decision held that Native Americans who use peyote in their religious ceremonies were not exempt from the narcotics law that applies to everyone else. Although RFRA was triggered by the *Smith* case, its purpose was never specifically directed at protecting American Indian religious freedom.

The coalition rallied Congress to pass a law prohibiting the government from enforcing a law that substantially burdened religious exercises without first demonstrating a "compelling" need to do so and without using "the least restrictive means" possible.

RFRA restored the "compelling interest" requirement wherein governments would have to show an overriding public interest was being served by interfering with a religious practice. This requirement was removed by the Supreme Court in the Oregon peyote case.

In reality RFRA solved the problems of mainstream religious communities, but did not resolve the issues faced by Native Americans who wanted protection of traditional forms of worship, including sacred sites and religious materials. Some senators and representatives believed RFRA would take care of the Indian problems. At the time Congress was considering RFRA, it also was considering another bill—the Native American Free Exercise of Religion Act of 1993 (NAFERA)—that aimed to protect traditional forms of worship practiced by Indian peoples. The introduction of this bill by Senator Daniel K. Inouye (D-Hawaii), chairman of the Senate Committee on Indian Affairs, culminated nine congressional hearings held throughout the country, chaired by Senator Inouye.

After working on extensive amendments to NAFERA with the Clinton administration, tribes, and leaders of the coalition in the summer of 1994, Senator Inouye introduced new legislation that included cultural protection as well as religious protection. This act specifically protected sacred sites, sacramental use of peyote, prisoners rights, and ceremonial use of eagle feathers and other animal parts. No action was taken on the bill due to mounting concerns regarding sacred sites. But a team, an unprecedented coalition of Native American Church leaders, tribal leaders, and Native American Rights Fund attorneys, came together to develop a strategy for the enactment of separate peyote legislation.

Eventually, Congress passed and President Clinton signed, on October 6, 1994, the landmark legislation—the AMERICAN INDIAN RELIGIOUS FREEDOM ACT AMENDMENTS OF 1994—guaranteeing American Indians the right to use the sacrament of peyote in traditional religious ceremonies.

On June 25, 1997, the U.S. Supreme Court declared RFRA unconstitutional in *CITY OF BOERNE V. P.F. FLORES.* (See also NATIVE AMERICAN CULTURAL PROTECTION AND FREE EXCERCISE OF RELIGION ACT OF 1994.)

REMAKING RITE *Navajo (Dineh)* A healing ceremony and rite in which wooden figurines that have curing functions are made. When personal life has been disrupted, one may correct a situation by ceremonial means of the remaking rite, in which the inner form of an offended animal or other entity is re-created and restored to its former condition. The prayer act in a remaking ceremonial communicates the intentions of the communicant who beseeches a Holy Person, to whom the prayer is directed, to make a proper response, a reestablishment of the right order in the world and restoration of health and peace. The rite is an act of creation, or re-creation, based on the model of the original creation. Referred to as "dolls" by the Navajo, the wooden figurines are carved by Navajo (Dineh) singers or assistants and placed near ruins as part of the ceremony. They have human forms and are decorated with jewels, fabrics, and paint to give them specific identities. Following placement at a ruin, there is a continued relationship between the figurine and patient until the figurine loses curative powers. Other than natural weathering, other forms of destruction or removal are not condoned, and a figurine is left where it has been placed. (See also SACRIFICIAL FIGURINES.)

RENVILLE, ISAAC *(c. 1840–1919) Dakota* An ordained minister of the Dakota presbytery. The son of a trader, he was born to Winona, a full-blood Dakota, and Antoine Renville, a mixed-blood Dakota, at Lac qui Parle in Minnesota Territory. Renville was educated at the Lac qui Parle mission established by THOMAS S. WILLIAMSON and at the Hazelwood mission developed in the region by STEPHEN RETURN RIGGS. At the time of the Dakota War of 1862, he was a member of the tribal farming group led by PAUL MAZAKUTEMANI. Renville was an active participant in the peace party during the war, which was precipitated by a number of factors among the Eastern Dakota people, including great land losses, poverty, and government failure to honor treaty agreements. He was selected to serve as a scout in 1863 under Colonel Henry H. Sibley, the army officer who led military campaigns against tribal opponents in Minnesota and eastern Dakota Territory. After settling on the Sisseton Reservation in South Dakota in 1867, Renville received a land allotment there in 1875. He received his license to preach from the Dakota presbytery in 1878 and was ordained the following year. He then became a pastor, serving at churches in the presbytery. Renville died in 1919. Several of Renville's relatives also became ministers, including his uncle JOHN B. RENVILLE and his cousin VICTOR RENVILLE.

RENVILLE, JOHN B. *(1831–1903) Dakota* The first Dakota minister to be ordained by the Presbyterian Church. He was born to Mary and Joseph Renville, Sr., an influential trader, at Lac qui Parle, Minnesota Territory, in October 1831. After attending the mission school established by THOMAS S. WILLIAMSON there, he was sent to a college in Illinois. Renville served as a teacher at the Upper Sioux Agency at Yellow Medicine in Minnesota Territory. Its jurisdiction included Sisseton and Wahpeton band members in Dakota Territory. During the Dakota War of 1862, when Dakota under Little Crow and other leaders fought against Euro-American settlers and military forces, Renville and his wife were taken captive, but were later released.

Renville was ordained a few years later, in 1865, and died on the Sisseton Reservation in South Dakota in 1903. Other family members also become ministers, including his nephew ISAAC RENVILLE and his cousin VICTOR RENVILLE.

RENVILLE, VICTOR *(1849–1927) Dakota* An Episcopal priest who was born to Mary and Gabriel Renville at Lac qui Parle in Minnesota Territory on November 13, 1849. Renville attended school at the mission established by the family of THOMAS S. WILLIAMSON. The family eventually settled at the Upper Sioux Agency at Yellow Medicine along the Minnesota River. When the Dakota War of 1862 broke out between Dakota forces and Euro-American opponents, the Renvilles stayed in vacant agency buildings. Along with other mixed-bloods, they became captives but were later released at Camp Release. In 1866 Renville worked with his father as a scout, and the following year the family moved to the Sisseton Reservation in South Dakota. After marrying Mary Roy on July 5, 1870, Renville later took land there. He became a member of the Episcopal Church in the 1880s and was ordained to the priesthood by WILLIAM HOBART HARE on June 26, 1895. Renville served at churches in the Sisseton area until his retirement in 1925. He wrote "A Sketch of the Minnesota Massacre," which was published in *Collections of the State Historical Society of North Dakota* in 1923. He died in January 1927. Other family members also entered the ministry, including his cousins ISAAC RENVILLE and JOHN B. RENVILLE.

REPATRIATION Native American tribes are demanding the return of skeletal remains, burial goods, and sacred objects that rightfully belong to them. Some sacred objects have been sold by the original owners. Some objects included in the spoils of war after military battles have fallen into museum hands. Many sacred objects were stolen from original Native owners. In other cases, religious property has been sold by Native people who did not have ownership or title to the objects. Many sacred objects were taken from Native American graves located on Indian and pub-

lic lands and eventually some of them have entered into the possession of museums.

Since 1906, federal statutes protecting "archaeological resources" on public lands have classified dead Indians and tribal burials on federal lands as "federal property." This classification of Indian dead as "resources" and the conversion of humans into property have resulted in injustices against Indian people, as thousands of Indian burial sites have been dug up since 1906 under federal permits. Many tribes who have requested the return of sacred objects have been ignored by museums. Some institutions, however, have cooperated. In 1980 the Denver Art Museum returned a WAR GOD to the Zuni Bow priests that was stolen from them and later donated to the museum. The Heard Museum in Phoenix, Arizona, returned kiva masks to Hopi elders, and the Wheelwright Museum in Santa Fe, New Mexico, returned 11 MEDICINE BUNDLES to Navajo practitioners. The State Museum of New York at Albany returned 12 old and revered WAMPUM belts to the Iroquois people. The Museum of the American Indian in New York City returned 11 Iroquois wampum belts to their home at the Six Nations Reserve at Grand River, Ontario, and also returned the WATERBUSTER CLAN BUNDLE to the Hidatsa clan that petitioned for its return. Harvard's Peabody Museum returned the OMAHA SACRED POLE to the Omaha people. Stanford University, the University of New Mexico, Seattle University, and the University of Nebraska have also returned thousands of human remains to tribes.

On April 14, 1992, the Heard Museum returned to a Hopi religious society a ceremonial war shield that had been stolen 20 years earlier. On September 11, 1992, the National Museum of the American Indian (NMAI) approved the return of nine potlatch objects to the Kwakiutl of British Columbia. These objects had been confiscated by the Royal Canadian Mounted Police in 1921. After more than 125 years in the collections of the Army Medical Museum and the Smithsonian's National Museum of Natural History, on July 10, 1993, the Cheyenne people in Oklahoma buried the remains of 18 Cheyenne people. Since 1991, the Repatriation Office of the Museum of Natural History has fulfilled several repatriation requests. In addition to the Cheyenne repatriation, the remains of 12 individuals were returned to the Chugach and Eyak people of Prince William Sound. In October 1993, the NMAI trustees repatriated 87 sacred objects to the pueblo of Jemez. The religious leadership of the pueblo, a traditional theocracy, negotiated the terms of the repatriation, including the selection of one item, a war shield, permitted to be photographed and published. In July 1996, 74 sacred belts and strings of *anakoha* (wampum) were returned to the Haudenosaunee Confederacy by the National Museum of the American Indian. On September

Repatriation of human remains, grave goods, and sacred objects. On May 26, 1989, in Browning, Montana, members of the Blackfeet tribe conducted a burial ceremony for 16 of their ancestors' remains, returned in September 1988 from the Smithsonian Institution. The Native American Rights Fund estimates that more than 600,000 "specimens" are held by museums, universities, historical societies, and private collections across the country. *Photograph by Leslie Logan. Smithsonian Institution.*

28, 1997, the remains of Long Wolf, a Lakota, were reinterred on the Pine Ridge Reservation in South Dakota. In 1886, he left his people to work in Buffalo Bill Cody's Wild West Show. He died of pneumonia in 1892 while performing at Earl's Court in west London, England. One hundred and five years after his burial in West Brompton Cemetery, an Englishwoman discovered his grave, which set in motion the repatriation of Long Wolf's remains.

At the same time, there is opposition to Native American efforts to reclaim ancestral remains and sacred objects among some physical anthropologists, archaeologists, state historical societies, museum directors and curators, National Park Service officials, and groups such as the Society for American Archaeology. For example, the Grand Council of the Iroquois Confederacy drafted a policy statement in March 1981 requesting the return of all masks to firekeepers of the Iroquois League and sent it to directors of museums. Some museums removed the FALSE FACES from exhibition, but others simply ignored the request. In November 1989

President George Bush signed the NATIONAL MUSEUM OF THE AMERICAN INDIAN ACT that requires the Smithsonian Institution to repatriate some of its 18,000 skeletal remains and thousands of associated funerary objects to requesting tribes for reburial. Tribes must notify the Smithsonian of their interest in the remains, and when evidence links the remains to tribes, the bones must be returned to the tribes for reinterment. Funerary objects are subject to repatriation under the same standards where they are associated with specific remains or grave sites. A 1990 landmark act, the NATIVE AMERICAN GRAVES PROTECTION AND REPATRIATION ACT, gives tribes legal procedures to reclaim culturally identifiable remains, funerary objects, and sacred objects from museum collections.

Decisions on repatriation vary among tribes. For example, the Confederated Tribes of the Umatilla Indian Reservation (CTUIR) adopted a policy to repatriate and reinter all human remains and associated and unassociated funerary objects that have been identified as originating from lands within the CTUIR's boundaries. The Zuni, on the other hand, have concluded that they will not seek repatriation of human remains in museum collections, but they have taken the position that the remains may not be exhibited to the public.

A number of options exist for the final disposition of repatriated objects. Objects may be returned to religious leaders, to specific social groups—such as clans—for their traditional use, or to an individual or lineal descendant who can demonstrate legitimate claims to them. In these cases, tribes assume no further responsibility for the repatriated objects unless they adopt legislation prohibiting the removal of cultural properties from their territorial jurisdiction. Those tribes that wish to ensure perpetual ownership of their cultural properties have adopted statutes that expressly prohibit the removal and sale of sacred and cultural objects from tribal ownership. For example, in 1976, the Chilkat (Tlingit) Indian Village of Klukwan in Alaska adopted the following "Artifacts Ordinance":

> No person shall enter onto the property of the Chilkat Indian Village for the purpose of buying, trading for, soliciting the purchase of, or otherwise seeking to arrange a removal of artifacts, clan crests, or other traditional Indian art work owned or held by members of the Chilkat Indian Village or kept within the boundaries of the real property owned by the Chilkat Indian village, without first requesting and obtaining permission to do so from the Chilkat Indian Village Council.
>
> No traditional Indian artifacts, clan crests, or other Indian art works of any kind may be removed from the Chilkat Indian village without the prior notification of and approval by the Chilkat Indian Council.

(See also AMERICAN INDIAN RITUAL OBJECT REPATRIATION FOUNDATION.)

REQUICKENING ADDRESS *Iroquois* A rite of the Condolence and Installation Council of the Iroquois Confederacy that has symbolic power to restore life as well as power to lift up the minds of those depressed by grief. It consists of "words" or messages, each of which is accompanied by a string of wampum. There is a general form of the address, but speakers can vary the order of the "matters" or "words." The address is delivered by a speaker for the clear-minded side of the tribe and one for the bereaved side. Each section describes a hurt arising from grief caused by death, then mentions that the hurt affecting those present is either removed or healed and the people restored to their former condition. At the conclusion of each section, the orator delivers one of the 15 "sympathy strings" of wampum to the mourning side. The number of sections differs from Iroquois group to group. In ritualistic phrases, the address

sets out in detail the evils and wounds that befall a stricken people and asserts that it counteracts these evils and restores to life the people in the person of their newly installed chief. (In Iroquois polity, an office never dies, its bearer dies). On some reserves, the address is called "Fourteen Matters" because it is accompanied by fourteen strings of wampum. (See also CONDOLENCE CEREMONY.)

RETREAT *Pueblo* When rain or community health is needed, medicine societies or priesthoods retire to their kivas, or ceremonial houses, where they remain for four, eight, or 16 days, observing fasts from certain foods, observing abstinence from sexual intercourse, and performing rituals. Zuni priest kachinas go into retreat before they impersonate spirits. The more sacred the impersonation, the longer the retreat.

REVITALIZATION MOVEMENT A deliberate, organized effort on the part of members of a society to restore, renew, or perpetuate elements of its culture. Many of these movements developed among Native American groups as they experienced dispossession, removal, and other assaults on their way of life. Holy men and women, who interacted with the spirits, provided spiritual guidance. They offered hope that the land would be restored, that the buffalo and other game would return, and that their oppressors would disappear. These spiritual leaders emphasized a return to Native traditions and a rejection of destructive ways, including alcohol consumption, introduced by the newcomers. After communicating with the spirits, many of them taught new doctrines, ceremonies, and songs. Other traditions, nearly obliterated, were brought back and reinterpreted. Many of the leaders of revitalization movements were key figures in Native resistance efforts. Related terms include *nativistic movement, revivalistic movement,* and *messianic movement.* Some of the movements and leaders included in this volume are: ABISHABIS, CHEROKEE RELIGIOUS REVIVAL OF 1811 TO 1813, the DELAWARE PROPHET, GHOST DANCE OF 1870, GHOST DANCE OF 1890, HANDSOME LAKE, JAKE HUNT, KENEKUK, KOTIAKAN, REDBIRD SMITH, SKOLASKIN, SMOHALLA, TENSKWATAWA, and WABOKIESHIEK.

RICHMOND, JOHN P. *(1811–1895)* Methodist missionary and physician. Richmond went to Oregon Territory in 1839 at the invitation of the missionary JASON LEE and superintended the Nisqually Indian Mission in the Puget Sound area, the first Methodist efforts in present-day Washington State. He left the region in 1842, eventually working at posts in Illinois, Mississippi, and Dakota Territory.

RIDE-IN AND WAR DANCE *Shawnee* A sacred ceremony believed to have been originated by OUR GRANDMOTHER, the

Shawnee female deity. It is generally held in August by the Kishpoko or Kishpokotha division of the people, and it includes a ceremonial horseback parade and a war dance. The ceremony is formally announced a few days in advance at a Shawnee Arbor Dance, which is held to prepare the arbor area. Among the principal participants are a head warrior and four other warriors who must meet certain requirements, including service in the military forces overseas and the completion of a "making of warriors" ceremony upon their return home. The ritual activities involve the opening of a medicine bundle at a distance from the grounds by qualified individuals, an early morning horseback parade around the camp to the accompaniment of a water drum and singing, dancing, the recitation of war deeds followed by tobacco offerings to honored elders, ceremonial feasting, and a closing prayer. Participants include other divisions of the Shawnee as well as members of the Kickapoo tribe. (See also BREAD DANCE; BUFFALO DANCE; DEATH FEAST; GREEN CORN DANCE; RITUAL FOOTBALL GAME.)

RIGGS, ALFRED LONGLEY *(1837–1916)* Congregational missionary to the Santee Dakota. Riggs was born to Mary and STEPHEN RETURN RIGGS at Lac qui Parle mission, founded by THOMAS S. WILLIAMSON, in Minnesota Territory. After graduating from Knox College in Galesburg, Illinois, he attended the Theological Seminary of Chicago from 1860 to 1862. He later began working at the Niobrara mission, which was established in 1866 among the Santee people removed to Nebraska after the 1862 Dakota conflict in Minnesota. Riggs started the Santee Normal Training School, the first Indian high school, where Dakota students were instructed in their own language. The Niobrara mission also produced a newspaper called *Iapi Oaye* ("The Word Carrier"), the successor of an earlier publication, *The Dakota Friend,* founded by the missionary GIDEON POND. Edited by Riggs after 1877, its printing was done on the school press. The missionary worked among the Santee until he died in 1916.

RIGGS, STEPHEN RETURN *(1812–1883)* Congregational missionary to the Dakota. Born in 1812 in Steubenville, Ohio, Riggs attended Latin school in Ripley, Ohio, and Jefferson College in Pennsylvania, where he earned his B.A. degree in 1834. After a year at Western Theological Seminary in Allegheny, Pennsylvania, he was licensed by the Chillicothe presbytery in 1836 and served as a minister in Hawley, Massachusetts, until the following year. The same year Riggs married Mary A. C. Longley on February 16, 1837. The couple journeyed to Minnesota Territory and began missionary work at Lac qui Parle with the Wahpeton band of Dakota. Assisted by Joseph Renville, a mixed-blood

trader, they began studying the Dakota language and preparing translations. Riggs served as a missionary at Lac qui Parle (1837–43, 1846–54), Traverse des Sioux (1843–46), and Hazelwood (1854–62) along the Minnesota River. By 1863 he and other missionaries had produced a number of Dakota-language publications, including: *The Dakota First Reading Book* (1839); *Wowapi Mitawa: Tamakoce Kaga* (1842), a primer; biblical translations (1842 and 1843); *Dakota Tawoonspe* (1850), two books of Dakota lessons; *Grammar and Dictionary of the Dakota Language* (1852), which combined the work of SAMUEL W. and GIDEON POND, JEDIDIAH D. STEVENS, and THOMAS S. WILLIAMSON and was published by the Smithsonian Institution; *Dakota Odowan* (1853, 1855, 1863, 1869), a hymnal; *The Pilgrim's Progress* (1857); *The Constitution of Minnesota* (1858); and a primer for prisoners of the 1862 Dakota conflict in Minnesota.

Riggs later moved to Beloit, Wisconsin, where he organized a mission and school among the Santee who were imprisoned and displaced during the period of conflict. He remained at Beloit, serving as a superintendent overseeing Dakota missions, until 1863. There he also continued to work on translations: *Dakota Wiwicawangapi Kin* (1864), a catechism; the New Testament from the Greek to the Dakota (1865); primers (1866, 1867, 1868); the book of Psalms from the Hebrew (1869); a model first reader (1875); Guyot's *Elementary Geography* in the Dakota (1876); a large part of the Bible (1877); and *Dakota Wowapi Wakan: The Holy Bible in the Language of the Dakotas* (1880). Other writings, besides translations, included *The Gospel among the Dakotas* (1869); *Mary and I: Forty Years with the Sioux* (1880); and numerous newspaper and journal articles. He also edited *Iapi Oaye,* the Dakota language newspaper, from 1873 until his death. Riggs continued to visit the Dakota missions until his death at Beloit on August 14, 1883. Several of his nine children worked in the mission field, including ALFRED LONGLEY RIGGS and THOMAS LAWRENCE RIGGS.

RIGGS, THOMAS LAWRENCE *(1847–1940)* Congregational missionary to the Dakota. Riggs was born to Mary and STEPHEN RETURN RIGGS at Lac qui Parle in Minnesota Territory in 1847. Along with his brother ALFRED LONGLEY RIGGS and other siblings he learned to speak the Dakota language as a child. Riggs was a graduate of Beloit College and Chicago Theological Seminary. Ordained to the ministry, he worked for a year in the South before joining the Dakota mission. In 1872 he established Hope Station under the auspices of the AMERICAN BOARD OF COMMISSIONERS FOR FOREIGN MISSIONS. Two years later he began the Oahe Mission (Ti Tanka Ohe) in the Peoria Bottom located east of the

Missouri River. By 1880 the mission's area included the Standing Rock Reservation in the Dakotas and 15 substations. In 1883 Riggs also established a boarding school at the mission, and it remained open until 1914. He continued his missionary efforts until illness forced his resignation in 1918. After retiring, Riggs maintained some involvement in the mission's work. He died on July 6, 1940, at his Peoria Bottom home.

RITUAL FOOTBALL GAME *Shawnee* A sacred ritual consisting of a number of football games played by men against women that are believed to be pleasing to OUR GRANDMOTHER, the Shawnee female deity, as well as to the Thunderbirds, and conducive to bringing rain and fertile crops. The first football game begins the Shawnee ceremonial year and the team that loses is required to provide wood for the spring BREAD DANCE that follows. A ball made with buckskin stuffed with deerhair is tossed in the air in the center of the playing field to start the game. The ritual, in which both young and old participate, has different rules for males and females. Men and boys are permitted to move the ball only with their feet, while women and girls are allowed to carry it in their hands. Each side tries to score by moving the ball through the opposite team's goal. The first game generally takes place at the end of April or the beginning of May and the last one in June. When the ritual ends, the ball is either destroyed or put away until the next year. (See also BUFFALO DANCE; DEATH FEAST; GREEN CORN DANCE; RIDE-IN AND WAR DANCE.)

ROADMAN (Road Chief) Leader of all all-night PEYOTE ceremony or peyote meeting. The term *roadman* comes from the *peyote road,* represented on the ceremonial altar by a line. It is believed that concentration on the peyote road will lead the prayers of the worshipers to the Creator. Often, roadmen are also medicine men, and many hold other leadership roles. They learn to conduct peyote ceremonies from attending services, from other roadmen, and from the experience of taking on the duties of the role. They then teach others who are interested in learning the necessary skills. For some, being a roadman is full-time work, but others combine it with other roles. Generally, roadmen are paid for their services with gifts, since no set fees are charged. The roadman is assisted during the ceremonies by a chief drummer, whose duties include providing drum accompaniment to the singing of sacred songs; a cedarman, who places cedar in the fire to consecrate ritual objects; and the fireman, who builds and tends the ceremonial fire, among other responsibilities. Roadmen included in this volume are JAMES BLUE BIRD, BILLY CHIWAT, JESSE CLAY, TRUMAN DAILEY, ELK HAIR, ALBERT HENSLEY, JOHNATHAN KOSHIWAY, OLIVER LA

MERE, BEN LANCASTER, SAM LONE BEAR, SAM LONG, QUANAH PARKER, PINERO, JOHN QUAPAW, JOHN RAVE, REUBEN SNAKE, EMERSON SPIDER, FRANK TAKES GUN, JACK THOMAS, WILLIE THOMAS, and JOHN WILSON. The peyote leader is also called a Road Chief. (See also NATIVE AMERICAN CHURCH; PEYOTE RELIGION.)

ROBERTS, JOHN *(c. 1853–1949)* The first Episcopalian missionary to the Arapaho and Shoshone people in Wyoming. Roberts was born in Wales and was educated at a local grammar school. He completed his degree at Oxford University and was ordained to the Episcopal ministry at Lichfield Cathedral. After serving as a missionary for two years at a leper colony in the West Indies, he traveled to the United States. The bishop of Colorado and Wyoming sent him to establish a mission among the Arapahoe and Shoshone. Roberts arrived at Fort Washakie in the region in 1883, beginning a misionary career there that was to last for 40 years. He started the first government school on the Wind River Reservation in Wyoming and served as the principal for many years. Roberts initially met with limited success in converting the Native people, including JOHN TREHERO, to Christianity. After studying the Arapaho and Shoshone languages, he began producing religious translations. Assisted by Michael White Hawk, he translated the Gospel of Luke into Arapaho. Besides completing other publications in that language, he worked on a catechism and additional materials in Shoshone. During his tenure as missionary, he buried Sacajawea, the famous guide of Lewis and Clark, on her death in 1884. He also baptized Chief Washakie and obtained land from him for a school. Roberts was known to the Native people as Dambavie, meaning "elder brother." His tenure in the region included work among non-Indians and service as an army chaplain for 20 years. Roberts died in 1949 at the age of 96. His writings included an account of the early life of SHERMAN COOLIDGE, entitled "Desthewa, the Young Arapahoe."

ROBERTS, TUDY (Tu:di, "To Stretch") *(1882–1957) Shoshone* Highly respected medicine man and leader of the GHOST DANCE OF 1890 in the Sage Creek area of the Wind River Reservation in Wyoming. Roberts possessed the ability to heal such illnesses as colds and measles as well as paralysis but only doctored a person after he had received spiritual help and instructions in a dream. Roberts attributed his powers to the many different spirits who liked and appeared to him. He described waking visions as more powerful than dream visions. Besides his curing abilities, Roberts received powers to become bullet-proof and to predict the weather. Roberts also initiated and led SUN DANCE ceremonies, receiving authority to do so in a vision. He held Ghost Dances at Sage Creek as recently as the 1950s, conducted once or twice during the year. Roberts and his family sponsored the sacred dance, which was held four nights in succession when there was a full moon. He indicated that the dead sang with him at that time. The observances were said to include elements of the Shoshone FATHER DANCE. The Ghost Dance leader died in 1957. His name also appears as Toorey Roberts. Other adherents of the Ghost Dance on the Wind River Reservation included EMILY HILL, NADZAIP ROGERS, WILLIAM WASHINGTON, and WHITE COLT.

ROBERTSON, ANN ELIZA WORCESTER *(1826–1905)* Presbyterian missionary and linguist among the Creek. Robertson was born on November 7, 1826, at the Cherokee Nation's Brainerd mission in Tennessee. When Ann Eliza was an infant, the family moved to the Cherokee capital in New Echota, Georgia. Her father, the well-known Congregational missionary SAMUEL AUSTIN WORCESTER, was later imprisoned for challenging the state of Georgia's claim to jurisdiction over Cherokee territory. The family resettled in Indian Territory (present-day Oklahoma) following removal of the Cherokee, and Ann Eliza was educated at home and then at the Park Hill mission established by her parents in 1836. She also enrolled in Vermont's St. Johnsbury Academy at the age of 16. Upon her return home in 1847, she taught at Park Hill. Two years later she accepted an appointment to teach at the new Tullahassee Manual Labor Boarding School sponsored by the Creek Nation and the Presbyterian BOARD OF FOREIGN MISSIONS. After her marriage to WILLIAM SCHENCK ROBERTSON, Ann Eliza joined his Presbyterian denomination. Besides teaching, she helped prepare Creek translations for publication. The Robertsons' missionary work was disrupted in 1861 when the Creek Nation closed its boarding schools during the Civil War. They moved to the North for five years and returned to Tullahassee in December 1866 and found that the school had to be rebuilt. It reopened in 1868 but burned down several years later in 1880. Following her husband's 1881 death, Ann Eliza moved to Muskogee, where she lived with her daughter Alice, and continued to work on Creek translations, assisted by JAMES PERRYMAN. In 1887 she completed her translation of the New Testament, her proudest accomplishment, but continued to revise it. By the time she died, the fifth edition was nearly finished. Her other publications included translations of Genesis, Psalms, and a hymnal. In 1892 she was awarded an honorary doctorate by the University of Wooster in Ohio. Ann Eliza died on November 19, 1905, and was buried at Park Hill. Among her children were three daughters, all of whom taught in the tribal mission schools, and a son. One daughter, Alice May Robertson, became the second woman

elected to the U.S. Congress and another, Augusta, married a Creek rancher.

ROBERTSON, WILLIAM SCHENCK *(1820–1881)* Presbyterian missionary to the Creek people in Indian Territory (present-day Oklahoma). Robertson was born in Huntington, New York, on January 11, 1820. After graduating from Union College in Schenectady with a master of arts degree in 1843, he taught in New York for several years. In 1849 he began working at the Tullahassee Manual Labor School in the Creek Nation under the auspices of the Presbyterian BOARD OF FOREIGN MISSIONS. Besides serving as a missionary teacher, Robertson worked as a farmer, minister, and physician. In 1850 he married ANN ELIZA WORCESTER, who began studying the Creek language and serving as a teacher at the mission. Robertson later completed educational and religious materials in the Creek language, including the *First Reader* (1856) and the *Second Reader* (1871) which were coauthored with DAVID WINSLETT, a Creek. Assisted by other Creek translators and by his wife, he also worked on translations of books of the New Testament. When the mission closed during the Civil War, Robertson and his family lived in the North for a period of five years. Before returning to the Creek Nation at the end of 1866, he was ordained a Presbyterian minister. Tullahassee mission was reopened in March 1868. Robertson later served as the editor of *Our Monthly,* a newly established bilingual newspaper at the school. He continued his missionary work among the Creek people until his death on June 16, 1881.

ROBINSON, FRED *(c. 1861–1941) Assiniboine* Leader of the GHOST DANCE OF 1890 among the Dakota people in Saskatchewan. Robinson, who was from Wolf Point, Montana, learned the Ghost Dance after the turn of the century. His teacher in the fall of 1902 was KICKING BEAR, one of the Lakota emissaries sent by his people to meet with the Paiute holy man WOVOKA in Nevada. After being widowed twice, Robinson married a Dakota woman, Agnes, a member of the White Cap Reserve near Saskatoon, Saskatchewan. He moved to her property on the reserve and helped her tend the cattle she owned. Robinson taught the Ghost Dance there but was unable to attract followers because of the strong presence and influence of the Methodists and the model mission they had established.

Robinson succeeded in gaining adherents to the religion in another Dakota community, Sioux Wahpeton Reserve, also called Round Plain Reserve, located near Prince Albert, Saskatchewan. Because Canadian officials and missionaries opposed the Ghost Dance, the congregation could not practice it openly. Although the religious practice was believed to have ended years earlier, it survived into the 1960s at Round Plain. At that time Henry Two Bears, an elderly Dakota man, was the leader of the congregation. In 1961, Two Bears, who was in his eighties, provided an oral account of his religion to the anthropologist Alice B. Kehoe. He spoke in Dakota, as he believed sacred knowledge must be told in the Native language, and provided a shortened version of the Ghost Dance's origins and beliefs. New Tidings or Woyaka Teca in Dakota is the name given to the Ghost Dance teachings and congregation on the Sioux Wahpeton Reserve. Ritual elements of the faith, which taught each practitioner to lead a "clean, honest life" and reinforced Native traditions, included daily prayers, the singing of sacred songs, the use of the pipe, sweet grass incensing, the wearing of Ghost Dance shirts to protect those who wore them from evil, and the sharing of a feast of meat, corn, berries, and rice.

Robinson died in November 1941 when he was about 80 years old. One of the few surviving records about him is a letter he wrote to Wovoka in 1909 requesting sacred paint and spiritual assistance. Although the dancing associated with the religion reportedly ended about 1950, other practices of the faith persisted.

ROCK BABY *Kawaiisu* In Kawaiisu belief, Rock Baby lives in the rocks and creates pictographs. As work on the drawings is ongoing, it is said that humans can sometimes see changes on return visits. Touching or photographing the pictographs is believed to result in disaster. Seeing or hearing Rock Baby also foreshadows tragedy. (See also LITTLE PEOPLE; MEDICINES [Kawaiisu].)

ROE, WALTER C. *(?–1913)* Missionary of the Reformed Church in America among the Arapaho and Cheyenne people in Indian Territory (present-day Oklahoma). Roe was educated at Williams College in Massachusetts, where he received his doctor of divinity degree. After serving as the pastor of a Presbyterian church in Dallas, Texas, he began working at Segar Colony in Indian Territory in 1897 under the auspices of the Women's Executive Committee of the Reformed Church. Dr. Roe and his wife went there at the invitation of the Reverend FRANK HALL WRIGHT, a Choctaw missionary who had organized the newly established Columbian Memorial Mission. The missionaries preached in the church and at camp meetings and provided Sunday school and Christian Endeavor activities as well as medical and social services. The Roes also established the nondenominational Mohonk Lodge at Segar Colony. Its services included providing instruction in homemaking and the care of the sick. Besides their extensive involvement in the Indian reform movement in the United States, they were interested in providing missionary services to Native people in South

American countries. The family also became known through the work of their prominent Winnebago (Ho-Chunk) protegé Henry Roe Cloud (who had adopted their surname), who graduated from Yale University in 1910 and from Auburn Theological Seminary in 1913. Dr. Walter C. Roe died on March 12, 1913.

ROGERS, NADZAIP *(1871–1952) Shoshone* Medicine woman and Ghost Dance adherent. Rogers once said that her soul traveled to heaven while she slept. She knew the way there and had also seen the dead in her dream. Rogers continued believing in the Ghost Dance until the end of her life. (See also HILL, EMILY; ROBERTS, TUDY; WHITE COLT.)

ROLL CALL OF THE CHIEFS *Iroquois* A rite that begins the CONDOLENCE CEREMONY in the longhouse in which the names of the original founders of the Iroquois League, preserved as titles of office, are recited. The names are grouped, with the Mohawk chiefs mentioned first, then the Oneida, Onondaga, Cayuga, and Seneca. The refrain *hai, hai,* repeated after each group, is said to be the cry of the souls, and its repetition consoles the spirits of the dead. The roll call is also repeated at a preliminary rite of greeting called "at the wood's edge" at a fire kindled a short distance from the longhouse before the Condolence Ceremony begins. At the Six Nations Reserve in Canada, the roll call is chanted as the two divisions of the tribe, the bereaved and "clear-minded" sides, make their way to the longhouse after the rite "at the wood's edge."

ROMERO, JUAN DE JESUS (Deer Bird) *(1874–1978) Taos Pueblo* Cacique of Taos Pueblo. Romero fought the United States government for the return of BLUE LAKE, in New Mexico, whose sacredness to the Taos people is incalculable. Deer Bird was 32 years old in 1906 when the government seized Blue Lake. He began a campaign that year for the return of the land. Decades later, he took his case to Washington and appealed to President Richard Nixon directly. Finally, through his efforts, in 1971 the president signed a bill returning Blue Lake watershed and 48,000 surrounding acres to the pueblo.

ROOSTER PULL (Gallo) *Pueblo* Ritual fusing Indian and Spanish cultures. Horsemen fight with roosters until the roosters are torn to pieces, bringing good luck and rain to the pueblo. The Gallo ritual dramatizes episodes in the stories about Santiago, the Spanish saint who impressed the Keresan peoples and has become one of their beneficent spirits.

ROOT FEAST *Confederated Tribes of Warm Springs Reservation of Oregon*   This principal FIRST FOOD OBSERVANCE is a ritual gathering, serving, and eating of traditional foods at which people give thanks to the Creator and bless the roots. In April, women unearth three different roots, accompanied by ritual and prayer songs. The roots are boiled in pots on longhouse stoves on the morning of the feast. Root diggers, along with fishermen and hunters, who also provide food for the celebration, carry their food around the longhouse, and set it before friends and guests. The names of each food are called out, and people eat tiny ritual portions. After the feast people rise, face east, and pray. The celebration sanctions the harvest of certain plants, and families are free to gather food for their own use. There are also feasts for two other Native foods, huckleberries in August and wild celery in both late winter and late spring.

ROUND DANCE *Great Basin*   A dance of great importance in the religious and social ceremonies of the Paiute, Shoshone, and other Great Basin Native groups. One form consisted of alternating male and female participants who formed a circle around a center tree or post. Facing inward, they linked arms or fingers and danced in a clockwise movement. The Round Dance was sometimes held for several nights in succession. A number of names and purposes have been associated with it, depending upon the period and the location. Examples include seed dance, pine nut dance, and grass or spring dance. The Round Dance was also associated with prayers for health, for the return of the fish and other foods and for the welfare of the people, plants, and animals. Among some groups it was performed in conjunction with mourning ceremonies, at pinyon or other harvests, and in conjunction with communal rabbit or antelope hunts. The Ghost Dance prophets from the region also built upon the traditional Round Dance form in their religious rituals. It continues to be held in a variety of settings in the present day. (See also FATHER DANCE; GHOST DANCE OF 1870; GHOST DANCE OF 1890.)

ROUND DANCE (woman's dance, old time dance) *Plains Ojibway*   A dance once associated with the principal women's dancing society of the Plains Ojibway. Eight women owned the dance and performed its rituals in honor of the sacred powers above. Origins of the Round Dance have been traced to an elderly woman on the Turtle Mountain Reservation in North Dakota. The women's dancing society included a man, who served as a drummer, in its membership. A ceremony performed by the eight women opened with a song warning nonmembers not to participate. The members, who dressed alike in black, then danced. After singing another song, other people, both men and women,

were able to participate. The ceremony later closed as it had opened, with the same performances by the society members. The Round Dance is said to continue to be performed, often in association with the GRASS DANCE, but without the opening and closing rituals of the women's dancing society. Other names include "woman's dance" and "old time dance." (See also TEA DANCE; TRADE DANCE.)

RUDDER, MARK *(fl. 1890s) Pawnee*   A Skiri band leader of the GHOST DANCE OF 1890. Rudder was instrumental in the establishment of the Seven Brothers of the Crow, an organization of men who sang the sacred songs of the GHOST DANCE OF 1890 and the GHOST DANCE HAND GAME. The group alternated singing with the Seven Eagle Brothers, another association of singers formed earlier. The Crow Brothers organization was established as a result of a young woman's vision. Besides developing the ceremonial ornamentation of the group, Rudder served as the lead Crow. He also selected the other six singers and chose a woman named Mrs. Cover as the "Mother" of the Seven Brothers of the Crows. Other adherents included MRS. GOODEAGLE, MRS. WASHINGTON, and FRANK WHITE.

RUNDLE, ROBERT TERRILL *(1811–1896)*   Wesleyan Methodist missionary in Saskatchewan. Rundle was born to Grace and Robert (Carvosso) Rundle in Mylor, England, on June 11, 1811. In 1837 Rundle attended business school at Botreaux Castle and two years later entered the ministry. He underwent two months of training, then accepted a missionary post in Saskatchewan. Rundle and three other Methodists received invitations from the Hudson's Bay Company to set up missions in the region. A short time after his March 8, 1840, ordination, he traveled to North America. Rundle was accompanied on the journey by GEORGE BARNLEY and WILLIAM MASON, fellow missionaries. He spent a number of months at the Norway House (Manitoba) mission, then traveled to Fort Edmonton in the Saskatchewan district. The first Methodist missionary there, he served as chaplain for the Hudson's Bay Company. Rundle's circuit was extensive as he traveled among diverse Native groups, including Cree, Assiniboine, Stoney, Blackfeet, and Métis. He generally served Fort Edmonton, Lesser Slave Lake, and Fort Assiniboine during the winter months and visited other areas the rest of the year. In 1844 and 1847 Rundle traveled as far as the Rocky Mountains. His Native assistants included William Rowland, a mixed-blood translator, and Benjamin, the son of the Cree chief Maskepetoon. In 1847 Rundle sustained an injury to his arm when he fell off a horse. After leaving for England the following year to obtain medical treatment, he did not return to North America. His position at Fort Edmonton was later filled by his brother-in-law

THOMAS WOOLSEY. Rundle died on February 4, 1896, in Garstang, England.

RUPERT, HENRY (Henry Moses) *(1885–1973) Washoe* A Washoe shaman who healed both Native and non-Native people. Rupert was born to Susie John and Pete Duncan in 1885 in Genoa, Nevada. His father abandoned the family early in Rupert's life and his mother was absent much of the time earning a living as a domestic worker. The household was managed by Rupert's sister, Annie Rube, who was married to Charley Rube, an antelope shaman, a shaman who in earlier times had the responsibility of "singing" the antelope to sleep during Washoe antelope drives. Rupert spent much of his childhood in the company of the antelope shaman and another relative, his uncle Welewkushkush, a well-known shaman. At the age of eight, Rupert's schooling began. He was sent to the Stewart Indian School near Carson City, Nevada, where he began a highly regimented program of forced acculturation. Although he ran away three times, he eventually stayed at the school until he was 18 years old. Besides mastering academic subjects, he learned the printing trade. After leaving the Stewart Indian School, he served as a typesetter on the *Reno Evening Gazette* for 10 years.

As a child, Rupert began having dreams that marked him as a potential shaman. At the age of 17, while he still attended boarding school, one dream experience definitely marked his future as a healer. In the dream Rupert learned that water would be his spirit helper, the being who would provide spiritual power, assistance, and instruction. He also learned that he would be able to control the weather. Rupert began healing his first patient when he was 22 years old. He acquired his second spirit helper, a young Hindu, about the same time. While visiting a Carson City high school, Rupert saw a Hindu skeleton whose spirit later "got on" him. The Washoe shaman then had to reconcile the conflicting demands on his two spirit helpers for primacy in healing. As accounts of Rupert's curing success spread, he began to acquire patients from many different ethnic groups. He treated Washoe, Paiute, Shoshone, Hawaiian, Filipino, Mexican, and Euro-American patients. At the age of 57, Rupert became a shaman on a full-time basis. He later cured a Hawaiian healer, George Robinson, who, in return, gave Rupert a Hawaiian spirit healer. Rupert died at the age of 88, a highly respected, innovative healer who was identified as the last shaman among the Washoe. Rupert was also called Henry Moses.

SACRED ARROW KEEPER'S WOMAN *Cheyenne* The wife of the keeper of the SACRED ARROWS, which were brought to the Cheyenne people by the great prophet SWEET MEDICINE. The Sacred Arrow keeper's wife's position is a holy one. The person who fills it carries out specific sacred duties as originally taught to the people. The keeper's wife fulfills the role related to the Sacred Arrows that was first held by the holy woman who accompanied Sweet Medicine to NOAHA-VOSE, or Bear Butte.

SACRED ARROWS *Cheyenne* The most sacred possession of the Cheyenne people. The four arrows were bestowed upon SWEET MEDICINE, the great prophet of the Cheyenne, by the Supreme Being, MAHEO, at NOAHA-VOSE, the sacred mountain. During the time that Sweet Medicine lived among the Cheyenne people, he gave them the Sacred Arrows as well as teachings, laws, and prophecies. The Sacred Arrows are known to the Cheyenne as Maahotse (also Mahuts) from Maheo. Besides blessing the people and uniting them as Cheyenne, the Sacred Arrows represent male power. Two of them are man arrows and two are buffalo arrows.

Described as one of the two covenants of the Cheyenne (the other is the SACRED BUFFALO HAT), the Sacred Arrows are considered the living manifestation of spiritual power. In the early days, when the Sacred Arrows and the Sacred Buffalo Hat were taken into battle, they were said to possess the power to blind the enemy. One of the worst tragedies in the history of the Cheyenne people was the capture of the Sacred Arrows by the Skidi Pawnee about 1830, when WHITE THUNDER was keeper, unleashing a long period of

catastrophe. New Arrows were made with the assistance of the holy men BOX ELDER and CRAZY MULE.

As instructed by Sweet Medicine, the Sacred Arrows are renewed whenever the people experience illness or trouble, in ceremonies described as "the supreme act of Cheyenne worship." They are also renewed when one Cheyenne is murdered by another. Such killing is believed to bring blood to the Sacred Arrows, requiring their renewal and the restoration of unity to the people. In the early years the ceremonies, said to be the same as those first learned by Sweet Medicine at Noaha-Vose, were pledged by one of the chiefs of the Council of Forty-four, but during the reservation period that practice changed.

Any Cheyenne man who met other essential requirements was permitted to vow the ceremonies. Besides preparing spiritually, the pledger gathered together gifts, offerings, and food. Traditionally, he could announce the upcoming renewal of the Sacred Arrows after the first thunder was heard in the spring. When the renewing rites were held during a given year, other ceremonies were not to take place until after their completion. The extensive rituals, performed by the Sacred Arrow priests, generally include four days of preparations and four days for the renewing ceremonies.

Early keepers of the Sacred Arrows were STONE FOREHEAD and BLACK HAIRY DOG. In the 20th century, keepers have included MEDICINE ELK, EDWARD RED HAT, and BALDWIN TWINS. The keeper is assisted in his duties by SACRED ARROW KEEPER'S WOMAN.

SACRED BOW SOCIETY See BLACK ROAD

SACRED BUFFALO HAT *Cheyenne* The Sacred Buffalo Hat is one of the holiest possessions of the Cheyenne people. It is perceived as a living manifestation of supernatural power and represents the second holy covenant of the Cheyenne, after the SACRED ARROWS. In the Cheyenne language, the Sacred Buffalo Hat is known as Esevone, referring to a herd of female bison. The hat was brought to the people by Tomsivsi, or ERECT HORNS, the great prophet or culture hero of the Suhtaio, who received it from MAHEO, the Supreme Being, at a sacred site in the north. The Cheyenne received the Sacred Buffalo Hat and the SUN DANCE ceremonies from the Suhtaio when the two tribal groups united. With the spiritual gift of the Sacred Buffalo Hat, the horned scalp of a female buffalo, the people received blessings of renewal and plenty.

During an early period when the Sacred Buffalo Hat and the Sacred Arrows were carried into battle, the Cheyenne believed their powers blinded the enemy and protected the Cheyenne warriors. In 1874 a dispute over the Sacred Buffalo Hat arose among the Cheyenne. When the keeper, Half Bear, died, his son, COAL BEAR, was absent, and the Sacred Buffalo Hat passed into the hands of a temporary keeper, who refused to relinquish the hat to Coal Bear upon his return. Coal Bear eventually retrieved the Sacred Buffalo Hat, but it had been damaged. Its desecration represented a terrible tragedy in the history of the people and followed the loss of the Sacred Arrows in 1830.

Coal Bear's son, SAND CRANE, also became a keeper, as did his granddaughter, JOSEPHINE HEAD SWIFT LIMPY, who was succeeded in the role by JOE LITTLE COYOTE. Today, the Sacred Buffalo Hat is ritually cared for by its present-day keeper among the Northern Cheyenne in Montana, assisted by SACRED BUFFALO HAT WOMAN.

SACRED BUFFALO HAT WOMAN *Cheyenne* The wife of the keeper of the SACRED BUFFALO HAT, Esevone, which was given to the great Suhtai prophet ERECT HORNS. The Sacred Buffalo Hat Woman's position is a holy one. The person who fills it assists the keeper in ritually caring for Esevone and the Sacred Buffalo Hat Lodge.

SACRED FIRE *Southeast* The sacred fire is basic to the religious practices of the Cherokee, Chickasaw, Creek, Seminole, Yuchi, and other southeastern Native groups. Each group has its own account of the fire's origins and rituals, but they generally include the following elements: a divine origin associated with the sun, the use of four logs oriented in the four directions and forming a cross, preparation and maintenance by firekeepers and their assistants, and rekindling during the GREEN CORN CEREMONY. The sacred fire, generally built in the center of the square ground, serves as the focal point for dances and other religious or ceremonial activities.

Sources indicate that some southeastern groups kept a perpetual fire while others annually renewed it during the Green Corn Ceremony. (See also BLACK DRINK; "GOING TO WATER"; SCRATCHING CEREMONY; STICKBALL GAME; STOMP DANCE.)

SACRED FORMULAS *Cherokee* Prayers, songs, prescriptions and other sacred knowledge of the Cherokee people. Approximately 600 of these formulas were collected by the ethnologist James Mooney among the Eastern Band of Cherokee Indian in North Carolina in 1887 and 1888. They were written by Cherokee priests in the Sequoyan syllabary and maintained for their private use. Topics covered include medicine, plants, hunting, fishing, love, war, agriculture, council, ball games, and self-protection. Manuscripts were obtained from SWIMMER, BLACK FOX, GAHUNI, and other Cherokee priests or their families by Mooney for the Bureau of American Ethnology.

SACRED OBJECTS Sacred objects generally originate as spiritual gifts to an individual, family, society, clan, or an entire tribal group. They are sometimes made as instructed in a vision or dream, ritually inherited or purchased, given by a sacred being or associated with a venerated religious leader. Sacred objects have also been known to manifest themselves in nature to a certain person by their sacredness. They generally come from animals, birds, plants, fish, and other life forms in creation. These may be kept, worn, or carried. Examples include beaks, claws, fangs, feathers, furs, hides, quills, shells, tusks, stones, rocks, and corn ears. Sacred objects may be owned and/or kept by individuals, families, societies, clans, or entire tribal groups. They are generally ritually cared for according to spiritual instructions and formal training by a qualified religious teacher.

Sacred objects that are integral components of tribal ceremonials may include corn ears, dolls, fans, eagle talons or feathers, masks, pipes, rattles, drums, scrolls, medicine bundles containing hundreds of articles, distinctly shaped rocks, ceremonial clothing, and different parts of animals or plants. Sacred objects require care according to spiritual instructions before and after their use; some require periodic offerings of tobacco, cedar, or cornmeal. There are restrictions on actions in the physical presence of sacred objects.

It is generally believed that persons who lack ritual authority to handle sacred objects yet do so will bring about harmful consequences.

Aleut and Inuit

Aleutian and Inuit people use sacred objects, called amulets, charms, and talismans by non-Indians, to ward off danger and bring good fortune in every undertaking. They believe that the objects contain spiritual power that they can enlist to serve them. A sacred object may be a naval string, part of an animal's body, a quartz crystal, a mask, certain words or phrases, formulas or songs. Practically every traditional Inuit and Aleut, from infancy to old age, possesses a number of sacred objects. They acquire them through gift, purchase, transfer, inheritance, or personal acquisition. Aleut and Inuit generally conceal their sacred objects somewhere on their bodies.

Pueblo

Among the Pueblo, sacred objects may include concretions of plant or animal material and carvings in shell, stone, or wood in any form used to assist people in hunting, diagnosing, and curing diseases, initiations, war, propagation, and the detection and protection against witchcraft. Pueblo people believe that a sacred object contains a living power that, if treated properly and ceremonially fed (usually with cornmeal), will give help to its owner. An individual, clan, medicine society, or tribe may own a sacred object. When not in use, it must be protected and kept in special containers and in special dwellings. Practitioners in tribes in the Southwest make and use these sacred objects, but the Zuni have the reputation of being the most skillful at carving them.

Hopi

Perfectly formed ears of white corn, which symbolize life and authority, are the central item of every Hopi ceremonial. These sacred objects, called *tiponi,* belong to a clan or society, and the leader keeps them in his house, where they are blessed by cornmeal and fed with pinches of food each day. The name also denotes the person with the spiritual authority to conduct the rites at the altar.

Keresan

A perfect ear of corn represents the mother of the Keresan pueblos. A perfect ear of corn, the guardian of infants, is given to a man at the time of his initiation. Through the corn ear sacred object, medicine people secure the corn mother's spiritual power and blessings to bestow on people. The representative of the corn mother accompanies a person throughout life and at death is destroyed. Associated with health and curing, a corn ear is placed beside an ill patient. The Keres word is spelled variously Iariko, Iarriko, Iatik, Iatiku, and Iyatiku.

Zuni

A large part of Zuni ceremonialism centers about the veneration of sacred objects. Some are perfect ears of corn, called *ettowe,* which are the sacred objects of RAIN PRIESTHOODS. They are of indescribable sanctity and in them rests the welfare of the Zuni people. Each medicine society has its own sacred objects kept in the clan-associated household. Each society member has his or her own corn ear object as well,

which is never borrowed or passed on. It is broken up at the owner's death. These sacred objects contain living forces that, if treated properly, will give help to its owner. There are periodic offerings of cornmeal made to all sacred objects, and at stated times, they are removed from their resting places and honored. Objects are powerful themselves, but they are also the means of reaching the more powerful spiritual forces. (See also Subject Index for other sacred objects described in this volume.)

SACRED PIPE The Sacred Pipe is a religious object central to belief, ritual, and ceremony across Native North America. Of considerable antiquity, some tribal groups trace its spiritual origins back to the time of creation or to the period of a great deluge, as spoken of in their oral traditions. Early European observers, as well as archaeological evidence dating some pipes back thousands of years, corroborate this sacred object's long history in Native religious life. Examples include Jacques Cartier's account of pipe smoking in the St. Lawrence region in 1535, Samuel Champlain's welcome by the Montagnais who passed him a pipe after he arrived among them in 1603, and an account by Father ANDREW WHITE of a pipe ritual in Maryland in 1633. Father JACQUES MARQUETTE noted in 1673 that through the pipe's use, tribal differences were ended, alliances formed or strengthened, travelers safeguarded in distant or enemy territory, weapons deflected, and strangers greeted. Europeans used the pipe themselves to gain the upper hand in trading, proselytizing, and forming treaties. Knowing the Native respect for it, they manipulated the religious practice to their own advantage. The geographic range of the Sacred Pipe and its rituals has been identified as including most of the North American continent. The Native origins, traditions, and types of pipes are just as extensive. Among the most sacred are those that originated as spiritual gifts to the entire tribal nation. The well-being or the very existence of the group is linked to the supremely holy pipes of this nature. They are generally ritually cared for by qualified individuals or keepers and are rarely exposed to view. Individual Sacred Pipes may also be associated with certain venerated leaders, particular religious ceremonies or movements, and historic events. Their origins may sometimes be traced to holy beings who bestowed them upon the people, to spiritual instructions given to individuals during visions, and to particular animals, feathered creatures, and other beings. Some are believed to have such spiritual power that only a particular medicine person may safely use them.

The origins and instructions for particular Sacred Pipes generally determine their ownership, keepership, rituals, and other elements of their use and care. One holy man from the Plains region identified a number of pipes that were used only for specific ceremonial purposes. These included one used for praying with the people, the SUN DANCE pipe, the preamble pipe used by one individual before council meetings, the peace pipe smoked during council meetings, the sweat lodge pipe or the medicine man pipe, the eagle pipe, and the woman's pipe. He also noted others, such as the buffalo pipe, the rain pipe and the trance pipe. Ownership and/or keepership of pipes also vary. Some are owned by individuals, families, clans, societies, bands, or by the entire tribal group.

The shapes and types, including the separate-stemmed pipe, reflect differing religious use. The bowls of the pipes are generally made from black or red stone and the stems from wood. Much of the stone used to make pipes came from the PIPESTONE quarry in Minnesota. Other materials and colors are also used. The bowls sometimes include inlay decorations or carved figures. The stems may be wrapped with porcupine quills, animal fur, beadwork, cloth fabric, or other materials. The stems may also have feathers or other sacred objects attached to them. Unadorned Sacred Pipes exist as well. A pipe may be made a particular way according to spiritual instructions received in a vision or dream.

The bowl of the Sacred Pipe is generally symbolic of the life-giving and life-sustaining female, the woman and the earth. Its colors, shapes, hollows, and other features are also linked to this symbolism. The substance of the bowl, often stone or clay, comes from Mother Earth. The stem of the Sacred Pipe is also symbolic. Representations attributed to it include male energy, all growing things, a person's voice, the road or path of life, and life itself. When the male stem and female bowl are joined, the Sacred Pipe becomes ritually active and powerful. The two components only come together in religious use. Otherwise they are kept separated.

TOBACCO, including Nicotiana varieties and varieties made from the inner bark of particular trees, is a sacred plant fundamental to the pipe and its rituals. It is offered to the spirit world not only through ceremonial smoking but by direct placement on the earth, in the water, in the fire, or in other places. During a Sacred Pipe ceremony, each participant becomes part of a sacred circle of prayer. The ritual is conducted by a qualified person who makes the necessary preparations and offers the pipe to the four directions (or semi-cardinal directions), the earth and the sky. The leader then passes it to each person taking part in the ceremony, generally in a sunwise (clockwise) direction. Other ritual elements include the singing of sacred songs and smoke consecration. The Sacred Pipe continues to be central to Native religious practices in the present day. (See also WHITE BUFFALO CALF WOMAN.)

SACRED POLE *Chickasaw* According to a Chickasaw migration account, the sacred pole guided the people as they sought a homeland. They began their search during a prehistoric period when they lived in the place of the setting sun. The sacred pole, carried by Chickasaw holy men, guided each day's journey. When the people stopped to sleep, the pole was placed in the ground in an upright position. At night it mysteriously moved about. The following morning, the pole's orientation guided the Chickasaw as to the direction to travel. Directed eastward, they eventually arrived at the Tennessee River. When the people awakened, they saw that the sacred pole remained upright. They then settled in the area, building homes and planting corn. When the holy men later observed the sacred pole pointing westward, the people again journeyed under its guidance. As directed, they resettled in what is now northeastern Mississippi.

SACRED POLE, OMAHA   See OMAHA SACRED POLE

SACRED ROCK MEDICINES *Crow* Venerated medicines known as Bacoritse in the Crow language. According to belief, they originated with the Rockman, one of the first people on Earth, and his wife, the Tobacco Plant Woman. Old Man Coyote and the Rockman later gave the Sacred Rock Medicines to the Crow people along with the SWEAT LODGE, the SUN DANCE and the tobacco-planting ceremony. Because they came from the marriage of a man and a woman, the Bacoritse are also male and female and are able to multiply. A spirit being, personifying a particular rock, may appear to a person in a dream. The dreamer may then receive sacred instructions and knowledge, including where to locate the Rock Medicine, whether it is male or female, powers and rituals associated with it, and any requirements or taboos involved in keeping it. Offerings and prayers are made to the Bacoritse, which are revered for their holiness and treated with the proper care and respect.

SACRED SCROLLS *Ojibway* Pictographic writings or drawings, generally etched on birch bark, to record sacred knowledge. These varied in form from folded strips to rolled scrolls. Types of knowledge recorded included sacred songs, dreams, and MIDEWIWIN instruction charts. Created, kept, and interpreted by qualified individuals, they served as mnemonic aids to recall and to transmit knowledge from the oral tradition. It was generally the practice of Midewiwin priests to bury or burn their scrolls before they died if they had no qualified successor. (See also REDSKY, JAMES, SR.)

SACRED SITES Traditional practices of Native Americans are inseparably bound to land and natural formations. For millennia Indian peoples have worshiped at natural sites that are part of the land—natural, not built, sanctuaries. Sacred places include mountains, lakes, piles of rocks, unusually shaped mounds, middens, caves, burial grounds, rock art sites, ceremonial grounds, doctoring sites, and medicine or training sites. These are places where spirits most often reveal themselves. Traditional accounts relate the sacredness of certain places as the place of creation of specific tribes, the locations of important revelations, and as places essential to the entrance to the next life. A sacred area can also be a site from which plants, herbs, minerals, and waters possessing healing powers may be taken and where people communicate with the spirit world by means of prayers and offerings. In North America, some sites include BADGER-TWO MEDICINE, BEAR BUTTE, BIG MOUNTAIN, BLUE LAKE, COSO HOT SPRINGS, KOLHU/WALA-WA, KOOTENAI FALLS, MAT FAAR TIIGUNDRA, MOUNT ADAMS, MOUNT GRAHAM, and SAN FRANCISCO PEAKS.

In these locations, people relate in a sacred manner to ancestors and relations, humans, plants or animals, and all of the most significant sacred powers. Ceremonies, vision quests, prayers, fasts, or pilgrimages must take place here. The efficacy of these sacred sites depends on the physical conditions. Spraying and logging trees; altering the terrain through dams, fencing, and other methods; building roads; tourism; and vandalism damage the sacred nature of the land.

A number of tribes have sacred sanctuaries on lands now under federal or state control. Many sacred grounds required for certain seasonal ceremonies have been fenced off, leaving Indians without access to these places. For many tribes, there is no alternative place of worship. Native Americans cannot substitute another site for one considered sacred. Sacred places have been threatened by logging and mining operations, hydroelectric plants and other public works projects, Forest Service regulations, urban housing, highways, and other dangers. Law makers and judges have weighed Indian constitutional rights for free exercise of religion against the right to regulate property in the interest of the public. In some cases, sacred lands have been protected or returned to Indian peoples. In others, decisions have threatened the free exercise of Indian religions. Some of the cases included in this volume are: *BADONI V. HIGGINSON, FOOLS CROW V. GULLET, LYNG V. NORTHWEST INDIAN CEMETERY PROTECTIVE ASS'N, SEQUOYAH V. TENNESSEE VALLEY AUTHORITY, UNITED STATES V. MEANS,* and *WILSON V. BLOCK.*

(See also subject index for other sacred sites.)

SACRIFICIAL FIGURINES *Navajo (Dineh)* Figurines of dolls and their prayersticks that are reproduced for sacrificial offerings to spirits. Like other sacrificial offerings, they are deposited in spots that are easily accessible to spirits. There are certain requirements regarding the materials from which they must be made, the kind and number of jewels to be added, their sizes, type of sticks, colors, decorations, and places of deposit. There are songs and prayers that accompany their preparation and deposit, all sanctioned by tradition and religiously observed. Sacrificial figures are made because a person has offended the spirit form of an animal. Because of his or her wrongful actions, the spirit is "exercising a hold" on the transgressor through sickness, which informs the offender that the spirit must have a sacrifice to rid the patient of the spirit's hold. It is believed that reproducing the cause of illness is a safe remedy and will placate the spirits. An offense against a bear, for example, can be atoned for by making a bear figurine. Sacrificial figurines are designed for minor offenses, and Navajo (Dineh) CURING CEREMONIALS are designed for major offenses. Singers furnish the jewel fragments, feathers, colors, tobacco, reeds, and other things required for the figurine and prayerstick offerings. Singers are compensated with food, pollen, goats, sheep, and money for their services. (See also REMAKING RITE.)

SAGUARO FESTIVAL *Tohono O'odham (Papago)* A July ceremony observed in Arizona and Mexico that marks the beginning of the rainy season and involves the making and drinking of cactus wine. Women collect the fruit of the giant saguaro cactus, boil the pulp, strain the juice through a basket, pour the syrup into jars, and place them in a ceremonial RAIN HOUSE, as it is called, during the ceremony. The village headmen and assistants preside at the fermentation of the liquor inside the house while people dance and sing in a large circle outside. The "sit and drink" drinking ceremony takes place on the third day to wet the earth. The ceremony takes place on the dance ground outside the council house before a gathering of both sexes and all ages from home and neighboring villages. The men of the village pass the sacred wine around in large baskets. The village headmen recite long poems during the ceremony that explain how the cactus wine produces clouds, rain, and corn.

SAINT'S DAY FIESTA (Pahko) *Yaqui* A celebration by the town's people in the town plaza to honor the patron saint of the town or of the church. Like other Yaqui ceremonies, the fiesta combines Christian and Native elements. The fiesta, administered by the Pahkome, requires the organization of two separate and competing fiestas, each of which proceeds separately through the traditional ritual sequences but which come together under church sanction in the final phase. A large part of, if not all, the people of a town are drawn into the fiesta competition. The Saint's Day fiesta follows in its general form the pattern of a PAHKO, a household fiesta. The fiesta includes feasting, clowning, and PASCOLA DANCERS and DEER DANCERS. At the climax of the Saint's Day fiesta there is a ritual drama of the defeat of the Moors by the Christians enacted by the two opposing groups of the Pahkome.

SALT Salt has been ascribed ritual uses by many different tribes. In the Southeast, salt has been used as a love charm in the GREEN CORN DANCE and various BUSK ceremonies. It figures in traditional mortuary customs of Cherokee and Pueblo peoples and in curing ceremonies at Isleta and Laguna Pueblos. There are salt taboos during certain ceremonies among peoples in the Southeast, Southwest, and Northeast.

In the Southwest, the Hopi, Zuni, Navajo, and Rio Grande pueblos and Tohono O'odham religious practitioners conducted expeditions and a religious ceremony to gather salt. Leaders with certain duties arranged the date of the trip, prayed for a successful journey, and taught rituals for collecting the salts and songs appropriate for the undertaking. Initiates, generally men, went on salt trips while women prayed for success, performed rituals, and then distributed the salt upon the return of the salt gatherers.

The Navajo made trips to Zuni Lake in early July or in November to ritually gather salt for ceremonial purposes. Any person knowledgeable about ritual formulas could lead a party. Members of the group spent four days ritually preparing for the journey, which included cleansing and continence. The journey usually lasted four days and was accompanied by prayer and song. The salt gathering itself was accompanied by rituals.

The Tohono O'odham received personal power by going on an annual salt pilgrimage in the summer to the Gulf of California. Salt pilgrims were purified, and the journey was hedged with ceremonial restrictions from the time it was proposed until long after completion. Pilgrims, who might be as young as 16, had little food, water, or sleep on the journey and were not permitted to talk. The trip had to be repeated four successive years, and after the 10th journey, a man could lead others. Preparations were made in advance, and all equipment had to be new. On the morning of the fourth day, the pilgrims reached the beach. The young men ran, some experiencing personal visions, and made offerings of prayersticks and cornmeal before gathering the salt. Without looking back, they returned home and distributed the salt. After being purified, they retreated for a period of time awaiting visions that made them "Ripe Men." The pilgrimage symbolized the quest for life as bringing salt back from the ocean to a desert environment—bringing new life, in the form of moisture, to the Tohono world. The salt expeditions brought communities together, since everyone was involved in the undertaking. The pilgrimage transformed pilgrims from youths to men. Those who did not go provided moral support at home by singing and praying. The collection of salt was a ritual occasion, and the salt gatherers abstained from sexual intercourse before leaving and upon their return home as well as for a period after their return. Each Native group has different stories concerning the salt deity.

SAN FRANCISCO PEAKS In Coconino National Forest in Arizona, a sacred site to the Navajo, Hopi, Apache, and Zuni. Traditional Navajo (Dineh) believe the peaks include one of the four sacred moutains that mark the boundaries of their homelands. They believe the peaks are the home of specific spirits as well as the body of a living spiritual being. Practitioners collect herbs from the peaks for use in religious ceremonies to heal Navajo people, and ceremonies are performed there as well. Traditional Hopi believe that for about six months of the year kachinas reside at the peaks and that their activities there create rain and snow that sustain the villages. Hopi, who have many shrines in the peaks, collect herbs, plants, and animals there for use in religious ceremonies. A 777-acre portion of the peaks, known as the Snow Bowl, has been used for downhill skiing since 1937 when the U.S. Forest Service built a road and ski lodge. In 1979, the Forest Service of Coconino National Forest issued a decision to permit moderate development of the Snow Bowl. In 1980 the Forest Service regional supervisor approved the proposal to pave an access road to the area. The Hopi initiated a lawsuit, WILSON V. BLOCK, to halt development. (See also SACRED SITES for related cases in this volume.)

SANAPIA (1895–1968) Comanche   Comanche medicine woman. Sanapia was born in the spring of 1895 at Fort Sill, where her family had traveled for rations. She attended the Cache Creek Mission School in southern Oklahoma for seven years and then began four years of training to become an eagle doctor, a medicine person spiritually assisted by the eagle. By the time she was 17, she had completed instruction but could not begin doctoring until after menopause. During the training period she was observed by her mother, maternal uncle, maternal grandmother, and paternal grandfather, who each had to give their final approval through a blessing ceremony. In addition to studying medicine plants and the diagnosis and treatment of illnesses, she learned the proper conduct of doctors and assisted her teachers, her mother and uncle, when they treated patients.

Sanapia was influenced by three different religious traditions within her family. Her father was a Christian, her mother and maternal uncle were eagle doctors, and her uncle and grandfather were peyotists. Sanapia's medicine practice included treatment of "ghost sickness," a condition believed to derive from contact with ghosts. Besides utilizing herbal medicines, she obtained assistance through her spirit helper, the eagle, and through her medicine song. Sanapia told her story to David E. Jones, an anthropologist she adopted as a son, in the late 1960s. At that time she was the last surviving eagle doctor and was considering passing on her spiritual knowledge and power to one of her children or grandchildren. Jones wrote of her medicine way in *Sanapia: Comanche Medicine Woman* (1972). Sanapia was a pseudonym. Her real name is not known.

SAND ALTAR WOMAN *Hopi* Earth mother said to be the wife of the deity MASAU'U and sister of the GERMINATOR (Muingwa). She is sometimes thought of as the mother of humanity and spoken of as the mother of kachinas. (See also KACHINA.)

SAND CRANE *(c. 1873–1950) Cheyenne* Keeper of Esevone, the SACRED BUFFALO HAT of the Cheyenne people. Sand Crane's father was COAL BEAR, and his mother was Glad Traveler. (One source lists his mother's name as Morning Star or Rabbit Woman.) Coal Bear served as keeper of the Sacred Buffalo Hat until his death in 1896, but it was not until 38 years later that his son Sand Crane assumed the role. Sand Crane was married to an Arapaho woman who was initially opposed to her husband becoming the caretaker of Esevone. Known for his devotion to continuing the sacred ways of his people, he taught the Suhtaio SUN DANCE to a number of young men who later served as priests of the ceremony. The keeper's determination and training resulted in a new generation of religious leaders making certain that the sacred traditions continued. Those who received Sand Crane's teachings became respected Sun Dance instructors among their people. Sand Crane is also remembered for helping conduct the last MASSAUM CEREMONY among the Northern Cheyenne in 1911. His account of the gift of the Sacred Buffalo Hat to the Cheyenne (in a Mari Sandoz manuscript) is in keeping with a tribal variation that is earlier than other accounts of ERECT HORNS. After Sand Crane's death in March 1950, his brother Head Swift became Esovone's keeper.

SANDPAINTING A ceremonial ritual practiced among Pueblo, Navajo, Apache, Cheyenne, Arapaho, and peoples in southern California. *Sandpainting* is a misleading term because there is no paint, no brush, and no fluid medium. Handfuls of dry material are sprinkled from between the thumb and forefinger to form the figures of the "painting." Pueblo make their sandpaintings of sand or ocher of various colors, corn pollen, pulverized flower petals, and green leaves in private kiva rituals; Cheyenne and Arapaho make theirs during SUN DANCE ceremonies. In southern California, sandpaintings made on the ground are an important part of

initiation ceremonies or puberty rituals. The ground paintings represent abstract forms of the universe in which spiritual and astronomic phenomena are depicted. The Apache make one large, complex sandpainting inside a circular enclosure of boughs, opening to the east, and the sandpainting is destroyed before sundown. The Navajo may make more than one during a ceremony.

The Navajo are well known for their large, elaborate sandpaintings. Also called dry paintings, the ritual is part of some, but not all, religious ceremonies performed to cure an ailing person, cast out evil, or bless and harmonize a person with nature. They are holy, temporary altars made on the ground or floor of the ceremonial hogan, blessed by pollen and cornmeal offerings, upon which a patient sits while the singer or his assistant performs certain rites. A singer consults with the family and patient and selects from various sandpaintings prescribed for the ceremonial those that seem appropriate to the illness and its cause. A sandpainting is part of a ceremonial that may continue for one to nine days.

Each painting is linked to a particular ceremonial and the traditional creation story upon which the ceremonial is founded. It is believed that in the beginning, HOLY PEOPLE prescribed the construction, composition, and ritual designs of the paintings. They gave up the sandpainting to the protagonist of each origin story, who in turn taught it to Earth People. The sandpainting reproduces the painting acquired by a chant hero from the spirits on one of his adventurous journeys. Sandpaintings symbolize the creation and history of the spirits, ancestors, and humans and commemorate episodes in the story of a chant hero.

A sandpainting can be very small, a foot or less in diameter, or very large, 20 feet or more across. It can be circular, squarish, or an elongated rectangle. The time required for making a painting depends on its size and complexity as well as on the number of artists employed. For example, a large painting may require 15 men during most of a day. A six-foot painting may be completed by four to six men in three to five hours. The colors for the designs are most often pulverized charcoal, gypsum, ocher, and white, yellow and red sandstone. The technique involves the singer or his assistant picking up some of the material in his hand, holding it near the surface to be decorated and allowing it to flow between his thumb and flexed index finger as he delineates the pattern. The sandpainting is replicated according to the memory of the officiating singer. The singer aims to reproduce exactly without alteration the prescribed sacred designs that spirits taught to a chant hero who memorized them and inaugurated that particular ceremony for earth people. No visual record is kept, but hundreds of patterns are known to exist.

There are two common patterns of composition. The first has long rows of figures side by side with an encircling element around three sides and open to the east side where two elements (animals or objects) guard the opening. The second arrangement has a center that represents a geographical setting (mountain, lake, water, home of the spirits, or the place of emergence) for the location that is an important element in the chant. Sandpaintings may include images of holy people in a row or multiples of four to represent augmented power. There are many symbolic elements in the paintings. These may include stylized human beings, arrows, lightning, snakes, earth, sky, wind, rain, clouds, rainbows, stars, comets, thunder, water monsters, animals, plants, herbs, seeds, pollen, and the underworld. Most major powers are represented as pairs. Sandpaintings emphasize the cardinal points, the four corners of the earth where the four sacred mountains stand, four seasons, and four parts of day. White, blue, yellow, and black are associated with the time of day, season of the year, stage of a person's life, and the underworlds from which the original beings emerged. Generally, some guardian—rainbow, lightning, or arrows—encircle three sides of the picture with an opening to the east.

The finished sandpainting provides a physical form in which the Holy People manifest their presence. The singer sprinkles cornmeal on the painting and on the person for whom the ceremony is being performed; the ailing person sits in the middle of the sandpainting facing east. Identification with the Holy People in the painting (who have a connection with the cause of the illness being treated) is accomplished by the singer transferring sands from parts of the painted figures to corresponding body parts of the person sitting on the painting. The spirits are called to the hogan by their portrayal in the sandpainting and they imbue the painting with their power and strength, curing in exchange for the offerings of the patient and singer. The patient is made one with the Holy People and shares their power.

When this identification is complete, the sands are removed and returned to nature. The sandpainting is therefore made and destroyed within the day. For many years, Navajo sandpaintings have been made as permanent, secular items. Beginning in the late 1880s, sandpaintings have been reproduced outside their ceremonial context, in books about Navajo religion, in Navajo weavings, in rugs and on fabrics. Sandpaintings have been drawn, painted, filmed,

Navajo sandpainting. John Burnside demonstrates sandpainting at a Navajo craft show in July 1963. *Photograph by Paul V. Long. Museum of Northern Arizona.*

Dennis Roger demonstrates Navajo sandpainting in 1990 to students at Quincy Elementary School in Topeka, Kansas. *Topeka Capital-Journal.*

photographed, demonstrated, and made into jewelry and wall decorations. While some Navajo are indifferent, many oppose the commercialization of sandpainting designs that the Holy People never intended to be made permanent.

SANTORA *Yaqui* A standard set of representations of religious figures introduced to the Yaqui by the Jesuits and including Jesus, Mary, patron saints of church and town, and the statue of the Holy Trinity. All of the figures are carefully clothed and tended to by organized groups of men and women and are treated with reverence. The figures represented by statues are regarded as "living" in the church of a town.

SAWYER, DAVID (Kezhegowinninne, "Skyman," "Man of the Sky" or "One Who is Exalted") *(c. 1812–1889) Mississauga (Ojibway)* Methodist lay preacher, teacher and chief. Born to Chief Joseph Sawyer (Nawahjegezegwabe)

and his wife Jane (Wetosy), Sawyer was a member of the Eagle clan, and his people belonged to the Credit band of Mississauga located above Lake Ontario in Upper Canada. He was influenced by the preaching of his cousin PETER JONES, the Native missionary, and was baptized into the Methodist Episcopal Church as David Sawyer in 1825 by the Reverend ALVIN TORRY. Sawyer, who was later affiliated with the Wesleyan Methodist Church, then began his life-long commitment to the faith. After completing his mission school education, he became an assistant to Peter Jones.

In 1829 Sawyer started teaching at the Lake Simcoe mission in Ontario and a year later began working with the Matchedash band located on Georgian Bay. Besides serving as an interpreter to the white Methodist missionary in the area, he preached to the people in the Ojibway language. In 1832 he and two other Credit band members traveled to Sault Ste. Marie on a mission for the church. Sawyer was later sent to the Saugeen community on Lake Huron and the Muncey area in Middlesex County, where he taught and interpreted. Upon his return home, the Credit band council appointed him to a paid position. Sawyer was later adopted by the Newash band, located near Owen Sound, which consisted of both Ojibway and Potawatomi members. He was given land and a house in exchange for assisting them in their dealings with the government. In 1852 Sawyer was ordained by the Wesleyan Methodist Church "for special purposes." Three years later the Newash band passed a resolution naming him chief, but the government's Indian Department, which feared his Methodism would heighten religious tensions among the Catholics and other factions in the community, refused to endorse the appoinment. In 1861, Sawyer went to the New Credit Reserve located in the corner of the Grand River Reserve near Brantford, Ontario, and when his father died two years later he became head chief. He served in the position for about 25 years. Sawyer died on November 11, 1889. He was married to Anna Springer, and their family included at least three sons and one daughter.

SCHWEIGMAN, BILL (Eagle Feather) *(b. 1914) Lakota* Medicine man. Schweigman was born on July 10, 1914, in Rosebud, South Dakota. His paternal grandfather, Joseph Peter Schweigman, was a German who emigrated to America from Hamburg and later married Millie Pino, a Lakota. Schweigman's father, who served as chief of police on the Rosebud Reservation, died in 1922. His mother, Annie Eagle Feather, a Brulé from Rosebud, married John Good Elk, and the family moved to St. Francis, South Dakota. Schweigman then began attending the local Catholic school. After marrying Hazel Flory of the Crow Creek Reservation in 1936, he began studying to become an Episcopal lay reader. They later lived in California, where he supported the family by working as an electrician. In 1963 Schweigman had a heart attack and eventually lost his employment because of his physical condition. The family returned to South Dakota, settling at St. Francis. As early as 1931, he was told during a YUWIPI meeting that he would become a holy man. Schweigman began participating in the SUN DANCE in 1956 and continued his involvement each year. Besides being named traditional chief of the Sioux Nation Sun Dance Association in 1960, he was made a holy man by FRANK FOOLS CROW and JOHN (FIRE) LAME DEER the same year. Schweigman then became a practicing medicine man. Assisted by his wife, he served as a Sun Dance intercessor as well as a Yuwipi man.

SCRATCHING CEREMONY *Oklahoma Seminole and Creek* A sacred rite believed to be beneficial to good health. It is performed during the GREEN CORN CEREMONY after ritual medicine taking and washing. The upper arm, lower arm, and the back of each calf are each scratched four times. Early scratching implements included thorns or pins in a wood frame, but steel needles are now in use for this purpose. Small children, very lightly scratched, are sometimes included in order that they may receive the benefits of the rite. After the ritual scratching, the women and children rinse with water and are free to break their fasts. The men are scratched by the same procedure, but their scratches are not as lightly done and they may choose to add an X on the chest in addition to the marks on their arms and legs. An older male relative may carry out the rite for a woman and her children, but the men are generally scratched by the medicine man. This religious practice is also found among other southeastern tribal groups.

SEA WOMAN *Inuit* A female spirit living in the depths of the sea; the mother and protector of all sea mammals. There is a wide variety of names used by different groups in the central Arctic that refer to the "old woman of the sea." Baffin Islanders call her Sedna; northwest of Hudson Bay, she is called Nuliayuk; Copper Inuit use the name Kannakapfaluk; and Iglulik call her Takanakapsaluk. As ruler of the sea, Sedna withholds sea mammals as game if humans offend the regulations she has laid down regarding hunting, mixing products of land and sea, and ritual cleanliness and diet.

SEDNA CEREMONY *Baffin Island Inuit* Performed in autumn, the central feature of this ceremony involves an *angakok* (shaman) in the role as intermediary between people and spirit forces. When the *angakok* enters a trance, his spirit flies to a place where Sedna dwells, doing battle with her to capture seals. The ceremony also features the confessions to the shaman of taboo transgressions and a tug of war between people born in winter and those in summer, which determines the amount of food available for people. The ceremony is designed to drive away boisterous weather typical at that season and to secure better hunting.

SEED PLANTING CEREMONY *Iroquois* A one-day ceremony held in late April, early May, or June at the time corn is planted. The faithkeepers gather vegetable seeds from houses, take them to the longhouse and soak them. The purpose of the ritual is to bless seeds so they will grow, thank the spirits of the life supporters (corn, beans, squash, and all garden vegetables) and the Creator, and ask all spirit forces to take care of the crops and water them. The ceremony informs women that it is time to plant again and to ask for the help of the food spirits and rain for the coming season. (See also IROQUOIS CALENDRICAL CEREMONIES.)

SELECTED WOMEN (The Selected Ones.) *Cheyenne* Women who worked in guilds to create sacred quillwork, later beadwork, for clothing and lodges. Each guild, consisting primarily of holy women, possessed a sacred bundle. Other Plains groups established similar societies. (See also SOCIETIES.)

SEMMENS, JOHN *(1850–1921)* Methodist missionary. Born on January 9, 1850, in Perron Downs, Cornwall, England, Semmens was reared in Bruce Mines, Ontario, and educated at Victoria College in Toronto. In 1872 he was sent to Norway House in Manitoba and eventually served at a number of Canadian mission posts, including Cross Lake, Nelson House, and Berens River. He was chosen in 1895 to establish an industrial school in Brandon, Manitoba, for Native children and later worked for the Department of Indian Affairs. While serving as an Indian agent, he discounted an accurate report of starvation among Sandy Lake Natives made by the Reverend FREDERICK GEORGE STEVENS, another Methodist missionary. Semmens also served in a treaty commission role between 1909 and 1910. He wrote *Mission Life in the Northwest,* a book that includes condemnations of Native beliefs and practices.

SEQUOYAH V. TENNESSEE VALLEY AUTHORITY (480 F. Supp. 608 [E.D. Tenn. 1979], 620 F. 2d 1159 [6th Circ.], cert. denied, 449 U.S. 953 [1980]) *(1980)* This case began in 1979 when the Eastern Band of Cherokee Indians, the United Ketooah Band of Cherokee, and three Cherokee individuals jointly petitioned the district court for the eastern district of Tennessee for an injunction to halt the Tennessee Valley Authority from completing the Tellico Dam and Reservoir on the Little Tennessee River. The project, with a long history of opposition from environmentalists and other groups, was opposed by the plaintiffs because it would destroy sites of profound significance to their people. The valley of the Little Tennessee River was the location of Seven Towns, the historic center of the Cherokee Nation, where hundreds of archaeological sites of worldwide importance are situated. The plaintiffs contended that the actions of the Tennessee Valley Authority would abridge their freedom of religion under the First Amendment of the United States Constitution. The Tellico Dam project would deny them access to the area and its sacred sites and historic villages, inundate the burial grounds of their ancestors, and disturb the relationship between the physical and spiritual worlds. The plaintiffs noted that the Cherokee, who had been forcibly removed to Indian Territory (Oklahoma) by the United States Government in the 19th century, continued to have religious, cultural, and historic ties to their ancestral homeland in the Southeast. Ammoneta Sequoyah, a

78-year-old Cherokee medicine man and the lead plaintiff, stated that he had gone to Chota and other sacred places in the valley of the Little Tennessee River all of his life. He testified that the flooding from the Tellico Dam project would result in the loss of medicine gathering sites, sacred knowledge, and spiritual power and strength. The district court denied the Cherokee plaintiffs' motion for an injunction and ruled to dismiss the case. The court held that their lack of a property interest in the Tellico area precluded the advancement of a First Amendment claim.

On appeal the Sixth Circuit Court of Appeals affirmed the decision, ruling that the Cherokee plaintiffs had failed to prove that the location was central and indispensable to the practice of their religion. The court reasoned that religious concerns were separate from cultural or historical interests. Invoking the AMERICAN INDIAN RELIGIOUS FREEDOM ACT OF 1978 or the National Historic Preservation Act could not overcome the congressional mandate to complete and operate Tellico Dam. In 1980 the United Supreme Court denied *certiorari,* declining to hear the case. (See Subject Index for other legal cases listed in this volume.)

SERGEANT, JOHN *(1710–1749)* Congregational missionary to the Housatonic Indians in the area of present-day Berkshire County, Massachusetts. He was born in Newark, New Jersey, and following his graduation from Yale in 1729, Sergeant served as a tutor at the college and studied theology. He began preparing to minister to the Housatonic after the SOCIETY FOR THE PROPAGATION OF THE GOSPEL IN NEW ENGLAND offered him the post in September 1734. Wishing to finish out the school year at Yale, he compromised by spending two months at his new post to get missionary work started. He had the Indians construct a building between their settlements in present-day Sheffield and Stockbridge for use as a school and church, then left Timothy Woodbridge, who was to assist him, in charge while he returned to New Haven. Two young Indian boys accompanied Sergeant to Yale, where they lived with him while learning English and teaching him their Native language. Sergeant began his missionary work on a permanent basis in July 1735, and a short time later, on August 31, he was ordained a Congregational minister in Deerfield, Massachusetts. To "civilize" the Indians he combined an emphasis upon farming with instruction in English and religion. With assistance from the Massachusetts General Court, which in 1736 granted land for the Indians to move to from two settlements, Sergeant turned the newly founded Stockbridge into New England's most impressive Christian Indian settlement. Besides baptizing 182 of 218 inhabitants and receiving 42 as church members during his 14 years as a missionary, he also emphasized education. With help from

English benefactors, he tried a number of approaches to schooling Indian youngsters. Some attended Woodbridge's classes while others were placed with English families where it was thought they made better progress in their studies. One of Sergeant's main ambitions was the establishment of a "Charity-House," or boarding school, where Indian children could be instructed in business and industry, as well as in reading and writing and matters of religion. Although he had publicized this plan in 1743, the boarding school was not constructed until a few days before his death in 1749. Sergeant gained the respect of the Indians with his mastery of their language. He translated biblical passages and other religious works into Mahican with the assistance of JOHN QUINNEY. Sergeant was married to Abigail Williams on August 16, 1739. The couple had two sons, one of whom also served as a missionary to the Indians, and a daughter. Sergeant died on July 27, 1749.

SERRA, JUNÍPERO *(1713–1784)* Franciscan missionary considered the architect of the CALIFORNIA MISSION SYSTEM, a 600-mile long chain of 21 missions. Born in Spain, Serra was a theologian and professor of philosophy before he was transferred to Mexico in 1749. Inspector-General José Galvez, who had been sent to Mexico to effect administrative reforms, requested that Serra convert Indians of the northern regions to Christianity for the Spanish Crown. Between 1752 and 1758, Serra helped build five missions, still used in the 1980s. In 1769, when Spain occupied Upper California, Serra and other friars joined the Portola expedition in its efforts to colonize Upper California. Serra founded the first California mission, San Diego de Alcala, in 1769 and founded and assigned names to eight more by 1782, laying the groundwork for the entire chain of missions. Serra prescribed in detail written regulations about the daily routine to be followed at each mission. He condoned lashing Indians who disobeyed. His records show that he baptized more than 6,000 Indians and confirmed more than 5,000.

Efforts to sanctify Junípero Serra began in the mid-1700s and continue today, spearheaded by Catholic clergy and lay people. California Indians, several tribes, some historians, the American Indian Historical Society, and others oppose Serra's being declared a saint, arguing that he oversaw the system that uprooted tribes, seized Indian lands, forced conversions, and worked Indians for no pay. There are historians who argue that some of the allegations against Serra are untrue or exaggerated. In 1985, Serra was declared venerable. In 1988, he was beatified.

SETTEE, JAMES *(c. 1809–1902) Swampy Cree* Nineteenth-century Anglican missionary and priest. Settee was born at Nelson River in present-day Manitoba and became a Christian through the influence of one of the first missionaries in the region. As a child, he received instruction from the Reverend JOHN WEST. In 1833 he worked as a catechist at St. Peter's settlement near present-day Winnipeg. Settee and James Beardy, another Native convert, later established Lac la Ronge and Lac la Crosse mission stations among the Cree in 1846. Their efforts in the region followed those of HENRY BUDD, the missionary who had established Anglican efforts at The Pas (Manitoba) in 1840. Settee later studied at Bishop's College, Red River (present-day Winnipeg), and was ordained by the bishop of Rupert's Land in 1853. Three years later he attained priests' orders. Settee worked among Native people under the auspices of the CHURCH MISSIONARY SOCIETY for more than 50 years. The society placed him on retirement at the age of 75, but he continued his religious efforts after that period. Settee died in Winnipeg on March 19, 1902, at the age of 93. His son JOHN R. SETTEE also became a missionary. (See also SETTEE, RURAL DEAN.)

SETTEE, JOHN R. *(fl. 19th century) Swampy Cree* An Anglican missionary who was the son of the Reverend JAMES SETTEE. He served as a catechist for a long period of time before his 1885 ordination. Settee, who was sent to establish a mission station at Moose Lake, left Prince Albert (Saskatchewan) with his family in a small boat he had built. Upon their arrival he constructed a log house that served as a mission station and church. Settee was later ordained by the bishop on the basis of his work at Moose Lake. He eventually served at Sandy Lake and at Cumberland, where he died.

SETTEE, RURAL DEAN *(fl. 19th century) Swampy Cree* A 19th-century Anglican missionary in Canada who was born in the Hudson Bay area in the early 1800s. Described as "a native of pure blood," Settee was educated at the Church Mission School, which later became St. John's College in Winnipeg. He was ordained in the holy orders of the Episcopal Church in 1854. His early missionary work covered a large region, extending from the Missouri River to Hudson Bay and to the Isle la Croix District in the west. The native missionary, who was also fluent in English, preached to Native people in the Cree and Saulteaux languages. The *Manitoba Free Press* reported on August 31, 1883, that the Reverend Settee was in Winnipeg on a visit from Prince Albert (Northwest Territories), where he had been working among Native people for the previous four years.

SEVEN SACRED RITES OF THE LAKOTA *Lakota* Sacred ceremonies foretold to the Lakota by WHITE BUFFALO CALF WOMAN, a holy woman who appeared among the people. They include the SWEAT LODGE CEREMONY (Inikagapi), the VISION QUEST (Hanbleceya, "crying for a vision"),

GHOST KEEPING CEREMONY (Wanagi yuhapi), the SUN DANCE (Wi wanyang wacipi), the HUNKA CEREMONY ("the making of relatives"), GIRL'S PUBERTY RITE (Isnati awicalowan), and the THROWING OF THE BALL CEREMONY (Tapa wankayeyapi). The Lakota people have a rich, diverse array of ceremonies beyond these seven sacred rites, including those that originated in visions.

SHABAZZ V. BARNAUSKAS 600 F.Supp. 712 (1985) In this case, appendixed to *Shabazz v. Barnauskas*, an American Indian inmate in the Florida State Penitentiary charged that the institution's hair length regulation violated his rights under the First Amendment and under the AMERICAN INDIAN RELIGIOUS FREEDOM ACT OF 1978. The court ruled that the maintenance of penal security in the public's interest outweighed the First Amendment rights of the plaintiff. (See Subject Index for other cases in this volume regarding the religious freedom of Native Americans.)

SHADES OF THE DEAD *Inuit* Spirits of the dead to whom Inuit show deference. It is believed that the human soul continues to exist after the end of life as an entity capable of taking part in the affairs of the living. The spirits of dead animals persist as well. (See also MOURNING OBSERVANCES; NAME-SOUL; PERSON; SOUL.)

SHAKING TENT CEREMONY *Algonquian* A ceremony practiced among Algonquian groups for the purpose of healing, divining, and prophesying. It was conducted by a SHAKING TENT SHAMAN, who possessed a number of powers, including the ability to summon and communicate with spirits. The presence of the spirits in the lodge would cause it to shake violently, hence the name of the ceremony.

The shaman sought spiritual assistance for a number of purposes, including to diagnose and treat illness, to find lost persons or objects, to determine the well-being of absent friends or relatives, and to prophesy future events. Preparations for the shaking tent ceremony generally included fasting, praying, offerings, and sweat lodge purification. The shaking tent shaman was often bound hand and foot with the strongest thongs and suspended within the lodge, to be released by the spirits. Different voices and animal sounds could sometimes be heard during the ceremony as well as rapid conversation between the shaman and the spirits in an archaic version of the Native language. Other characteristics of the ceremony included the singing, accompanied by a drum and rattle, of personal dream songs at intervals during the ceremony, the attainment of a trance state by the shaman, and sparks of light indicating the presence of spirits in the lodge. The shaman generally performed the ceremony alone in a tent or lodge built for the purpose.

The ceremony has been described among the Cree, Menominee, Montagnais, Ojibway, Ottawa, Saulteaux, and other Algonquian groups in the United States and Canada. Early missionaries attributed the practice to paganism and attempted to discredit the shaman and to obliterate the ceremony.

SHAKING TENT SHAMAN *Algonquian* A particular type of shaman among the Ojibway, Ottawa, Cree, Montagnais, Menominee, Saulteaux, and other Algonquian groups in the United States and Canada, this spiritual leader was generally a male and communicated with the spirits to heal, divine, or prophesy. He often demonstrated his power through the SHAKING TENT CEREMONY, in which spirits summoned by him indicated their presence by violently shaking the ceremonial lodge. The shaman received his calling to the vocation, in part, through dreams and visions, but he also underwent difficult preparations. His services were often sought by tribal members who needed assistance locating lost friends, relatives, or objects, as well as for healing physical and mental ailments. The shaman sometimes recorded his ritual in pictographs etched onto birch bark to serve as a mnemonic device, especially when the number of his dream songs had increased. The shaking tent shaman was highly respected among his people for the great spiritual powers he possessed. The practices of some of these shamans, like CARIGOUAN and ETIENNE PIGAROUICH, were described by a number of European-American observers who were both repelled and fascinated by the "magic" they described, and the early Jesuits sometimes made wagers with them to try to prove them false. In the Ojibway language, the shaking tent shaman is variously called Jessakkid, Djasakid, or Tcisaki. In English, he was also termed a diviner, juggler, or conjurer. (See also MEDICINE MAN/WOMEN; SHAMAN, TUBE-SUCKING SHAMAN.)

SHALAKO CEREMONY (House Blessing Ceremony) *Zuni* An annual religious ceremony held before the Zuni new year or winter solstice, during the last part of November and the first part of December, according to the time schedule set by Zuni religious leaders. The ceremony involves prayer, dances (representations of prayers of thanks for the Creator), singing, and races (endurance tests). The ceremony is a sacred and dramatic interpretation of what tribal religion means to the Zuni.

The arrangements and appointments of the participants for the Shalako ceremony are made at the preceding New Year. The rain chiefs appoint spirit impersonators who meet throughout the year to learn prayers, dance, make ritual sacrifices, go into retreats, make pilgrimages, offer monthly prayersticks, run foot races, fast, and abstain from sex. Eight days before the Shalako, 10 KOYEMSHI (mudheads) make a public announcement that the ceremony will be held and then go into seclusion. Four days before Shalako, LONG HORN makes a public announcement.

The all-night ceremony, called the Shalako Dance, is held in special Shalako houses. Larger than ordinary homes, the houses are built by families who are sponsoring the mudheads, Long Horn, and Shalako during the ceremony. Ideally, eight houses are built, one for each of the six Shalakos, one for the mudheads, and one for the Long Horn.

When six Shalakos, giant-sized masked messengers of rain spirits, arrive, they plant PRAYERSTICKS in shrines and go to host homes where they perform rites and are entertained. They bless the houses constructed in their honor and offer prayers that Zuni may enjoy fertility, long life, and prosperity. The Shalako depart for their homes in the west following ceremonial races, a test of whether the Shalako men have kept their sacred vows during the year they were

in office. During the week following the departure of the Shalakos, kivas perform night KACHINA DANCES. On the final day of the week, clan member compensate the mudheads for their year of service. The mudheads' departure completes the Shalako festivities.

The Shalako ceremony is followed by a 10-day fasting period called TESHKWI.

SHAMAN Intermediaries to the spirit world; originally a term given to tribal specialists, medicine men, or exorcists by the Tungus of Siberia, from which it was extended to similar individuals among Indian tribes of North America. Shamans are individuals, both men and women, who due to illness, dreams, visions, or some inborn sensitivity or need directly experience the presence of spirits, whether those of living persons, plants, animals, other environmental features, or ghosts of the dead. The dreams or visions the shamans receive give them direct experience of sacred knowledge. Shamans may

Shaman. A religious figure among the Algonquian-speaking Indians was the shaman, or medicine man. The drawing shows an Algonquian shaman preparing his medicine. He sings sacred songs as he mixes various ingredients together, while shaking a rattle. *Library of Congress.*

also have special power if they have recovered from illness that brought them close to death. They journey from the world of the living to the spirit world of the dead and then return to the living. Shamans are also capable of altered states of awareness and are able to travel beyond ordinary boundaries of experience. They see over great distances and can travel inward to learn the way the human body and mind work. New shamans seek and pay shaman practitioners for guidance and training and must complete a course of action to gain control of forces that could make life miserable for them. This course may include fasting, vision questing, and confrontations between the shaman and spirit forces. The spiritual and physical training, which may take years, is essential to learn how to draw on the spirit helpers to assist in cures.

In general, shamans throughout North America compose special healing songs and put themselves into trances. In this way, they foretell the future, predict game movements, travel after souls, seek lost objects, and diagnose and cure illness, aided by spirit helpers with whom they communicate, whether they be spirits of earth, air, or sea. One of the most important ways shamans use their knowledge is to diagnose the cause of illness by "seeing," a sort of X-ray technique. During trance states, an assistant or interpreter may record the spiritual dialogues that take place and what the spirits prescribe for the patient as the shamans themselves lose all memory of the event.

Because shamans control many powerful forces, which can be used for constructive or harmful purposes, they are often feared as witches, individuals who prefer to use power to destroy others. Shamans have been suspected of being witches as often as they have been respected for their healing powers. Traditionally, shamans have been clairvoyants, mystics, herbalists, diagnosticians, hunters, dancers, singers, storytellers, artists, and physicians. In Western terms, a shaman is a philosopher, surgeon, priest, botanist, teacher, and psychologist. The practices of shamans can vary among tribal groups. Tribal names vary as well because *shaman* is generally not a term used by tribal people.

Apache

Apache shamans master a body of ceremonies to equip them to deal with life's hardships and act as intermediaries between people and spirits. They conduct puberty rites, paint masked dancers, or direct helpers who paint while the shamans pray and sing. The shamans receive details of ceremonies they are to conduct—the songs, prayers, ritual gestures, design elements, ritual objects—in dreams or visions in which spirit helpers appear, in some shape, and reveal the information, usually at the spirit's "holy home." Most frequently, shamans use spirit power to diagnose and heal disease. They sing and pray to determine the cause of

ailments and to learn what to do to cure them. They also locate lost persons or objects, bring success in hunting, love, and games. There are dream shamans who are consulted when someone has bad dreams. (See also APACHE POWER CONCEPTS.)

California

In northern California, shamans, usually women from Hupa, Shasta, Chilula, Wiyot, and men from Yuki, speak directly to spirits and use spiritual power to diagnose and cure disease caused by the presence in the body of some hostile object. Called "doctors" in English, they remove disease-causing objects, usually by sucking or by massage, singing, dancing, brushing, blowing tobacco smoke or breath, or administering plant or herbal medicine while either in or out of a trance. They are also said to ward off ghosts, expel evil forces, control weather, and are clairvoyant in seances. They find lost or stolen articles and predict the future. Among northwestern California tribes, the power of shamans comes from maintaining "PAINS" (disease objects) in their bodies. These pains are implanted in pairs during dreams by a guardian spirit. Afterward, there is long and rigorous instruction by older shamans during which the novices tame the pains. Strong doctors acquire many pairs of pains, but the strongest ones are the first two pairs. The instruction culminates in a doctor's (kick) dance, an initiation ceremony in which the shaman displays his or her power in a sweathouse. After the performance, the shaman can heal the sick, usually for a fee, by using his or her power for controlling the "pains" by sucking them from the patient's body, vomiting them up, and sending them away.

Inuit

Called *angakok* by people in the central Arctic, shamans are predominantly men, although among the Copper, Padlimiut, Iglulik, and eastern Baffin Island, women may be shamans as well. Their apprenticeship varies from a few days to as long as five to 12 years, during which novices experience tremendous hardships in order to learn how to control spirit helpers. A common feature of the training is "dying" and "coming back to life." In theory, anyone can become a shaman after the proper dream experience (because every Inuit is believed to have the ability to deal directly with the spirit world), but in fact the role is often passed from father to son or from a man to a close relative in the new generation. Their practices are applied to curing sickness from spiritual causes, predicting the future, finding lost objects, influencing the weather and supply of game, providing sacred objects for people desiring them, and conducting rites and observances related to the food supply. The prestige of the shamans rests on their demonstrated possession and alliance with spirit powers who assist them.

They reveal these powers by holding seances in which they travel on spirit flights over long distances to the land of the dead, to the Moon, or under the sea while their bodies are bound up, wrestle with hostile powers sent by rival shamans, and speak with corpses.

Inuit shamans are believed to be allied with helping spirits, called TUNERAKS. As a rule, shamans possess several helping spirits that they summon to the site of the performance with the help of songs they compose or obtain from other shamans and by drumming on a tambourine-type drum. The song reflects the rapport between the shaman and helping spirits. During performances, they dance while wearing masks that represent their spirits. Shamans go into trances in which they are believed to be under the control of powerful spirits. Shamans are greatly feared because they can cause illness and have the power to bring misfortune and death to an individual or community.

North Pacific Coast

Among these groups, shamans are men or women, not usually of high birth, who have obtained spiritual power for prediction, exposing witches, controlling weather, and diagnosing and curing diseases caused by intrusion of small objects sent by enemies and disease caused by soul loss. They inherit their roles and acquire them in quests in the woods where spirits are encountered or by possession by a spirit. Animals and fish that figure in shamanic objects include land otters, bears, mountain goats, frogs, devilfish, and other animals. Shamans summon their spirit helpers usually by singing their songs, drumming, and dancing until the spirits enter their bodies and speak through them in sacred language. Shaman regalia and ritual objects (rattles, masks representing spirit helpers, headbands, neck rings, boards painted with ritual designs, and necklaces) vary.

Pima (Akimel O'odham) and Tohono O'odham (Papago)

Called *ma:kai,* this shaman is recruited by animal spirits and specializes in diagnosing and curing STAYING SICKNESS found among Pimans. A *ma:kai's* heart, gifted with special knowledge, sensitivity, power, and training uses an eagle feather to wave smoke over a patient's body, a rattle, crystals, and other tools. The shaman keeps secret his spirit helpers, summoned by night-long diagnostic sessions called *doajida* in which shamans sing to them. The shamans also identify sickness by "illuminating" it with tobacco smoke blown over the patient's body during a *doajida,* after the singing of *doajida* songs, or during the daytime. After the songs, shamans make difficult diagnoses with help from their spirit aids. They identify and separate the "strengths" of dangerous objects in the patient's body one by one, moving them back from the heart to points of entry and sucking each one out.

Many other groups have shamans, which they call by a variety of names. (See also DIAGNOSTICIAN; HAND TREMBLER; MEDICINE MAN/WOMAN; MEDICINE SOCIETIES; SHAKING TENT SHAMAN; TUBE-SUCKING SHAMAN; Subject Index for individuals listed in this volume.)

SHAMANS' SOCIETY *North Pacific Coast* One of the DANCING SOCIETIES of Kwakiutl-speaking and other groups that dramatizes encounters with monster-like spirits. Members of this society inherit the right to perform these dances from their ancestors. Each group, according to traditional family history, has its own series of dances. Each performance calls for the principal performers (novices) to go into hiding for some time. They are said to be kidnapped by spirits that bestow spiritual power on them. When they reappear, they are possessed by a particular spirit. The public and private parts of the ceremony exorcise the monstrous spirits possessing the novices. The public rites end with the "taming" of the novices and a POTLATCH, after which the novices undergo long purification rites. The dancers wear insignia of the society, which include elaborate headbands and neck, arm, and leg rings made of dyed red cedar bark. (See also HAMATSA DANCE; SHAMANS' SOCIETY [Nootka].)

SHAMANS' SOCIETY *Kwakiutl* See HAMATSA DANCE

SHAMANS' SOCIETY *Nootka* One of the DANCING SOCIETIES of the Nootka. The Wolf Society performs the Wolf Dance, a complex of performances, feasts, and potlatches related to a series of dances among the Kwakiutl. The ritual, which usually takes place in winter, is hosted by a chief, who usually only hosts one during his lifetime. It enacts the seizure (kidnapping) of novices (principal performers who are children) by men impersonating wolf spirits and the bestowal of ancestral rites and powers on them. The rite varies from place to place, each Nootkan tribe having its own traditional account of how its ritual originated. The children are concealed for several days during which they are taught the rituals and rites of their family and village while villagers feast and dance and play pranks. For several days, different groups of dancers, according to age, imitate natural phenomena, animals, and people. Search parties are organized by villagers to rescue the children from their captors. The children, whose faces are painted, are paraded through the village to "tame" them. Finally, the novices demonstrate their spiritual gifts from the wolf spirits by singing hereditary spirit songs, dancing, displaying society insignia (cloaks and kilts of hemlock branches, headbands), or announcing the hereditary names they have received. The potlatch ends the public performance and is followed by purification rites for the children, including minor restrictions on their activities and the burning of hemlock branch apparel. Special rules of conduct are in force during the ceremonial. People sit without regard to rank, avoid certain words, and do not eat alone. In the early 20th century the Canadian government legislated against the Nootka dance. The ceremonial has been shortened in the 20th century. (See also HAMATSA DANCE; SHAMANS' SOCIETY [North Pacific Coast].)

SHENANDOAH, LEON *(ca. 1915–1996) Onondaga* Tadodaho (spiritual and political leader) of the centuries-old Six Nations Confederacy (Iroquois). Shenandoah, whose mother was a Faithkeeper, was originally of the Eel clan of his people. At the age of three or four, he had boiling water accidentally spilled on his back, an incident that nearly caused his death. The Seneca man who treated him with ceremony and medicine foretold that Shenandoah would grow to have a high position involving many people.

Shenandoah was elected Tadodaho in 1969, assuming a leadership position that originated centuries ago in the Great Law of Peace of the Six Nations Confederacy. The duties and responsibilities of the position include presiding over meetings of the Grand Council, composed of condoled chiefs, or sachems, of the member nations of the Haudenosaunee (Iroquois), or People of the LONGHOUSE (Cayuga, Mohawk, Oneida, Onondaga, Seneca, and Tuscarora). In an address to the General Assembly of the United Nations delivered October 25, 1985, Shenandoah spoke of the Creator's words given to "the first United Nations—the Haudenosaunee" concerning some of the responsibilities of leaders:

> The Chiefs of the Haudonosaunee shall be mentors of the people for all time. The thickness of their skins shall be seven spans; which is to say that they shall be proof against anger, offensive action, and criticism. Their hearts shall be full of peace and good will, and their minds full of a yearning for the welfare of the people. With endless patience, they shall carry out their duty. Their firmness shall be tempered with a tenderness for their people. Neither anger nor fury shall find lodging in their minds, and all their words and actions shall be marked by calm deliberation.

Shenandoah's status as Tadodaho in effect nullified his Eel clan affiliation. He noted: "It's made out that way so that then I cannot favor any particular clan, or even my own mother—if she's wrong, she's wrong."

Described as a "gentle, soft spoken, humble holy man," ˙nandoah's adherence to the Great Law of Peace of his ˙˙ was steadfast. Whether representing his people be- ˙˙ ˙ber nations composing the Haudonosaunee or ˙˙national tribunals, such as the World Confer- ˙˙nous Peoples in Rio de Janeiro in 1992, he

was an eloquent spokesperson for peace and for the rights of the natural world.

During his nearly 30-year tenure as Tadodaho, Shenandoah faced many challenges. He stood firm against forces that would diminish Iroquois sovereignty or the cultural ways of his people, including get-rich schemes associated with casino gambling. Shenandoah commented in an interview with author Sandy Johnson: "We still carry on our old ways. We are governed by the clan mothers' chiefs, and that's what makes us strong. We are different from the European people because we don't ask for help from the outside. That's what gives us power, because we're not dependent on other governments."

Shenandoah lived most of his life on the Onondaga Reservation, near Syracuse, New York. His last official act took place on July 4, 1996, when the Iroquois celebrated the REPATRIATION of 74 wampum belts from the National Museum of the American Indian. Once asked, "What is the greatest power?" Shenandoah replied, "The greatest power is the Creator. But if you want to know the greatest strength, that is gentleness." In other comments, he noted: "It's said that we're all visitors. That none of use stays here forever. The time is set, but nobody but the Creator knows when we're all going to go. So that's our whole outlook—we're visiting and trying to make the best of it." Shenandoah died on July 22, 1996, at Syracuse University Hospital. Paying homage to him during burial services at Onondaga, mourners included "the largest assemblage of Iroquois in modern times," according to Doug George-Kanentiio, Akwesasne-Mohawk, a *News from Indian Country* journalist.

SHIPAPOLINA *Zuni* A sacred place that is home to POSHAYANKI and his followers as well as to the BEAST GODS, animal curers, and some KACHINAS.

SHIPAPU (sipapu, shipapulima). *Pueblo* In Pueblo religion, a small hole in the floor of a KIVA that denotes the umbilical cord leading from Mother Earth. It symbolizes the place of the people's emergence from the previous underworld. The *shipapu*, the name varying with the language of the tribe, also represents the center of the cosmos, an earth navel and the seat of the CORN MOTHER.

SHIWANA *Keresan pueblos* Spirits of the dead who become spiritual cloud beings and bring rain. They are mostly benevolent, but if offended, they may choose not to appear, which results in drought. One kind of *shiwana*, which lives at Wenima in the west, is protected by ceremonial precautions, and outsiders are not permitted to see it impersonated. Another kind of *shiwana* lives in the south, has fewer ceremonial precautions surrounding it, and permits outsiders to see it impersonated. These do not bring rain like the other *shiwana,* and their regalia is different as well. *Shiwana* is a comparable term to KACHINA.

SHORT BULL (Tatanka Ptecela) *(mid-1800s–1924) Lakota* Brulé holy man who was the apostle of the GHOST DANCE OF 1890 among his people. Born in the mid-1800s, Short Bull was a member of Chief Lip's band of Lakota, located on Pass Creek between Rosebud and Pine Ridge in Dakota Territory. Before achieving prominence as a Ghost Dance leader, he had fought at the Battle of the Little Bighorn and in intertribal wars. Short Bull was one of the delegates chosen by Lakota leaders to visit WOVOKA, the Paiute holy man, in 1889 to learn of his teachings firsthand. He traveled to Nevada with his brother-in-law KICKING BEAR and other emissaries. After meetings with Wovoka, they returned home the following year and began teaching the sacred beliefs and songs of the Ghost Dance. Although warned to stop practicing the new faith by government authorities, Short Bull persisted. He prophesied the date of a new world to come, when the Indian dead would be returned to life, the buffalo restored, and the whites would vanish. Short Bull advised his followers to continue dancing and not to fear the soldiers who opposed them as their sacred Ghost Dance garments would protect them. With the appearance of federal troops to stop the religious movement, Lakota Ghost Dancers fled to an area of the Badlands known as the Stronghold.

By December 1890, the furor over the Ghost Dance culminated in tragedy in Dakota Territory. James McLaughlin, the government agent at Standing Rock who feared the influence of SITTING BULL, the Hunkpapa holy man, on the reservation, ordered Sitting Bull's arrest. Sitting Bull had resisted efforts to impose Christianity and "civilization" on his people and fought against relinquishing Lakota lands. Although Sitting Bull was not a Ghost Dance leader, he had invited his nephew Kicking Bear to conduct the sacred dance at Standing Rock after Kicking Bear's return from visiting Wovoka in Nevada. The Hunkpapa holy man was murdered on December 15, 1890, when fighting erupted between his followers and the tribal policemen sent to carry out McLaughlin's order. Upon learning that Sitting Bull had been murdered and fearing for the safety of his people, Big Foot, the Minneconjou leader, led a band of Lakota, including Ghost Dancers, to seek protection from the Lakota leader Red Cloud on the Pine Ridge Reservation. Federal troops, who intercepted the group on its journey, subsequently slaughtered Big Foot's band at Wounded Knee in South Dakota on December 29, 1890.

Lakota Ghost Dancers surrendered to Nelson A. Miles the following month and Short Bull, Kicking Bear, and

Short Bull (Tatanka Ptecela). A Lakota holy man who was the apostle of the Ghost Dance of 1890 among his people. *National Anthropological Archives, Smithsonian Institution.*

other adherents were incarcerated at Fort Sheridan in Illinois to serve a two-year sentence. In the spring of 1891 Buffalo Bill Cody obtained their release to travel abroad with his Wild West Show for two years. One of their stops included Washington, D.C., where their photographs were taken for the Smithsonian Institution. Upon his return from the tour, Short Bull lived on the Pine Ridge Reservation and was affiliated with the Congregational Church. In interviews about the religious movement, he stated that he had taught peace as a Ghost Dance leader. Short Bull was also one of the holy men who contributed sacred knowledge to JAMES R. WALKER, the physician at Pine Ridge. The Ghost Dance apostle died in 1924.

SHRAMAIA *(fl. 19th century) Skin* A Washani dreamer-prophet identified as one of the three great Native religious leaders, along with LISHWAILAIT and SMOHALLA, in the Dallas area of present-day Washington State in the mid-19th century. Shramaia was believed to have died and returned to life before becoming a religious leader at Skin in the middle Columbia River region. The Wishram, as well as people from the upper Columbia River, attended his gathering which were held in the cedar house where he and his family lived. In his dream, Shramaia was shown four roads associated with the whites, Catholics, Methodists, and Native people. These roads, each with a corresponding color, ran north and south. Shramaia taught that whites would bring another law, construct buildings, and turn against Indian people. Besides interpreting the four roads, Shramaia incorporated other teachings and objects from his dream. He made a cedar flagpole with a sacred bird on top and placed it in front of his house. The people were summoned to the Sunday gatherings with a drum and a bell. Other elements of Shramaia's beliefs included dancing and giving thanks for abundance.

SHU'DENACI (Smoked Yellow) *(fl. 19th century) Omaha*
The last keeper of the OMAHA SACRED POLE who also served as a chief. Changes brought about by contact with the dominant white culture had taken a toll on the practice and continuity of tribal traditions. Therefore, Shu'denaci and other Omaha elders were faced with the serious problem of deciding what to do with the Sacred Pole and other objects. Destroying them, when they had sustained the tribe for generations, was out of the question. Instead, a decision was reached that they should be buried with their keepers. Fearing that the full story of the Omaha would be lost, the ethnologists Alice C. Fletcher and Francis La Flesche began efforts to prevent the burial plan from being carried out. Shu'denaci agreed to relinquish the Sacred Pole to them for transfer to the Peabody Museum at Harvard University for safekeeping. In 1888, when La Flesche secured the pole, he became the first person to touch it outside of its hereditary keepers. Although he consented to reveal the accompanying sacred story of the pole, Shu'denaci had misgivings about doing so. He began to speak after Joseph La Flesche, the father of Francis La Flesche and the former principal chief, promised to bear any punishment that might result from revealing the information. Three people met with Shu'denaci to obtain the story, including Joseph and Francis La Flesche and Alice Fletcher. At the end of three days, when the keeper's words had been recorded, Joseph La Flesche became ill. Within two weeks he lay dead in the same room in which the Sacred Pole's story had been revealed. The keeper's name also appears as Yellow Smoke. (See also MON'HIN THIN GE.)

ˈNGER *Navajo (Dineh)* See DIAGNOSTICIAN

ᵖOLE BALL GAME *Oklahoma Seminole and Creek* A
ᵈ in the tribal religion. Its object is to hit a cow
ᵍy target at the top of a single tall pole with a
played by the males versus the females,

and it includes participants from all age groups. The men and boys are required to use a pair of ballsticks, but the women and girls are allowed to use their hands to carry and throw the ball. The most points are scored for hitting the target, but others are granted for hitting the pole above a designated band. One person tosses the ball into the air to start the game and keeps score for both sides. The single pole ball game is frequently played before and after a nighttime STOMP DANCE. Believed to be of considerable antiquity, the game helps prepare the male players for the more formal and less frequent STICKBALL GAME. The game ends after one team has scored 30 points.

SITTING BULL (1) (Hana'cha-thi'ak) *(c. 1854–c. 1932)*
Arapaho Apostle of the GHOST DANCE OF 1890. Born about 1854, Sitting Bull was originally a southern Arapaho who was known as Bitaye, or "Captor," during his childhood. When he was about 10 years old, he moved to the tribe's northern division. He was named Hana'cha-thi'ak on reaching adulthood. At the end of 1889 Sitting Bull traveled to Nevada with a large delegation of Lakota and Cheyenne emissaries, including SHORT BULL and KICKING BEAR, to meet WOVOKA, the Paiute messiah. Sitting Bull began teaching the Ghost Dance among the southern Plains people, using sign language to instruct those from different tribes. In September 1890 he led the largest such dance held in the south. Attended by approximately 3,000 Apache, Arapaho, Caddo, Cheyenne, Kiowa, and Wichita participants who danced each night for about two weeks, it took place near present-day Darlington, Oklahoma. This Ghost Dance also saw the first trances among adherents in the region and demonstrations of Sitting Bull's spiritual power, including the ability to cause a trance by pointing his eagle feather at a person. At the height of his influence he was almost as highly esteemed as the holy man Wovoka himself. Convinced that land sold through a treaty would be restored by the messiah, Sitting Bull advised Left Hand, the Arapaho leader, to agree to sell. Despite threats from opponents, other adherents also signed the transaction. Sitting Bull defended the Ghost Dance religion in a debate with WOODEN LANCE, the Kiowa leader, at a council held at Anadarko agency in Indian Territory on February 19, 1891. The debate represented a challenge, not only to the Arapaho apostle's leadership, but to the hope of his followers. Sitting Bull and other delegates returned to Nevada in October 1892 for another visit to Wovoka, who advised them to stop practicing the Ghost Dance. Although some adherents refused to accept the message, the religion continued to decline. Sitting Bull lost influence, especially after the Arapaho and Cheyenne land lost by treaty was not restored. He died about 1932 in Carlton, Oklahoma.

SITTING BULL (2) (Tatanka Yotanka) *(c. 1830s–1890)*
Lakota Noted Lakota medicine man and leader of the
Hunkpapa division of the Teton. Born in the 1830s at a site
known as Many Caches, along the Grand River in present-day South Dakota, as a youngster Sitting Bull was
known as Jumping Badger and as Slow, for his thoughtful
deliberations. As early as the age of 10, he demonstrated
hunting abilities while pursuing buffalo calves. After counting his first coup on the body of an enemy when he was 14,
he was honored with the same name as his father, Sitting
Bull, a subchief, also called Four Horns. He further distinguished himself by attaining membership in the Strong
Hearts, a prestigious warrior society. In 1856 he took charge
of the organization after killing a Crow chief and sustaining a
gunshot wound that caused him to limp.

When the U.S. military ordered Lakota and other Northern Plains Indians, who had not done so, to report to Indian
agencies by the end of January 1876, Sitting Bull, and other
so-called hostiles, refused to obey the order, preferring freedom to confinement on reservations under the control of
the government. Federal troops were then sent against the
Hunkpapa holy man, his followers, and their tribal allies at
their encampment on the Little Bighorn River.

As the government's soldiers advanced, the Hunkpapa
leader participated in a SUN DANCE and had a vision that
foretold the outcome of the ensuing battle. The defeat of the
Seventh Cavalry under Lt. Col. George A. Custer at the Battle of the Little Bighorn on June 25, 1876, prompted extensive reprisals against Lakota and Cheyenne participants.
Many were forced onto reservations, but Sitting Bull and
some of his followers escaped to Canada. He remained there
until surrendering at Fort Buford in present-day North Dakota on July 19, 1881, under a promise of amnesty. Although led to believe that he and his remaining followers
would be taken to the Standing Rock Reservation in the Dakotas to rejoin family and friends, they were confined at
Fort Randall in present-day South Dakota until 1883.

Fearful of Sitting Bull's influence, the reservation agent
sent him on a number of trips after his return home. In 1883
he attended the opening of the Northern Pacific Railroad in
Bismarck, North Dakota, and led the last buffalo hunt organized among the Teton. The following year he toured St.
Paul and other cities. In 1885 he traveled with Buffalo Bill
Cody's Wild West Show across the eastern part of the country and into Canada.

Sitting Bull continued to resist U.S. policies, however,
influencing his people not to agree to treaties that would
break up the great Sioux reservation. KICKING BEAR introduced the GHOST DANCE OF 1890 on the Standing Rock
Reservation on October 9 in Sitting Bull's camp at his invitation. The religious movement soon gained adherents and

caused fear of an uprising among the whites. Sitting Bull's
arrest was ordered by the secretary of the interior, setting in
motion the events of December 15, 1890, when he was
shot and killed by Indian policemen Red Tomahawk and
Bullhead, sent by the agent to take him into custody. The
medicine man's son, Crow Foot, and several others, both
ghost dancers and Indian police, were also killed during
the confrontation.

Sitting Bull was buried at Fort Yates, North Dakota,
but was reinterred in 1953 near Mobridge, South Dakota.
At the time of his death he had two wives, one known as
Pretty Plume, and was the father of nine children. A leader
who symbolized Indian resistance to white domination,
Sitting Bull remains one of the most famous Native Americans. Although known as a leader, he was also a holy man
of great spiritual power.

SITTING IN THE SKY (Papamekesickquap) *(?–1907)*
Cree-Saulteaux A shaman and clan leader who may have
been the son of Long Legs, a hunter from the area of the upper Severn River in present-day northwestern Ontario. By
the 1870s Sitting in the Sky served as the leader of the Crane
clan, located near Cliff Dweller Lake, which later became
known as North Spirit Lake. References to him by fur traders
indicate his importance to the well-being of his people. Sitting in the Sky was elderly when he died in 1907.

SIX CHEROKEE FESTIVALS *Cherokee* Six of the greater annual festivals or religious observances described by the
19th-century missionary DANIEL SABIN BUTRICK and other
early observers of the Cherokee Nation before the forced removal of the tribal group from the southeastern Appalachian
region to Indian Territory (present-day Oklahoma). The observances included the FIRST NEW MOON OF SPRING
FESTIVAL, the PRELIMINARY GREEN CORN FEAST, the
GREEN CORN FEAST, the GREAT NEW MOON FEAST, the
CEMENTATION, OR RECONCILIATION, FESTIVAL, and the
EXALTING, OR BOUNDING, BUSH FEAST. They were held at
the capital of the Cherokee Nation. The ancient capital,
Chota, or Great Echota, was located on the south side of
the Little Tennessee River below Citico Creek in Tennessee.
New Echota in northwestern Georgia also served as the
capital for a number of years before removal. The participants of the festivals included the Uku, or priest, seven
prime counselors, and the people from all seven Cherokee
clans. Besides the six festivals held at the capital town, others were conducted at the local level. These included observances held every seven days, quarterly, at the new moon,
and during a calamity or epidemic. A sacred Uku or
OOKAH DANCE was also conducted every seven years. The
Cherokee ceremonial calendrical cycle had both lunar and

solar reckoning with the new moon, for instance, indicating the period for particular religious observances. (See Subject Index for other Cherokee festivals and ceremonies included in this volume.)

SIX DIRECTIONS The six directions, the four cardinal points plus zenith (above) and nadir (below), permeate traditional Native American thinking and activity. Depending on the tribe or pueblo, the directions are associated with specific colors, corn, animals, birds, mountains, plants, trees, seasons stones, shells, and spirits. In sprinkling meal, pollen, other OFFERINGS, or smoking rituals with the SACRED PIPE, and in ceremonies and ritual games, the six directions are observed.

SIX NATIONS MEETING (CONVENTION) *Iroquois* A Six Nations convention is one of the meetings of the circuit that begins every fall and at which the entire CODE OF HANDSOME LAKE, the Seneca prophet, called the "good word" or "good message," is recited in longhouses, independent of the calendrical ceremonies. The meetings were created in the 1840s under the guidance of Jimmy Johnson, Handsome Lake's grandson. These Six Nations meetings ensure that the entire code is preached in each longhouse at least once every two years. In September, representatives from the various longhouses meet at Tonawanda, New York, to arrange the fall meetings. The meetings always start with the TONAWANDA LONGHOUSE, after which they proceed to other participating longhouses. The schedule of visits to longhouses differs from year to year. The first day of a Six Nations meeting, called the handshaking, includes a reception for the visiting delegates who present their credential strings of WAMPUM. The first morning's recital tells the story of the death and rebirth of HANDSOME LAKE and is followed by a FEATHER DANCE and a meal. In the afternoon there is an "interpretation" of portions of the morning's text and a CONFESSION RITE. In the evening, there are social dances. The remaining three days follow the same pattern. During the second, third, and fourth mornings, when the "good word" is preached, people drink a strawberry drink from a dipper. The preacher completes the code the fourth morning. In the evening, the last social dance, "shoving off the canoes," is held.

SKANUDHAROVA *(1642–1657) Huron* Believed to be the first Native girl to have entered Catholic religious life. Skanudharova was born in the Huron village of Ossossane, the daughter of a leading chief whose family had been the first of that nation to become Christians. Skanudharova lived with Ursuline nuns at Quebec and in 1650, when the nuns' house burned, she was taken to Hotel-Dieu in

Quebec where she learned French. She was admitted to the novitiate in 1657 and was given holy garb and the name Tousles-Saints. She took her vows before she died. She is buried at Hotel-Dieu in Quebec with other nuns.

SKOLASKIN (Kolaskin) *(c. 1839–1922) Sanpoil* Nineteenth-century dreamer-prophet from the Sanpoil tribe in the Pacific Northwest's Columbia Plateau region. Skolaskin was born about 1839 in a small community upriver from the tribe's Whitestone Village. As a young man, Skolaskin suffered a malady that crippled his legs and required him to use a staff. The exact cause of this crippling cannot be identified because of conflicting accounts attributing it to injury, illness, or revenge. His convalescence was extensive. This event was pivotal in shaping Skolaskin's life as a prophet, for his illness and recovery may have been the basis for a religious experience whereby he visited the spirit world.

Skolaskin's religious influence over his people was reinforced by their fears of the encroaching white presence in the region. His message of escape and salvation offered hope not only from this threat to their way of life but from catastrophes such as the earthquake of 1872. Besides preaching against drinking and stealing, the prophet banned gambling, a traditional practice of Native cultures. Unlike the prophet SMOHALLA, whose followers participated in the WASHAT DANCE, Skolaskin preached against dancing. In contrast to the FEATHER RELIGION and the INDIAN SHAKER RELIGION, Skolaskin performed no curings in his services, which were held on Sundays as well as other days of the week. A church constructed about 1877 included a congregation of Whitestone villagers, others who traveled there to hear him and those who gathered when he went to the lower Sanpoil River area to preach.

Skolaskin's rise to prominence in 1872 was not to last. Opposition from Catholic missionaries, government officials, and rival tribal leaders such as Moses, a Sinkiuse chief, and Chief Joseph of the Nez Perce eroded his influence. Viewed as an obstacle to government plans for assimilating his people on the Colville reservation in Washington, Skolaskin was removed by Interior and War Department officials. He was arrested on November 21, 1889, and later taken to the military prison on Alcatraz Island in San Francisco Bay. After signing a pledge on June 22, 1892, to change his ways, Skolaskin was finally released. His leadership and power diminished by his imprisonment, the prophet eventually made a number of concessions to the dominant culture. Besides having his long braids cut, he converted to Catholicism on May 30, 1918, and was christened "Frank." Skolaskin died on March 30, 1922, at his home near Snuke'ilt and was buried in his yard. When Lake Roosevelt threatened to flood his grave, his remains were reburied in Keller, Washington. Skolaskin is also identified as Kolaskin.

SLAYER OF MONSTERS *Apache* The foremost Apache culture hero who once lived on earth. At rare times, he still appears in the shape of some animal or wind or other guise, to aid people. He is important in war power and mentioned in almost every ceremonial song cycle.

SLOCUM, JOHN (Squ-sacht-un) *(fl. 1880s) Squaxin* Founder of the INDIAN SHAKER RELIGION of Puget Sound. Little detail is known about Slocum's life, his exact birthdate, where he was born or when he died. In 1881, when Slocum was about 40 years old, he became ill and apparently died. During his wake, he revived and began to speak to those assembled, confirming his death and resurrection. He related that his soul had left his body and gone to the promised land, where it had been turned away. The errors of his life were revealed to him, and he was instructed to return to earth to carry out a mission among the Indian people. He announced that a church had to be built immediately and that he would begin preaching.

About a year later, Slocum had a second serious illness. His wife, MARY THOMPSON SLOCUM, found him near death and surrounded by relatives and neighbors. As she approached her husband's bed, she was shaking uncontrollably. His subsequent recovery was attributed to Mary Slocum's shaking or seizure, interpreted as a sign of divine power. "Shaking" then became important to the religion, especially in ceremonies for the ill.

SLOCUM, MARY THOMPSON *(fl. 1880s) Squaxin* Introduced the practice of "shaking" into the INDIAN SHAKER RELIGION founded by her husband, JOHN SLOCUM. About a year after John Slocum's first religious episode in 1881, he again fell ill and was expected to die. The crisis of his condition precipitated uncontrollable trembling in Mary when she first approached him. His subsequent recovery was attributed to the shaking, which was interpreted as a sign of divine power and became an important aspect of the religion. A short time later, Mary Slocum had another revelation that instructed her to teach Shakers to wear special clothing during curing rites, white dresses for women and collarless shirts for men. She also advocated a clockwise movement in Shaker rituals, attempted to enshrine the creek where she first experienced "shaking," and taught a particular tableware arrangement to adherents. After John Slocum's death, Mary carried on the religion but did not become a minister. At the end of her life, she is said to have become disillusioned with the internal strife of the church.

SMALL ANKLE *(?–1888) Hidatsa* A medicine man who became the keeper of the Maa-duush, the sacred WATERBUSTER (MIDIPADI) CLAN BUNDLE, believed to have originated as a gift from a supernatural being who had joined the human race. Passed down through generations of keepers, ownership was acquired through ritual purchase by a Midipadi clan member. A transfer generally occurred after a keeper became elderly and could no longer carry out the necessary obligations associated with it. Small Ankle purchased the sacred bundle from MISSOURI RIVER, who had helped to lead their people upriver to Like-a-Fishhook village after their villages at the mouth of the Knife River in present-day North Dakota were struck by smallpox in 1837. The new keeper was a member of a prominent family. His father, Big Cloud, was another leader in the migration to Like-a-Fishhook, and Buffalo Bird Woman, his daughter, and other relatives had acquired rights to sacred ceremonies. Because Small Ankle's earth lodge housed the ancient bundle, stored in a wooden shrine, it was treated with particular honor and respect. His grandson, EDWARD GOODBIRD, described the area between the central post and the shrine as holy: "It was therefore not permitted to walk between the post and the sacred Bundles." When Small Ankle died in 1888, he was still the keeper. His son, Wolf Chief, who became custodian of the objects, was ineligible to assume the role as he belonged to the Prairie Chicken clan on his mother's side of the family, not the Midipadi, and he was a Christian convert. In 1907 Wolf Chief sold the shrine, accompanied with data about its history and use, to the anthropologist Gilbert L. Wilson, who collected it for George Heye, founder of the Museum of the American Indian in New York City. Members of the Midipadi clan were outraged by the sale and petitioned the museum for its return. In 1938, in one of the first successful repatriations of Indian sacred objects, the ancient bundle was reluctantly returned.

SMILEY, ALBERT K. *(1828–1912)* Quaker organizer and host of the Lake Mohonk Conference of Friends of the Indian from 1883 to 1912. Influential reformers or "friends of the Indian" met at the conference at Smiley's resort hotel near New Paltz, New York, each fall to discuss issues and proposals for assimilationist policies and programs affecting American Indians.

Smiley was born in 1828 in Vassalboro, Maine, to Quaker parents and was graduated from Oak Grove Seminary, a Friend's preparatory school, in 1845, and then entered Haverford College outside Philadelphia in 1848. He pursued a career in education, returning to Haverford in 1859 for master's degrees. Smiley served as principal of Rhode Island's Providence Friends School from 1860 to 1879. Because New England's Orthodox Friends had no professional clergy during this period, Smiley's teacher and principal role was as close to that status as existed. He purchased his resort in 1869 and convinced Alfred, his twin brother, to manage it while he continued as a principal to meet expenses. It was not until 1879 that Albert took over its full-time operation.

During that same year, with his appointment to the federal government's board of Indian commissioners, he began his involvement in American Indian affairs. The first Lake Mohonk conference was held from October 10 to 12, 1883 with 12 men in attendance. It grew in size and influence to include government leaders, church missionaries, military officers, school administrators and teachers, private philanthropists, and noted scholars. Smiley selected guests, paid their expenses, and chose the leader of each conference. Besides serving the longest term of any member of the Board of Indian Commissioners (1878–1912) during its 64-year history, he was a representative of the New York annual meeting to the Associated Executive Committee of Friends on Indian Affairs, from 1886 to 1898. Among Quakers, according to one author, only William Penn held greater national recognition until Smiley's time. His reputation stemmed primarily from the Lake Mohonk conferences, which were carried on after his death on December 2, 1912, by other family members until 1929.

SMITH, REDBIRD (1850–1918) *Cherokee* The leader of a nativistic movement and a principal chief. Smith was born on July 19, 1850, during his family's move from Arkansas to the Cherokee Nation in Indian Territory (present-day Oklahoma.) His mother was the daughter of a German miller and a full-blood Cherokee from the Wolf clan. His father, Pig Smith, a traditionalist full-blood who became active in politics and served in the Cherokee government, acquired his name from his trade as a blacksmith. The family settled in the Illinois district of the Cherokee Nation. In 1859, nine years after Redbird was born, the Keetoowah Society was formed as a resistance organization of traditionalist Cherokee. Its organizers included the Baptist missionaries EVAN JONES and JOHN BUTTRICK JONES. Meeting at night and in secret, the organization became known as the Nighthawk Ketoowah Society. The Smith family became active participants and leaders in the movement.

Pig Smith selected Creek Sam, a visionary of Natchez descent, to spiritually instruct and guide his son. Redbird Smith was later chosen by members of the Keetowah Society to help regain what their people had lost. One of the organization's first efforts was to obtain sacred WAMPUM belts from a former chief's son and to have them interpreted by the elders. Other activities included the revival of traditional dances and ceremonies. The members resisted the Curtis Act of 1898 and its provisions, which included the abolishment of tribal governments and the allotment or division of tribal lands into individual parcels in Indian Territory. The federal legislation affected the Cherokee as well as the Chickasaw, Choctaw, Creek, and Seminole.

In 1902 Redbird Smith and other traditionalists were imprisoned by the Indian office in an effort to break up the resistance movement. Members of the Keetoowah Society then withdrew from tribal political participation and turned to the religion of their people to sustain them. Smith established a ceremonial ground, now named for him, in his home community in 1902, and more than 20 others emerged in other settlements within a year. His leadership contributed to the survival of Cherokee sacred ways that otherwise would have been lost. Smith was elected to the office of principal chief by his people in 1908. He also helped organize the Four Mother's Society among the Cherokee, Creek, Chicksaw, and Choctaw. Its purpose included continuing the struggle for tribal cultural and political survival. Redbird Smith died in 1918.

SMITH, STANLEY (*fl. 1940s*) *Creek* Baptist missionary who was sent to Florida in 1943 by the Muskogee, Wichita, and Seminole Baptist Association based in Oklahoma. Smith was from the Creek town Arbika and had been a boxer. Described as an eloquent preacher, he succeeded in gaining converts among the Florida Seminole where others had failed. Upon his arrival, Smith found a membership of 11 people and three active participants in the Seminole church. He preached in the Creek language, making his first conversion in 1944. After converting JOSIE BILLIE, a traditional medicine maker, at a revival on the Big Cypress Reservation on January 2, 1945, 37 other Native people followed. In 1947, the same year Smith transferred his affiliation to the Southern Baptists, his baptisms numbered 197 Florida Seminole.

SMOHALLA (Dreamer) (*c. 1815–1895*) *Wanapam* Nineteenth-century dreamer-prophet associated with a revitalization movement among Native people in the Pacific Northwest's Columbia Plateau region. Born between 1815 and 1820 in the Wallula area of present-day Washington State, Smohalla belonged to the Shahaptian Wanapam (also Wanapum; called Sokulk by Lewis and Clark) tribal group. At birth he was called Wak-wei or Kuk-kia, meaning "arising from the dust of the earth mother." After achieving prominence as a spiritual leader, he became known as Smohalla (also Shmoqula, Smuxale, Smowhalla), also defined as "preacher." Still other names associated with him include Yuyunipitqana, "the Shouting Mountain" and Waipshwa, "Rock Carrier."

Following political conflicts with the Wallawalla chief Homily (Homli), Smohalla and his followers moved to the more isolated area of P'na Village at the foot of Priest Rapids in present-day Yakima County, Washington. Already distinguished as a warrior, Smohalla began to preach his revitalization doctrine, which emphasized a return to tribal traditions and beliefs, about 1850. The rapid spread of his teachings is said to have contributed to the confederation of tribes in the region against white expansionism in the Yakima War of 1855–56. Precipitated by government plans to confine Native people to small reservations, the war was fought by a coalition of Indians opposed to the assault on their land base and traditional cultures. Shortly after the war, Smohalla is said to have fought with Moses, a Sinkiuse chief, and was nearly killed. Presumed dead, he revived enough to escape by boat.

It is said that he then set forth on a journey. According to this account, he traveled as far south as Mexico, returning by way of Arizona, Utah, and Nevada. When he reached home, he reported to the people that he had been to the spirit world. However, this version was discounted by Wanapam elders and descendants of Smohalla, who argued instead that his communication with the spirits is said to have occurred while he was mourning the loss of a beloved child. Already known as a medicine man, the teachings he acquired at this time established him as a prophet. Smohalla exhorted his followers, eventually numbering about 2,000, to return to the ways of their ancestors and to relinquish the teachings and goods of the intruders. One of the best known of a series of prophets in the area, he revived the WASHANI RELIGION and WASHAT DANCE (RELIGION) traditions while introducing other features from his dream or vision. Adherents included Chief Joseph and his Nez Perce followers as well as Native people from other tribes in the region. One of his chief supporters and assistants was KOTIAKAN, a Yakama prophet, who helped him in the revitalization movement. Despite government opposition and interference, Smohalla practiced his religion until the end of his life. After his death in 1895, he was succeeded by his son YOYOUNI (also Yo-Yonan), then by his nephew PUCK HYAH TOOT. They carried the Smohallan beliefs into the 20th century.

SMOKE HOUSE *Coast Salish* Also called a longhouse or a big house, this wooden plank structure serves ceremonial functions in Coast Salish communities. The hall is lined with rows of benches.

SMOKE LODGE CEREMONY *Cree* A sacred ceremony reintroduced among the Montana Cree by a young man who had vowed to renew its practice upon his safe return from World War II. It is believed that the Smoke Lodge was first given to the people by a man named Bear Child, who had

been lost in the woods as a baby and rescued by a bear. Thriving under the prayers and powers of his grandfather, the bear, he had quickly grown to manhood. The bear eventually foretold his own death at the hands of one of the people and instructed Bear Child how to continue communicating with him when that happened. After the bear had died, the young man went to a tipi constructed for him away from the camp where he sang songs and guarded against being looked at by a woman. When the taboo was broken and a woman looked into his tipi, Bear Child prepared to leave and to rejoin the bear forever. Before departing, he gave the people a new ceremony, the Smoke Lodge, which was intended to help them. Besides teaching them sacred songs to be sung with a rattle, he told them to provide abundant food during the observance. Bear Child then disappeared, and the ceremony was held according to his instructions. In the lodge or double tipi in which it is held, leaves are not trimmed from the top of the poles. Ritual elements include a night-long service, prayers to the leading Spirit of the Bear, the singing of sacred songs, the use of rattles, and the provision of berries as part of the feast. The Smoke Lodge, which comes after the SUN DANCE in the ceremonial cycle, is generally conducted to fulfill a vow.

SNAKE, REUBEN (Kikawa Unga, "To Rise Up") *(1937–1993)* *Winnebago* ROADMAN and activist. A member of the Winnebago Tribe of Nebraska, Reuben Snake was the fourth child of Virginia Greyhair and Reuben Harold Snake. Young Reuben was baptized into the NATIVE AMERICAN CHURCH a few months later and given an ancient Winnebago Snake clan name, Kikawa Unga, "to rise up." His early years were spent in a woodland area along the bluffs of the Missouri River, but he later lived in Iowa and Wisconsin after the breakup of his parents' marriage. His education was conducted in part at an assimilationist boarding school run by German-speaking Swiss missionaries at Neillsville, Wisconsin.

In 1954, Reuben joined the U.S. Army as a Green Beret under the Berlin command. Upon receiving an honorable discharge in 1959, Reuben Snake pursued his education at a time when many universities were turning away young Native Americans. He attended Northwestern College in Orange City, Iowa, the University of Nebraska in Omaha, and Peru State College in Nebraska. Eventually, Reuben was awarded an honorary degree, doctorate of humanities, by the Nebraska Indian Community College in 1989. The course work that Reuben completed enabled him to fill a variety of positions that advanced the social conditions affecting American Indian people.

Chairman of the Winnebago Nation of Nebraska for a decade, Reuben's major accomplishment was to bring the tribal government out of debt and turn it into a thriving and resourceful multimillion-dollar enterprise that was responsive to community needs. As a spokesperson for the Winnebago people, he was responsible for fostering intergovernmental relations at the federal, state, and local levels.

Due in large part to his success within his own tribal community, Reuben was elected as president of the National Congress of the American Indian (NCAI), the nation's oldest and largest Indian organization. Reuben's advocacy helped develop and enact legislation such as the AMERICAN INDIAN RELIGIOUS FREEDOM ACT OF 1978, the NATIVE AMERICAN GRAVES PROTECTION AND REPATRIATION ACT, and the Native American Language Act. In 1976, Congress appointed him chairman of Task Force XI of the American Indian Policy Review Commission, the Task Force on Drug and Alcohol Abuse. In 1989, Senator Robert Kerrey of Nebraska hired Reuben to serve as a legislative assistant with responsibilities involving all Native American affairs.

Reuben served as the dean for the Center for Research and Cultural Exchange at the Institute of American Indian Arts (IAIA) in Santa Fe, New Mexico. Much of this work focused on American Indian history, comparative cultures, Native cultures, Native religions and practices, cultural rights, and tribal government. Every week, he conducted Sunrise Services to foster understanding of blessings from the Creator that everyone on earth should enjoy. He perfected his skills as an orator on such subjects as cultural resources and indigenous rights, while traveling extensively throughout the United States and internationally on behalf of IAIA. He so inspired others that the Sikhs, an international religious group with more than 60 million members, awarded Reuben the World Peace Award for his humanitarian efforts.

In Reuben Snake's final days, he worked tirelessly to advocate for the introduction of legislation to protect the religious freedom of Native Americans. Immediately after the Supreme Court's 1990 ruling in *EMPLOYMENT DIVISION, DEPARTMENT OF HUMAN RESOURCES OF OREGON, ET AL. V. SMITH ET AL.*, the Native American Church organizations of the Omaha and Winnebago tribes asked Reuben to take the lead in overturning the Supreme Court's devastating ruling. In a September 29, 1990, speech Reuben Snake delivered at the future site of the National Museum of the American Indian on the Mall in Washington, D.C., he said:

> The U.S. Supreme Court reversed a long line of settled cases in order to rule that the use of the sacrament of Native American worship, the holy medicine, peyote, is not protected under the First Amendment of the Constitution. They said, in our case, our religious exercises, our form of worship, the use of our holy sacrament, is not protected by the Constitution. The Court said that Native Americans, who have enjoyed religious liberty on the land since before

the Pilgrims fled here, are no longer entitled to religious liberty. This trampling of Native American religious liberty is intolerable. Our people have been using the holy medicine, peyote, for thousands of years.

> For the last twenty years, the American people have been suffering an epidemic of abuse of refined chemical drugs like cocaine, heroin, amphetamines, PCP, and so forth. American cities are crawling with violence and crime. This is a terrible tragedy, and this kind of drug abuse is also a problem for some Indian youth. But there is no peyote drug problem. I defy the justices of the Supreme Court to find newspaper reports of drive-by shootings in connection with the holy medicine. I challenge anyone concerned about the problem of drug abuse to find examples of dope peddlers selling the holy medicine in America's school yards and play grounds. The idea is preposterous. We don't have a peyote abuse problem in the Nation.

In 1992, Reuben testified at oversight Senate hearings in Portland, Oregon, that laid the groundwork for the introduction of the Native American Free Exercise of Religion Act of 1993 that aimed to protect traditional forms of worship practiced by Indian peoples.

Reuben Snake died on June 29, 1993, more than a year before President Bill Clinton signed into law the AMERICAN INDIAN RELIGIOUS FREEDOM ACT AMENDMENTS OF 1994 to protect the traditional use of peyote by Indians throughout the United States for religious purposes.

Besides NCAI, Reuben Snake served in the following organizations: the First Nations Development Institute, the Native Research and Policy Institute, the Seventh Generation Fund, the American Indian Law Resource Center, the American Indians for Opportunity, the International Circle of Indian Elders and Youth, the 1992 Alliance, the American Indian Ritual Object Repatriation Foundation, and the Native American Religious Freedom Project. The latter organization worked with the Pentagon to implement a draft rule in 1997 that permitted Native American soldiers to use peyote for religious ceremonies. Reuben also served on the United Nations Committee on Human Rights. (See also PEYOTE AND PENTAGON RULE; PEYOTE RELIGION.)

SNAKE-ANTELOPE CEREMONY (Snake Dance) *Hopi* A

16-day ancient sacred dance performed in villages every two years in August. The Snake-Antelope ceremony alternates with the FLUTE CEREMONY in each village to present ceremonies that are petitions to rain spirits to send moisture. Performed by the Snake-Antelope Society, the dance is an elaborate prayer for rain and a bountiful harvest in which reptiles, ritually gathered from the fields in each of the four directions, are entrusted with prayers of the people, which are to be borne by them to the spirits who bring rain to Hopi crops. There are private rites in kivas and public rites in plazas. The public ceremony of the Snake Dance, in which snakes are carried about the plaza, has intrigued visitors for more than 100 years. At the end of the ceremony, the snake society members return the snakes to the desert and release them in four directions to carry messages of prayer to the spirit world. The functions of the ceremony are broad, related to hunting, war, cure of snakebite, lightning shock (snakes resemble lightning), and other ailments, as well as a plea for rain and crops. At times, the public ceremony of the Snake Dance is closed to guests because village leaders fear that tourists mar the event and threaten the survival of the Hopi faith.

SNOQUALMIE FALLS *Snoqualmie* A sacred site to the Snoqualmie and other coastal tribes in western Washington State. Central to the culture, beliefs, and spirituality of many tribes, Snoqualmie Falls is a traditional burial site and place where prayers are carried to the Creator.

Much of the Snoqualmie Falls, near Seattle, has been developed into hydroelectric facilities as part of Puget Power, now merged into Puget Sound and Energy. The flow of water that would pass over Snoqualmie Falls has been diverted to an electricity generating plant, blasted into rock behind and beneath the falls. The Snoqualmie believe both the blasting and the diversion of the waters has desecrated their sacred site. Currently the company that receives an annual license to operate the hydroelectric facility, is waiting for approval of a 40-year operating license by the Federal Energy Regulatory Commission, the agency responsible for determining whether and under what conditions to issue a new license. A coalition of the Snoqualmie Tribe, Church Council of Greater Seattle, and Washington Association of Churches has proposed decommissioning the power project.

SNOW, JOHN (Intabeja Mani, "Walking Seal") *(b. 1933) Stoney* Religious and political leader. Snow was born on the Stoney Reserve in Morley, Alberta, in January 1933. He was the fifth of 11 children born to Chief Tom Snow and his wife, Cora. Snow began attending a residential school operated by the United Church of Canada at the age of eight and remained there until he turned 16. He converted to Christianity in 1957 and a year later began attending the Cook Christian Training School in Phoenix, Arizona. After graduating in 1962, he enrolled in St. Stephen's Theological College in Edmonton to further prepare for the ministry. He was ordained the following year and began working with both Native and non-Native congregations. Snow later attended Arizona State University and during that time ministered to Apache and Pima (Akimel O'odham) congregations under the auspices of the U.S. Presbyterian Church. After working among the Cree people in Alberta, he returned to his own people in 1968 and was elected as chief a short time later. Among the issues facing him were a school crisis and the planned construction of the Bighorn Dam Project on traditional lands in the Kootenay Plains area of Alberta. By the time Snow assumed the leadership role in January 1969, work on the dam had already begun. Tribal efforts to stop construction were to no avail. After the first Indian Ecumenical Conference was held at Montana's Crow Agency in 1970, subsequent gatherings were hosted on the Stoney Reserve at Chief Snow's invitation. His book, *These Mountains Are Our Sacred Places,* was published in 1977.

SNOW SNAKE *Iroquois* A ceremonial game or rite, "playing sticks" is performed primarily for curing. Players bring snow snakes into the home of an ailing person for prayer and tobacco burning. Afterward, players go out and play the game. The Iroquois dug trenches in hillsides and iced them with water. They sent spears or miniature canoes down the runs and wagered to see how far they would slide onto the flats below. The person cured by the performance of this ceremony becomes a member of the society. The rite has developed into a national sport of the Iroquois today.

SOCIETIES *Plains* Among the Plains groups an extensive system of societies, or organizations, existed, generally rooted in religious belief and practice. Many of them originated as spiritual gifts received in a vision and were established in accordance with divine instructions. Purposes of the various societies included maintaining sacred history, healing the sick, treating the injured, defending the people and their territory, performing sacred ceremonies, keeping sacred knowledge and objects, advising the governing council and carrying out specialized roles in their communities. Each society had specific membership requirements. Some consisted of individuals who became eligible for membership after attaining a certain age and/or accomplishment. Others became members by invitation, purchase, or inheritance. Still others consisted of individuals who had all dreamed of the same phenomena or being. Organizations existed for males and females separately as well as together. Women's societies included religious, healing, planting, and warrior as well as quillmaking and other art guilds. Plains groups had both age-graded and non-graded warrior societies, healing societies, and strictly religious societies. Many of them disappeared because of assimilationist pressures, the loss of buffalo, and other factors. However, others either survived or were revived and continue their sacred songs, dances, and other roles in the modern day. (See Subject Index for societies included in this volume.)

SOCIETY FOR PROMOTING CHRISTIAN KNOWLEDGE

(S.P.C.K.) A voluntary society founded in 1698 by the Anglican clergyman THOMAS BRAY and four laymen to promote the establishment of schools and to disperse Bibles and other religious works in England and abroad. While recruiting missionaries for colonial posts, Bray became aware of the need for providing books to clergymen who could not afford to buy them. By 1699 he had gathered approximately 30 collections, with over half of them in the colony of Maryland, some of which eventually served both laity and clergy. The society's efforts have also contributed to the building of schools and colleges. Although some of its work has been taken over by the National Society and the SOCIETY FOR THE PROPAGATION OF THE GOSPEL IN FOREIGN PARTS, the S.P.C.K. continues to conduct missionary endeavors and to produce books and pamphlets through its publishing house.

SOCIETY FOR THE PROPAGATION OF THE GOSPEL IN

FOREIGN PARTS (S.P.G.) An Anglican society organized in 1701 by THOMAS BRAY and others to support missionary efforts and to augment the work of the SOCIETY FOR PROMOTING CHRISTIAN KNOWLEDGE. Its objectives included ministering to Church of England members overseas and evangelizing among "non-Christian races." In the 18th century the society primarily served the American colonies, Canada, and the West Indies. By the 19th century its influence had spread to Africa, Australia, India, and the Far East. In most countries, where the S.P.G. operated, the churches are now independent of the organization and obtain staff members from within their own borders. Britain still provides funding and staffing in some areas, however, especially in Africa, Asia, and the West Indies. The S.P.G. and the (Anglican) Universities' Mission to Central Africa (U.M.C.A.) joined together in 1965 as the United Society for the Propagation of the Gospel (U.S.P.G.).

SOCIETY FOR THE PROPAGATION OF THE GOSPEL IN NEW

ENGLAND The first Protestant missionary society. Established in London by an act of Parliament in 1649, it was brought about through the influence of JOHN ELIOT and THOMAS MAYHEW and their efforts to Christianize the Native people in Massachusetts. The society was rechartered after 1660 as the Company for the Propagation of the Gospel in New England and Parts Adjacent in North America and became known as the New England Company. It supported most of the mission work in America prior to the American Revolution, including the activity among the New England PRAYING INDIANS. Colonial commissioners were initially drawn from the United Colonies of New England, then from clergymen and laymen in the Boston area. The association was the forerunner of other voluntary societies incorporated to finance missionary work, including the SOCIETY FOR PROMOTING CHRISTIAN KNOWLEDGE, founded in 1698, the SOCIETY FOR THE PROPAGATION OF THE GOSPEL IN FOREIGN PARTS, founded in 1701, the Society for the Propagation of the Gospel among the Indians and Others in North America, and the Moravian Society for Propagating the Gospel among the Heathen, both founded in 1787. (See subject Index for missionaries affiliated with the society included in this volume.)

SOCIETY OF WOMEN PLANTERS Iroquois This society returns thanks to the "three sisters," corn, beans, and squash, called Our Life Supporters. The women perform in the longhouse during the MIDWINTER CEREMONY and GREEN CORN festival.

SOHAPPY, DAVID (c. 1921–1991) Yakama A contemporary healer in the traditional FEATHER RELIGION. Sohappy and other Native people were arrested in 1982 and charged with conspiracy to catch and sell salmon illegally. The arrest, made under a federal "sting" operation of the National Marine Fisheries Service, resulted in his conviction under poaching laws. Although the charges against many of the other people were either dropped or reduced, Sohappy received the maximum five-year penalty. He and his son, David Jr., were incarcerated at the Geiger Correctional Center in Spokane, Washington. An elder of the Wanapum band who lived near Cook's Landing, Washington, Sohappy had been fishing in the Columbia River since the age of five. A salmon drought, believed by the authorities to be caused by the Native people, was later attributed to fluoride contamination from an aluminum plant. Under an 1855 treaty the Yakama had ceded 9 million acres of land but had retained the right to take salmon "in usual and customary places." Sohappy, a traditionalist who defended Native fishing rights, had earlier filed a 1968 lawsuit that contributed to a Supreme Court decision reaffirming those rights. He continued to follow his religious beliefs in fishing for salmon as he had always done. Sohappy died in May 1991.

SOLSTICE CEREMONIES Pueblo Rites to observe the solar solstice in both summer and winter. The sun's arrival at its house at winter solstice is celebrated in ceremonial ways that differ from pueblo to pueblo. The rites are built around the sun, the coming new year, and the rebirth of vegetation in the spring. The summer solstice is observed, as the calendar turns back to winter, but the most important ceremonial celebration everywhere is the winter turning back to summer. People are involved in summer's work and the spirits leave during the growing half of the year so people can focus on crops. Winter solstice rites include RPAYERSTICK MAKING,

retreats, altars, emesis, and prayers for increase. The Hopi winter solstice ceremony is called SOYAL.

SOMILPILP (Red Shirt) *(fl. 19th century) Palouse*   A 19th-century prophet who was a contemporary of the religious leader SMOHALLA. Somilpilp carried his Washani teachings to several bands of Nez Perce and to the Umatilla people. (See also MEXISTET)

SORCERY   A branch of WITCHCRAFT. Sorcerers were known to make images of a victim in clay or from wood and then to "kill" or "torture" the effigy. Sorcerers also obtain a bit of a victim's clothing or personal offal, bury it, and recite a spell, after which the victim is said to die in four days. Sorcerers, among other deeds, use both poison and shooting objects to cause sickness, death, and destruction of personal property. Some believe sorcerers have a power that assists them. Sorcery is carried out against people, animals, crops, and other property, usually at night. Victims may recover from illness with the recovery of the bit of clothing, body dirt, or other materials.

SOUL   According to the traditional beliefs of many Native peoples in North America, individuals have at least two souls; however, traditional Pueblo believe in a unitary soul, and among the Yuchi and Sioux tribes there is a belief in four souls. Every healthy individual has one soul linked to breath and life that dies with the body and another, called a free soul, that leaves the body in dreams or vision states, often traveling to distant places and on occasion visiting the land of the dead. Disease, even deaths, may be caused by the loss of the free soul, which may have wandered off or may have been carried away by malevolent spirits, especially those of the dead. A shaman goes into a trance and sends his or her soul to retrieve the runaway soul. Sometimes, shamans face the opposition of the dead and must battle for the soul with the inhabitants of the other world. Shamans also guide souls of the deceased to the land of the dead. Indians also believe that "inanimate" objects (stones, plants, and so forth) and animals have souls. Tribes picture the afterworld to which souls of the deceased journey in different ways, according to their own surroundings and experience. There are detailed descriptions of the land of the dead among almost all American tribes. Usually, the land of the dead is the reverse of the land of the living, with day and night and seasons reversed. The dead live very much as they had while alive—eating, dressing, playing, and living in dwellings as during their previous existence. (See also SOUL [Inuit]; SOUL RECOVERY CEREMONY.)

SOUL *Inuit*   In general, traditional Inuit believe that each person has more than one soul. Some count three: one, an immortal spirit that leaves a person's body at death and goes to live in the spirit world; another, the breath of the spirit of life, a soul that ceases to exist at death; and a third that abides in a person's name (the NAME-SOUL) and persists after death and is reincarnated through the custom of naming babies after relatives who have recently died. An essential aspect of a person is therefore reborn in the next generation through these newborn children who receive both the name and with it the soul of the recently deceased person. For Inuit and Aleut, the name provides the child with strength to survive infancy. For Inuit of central and eastern Arctic areas, it provides a person with a guardian spirit during life. Inuit believe souls reside in human beings, animals, and inanimate objects and can change into other forms, such as demonic spirits. For humans and nonhumans, the soul remains in the vicinity of the body for a specified time after death before going to another world to await rebirth. The nature of this other world varies from group to group. The Inuit generally believe that the destination of the soul after death depends partly on how the person dies. Souls are invisible except to certain shamans, and they have the power to come and go from the body while the latter is alive during sleep, trance, or coma. The departed souls of people and animals have power to influence other souls, therefore, they can affect the game supply. (see also MOURNING OBSERVANCES [Inuit]; PERSON.)

SOUL RECOVERY CEREMONY *Coast Salish*   Also called the spirit canoe ceremony, this elaborate rite, which differs from group to group, is held during the winter at night in a plank house. The ceremony is enacted to recover a lost soul and includes singing, drumming, feasting, speech making, and gift giving and is officiated by several shamans acting together. They travel to and from the land of the dead, with other tribal members helping them in thought and song. The ritual is intended to cure someone who is wasting away, a sign that an invisible part of a patient, the free soul, has been taken away by ghosts to the land of the dead to await his or her final demise. The soul stolen by the dead can only be recaptured through an elaborate ceremony that involves combat with the dead for the possession of the soul.

This ceremony is one of the few occasions when a group of shamans, usually rivals, cooperate with each other for the good of the patient and the community. The doctor's paraphernalia includes painted planks, poles, and small cedar carvings that represent immortals who make the journey to the world of the dead and give the shamans the power to go along. The shamans' journey involves stops to hunt, fish, pick berries, and collect resources on a vehicle fitted for water, meadows or mountain travel. Eventually, they reach the land of the dead, recover the soul, and fight off ghosts. The doctors return, bringing the soul back to the patient.

The ceremony commemorates an ancient enactment of a collective shamanic boat journey to the land of the dead. The Salish spirit canoe of old retraced the voyage of the deceased person's soul, for in the past the dead were buried in the southern Coast Salish area in a canoe that journeyed to the other world.

SOUP DANCE *Oklahoma Seminole and Creek* The final all-night dance of the ceremonial year at a Seminole or Creek "square ground," or ceremonial center. It may have derived from an earlier Horned Owl Dance, a ceremony that was similar to the Shawnee BREAD DANCE. The Soup Dance is basically a STOMP DANCE, but it includes other features. Two women are appointed to ritually prepare soup from wild game for the dance, and it is served, with corn bread, to the participants as morning approaches. The Soup Dance concludes with the performance of a Morning, or Drunken, Dance, named for the time it occurs and for the excitement, not the inebriation, of the dancers. In the annual ceremonial cycle, the Soup Dance follows the Stomp Dance, GREEN CORN CEREMONY, and STICKBALL GAME.

SOUR SPRINGS LONGHOUSE *Iroquois* Longhouse at the Six Nations Reserve in Canada. This longhouse decides, independently of the September SIX NATIONS MEETING at TONAWANDA LONGHOUSE, whether it will participate in that season's circuit of recitations of the CODE OF HANDSOME LAKE. The longhouse exemplifies local autonomy at one of the "home fires" (longhouses) as representatives of Sour Springs decide themselves upon the need and suitability of the convention each year.

SOYAL (Winter Solstice Ceremony) *Hopi* This great tribal ceremony at winter solstice in December is dedicated to giving aid and direction to the sun, which is ready to "return" and give strength to budding life. This ceremony is designed to regulate and control Hopi life and involves all the men and households of the village. In full form, Soyal lasts 20 days, which include days for making PRAYERSTICKS and depositing them in shrines, purification, rituals, and a concluding rabbit hunt, feast, and blessing rites. A single impersonator, Soyal Kachina, represents the first KACHINA of the year to return and "opens" the kivas and allows the return of other kachinas. The Soyal Society controls Soyal, and the Two Horn, One Horn, Flute, and Powamu Societies also participate. The main rituals are conducted in the chief kiva by the Soyal chief, joined by members of other kivas, who assemble there to help the chief perform the ceremony. Countless prayersticks are made and presented to relatives and friends for well-being during the ceremony, and many are placed in fields and orchards or with livestock and in houses.

SPALDING, ELIZA HART (1807–1851) Pioneering missionary in present-day Idaho. Eliza was born in 1807 near present-day Berlin, Connecticut. After her family moved to New York State, Eliza attended an academy in Clinton and then taught school. In 1826 she joined a Presbyterian church located in a town nearby. She began a correspondence with HENRY HARMON SPALDING of Prattsburg, New York, in 1830 and married him in 1833. They decided to accompany Dr. MARCUS WHITMAN and his bride, Narcissa, to Oregon Territory. NARCISSA WHITMAN became the first white woman to cross the Rocky Mountains. The Spaldings settled at Lapwai, near what is now Lewiston, Idaho, among the Nez Perce people. The couple studied the Native language, promoted Christianity and built their mission. Eliza's work included teaching spinning and weaving at the school they established. Tensions with the Whitmans, who had settled among the Cayuse Indians at Waiilatpu station, nearly caused the AMERICAN BOARD OF COMMISSIONERS FOR FOREIGN MISSIONS to end the Spalding assignment at Lapwai. Although a mission station was initially welcomed by Nez Perce, by the mid-1840s they had become angry over the increasing numbers of white settlers arriving in the area. However, when the Whitman missionaries were killed by Cayuse, Nez Perce friends warned and protected Eliza during her husband's absence. Soon after the destruction of the Waiilatpu mission, the Spaldings moved to the Willamette Valley, where they staked a claim near what is now Brownsville, Oregon. Eliza Spalding died there in 1851 at the age of 43. In 1913 she was reinterred next to her husband's grave at Lapwai.

SPALDING, HENRY HARMON (1803–1874) A Presbyterian missionary who established a pioneering mission among the Nez Perce people in 1836 at Lapwai above present-day Lewiston, Idaho. Born on November 26, 1803 in Bath (now Wheeler), New York, he was the son of Howard Spalding. His mother, whose identity is uncertain, turned him over to a foster family when he was 14 months old. He was educated in Ohio at Western Reserve College, graduating in 1833, and Lane Theological Seminary. Spalding was ordained on August 27, 1835, and he and his wife, ELIZA HART SPALDING, began their journey to the Northwest the following year. Upon their arrival they began the work of establishing a mission. Besides constructing buildings and introducing Christianity, Spalding's activities included initiating agricultural efforts and establishing a school. He later acquired a printing press, the first in the area, and published the Gospel of Matthew and other works in the Nez Perce language. In 1838 other workers arrived under the auspices of the AMERICAN BOARD OF COMMISSIONERS FOR FOREIGN MISSIONS (ABCFM).

After receiving reports of dissension within the missionary group, the ABCFM sent a letter ordering Spalding's dismissal and other changes in 1842. Another missionary, MARCUS WHITMAN, left for Boston to request that the board rescind its action, but by the time he arrived it had already reconsidered. Spalding remained at Lapwai until the Waiilatpu station was attacked in 1847. He then moved to the Willamette Valley, where he built a home and school. Although he returned to Lapwai in 1862 as a teacher, he left in 1865 after having conflicts with federal officials. In 1871 Spalding rejoined the Nez Perce under both government and missionary appointment but encountered the same difficulties. He died on August 3, 1874, at Lapwai. He and his first wife, Eliza, had four children during their years among the Nez Perce. After Eliza's death, Spalding married Rachel Smith.

SPEAKER *Iroquois* An individual who delivers traditional addresses, such as the THANKSGIVING ADDRESS and the TOBACCO INVOCATION, and extemporaneous moral exhortations at the longhouse (excluding the CODE OF HANDSOME LAKE, which is recited by "preachers") in Native languages. Each longhouse community has one or more speakers, who are always male, on each side (MOIETY). The ability to speak is believed to be a gift from the Creator, and although the abilities are a matter of natural endowment, the individual seeks guidance from other experienced men. The speaker who begins speaking at different times of life, usually speaks several languages but prefers one for formal speaking. No speaker's performance is precisely like any other. Longhouse speakers do not deviate from the general sequence of spiritual beings addressed in the Thanksgiving Address, but they do vary their words.

SPENCER, FRANK (Pongi Weneyuga, Dr. Frank, Tsawenega) *(?–c. 1910–1920) Paiute (Paviosto, Numu)* Prophet and proselytizer of the GHOST DANCE OF 1870. Weneyuga, a disciple of the Ghost Dance leader WODZIWOB, was from Nevada. He took the doctrine of the religious movement to a number of Paiute groups as well as to the Washoe in the Carson City and Reno areas. After visiting the spirit world during a trance, he returned with a number of prophecies. He predicted that the Indian dead would return to life, that whites would disappear from the land and that earthquakes and flooding would occur. Ritual features utilized by Spencer, called Weneyuga by the Washoe after a word in one of his songs, included preaching the Ghost Dance doctrine, the singing of sacred songs learned during a trance, performances of the Paviotso (Numu) Negaba, or Round Dance, by participants at the gatherings and face and body painting. The prophet was known to carry a sacred staff and to demonstrate some of his powers for his followers. Weneyuga led the Ghost Dance for about five years. Later in his life he was known as a healer or curer. He died at Fort McDermitt sometime between 1910 and 1920. One source identified the prophet's Paiute name as Pongi. Other names included Dr. Frank and Tsawenega.

SPIDER, EMERSON, SR. *(fl. 20th century) Lakota* State high priest of the NATIVE AMERICAN CHURCH in South Dakota who is an adherent of the Cross Fire Peyote Way. Spider, from the Porcupine community of the Pine Ridge Reservation in South Dakota, is descended from a family involved with peyotism since its inception among the Lakota. Jessie Black Bear, his mother, was the daughter of William Black Bear, the first headman of the Native American Church in South Dakota. The Black Bear family lived in the community of Allen, where the first PEYOTE church in the state was established. The Spider side of the family lived in the Porcupine community. His father, the son of an Episcopal minister, was initially opposed to the use of peyote but eventually succeeded Black Bear to the peyotist's headman position and held it until his death at the age of 66. Spider assumed the role in about 1965. In a 1982 interview, later published in *Sioux Indian Religion* (1987), he provided information about his religious beliefs and practices. By then, he had served as high priest or bishop for 17 years.

Spider attended school at Holy Rosary Mission on the Pine Ridge Reservation until the fifth grade. He remembered encountering opposition to peyotism there from some of the teachers and other students. In his interview he credits peyote with healing family members, including his mother and father, of serious illnesses. JAMES BLUE BIRD, a Lakota ROADMAN influenced by Winnebago peyotists, organized the religion into a church in Allen, South Dakota. When practitioners first began using peyote in Allen, the police would disrupt services and confiscate their drum and peyote. In 1916 a court case, *U.S.A. v. Harry Black Bear*, was heard in Deadwood, South Dakota. Peyotists, including members of Spider's family, had been caught using peyote and turned in to the authorities. At that time his mother was a young child who had been treated with peyote at home for the tuberculosis that had stricken her in boarding school. Her recovery, after she had been expected to die, was used as proof of peyote's positive value at the trial. The charges in the case were dismissed.

Before assuming the state leadership role in his religion, Spider served as a leader helper, candidate leader, community minister, and an assistant to his father. At the time of his interview, Spider had ordained a number of peyote roadmen, or leaders, as ministers. He indicated that some of them worked on the three South Dakota reservations—Pine Ridge, Rosebud, and Yankton—where the Native American Church is found. His church, built at Porcupine not long before his interview and incorporated in 1979, is called the Native American Church of Jesus Christ. According to Spider, the Peyote Way of worship is known in the Lakota language as Pejuta yuta okolakiciye, "medicine-eating church."

SPIRIT ADOPTION CEREMONY (Fourth Night Feast) *Iutelo (Six Nations Reserve, Canada)* A complex ceremony to carry on the living identity of a deceased Tutelo. The ceremony is held in the winter season while vegetation is dormant (on the ninth night after death or within a year after death). The spirit of the deceased is recalled for the night of the ceremony and his/her qualities, name, and tribal membership are adopted, or reincarnated, in a living substitute. That individual is bound to observe all Tutelo cultural traditions and upon death, his or her Tutelo nationality is transferred to another person. The individual may be Iroquois, but the ceremony bestows genuine nationality, regardless of birth, and sustains the Tutelo people (whose nation was adopted by the Iroquois League in 1753). The ceremony, sponsored by the family of the deceased, is performed in private homes or one of the longhouses. The family provides a new outfit of clothing for the adopted person worn throughout the ceremony, and a chain of Tutelo wampum. The mourners choose the person to be reclothed and adopted in the name of the deceased who must be the same gender. Active participants in the ritual include a caretaker who has responsibility to be custodian of the adopted person and supervise him or her in each movement of the ritual; a cook who prepares food and drink for the feast; a fire keeper who maintains the fire in two stoves in the longhouses; a drummer, rattler, and singers who perform during the 10-hour ritual; and a speaker who converses in the Tutelo language to the adopted person during the ritual. The ceremony is preceded by four days of preliminary observances in which the entire ritual is rehearsed to ensure its correct performance on the actual ceremonial night, called the fourth night feast. People maintain this ritual that is pleasing to the dead and believe its discontinuation could cause harm.

SPIRIT DANCE CEREMONIAL *Salish* A major winter ceremonial in southern British Columbia and northern Washington. The ceremony involves the initiation into spirit dancing of a person with spirit illness, prescribed by a shaman as a healing process. Possession by GUARDIAN SPIRITS is seen as causing spirit illness, curable only by spirit dancing. The ceremony lasts from four days to a few weeks, depending on the candidate who is trying to find his or her song and dance, the purpose of the initiation process. The candidate enters an altered state in seclusion in the longhouse by a combination of fasting and kinetic, tactile, acoustic, and painful treatments alternated with restricted mobility and sensory and sleep deprivation. The candidate's relatives and people all over the Coast Salish area participate by drumming and singing for him or her, assisting in ritually prescribed ways, cooking for guests invited to the dance debut and, witnessing and paying their respects to the spirit power that the candidate represents. Spirit dancers, both male and female, experience unanimous group support when they express their "power" at future ceremonies. From November to April, the initiated, ritualists, kinfolk, and other families prepare and execute the ceremonial by acting as "baby sitters" (initiated dancers who keep the candidate awake), witnesses, drummers, singers, speech makers, seamstresses, and cooks. During the ceremonials, initiates express in public the final forms of their dances and songs, showing power granted by the spirit. Once the initiate has found his or her song, he or she is invested with regalia, a new dancer's hat, and a pole. Sometimes there are annual visits by the now-controlled spirit, who desires public exhibition by its owner in winter, necessitating the repetition of the Spirit Dance. In every winter season, and at every dance, the spirit dance relives the process of his or her past initiation, with spirit illness, death, and rebirth, manifesting the spirit power he or she had learned to control. Washington Territory formally outlawed spirit dancing in 1871 by decree of the Superintendent of Indian Affairs. In British Columbia, the 1884 CANADIAN INDIAN ACT initiated legal sanction against spirit dancing. During the 1960s, there was a resurgence of spirit dancing in Fraser Valley, British Columbia, and northern Washington.

SPIRIT FLIGHT *Inuit* See SHAMAN

SPIRIT LODGE RITUAL *Cheyenne* A sacred ritual that can be traced to the spirit lodge of NOAHA-VOSE, the sacred mountain, where SWEET MEDICINE, the prophet, was instructed by the Creator. One of its several forms, performed today, is conducted by a priest or shaman to summon the spirits for information and assistance, sharing similarities with the practices of a SHAKING TENT SHAMAN of other Algonquian tribal groups as well as the Lakota YUWIPI ceremony. The ritual was conducted independently or as a part of other ceremonies, including the renewing of the SACRED ARROWS. Conducted in a spirit lodge, it generally included the ritual binding of the shaman, the singing of sacred songs, summoning of the spirits, the arrival of the spirits, the untying of the shaman and communication with the spirits. The shaman not only obtained answers to questions of great importance during the ritual, but received prophecies.

SPRING RITE (Wedam) *Maidu* A ceremonial gathering that occured in the spring in which the Maidu asked the Creator for protection against snakes and bears while picking roots, berries, and other resources in the hills. Prayers and thanksgiving to the Creator were important parts of the Wedam. Women begin the rite by dancing, decorated with flower blossoms and greenery.

STAR DOCTOR (Pahalawasheschit, "Five Shades," Haslo) *(fl. 19th century) Palouse* A legendary medicine man who was known to have strong spiritual powers. In 1877 he joined the Nez Perce anti-treaty forces fighting under Chief Joseph's leadership. Star Doctor was captured and sent to Indian Territory (present-day Oklahoma) along with other members of the band. He eventually escaped and made his way back to the Northwest. Friends thought he had been killed during the war; upon his return, they recognized and greeted him, but he did not respond to his former name. He then became known as Star Doctor, and no one revealed his identity to the authorities. After the war period he lived mainly on the Umatilla Reservation in Oregon, where he became a renowned medicine man. Described as the last Palouse there, he was called "Old Man Star" in later years. He maintained the WASHANI RELIGION, keeping its beliefs alive while missionaries and agents opposed their practice. Star Doctor claimed that he had as many as 25 wives during his lifetime. Known as Five Sack to non-Indians, another name for the medicine man was Haslo.

STAR GAZING *Navajo (Dineh)* One method used by a Navajo (Dineh) practitioner who diagnoses a sickness when the cause of disease cannot be determined by obvious symptoms and who determines the proper form of ceremonial activity to be employed to cure the patient. The skill of star gazing must be learned from another practitioner. The ritual may also include SANDPAINTING. (See also DIAGNOSTICIAN; HAND TREMBLER.)

STATE V. SOTO (210 Or. App. 794, 537, P. 2d, 142 [1975]) *(1975)* A state case involving the arrest of Roland Soto, a six-year member of the NATIVE AMERICAN CHURCH, for possessing PEYOTE in the state of Oregon. During a pretrial conference, the judge disallowed evidence pertaining to the defendant's religious beliefs. Soto's First Amendment challenge failed, and his conviction was upheld by the Oregon Court of Appeals. The court asserted that the state had the right to restrict religious practice but not religious belief. (See also PEYOTE RELIGION; PEOPLE v. WOODY; Subject Index for related legal cases included in this volume.)

STATE OF ARIZONA V. JANICE AND FRED WHITTINGHAM (Arizona, Super. Ct., Ct. App., Sup. Ct., U.S. Sup. Ct., 1973) *(1973)* An Arizona state PEYOTE case involving the arrest of Janice and Fred Whittingham

during a NATIVE AMERICAN CHURCH service at which their marriage was being blessed. The ceremony, held on October 18, 1968, was disrupted by the police and the couple arrested. The Whittinghams were originally convicted by a superior court in Coconino County, Arizona, of violating a state statute prohibiting possession of peyote. On appeal, the court noted the First Amendment right to the practice of religion without government interference absent a compelling state interest. It further noted the long history of peyotism and its large number of followers, rejecting the state's argument that enforcement of peyote regulation would be difficult when exceptions were made. Indicating that it had been guided by the California Supreme Court's decision in *PEOPLE V. WOODY,* the Arizona Court of Appeals found the defendants immune from prosecution under the state statute. It also indicated that legislatures in other states had made statutory exceptions to their general drug regulations for the religious use of peyote. The court found:

> The State of Arizona's interest cannot be of such a different quality or nature than those jurisdictions that have acknowledged an exception within their criminal codes for the sacramental use of peyote in a bona fide religious ceremony.

This case and *People v. Woody* are considered landmark cases that address the First Amendment issue of freedom of religion against a state's regulation of drugs. (See also PEYOTE RELIGION; Subject Index for related cases included in this volume.)

STATE OF ARIZONA V. MARY ATTAKAI (No. 4098, Superior Court, Coconino County, 1960) *(1960)* This 1960 Superior Court case set a legal precedent for the religious use of PEYOTE in the state of Arizona. Mary Attakai, a Navajo (Dineh) peyotist, was arrested on October 29, 1959, in Williams, Arizona, for possession of peyote, after she had filed a complaint against her brother for disorderly conduct. He had retaliated by telling the arresting officer that she had peyote in her home. The peyote was found and Attakai was charged with possession and was jailed. At her trial on July 25 and 26, 1960, in Flagstaff, Arizona, she was represented by Herbert L. Ely, an American Civil Liberties Union attorney, before Judge Yale McFate. The judge, who found the Arizona statute prohibiting peyote unconstitutional as applied to Attakai's religious beliefs and acts, dismissed the complaint and released the defendant. According to Omer C. Stewart, who served as an expert witness for the defense, the Arizona Supreme Court dismissed an appeal of the case on April 25, 1961. The state law prohibiting peyote remained in effect, but Judge McFate's ruling established a precedent for religious use of the substance in Arizona. (See Subject Index for other cases involving peyote use included in this volume.)

STATE OF NEW MEXICO V. ROBERT DAN PEDRO (Case Number 660, State Court of Appeals, 1971)

(1971) In this New Mexico case, Robert Dan Pedro, an Arapaho, was convicted for possession of PEYOTE in Chaves County District Court. He had been carrying Native medicine, as advised by an Arapaho doctor, to protect himself from harm. Without Pedro's realizing it, a significant part of the medicine was peyote. Though he was not a member of the NATIVE AMERICAN CHURCH, which uses peyote in religious ceremonies, his conviction was reversed by the New Mexico Court of Appeals. The court held that there was no evidence of criminal intent and that the peyote had been given in good faith for healing purposes. (See also PEYOTE RELIGION; Subject Index for related legal cases included in this volume.)

STATE OF WASHINGTON V. ROBIN H. GUNSHOWS, ET AL. (Superior Court, County of Ferry, October 11, 1978)

(1978) A state case in which peyotists Kenneth Little Brave (Lakota), Roger Eagle Elk (Sioux), and Robin H. Gunshows (Colville) were arrested after being stopped for a traffic violation on August 30, 1978. Charged with violating the U.S. Drug Abuse Control Act of 1965 by possessing PEYOTE, the defendants were jailed because they were unable to meet the $5,000 bail required of each. It was pointed out in court that the Federal Drug Enforcement Administration's interpretation of the law exempted peyote when it was used in a bona fide religious ceremony and that many states had also adjusted their laws to allow such use. Judge B. E. Kohl of Ferry County Superior Court then dismissed the charges against the defendants, who had been incarcerated for 13 days, and ordered that the peyote buttons confiscated from them be returned. According to Omer C. Stewart, the noted anthropologist asked to testify at the trial, the state of Washington did not amend its drug law to exempt peyote for religious purposes as a result of the case and peyotists are still subject to arrest. (See AMERICAN INDIAN RELIGIOUS FREEDOM ACT; NATIVE AMERICAN CHURCH; PEYOTE RELIGION; Subject Index for related legal cases included in this volume.)

STAYING SICKNESS Pima, (Akimel O'odham) and Tohono O'odham (Papago)

The medicine theory of Pima and Tohono O'odham. Pima believe that "staying sickness" has always existed and always will, that it was created along with the Pima and affects no other peoples and that it is not contagious. Pima perceive that 38 or so dangerous objects (bear, deer, dog, lightning, mouse, owl, rattlesnake, wind, and so forth) outside the body have a "way." A human must observe certain rites when encountering those objects, as specified by rites set down at the time of creation. One gets a staying sickness by transgressing a way, not by simply encountering one of the objects. After the transgression, the "strength" of the dangerous object will enter the body to produce symptoms of disease. The "strength" is a liquidlike substance that a shaman can suck out and that, if left unattended, will permeate the entire body. Each kind of strength produces distinct symptoms while it exists in the body as a liquid. (See also SHAMAN.)

STEAD, ROBERT *(fl. 20th century) Lakota*

A contemporary medicine man who is a member of the Rosebud Reservation and lives in the community of Ring Thunder, South Dakota. He participated in a 1982 symposium where he provided an account of Lakota religious traditions in modern-day life. Stead recalled having spirituality within himself at the age of eight or nine but, as a young boy, abusing his powers. He was able to achieve A's in school without studying, to answer problems without effort and to excel in athletics although he was physically small. About eight medicine men eventually told him that because he had been chosen he would have to go on a VISION QUEST. Although he was fearful, he prepared for one month, then perservered for four difficult days and nights by praying with the pipe.

In his practice today Stead specializes in treating people afflicted by strokes or paralysis. A description of one of his healings included four nights of YUWIPI meetings for a woman whose face was paralyzed on one side. Many people go to him for assistance, and he has traveled to 33 reservations, treating not only members of his own group but individuals from other nationalities. Stead stated that he has to live a particular way, with humility and without hurting others. He stated that he does not try to influence anyone to join his traditional religion and that he cannot be prejudiced or discriminate against others, spread gossip, say or do bad things, or drink. Stead was introduced at the symposium by his apprentice, Kenneth Oliver, who spoke about the virtues associated with traditional Lakota religion.

STEINHAUER, HENRY BIRD (Shahwahnegezhik) *(1816–1884) Ojibway*

A Wesleyan Methodist missionary, interpreter and teacher for more than 40 years. Born near Lake Simcoe in Ontario, Shahwahnegezhik was about 10 years old when he was exposed to Christianity by Methodist missionaries in the area. On June 17, 1828, he was among the 132 Native people baptized by the Reverend WILLIAM CASE and PETER JONES at Holland Landing. Shahwahnegezhik attended the Methodist mission school at Grape Island in the Bay of Quinte, where he took the name Henry Steinhauer from a Philadelphia philanthropist who paid his expenses. In 1829 he was among seven Native youngsters chosen by the Reverend Case to travel on a fund-raising tour of the United

States as "specimen trophies of the victories won by Methodism." Steinhauer's portrait, entitled "Sketch from Nature," was painted by the artist John Neagle in Philadelphia that year. He attended New York's Cazenovia Seminary from 1832 to 1834 and later the Upper Canada Academy at Cobourg, which is now Victoria College.

Steinhauer worked as a teacher from 1834 to 1836 and from 1838 to 1840 before he was asked by JAMES EVANS to accompany Evans on a mission to the West. In 1840, when the Methodist missionary effort began among the Cree and neighboring tribes, Evans went to Norway House, but Steinhauer and another missionary, WILLIAM MASON, stopped at Lac La Pluie, Ontario. Steinhauer's work included translating the liturgy into the Ojibway language and helping open a small school. The Ojibway missionary joined Evans a few years later at Norway House, where he was placed in charge of a nearby school and began studying the Swampy Cree language. He completed translations of Scripture into Cree syllabics, continuing the work alone when Evans returned to England in 1846.

Steinhauer established a new mission in 1850, at a Hudson's Bay Company post, Oxford House, located between York Factory and Norway House. In 1854 he traveled to England, where he remained for six weeks, making presentations to missionary societies and other audiences about his work. After returning home he was ordained by the Canadian Conference in London, Ontario, in 1855, together with THOMAS WOOLSEY, with whom he would later establish Victoria Mission. He was sent to Lac la Biche the following year and later moved near Whitefish Lake. Besides conducting religious services, he traveled with community members on buffalo hunts and worked to establish a school, homes, and gardens.

After another transfer in 1873 to the Woodville mission in Alberta at Pigeon Lake, Steinhauer returned home to Whitefish the following year. In 1876 he succeeded in obtaining government support for his school, the first Protestant Indian school in the district to receive such a subsidy. A few years later, in 1880, he traveled to eastern Canada for a year on a fund-raising tour. Steinhauer considered Native workers essential to the mission field because of Indian distrust of foreigners. He was married to Jessie Mamanuwartum, a Cree, in 1846 and they had several children. Two of his children, Egerton and Robert, prepared for the Methodist ministry but without much support from the missionary society. One of his daughters, Abigail, married missionary JOHN MCDOUGALL. His reminiscences, "Beginning at Whitefish Lake," were printed in *Missionary Outlook*. Steinhauer died on December 30, 1884. Methodist missionary JOHN MACLEAN published an account of Steinhauer's life and work. (See also COPWAY, GEORGE; SUNDAY, JOHN.)

STEINMETZ, PAUL B. *(1928–   )* A contemporary Jesuit priest who worked among the Oglala Lakota on the Pine Ridge Reservation in South Dakota from 1961 to 1981. Born in St. Louis, Missouri, in 1928, Steinmetz was educated at St. Louis University, the University of Aberdeen in Scotland, and the University of Stockholm, Sweden, where he studied under the religious scholar Åke Hultkrantz and received his Ph.D. in 1980. He introduced a number of innovations during his tenure at Pine Ridge, including the renaming of the local parish from St. Elizabeth to Our Lady of the Sioux and the decoration of the church with Lakota symbols such as a tipi, an "Indian-featured Christ," an eagle, and the SACRED PIPE. Father Steinmetz prayed with the pipe as a priest for the first time on November 6, 1965, at the funeral of Rex Long Visitor, an Oglala from Slim Butte. During the ceremony he separated the parts of the pipe to symbolize death, then later reconnected them as a sign of the Resurrection of Christ. Although members of the community subsequently questioned whether this use of the pipe was proper, John Iron Rope, the YUWIPI man consulted, expressed his approval. Father Steinmetz then began praying with the Sacred Pipe often.

He recognized the funeral of Benjamin Black Elk, son and interpreter of the famous holy man BLACK ELK, as a significant occasion to bring together Lakota and Christian traditions during the period he was at Pine Ridge. Father Steinmetz served as the main celebrant during the requiem mass, praying at the grave with the Lakota holy man FRANK FOOLS CROW. Besides his friendships with Frank Fools Crow and John Iron Rope, Steinmetz developed relationships with other influential medicine men, including PETER CATCHES and GEORGE PLENTY WOLF. Father Steinmetz participated in a SUN DANCE in 1971, an action that met with opposition from a number of Native people. He indicated that Frank Fools Crow had asked him to join him in prayers during the ceremony. In 1974 Father Steinmetz also participated in a two-day Pipe fast supervised by Catches.

Besides his religious work with Lakota Catholics, Father Steinmetz has prayed with members of the NATIVE AMERICAN CHURCH and The Body of Christ Church on the reservation. He has also conducted field work among the Oglala Lakota people on their contemporary religious identities. In 1975 he presented a Papal Blessing from Pope Paul VI to the Native American Church at Pine Ridge after a trip to Rome. Father Steinmetz has been associated with St. Rita Church in Wellington, Florida. His publications include *Pipe, Bible, and Peyote Among the Oglala Lakota* (1990).

STEVENS, FREDERICK GEORGE *(1869–1946)* A Methodist missionary to Native groups in Canada. Born near Marksdale, Ontario, on October 9, 1869, Stevens became a devout adherent of Christianity. In 1891, he gradually turned to religious work in the Indian mission field. In 1897 he was sent to Oxford House, Manitoba, to work with EDWARD PAUPANAKISS and others, and two years later he became the first missionary to visit Algonquian clans at the headwaters region of the Severn River. Stevens was forced from his post in 1902 following his report of deaths numbering between 20 and 30 Sandy Lake Natives by starvation; officials considered his account a fabrication. After going to Fisher River, Manitoba, in 1907, he made a few return visits to the Caribou Lake area until the Manitoba Methodist Conference ended his travels in 1920. Stevens translated many hymns into the Cree language. A number of them were published in his Cree primer, "The Spiritual Light." Nan Shipley's book, *Frances and the Crees,* is about Stevens's wife, Frances Pickell, and her experiences at northern missions. Stevens remained at Fisher River until 1940. He died at Norway House, Manitoba, in August 1946.

STEVENS, JEDIDIAH D. *(fl. 1830s)* A Congregational missionary who worked among the Dakota at Lake Harriet in present-day Minnesota. He taught about three years in the Stockbridge mission at Green Bay and studied theology until a New York presbytery licensed him to preach. When two Dakota mission stations were established by the AMERICAN BOARD OF COMMISSIONERS FOR FOREIGN MISSIONS in 1835, THOMAS S. WILLIAMSON was assigned to one at Lac qui Parle on the Minnesota River, and Stevens was sent to the other at Lake Harriet. He remained at the mission for only a few years, until 1839, mainly because of conflicts with SAMUEL W. AND GIDEON POND, other early missionaries in the area. Stevens assumed a superior position based on his ordination, expecting Gideon to build a mission station for him while he devoted time to studying the Dakota language. The dissension, written about in correspondence to the ABCFM, prompted Samuel Pond to complete the necessary studies for ordination, and Stevens to leave the mission for the post of farmer among the Dakota people.

STEWART, JOHN *(1787–1823)* A Methodist missionary to the Wyandot in Ohio. Born in Powhatan County, Virginia, to free African-American parents, at the age of 21 Steward moved to Marietta, Ohio, where he worked at odd jobs. In the spring of 1816, after receiving divine inspiration to spread the gospel among the Indians, he left to carry out his mission. Stewart initially stopped at Pipetown on the Sandusky River, where he preached to the Munsee Delaware. Although he was invited to stay, he traveled to Upper Sandusky and began working among the Wyandot people. He preached the Methodist faith and began to win converts despite the fact that he was not an ordained minister and that

some people believed him to be a runaway slave. His success has been attributed, in part, to his religious fervor and melodious singing. He also had the assistance of an interpreter, Jonathan Pointer, a black man captured in childhood who had learned the Wyandot language. Although white traders tried to convince the Wyandots that they should drive him out, Stewart was defended by the subagent and interpreter William Walker. The missionary succeeded in converting some Native leaders, although others resisted his efforts. Following the ceding of most of their land in Ohio to the United States in 1817, the Wyandot adopted Stewart into the tribe. He also received a section of land for his mission and a share of tribal annuities. In 1819 the missionary received a visit from the Reverend Moses M. Henkle, who subsequently licensed Stewart to preach and placed his mission under Methodist jurisdiction. Two years later the denomination sent the Reverend JAMES BRADLEY FINLEY to assist Stewart's missionary efforts among the Wyandot. When the tribe sold their remaining Ohio lands in 1842, the mission closed.

STICK DANCE (Feast for the Dead, Hi'o) *Alaska Athabascan* Ancient week-long, mortuary and grief ritual of Alaska Athabascan Indians that honors dead men of the village. Held in March, the dance is believed to have the power to help lay to rest the spirits of dead men as well as transfer the identity of the deceased to the men who helped dig the graves, dress the bodies, and compose the songs for the dead. The widows sponsor the dance with the assistance of relatives. The week of ceremonies and festivities includes gift exchanges, dogsled races, feasting, speech making about the deceased, dancing, the singing of privately owned mourning songs by the widows, and drumming. The food and gifts of clothing compensate the men for their help in burying the dead; the dancing and singing provide emotional release after winter; and friendships are renewed when village people get together for the ceremony.

The dance takes its name from the 15-foot-long stripped spruce pole men carry into the community hall on the fifth evening. Once the pole is lashed into place and decorated with ribbons and furs by women, night-long pole dances take place along with ritual songs (13 today now that one has been forgotten), called *hi'o keleka,* that honor the deceased. The pole is torn free from its moorings above and danced around the entire village, returned to the community hall and reattached to the beams above. On the final evening, the honored men (who represent the dead) are formally fed and ritually dressed in new clothes representing the deceased, and the other gifts are distributed to community members. The honored men who have assumed the identity of the dead visit friends in the village to say goodbyes. At the end of the week, the young men break up the spruce pole and toss pieces into the Yukon River.

It can take months, even years, for a family honoring its deceased members to prepare for a stick dance, which involves saving up gifts to distribute, choosing people who will represent the dead, and making clothes that symbolize the identity of the deceased. Friends and relatives from other villages who come to the stick dance share traditional foods (moose, salmon, beaver, rabbit, ptarmigan) at a feast called a POTLATCH.

STICK GAME DANCE *Blackfeet* A sacred religious ceremony in which the stick game, a guessing game, was played as part of the ritual activities. Big-spring, a Piegan man, acquired a bundle containing a stick game set from a member of the Gros Ventre (Atsina) tribe in 1909. He gave it to a relative named Fish who later dreamed about the game and its spiritual powers. The ceremony, at which prayers were offered to the Creator, could be initiated in case of sickness, whereby a person made a vow to provide a feast for the owner of the stick game bundle or medicine bundle if the afflicted person recovered. It was held at night, although the ordinary game was played at other times, and everyone present, including men, women, and children, could participate. The owner of the stick game dance bundle selected a woman and a man,

gave them each 10 sticks, prayed for them, and symbolically painted their faces. These individuals, the guessers or leaders on opposing sides, then selected other participants, and games were played to the accompaniment of singing and drumming. After the completion of each guessing game, when one side had obtained all the sticks, the winners danced while the losers remained seated. The ceremony concluded with a feast, generally after eight games, and the last two guessers in the stick game had to pass the food around. (See also ALL-SMOKING CEREMONY; BLACK-TAILED DEER DANCE; CROW-WATER SOCIETY; DANCE FOR THE SPIRITS OF THE DEAD.)

STICKBALL GAME *Oklahoma Seminole and Creek* Called the "little brother of war," the stickball game is one of the high points of the ceremonial cycle, generally held annually in September. The object of the game is to move the ball with sticks through goals on opposite ends of the playing field. Players, men and boys, are presently selected in such a way that they may be on either the sponsoring town's team or on the visiting town's team. The game is rough and often results in broken bones. Ritual preparations include medicine taking and dancing at the ceremonial square ground, or religious centers, each night for a week or more, fasting 24 hours before the match, and dancing by the women the

Stickball game. Layout of the stickball game field. The field is about 150 yards in length. The line midway between the two goals is where the lineup, war speeches, and tossup take place. *Pen-and-ink sketch by Oklahoma Seminole Willie Lena, 1982. From* Oklahoma Seminoles. Medicines, Magic, and Religion, *by James H. Howard, in collaboration with Willie Lena. Copyright © 1984 by the University of Oklahoma Press.*

night before the game for the purpose of strengthening the home team's "medicine" and weakening that of the opposition. On the morning of the game, each team "goes to water" or for ritual cleansing in a river or lake. The players, assisted by medicine men, are then painted and begin putting on stickball game regalia. After being ritually "doctored" and scratched, they go to the playing field and perform the Ball Game Dance. After a speech, the ball is thrown into the air in the center of the field, and the game begins. Whenever the ball nears the goal, two designated females perform the "calling of the ball" ritual to the accompaniment of a rattle and a water drum. The game generally ends with speeches, a Ball Game Dance by the winning team, ritual washing, and lunch. The Stickball Game is also called the Match Ball Game or Match Game. It follows the STOMP DANCE and the GREEN CORN CEREMONY, and the annual ceremonial cycle concludes with the SOUP DANCE. (See also "GOING TO WATER.")

STILLDAY, THOMAS, JR. *(1934–) Ojibway* First religious practitioner outside of the Judeo-Christian tradition to serve as official chaplain of the Minnesota legislature. Stillday, a leader in the MIDEWIWIN religion, was born on Minnesota's Red Lake Reservation in 1934. Growing up in the cultural and religious ways of his people, he later served for 12 years in the army. His military service included work as a combat engineer during the Korean War, where he and other Ojibway used their Native language as a code in radio communications. Stillday also studied elementary education for a time at the University of Minnesota-Morris and worked as a commercial fisherman and in logging and road maintenance. He continued to practice his religion and gradually rose to the top leadership role of his local community.

Consistent with the legendary privacy of the Midewiwin religion and at Stillday's request, his opening prayer in the Minnesota senate on February 13, 1997, was neither photographed nor filmed. Stillday also declined to speak about specific tenets or ceremonies of his faith. Explaining how his religion has neither physical church or temple nor regularly scheduled meetings, he noted that "Jesus did it the same way." Stillday was appointed to his two-year chaplain position by Senate Majority Leader Roger Moe, Democrat-Farmer-Labor Party–Erskine, whose district includes the Red Lake and White Earth Reservations. Paid only in expenses, Stillday's official duties include opening sessions occasionally during his two-year term. His appointment is a historic first, with an indigenous religion officially represented for the first time in 139 years of statehood.

STIRRING ASHES RITE *Iroquois* A new fire rite that marks the formal opening of the MIDWINTER CEREMONY. This rite addresses and thanks the Creator for life and health at the midwinter season. Performed the first and second or second and third days of the New Year, two chiefs appointed by the head officer, one from each of two moieties, stir ashes in the east and west fires of the longhouse with special maple wood paddles with a clan emblem. They sing as they walk from one fire to the other. An appointed speaker opens the ceremony and concludes it with a prayer of thanksgiving. Afterward, the two chiefs circle the houses, stirring ashes and singing and praying. After repeating the longhouse ritual, people stir the ashes with paddles of their own clan.

STOMP DANCE *Oklahoma Seminole and Creek* The Seminole or Creek ceremonial cycle begins in the spring with this all-night dance. The name *Stomp Dance* refers to the nighttime dances held at the square ground, or religious center, as well as to a specific dance form. It has also been referred to as the Seminole and Creek national dance. The participants include a leader, assistants, and one or more "shell-shaker girls" who wear leg rattles and provide rhythmic accompaniment during the performance. The ceremonial observance involves sacrificing meat to the sacred fire at the center of the grounds, taking medicine, and "GOING TO WATER," or to a river for ritual cleansing. After the first Stomp Dance in the spring, others are conducted in May and June. They are preliminary to the GREEN CORN CEREMONY, the principal observance of the ceremonial year, held in June or July. A Stomp Dance is also held in August and it is followed, in September, by a STICK BALL GAME. The cycle concludes with a SOUP DANCE. As well as a variety of stomp dance songs, other dances may be performed at intervals during the night. These include the Bean Dance, the Doublehead Dance, the Duck Dance, the Four Corner Dance, the Fox Dance, the Friendship or Love Dance, the Garfish Dance, the Long Dance, and the Mother Dance.

STONE FOREHEAD (Hohonai'viuhk' Tanuhk; Man Who Walks With His Toes Turned Out, Medicine Arrow) *(c. 1795–1876) Cheyenne* A venerated holy man who served as keeper of the SACRED ARROWS of his people from 1849 until his death in 1876. Stone Forehead, a member of the Ivistsinih'pah, or Aorta, band, was noted for possessing extraordinary spiritual powers. He was also an honored warrior who led war parties and captured horses. When he assumed the sacred role, he became a man of peace as required of the keeper. During the period he served as keeper of the Sacred Arrows, his people and their traditional way of life came increasingly under attack with the influx of outsiders to their territory, and Stone Forehead assumed other leadership roles, including that of head chief in 1851 when he was one of the signers of the Great Treaty at Horse Creek. The parties to the treaty included representatives of the U.S. government and Plains tribal groups and the agreement included provisions on territorial boundaries and rights of way as well as pledges of peace and friendship. With his people under siege by the military, Stone Forehead eventually concluded that peace would only be possible if the invaders were driven out. He was determined not to relinquish tribal territory or be confined to a reservation. Stone Forehead traveled between the Northern and Southern bands of his people during this period to bless them with the presence of the Sacred Arrows. It is believed that while traveling to the north one winter he transformed those in his party into buffalo to avoid detection by approaching soldiers.

Stone Forehead's prophetic warning to Lieutenant Colonel George Armstrong Custer was remembered by the Cheyenne people after the Battle of Little Bighorn. In 1869 Custer had smoked the pipe with the arrow keeper and other Cheyenne in the Sacred Arrow lodge, promising not to fight against them. Stone Forehead, speaking quietly in Cheyenne, told Custer that the outcome of treachery would be the death of him and his entire command. Putting ashes from the pipe bowl on Custer's boots, he warned him that Maheo, the Creator, would thus destroy him if he went against the pipe.

Stone Forehead died in 1876 among the Northern Cheyenne people. He died before he could carve sacred symbols on the chest of the next keeper with a flint knife, offering the flesh removed to MAHEO, the Creator, and the Sacred Powers, or spiritual beings, as customary; his son and successor, BLACK HAIRY DOG, was away at the time. The practice was then discontinued after that period. Stone Forehead was also known as Man Who Walks With His Toes Turned Out and Medicine Arrow. Besides Black Hairy Dog, his family included two other sons, Tall Wolf and Fox Tail.

STRAWBERRY FESTIVAL *Iroquois* Held in mid-June, when strawberries are ready, for one morning until noon, this is a first fruits ceremony that gives thanks for all berries and new life. The juice of the berry is drunk by young and old, and the Creator and spirit forces are thanked for the first fruits of the year and implored to allow all growing things to reach fruition. This ceremony combines first fruits and spring renewal with moral lessons. Preachers recite the CODE OF HANDSOME LAKE and give sermons concerning the behavior of people.

STRIKING-A-STICK DANCE *Iroquois* A dance imported from the southern Plains. Connected with the ancient custom of warriors reenacting their exploits on their return after they had struck a center pole. Its purpose is to cure disease of any kind in the home or the longhouse. The dance functions as a cure in the MIDWINTER CEREMONY and in private ritu-

als. The dance is also considered an invocation to the sun and, in the spring, an invocation to bring rain.

SUN *Navajo (Dineh)* An important Holy Person (and husband of CHANGING WOMAN) that is symbolized throughout Navajo (Dineh) religion and dominates the other deities.

SUN *Pueblo* The sun is viewed as a power for fertility and the giver and source of life that, along with the moon, establishes the calendar. The Pueblo year is divided into two halves, based in part on the sun's movements. Pueblo peoples differ as to whether the sun always existed, whether it was created by a supreme force, or whether it may have been called upon to rise. The sun is personified in many Pueblo stories and thought of as beginning his travels in the east and passing to the west where, in setting, he is said "to go home." The traditional practice of presenting newborn children to the sun exists in the pueblos.

SUN AND MOON CEREMONY *Iroquois* Short ceremonies held after SEED PLANTING at the end of May that are scheduled for the same day. The sun ceremony offers thanksgiving to the sun and appeals to it for continued blessings of the heat and warmth that plants need in order to grow. The moon ceremony offers thanks to the moon and appeals to it to continue to provide for good crops and a satisfactory planting season.

SUN DANCE *Plains* The Sun Dance is one of the best known and most spectacular religious ceremonies of Native North America. It was conducted among the buffalo-hunting tribal groups of the Plains region, including the Arapaho, Arikara, Assiniboine, Blackfeet, Cheyenne, Comanche, Crow, Eastern Dakota, Gros Ventre (Atsina), Hidatsa, Kiowa, Lakota, Mandan, Ponca, Plains Cree, Plains Ojibway, Sarsi, Shoshone, and Ute. The popular term, *Sun Dance,* is a misnomer. It is generally traced to the English translation of the Lakota name, Wi wanyang wacipi ("Sun gazing dance"). Other groups have different names for the observance, generally without reference to the Sun. The Arapaho name is translated as "Offerings Lodge," the Cheyenne as "New Life Lodge," the Plains Cree as "Abstaining from Water Dance," and so on.

In addition to differences in name, other variations exist in origin of the dance, purpose, and ritual from group to group. The Cheyenne people, for example, trace the sacred ceremony to the venerated Suhtai prophet ERECT HORNS. Among the Lakota, the Sun Dance is one of the SEVEN SACRED RITES foretold by WHITE BUFFALO CALF WOMAN and taught to a holy man in a vision. The sacred ceremony is held to pray for the renewal of the people and the earth, to give thanks, to fulfill a vow, to pray for fertility and plenty, to protect the people from danger or illness, and for other religious purposes. The time for the Sun Dance was traditionally determined by natural indicators, such as when the chokecherries began to ripen, when the trees were in leaf, when the buffalo were fat or "When the moon is rising as the Sun is going down." It traditionally brought scattered tribal bands together during the summer for social as well as religious activities. The annual Sun Dance period was a time for renewing friendships, exchanging information, visiting relatives, holding traditional games, and conducting council meetings. Among some groups the sacred ceremony included four days of preliminary preparations and four days of rituals.

The Sun Dance generally includes sweat lodge purification, the preparation of male pledgers by instructors, prolonged fasting, and dancing by the participants before a sacred pole. Some ritual elements were found in some groups but not in others. For example, the Kado, or Sun Dance, of the Kiowa did not include flesh piercing, as the people believed that any shedding of blood during the sacred ceremony would bring misfortune. Other ceremonial features identified in some groups but not others included buffalo hunts, sham battles, buffalo tongue feasts, the piercing of children's ears, a sun-gazing dance during the course of the rituals, and the use of symbolic images. The Sun Dance reinforced such values as bravery, generosity, fortitude, and honesty. Participants included priests, instructors, assistants, singers, pledgers, and the sponsor. The ceremony generally has both nonpublic and public phases in its performance.

Descriptions of the Sun Dance by outsiders began in the early 1800s. In 1805 Charles Mackenzie referred to it as a "Great Festival," and the artist George Catlin observed it among the Lakota in 1833. Many other accounts followed, often sensationalizing the ceremony. Missionaries and government agents in the United States and Canada eventually condemned the Sun Dance, and it was officially banned in both countries. Subject to arrest, practitioners were forced to discontinue the ceremony or to practice it in secret. With the confinement of people to reservations, travel was possible only with official permission or in secret. This prevented members of distant bands from gathering, as they traditionally had, for the ceremony. The decimation of the life-sustaining buffalo also had a devastating impact on both the livelihood and the religion of the people.

Some missionaries and agents were particularly repressive against the Sun Dance. Among the Southern Blood in Canada, the agent not only refused to give the practitioners beef tongues with their treaty rations but also ordered them cut up to render them ceremonially useless. Other pressures by the same individual in the 1890s included holding an officially sponsored sports day to compete with the ceremony, threatening to deny employment to a traditional religious leader, and invoking the CANADIAN INDIAN ACT before it actually applied to the Sun Dance. The situation on the United States side of the border was similar. The Sun Dance became a punishable offense of the COURTS OF INDIAN OFFENSES, established by the U.S. government in 1883. Penalties for offenders included the withholding of treaty rations and imprisonment. This official ban did not end until John Collier, the U.S. Commissioner of Indian Affairs, issued CIRCULAR NO. 2970 on Indian religious freedom in 1934. During the 19th century the Sun Dance is said to have ended among the Crow in about 1875, the Gros Ventre in about 1884, the Kiowa in 1890, and among Teton Lakota bands in 1881, 1882, and 1883.

The Sun Dance survived among many Plains groups into the 20th century because of a combination of factors. Their determination to maintain the sacred ceremony was manifested in a number of ways. Native people made direct requests to government officials on a regular basis for permission to conduct it, agreed to eliminate or change objectional aspects of the observance, incorporated Sun Dance elements into other ceremonies, conducted it under a new name, and risked imprisonment and other penalties for holding in in secret. The Blackfeet changed the time of their observance to coincide with the patriotic Fourth of July celebration, incensing one of the resident missionaries. He wrote an article entitled "The Fourth of July Dishonored" in which he noted that the Blackfeet name of the day was Umnarkatviksistsikui, or "Big Holy Day."

The Cheyenne held the ceremony under a new name, the Willow Dance, until permission for that was also denied. A study of the Cheyenne Sun Dance by the scholar Margot Liberty identified several factors that contributed to its survival. These included firmness of purpose on the part of the practitioners, inconsistent federal enforcement, the isolation of the northern reservation, sharing of ritual information among the Northern and Southern branches of the Cheyenne as well as with the Arapaho, the use of mnemonic devices by the tribal group to record ceremonial information, compiling and maintaining records, a wide enough knowledge of the practice to prevent irrevocable loss when a priest or other key figure died, and the interdependence of Cheyenne institutions.

Some groups who lost the Sun Dance during the long period of suppression have reintroduced it in the 20th century. The modern-day practitioners continue to pray for the regeneration of the earth, the continuation of the people, the recovery of those suffering from illness, the safe re-

Sun Dance. The Northern Cheyenne delegation to Washington in 1914 that sought permission from the government to hold the Sun Dance. Left to right, standing: Willis T. Rowland, Lone Elk, Samuel Little Sun; seated: Jacob Tall Bull, Thaddeus Red Water, Big Head Man. *National Anthropological Archives, Smithsonian Institution.*

turn of loved ones, and for other spiritual blessings just as their ancestors did at past ceremonies.

SUN DANCE (Wiwanyag Wachipi, "Dance Looking at the Sun") *Lakota* One of the SEVEN SACRED RITES foretold by WHITE BUFFALO CALF WOMAN. According to the holy man BLACK ELK, the Wiwanyag Wachipi, or SUN DANCE, originated in the vision of a man named Kablaya. Before beginning the ceremony, he told the people that four days of preparations were necessary. These preliminary activities included gathering the required objects, teaching holy songs to designated singers, selecting persons to scout for a sacred cottonwood tree, choosing a man for the honor of counting coups on the tree, and ritually cutting, transporting, and positioning it in a prepared location in the ceremo-

nial area. Besides consecrating the objects to be used in the ceremony, he prayed with the SACRED PIPE. He also ritually painted the sacred tree and prepared holy objects for it, including a buffalo calf skin, a bag of tallow, a small choke-cherry tree, and symbolic representations of the buffalo and a man. After the tree was raised, a sacred lodge representing the universe was built around it according to the holy man's instructions. The participants then received further teachings in a sweat lodge purification ceremony. They each vowed flesh offerings or sacrifices on behalf of the earth, the people, winged creatures, and for other purposes.

Ritual elements of the Sun Dance included fasting, purification, and dancing before the sacred tree. One aspect of the ceremony included piercing the flesh of the male dancers who had pledged to undergo the sacrifice.

Conducted by a holy man on the final day of the Sun Dance, the process was done in various ways. Mato-Kuwapi (Chased-by-Bears), a Dakota from the Santee-Yanktonai bands, provided an explanation of the piercing or flesh offerings to the ethnologist Frances Densmore, who included it in her publication *Teton Sioux Music*. Mato-Kuwapi stated: "A man's body is his own, and when he gives his body or his flesh he is giving the only thing which really belongs to him." The participants concluded the sacred ceremony with sweat lodge purification.

After the first Sun Dance taught to the Lakota by Kablaya, they continued to hold it each summer in June or July. During the course of the four-day Sun Dance, other ceremonies often took place. In one of them, families could have their children's ears pierced. This ritual act, often done to fulfill a vow, symbolically connected the youngsters and the dancers who had undergone piercing.

The Sun Dance, condemned by missionaries and agents among the Lakota and other Plains groups, became a punishable offense of the COURTS OF INDIAN OFFENSES in the 19th century. In the present day, the sacred ceremony continues to be held in Lakota communities.

SUN DANCE (Young Dog's Dance) *Pawnee* A ceremony introduced to the Pawnee by a tribal member named Medicine Chief who learned it while living among the Ree or Arikara people. It originated with a young man from that group who was isolated while trapping eagles according to custom. After hearing drumming, he investigated and found that it came from a lake. He remained at the water's edge praying, finally hearing the music again at night and seeing animals and birds swimming. By the fourth night the young man, who had been fasting, fell asleep. When he awakened, he was in a lodge with many people. The leader, representing a dog, told him that each person there represented an animal. They then taught him a dance, whose benefits included aid in wartime, telling him to take it to his people. Each animal gave him a special skill and bestowed sacred gifts upon him. The young man returned home and introduced the teachings to the people. Medicine Chief, who learned the sacred dance and its rituals, took them to the Pawnee people. He served as the leader of the Young Dog's Society, instructing those who qualified. The four-day ceremony includes fasting, piercing, and looking at the sun or moon while dancing.

SUNDAY, JOHN (Shahwundais, "God of the South" or "Sultry Heat") *(c. 1795–1875) Mississauga (Ojibway)* Methodist missionary and chief. Shahwundais, a Mississauga from Upper Canada, was born near the Black River in New York State. A veteran of the War of 1812, he turned to Christianity after the Canada Conference of the Methodist Episcopal Church had begun efforts to convert Native people in the region in 1824. Following his conversion, he acquired Euro-Canadian educational skills through his involvement with missionaries. In 1826 he was one of the Native people who signed a lease of the tribal lands used for a mission established at Grape Island in the Bay of Quinte by WILLIAM CASE. Sunday assisted in establishing a model settlement, where Native people were to follow Christian teachings, to farm and to pursue other "civilized" ways. He remained at Grape Island a short time and then served as a missionary among the Mississauga in Upper Canada and the Ojibway in Michigan. In 1833 Sunday, GEORGE COPWAY, and other Native workers established a mission at L'Anse and, two years later, another one at Ottawa Lake, both in Michigan. After he was ordained in 1836, he toured Great Britain to raise funds for Methodist missions. While there, he was presented to Queen Victoria and addressed a number of congregations and other audiences. Sunday, who had also traveled on a missionary tour of the United States, returned to his work at various stations in the region. He remained at Alderville, Ontario, one of his missions, upon retiring in 1867. As a Mississauga chief, Sunday was reportedly as eloquent at defending the land rights of his people as he was at preaching. He addressed his people in their own language, as he never acquired fluency in English. The Native pastor continued exhorting the Native people even while blind and close to death. Sunday died on December 14, 1875, in Alderville.

SUPPLICATION FOR LONG LIFE *Gros Ventre (Atsina)* A ceremony described by a Gros Ventre elder, Ben Horseman, who recalled it in 1967 in an interview with a writer. It was held for a boy when he was about six years old. The child's mother would approach a respected elder with gifts, asking that he conduct the ceremony. If agreement was reached, the necessary preparations were made. On the day of the ceremony, the elder and the boy went alone to a hilltop where it was to be held. He smudged or consecrated the child himself and the ritual objects, including a knife and bison skull. A flesh offering was taken from the boy's arm and offered to the Supreme Being. The elder then prayed that the child would be blessed with a long life. He concluded the ceremony by offering the boy words of wisdom.

SUTKWEWAT *(fl. 19th century) Walla Walla* A WASHANI RELIGION preacher from the Wallula area of Washington Territory and a contemporary of the 19th-century religious leader SMOHALLA.

SUYETA ("The Chosen One") *(c. 1825–?) Cherokee* A Baptist minister who preached to a congregation of his own people. During the Civil War Suyeta served the Confederacy as a fourth sergeant in Company A of the Sixty-ninth North Carolina. He later provided information to the ethnologist James Mooney, discussing mainly secular topics. He did not speak English, according to Mooney, "but by an ingenious system of his own has learned to use a concordance for verifying references in his Cherokee bible." (See also BLACK FOX; GAHUNI; SWIMMER.)

SWEAT LODGE CEREMONY This ceremony is nearly universal among American Indian tribes, from coast to coast and in Alaska, across Canada and in Mexico today. A sweat bath is one of the main ways by which ritual purification is achieved. The sweat lodge itself varies from tribe to tribe, but typically it is a small, dome-shaped structure between six and 12 feet in diameter, constructed of saplings and covered with canvas, hide, or blankets. An area of the dirt floor is excavated and lined with stones heated by a fire built outside the sweat lodge. The stones are chosen for their durability and capacity to absorb and hold heat. Water is poured over the heated stones after the opening is closed, generating steam. The construction of a sweat lodge is accompanied by prescribed rules and observances. The sweat lodge ceremony serves several purposes. It is a religious rite to purify the body and a medical treatment to cure ailments or to prevent ill health by influencing the spirits. It serves a social function in instructing the young in the culture, traditions, and knowledge of the tribe by older people. Although the sweat bath can be regarded as a sacred rite in itself, it is sometimes part of a larger religious ceremony. It is conducted as a purification in preparation for the SUN DANCE ceremony, the NATIVE AMERICAN CHURCH peyote ceremonies, and other ceremonies. The sweat bath ceremony is such a central part of the religious beliefs and rites of tribes that it is inconceivable that an Indian could practice his religious life in the traditional Indian way without having access to a sweat lodge. Yet requests by Indian inmates at state, federal, and local prisons for sweat lodges are routinely denied. Attorneys represent Indian inmates in compelling prison authorities to allow the use of sweat lodges, which pose no security problems. After a four-year battle with Utah officials over its sweat lodge ban, a federal judge ruled that the ritual was protected by the U.S. Constitution. Utah State Prison inmates celebrated the sweat lodge ceremony on July 8, 1989. The Arizona Department of Corrections has had sweat lodge ceremonies operating throughout the prison system for a number of years.

SWEAT LODGE RITE (Inikagapi; i, "by means of"; ni, "life" or "breath"; kagapi, "they make" or "cause") *Lakota* One of the SEVEN SACRED RITES OF THE LAKOTA PEOPLE. Conducted in a sweat lodge, it is both a ritual in itself and one associated with other ceremonies. It serves a number of

Sweat lodge and church at Wounded Knee, South Dakota, the site where Lakota men, women, and children were massacred by federal troops sent to suppress the Ghost Dance of 1890. *Photograph by Richard Erdoes.*

purposes. Besides purifying and strengthening a person before an important undertaking, it helps heal the sick. The sweat lodge rite is also held before and after other ceremonies as preparation for both entering and leaving the realm of the sacred. It is conducted by a holy person who makes certain that it is carried out as ritually prescribed, and it includes praying, singing and the use of the SACRED PIPE.

Constructed with willow saplings, the sweat lodge framework is covered with robes, blankets, or canvas before the rite begins. Symbolic of the entire universe, the two-legged, four-legged, and winged creatures are all represented in the sweat lodge. In the center is a place for the sacred "fire without end," which is tended by one person. The heat in the lodge is intense, as steam, symbolizing the breath of life, rises from the red hot rocks. During the sacred rite, the entrance flap is only opened as prescribed to let in cool air. Depending on the size of the lodge, six or seven people participate at a time.

Both males and females may undergo sweat lodge purification, but they generally do so separately. After smoking the Sacred Pipe for the fourth and last time, the sacred rite concludes with the words, *Mitakuye oyasin,* meaning "all my relatives."

SWEET GRASS HILLS Sacred site of the Assiniboine, Blackfeet, Chippewa, Cree, Gros Ventre (Atsina), Salish-Kootenai, and many tribes in Canada. The Sweet Grass Hills, which straddle the U.S.–Canadian border and extend into northern Montana, have traditionally been a place for ceremonies and spiritual retreat. According to Curly Bear Wagner, the Blackfeet tribal historian, the hills are the place where prayers are gathered before they go up to the Creator. Mining companies have been interested in the minerals buried in the buttes of the Sweat Grass Hills. In the summer of 1993, the Bureau of Land Management (BLM), responsible for the stewardship of U.S. public lands, issued a two-year segregation order on the hills during which time exploration of minerals was prohibited on these federal lands.

In 1995, the BLM released a "Draft Sweet Grass Hills Amendment and Environmental Impact Statement" in which the agency withdrew all mining of minerals located on federal land under emergency withdrawal authority for another two-year period. It withdrew from mining operations only 6,328 acres in the hills, identified as an "Area of Critical Environment Concern," rather than the full study area of 19,700 acres whose subsurface rights are owned by the government. Under the 1872 Mining Law, mining companies are allowed to stake claims and mine federal lands for as little as $5.00 per acre. The BLM is not empowered to deny permits to mining companies, some of which use the process of heap leach mining. This process allows entire mountains to be dynamited, leveled, crushed, and the ore leached with cyanide to recover gold particles.

Although there is a federal moratorium on mining or mineral exploration, the BLM has ruled that eight of the 14 claims held by E. K. Lehman of Duluth, Minnesota, are valid and may be sufficient to justify a small gold mine.

SWEET MEDICINE *Cheyenne* The venerated prophet, or culture hero, of the Cheyenne people. According to tradition, Sweet Medicine met with the Creator, the FOUR SACRED PERSONS, and the Sacred Powers in a lodge on NOAHA-VOSE, the sacred mountain, where he received spiritual teachings and gifts of immense power. Upon returning to the people from his pilgrimage, he began instructing them in the sacred laws, prophecies, and ceremonies he had been given. Sweet Medicine also brought back the four SACRED ARROWS, his holiest gift to the Cheyenne. The prophet remained among the people for four long lifetimes, aging through the seasons of each year then becoming youthful again in the spring. During that period he taught many sacred ways, including rituals, ceremonies, beliefs, and skills. Besides serving as the first keeper of the Sacred Arrows, Sweet Medicine founded the Kit Fox, Elk-Horn Scrapers, and other societies. The chiefs, or governing body of the Cheyenne people, which became the Council of Forty-four, can also be traced to the prophet and his teachings. Before Sweet Medicine died, he gathered the people around him and prophesied the changes to come. Sweet Medicine's Cheyenne names include Mut'si-i'u'iv (the prophet) and Nizhevoss (Eagle's Nest). The people also called him Sweet Root Standing. Traditionally, only priests told narratives of the prophet, taking four nights to do so. An account of his life and Cheyenne sacred ways was written by PETER JOHN POWELL and published in 1982.

SWIMMER (A yun'ini) *(c. 1835–1899) Cherokee* A venerated traditional priest and doctor. Swimmer, an Eastern Cherokee, lived among his people in North Carolina. In-

Swimmer. A Cherokee priest, doctor, and "storehouse of Indian tradition," according to ethnologist James Mooney. *National Anthropological Archives, Smithsonian Institution.*

structed in holy ways, he became recognized as an authority on Cherokee traditions. He maintained a record of sacred knowledge, including songs, prayers, and formulas, in the Cherokee language. Swimmer later astonished the ethnologist James Mooney by showing him a book of writings he had authored. The original manuscript was procured from the priest for the library of the Smithsonian Institution's Bureau of American Ethnology. Swimmer served as Mooney's principal informant, providing him with the major portion of his data on the Cherokee. Besides describing him as an "antiquarian and patriot," the ethnologist referred to Swimmer's mind as "a storehouse of Indian tradition." He also noted that Swimmer possessed a musical voice and the ability to imitate bird and animal sounds. The holy man was active in his community and was a principal participant in the Green Corn Dance, ball games, and other ceremonies. During the Civil War Swimmer served as a second sergeant to Cherokee Company A, Sixty-ninth North Carolina Confederate Infantry, Thomas Legion. He did not speak English, maintaining his traditional Cherokee ways until his death in March 1899 at the age of about 65. Mooney stated: "Peace to his ashes and sorrow for his going, for with him perished half the tradition of a people." (See also BLACK FOX; GAHUNI; SACRED FORMULAS; SUYETA.)

SWORD, GEORGE (Miwakan) *(c. 1847–?) Lakota* A 19th-century Oglala holy man who provided extensive information on Lakota culture and religion to JAMES R. WALKER, the agency physician on the Pine Ridge Reservation in South Dakota between 1896 and 1914. Sword agreed to instruct Walker in the sacred ways because "the Gods of the Oglala would be more pleased if the holy men told of them so that they might be kept in remembrance and all the world might know of them." He wrote his narratives in Lakota and included an autobiographical account in which he identified his credentials to speak about traditional ways. Sword was a *wicasa wakan* (holy man) and a *pejuta wakan* (medicine man) who had conducted traditional ceremonies, including the SUN DANCE, and was one of the Bear medicine people. He was also a warrior and *blota hunka,* war party commander, who fought against both Indian and white enemies and knew the ceremonies related to warfare. Since he had served as a *wakiconze* (magistrate), he knew the customs associated with that position as well. As a buffalo hunter, he also knew the ceremonies corresponding to that activity. After traveling to Washington, D.C., and other cities, the holy man became convinced that whites could not be driven out and later assumed roles reflecting the changes introduced among his people. He served as a captain of the Indian police, as a judge for the COURTS OF INDIAN OFFENSES, and as a deacon in the Episcopal Church on the Pine Ridge Reservation. Sword could understand English although he could not speak it. His extensive writings and instructions to Walker from firsthand experience, together with those of FINGER, RED HAWK, and THOMAS TYON, are a unique and valuable legacy. Sword died sometime before 1915. Walker referred to him at times as Long Knife.

TABLITAS *Pueblo* Thin headboards of wood decorated with symbols of clouds, Sun, and stars worn by Pueblo women during the CORN DANCE. When a kiva head requests men in his kiva to prepare and decorate *tablitas* for a dance, he accompanies his request with a gift of tobacco or cornmeal. Since *tablitas* are the product of a ceremonial request, they are sacred and due respect not accorded ordinary objects.

TABOO A Polynesian term (*tabu*) now applied in North America to a number of religious regulations observed at definite periods of life and in connection with important undertakings, either by individuals or by groups. There are restrictions for women during their reproductive life concerning puberty, menstruation, and childbirth. Boys and girls observe regulations at puberty and during ceremonial initiations. Relatives of a deceased individual, hunters (who cannot kill animals relating to their totem), shamans "showing their power" in any manner, novices being initiated into societies, participants in society or tribal ceremonies, and boys seeking guardian spirits all observe regulations concerning their behavior. There are restrictions in behavior around SACRED OBJECTS and on pilgrimages. The telling of stories and playing games at certain seasons are also taboo. Prohibitions include abstaining from hunting, fishing, war, women, sleep, certain kinds of work, and eating particular foods. In many traditional religions among American Indians, the name of a dead person is not uttered unless in an altered form or following a considerable period after death. Some people believe that misfortune or illness will result if regula-

tions are ignored. It is also believed that transgressions through engaging in taboo activities displease the spirits.

TAHIRUSSAWICHI *(c. 1830–?) Pawnee* A priest and keeper from the Chawi band of the Pawnee tribe who was the source of information on the intricate Calumet ceremony, or HAKO CEREMONY, for the ethnologist Alice C. Fletcher and her collaborator, James R. Murie. A respected holy man, Tahirussawichi's life was dedicated to maintaining the sacred objects and ceremonies in his keeping. He was a *ku'rahus,* or doctor, whose work included treating the sick through his knowledge of curative herbs and roots. He also accompanied the Hako when it was taken to the Omaha, thus becoming friends with that tribe's leaders. They influenced him and other Pawnee to trust Fletcher, and in 1898 Tahirussawichi began working with her. The ethnologist had tried for 15 years to obtain information about the ceremony. After the death of the only Omaha man who knew the rituals, she was eventually able to secure them from the Pawnee. Tahirussawichi was about 70 years old during the period he worked with Fletcher and Murie. He preferred living in the traditional way, stating, in *The Hako: A Pawnee Ceremony:* "The sacred articles committed to my care must be kept in an earth lodge, and in order that I may fulfill my duties toward them and my people, I must live there also, so that as I sit I can stretch out my hand and lay it on Mother Earth." Tahirussawichi traveled to Washington, D.C., with Murie in 1898 and again in 1900 for meetings with Fletcher. On his first trip he was shown the Capitol and the Library of Congress. Fletcher wrote that although their beauty gave him pleasure, "they did not appeal to him, for such buildings . . . were unfitted to contain the sacred symbols of the religion of his ancestors, in the service of which he had spent his long life." It took Fletcher and Murie four years to complete work on the Calumet ceremony, in part because of the time it took to overcome Tahirussawichi's scruples about revealing sacred subjects. He eventually provided a complete account of the rituals "so that the ceremony known among his people can be preserved."

TAH'-LEE *Kiowa* Tah'-lee, meaning "boy" in the Kiowa language, is the supernatural half-boy who gave the people their 10 sacred medicine bundles. One account states that a couple watched over their baby girl with great care, but on one occasion they left her with a friend who placed her cradleboard in a tree. The child crawled out to pursue a beautiful bird she had spotted on a limb, following it as it ascended. Eventually the tree grew into the sky, and the child found herself in a strange new place. She was transformed into a woman and the bird into a man, the Sun, and they eventually had a boy together. The woman, lonely for her people, later dropped a rope through a hole she had discovered and started down with her child. Before they reached the ground, the Sun realized her absence and threw a ring or game wheel down that killed her. Their son lived on earth where he was cared for by a grandmother spider until the time he tossed a ring into the air that cut him in two when it came back down. The resulting half boys remained on earth for a time, but one eventually disappeared into Wyoming's Spear Lake and the other transformed himself into 10 sacred medicines as an offering to the people. Because of a similarity with the Kiowa word *taw-lee,* meaning "paternal grandmother," these bundles have been incorrectly called the "ten grandmothers."

TAI-MAY *Kiowa* Tai-may, the image of a human figure, is the sun-power symbol for the SUN DANCE of the Kiowa and one of their most sacred objects. According to belief, it was first acquired by an Arapaho man during a Crow Sun Dance. During the ceremony the Sun Dance priest observed that the man, who was poor and without possessions, prayed a long time before the Tai-may. Taking pity on him, the priest gave him the sacred object. With the Tai-may, the Arapaho man acquired powers, and his fortunes changed. During another Crow Sun Dance, however, the sacred object was stolen from him by Crow who resented his having it. The Arapaho man later duplicated or recovered it and took it with him when he married a Kiowa woman and lived among her people. Seeing its great power, the Kiowa adopted it, and it has been with them since about 1765. By tradition its keepers, descendants of the Arapaho man and his wife, have Arapaho blood. One of

A-Mah-ah, Kiowa Tai-may keeper from 1894 to 1939 and wife of Chief Heap-of-Bears. *Fort Sill Museum, Oklahoma.*

them, A-mah-ah, served in the position from 1894 until her death in 1939. The Tai-may, the sacred symbol of the Skaw-tow, or Sun Dance, is cared for by its present keeper.

TAKES GUN, FRANK *(fl. 20th century) Crow* Elected vice president of the NATIVE AMERICAN CHURCH OF THE UNITED STATES in 1944, Takes Gun was one of the organization's first officers and the only official selected from outside the state of Oklahoma. He was reelected to the post until 1956, when the organization held its first election as the newly named Native American Church of North America, and he was chosen as president. Interested in the legal problems concerning the use of PEYOTE, Takes Gun devoted efforts to establishing and maintaining religious freedom for the church. Under his leadership, tribes were encouraged to incorporate peyote churches under the laws of their states in order to gain further protection. He assisted with incorporations in Utah, New Mexico, Arizona, Colorado, California, and Nevada as well as in Canada. Takes Gun subsequently worked for many years to convince the Navajo (Dineh) tribal council to legalize peyotism on its reservation. Furthermore, he sought aid from the American Civil Liberties Union and other organizations for the defense of David S. Clark, Mike Kiyaani, Mary Attakai, Jack Woody, and other Indians arrested for using peyote. Under Takes Gun's administration, the Native American Church of North America made progress in its efforts to gain religious freedom for its adherents. After the Navajo tribal council amended its anti-peyote ordinance to allow the religious use of peyote on the reservation in 1967, the need for his assistance on legal problems diminished in that area. For a period of time, Takes Gun's primary support came from Navajo peyotists who recognized his efforts on their behalf.

TALKING GOD *Navajo (Dineh)* One of the HOLY PEOPLE and leader of the YEIS. Talking God acts as mentor and monitors, guides, and directs human life. This foremost deity, who can travel on rainbows, answers questions that Earth Surface People cannot.

TAMANOUS (Black Tamanous) *Coast Salish (southern Puget Sound, Washington)* Term from a regional trading vocabulary called Chinook Jargon referring to anything associated with the spiritual. The term also refers to a society with initiation rites in which society members and initiates have blackened faces during the ceremony. The Canadian Indian Act of 1884 (potlatch law) made participation in the Indian dance "known as the 'Tamanawas' . . . guilty of a misdemeanor and . . . liable to imprisonment for a term of not more than six nor less than two months."

TA-NE-HADDLE (Running Bird) *(fl. late 19th–early 20th centuries) Kiowa* One of the last Kiowa buffalo medicine men. Known as Pauahty (Walking Buffalo) as a young man, he later gave the name to a relative and took Ta-ne-haddle as his second name. The Buffalo Medicine Cult Dance, or P'-haw-eey-ghun, in which he participated, originated as a gift to a Kiowa woman who had escaped from captivity among the Pawnee. As she was traveling, she was caught in a big storm and found shelter inside a buffalo carcass. Upon her return home, she took the buffalo power she had received to the people and subsequently gave separate sacred bundles to Kiowa medicine men. The Buffalo Medicine Cult Dance is believed to have started in 1822 and to have lasted until the early 20th century. Ta-ne-haddle's son observed what may have been the last performance of the ceremony, conducted by his father and five other official medicine men in 1914.

TANENOLEE (Danenolee, Dunenolee) *(fl. mid-19th century) Cherokee* A 19th-century Baptist minister. Baptized in 1830, Tanenolee began serving as an exhorter in 1834. During the removal of the Cherokee from their homelands to Indian Territory (present-day Oklahoma) he assisted the Reverend JESSE BUSHYHEAD and the Reverend EVAN JONES in leading detachments of Cherokee from their southeastern homeland to Indian Territory. Upon their arrival he assisted by ministering to the people and helping them resettle and rebuild. Tanenolee, who was ordained in 1843, eventually served as pastor at Taquohee, Dsiyohee, and Long Prairie. A paid assistant of the Baptist mission board for a period of time, he was also elected to the Cherokee Nation's legislature. Tanenolee was closely associated with the missionary work of the Reverend Evan Jones and his son JOHN BUTTRICK JONES. Tanenolee, an abolitionist, may have been killed in 1862 by Cherokee forces supporting the Confederacy. He is also called Danenolee and Dunenolee.

TANOAN MOIETY CEREMONIAL ASSOCIATIONS *Tewa, Tiwa, Towa.* These Pueblo associations, which serve a curing function, also maintain the annual solar calendar and announce dates for fixed ceremonials during the year. They organize and direct large communal dances and ceremonies, coordinate purification and cleansing rites for the village conducted by medicine associations, coordinate communal hunts conducted by hunt associations, coordinate warfare ceremonials conducted by war associations, organize and direct planting and harvesting activities, do tasks toward cleaning and constructing irrigation ditches, repair and construct communal kivas, cleanse the plaza for communal ceremonies, and nominate and install secular officers. Women may join these associations; however, their roles are as food preparers and carriers for the men when the associations are in RETREAT. Membership is lifelong. One joins a moiety association by dedicating a sick child, by recovery from an illness and vowing membership, and by ritual capture. (See also TANOAN MOIETY CEREMONIAL ORGANIZATION.)

TANOAN MOIETY CEREMONIAL ORGANIZATION *Tewa, Tiwa, Towa* A religious organization composed of two groups. Both groups, or moieties, named Summer and Winter, transfer religious responsibility from one to the other as the seasons change at the equinoxes. The head of the winter moiety rules the village during autumn and winter, and the summer moiety chief rules during spring and summer. The annual calendar of religious dances and other activities is planned and divided according to this fundamental alternation. Associated with the moieties are two caciques, summer and winter KACHINA societies, and two rectangular kivas in which many rituals are enacted. Kivas are used by the Winter and Summer managing societies, the pinnacle of the moiety religious hierarchy, responsible for performing certain religious duties. A CACIQUE who heads each moiety is responsible for the direction of secular affairs and religious proceedings. Moiety membership is inherited from the father, but it is changeable and accompanied by reinitiation into the new moiety. Rituals involving winter spirits are sponsored by the winter moiety and only members of this moiety may impersonate winter spirits; members of the summer moiety sponsor summer rituals and impersonate summer spirits. (See also TANOAN MOIETY CEREMONIAL ASSOCIATIONS.)

TANOAN PUEBLOS There are three Tanoan language subgroups, the Tiwa in the north and south of the Rio Grande valley, and Tewa and Towa in the center of the valley. The southern Tewa, or Tano, fled to the Hopi country and occupy the Hopi-Tewa pueblo called Tewa Village, which is adjacent to Walpi and Sichomovi on First Mesa in Arizona. (See also TEWA PUEBLOS; TIWA PUEBLOS; TOWA PUEBLO.)

TATE, CHARLES MONTGOMERY *(c. 1853–1933)* Methodist missionary to Native people in British Columbia. Tate was born in England and spent his early years there as a butcher's apprentice. When he was 17 years old, he left for British Columbia's caribou fields to mine for gold. After hearing in Victoria that the caribou gold was a myth and no fortunes were to be made, he traveled to Nanaimo, where he worked in the coal mines until a strike ended his employment. Tate then began visiting the Native people in the area and teaching them English. He eventually obtained a paid position as their teacher. Tate was ordained in 1879 during Victoria's first Methodist conference. His missionary efforts included translating religious materials into the Chinook jargon and establishing an Indian boarding school, which later became known as Coqualeetza Institute. During his long period of missionary service, he worked among the Tsimshian, Bella Bella, and other Native groups. He died in 1933 at Vancouver at the age of 80.

TAVIBO ("White Man," Numu-tibo'o) *(c. 1835–c. 1915)* *Northern Paiute (Numu, Paviotso)* A prophet and leader who was the father of WOVOKA, originator of the GHOST DANCE OF 1890. Also known as Numu-tibo'o ("Northern Paiute-White Man") information about Tavibo is sketchy. The prophet was said to have been born near Walker Lake in present-day Esmeralda County, Nevada. He may have fought against Euro-American encroachment on Great Basin lands in the Pyramid Lake War of 1860, the Owens Valley War of 1863, or the Bannock War of 1875. Tavibo was initially identified as the originator of the GHOST DANCE OF 1870, but WODZIWOB, another prophet, was shown to be the founder of that religious REVITALIZATION MOVEMENT. Tavibo, however, is believed to have participated in the Ghost Dance religion of the period. When his people suffered from the encroachment of outsiders on their land, they looked to him and other religious leaders for relief.

Several revelations were attributed to Tavibo. He was said to have gone into the mountains in search of spiritual guidance, returning with prophecies. He prophesied that the intruders would be swallowed up in an earthquake but the Native people would be saved. Native Americans would then be able to enjoy the fruits of the earth, including possessions left by the offending invaders. A second prophecy revealed that the disaster would engulf everyone but that the Indians would be resurrected within a few days, forever enjoying the earth and an abundance of game, fish, and piñon nuts. Tavibo attracted followers not only among his own people but from the Shoshone and Bannock tribes. When the faith of his followers began to wane, the prophet again returned to the mountain to fast and to pray in solitude. The message of his third revelation was said to have been that only believers in his prophecy would be resurrected. Besides the gift of the prophecy, Tavibo's other spiritual powers included being bulletproof and possessing healing abilities as a medicine man.

Although Tavibo's death is generally cited as 1870, other evidence indicates that he lived well into the 20th century. His beliefs and practices became the foundation upon which Wovoka would build the influential Ghost Dance of 1890. One of Tavibo's wives was Tiya, identified as Wovoka's mother. The Paiute name *Tavibo* or *Numu-tibo'o* may have derived from the prophet's involvement in war against Euro-Americans. *Buckskin,* a name in English, was also attributed to the prophet.

TEA DANCE *Plains Ojibway* A dance described in connection with a women's dancing society on the Turtle Mountain Reservation in North Dakota. The society was said to have originated with a tribal member named Simakwa, or Rising Sun Woman, after she received spiritual instructions for it in a dream. Regalia included the wearing of yellow dresses by the female members and the use of four lances. The Tea Dance of the society shared similarities with another women's dance, the ROUND DANCE. Male participants included a singer and two ritual waiters. During the course of the Tea Dance the participants drank strong tea at a particular point in the performance. An Ojibway name for the dance was translated as "acting like drunk." The Tea Dance was also referred to as a "worship dance." The society was reported as obsolete, with only two members remaining, in more recent times. (See also TRADE DANCE.)

TEHORENHAEGNON *(fl. early 17th century) Huron* A medicine man called one of the "two greatest sorcerers in the country" by the Jesuits who described some of his practices between 1628 and 1637. Failing to fulfill his promises of rain in 1628 and later in 1635, he claimed that the cross in front of the Jesuit house at Toanche II and at Ihonatiria was the cause of misfortunes, including the fires that had destroyed three villages. During the smallpox epidemics of 1637, he told of obtaining a secret remedy from the spirits after nearly two weeks of fasting. Villagers at Ossossane (La Conception) then requested his help. Tehorenhaegnon sent Saossarinon, an associate, endowing him with his power and giving him his bow and arrow to take along. To ward against disease, three days of feasting were required of those who participated. While the men sang and danced the first night, Saossarinon visited the homes of the sick. At dawn he entered the ceremony following a person bearing Tehorenhaegnon's bow and a container of water to be used for sprinkling those who were ill. After fanning participants with a turkey wing and giving them a liquid to drink, Saossarinon withdrew and a feast was held. The women then sang and danced without participating in the feast. The second day's feast was given by Saossarinon, but none was held on the third "for lack of fish." Before leaving, he taught the remedy to two Ossossane villagers and gave them turkey wings representing his power. Later a messenger was again sent to Tehorenhaegnon after the ceremonies resulted in only partial success. Saossarinon returned to Ossossane but did not visit the sick, requiring instead that they come to him. Tehorenhaegnon's reputation reportedly dwindled when his methods failed to stem the ravages of the epidemics.

TEKAKWITHA, KATERI (Catherine Tekakwitha) *(1656–1680) Mohawk* Called "Indian Saint" and "Lily of the Mohawks," she was born in 1656 near Auriesville, New York. The daughter of a Mohawk man and a Christianized Algonquian woman, she lost her parents in childhood in a smallpox epidemic. She grew up in a village near present-day Fonda, New

York, and met Jesuit missionaries around 1667. Determined to embrace the new religion despite her uncle's opposition to Christianity, she was baptized in 1676. She fled in 1677 to an Indian mission in upper Canada where she practiced her new religion. She received her first communion on December 25, 1677, at the mission of St. Francis Xavier du Sault near the Christian community of Mohawk called Caughnawaga by Indians. She practiced austerity, fasted two times a week, performed penance, and vowed chastity. She tortured herself by being flagellated with willow rods, sleeping in beds of thorns, and holding brands between her toes so she could suffer. She established a remarkable reputation for sanctity. In 1679, she began a modest convent at the mission patterned after the Hospital Sisters of Ville-Marie in Montreal. Kateri Tekakwitha died April 17, 1680. There are numerous biographies of her, all based on contemporary accounts. In 1943, she was declared venerable by Pope Pius XII, and in 1980 she was beatified by Pope John Paul II. The Jesuits have a shrine to her at her Auriesville home and the Franciscans have a shrine to her at her second home of Fonda. She is honored as well at the Kahnawake Reserve in Quebec. There is an organization named after her, and Indian Catholics want her to be declared a saint.

TEKAKWITHA CONFERENCE Begun in 1939 by a small group of non-Native missionaries working among Indian communities in the northern United States, the organization has grown into a nonprofit corporation dedicated to Indian concerns and making the Native American presence known to the American and Vatican Catholic hierarchy. The conference is a year-round organization headquartered in Great Falls, Montana, with youth programs and a nationwide newsletter. There have been annual conferences since the first, which convened in Fargo, North Dakota, in 1939. Although meeting in the name of a Native American woman, the conference saw no participation by Native Americans or by women during its first years. In 1973, a small group of sisters broke the barrier and joined. In 1977, at the 38th annual conference in South Dakota, the conference opened itself to full participation by Native American Catholics. In 1980 the Conference expanded its regional role and became a national movement supported by the BUREAU OF CATHOLIC INDIAN MISSIONS. Participation in the conference now includes Catholic bishops, priests, sisters, brothers, deacons and laity, Native Catholics from more than 150 tribes, and Native priests, sisters, laity, and ordained deacons. Annual meetings since 1980 have grown to include more than 3,000 participants, mostly Indian, dialogue on Native American liturgy, ministry, family life, catechesis, advocacy, education, and ecumenical cooperation. Among the programs and objectives of the conference is "Native Spirituality," which encourages Indians and tribes to tell their own stories and histories. The conference supports the movement for the sainthood of the Blessed KATERI TEKAKWITHA but lobbied against the beatification of Father JUNÍPERO SERRA because of the oppressive mission system he established. The conference newsletter printed articles that charged California missionaries with mistreatment of Indians over the decades in which the missions functioned. The conference is now a strong voice before the Catholic Church and the federal and state governments.

TEN GRANDMOTHERS See TAH'-LEE

TENSKWATAWA ("The Open Door," the Shawnee Prophet) *(1775–1836) Shawnee* The Shawnee Prophet. A holy man whose religious movement, which attracted thousands of Indian people, was used by his brother Tecumseh to forge an intertribal confederacy prior to the War of 1812. Tenskwatawa was born a triplet with two brothers in early 1775. He grew up without his parents, as his father had died before his birth at the Battle of Point Pleasant in October 1774 and his mother either returned to her people or accompanied the Kispokothas west when they left Ohio in 1779. Other Shawnee, including Black Fish, a war chief, and Tecumpease, a married sister, took care of the children. Tecumseh, seven years older than Tenskwatawa, was also affected. Perhaps because of Tenskwatawa's insecure childhood, he boasted about himself and became known as Lalawethika (the rattle or noisemaker). During a childhood accident, the youngster lost the sight of his right eye while playing with a bow and arrows. A taste for alcohol, acquired in adolescence, increased Lalawethika's boasting and earned the disdain of other Shawnee. In August 1794 he participated in tribal opposition to "Mad Anthony" Wayne's legions at the Battle of Fallen Timbers. In the decade after the Treaty of Greenville, which was signed in 1795 and forced tribal groups to relinquish their claims to most of Ohio, the young Shawnee took a wife and fathered several children.

In 1804 or 1805 Lalawethika became ill and was believed to have died. Before his funeral arrangements were completed, he revived and told the people assembled that the Master of Life had sent two young men to carry his soul to the spirit world. There, he had been shown the past and the future. Permitted to look at paradise, he described it as a rich country with plenty of game and fish and which possessed fine hunting grounds and cornfields, where the spirits of good Shawnee would go. Lalawethika also described the fiery torture that would await the souls of evildoers. He vowed to give up his sinful ways and to quit drinking. His name would be Tenskwatawa to symbolize leading his people through the "open door" to paradise. In the months to

Tenskwatawa. Open Door, known as the Shawnee Prophet, and brother of Tecumseh, in a painting from 1830. Portrait by George Catlin. *The National Museum of American Art, Smithsonian Institution, Gift of Mrs. Joseph Harrison Jr.*

follow he had additional visions and further developed his religious doctrines, which he taught to fellow Shawnee and then to members of other tribal groups. In late November 1805, Tenskwatawa met with Shawnee, Ottawa, Seneca, and Wyandot delegations at Wapakoneta on the Auglaize River to expound on his religion. He declared that his sole purpose was to reclaim Indian people from bad habits and to have them live in peace with everyone. He denounced a number of practices, including consumption of alcohol, intertribal violence, polygamous marriages, and promiscuity.

Although against many tribal customs, Tenskwatawa's beliefs were essentially nativistic. His followers were encouraged to return to the communal life of their ancestors and to relinquish white technology. They could be friends with European allies such as the British who had been created by the Master of Life but not with the American enemies, because they had been made by "another spirit." The Shawnee Prophet warned that opposing him meant opposing the Master of Life, and those who did so would be suspected of witchcraft. Converts were asked to confess their sins and to confirm their regeneration by the ritual of "shaking hands with the Prophet." Tribal bitterness and desperation over dispossession of their land to the United States increased the number of converts, who placed their trust in a religious solution and the Prophet. As resentment against the United States increased, he gained followers among the Kickapoo, Winnebago (Ho-Chunk), Sac, Miami, and other groups.

For four years, from 1805 to 1809, Tenskwatawa dominated the Indian movement, attracting adherents to Greenville, Ohio, then to Prophetstown on the Wabash. After the Treaty of Fort Wayne at which the Indians ceded more than 3 million acres of land in Indiana and Illinois to the United States in 1809, Tenskwatawa's followers shifted their focus to Tecumseh's political-military strategy. The Indian retreat from the Battle of Tippecanoe, fought on November 7, 1811, was a devastating defeat for the Prophet who had assured his followers of victory. His religious movement ended with his flight to Canada after the Battle of the Thames in 1813. In exile there for a decade, he eventually became alienated from the British because of the government's Indian policies and returned to Ohio after agreeing to assist Governor Lewis Cass in his efforts to remove Shawnee west. His influence diminished, the plan offered Tenskwatawa an opportunity to return to the United States in a leadership role as well as the possibility that removal to an area away from white encroachment and influence would be beneficial to the Shawnee. In 1828 emigrant tribal bands subsequently established small villages along the Kansas River. A few years later, in 1832, Tenskwatawa posed for the artist George Catlin, who portrayed him in traditional garments and wearing symbols of his religious movement. The Shawnee Prophet died in November 1836 and was buried somewhere in what is now Kansas City, Kansas.

TENTH DAY FEAST *Iroquois* A traditional ritual held 10 days after the death of an individual. The elements consist of a speech, distribution of the personal effects of the deceased, and a feast. On the 10th day, the spirit, ghost, or soul of the deceased leaves and travels along the path of the soul to the afterworld. After the funeral and burial, the matrilineal clan of the deceased begins preparations for the feast, which includes plans for distributing the personal property of the deceased at the feast to prevent the ghost from returning to bother the living. An extra place is set for the deceased to constitute "feeding the dead." Feasting is confined to the passing of food at the end of the property distribution, and the deceased accumulates a share of the food, which is kept until morning. Unless the feast is shared, it is not valid. Seating rules are observed, and special people speak, cook, and pass food. Sometimes families have a one-year feast at which the deceased is "fed" one more time. It occurs on the first anniversary of death, for it is believed that the soul of the dead returns to earth on this day. This one-year feast is less formal.

TERRY, JOSHUA *(1825–?)* A missionary of the Church of Jesus Christ of Latter-day Saints who served as the president of the Shoshone mission for his denomination. Born in Home District, Canada, in 1825, he achieved a number of high offices in his church after his baptism on June 20, 1840. Besides being ordained as a teacher in Nauvoo, Illinois, and as a Mormon "seventy" in Salt Lake City, he was named as president of the Shoshone mission in 1881 and as a patriarch on May 5, 1901.

After experiencing persecution in Missouri, Terry left the area in 1847. Settling in Salt Lake City, he engaged in a number of pioneering activities, including helping construct a fort in the area. He later lived in Idaho and Wyoming as well. Besides his religious involvement with Indian people, he traded with them for about nine years. Terry and his family eventually settled in present-day Draper in Salt Lake County, Utah, where he served as a justice of the peace. Terry's family included 16 children. One of his wives was a Shoshone woman, and their son George became a tribal chief.

TESHKWI (Deshque, "Sacred" or "Forbidden") *Zuni* A 10-day period of quiet in late December following the SHALAKO CEREMONY when the year ends. All people refrain from smoking outside or driving in cars. No light is permitted outdoors, and businesses are closed. People make ceremonial offerings to the spirits, meditate, and pray to the Creator for continued blessings to be given to them for the year ahead. Men, women, and children abstain from certain foods for at least four days. The 10-day period begins after the North Priest's announcement of prayerstick cutting and ends in "middle time," or the winter solstice. After the fast is over, the new year begins. There is also a four-day summer Teshkwi.

TETERUD V. GILLMAN, TETERUD V. BURNS (385 F. Supp. 153 [S.D. Iowa 1974], aff'd, 522 F.2d 357 [8th Circ. 1975]) *(1975)* Jerry Teterud, a Cree inmate of the Iowa State Penitentiary, challenged a prison regulation that prohibited Native American inmates from wearing long braided hair. Teterud contended that the regulation violated his religious freedom, freedom of expression, and equal protection rights under the First and Fourteenth Amendments of the United States Constitution. The district court found Teterud's religious beliefs to be sincere and held that the penal institution's administrative and security concerns about hair length could be addressed in less restrictive ways. The court ruled that the regulation unconstitutionally infringed upon the First Amendment rights of Teterud to freely exercise his religion. On appeal, the Eighth Circuit Court of Appeals affirmed, ruling that it was not necessary to prove that the wearing of long braided hair was an "absolute tenet of the Indian religion practiced by all Indians . . . Proof that the practice is deeply rooted in religious belief is sufficient. It is not the province of government officials or court to determine religious orthodoxy." (See also *HATCH V. GOERKE; NEW RIDER V. BOARD OF EDUCATION; UNITED STATES EX REL. GOINGS V. AARON;* Subject Index for related legal cases included in this volume.)

TEWA CEREMONIALISM The central theme in Tewa ceremonialism is seeking, finding, regaining, and renewing life. Tewa song images, dance gestures, and regalia symbolize this theme of new life and are viewed as mechanisms for revitalizing the community. Tewa define spatial dimensions of their world. Their songs and gestures refer to cardinal directions, each of which is designated by a color, animal, bird, mountain, and natural phenomena. Their dance circuit patterns reflect a cyclical concept of time. There is a clear distinction made between winter and summer, two ceremonial halves. Winter is the time for nonagricultural activities, especially hunting, and summer is the time for planting and harvesting corn and other crops. The ritual cycle reflects this distinction. At the basis of the Tewa world view is a dual organization of Tewa ritual and society, a duality expressed in winter and summer, material and spiritual. The winter-summer division is given form in Tewa landscape, with north and east associated with winter and south and west associated with summer. Spiritual figures, clowns, lakes, mountains, hills, minerals, and shrines are associated with winter and summer as well. Spirit impersonators dress, dance, and behave in terms of the season to which they belong. (See also PUEBLO CEREMONIALISM; TANOAN MOIETY CEREMONIAL ORGANIZATION; ZUNI CEREMONIALISM.)

TEWA PUEBLOS Tewa is one of the three subgroups of the Tanoan language family. There are six Tewa villages on the upper Rio Grande above Santa Fe, New Mexico: San Juan, Santa Clara, San Ildefonso, Tesuque, Nambe, and Pojoaque. The Tewa village of Hano is on the Hopi First Mesa. (See also TIWA PUEBLOS; TOWA PUEBLO.)

THANKSGIVING ADDRESS *Iroquois* A traditional speech delivered by men in an Iroquois language; a central prayer that opens and closes almost every Iroquois ceremony except those honoring the dead. This address conveys the Iroquois view and organization of the world. The SPEAKER first thanks the Creator for permitting the gathering and urges people to be thankful for each other and then moves to the sets of thanksgiving. The speech mentions a graded hierarchy of spirit forces that must be remembered and honored. There is a particular sequence of spirit beings listed in the speech, from spirits of the earth (terrestrial) to spirits in the sky (celestial) to spirits beyond the sky and ending with the Creator. After passages, the Iroquois use an Iroquois phrase meaning "Yes, I agree with what you are saying." The first part of the speech is devoted to things below, on this earth. Speakers mention people, the earth, waters (springs, streams, rivers, lakes), plants on earth (grasses, berries, medicine herbs, weeds, bushes, saplings, trees, forests), cultivated foods called "our sustenance" (corn, squash, beans), animals, and birds. The next part of the speech deals with the wind and thunderers, sun, moon, and stars followed by the Four Messengers or Beings (messengers from the Creator to HANDSOME LAKE), Handsome Lake himself, and then the Creator. The Thanksgiving speech may be short (less than a minute) or long (around three quarters of an hour). A short version begins every ceremony and a long one is spoken at the GREEN CORN ceremony. Different speakers use slightly different versions (and the same speaker varies the words each time he gives the speech). Each speech is similar, however, because it follows the general sequence of "thanks upward," from Earth to the Creator. (See also IROQUOIS CEREMONIALISM.)

THANKSGIVING (DRUM, SKIN) DANCE *Iroquois* One of the FOUR SACRED CEREMONIES belonging to the Creator. It takes its name from the skinheaded water drum on which a singer beats out a rhythm for the dancers. This ceremony returns thanks to the Creator for all benefits. People wear regalia befiting a ceremony addressed to the Creator. A short version of the dance begins every ceremony, and there is a long one performed at the GREEN CORN and the MIDWINTER CEREMONY.

THOMAS, JACK (c. 1850–?) *Delaware (Lenni Lenape)* PEYOTE leader who also served as a chief of the Delaware (Lenni Lenape) band located near Anadarko, Oklahoma. Thomas had known JOHN WILSON, the Caddo-Delaware originator of the Big Moon peyote ceremony, and devoutly believed in his ritual. In the late 1920s or early 1930s, when he was about 80 years old, he was interviewed by the ethnologist Vincenzo Petrullo and provided an account of his religious beliefs. While working as a policeman, Thomas said, he attended peyote meetings after becoming ill. Although he recovered, he was stricken again when he returned to work and nearly died. He was hospitalized but eventually ran away and went to his brother, who held a peyote meeting for him. Thomas learned that his police work, arresting people, was making him sick, and after his recovery he did not return to it. He became an adherent of the PEYOTE RELIGION and relinquished his previous way of life.

THOMAS, WILLIE (*c. 1869–?*) *Delaware (Lenni Lenape)* A renowned PEYOTE leader in Anadarko, Oklahoma, whose conversion to the PEYOTE RELIGION occurred after an extraordinary experience. Sometime around the turn of the century Thomas became very ill and was taken to peyotists for help. Although it was believed that he died during the ceremony, the participants did not have him buried, and he returned to life after three days. He became a devout believer in the power of peyote as a result of this experience and later developed his own variation of the Big Moon peyote ceremony of JOHN WILSON. When he was interviewed by an ethnologist in the early 1930s, he had been a peyotist for more than 30 years. (See also QUAPAW, JOHN.)

THOSE-WHO-DESCEND-FROM-THE-HEAVENS *North Pacific Coast* A dancing society that emphasizes encounters with star, cloud, bird, and other spirits associated with the skies. Novices are "called down" from the sky world to which they have been taken. The society's insignia consists of ornaments of bleached cedar bark. The ceremony has quiet, stately dancing with masks and other paraphernalia. These spirit impersonators lack the violent characteristics of the SHAMANS' SOCIETY dancers. (See also DANCING SOCIETIES.)

THROWING OF FLOWERS *Yaqui* Flowers (*sewam* in Yaqui) thrown during the WAEHMA ceremonial. It is one of the final ritual activities in the series sustained from the first Friday in Lent. The flowers symbolize the destruction of Chapayekas (see YAQUI CEREMONIALISM), who are weakened by the powers of the pelted flowers, and the triumph of the church. The immediate effect is the destruction of evil power residing in the Chapayeka masks and the military insignia of the Soldiers of Rome. The culmination of the Waehma ceremonial, the symbolic acts of throwing flowers, ends the seven weeks of ritual expression and ceremonial effort. The Yaqui believe that flowers are symbolic of grace because when blood fell from Christ's wound to the ground, flowers grew on the spot.

THROWING OF THE BALL CEREMONY *Lakota* The last of the SEVEN SACRED RITES OF THE LAKOTA, foretold by WHITE BUFFALO CALF WOMAN. According to an account given by BLACK ELK, the ceremony originated in a vision in which a holy man, Moves Walking, saw it performed by a young buffalo calf who was transformed into a human being. Moves Walking taught it to the people after the necessary preparations, prayers, and offerings were made. During the sacred rite a young girl stood in the center of four teams gathered at each of the four directions (north, south, east, and west). She tossed a ball, made from buffalo hair covered with hide and painted to symbolize the universe, first to the peo-

ple in the west. The person who caught it offered it to the earth and sky and the four directions before returning it to the girl. The action was repeated until the ball had been thrown and caught in all four directions. The young girl concluded by tossing it into the air for everyone to try to catch. The rite was believed to represent the ages of a person's life, the ball to symbolize the universe or knowledge, and the efforts to catch it the struggle to break free of ignorance.

THUNDER DANCE *Iroquois* Scheduled in times of drought or held in spring when thunder is first heard, the rite held in the morning or afternoon welcomes back the thunderers (grandfathers) and includes a TOBACCO INVOCATION, a LACROSSE game, and a LONGHOUSE dance in which children represent thunder spirits. This one-day ceremony is performed again in honor of the thunderers during summer. The purpose is to implore the thunderers to travel through the country, water the fields, control the winds, and continue their duties of restraining pesty animals. This dance is also a farewell because the grandfather thunderers leave during winter and go to another part of the world to do their duties. Playing lacrosse, circumscribed by rituals before and after the game in the longhouse, is believed to cure thunder-related diseases.

TIAWIT (*fl. late 19th century*) *Yakama (Yakima)* A dreamer-prophet who appeared after SMOHALLA, the 19th-century religious leader. Tiawit, who adhered to the WASHANI RELIGION, preached at Satus on the Yakama (Yakima) reservation in Washington State. He was said to have each participant dance with a plate. A dark spot would sometimes appear on it, indicating evil in a person.

TIMS, JOHN WILLIAM (*c. 1858–1945*) Anglican missionary among the Blackfeet and Sarcee people in Canada. He was the son of John Tims, a boat-builder in England, and his wife Sarah. Tims started learning his father's trade, but in 1879 he enrolled at Islington and began preparing to become a missionary. He was ordained four years later at St. Paul's Cathedral. Tims then left for the Blackfeet Reserve in Canada, arriving in July during a SUN DANCE. After meeting Crowfoot, the head chief, he journeyed to Old Sun's band and started his missionary work. He began studying the Native language and later devised a writing system and wrote a grammar and dictionary. During his 12 years among the Blackfeet he was instrumental in organizing a school. In 1895 he was sent to the Sarcee Reserve near Calgary in southern Alberta, where he remained as a missionary for 35 years. His efforts included building a church and serving as archdeacon of Indian missions. He was also instrumental in establishing Calgary's Anglican diocese. Tims later became archdeacon of Calgary, holding the position for 15 years and continuing to oversee Indian mission work in the area. During his career he became recognized as an authority on the Blackfeet language. He was assisted in his missionary work by his wife, Violet Winifred Woods. Archdeacon Tims died in 1945 at the age of 87.

TIPI WAY CEREMONY   See PEYOTE RELIGION (Half-Moon ceremony)

TIWA PUEBLOS   One of the three subgroups of the Tanoan language people. There are four villages. Two of these, Taos and Picuris, are both in northern New Mexico, and Isleta and Sandia are near Albuquerque, New Mexico. The northern and southern groups speak dialects that are not mutually understandable. (See also TEWA PUEBLOS; TOWA PUEBLO.)

TOBACCO   For thousands of years, tobacco has been used among the hundreds of tribal groupings in both North and South America. Researchers have concluded that precontact tobacco use originated among Native peoples of South America, then spread through Central America, and later to North America.

Some forms of tobacco grew wild; others were cultivated. In times prior to European contact, the most commonly used species of tobacco was *Nicotiana rustica,* used primarily by American Indians in the eastern United States and throughout the Great Plains. Often Native peoples mixed tobacco with other substances such as parts of the bark of the willow, dogwood, sumac, bearberry, rose, and leadplant, in addition to the leaves and small stems of these plants, as well as herbs or oil to form a milder substance called *kinnikinnik* in the Algonquian languages and *chan sha'sha* in the Siouan language. In most languages, the term applied to the mixture meant "mixed" or "mixed by hand."

Aboriginal tobacco was in small supply and was sacred. There were gender differences in the growing of tobacco. Women generally were not allowed to participate in its cultivation, although they were responsible for other crops, thus affirming its distinctive sacred status. Among the Plains tribes, there were tobacco societies. Initiation into their ranks was required before members could sow tobacco. Duties of initiates included sweat lodge rituals, the selection of medicine, and the planting of sacred tobacco, all of which were executed with the greatest ritual and care.

Tobacco was used in agricultural rites. It was used in the harvesting of crops and to bless the harvest. The rising tobacco smoke was regarded as a means of communicating with the spirit world. Tobacco smoke was also an important visual symbol of contact with the supernatural world. The Haudenosaunee (Iroquois) believed the ascending smoke carried their petitions to the Creator. Tobacco was commonly used to bind agreements between tribes, and it often accompanied invitations to individuals or families. Tobacco was also given as payment to a sacred practitioner.

In addition to its ceremonial use, many different tribes used tobacco, especially its active component, nicotine, medicinally and in medical ceremonies. It was chewed as a remedy for toothaches and was used to treat earaches. Open wounds and insect or snakebites were treated with tobacco because of its presumed analgesic properties. It was also used to treat ailments such as asthma, rheumatism, convulsions, intestinal disorders, childbirth pains, and coughs. Healers used tobacco as a fumigation to drive disease away from a patient's body.

Native American people believe that tobacco, used at the right time, the right place, and in the right way, helps in the spiritual development of a good person. Some tribes still have sacred people who know the proper way to plant, pick, prepare, and use tobacco. Today traditional Native people use tobacco as a sign of respect and as an offering when praying to the Creator. By placing tobacco in a fire while praying, the smoke that rises carries their prayers to the Creator. Sometimes tobacco is smoked in a pipe, used in crumbled leaf or seed form, or as a paste. Sometimes it is sprinkled around young corn plants. When someone wishes to show respect to a healer or elder, tobacco is given. Traditional healers use tobacco to help cure illnesses. When people travel to a foreign area and wish to pay respect to the ancestors of that land, they offer tobacco to the earth. No matter what form it takes, this kind of tobacco use is sacred to Native people. (See also TOBACCO SOCIETY.)

TOBACCO INVOCATION *Iroquois*   Addressed to the Creator, this speech contains sections similar to those in the THANKSGIVING ADDRESS, based on the graded hierarchy of spirit forces, and is performed twice a year, during the MIDWINTER CEREMONY and during the summer. A chant accompanies the tobacco offering. The tobacco is esteemed by the Iroquois as one of the blessings bestowed on them by the Creator and viewed as a helper to aid people in communicating with the Creator. It is burned, usually in a stove or fireplace, as well as smoked, as an offering to carry messages to the Creator and other spirits. The offering is a form of pledging a sincere mind and heart. The tobacco used in the ceremonies is grown and cured by the Iroquois for sacred purposes. The contents of the tobacco invocation depend on the occasion.

TOBACCO SOCIETY *Crow*   A sacred society believed to have been organized after a mystical star being appeared on earth and transformed itself into the holy tobacco plant. The

Tobacco Society was considered beneficial to the welfare of all of the Crow people. Its membership included both men and women. Initiates were ritually adopted into the society after receiving instruction from their sponsors, completing the required preparations and assembling payment fees. The holy or medicine tobacco associated with the society is distinct from that grown for ordinary use. It is ritually planted, cared for, and harvested by members of the society. Many subdivisions, or chapters, of the society developed over time, generally as the result of visions. Each chapter possessed unique features, including sacred songs, symbols and ceremonies. It is said that in the early years membership in the Tobacco Society was restricted to a small number of people, most of whom were elders.

TONAWANDA LONGHOUSE *New York Iroquois* The LONGHOUSE near Akron, east of Buffalo, New York, is the headquarters, or "head fire," of the HANDSOME LAKE RELIGION, an association of all 11 Iroquois longhouses in a united religious body. This longhouse has become the religious center for all Iroquois followers of the Handsome Lake religion. Located on the Seneca reservation, the wampum strings that HANDSOME LAKE himself held as he preached are kept here. Here the best preachers are qualified for interlonghouse speaking. Every fall, in September or October, delegates from each of the other 10 Iroquois longhouses assemble at the Tonawanda longhouse to arrange that fall's itinerary of SIX NATIONS MEETINGS and to hear their prophet's message recited before it is preached elsewhere. At Tonawanda, in the 1840s, under the guidance of Jimmy Johnson, Handsome Lake's grandson, a version of the CODE OF HANDSOME LAKE developed that is close in form to the published code. The Tonawanda version has become the standard by which other speakers' versions are now judged. This version is carried from village to village in the fall of each year.

TONGUE RIVER VALLEY Sacred site of the Northern Cheyenne. Located in southeastern Montana, the Tongue River valley forms the eastern boundary of the Northern Cheyenne Indian Reservation. The Northern Cheyenne people have regarded the area as a spiritual sanctuary for VISION QUESTs, cloth and tobacco offerings, afterbirth ceremonies, and the production of medicinal plants. It is also the location of many burial sites.

The valley is threatened by the proposed extension of the Tongue River Railroad. This project is directly linked to the expansion of strip-mining for coal and the clear-cutting of timber in southeastern Montana, which will include 13 massive coal mines.

TOOHULHULSOTE ("Sound," Toolhoolhoolzote, Tulhulhutsut) *(c. 1810–1877) Nez Perce* A dreamer-priest and leader of his people who lived near the mouth of the Salmon River in present-day Idaho. Toohulhulsote's beliefs, similar to those of the prophet SMOHALLA, led to his refusal to sign the Treaty of 1863, which included provisions to cede Nez Perce lands to the U.S. government. He later served as a spokesman representing Lower Nez Perce bands at a council with army officer General Oliver Howard. During a meeting in 1877 Toohulhulsote gave his reasons for not agreeing to sell or relinquish the land. Besides stating that the earth was his mother and a part of himself, he said that people should subsist on its natural bounty without disturbing it. He also stated that the earth's sovereignty could not be sold or bartered. Howard ordered Toohulhulsote's arrest at Fort Lapwai, Idaho, releasing him only after those of his people who opposed the ceding of Nez Perce lands agreed to go to a reservation by June 14, 1877. Toohulhulsote later served with Chief Joseph (the younger) in the Nez Perce War of 1877. The dreamer-priest was instrumental in the Indian victory at the Battle of the Clearwater on July 11, 1877, but he later died at the Battle of Bear Paw on September 30, 1877. He is also called Toohoolhoolzote and Tulhulhutsut.

TORRY, ALVIN *(c. 1798–?)* The first Methodist missionary sent to the Grand River area in Ontario. An American, Torry began his ministry in 1817. After working on a circuit in New York State, he traveled to Canada in 1818. He was associated with the Long Point, Westminster, and Ancaster circuits until 1821. After an assignment at Lyon's Creek, he was sent to the Grand River area by the Reverend WILLIAM CASE in 1822. At first the 24-year-old Torry was unable to convert any of the Iroquois people. It was not until he met PETER JONES and other Native converts that he became more successful, converting Jones's cousin DAVID SAWYER and others. Torry then organized a Methodist Indian society, and its members constructed a building to serve as a church and school. The Anglican Mohawk were said to attribute the shouting and crying of the new Christian converts to the use of wolf medicine by the Methodist missionaries. Torry, accompanied by the Reverend Peter Jones as interpreter, went on his first missionary tour in the region in 1825. They preached to the Munsee people at Moraviantown on the Thames River and to an Ojibway band nearby. In 1828 Torry returned to New York, where he worked in the Ontario district. He wrote *Autobiography of Alvin Torry*, which was published in 1864.

TOTEM An animal, plant, or other natural being that serves as the symbol or emblem of a clan or extended family among many tribal groups. According to Frederick Hodge (whose two-volume *Handbook of American Indians North of Mexico,* 1907–1910 gives brief descriptions of the origin and derivation of words whenever they are known), *totem* is derived from *ototeman,* a word belonging to the Ojibway language and other cognate Algonquian dialects. According to Hodge, the word signifies "his brother-sister kin." In his 1990 book *Ojibway Heritage,* Ojibway scholar Basil H. Johnston defines *dodaem,* or totem, as "that from which I draw my purpose, meaning, and being" and states that "the bonds that united the Ojibway-speaking people were the totems." He further asserts that the feeling of oneness among people who occupy a vast territory is based not on political, economic, or religious considerations but on totemic symbols that "made those born under the signs one in function, birth, and purpose." This means that men and women belonging to the same totem regarded one another as brothers and sisters having kinship obligations to each other.

The Abbé Thavenet, a missionary to the Algonkin at Lake of the Two Mountains, Canada, in the early part of the 19th century, wrote an explanation of the use and meaning of the stem *ote* in *ototeman:*

> It is to be presumed that in uniting into a tribe, each clan preserved its *manitou,* the animal which in the country whence the clan came was the most beautiful or the most friendly to man, or the most feared, or the most common; the animal which was ordinarily hunted there and which was the ordinary subsistence of the clan, etc.; that this animal became the symbol of each family and that each family transmitted it to its posterity to be the perpetual symbol of each tribe. One then must when speaking of a clan designate it by the animal which is its symbol.

Hodge discusses the shift in meaning of the term *totem* by discussing how it has been indiscriminately applied to any one of several classes of imaginary beings that are believed by a large number of the Indian tribes and peoples of North America to be the guardian or the patron saint or being of a person or of an organization of persons. He concludes that since *totem* has come to signify the protector of a person, a clan, society, or tribe, it also denotes the name, crest, or symbol of a clan, person, society, or tribe.

In North America, there is a certain feeling of affinity between a kin group or clan and its totem. There are taboos against killing clan animals, as humans are kin to the animals whose totems they represent. In some cases totem spirits are clan protectors and the center of religious activity.

TOWA PUEBLO One of the three subgroups of the Tanoan language family, there is a single surviving town, Jemez, located up the Jemez River, near Zia. The Towa once included the large and well-known Pecos Pueblo. (See also TEWA PUEBLOS; TIWA PUEBLOS.)

TRADE DANCE *Plains Ojibway* A ceremony generally held for four nights early in the winter season. Its purpose is to secure a snowfall to enable the people to track and obtain game. It is pledged by an individual who may conduct it if qualified. Otherwise, assistance is obtained from a person with the right to hold it. The Trade Dance honors Pakahk, the mystical skeleton being and spirit who helps hunters in Cree and Plains Ojibway belief. The ceremony opens with four men who are posted with rifles outside of the lodge at the four directions, or cardinal points. When the opening or first song is sung, the man in the north position fires. This is repeated at the second song by the man in the east and continues in the remaining two directions. The firing symbolizes the number of nights the ceremony is held. If the rifle misfires at one point, the observance is held for three nights only. The Trade Dance may be extended by contributing a horse at the ceremony for each additional night. During the Trade Dance a participant dances up to another person in the lodge and presents a gift. The recipient later returns a present to that individual. On the final night, offerings are made to Pakahk. (See also ROUND DANCE; TEA DANCE.)

TRAVELING RITE *Iroquois* The rite refers to members of the FALSE FACE SOCIETY and HUSK FACE SOCIETY who travel, usually by car, from the longhouse to homes of longhouse members in order to chase away disease from the house. The visit, in the spring or fall, begins with the entrance of the unmasked leader of the group, carrying ritual paraphernalia symbolizing the False Faces and the Husk Faces. First, the members of the Husk Face Society tumble into the house and dance, carrying sticks, branches, or cornbread paddles. They function as messengers for the members of the False Face Society, who next roll in and dance and rub their rattles on house furnishings. The False Faces exorcise disease from the home by scattering about wood ashes from the home fire, entering each room, rubbing the woodwork with large rattles, and voicing their nasal whinnies. At the end of the purification, people in the house hand over tobacco to the leader. After the False Faces spiritually cleanse the individual homes, they return to the longhouse. The whole procession, going and coming, is accompanied with songs appropriate to the False Face Society. Not every Iroquois community performs the rite.

TREHERO, JOHN (Rainbow, Truhujo, Treeo, Middle of the Belly) *(c. 1883–1985) Shoshone* A medicine man and SUN DANCE chief who reintroduced the Sun Dance on the Crow Indian Reservation in Montana in 1941. Trehero was the son of a full-blood Shoshone mother and a part-Mexican father. When he was about six years old, his father died, and other family members sent him to a government boarding school in White Rock, Utah. Trehero remained there for less than two years then returned to Fort Washakie, Wyoming, and enrolled in a mission school. At about age 19, he completed the eighth grade. Besides working as an interpreter and policeman, Trehero hauled wood and coal and owned herds of cattle and sheep for a time.

Although he had been baptized at the age of 14 or 15 by the Reverend JOHN ROBERTS, the Episcopal minister in charge of the mission school he attended, Trehero was primarily interested in the traditional religious practices of his people. He learned about the Sun Dance and its beliefs from his maternal relatives and participated in the sacred ceremony for the first time when he was 18 years old. He also turned to peyotism, but eventually received visionary instructions that led him to reject the practice. Trehero acquired hereditary Sun Dance medicine bundles from his mother, a descendant of Chief YELLOW HAND, two years before her death in 1922.

Vying for religious leadership among the Shoshone people, Trehero eventually became very influential on the Crow Indian Reservation where he had relatives and where he had lived for about five years. In 1938 Trehero conducted a Sun Dance at Fort Washakie, and it was attended by visiting Crow, including WILLIAM BIG DAY. Big Day subsequently invited him to the Crow Indian Reservation, where he reintroduced the Sun Dance in 1941. The last 19th-century Sun Dance among the Crow is believed to have been held in 1875. Trehero served as mentor and instructor to Big Day before breaking with him, but by then had the support of influential Crow leaders.

During his long tenure, Trehero trained many medicine men, introduced innovations to the Sun Dance, and healed people. By 1967, when Trehero was in his eighties, he began to consider retiring and eventually transferred his medicine powers and religious leadership to THOMAS YELLOWTAIL. In 1975 his blessings were still sought by the younger Crow leaders he had instructed. Besides the other spiritual powers he possessed, he was credited with receiving a cure for epilepsy from the Water-Ghost-Being, a spirit helper. After Trehero's first wife died in 1915, he married Deborah Kagawoh, who had three children from a previous marriage. There is disagreement on the spelling of his name, which also appears as Truhujo or Treeo, and on his birthdate. He also had a Crow name, Middle of the Belly. Trehero died in January of 1985 in Wyoming.

TROTT, JAMES JENKINS *(1800–1868)* One of the first Methodist missionaries to the Cherokee people. Trott was born in North Carolina but moved to Tennessee in 1815. Within two years of joining the Methodists in 1821, he be-

came an assistant circuit rider of the denomination. In 1827 the Tennessee Methodist Conference assigned him to a circuit in the Cherokee Nation and the following year he married a mixed-blood tribal member, Sallie Adair, who lived near his mission at New Echota, Georgia. At a meeting held on September 25, 1830, Trott and other Methodist missionaries passed a resolution opposing the removal of the Cherokee to Indian Territory (present-day Oklahoma). Their protest may have prompted a similar action by Presbyterian workers in the field three months later. The Methodist missionaries, however, were unable to obtain the support of their board, the Tennessee Conference of the Methodist Episcopal Church. Trott was arrested on May 31, 1831, for violating a law requiring whites residing in the Cherokee Nation to swear an oath of allegiance to the state of Georgia in order to obtain a license to continue living and preaching there. After a forced march of 110 miles to Camp Gilmer, Trott was imprisoned for four days then released after posting a bond, as required, with orders to stay out of the area of the Cherokee Nation within Georgia boundaries. Trott was arrested again on July 6, 1831 while visiting his wife and children at New Echota. He repeated the 110-mile march to prison, this time accompanied by SAMUEL AUSTIN WORCESTER, Dr. ELIZUR BUTLER, DICKSON C. MCLEOD, and several other men who had also violated the Georgia law. They were eventually sentenced to four years at hard labor at a trial held on September 15, 1831, in Lawrenceville, Georgia. All but Worcester and Butler accepted pardons. Trott was released after agreeing not to return to Georgia. His wife died within days of his release, and he left the Methodist denomination several weeks later. He became an adherent of the Campellites, or the Disciples of Christ, then served as an itinerant preacher in the South. Although he did not initially follow the Cherokee to Indian Territory, he worked among them in 1856 until the Civil War intervened and again in 1866. Trott died in Nashville in 1868.

TSO, HOLA *(fl. 1940–1956) Navajo (Dineh)* Councilman and peyotist who spoke in defense of PEYOTE on June 3, 1940, when the Navajo tribal council deliberated its anti-peyote ordinance. The only peyotist at the meeting, he requested additional evidence and medical testimony about the plant. By informing the council that he had attended a peyote meeting conducted by Alfred Wilson, president of the NATIVE AMERICAN CHURCH, Tso indicated having firsthand experience with peyotism. Despite his efforts, the Navajo anti-peyote ordinance passed by a vote of 52 to 1. When the tribal council voted to reconsider the ordinance in 1954, Tso rejected the council's offer to defend peyote for five minutes on the grounds that it was insufficient time. Although other testimony was provided in defense of peyotism, the tribal council failed to act, and the anti-peyote ordinance remained in effect. The following year Tso and other peyotists petitioned the council to amend the ordinance, but that effort, and subsequent efforts, failed. In 1956, Tso was elected vice president of the Native American Church of North America. He also assisted peyotists, such as Mike Kiyaani, arrested under the Navajo anti-peyote ordinance.

TUBE-SUCKING SHAMAN A shaman who cures illnesses by ritually sucking or blowing into small tubular bones applied to the affected area of a patient's body. The shaman generally communicates with the spirits while performing the cure to find out the cause of the problem and how to remedy it. Some individuals receive these unique healing abilities from a dream or vision experience. Other requirements for the role generally include an apprenticeship with a qualified teacher, the observance of spiritual instructions and restrictions on behavior, such as abstention from certain foods. Some are blessed with other spiritual gifts, such as a knowledge of herbal cures or other powers. In a 1929 publication, the ethnologist Frances Densmore described an Ojibway *djasakid*, or SHAKING TENT SHAMAN, who wore a long string of bones, indicating that he had acquired "unusual proficiency" with the bone-sucking healing technique. Once a widespread method of curing among shamans of many tribal cultures, it is not known how prevalent it is today. Another name in English is *bone-sucking shaman*.

TUNERAK (Tornait, Tunarak, Tuŋak, Tuŋalik, Tuŋhak, Tunraq) *Inuit* Spirit aids of shamans that resemble giants, dwarfs, half-beings, or malevolent beings not in any way connected with the spirits of living creatures or objects. They have human qualities, often live like Inuit but are unavailable to ordinary people. Whatever their form, the spirit aids are a large source of shamanistic power. They escort shamans' souls beneath the sea, to the Moon or to Sila, the air spirit. Bering Sea Inuit believed the *tunerak* were a supreme deity that controlled animals and lived in the moon. They sent their shamans to him to plead for game and other favors. If displeased, the spirit could punish people by withholding animals.

TUNKANSHAICIYE ("Sacred Stone That Paints Itself Red" or Solomon Tunkanshaiciye) *(1833–1910) Dakota* Presbyterian minister. Born at Lac qui Parle in Minnesota Territory in 1833, Tunkanshaiciye was educated at the mission school established there by THOMAS S. WILLIAMSON. In 1858 he became a member of the church at Hazelwood, a mission that had been developed by the Reverend STEPHEN RETURN RIGGS. During the Dakota War of 1862, which was fought between Eastern Dakota forces and Euro-American opponents, Tunkanshaiciye was accused of participating in several battles. The war had erupted because of a number of factors, including a greatly reduced land base, failures of the government to uphold treaty agreements, corrupt officials and traders, and conditions of hunger and illness among the Dakota people. Tunkanshaiciye was one of more than 300 Dakota men sentenced to die by a military tribunal, but received a reprieve after President Abraham Lincoln reviewed the trial records and found that most of the evidence was insufficient. Lincoln reduced the number of death sentences, and 38 Dakota men were eventually hanged on December 26, 1862, in Mankato, Minnesota—the largest mass execution in United States history. Other accused, including Tunkanshaiciye, were incarcerated at Davenport, Iowa, where many of the prisoners died during their three-year incarceration. Missionaries who had worked among the Dakota people in Minnesota visited the Dakota inmates and continued to proselytize. After being imprisoned from 1863 to 1866, Tunkanshaiciye received his license to preach in 1867 and was ordained a year later. He then served in pastorates on the Sisseton Reservation in South Dakota. In 1879 he traveled to Manitoba to work among Dakota refugees from the United States. He returned to Sisseton in 1890, serving as pastor of the Buffalo Lake church. Tunkanshaiciye died in 1910.

TWINS, BALDWIN (Scabby) *(c. 1874–1964) Cheyenne* Keeper of the SACRED ARROWS of his people from 1936 to 1956. Twins, a Southern Cheyenne, was the son of Yellow Calfskin Shirt. In 1945 he took the Sacred Arrows to NOAHA-VOSE, the sacred BEAR BUTTE, to offer prayers of thanks for peace after World War II. Until then, the arrows had not left the Southern Cheyenne in many years. Twins later returned to the north with the Sacred Arrows for ceremonies in 1948 and 1953. In 1956, prompted by a number of concerns, he decided to turn the Sacred Arrows over to a religious leader among the Northern Cheyenne. As the transfer was carried out without the involvement of the military societies and chiefs, as required, the decision was not allowed to stand. A delegation, designated by the Cheyenne authorities, returned the Sacred Arrows to the south.

TWO HORN SOCIETY *Hopi* This society, which directs rituals of the WUWUCHIM CEREMONY, is considered to be the most important of the societies participating in the ceremony. The Two Horn priests' first significant ritual during

Baldwin Twins, keeper of the Sacred Arrows of the Cheyenne from 1936 to 1956, in a 1908 photograph. *National Anthropological Archives, Smithsonian Institution.*

Wuwuchim is the NEW FIRE CEREMONY. The two horns are the symbol of the society's spirit.

TYLER, LEONARD *(1864–1913) Cheyenne* A Southern Cheyenne who introduced peyotism in Montana and also served as an elder in the Reorganized Church of Jesus Christ of Latter-day Saints. The son of a chief, Tyler was educated at the Carlisle Indian School in Pennsylvania (1880 to 1883) and Haskell Institute in Lawrence, Kansas. He became a farmer, stock raiser, and businessman. In 1902 he was described as a large land owner who was well known across the state of Oklahoma for his "phenomenal success" in the stock-breeding industry. Tyler reportedly learned his PEYOTE ceremony from Kiowa practitioners in 1884 to 1885, later adopting his own fireplace, or moon. He was subsequently identified as a chief and medicine man as well as an apostle of peyotism among the Northern Cheyenne in Montana. The Bureau of Indian Affairs was informed of his role with peyote, both as a missionary and a supplier, in reports sent from Oklahoma, Montana, and Texas. Tyler continued as a peyotist until his death in 1913.

TYON, THOMAS (Gray Goose) *(c. 1855–?) Lakota* An Oglala interpreter and informant to JAMES R. WALKER, an agency physician who studied Lakota religion on the Pine Ridge Reservation in South Dakota. Tyon was a mixed-blood and Christian who served as a government farmer in the White Clay district of Pine Ridge. Literate in the Lakota language, he used the phonetic system developed by early missionaries to the eastern Santee band of his people to record information for Walker. In 1911 he wrote narratives based on material acquired in interviews with older Oglala holy men. His contributions included information on the SUN DANCE, the Lakota kinship system, and men's societies. In a 1915 letter, Walker wrote that Tyon and GEORGE SWORD, his "most valued" and "most depended upon" informants, were no longer living. In Walker's writings Tyon is at times referred to as Gray Goose. Other Lakota who provided material for Walker included FINGER and RED HAWK.

UNITED FOREIGN MISSIONARY SOCIETY A missionary society organized in July 1817 in New York City by the general assembly of the Presbyterian Church, the general synod of the Reformed Dutch Church, and the general synod of the Associated Reformed Church. Its purpose was to spread the gospel among the "heathen" and "anti-Christian" of North America, South America, and other areas of the world. The United Foreign Missionary Society was later transferred to the AMERICAN BOARD OF COMMISSIONERS FOR FOREIGN MISSIONS after a merger was proposed on August 15, 1825.

UNITED STATES EX REL. GOINGS V. AARON 350 F. Supp. 1 (D. Minn. 1972) A Minnesota district court case in which an Oglala Lakota inmate in federal prison refused to have his hair cut because he had taken a religious vow to wear it long. The man, who was punished by the authorities for his refusal, contended that by breaking such a vow he would be subjected to serious consequences. The court found the prison's regulation on hair length reasonable and questioned the sincerity of the plaintiff's beliefs. It indicated that the inmate had not followed American Indian customs for 26 years, that no other Native person at the correctional institution had requested to follow the same custom, and that he could renew his vow upon his scheduled release from incarceration 55 days after the trial. (See *HATCH V. GOERKE; NEW RIDER V. BOARD OF EDUCATION; TETERUD V. GILLMAN;* Subject Index for related legal cases included in this volume.)

UNITED STATES V. DIAZ (368 F. Supp. 856 [D. Ariz. 1973], rev'd, 499 F.2d 113 [9th Cir. 1974]) *(1974)* This 1973 case is said to be the only one reported in federal courts as litigated under the ACT FOR THE PRESERVATION OF AMERICAN ANTIQUITIES, a 1906 law making it illegal to appropriate, excavate, or otherwise harm any object of antiquity on government lands. The case involved Ben Diaz, who was convicted by a United States magistrate of appropriating religious masks from a cave located on the Apache San Carlos Reservation in Arizona. On appeal, the issue of whether the masks, made in 1969 or 1970, were "objects of antiquity" was addressed. The district court affirmed the conviction, accepting the testimony of an anthropologist from the University of Arizona who stated that "objects of antiquity" could include recently made items if they were connected to long-standing religious or cultural traditions. Other testimony indicated that the masks were sacred objects that were placed in remote areas because they were not to be removed from the reservation and were to be handled solely by qualified medicine men. Diaz appealed to the Ninth Circuit Court of Appeals and the decision was reversed. The appeals court held that the Act for the Preservation of American Antiquities was unconstitutionally vague and that it failed to define key statutory terms. It was unclear whether recently made objects were to be protected, because the statute did not include a clear definition of "antiquity." (See also Subject Index for other legal cases included in this volume.)

UNITED STATES V. JONES (449 F. Supp. 42 [D. Ariz. 1978]) *(1978)* A 1978 case in which the Arizona district court pointed out the weakness of the ACT FOR THE PRESERVATION OF AMERICAN ANTIQUITIES. The defendants were arrested with clay pots, bone awls, stone metates, and other artifacts after they were seen digging among American Indian ruins. They were indicted on charges of theft and malicious mischief because the prosecutors realized that a conviction under the 1906 Antiquities Act would not be upheld. Finding that the Antiquities Act was "the exclusive means through which the government could prosecute" a defendant for acts encompassed by the statute, the charges were dismissed. (See also AMERICAN INDIAN RELIGIOUS FREEDOM ACT OF 1978; ARCHAEOLOGICAL RESOURCES PROTECTION ACT; *UNITED STATES V. DIAZ*; Subject Index for related cases in this volume.)

UNITED STATES V. MEANS (627 F. Supp. 247 [D.S.D. 1985]) *(1985)* This case started in 1981 with the application by Russell Means and other Lakota for a special use permit to establish Yellow Thunder Camp, a "religious, cultural and educational community" on 800 acres in Black Hills National Forest in South Dakota. When the request was denied by the Forest Service, a legal battle ensued in federal district court. The Lakota charged that denial of the permit violated their rights under the First Amendment, the AMERICAN INDIAN RELIGIOUS FREEDOM ACT OF 1978, and the Fort Laramie Treaty of 1868. Findings in the case revealed that the Black Hills National Forest had received 61 applications for special use permits five and one half years before the dispute. Fifty-eight, all made by non-Indians, were approved, and three, made by Indians, were denied. Several hundred private and semi-private uses, including other church camps, had been permitted in the area but none by Indians. The court ruled that the denial of the special use permit for Yellow Thunder Camp was arbitrary and capricious and that Forest Service policies had the effect of discriminating against Indians. Although the Lakota prevailed in district court, the case was appealed to, and reversed by, the Eighth Circuit Court of Appeals. (See also Subject Index for related cases in this volume.)

UNITED STATES V. TOP SKY (547 F.2d 483 [9th Cir. 1976]) *(1976)* In this case a Chippewa-Cree who made sacred objects for use in American Indian religious ceremonies was charged with violating the BALD AND GOLDEN EAGLES PROTECTION ACT by selling an eagle feather fan and bustle to undercover federal agents. In ruling to uphold the conviction, the court held that the defendant's free exercise of religion claim had no standing because the charge was based upon the sale of the feathers. It found only a commercial interest asserted in the case without a showing that the law's operation was coercive to the religious rights of the defendant. (See also AMERICAN INDIAN RELIGIOUS FREEDOM ACT OF 1978; Subject Index for related cases in this volume.)

UNITED STATES OF AMERICA V. BUERK (No. A. 77–121 [N.D.W.D. Ohio, Opinion and Order, Jan. 16, 1979]) *(1979)* In this case the defendant, a non-Indian, had been convicted of violating the ENDANGERED SPECIES ACT OF 1973 by possessing federally protected bird feathers. Given the defendant's participation in Native American religious ceremonies, the court ordered the charges dismissed in accordance with the AMERICAN INDIAN RELIGIOUS FREEDOM ACT OF 1978.

UNMARKED HUMAN BURIAL SITES AND SKELETAL REMAINS PROTECTION ACT (Nebraska Legislative Bill 340) *(1989)* Legislation enacted in 1989 that requires museums and other institutions in the state of Nebraska to return Indian skeletal remains and associated burial goods to the appropriate tribes for reinterment. Sponsored by Senator Ernest Chambers of Omaha, the precedent-setting law applies to human remains and grave goods as well as both private and state property. The Pawnee tribe supported the bill as part of a three-year struggle to rebury ancestral remains kept by the Nebraska State Historical Society. The Pawnee and other supporters of the legislation sought the same protection and respect for the Indian dead as that accorded the decedents of other groups in society.

Under the act, remains in state-recognized or state-funded institutions identified with a specific Indian family or tribe would be subject to reburial upon request. Another provision prohibits the unnecessary disturbance of unmarked graves and establishes penalties for trafficking burial contents within the state. In instances where road construction and other activities would cause disturbance to unmarked Indian burial sites, the law requires state authorities to contact the appropriate tribes and to comply with their decisions as to disposition. Other provisions of the act include terms and conditions of scientific study, a procedure for arbitrating disputed claims related to Indian remains, penalties for trafficking burial objects within the state, and the stipulation that private civil actions may be brought against those who violate the law. (See also Subject Index for additional entries concerning reburial and repatriation included in this volume.)

UPLEGGER, FRANCIS *(fl. 1919–1939)* A Lutheran missionary who served as superintendent of the Apache Indian Mission. Uplegger arrived on the San Carlos Reservation in Arizona in 1919, two years after his son Alfred, also a pastor, began working there under the auspices of the Wisconsin Synod. Besides establishing Grace Lutheran Church in 1921, they undertook other work among the Apache people. Francis ministered to people stricken with tuberculosis in the 1920s and 1930s, his efforts earning him the Apache name Iv Nashovd Hastin, "The Old Gentleman Missionary." He also studied the Apache language, eventually devising a writing system with the aid of Apache texts he had obtained from the Smithsonian Institution. Uplegger later compiled the first complete dictionary of the language. His linguistic efforts enabled him to create new Apache words to label and explain concepts foreign to the Native culture. He also completed religious translations, including hymns and prayers. When the tribal government drafted a new constitution, Uplegger served as adviser and secretary on the project. He held the superintendency of the Apache Indian Mission, which served the San Carlos and Fort Apache Reservations, for 20 years.

UTAH CLEAN AIR ACT AND PIPE CEREMONY EXEMPTION

(1995) On April 4, 1995, tribal elders from throughout Utah gathered in the Utah capitol rotunda for the ceremonial smoking of the pipe and to celebrate the traditional use of TOBACCO. The ceremony also celebrated Governor Mike Leavitt's signing of HB149, a bill that exempts American Indian religious leaders from the state law prohibiting smoking in public buildings. Because there was no exemption for religious ceremonies, even in churches or at annual gatherings of Indians at traditional powwows, the law directly infringed on American Indians' right to freedom of religion.

In sponsoring the legislation to exempt Indian religious leaders from the smoking ban, Representative Eli H. Anderson (Republican-Tremonton), maintained the infringement of religious freedom was never the intent of the legislature. After initial opposition from the Rules Committee, the bill passed overwhelmingly. Under the provisions of HB149, those American Indians who have been designated by their tribes as religious leaders or pipe carriers are allowed to conduct pipe ceremonies in a public building at the invitation of the owner of the public place.

On April 4, 1995, the state granted permission to Pete Littlejohn, a Shoshone pipe carrier from Ft. Hall, Idaho, to smoke the pipe inside the capitol. Clifford Duncan, former councilman of the Ute tribe, explained that it was not the spirit of tobacco alone that is meaningful to Indians but the many dreams and prayers reaching back through generations of ancestors. He said the Great Spirit touches the smoke rising from a traditional ceremony. (See also SACRED PIPE.)

UTTAMATOMAKIN *(fl. 1616–17) Powhatan* A 17th-century priest among the Powhatan people of Virginia. In 1616 Uttamatomakin traveled to England with a group that included Pocahontas, the daughter of Powhatan. Interviewed there by the Reverend Samuel Purchas, the Powhatan priest told him some of the religious beliefs of his people. Uttamatomakin indicated that four priests summoned Okeeus, their deity, into the temple through the use of a "strange" language not known to the "Common-people." When Okeeus arrived, he gave the priests and eight other principal people instructions and prophecies. Uttamatomakin revealed that the deity had foretold the arrival of the English. Okeeus had also told the priest when the Powhatan party traveling to England would return home. During the interview Uttamatomakin noted that the weather had delayed their departure to the date his prophecy indicated. Stating that he was too old to learn about Christian worship, he later became exasperated by the English proselytizers and opposed their beliefs.

UWANNAMI *Zuni* Spirit rainmakers, also called cloud beings, who live along the ocean shores and in springs. They pass over the upper regions, protected from view of people by cloud masks, through which they pour water. They travel as clouds, dew, fog, and rainstorms. The RAIN PRIESTHOODS join the *uwannami* after death. These spirits are different from the *KOKO* who also bring rain.

V

VENIAMINOV, IVAN *(1797–1879)* Russian Orthodox Church missionary. Born Ivan Popov in Irkutsk Province, Siberia, he was sent to the Russian Orthodox Seminary at Irkutsk at the age of nine. He went to Unalaska, one of the Aleutian Islands, in 1823, two years after becoming an ordained priest. He took the name Veniaminov in honor of a former bishop. He learned the Aleutian language and converted some Aleut to Christianity, taught them building trades, and trained them for employment with the Russian-American Company. He also encouraged traditional Aleut interests in art, music, and basketry. He founded a boys' school to teach reading, writing, and Christianity. He wrote the first Aleut-Russian dictionary and Aleut grammar, invented an Aleut alphabet and translated the liturgy, catechism, and gospel of Matthew into Aleut. While he lived with the Aleut, Veniaminov kept detailed records of their life and customs and left an Aleut ethnography. In 1825, he established the first Russian Orthodox church-school in the Aleutians at Iliaka. In 1834, he went to Sitka and worked among the Tlingit, converting some of them to Christianity. In 1838, he left for Saint Petersburg. Later, in 1840, he became a monk and was appointed bishop of the newly formed diocese based at Novo Arkhangelsk, Russia. In 1841, he founded a seminary and devoted himself for the next 27 years to educating the people of his diocese in Christian principles. He had the Holy Scriptures translated into Aleut, Yakut, and Kuril. In 1868, he became head of the Russian Orthodox Church in Moscow.

VILLAGE CHIEF (Kikmongwi) *Hopi* The supreme priest, or officer, in all Hopi villages. The position is lifelong, although a chief may be removed from office for incompetence. The village chief is supposed to watch over the people and protect them. He is usually selected from the Bear clan unless members of the clan have died out.

VISION QUEST A vision quest is the ritual seeking of communication with the spirit world by a solitary individual. It is conducted in an undisturbed natural setting, often at a site sacred to the tribal group. Generally, the individual ritually prepares under the guidance of one or more medicine people. Vision quest rites vary from one tribal culture to another, with differences including age, gender, and ritual elements. It may take place once at adolescence, repeatedly as part of long-term training during puberty, at adolescence and in adulthood, or in maturity only. In many cultures the vision quest is associated only with males, but in others females may also undergo the rite. The length of time an individual undertakes a vision quest also varies, many last from one to four days. Ritual elements identified in many cultures include praying with the SACRED PIPE, fasting from food or water, and taking offerings of tobacco, pieces of flesh, or other sacred gifts to the spirits. A vision quest may be undertaken for a number of reasons: to complete a puberty ceremony, to prepare for becoming a healer or shaman, to fulfill a vow, to participate in other ceremonies, and/or to seek spiritual guidance.

Individuals blessed during a vision quest may receive sacred ceremonies, names, objects, songs, prophecies, teachings, and/or spiritual powers from an animal, bird, or other being. Such powers may be related to specific healing, control of weather, or spiritual assistance during a difficult undertaking. The person may also receive teachings or prophecies that will entail great suffering and difficulty. Restrictions on behavior, such as abstaining from certain foods, and other requirements are also associated with spiritual instructions. The teachings may not be understood at the time but may gradually reveal themselves later in life. Not every individual has a vision during the quest. Some may repeat the quest at another time, but others may relinquish the effort. After the rite ends, the suppliant generally receives assistance from the medicine person. Some quests are undertaken for purposes other than vision seeking. For instance, vision quests have been differentiated from Pipe Fasts, where individuals pray and fast in much the same way but do not seek visions. (See also HANBLECEYA.)

WABAN ("East") *(c. 1604–c. 1676) Nipmuc* One of the PRAYING INDIANS believed to be the first Massachuset chief to embrace Christianity. Waban was born about 1604 in Musketaquid, present-day Concord, Massachusetts. He later lived at Nonantum ("I rejoice"), where he was appointed "chief minister of Justice" by authorities who appreciated his welcome of missionaries and the enrollment of his son in a colonial school. When JOHN ELIOT established the first praying town at Natick in 1651, Waban and his people moved there. In 1674 he was a principal leader in the community, which then consisted of 29 families. He was married to a daughter of Tahattawan (also Attawan), the sachem (chief) of Musketaquid. About two months before King Philip's War broke out in 1675, Waban warned a magistrate about Native plans to attack the colonists. In a subsequent warning he stated that the Wampanoag leader Metacom, or King Philip, and his followers "were only waiting for the trees to get leaved out that they might prosecute their designs with more effect." Waban may have been among the Native prisoners who were falsely accused and imprisoned during the conflict. He returned home ill in May of 1676. That year he also became a "ruler of fifty" in the community and later a justice of the peace. Waban died at the end of 1676 or the beginning of 1677.

WABENO ("Morning Star Man"; also "Men of the Dawn Sky") *Algonquian* A religious society found among the Menominee, Ojibway, and other Algonquian groups. Mani-festing their spiritual power, in part, through the manipulation of fire, the Wabeno shamans interpreted dreams, guided initiates through rituals, and healed the sick. The term has been variously interpreted as referring to the "red dawn sky," symbolizing fire, to the morning star as the source of sacred power, and to the all-night rituals that lasted until daybreak. Early on, it was a society that shared some similarities with the MIDEWIWIN, requiring fees and initiation and having both male and female members. Possessing particular spiritual powers, the Wabeno were known as fire walkers because of their ability to walk on or to handle hot coals. By concentrating on fire and singing sacred songs, they were able to enter a trance state and receive spiritual assistance in treating patients and divining, or foretelling, events. Using herbal preparations for protection, they were known to plunge their hands into boiling water or maple syrup without burning themselves. Capable of transformation, the Wabeno could assume animal form, such as the bear, and were sometimes observed at night as meteors. Another power attributed to them was their ability to become fox-like and shoot fire from their mouths while speaking. The *Jesuit Relations* described early Ojibway Wabeno who healed through fire manipulations and erotic dances. These practices, considered jugglery or witchcraft, were looked upon with disfavor by Christian missionaries. Wabeno are said to have become primarily associated with evildoing in some groups, using their spiritual powers to cause illness or even death. Feared and often blamed for misfortune, they were condemned as false or dangerous and reportedly died out among various groups.

WABINO THANKSGIVING CEREMONY *Cree* A ceremony described among Cree (also identified as Saulteaux or mixed-Algonquian) clans in the upper Severn River area in present-day northwestern Ontario. It was an annual ceremony held in the spring to give thanks to Manitou, the Creator, not only for surviving the winter season but for other gifts. The Wabino Thanksgiving Ceremony was conducted in the Wabinogamick, a religious lodge or longhouse. Ceremonial features included dancing by godchildren for the person who named them, dancing by the hunters who had killed moose, a thanksgiving to the fish essential to the survival of the people, a women's dance, and a dance by young boys. Before the Wabino ended, herbal medicine was prepared. Some of it was given to the people during the ceremony, and the remainder was saved for later use. On the last day, a feast was held. The Wabino concluded after several days with a SHAKING TENT CEREMONY and a final dance. The Wabino Thanksgiving Ceremony, one of four annual ceremonies, reportedly ended among the Native people in the Sandy Lake area in 1959.

WABOKIESHIEK ("The Light" or "White Cloud") (*c. 1794–1841*) *Winnebago (Ho-Chunk)-Sauk.* A medicine man known as The Prophet who was influential during the Black Hawk War. Born about 1794, he was half Winnebago and half Sauk. His community, known as "Prophet's Village," was located about 30 miles above the mouth of Rock River, the area of present-day Prophetstown, Illinois. Wabokieshiek favorably influenced Black Hawk, the Sauk and Fox leader, to continue his fight against the Americans. Wabokieshiek informed Black Hawk's emissary that his visions and prophecies foretold spiritual assistance in overcoming the enemy. Friend and adviser of Black Hawk, Wabokieshiek was blamed by the Sauk leader Keokuk for his role in the conflict. Following the Indian defeat at Bad Axe in 1832, The Prophet and Black Hawk were captured and transferred to Jefferson Barracks, near St. Louis, where they were incarcerated in irons. George Catlin, the artist, obtained permission to paint portraits of the prisoners. Catlin described The Prophet, whom he called Wah-pe-kee-suck, as "a very distinguished man, and one of the leading men of the Black Hawk party . . . about forty years old and nearly six feet high, stout and athletic." In 1833 the prisoners were taken to Washington, D.C., where they saw President Andrew Jackson and appealed for their freedom. Instead, they were incarcerated at Fortress Monroe in Virginia until their release two months later. Wabokieshiek returned to his people, living among the Sauk in Iowa until their removal to Kansas. At the time of his death, about 1841, he was living among the Winnebago. In addition to Catlin, R. M. Sully, another artist, painted Wabokieshiek's portrait.

WAEHMA *Yaqui* An intensive, sustained, collective ceremonial expression that reinforces the Yaqui town as a unit each year. The Waehma is the Yaqui version of the Christian religious drama the Passion. The story of the Crucifixion and Resurrection of Jesus is enacted as the basic struggle between good and evil in a complex integration of native ceremonial practices with Christian liturgy and beliefs. According to Yaquis, the Waehma started "in the very beginning." All the events of Lent and Easter, from Ash Wednesday through the Gloria, as well as Easter Sunday itself, are considered to be one ceremony commemorating the wanderings and sufferings of Jesus.

At least 30, usually more than 40, separate ceremonial occasions make up the elements of the Waehma, an intricate and structured set of rituals that define and annually reaffirm the nature of the relationships between people and spirit forces. The dramatic narrative of the Waehma is enacted everywhere in a town, within the church building, in areas immediately outside the church, in the plaza, and potentially in every household in the community and even at Yaqui households outside the town. The principal actors in the Waehma are the good soldiers, the infantry, the soldiers of Rome, and the LITTLE ANGELS (opponents of the infantry and soldiers of Rome). The latter are small boys and girls who wear white dresses and wreaths of FLOWERS on their heads. The central theme in the course of the seven-week ceremonial is the story of Jesus' last days on earth, of the evildoers who persecute and crucify him, and of the rise and fall of evil soldiers. For those participating in the Waehma, it brings positive good of sharing in a collective and dynamic spiritual community enterprise. See also YAQUI CEREMONIALISM.

WAKAN FEAST *Eastern Dakota* A feast described among 19th-century Eastern Dakota people. Wakan, or Holy Feasts, were held frequently, with a number of them sometimes occurring at the same time. Several men assisted in the ceremonies held before the feast, weeping in prayer and supplication. The guests were summoned by a messenger when the food was ready. After preliminary rituals, including the consecration of the participants' hands and knives in cedar smoke, the food was divided into equal portions and eaten. None of the foods could be carried off, and people unable to finish the meal were required to pay the host a fine, such as a pair of leggings. On departure, a guest addressed each of the remaining participants individually before leaving the home of the host. The people believed that holding frequent Wakan Feasts led to the greatest success in hunting. (See also HOLY DANCE; RED FISH.)

WALAM OLUM *Delaware (Lenni Lenape)* A pictographic record attributed to the Lenni Lenape. Walum Olum has been translated as "Painted Tally" or "Red Score." An English language version of this pictographic record was initially published in 1836 by Constantine Samuel Rafinesque as *The American Nations.* He based his manuscript on wooden sticks, engraved and painted with glyphs, that a "Dr. Ward" had obtained from Lenni Lenape people in Indiana. The Walam Olum includes an account of Creation, the story of a flood, and a record of Lenni Lenape migration millennia ago. Although at first questioning the authenticity of the Native chronicle, the anthropologist Daniel Brinton eventually concluded that it was genuine. However, the Walam Olum has continued to be debated since its publication. Some scholars question Rafinesque's linguistic skills and his knowledge of Lenni Lenape oral traditions. Others have commented that the Walam Olum, though it may be fabricated, expresses ideas drawn from authentic accounts and practices. Writings on birch bark or wood certainly existed among the Lenni Lenape and other Native groups. Brinton, assisted by Lenni Lenape scholars, later published the entire pictography as *The Lenape and Their Legends, with the complete text and symbols of the Walam Olum* in 1885. Today, these documents continue to be studied and are an ongoing controversy. (See also SACRED SCROLLS.)

WALKER, ELKANAH *(1805–1877)* Congregational missionary who established Tshimakain station near present-day Spokane, Washington. Walker was born to Jeremiah and Jane (Marston) Walker on August 7, 1805, in North Yarmouth, Massachusetts. Walker attended the Kimball Union Academy in Plainfield, New Hampshire, from 1832 to 1834 and the Bangor Theological Seminary in Maine from 1834 until his graduation in 1837. After applying to the AMERICAN BOARD OF COMMISSIONERS FOR FOREIGN MISSIONS, Walker received an appointment to join HENRY HARMON SPALDING and Dr. MARCUS WHITMAN at their stations in the Pacific Northwest. He was ordained at the First Congregational Church of Brewer, Maine, on February 14, 1838, and married Mary Richardson on March 5, 1838, before beginning his journey to Oregon Territory. The couple and their colleagues arrived at Waiilatpu station on August 29, 1838, nearly six months later. Walker and CUSHING EELLS, another missionary, were assigned to work among the Spokane people and established their station the following spring. Besides introducing Christianity, they began building, farming, teaching, and studying the Spokane language. Walker completed a primer in 1842, the only book printed in the Spokane language by the American Board missionaries. Tshimakain mission closed, along with the other ABCFM stations in the area, after the Whitmans and others were killed by Cayuse at Waiilatpu in 1847. During Tshimakain's period of operation no Native people became

members of the church established by the missionaries. Walker spent most of his remaining years at Forest Grove, Oregon, where he farmed and preached. He helped establish some of the first churches in the area and served trusteeships at Whitman College and Pacific University. Walker died on November 21, 1877. He and his wife had eight children, most of whom were born at Tshimakain mission.

WALKER, JAMES R. *(1849–1926)* Agency physician on the Pine Ridge Reservation in South Dakota for 18 years who, in the course of studying Lakota religion, became the only white man to be instructed as a shaman by traditional Oglala of the 19th century. Walker, born in 1849 near Richview, Illinois, was 14 when he enlisted as a private in the Union Army on January 29, 1864. After his discharge on August 31, 1865, Walker completed his schooling in Richview and attended Northwestern University Medical School and graduated with a doctor of medicine degree in 1873. He began his work with American Indians by overseeing a Chippewa subagency and serving as physician. Before his reassignment to the Pine Ridge Reservation on July 15, 1896, he also worked at the Colville Agency in Washington State from 1893 to 1896 and for a few months in 1896 at the federal boarding school in Carlisle, Pennsylvania.

At Pine Ridge, he focused his attention on the problem of tuberculosis. Deciding to work with traditional healers rather than against them, Walker began studying their treatment methods and exchanging medical information with them. As a result of this decision, he gained the trust of the Lakota, improved health conditions, and began the anthropological studies he would continue for the rest of his life. Walker's research began in earnest after anthropologist Clark Wissler visited the reservation in 1902 and proposed that he send Lakota material to him for the American Museum of Natural History in New York.

Walker became a medicine man in order to obtain sacred information about Lakota religion. Holy men collectively agreed to instruct him in order that the teachings "might be kept in remembrance and all the world might know of them" but only after agreement on Walker's part to certain conditions. He was required to choose a Buffalo medicine man as a teacher, to follow his instructions, and to pledge his word that he would not divulge sacred teachings until after the holy men had all died. Walker's instructors included influential leaders and shamans such as American Horse, Red Cloud, Bad Wound, No Flesh, Little Wound, Ringing Shield, FINGER, and RED HAWK, with GEORGE SWORD and THOMAS TYON serving as interpreters. Walker published a classic monograph, *The Sun Dance and Other Ceremonies of the Oglala Division of the Teton Dakota,* in 1917, and other writings but was unable to publish most of his primary material because of the secrecy pledge. These documents, dictated or written by Walker's instructors, have only recently become available through the Colorado Historical Society and are the basis for new studies of Lakota religion. After Walker's retirement from the Indian service on May 5, 1914, he retired to a ranch in Colorado. He died in 1926 at age 77.

WAMPUM *Algonquian and Iroquois* The word is shortened from *wampumpeag,* an Algonquian word meaning "strings of white beads." Sacred material of quahog clam shells made into cylindrical purple and white beads about one-half inch long and narrow in diameter was strung on sinews or fiber threads or woven into belts by Algonquian and Iroquois tribes. These tribes traditionally used wampum for decoration, as currency, and in ritual and ceremony. Wampum is used by the Iroquois in their religious and civil ceremonies. During the MIDWINTER CEREMONY, men, women, and children "touch" wampum (hold it in their hands) as they pledge their hearts in a CONFESSION RITE of sins and canceling of grievances. Each longhouse has a strand of shell beads that legitimizes it, comparable to the charter of a congregation. LONGHOUSE WAMPUM is displayed during the recitation of the CODE OF HANDSOME LAKE. The strings of wampum held by Handsome Lake himself as he preached are sacred and kept at the TONAWANDA LONGHOUSE in New York. It is told that they are so sacred that they are used only once every two years and only if the Sun shines and skies are cloudless. Today, wampum strings and belts are still regarded as sacred, and they are part of ceremonies of the Iroquois peoples. Many wampum belts are in U.S. and Canadian museums as well as in museums around the world. The Onondaga, an Iroquois people, have been successful in recovering their sacred wampum belts from the Museum of the State of New York in Albany. (See also ADOPTION STRING; AMERICAN INDIAN RITUAL OBJECT REPATRIATION FOUNDATION CONDOLENCE CEREMONY; REQUICKENING ADDRESS; SHENANDOAH, LEON SIX NATIONS MEETING.)

WANGOMEN (Wangomend) *(l. 1760s–1790s) Munsee* A Munsee prophet who emphasized a return to Native traditions and the relinquishment of European ways. Wangomen informed the Moravian missionary JOHN HECKEWELDER that he did not become a preacher on his own. Instead, he was chosen by the Great Spirit to teach his people, who were on the path to destruction, how to become reconciled to the Creator. The prophet condemned a number of Euro-American practices, including the enslavement of blacks and the use of intoxicating beverages. DAVID ZEISBERGER, another Moravian missionary, encountered Wangomen at Goshgoshing, a Delaware (Lenni Lenape) community located on the upper Allegheny River. According to an account by Heckewelder, the Munsee prophet became Zeisberger's enemy after hearing the missionary preach and finding that his teachings did not agree with his own. Wangomen used an "Indian Bible," or teaching chart, that depicted his religious teachings. This bible, or one similar to it, was described by a 1760 observer, John Hays, who noted its use at Asinsing in New York by an "old Preast," who read from it each day and sang to the rising sun. It is conjectured that Wangomen and the priest are the same person. Believing a conspiracy of witches existed, the Munsee prophet is said to have proposed a witch hunt in 1775, but the Delaware council rejected the plan. Wangomen continued preaching until the 1790s to the dismay of his rival David Zeisberger. Wangomen's name, also cited as Wangomend, is derived from a Delaware word meaning "to greet."

WAR AND SCALP CEREMONIES *Pueblo* War rituals among the Pueblo were concentrated in autumn and early winter. Ceremonies like the Zuni Scalp Ceremony dramatize the arrival of a war party. These and other ceremonies contain themes of symbolic violence or rebellion (mock battles between moieties or some other pair of opposing groups) that are most explicit and prominent during dramas of the winter solstice period. Alfonso Ortiz, Tewa scholar, argues that rituals of violence occurring at the change of seasons are intended for societal and cosmic regeneration and renewal. The acts that accompany the war ceremonies (new songs, distribution of seeds and/or prayersticks, new fire, bathing, games, and initiation rites for dead enemies) are intended to renew and regenerate nature. The rites also cleansed the scalper from danger from the slain enemy. It is believed some of these ceremonies have lapsed. There are organizations of women, such as the Tewa Women's Scalp Association, whose activities are closely connected with men's warrior associations.

WAR CAPTAIN *Keresan* Two living counterparts of the WAR TWINS, Pueblo culture heroes. The war captains bear their names in their official capacities and are selected annually by town chiefs, whom they assist. They are priests as well as chiefs, and they direct, control, and administer most ceremonies and act as executive officers in political affairs of the pueblo. They sanction all pueblo ceremonies, install a new CACIQUE and select his successor, a *gowiye,* and in some pueblos observe the sun to determine times for solstice ceremonies. They guard the pueblos from invasions and witches and guard ceremonials. They preserve and guard tribal traditions and punish pueblo members who transgress. Each war captain has a staff of office, presented annually to war captains by the cacique and returned to him at the end of the year when the term of office ends. The Zuni officials with similar functions to war captains are the BOW PRIESTHOOD.

WAR CEREMONIALS *Navajo (Dineh)* Now believed to be obsolete, these ceremonies were the Enemy Monster Way, sung for a night or two before going to war; the Monster Men Way, a war rite employed on or before an actual raid or war; and the Gesture Dance.

WAR DANCE *Iroquois* A men's dance performed at the MIDWINTER CEREMONY for curative reasons and during the summer for rain. The War Dance, STRIKING-A-STICK DANCE, and EAGLE DANCES form a group that has evolved from ancient war and peace rituals antedating the preaching of HANDSOME LAKE (1800). Possibly of Siouan origin and originally part of a war cycle, the dance addresses the patrons of war, sun, and thunder. The dance is likely to be long because of interruptions, one of its main features. At any hiatus in the dancing, a speech, serious or funny, may be made by anyone taking part. Any song may be interrupted by a male society member when he knocks a cane on the floor, arises to eulogize himself or others, and distributes small gifts to performers. There is a vestige of exploit narration, or boasting, in the speeches.

WAR DANCE *Navajo (Dineh)* A ceremony that takes place in summer and fall whose purpose is to free one from the power of one's enemies. The dance is a cure for all diseases that may have been contracted as a result of war or from seeing dead enemies.

WAR GODS (Ahayu:da) *Zuni* Also called war brothers and twin war gods. Sacred wooden statues placed in shrines that represent the twin brothers, sons of the Sun, who are guardians of the people. They are carved every year in an all-night ceremony at the winter solstice and taken to sacred shrines on mesa altars. The Ahayu:das serve as guardians for the people and land until relieved by new ones. The old ones remain in place until they return to the earth. In the late 19th century, scholars and museum collectors began taking or buying the statues. In 1978, the Zuni began to retrieve the statues, removed from the Zuni Reservation, after finding evidence that a 19th-century surveyor took a war god that ended up in the Denver Art Museum. Zuni Pueblo authorities assert that the war gods are created in a ceremonial process for the use of the entire tribe and that the pueblo owns them. No Zuni has the right to give them away or sell them and no outsider has permission by the tribe to take them. By 1990, the Zuni received 41 statues from 19 institutions and eight private collections, and they began discussions to re-

Zuni war gods. In 1990 the Museum of the American Indian in New York City returned two war gods to the Zuni Pueblo of New Mexico. Bow Priest Perry Tsadiasi carries the sacred objects out of the museum, followed by Head Councilman Barton Martza. *Photograph by T. J. Ferguson, courtesy of Institute of the NorthAmerican West.*

claim every war god image still known to be in an American museum or private collection, 15 in all, in three museums and several private collections. By the summer of 1991, it is believed the Zuni recovered the last of the war gods.

WAR TWINS *Pueblo* A pair of culture heros credited with saving people from monsters. Their names differ from pueblo to pueblo: Hopi—Pookong (elder) and Balonga (younger); Keresan—Masewa (elder) and Oyoyewa (younger); Zuni—Ahayu:da (elder) and Matsailema (younger). They are great hunters and warriors. The father of the twins is the sun, and there are a variety of mothers. They undergo a series of adventures that are somewhat similar from pueblo to pueblo. WAR CAPTAINS stand for these twins in Keresan pueblos today.

WARRIORS SOCIETY DANCES (Opi) *Pueblo* In the past, each pueblo had a warrior society, membership in which resulted from killing an enemy and taking a scalp in a ritual manner. Today, membership continues in these societies, although the original purpose has changed. WAR AND SCALP CEREMONIES still are performed.

WASHANI RELIGION *Columbia Plateau of the Pacific Northwest* *Washani* is a Shahaptian term meaning "dancers," also translated as "worship." A related word is *washat,* or "dance." Accounts vary on the origin and early history of the Washani religion. Some believe that it began with prophets, such as Watilki, a Wasco, while others think that it originated after a devastating epidemic. The anthropologist Leslie Spier theorized the existence of three different phases: an aboriginal version, a Christianized variation, and a revival by SMOHALLA and other dreamer-prophets. The dreamer-prophets had experienced a temporary death or vision, a visit to the spirit world and a return to earth with a message from the Creator. Some of the early religious leaders foretold the arrival of the Europeans, their articles and goods, and their treatment of Native people. They also pointed to natural signs, including earthquakes, to prophesy the end of the world. The prophets then taught the people how to prepare for the ensuing renewal of the world.

Smohalla, one of the prophets who later revitalized the Washani religion, advised his followers to return to Native traditions and to relinquish the ways of the intruders. He used flags and bells in his services and taught that Native people would arise from the earth on feathers after the world was returned to them. His beliefs were manifested in dances, including the WASHAT DANCE (RELIGION), ceremonies, and observances. The number seven was symbolized by Smohalla in a number of ways, including the star emblem of his shirt. There were also seven drummers in his ceremonies and seven women in each group who prepared the foods for the Feast of the New Food. Because religious services were held in longhouses, the Washani came to be called the Longhouse religion. It continues in the modern-day with a large array of ceremonies, including namings, weddings, feasts, memorials, and calendric observances or rituals. Other names include Seven Drum Religion and Indian Religion. An equivalent Chinook jargon term is *bum-bum,* also *pom-pom* in part of the region, which is derived from the tambourine used in the religion. Another name associated with the Washani is the PROPHET DANCE. It was coined by Spier, who believed that its practices were grafted onto the older medicine religion. Tribal groups identified with the beliefs include Cayuse, Klickitat, Nez Perce, Northern Paiute (Numu), Palouse, Sinkiuse, Tenino, Umatilla, Wallawalla, Wanapam, Wishram, and Yakama. The representation extended beyond the Shahaptian linguistic family; therefore, still other names are associated with the religion.

WASHAT DANCE (RELIGION) *Columbia Plateau of the Pacific Northwest* *Washat* is a Shahaptian term meaning "dance," and it is also translated as "worship." It has been described among the Wanapam people as the sacred dance revived by the prophet of the WASHANI RELIGION, SMOHALLA. Reintroducing it to the people at a longhouse on the Columbia River, he taught that it would restore the country and its belongings to them. Smohalla further taught that those who continued the purity of the people and their traditions would attain eternal peace and happiness. According to his teachings, the sacred song of the Washat Dance was to be sung every seventh day. Male and female participants were given eagle or swan feathers that were to help them rise up when the world turned. The Washat Dance also included seven drummers, sacred symbols, and feasts of salmon and other traditional foods. The Washat Dance includes a large complex of ceremonial activities related to rites of passage and calendar rituals. Practiced by the Yakama and other Native groups in the region, it continues in the present day.

WASHBURN, CEPHAS *(1793–1860)* Congregational missionary to the Cherokee people. Washburn, a native of Randolph, Vermont, attended the University of Vermont. He began his work among the Cherokee in 1819 at Brainerd Mission in Tennessee under the auspices of the AMERICAN BOARD OF COMMISSIONERS FOR FOREIGN MISSIONS (ABCFM). Washburn then devoted his efforts to the group of Cherokee people who had consented to move to Arkansas two years before, working with his sister Susanna and his missionary brother-in-law Alfred Finney on this endeavor. He and Finney traveled to the new location of this group in 1820 and arranged to establish a mission station there. After their transfer to the area the following year, they began the work of establishing Dwight Mission. The school and other programs of the missionary eventually grew, becoming influential in spreading Christianity and requiring a larger number of staff members. During the removal of Cherokee from their southeastern homeland, Dwight Mission became the base of missionary activities until other stations were established. Washburn wrote *Reminiscences of the Indians,* which was published in 1869.

WASHINGTON, JOE *(c. 1875–?) Delaware (Lenni Lenape)* A ROADMAN among the Eastern Delaware in Oklahoma whose faith in the PEYOTE RELIGION began when he was a child. In 1884, at the age of nine, Washington recovered from an illness during a meeting conducted for him by peyotists. Other family members also influenced his beliefs, including his uncle ELK HAIR, who was probably the earliest Eastern Delaware peyote leader. About 1885, while on a visit to the Delaware (Lenni Lenape) band near Anadarko, Elk Hair and other tribal members learned of the existence of the form of peyotism introduced by JOHN WILSON but rejected it because it incorporated elements of Christianity. Washington's creed, revealed to an ethnologist about 1929 or 1930, included his belief that peyote was to be used in the right way with one's mind on God and not for visions or for the wrong purpose. As an adherent of the traditional Delaware faith as well as peyotism, he emphasized the importance of continuing the BIG HOUSE CEREMONY of his people. Washington believed that different forms of worship were given to each group of people by God, all good in themselves, but that they should not be mixed.

WASHINGTON, MRS. *(fl. 1890s) Pawnee* A visionary who introduced new developments in the practice of the GHOST DANCE OF 1890 among the Pawnee. Initially Ghost Dances were introduced and led by the prophet FRANK WHITE among this tribal group, but a shift occurred in the religious movement away from domination by a single leader. Mrs. Washington inaugurated independent dances among the Skiri band of her people. Similar to other Ghost Dance participants, she experienced trances during performances of the dance. Washington had numerous visions of great complexity while in a trance state and received sacred knowledge at such times. Her visionary teachings were manifested in ritual changes and new developments, including the establishment of the Seven Eagle Brothers of the Skiri Ghost Dance, an organization of singers, in 1892 or 1893. (See also GHOST DANCE HAND GAME; GOODEAGLE, MRS; and RUDDER, MARK.)

WASHINGTON, WILLIAM (Pambiduwi:ji, "Long-Haired Young Man") *Shoshone* A prominent Ghost Dance leader on the Wind River Reservation in Wyoming. He was identified as leading the sacred ceremony later than WHITE COLT, a medicine man who lived from 1853 to 1936. Washington was in turn followed by a religious leader named John Dick. Other adherents to the Ghost Dance on the Wind River Reservation included EMILY HILL, TUDY ROBERTS, and NADZAIP ROGERS.

WASITECK See ABISHABIS

WATER DRUM A small drum, five to six inches in diameter, that accompanies dance rituals in a number of tribal groups. Its body is made of sections of wood fitted tightly together with a disc bottom and a stretched skin head that covers the top. The drum, watertight, holds a small amount of water. A stick bounced on the skin head produces a musical tone that accompanies the voices of singers. The DRUM, a spiritual entity, is treated with great respect.

WATERBUSTER (MIDIPADI) CLAN BUNDLE *Hidatsa* Sacred bundle believed to have originated as a gift from a supernatural being who had joined the human race. Passed down through generations of keepers, ownership had to be ritually purchased by a member of the Midipadi clan. Generally, a transfer took place after a keeper became elderly and could no longer carry out the responsibilities associated with it. One of its keepers, MISSOURI RIVER, used the bundle for guidance in planning Like-a-Fishhook village, where the people had journeyed after their former villages at the mouth of the Knife River were struck by smallpox in 1837. Before his death, Missouri River sold the privilege of being a keeper to SMALL ANKLE. As the keeper, Small Ankle's lodge was treated with particular respect because it housed the Maaduush, sacred objects of the bundle, stored in a wooden shrine. "The two skulls of the Big Birds' Ceremony made our lodge a sacred one, and we were not permitted to lounge or sport on the roof," his grandson, EDWARD GOODBIRD, wrote. When Small Ankle died in 1888, no member of the Midipadi clan had purchased the bundle. By then, the government agent outlawed traditional religious practices, and missionaries encouraged the destruction of sacred objects. After Small Ankle's wife died in 1901, their son, Wolf Chief, became responsible for the bundle. But as Wolf Chief was a Prairie Chicken, not Midipadi, clan member and descent was matrilineal, he therefore could not be a keeper. Furthermore, he had converted to Christianity. Despite his conversion, he could not bring himself to destroy a bundle of such sacredness to his family and tribe. In 1907 he agreed to sell it, with its stories and instructions, to the anthropologist Gilbert L. Wilson. Wilson, in turn, was collecting it for George Heye, founder of the Museum of the American Indian in New York City. The sale prompted a controversy because the bundle was the property of the Midipadi clan, not an individual, and its members were outraged. During the furor, Wilson's permit to enter the Fort Berthold Reservation in North Dakota was suspended. After Wolf Chief's death in 1934, the Midipadi clan petitioned the Museum of the American Indian to return their sacred bundle. In 1938 it was reluctantly returned, one of the first successful repatriations of Indian sacred objects. (See also MEDICINE BUNDLE, REPATRIATION.)

WATERS, GEORGE *(?–1923) Klickitat* Methodist minister and chief. Waters, the brother of Chief White Swan, attended the JASON LEE Missionary School located near Salem, Oregon. After his ordination in Portland in 1871, he served as a teacher and missionary. He taught in a boarding school on the Yakima Reservation in Washington and later built a church a few miles from Lapwai Agency in Idaho. Waters was also named an elder in the Methodist Church in Moscow, Idaho. After returning to the Yakima Reservation, he won an election to the office of chief in 1910. He remained in the position until his death in 1923. (See also WILBUR, JAMES H.)

WATKINS, EDWIN ARTHUR *(?–1881)* Church of England missionary whose Canadian mission stations included Ft. George on Hudson Bay (1856), Red River (1856–1860), and Cumberland (1860–1863). He also served at Portage la Prairie near Winnipeg after the death of Archdeacon Cochrane, his father-in-law, in 1866. Watkins worked on Cree translations, including the Gospels of John and Luke (1855), and compiled *A Dictionary of the Cree Language* (1865). Watkins died at Portage la Prairie, Manitoba, in 1881.

WEBBER, JAMES C. *(c. 1880–?) Delaware (Lenni Lenape)* A PEYOTE leader who was from the Eastern Delaware band in Dewey, Oklahoma. Although he had at first opposed the use of peyote as a religion or as a medicine, Webber was persuaded to attend a service during a long period of ill health. After participating in several meetings, he recovered from his illness and changed his mind about the practice. Webber used peyote for several years and eventually joined a Little Moon, or Half-Moon, peyote organization among the Shawnee people of White Oak Hills. He preferred the original version of the PEYOTE RELIGION rather than the variation proposed by JOHN WILSON, with its Christian features.

WESAW, TOM AND GEORGE *(fl. 20th century) Shoshone* Medicine men, SUN DANCE leaders, and PEYOTE roadmen from the Wind River Reservation in Wyoming. Tom Wesaw and his son George also became noted for their skill in using the traditional bone sucking technique with patients. After marrying, George moved to the Fort Hall Reservation in Idaho. He is active as a ROADMAN, traveling to meetings in other areas as well as carrying on religious work at home. (See also TUBE-SUCKING SHAMAN.)

WEST, EMILY J. *(1810–1899)* Episcopal missionary to the Dakota people in Minnesota Territory and Santee, Nebraska. West moved to the Minnesota area in 1856 to work in the mission field. In the fall of 1860 she began a missionary assignment at Redwood Agency, remaining there until fleeing to Fort Ridgely when the Dakota conflict of 1862 broke out. West subsequently worked at Santee Agency until

about 1878. She died on November 1, 1899, at her home near Herrick, Nebraska.

WEST, JOHN *(1778–1845)* Church of England priest who was the first Protestant missionary to the Red River Settlement at Fort Garry (Winnipeg). He was born in Farnham, Surrey, England, to Ann Knowles and George West, an Anglican clergyman, in November 1778. West became a deacon in 1804, was ordained two years later, and graduated with an M.A. from St. Edmund Hall, Oxford, in 1809. After his ordination, he was associated with curacies in Essex, where he became acquainted with the Reverend Henry Budd, a rector. West was appointed Hudson's Bay Company chaplain in 1819 and left England the following year. By the time he reached the Red River Settlement, he had recruited two young Cree children, including one he christened HENRY BUDD, for schooling. Working as Hudson's Bay Company chaplain and as a representative of the CHURCH MISSIONARY SOCIETY, he ministered to both Native and non-Native people. His emphasis was upon establishing an Indian mission school and extending his ministry to areas beyond Red River. He traveled to Brandon House, Fort Qu'Appelle (Saskatchewan), York Factory (Manitoba), and as far north as present-day Churchill, Manitoba. Intending to return to the Red River Settlement, West went back to England in 1823. He never returned, however, because his employment in Rupert's Land was terminated. Conflicts over the duties of his role as company chaplain and as a representative of the Church Missionary Society may have contributed to the decision to end his appointment in the area. His refusal to adapt his religious practices to the society at Red River also met with disfavor. West's successors in the area included DAVID THOMAS JONES and WILLIAM COCKRAN, who continued the missionary work he had started. West wrote *The Substance of a journal during a residence at the Red River colony, British North America; and frequent excursions among the north-west American Indians, in the years 1820, 1821, 1822, 1823* (1824). A second edition included *A journal of a mission to the Indians of the British provinces, of New Brunswick, and Nova Scotia, and the Mohawks, on the Ouse, or Grand River, Upper Canada* (1827). West died in Chettle, England, in 1845.

WHALE FEAST *Alaska Inuit* The principal ceremonial of Alaska Arctic Inuit owing to the importance of whaling among coastal peoples. The ceremonial activities included women preparing new clothes and new umiak (kayak) covers, a four-day period of taboos and restrictions in the ceremonial structure, the *KARIGI*, personal and group taboos on the water, and the use of numerous personal whaling objects necessary for success of the whaling expedition. The feast also included singing of songs during all stages of whaling, the ceremonial greeting of the beached whale, distribution of meat, a feast provided by the captain, a series of dances involving the entire community, masked dancing by men of the crew, and feasting in the *karigi* and outdoors. These activities were based on the belief that the whale allowed itself to be taken but had to be placated with proper treatment and the right kind of taboos. Whaling terminated in the spring with a festival marked by feasting and social events and competitive games.

WHALING RITUALS *Nootka* The Nootka have a variety of rituals associated with whaling. The chief undergoes rigorous ritual cleansing (fasting, bathing, and continence), construction of a shrine and nightly praying and chanting. The chief possesses a ritual that causes dead whales to drift ashore in the group's territory. From the beginning of the hunt, the whales are ritually treated. The harpooner and crew bathe, and the whaler's wife lies quietly on her bed. After the whale is brought in, a rite is performed over the "saddle," the strip of blubber over the back, in front of and behind the fin. It is cut off and carried to the whaler's house, adorned with cedar bark and feathers, and songs are sung in its honor. The saddle is cut into strips, and a feast is held that requires that all of the strips must be eaten in the whaler's house.

WHEELOCK, ELEAZAR *(1711–1779)* Minister of the second Congregational church in Lebanon, Connecticut, who founded Moor's Charity School for Indians in 1754 and Dartmouth College in 1769. Born on April 22, 1711, in Windham, Connecticut, Wheelock was educated at Yale College and graduated from there in 1733. He took up his ministerial position in 1735 and supported revival efforts of the Great Awakening of the 1740s. In addition to his parish duties, Wheelock tutored boys preparing for college, and in 1743 he began instructing SAMSON OCCOM of the Mohegan Nation, his first Indian student. From this experience, he expanded his work with Indians by establishing Moor's Charity School, named after benefactor Joshua Moor, in Lebanon, Connecticut. His educational plan included removing Native children from the "pernicious Influence of their Parents Example" and teaching them Christian civility. Although many of these children came from the New England tribes, the majority were Iroquois. About 67 Native students, generally between 11 and 14 years of age, attended the school before its move to Hanover, New Hampshire, in 1770. Wheelock became disillusioned with his inability to transform Indian children into Englishmen and -women and turned his attention to another project after Samson Occom and the Reverend Nathaniel Whitaker returned from a fund-raising tour for his Indian work with more than £12,000 in 1767. He used the money to found

Dartmouth College in Hanover, New Hampshire, for young Englishmen. Although Wheelock moved Moor's Charity School there, the school was overshadowed by his new project and finally closed in 1829. His shift to educating young Englishmen with funds raised for Indians caused a permanent rift with his "black son," Samson Occom, who stated: "I am very jealous that instead of your Semenary Becoming alma Mater, she will be too alba mater [white mother] to Suckle the Tawnees . . ." Wheelock became the first president of Dartmouth College and held that position until the end of his life.

WHEELWRIGHT MUSEUM Museum in Santa Fe, New Mexico. Formerly called the Museum of Navajo Ceremonial Art, the museum was founded in 1937, financed by the scholar Mary Cabot Wheelwright. She was permitted by the Navajo (Dineh) singer HOSTEEN KLAH to record many of his songs, and eventually, at Klah's urging, she agreed to erect a museum that would preserve his medicine knowledge and all the sacred objects of his ceremonial system. Klah mastered tapestry weaving, and he executed SANDPAINTING designs in tapestry, now housed at the Wheelwright museum as well.

WHIPPLE, HENRY BENJAMIN *(1822–1901)* First Episcopal bishop of Minnesota; noted for his missionary work among the Ojibway and Dakota in the region and for his advocacy of national Indian policy reform. Born in 1822 in Adams, New York, he attended local Presbyterian schools, then Oberlin Collegiate Institute in 1838 and 1839. Before studying for the ministry, Whipple joined his father's business, served as a school inspector and participated in Democratic state politics. Despite his Presbyterian upbringing, he leaned toward the Protestant Episcopal faith of his grandparents. After studying under the Reverend William D. Wilson of Christ Church in Sherburne, New York, Whipple was ordained an Episcopal priest in 1850. Following parish work in Rome, New York; Saint Augustine, Florida; and Chicago, Illinois, he was elected first Episcopal bishop of Minnesota in 1859. The following year he settled in Faribault with his family and resided there for the rest of his life. A few weeks after his arrival in Minnesota, Whipple visited Ojibway communities and began his work in the Indian mission field. He was assisted by Episcopal clergymen such as JAMES LLOYD BRECK, E. S. Peake, Joseph Alexander Gilfillan, and especially ENMEGAHBOWH, the Ojibway-Ottawa missionary upon whom his Ojibway mission work most depended.

Whipple began to appeal to state and national politicians to reform the Bureau of Indian Affairs after observing tragic conditions of near-starvation and government fraud in tribal communities. In 1860 he warned President James Buchanan that the circumstances among the Eastern Dakota could lead to an outbreak of war, an event that occurred two years later. The Dakota War of 1862, generally called the Sioux Uprising of 1862, was precipitated by factors arising out of the Dakota people's reduced land base, the failure of the government to honor treaty commitments, corrupt agents and traders, and conditions of poverty and illness. Under the leadership of Little Crow and other tribal leaders, raids were conducted against white settlers in the region that resulted in military reprisals against the Eastern, or Santee, Dakota. Besides ministering to the wounded and bereaved, Whipple appealed to President Abraham Lincoln for assistance. After more than 300 Dakota men had been condemned to die on war charges by a military tribunal, Lincoln reviewed the trial records and eventually signed death warrants for 39 men. Following the last-minute reprieve of one man, 38 Dakota were hanged at Mankato, Minnesota, on December 26, 1862, the largest mass execution in United States history.

The events surrounding the war in Minnesota, the work of establishing extensive missions and schools aimed at Christianizing and "civilizing" Native people, and visits to Civil War battlefields took a toll on Whipple's health. He went to Europe from 1864 to 1865 to recover, and the excursion became the first of many trips there to win support for his work. Upon his return, Whipple continued to press for Indian policy reforms, advocating individually owned lands with inalienable titles, adequate schools, improvement of the reservation system, and inspection of government agencies and personnel. As Whipple aged, his fame grew. In 1871 he was offered the bishopric of the Sandwich Islands by the archbishop of Canterbury, was presented to Queen Victoria in 1890, and attended an international conference as presiding bishop of the American church. In addition to his numerous other writings, his autobiography, *Lights and Shadows of a Long Episcopate,* was published in 1899 and reprinted several times. "Straight Tongue," as Whipple was called by the Indians, died on September 16, 1901, in Faribault.

WHITE, ANDREW *(1579–1656)* English Jesuit missionary. Born in England, he entered the Jesuit novitiate in 1607 at the age of 28. His ultraconservatism led his superiors to relieve him of his duties, and in late 1633, he sailed for the Maryland colony. He began missionary work with Indians in 1639. Living first with the Patuxent and then among the Piscataway, he introduced the gospel. He wrote a dictionary and grammar of the local Algonquian dialect and translated a catechism into that language as well. Within a year, he baptized Chitomachen, a Piscataway chief. His work angered Puritan Virginians who captured him and sent him back to England in 1645. His superiors did not wish him to return to missionary work.

WHITE, ELIJAH *(1806–1879)* A Methodist missionary-physician. White, a native of New York State, attended medical school in Syracuse. In 1836 he received an appointment from the Methodist denomination to serve as a physician to its missions in Oregon Territory. His missionary group arrived in the region the following year, supplementing the efforts of the Reverend JASON LEE. Following conflicts with Lee, White left his post in 1841. Shortly after returning to the East he was named to a position as Indian subagent with responsibility for the region west of the Rocky Mountains. He led a group of immigrants to Oregon Territory in 1842 and began his work as agent. During his tenure his efforts included drafting laws for the Nez Perce people and dealing with Indian reactions to encroachment on their lands and way of life. White also participated in the organization of the territorial government. He left the region in 1845 but returned a few years later to promote a new settlement. Although he received another appointment as Indian agent in 1861, he did not remain in the position for long. White later worked as a physician in California and died there in 1879.

WHITE, FRANK *(?–1893) Pawnee* Prophet of the GHOST DANCE OF 1890 who was a member of the Kitkahaxki band of his people. During visits to the Comanche and Wichita sometime after the fall of 1890, White used PEYOTE and also learned the doctrines of SITTING BULL, the Arapaho Ghost Dance leader. He returned home in the fall of the following year and began introducing the teachings among the South bands of the Pawnee. He taught Ghost Dance songs to singers and formed a group of seven leaders, giving them crow feathers to wear. Participants who wanted their faces painted before a dance would go to the sacred tipi of these leaders and have it done by the prophet in exchange for gifts. Initially White controlled the doctrine and interpretation of the dance among the Pawnee. Later a shift occurred, and any individual who had experienced trances could lead and teach. When agency officials learned of the Ghost Dance activities, White was told to leave the reservation. A large council of Native people was also warned that the dancing could not continue. When the Ghost Dance persisted, White was arrested and incarcerated. During that time Pawnee adherents were told that they could continue dancing if they agreed to take individual land allotments. White was released after about 12 days and returned home. He died in 1893.

WHITE BUFFALO CALF WOMAN (Ptehincalasanwin, White Buffalo Calf Maiden, White Buffalo Cow Woman, White Buffalo Woman) *Lakota* The holy woman who brought the Lakota people their most sacred possession, the BUFFALO CALF PIPE, and foretold the SEVEN SACRED RITES OF THE LAKOTA. According to belief, White Buffalo Calf

Woman first appeared to two young men who were out hunting. As they stopped to scan the area for game, they saw someone approaching in the distance. When the mysterious person drew nearer, they saw a woman of great beauty clothed in white buckskin. One of the young men expressed bad thoughts toward her, but his companion warned him that she was most likely *wakan,* or sacred. When the mysterious woman reached the hunters, she called to the one with evil intentions. After approaching her, they were both enveloped by a cloud. When it lifted, all that remained of the man were his bones and the snakes that had eaten him. The mysterious woman then told the other hunter to return home and tell his chief, named Standing Hollow Horn in the account given by BLACK ELK, to prepare for her arrival. Upon reaching the camp, the young man related all that had happened. As instructed, a large tipi was built, and the people gathered together. They then waited for the mysterious person to arrive. Soon some of the people saw the holy woman approaching in the distance. After entering the tipi, she walked in a sunrise (clockwise) direction then stopped before the leader. The holy woman took a bundle from her back, removing a pipe and a round stone.

She then gave the people sacred teachings. Beginning with the pipe, she explained its meaning and each of its components. She told the people that the pipestone bowl represented the earth, that the wood stem represented all of the earth's growing things, that a buffalo calf carved on the bowl represented all four-legged creatures, and that the pipe's 12 feathers, from the spotted eagle, represented all winged creatures. Whoever prayed with it would be joined to all other life in the universe. The holy woman also instructed the people about the stone, explaining that the seven circles on it stood for the seven sacred rites. She presented the first rite, stating that the other six would be revealed in time and that the SACRED PIPE was to be used in each of them.

After teaching the GHOST KEEPING CEREMONY, the first rite, the holy woman walked in a sunwise (clockwise) direction around the tipi, then left. While walking away, she stopped and sat down. When she stood up, the people saw that she had been transformed into a red and brown buffalo calf. The calf continued on, stopped, lay down and arose as a white buffalo. The white buffalo repeated the same actions, becoming a black buffalo. This buffalo bowed to each quarter of the universe and then vanished from view. There are several published accounts of White Buffalo Calf Woman, some including her other sacred teachings. She is also known as White Buffalo Calf Maiden, White Buffalo Cow Woman, and White Buffalo Woman.

WHITE BULL (Ice or Hail) *(c. 1837–1921) Cheyenne* Venerated holy man who also served as a warrior, chief, and scout during his lifetime. His father, North Left Hand, was said to have been banished for four years after being accused of murder by Cheyenne warrior society leaders. During his period of exile, North Left Hand joined the Apache and later the Arapaho people, marrying among each group. White Bull, identified as the son of North Left Hand and his Arapaho wife, eventually returned to the Cheyenne people. During his early years he was known as Ice, a name attributed to his grandfather as well as to his own ice-producing spiritual powers. At the age of 15 he fasted and prayed in the hills, receiving blessings from the spirits. He held membership in the Crazy Dog Society of his people but was expelled in 1858. The action was taken, not for something he had done, but because of an incident involving one of his relatives. He then joined the Elkhorn Scraper Society, maintaining that membership during his tenure as a warrior. In about 1860 the holy man made a war bonnet for the Cheyenne leader Roman Nose to protect him from bullets. A few years later, in 1867, he followed spiritual instructions to have himself buried in a pit with a large rock blocking the entrance. His escape became known as "Ice's miracle," and he received the name White Bull a short time later.

White Bull was among those in attendance at the Lakota SUN DANCE at which SITTING BULL, the Hunkpapa holy man, received his vision foretelling the Battle of the Little Bighorn. White Bull's only son, Noisy Walking, and other youths vowed a Suicide Warriors Dance, or Dying Dance, before the fight against the enemy. These young Cheyenne and Lakota warriors all died in the battle or its aftermath, sacrificing their lives for their people as they had pledged. White Bull survived the 1876 battle and became a scout the following year. His decision was attributed in part to sorrow over his son's death. The holy man became the first Cheyenne scout under the command of General Nelson A. Miles. White Bull's scouting duties included accompanying Miles against Lame Deer and his Minneconjou Lakota band in May of 1877.

In his later years, White Bull again demonstrated his spiritual powers. In 1908, during the Sun Dance, he produced hailstones to assist a participant who had collapsed. White Bull, greatly respected as a healer as well as a holy man, died on July 10, 1921.

WHITE COLT (Tosa Buŋkutua) *(1853–1936) Shoshone* A medicine man and Ghost Dance leader on the Wind River Reservation in Wyoming. White Colt is said to have experienced many trances, returning from the spirit world with teachings. One message he received was that the dead could not see the face of God until the arrival of Our Brother, or Jesus, among them. He also learned the Ghost Dances from the deceased, sponsoring them at Fort Washakie. It is believed that the sacred ceremony existed among the Shoshone people before White Colt's time. Other adherents to the Ghost Dance on the Wind River Reservation included EMILY HILL, TUDY ROBERTS, NADZAIP ROGERS, and WILLIAM WASHINGTON.

WHITE DEERSKIN DANCE *Northwest California (Hupa, Karok, Yurok)* Usually held in autumn, this ritual dance, part of a public ceremonial held during the WORLD RENEWAL CEREMONIAL CYCLE, aims to spiritually re-create and harmonize the individual, family, tribe, environment, and universe. People pray for bountiful fish runs and plentiful game, give thanks for food, and express gratitude to the Creator for sharing earthly resources. In a ceremony lasting 10 to 16 days, men wearing skins of albino or light-colored deer and hooked headbands and carrying long obsidian blades dance at ritually prescribed spots over the dance period. The dance gives the owners of the regalia, regarded as treasures, an opportunity to display their wealth in public. The type of hook demonstrated the wealth of the owner. Antler tips were of low value, undecorated sea lion teeth of moderate value, and painted and incised sea lion teeth of high value. The decorated deerskins were tribal property held in trust by the dancers. The dance required community cooperation: The women prepared food for the feast; spiritual leaders prepared the dance grounds; men prepared as dancers and singers. A vast amount of regalia had to be borrowed from tribal members and assembled for the dancers.

WHITE PAINTED WOMAN (Changing Woman, White Painted Woman) *Apache* Also called Changing Woman and White Shell Woman, White Painted Woman has existed from creation. She is an important and kindly deity that has control over fertility and the fruition of plants. She is represented in the GIRL'S PUBERTY RITE, an elaborate Apache ceremony.

WHITE THUNDER (Gray Thunder or Painted Thunder) *(c. 1763–1838) Cheyenne.* Keeper of the SACRED ARROWS. During White Thunder's tenure in the keepership, one of the greatest spiritual catastrophes occurred among the Cheyenne. The Sacred Arrows were captured by their enemies, the Pawnee, in an 1830 battle. This sorrowful event unleashed a long period of devastating misfortunes in the lives of the people. Although new arrows were made by BOX ELDER and CRAZY MULE under the guidance of the keeper, the Cheyenne continued to be affected by the loss. In 1835 White Thunder traveled with his pipe, without weapons, to the Skidi Pawnee. He and other Cheyenne met with Big Spotted Horse (also Big Eagle), the Pawnee chief who carried off the Sacred Arrows after their capture. During the visit, they succeeded in recovering one of the original arrows.

In 1837 White Thunder suffered an attack at the hands of Cheyenne Bowstrings, or Wolf Soldiers. As the renewing ceremonies of the Sacred Arrows had been pledged, the warriors could not leave on war parties until the ceremonies had been conducted. The Bowstrings had become impatient, insisting that the observances be held right away. When White Thunder quietly urged patience and turned down their demands, the warriors hit him with their quirts. The holy man agreed to hold the ceremonies but warned his attackers that they would suffer misfortune. A short time later, about 42 of the Bowstrings were killed in an encounter with the Kiowa and Comanche.

White Thunder, who died in 1838, is identified as the only keeper of the Sacred Arrows to be killed by enemies of his people. His death during a Cheyenne battle against the Kiowa and Comanche was attributed to the misfortunes resulting from the capture of the arrows. The holy man's family included his wife, Tail Woman, and his son-in-law, William Bent, who founded Bent's Fort. White Thunder did not leave a successor to become the new keeper. His name has also been translated as "thunder painted with white clay."

WHITEHORN V. STATE OF OKLAHOMA (561 P.2d 539 [1977]) *(1977)* In this case George L. Whitehorn was stopped by the authorities in Enid, Oklahoma, on January 5, 1975, because he did not have a valid automobile safety inspection sticker. As his driver's license had been suspended, the defendant was arrested and his vehicle impounded. PEYOTE was found during the arrest and he was charged with possessing a controlled dangerous substance. Whitehorn stated that he was a member of the NATIVE AMERICAN CHURCH (NAC) and that he had acquired a peyote necklace from his father, who had handed the sacred object down to him. Despite the presence of witnesses who testified in his defense, he was found guilty. The verdict, a two-year suspended sentence, was appealed and the Oklahoma Court of Criminal Appeals reversed the conviction after a determination was made that the defendant was in fact a member of the Native American Church and that the peyote was not possessed or used in a manner dangerous to the public. Citing *STATE OF ARIZONA V. JANICE AND FRED WHITTINGHAM* and *PEOPLE V. WOODY*, the appellate court ruled that the state possessed no compelling interest to prohibit the use of peyote by members of the Native American Church. It also held that peyotists did not have to prove official church membership to be immune from prosecution. The court concluded that as the state could not require rosters for any church, only a good faith showing by people of the legitimacy of their church affiliation was necessary. It stated:

> We wish to make it abundantly clear that we do not hold today that all members of [NAC] must . . . carry certificates of membership; we do hold that unless or until such time the legislature acts to exempt and provide for the administration of such exemption the question of membership in the Native American Church is for the trier of fact.

This decision has resulted in a case-by-case handling of the issue of the religious use of peyote. (See also PEYOTE RELIGION and the Subject Index for related cases included in this volume.)

WHITESHIELD, HARVEY (Hishkowits, "Porcupine") *(1867–?)* *Cheyenne* A Southern Cheyenne interpreter and teacher who was born in Indian Territory in 1867. The eldest son of Chief Whiteshield, he was educated at agency schools for five years before enrolling at the Carlisle Indian Industrial School in Carlisle, Pensylvania, in 1881. He later attended other schools in Indiana at Fort Wayne and Hanover and in Kansas at Lawrence. He began serving as an assistant teacher at the Mennonite mission school in Cantonment, Oklahoma, in 1893 and held the position for four years. Whiteshield also served as an interpreter at the mission and as the chief assistant to the Reverend RODOLPHE CHARLES PETTER, the Mennonite missionary who became an authority on the Cheyenne language.

WHITMAN, MARCUS *(1802–1847)* Presbyterian missionary-physician who established the Cayuse mission at Waiilatpu near Fort Walla Walla in the Pacific Northwest. Whitman, one of five children of Beza and Alice Whitman, was born on September 4, 1802, in Rushville, New York. When he was eight years old, his father died and he was sent to live with relatives in Cummington, Massachusetts. Whitman remained in that area for 10 years and at the age of 17 came under the influence of the Reverend Moses Hallock, a minister in Plainfield. A short time later, he returned to Rushville and began studying medicine under a physician, Dr. Ira Bryant. In 1825 and 1826 he attended the College of Physicians and Surgeons of the Western District of New York in Fairfield, then practiced medicine in Gainsboro, Canada, for several years. Whitman, who went back to Rushville in the fall of 1830 and began studying theology, returned to medical school in the fall of 1831 and graduated the following spring. He then served as a physician in Wheeler, New York, before becoming a missionary.

In 1834 Whitman applied for a position with the AMERICAN BOARD OF COMMISSIONERS FOR FOREIGN MISSIONS (ABCFM) but was turned down because of his health. It was not until the following year that he convinced the board to appoint him to the mission field. He traveled with another missionary, the Reverend Samuel Parker, on an expedition to present-day Idaho and Montana. After returning to the East, he worked on preparations to establish missions in the region. He also married Narcissa Prentiss (see below) a fellow Presbyterian, in 1836. The couple traveled westward with the missionary HENRY HARMON SPALDING and his wife, ELIZA HART SPALDING. During their pioneering journey, undertaken with the protection of the American Fur Company and the Hudson's Bay Company, the women became the first white females to cross the Rocky Mountains. After six and a half months of traveling nearly 4,000 miles, the missionaries arrived at their destination.

They began the work of establishing missions in the region, constructing buildings and providing religious and educational services. The Whitmans settled at Waiilatpu among the Cayuse, coming in contact with the Nez Perce and other neighboring tribal groups. Whitman also provided medical treatment to Native people, to the other missionaries, and to the growing number of Euro-Americans in the region.

In 1842 Whitman journeyed to Boston to voice opposition to a decision of his mission board to close Waiilatpu and other stations. Although the ABCFM had reconsidered and the posts remained open, more serious problems emerged. The couple remained at Waiilatpu, where they were blamed by Indians for the influx of whites to the region and for the arrival of a devastating measles epidemic. The physician's efforts to treat the Indians, who had no immunity to the disease, were ineffective and considered suspect. On November 29, 1847, a group of Cayuse raided the mission and killed 14 whites, including Marcus and NARCISSA PRENTISS WHITMAN. In the aftermath of the killing, the ABCFM missions in the region were closed and war was waged against the Cayuse by Euro-American settlers.

WHITMAN, NARCISSA PRENTISS *(1808–1847)* Presbyterian missionary who was one of the first white women to cross the Rocky Mountains. Born in Prattsburg, New York on March 14, 1808, Whitman taught in a district school there before going to the Far West. In 1834 her application for missionary work was rejected because of a policy against sending unmarried women to distant mission stations. It was only through her marriage to MARCUS WHITMAN in 1836 that she was able to work in the field under the auspices of the AMERICAN BOARD OF COMMISSIONERS FOR FOREIGN MISSIONS (ABCFM). She helped her husband establish the Cayuse mission Waiilatpu in Oregon Territory, which became one of the area's largest. Her work included supervising Waiilatpu's domestic affairs and conducting a school. Misfortunes and disappointments, including the accidental drowning of a two-year-old daughter in 1839, failing eyesight, and Native resistance to the gospel she preached, gradually diminished her enthusiasm for the work. Narcissa, her husband, and 12 other people were killed at Waiilatpu on November 29, 1847, by a group of Cayuse who retaliated against them for the increasing number of whites in the area and for failing to stem a measles epidemic.

WILATSI (*f. 19th century*) *Umatilla* A dreamer-prophet who lived during the time of the religious leader SMOHALLA and followed some of the same beliefs. Wilatsi lived on McKay Creek in Oregon. Like Smoholla, he was said to have been to the spirit world and have returned with sacred songs and teachings. He held fast to Native traditions, including a first foods feast that had to be held before food roots could be consumed in the spring. At his Sunday observances the people prayed and sang but did not dance. Walatsi was described as a stricter religious leader than LULS, an Umatilla prophet who practiced after him. The prophet's name also appears as Wiletsi.

WILBUR, JAMES H. (*1811–1887*) Methodist missionary-agent on the Yakima Reservation. Wilbur was born to Presbyterian parents in New York State on September 11, 1811. At the age of 29 he began serving as an exhorter and received his license as a Methodist minister two years later. In 1846 he was appointed to the Oregon mission, eventually building the first church in Portland and becoming the founder of Umpqua Academy. Wilbur became presiding elder of the Columbia River District after its establishment in 1859. When the district was expanded to include more territory, the Native people at Fort Simcoe in present-day Washington became part of the clergyman's jurisdiction. He was named superintendent of teaching by the Bureau of Indian Affairs in 1860 and Indian agent in 1864. Wilbur was known for banning Native traditional practices, including the religious faith of the prophet SMOHALLA as well as the stick and bone gambling game. He lost his government position for a brief time from 1869 to 1870 when the military resumed control of the reservation. Although he was accused of favoring members of his own religion in distributing supplies and other services, he was reappointed to the post in 1871. Before retiring in 1882, he oversaw the completion of a boarding school at Fort Simcoe. Father Wilbur, as he was called, died on October 8, 1887, at Walla Walla. He was married to Lucretia Ann Stebens in 1831. (See also WATERS, GEORGE.)

WILD RICE (*mahnomen*—from *manitou* ["spirit"] and *meenun* ["delicacy"]) A tall grass that grows primarily in shallow lakes, ponds, and rivers in the Great Lakes Region of the United States and Canada. Harvested in early fall, the food has such importance to tribes of that area that one, the Menominee, takes its name from it. In a Canadian Ojibway community, an elder conducts the annual preharvest ritual of gathering a handful of *mahnomen* from each of the bays where the band's families will pick the crop. When the elder returns, the *mahnomen* is cooked and divided among the harvesters. The first handful of *mahnomen* gathered is placed in the water with some tobacco and a prayer of thanksgiving made in appreciation for the food. Similar rituals, as well as feasts and festivals, are held throughout Great Lakes Native communities to express gratitude for the food and to share the bounty of the harvest.

WILLIAMS, ELEAZAR (*1788–1858*) *Mohawk* An Episcopal missionary who claimed to be the Dauphin of France, the lost prince Louis XVII. Williams was born one of about 13 children to Mary Rice Williams (Konwatewenteta) and Thomas Williams (Tehoragwanegen), probably near Lake George, New York. He grew up on the Caughnawaga Reserve outside of Montreal, Quebec. In 1800 Williams's father took him to Long Meadow, Massachusetts, for an Episcopal education against the wishes of his Catholic mother. After his teacher and benefactor, Nathaniel Ely, died in 1807, Williams lived in Mansfield and Long Meadow until he began studying for the mission field under the Reverend Enoch Hale of Westhampton, Massachusetts, on December 22, 1809. He continued his studies until 1812. During the War of 1812, Williams was appointed superintendent-general of the Northern Indian Department, obtaining valuable information for the Americans from Canadian Indians regarding the movement of British troops. He was wounded at the Battle of Plattsburgh in New York on September 14, 1814. After the war, Williams lived among the Oneida at Oneida Castle, New York, serving as an Episcopal catechist and continuing his theological studies with General A. G. Ellis. He convinced a number of people to convert to Christianity, obtained a grant of land for his own use, and convinced the Oneida to sell several hundred additional acres to raise funds for building a church and school.

Hoping to establish an empire with a single, supreme leader, Williams became involved with JEDIDIAH MORSE, the Ogden Land Company, and the War Department on a scheme to remove Iroquois people from New York State. Although Williams and a self-appointed delegation moved to Green Bay, Wisconsin, in 1823, the removal plan was officially rejected by Iroquois councils and eventually faltered. Failing to fulfill pledges he had made to persuade people to move, Williams was repudiated by the Oneida and lost support from missionary societies. The removal plan was partly realized under an 1832 treaty that relocated most of the Oneida people from New York to Wisconsin.

Little was heard from the preacher until 1853 when he claimed to be the lost Dauphin of France, Louis XVII, son of Louis XVI and Marie Antoinette. One account states that Williams was assured of his identity as the Dauphin of France by Prince de Joinville, son of Louis-Philippe, in 1841. Another source indicates that the idea for the claim may have started in Williams's youth, when he was told by a Catholic priest that he appeared to be part French. Williams also claimed that he had received lashings from a jailer in the Tower of the Temple in Paris. The Reverend John H. Hanson wrote an article, "Have we a Bourbon among us?" in 1853 and a book, *The Lost Prince,* in 1854 to support Williams's claim. Other authors, including A. G. Ellis and William Ward Wight, proved that the account was groundless. Eleazar Williams died on August 28, 1858, on the St. Regis Reservation, near Hogansburg, New York. His publications included an Iroquois spelling book in 1813, a prayer book in 1853, and an account of his father's life in 1859. Williams's part-Menominee wife, Mary Jourdain, was also rumored to have ties to French royalty.

WILLIAMS, ROBERT (?–1896) *Nez Perce* A Presbyterian missionary among the Nez Perce who was ordained in 1879. Williams attended the mission school opened by SUSAN LAW MCBETH in 1874 and became one of the first three Nez Perce to be ordained after completing the theological training McBeth provided. Williams became the pastor of the Presbyterian church at Kamiah, Idaho, and was later involved in a split with ARCHIE B. LAWYER, another Native missionary, and his followers in 1890. The differences of the two men included disagreement on the issue of eradicating tribal traditions. Lawyer, objecting to their total condemnation formed the Second Presbyterian Church of Kamiah as a result of the conflict.

WILLIAMS, ROGER (c. 1603–1682/83) Clergyman and founder of Rhode Island. Born in London to Alice (Pemberton) and James Williams, he completed his B.A. degree at Pembroke College, Cambridge, in 1627. After graduating, he continued his studies at the school for two years to prepare for the ministry. He took holy orders sometime before February 1629 and began serving as a chaplain. He and his wife left England for Boston on December 1, 1630. Williams soon angered the Puritan authorities, disagreeing with them on a number of issues. Besides criticizing civil involvement and interference in religion, he viewed the colony's royal charter as imperialistic and in violation of Native land rights. The General Court ordered him banished from the Massachusetts Bay Colony in 1635. Williams escaped arrest and went to the Narragansett Bay area. He eventually pur-

chased land from the grand sachem, Canonicus, and established a new settlement, Providence, in 1636.

Williams played an important diplomatic role in the Pequot War, using his influence to obtain Narragansett neutrality. He wrote about Algonquian life and language in *Key into the Language of America,* which was published in 1643. Williams was unique in that he did not attempt to convert Native people, explaining his views on the issue in *Christenings Make Not Christians* (1645). His skepticism of existing religions and their claims was reflected in his own choices. He became a Baptist for a short time, then a Seeker who remained Christian but followed none of the creeds.

During King Philip's War (1675–76), Williams served as a captain of a Providence colonial force against Native opponents, including Narragansett and Wampanoag. After the conflict, Williams continued to be active in colony affairs until his death.

WILLIAMSON, JOHN P. (1835–1917) Congregational missionary who lived and worked among the Dakota people for most of his life. Born at Lac qui Parle, Minnesota, he was the son of THOMAS S. WILLIAMSON, "the father of the Dakota mission." After graduating from Marietta College in 1857 and from Cincinnati's Lane Theological Seminary in 1860, Williamson was ordained by the Dakota presbytery in 1861. He began his mission work in Minnesota at the Lower Sioux Agency from 1860 to 1862 and at Fort Snelling from 1862 to 1863. In the aftermath of the Dakota War of 1862 and the expulsion of Dakota people from the state, Williamson went to the Crow Creek Reservation in Dakota Territory (1863 to 1866), then to the Santee Agency in Nebraska (1866 to 1869) with the refugees. In 1869 he established a mission on the Yankton Reservation in present-day South Dakota and remained there for the rest of his career. Williamson contributed to the numerous publications produced by his father, SAMUEL W. AND GIDEON POND, and the STEPHEN RETURN RIGGS family in the Santee dialect of the Dakota language.

WILLIAMSON, THOMAS S. (1800–1879) A Congregational minister who became known as "the father of the Dakota mission." Williamson, born in South Carolina in 1800, graduated from Jefferson College in Pennsylvania in 1820 and from Yale College in 1824 with a medical degree. After practicing medicine for nine years in Adams County, Ohio, he began studying theology in 1833. The following year, Williamson was licensed to preach by his local presbytery and left for the Upper Mississippi region under the auspices of the AMERICAN BOARD OF COMMISSIONERS FOR FOREIGN MISSIONS (ABCFM). He traveled as far as Fort Snelling and met with area agents and residents. His successful journey and favorable report back to the ABCFM led to the establishment of the first mission station among the Dakota people. Williamson was ordained in 1834 and began missionary work and established a mission school at the Lac qui Parle station on the Minnesota River the following year. One of his first students was PAUL MAZAKUTEMANI. Others educated at the school included SIMON ANAWANGMANI, JOSEPH NAPESHNEE, and TUNKANSHAICIYE. His colleagues there included JEDIDIAH D. STEVENS, who was assigned to the Lake Harriet station near St. Paul, SAMUEL W. AND GIDEON POND, and later STEPHEN RETURN RIGGS. They all contributed to the achievement of literacy in the Santee, or Eastern, dialect of the Dakota language and produced a wide array of translations, ranging from journals and textbooks to a grammar and dictionary. Their work dominated the Congregational and Protestant missionary field among the Dakota for a long period of time. Dr. Williamson's efforts were enhanced by his medical knowledge. He was also assisted by his wife, a daughter, and two sons. The Reverend JOHN P. WILLIAMSON, one of his sons, later worked among the Santee who were removed to Dakota Territory and Nebraska after the 1862 war in Minnesota.

WILLIER, RUSSELL (Mehkwasskwan, "Red Cloud")
(b. 1947) Cree   A Woods Cree medicine man and healer who was born on the Sucker Creek Reserve in northern Alberta and inherited the medicine bundle of his great-grandfather Moostoos. Willier grew up in a large family and attended Catholic mission school until he dropped out to help out at home. Although his father passed down the hereditary bundle to him when he was about 17, he did not begin studying the healing powers of plants until he was older. Willier learned from several medicine men in the area rather than under the apprenticeship of one teacher. He treats patients with herbal medicines, sweat lodge purification, religious ceremonies, and other healing practices.

After having a vision in which he was to serve as a leader in the revitalization of Native practices, Willier began to share his knowledge with three anthropologists who documented his treatment of psoriasis among non-Native patients in 1984 and 1985. The study was unprecedented and became controversial in both the Native community and among medical practitioners. Among the fears expressed by other Cree was that herbal prescriptions and combinations would become known and exploited and that Native religious beliefs would again be exposed to ridicule from the larger society. The president of Alberta's dermatological association wrote a letter in which he questioned the use of research funds for such a project. After consulting community elders and his spirit helpers, Willier proceeded because of his concern that many traditions were dying out and his hope

that Native young people, often lost to suicide, alcohol, and drugs, would benefit. He explained that herbal combinations were not given to outsiders and that patients would benefit from Native and non-Native practitioners working together. Since the study, Willier has worked with non-Native medical people on some of his cases. He has also organized a nonprofit organization called the Traditional Native Healing Society as a step toward fulfilling his dream of establishing a healing center on the reserve. He further hopes to attain the shaking tipi practice of his great-grandfather. An account of Willier's practices was published as *Cry of the Eagle: Encounters with a Cree Healer* (1989).

WILLOW DANCE *Cheyenne*
The Willow Dance was the new name given to the SUN DANCE by the Cheyenne during the missionary and government ban on traditional religious practices. In 1907 the four Old Man Chiefs and other tribal leaders met with the Bureau of Indian Affairs officials to protest the denial of their freedom of worship. They also sought permission to hold a Willow Dance. After the superintendent agreed to permit it on the condition that no "torture" be involved, the ceremony was held over the July Fourth holiday. In 1911, however, the government forbade the Willow Dance as well as the "animal dance" (MASSAUM). When the Cheyenne tried to have the religious observances reinstated, the agency superintendent instead proposed a fair where agricultural products could be exhibited. During the ban against the sacred ceremonies, the Cheyenne continued to petition for their reinstatement each year. The name of the Willow Dance is derived from the use of willows for wreaths and other purposes during the ceremony.

WILSON, EDWARD FRANCIS *(1844–1915)*
Anglican missionary. Born in Islington, England, in 1844, Wilson was the son of the Reverend Daniel Wilson. He came from a family of influential clerics, including a grandfather who served as bishop of Calcutta in India. Although he could have attended prestigious schools, Wilson was more interested in becoming a farmer. After spending his early years on an estate learning to farm, he was influenced to go to Canada by the bishop of Huron, Benjamin Cronyn. He took a course in theology at Cronyn's school, which became Huron College, and later worked under the auspices of the CHURCH MISSIONARY SOCIETY. Wilson was assigned to the Sarnia mission in Ontario from 1868 to 1873. He then freelanced as an educator and missionary, eventually founding the Shingwauk and Wawanosh boarding schools at Sault Ste. Marie. Wilson wrote *A Manual of the Ojebway Language* (1874) for the Society for the Propagation of Christian Knowledge. It was intended for use in training mission workers and was reprinted as recently as 1975. He also

wrote *Missionary Work among the Ojebway Indians* (1886) and other publications. Wilson retired from the mission field in 1893.

WILSON, JACK See WOVOKA

WILSON, JOHN *(c. 1840–1901) Caddo* Originator of the Big Moon peyote ceremony who was one-half Delaware (Lenni Lenape), one-fourth Caddo, and one-fourth French but is said to have considered himself Caddo and spoke only that language. During a two-week period in 1880, he used eight to 15 PEYOTE buttons while "learning from the peyote" how to direct a ritual. Generally called the Big Moon and later identified with the Cross Fire, Wilson's ceremony has also been called the Moonhead. Although he attributed its source to divine revelation, the basic structure was similar to the Lipan Apache ceremony taught to the Comanche and Kiowa. Differences from the Half-Moon peyote ceremony included Wilson's larger, horseshoe-shaped altar and more complex ceremonial arrangement. In addition, his ritual has been described as incorporating more Christian practices. Wilson was also a leader of the GHOST DANCE OF 1890 in Oklahoma for five or six years but subsequently returned to being a full-time peyote ROADMAN, or leader. Although he lived less than 50 miles from the prominent roadman QUANAH PARKER for 25 years, references rarely mention them together. John Wilson died in 1901 after he was struck by a train at a railroad crossing near the Quapaw reservation in Oklahoma. (See also CHIWAT, BILLY; PEYOTE RELIGION; PINERO.)

WILSON V. BLOCK, HOPI INDIAN TRIBE V. BLOCK, AND NAVAJO MEDICINEMEN'S ASSOCIATION V. BLOCK (708 F. 2d 735 [1983]) *(1983)* In these consolidated federal cases, Navajo (Dineh) and Hopi plaintiffs sought to prevent the U.S. Forest Service and the U.S. Department of Agriculture from expanding a ski area located in a mountain formation known as the SAN FRANCISCO PEAKS in Arizona. The site, on federal land in the Coconino National Forest, has critical importance to the religions of both tribes. For the Hopi, specific areas are considered sacred shrines and the peaks are believed to be the home of various kachinas. Similarly, the Navajo consider the mountain a holy being, one of four sacred mountains. For both, alteration of the natural order desecrates the peaks and interferes with, or precludes, traditional religious practices.

A 777-acre portion of the peaks, known as the Snow Bowl, has been used for downhill skiing since 1937 when the Forest Service built a road and ski lodge. In 1979, the Forest Service issued a ruling to permit moderate development of the Snow Bowl. In 1980, the Forest Service regional supervisor approved a proposal to pave an access road to the bowl area, and the Native American petitioners filed suit. The district court ruled that the planned ski bowl expansion did not violate the free exercise rights of the plaintiffs. It further ruled that taking the steps sought by the Indians would violate the establishment clause, which prohibits government endorsement or management of any single religion. On appeal, the District of Columbia Circuit Court affirmed the ruling. It found that the plaintiffs had not proved the San Francisco Peaks area indispensable to their religious practices and that government actions had only offended, not penalized, these religions and were therefore permissible. According to the court, the U.S. Forest Service had fulfilled the requirements of the AMERICAN INDIAN RELIGIOUS FREEDOM ACT OF 1978 by including the testimony of religious leaders in the preparation of its environmental impact statement for the Arizona Snow Bowl ski area project. (See also SACRED SITES and Subject Index for related cases included in this volume.)

WINDIGOKAN *Plains Ojibway* The Windigokan is a sacred CLOWN, or contrary. Its name is derived from the windigo, a feared cannibalistic being sometimes described as an ice giant in Ojibway belief. The Windigokan is also associated with the thunder being or thunderbird. Generally, windigo or thunder dreamers make up the society of dancers. Wearing masks with long noses and a costume usually made of burlap, they behave in an opposite or backward manner at sacred ceremonies, including the SUN DANCE. Some Plains Ojibway Windigokan societies also include a dancer known as the "hunter," who has a hunched back and carries a crooked bow and arrows. The sacred clowns became known for their healing powers and contrary antics. The Windigokan Society is said to flourish in the present-day on the larger reservations, its dancers primarily participating in the Sun Dance.

WINSLETT, DAVID *(c. 1830–1862) Creek* Presbyterian minister and interpreter. His mother, Hattie Ward, was a Creek woman from Old Hitiche town who had immigrated to Indian Territory (present-day Oklahoma) with her husband, a white man named Winslett, and their two daughters. They arrived at Three Forks, near present-day Muskogee, in February 1828, and David was born sometime after that. He attended school at both Coweta and Tullahassee missions and studied under the Presbyterian missionary, ROBERT MCGILL LOUGHRIDGE. In 1851 Winslett became a ruling elder of the Tullahassee school. He also served as an interpreter for the Reverend Loughridge and assisted him in translating religious works. Winslett, ordained as a Presbyterian minister on September 6, 1858, took charge of the Coweta mission. During the Civil War he served in the Confederate army, eventually becoming ill from exposure. After returning home on furlough, he died in 1862. Winslett was married to Mahala Perryman.

WINTER CEREMONIAL *Kwakiutl* Two religious rituals dominate the Kwakiutl winter ceremonials. The first involves the initiation of young people into DANCING SOCIETIES, each with its special ritual knowledge and privileges. The societies present dances that constitute the cycle of ceremonies. The most important ritual of the cycle is the HAMATSA DANCE based on oral tradition about the MAN EATER spirit. Other dance performances include the War Spirit and Forest Spirit. A second religious ritual features the capture by a creature and disappearance of the dancers from the ceremonial house. They later enter the house to participate in dances wearing regalia (headdresses, dancing blankets, and carved frontlets) and carrying rattles. At the end of the ritual, gifts are distributed to all attending, signifying the potlatch is over and the witnesses are paid. (See also WINTER CEREMONIAL [North Pacific Coast].)

WINTER CEREMONIAL *North Pacific Coast* A ceremonial complex observed by Bella Coola, Comox, Clallam, Haida, Kwakiutl, Lkungen, Nootka, Pentlatch, Quileute, Sanitch, Tlingit, and Tsimshian peoples. The ceremonials are held during winter, a sacred time of year when it is believed that spirits are closest to the villages and communion with spirits is more easily established. The stores of preserved food obtained during the summer months make it possible for people to feast and dance and celebrate their spirits.

At this time, the entire community is transformed spiritually. They put aside their family, tribal, and lineage affiliations. They put aside their summer names and assume a new set of personal ceremonial names. The lineage houses become ceremonial centers. The chiefs, the nobility, become religious leaders during the ceremonial season. They form into the shaman's society with its two ritual groups: the seals, who impersonate more than 50 spirits (the most important of which is MAN EATER), and the sparrows, who manage the ceremonial, all former seals. Within each group, there is a ranked order. During the ceremonial, DANCING SOCIETIES perform, each reenacting, through song and dance, ancestral encounters with spiritual donors of power, and dramatizing the concept of hereditary right to such experiences. The ritual theme involves the introduction, or initiation, of a novice to the spiritual donor that seizes him from the human realm. The novice returns afflicted with holy madness and is subsequently recaptured and returned to an ordinary state. The dramatizations of these ancient events simulate a spiritual reality through the use of face masks, whistles and other instruments, and red cedar bark rings worn on heads, around the neck, at wrists, and at ankles. Seating at the festivals follows dancing positions instead of families and clans.

The winter ceremonies involve feasting and gift giving called a POTLATCH. Winter dances and potlatching combine into elaborate ceremonies during which houses might be built and dedicated, totem poles raised, marriages made, names and titles given, the deceased memorialized and heirs installed, novices initiated into ceremonial dance groups, and ceremonial debts discharged. (See also WINTER CEREMONIAL [Kwakiutl].)

WINTER CEREMONIAL *Salish* The ceremonials involved performances by society members privileged to display evidence of a visitation from a spirit. Dances, characterized by a song sung to percussion accompaniment, were performed by individuals who derived inspiration from spirits through dreams, trances, or highly formalized initiations or who acquired their right to participate by inheritance, marriage, gift, or purchase. In both categories of dances, performers experienced a visitation from a spirit that gave the privilege of publicly displaying evidence of the spiritual encounter. Performances differed locally. (See also SPIRIT DANCE CEREMONIAL.)

WINTER SPIRIT DANCE *Confederated Salish-Kootenai (Flathead)* A sacred ceremony generally held for several days in midwinter. Ritual elements attributed to the Winter Spirit Dance include sponsorship by a qualified individual, the singing of guardian spirit songs, dancing by participants, performances by shamans, feasting and/or gift presentations. Descriptions of the ceremony by contemporary scholars resulted in controversy. One writer referred to the sacred observance as the Bluejay Dance and emphasized elements that were challenged as a misinterpretation. The opposition of the Native people to outside intrusion in the Winter Spirit Dance, a ceremony of great spiritual significance in their culture, has also been cited.

WITCHCRAFT A belief in witchcraft has been universal, but the term has had different meanings in different cultures and at different points in time. American Indians traditionally believe that spiritual powers may be manipulated for evil purposes. Witchcraft is one term applied to this use of power. Many believe SHAMANS can either use spiritual powers beneficially or to cause injury. Among some groups, witches are believed to cause illness either by stealing the heart of the victim or by shooting foreign objects into a victim. Witches also acquire hair, saliva, nails, bits of clothing, or personal belongings of the victim and treat them in certain ways that bring on sickness or some other misfortune.

They use narcotic plants or touch victims with the powder of corpse flesh. Witches are also believed to cause bad weather or any calamity that threatens tribal welfare, such as epidemics. Shamans, or medicine societies, cure the victims by sucking out foreign objects from the body or by retrieving the heart or engaging in mortal combat with the evil witches.

Traditional Navajo (Dineh), for example, believe there are various sources of evil, but the worst pertain to witchcraft and SORCERY. Navajo devote time to protecting themselves because witchery can victimize anyone. Many carry "witch medicine" to ward off attacks. There are traditional Navajo who believe there are malevolent men and women who learn witchery from parents, grandparents, or spouses in order to wreak vengeance, gain wealth, dispose of enemies, or injure wantonly. These witches travel undetected at night transforming themselves into wolves, coyote, bear, and other animals. Witches are believed to perform ceremonials using chants, SANDPAINTINGs, and masks, in which they plan concerted actions against victims. A witch's confession or death helps a victim recover as do prayer ceremonials, chants, especially the EVIL WAY, and plants. Some Navajo also believe there are wizards who practice witchery by injecting a foreign particle into the victim. They believe that witches also put certain plants into food or in cigarettes, a practice directed against the rich.

There has also been a long and intense involvement of Pueblo with witchcraft. Spanish colonial records from the early 17th century refer to witches and their activities, but the belief is grounded in ancient tradition. Witches are perceived to be powerful figures whose forms vary from pueblo to pueblo, either as owls, crows, coyotes, rats, and so forth, and who use their extraordinary knowledge to benefit themselves, the antithesis of Pueblo ethics. Traditional Pueblo peoples believe witches injure individuals or the entire community. They cause sickness, weather adversity, epidemics, crop destruction, and murder. Pueblo curing societies or the village CACIQUE work to overcome the injurious effects of witchcraft. According to traditional Pueblo belief, a bewitched person will die unless powerful forces counteract evil.

In the past, witch beliefs traumatized Pueblo communities. Zia declined in population at the end of the 17th century because witch phobia resulted in a large number of executions. Santa Clara as well declined in population during the end of the Spanish colonial period for the same reason. Witchcraft seriously disrupted Nambe Pueblo and reduced its population at the end of the 19th century. Zuni Pueblo also suffered from fear of witches during the late 1800s and had a string of trials and executions. The charge of witchcraft was not only brought against individuals but against entire towns and tribes. The people of the Hopi pueblo Awatobi were destroyed on grounds of witchcraft.

WODZIWOB (Gray Hair) *(c. 1844–c. 1873) Northern Paiute (Numu, Paviotso)* Prophet who originated the GHOST DANCE OF 1870 on the Walker River Reservation in Nevada. Wodziwob is believed to have visited the spirit world during a trance or temporary death and returned to life with sacred teachings. Besides giving his listeners messages from departed friends and relatives, he prophesied the return of the dead and spoke of the great fear that would follow that occurrence. Many people gathered to hear his teachings, including members of the Washoe and Mono groups. His disciple, FRANK SPENCER (Weneyuga), took the beliefs to other Paviotso groups and to the Washoe people. Spencer conducted the sacred dances and served as Wodziwob's messenger in some areas. TAVIBO, the father of WOVOKA, was another follower of Wodziwob and served as his assistant. Tavibo and Wodziwob are sometimes confused in accounts of their influence on Wovoka's life. Wodziwob began preaching his doctrine about 1869. Although the date of his death is generally cited at about 1873, one account indicates that he may have lived into the 20th century.

WOMEN'S SOCIETIES *Ponca* Societies, including the Pa-data, Ni kagahi EshonGa, and Pa-nin Ga, associated with ceremonial roundhouses established among the Ponca after their move to Indian Territory (present-day Oklahoma) in 1879. Each society, with specific membership requirements and prerogatives, assisted in maintaining tribal traditions. Pa-data ("No Sugar" or "Bitter Water") required that women qualify for particular membership positions by going through specific ceremonies. Ni kagahi EshonGa ("Chief's Daughters Dance") included the use of symbolic tattoos for members who qualified for membership through heredity and other means. Pa-nin Ga ("No Head" or "No Top of the Head") incorporated the use of special clothing as did the other two. Although men could sing to the drumming of the women's societies, only women could dance. A men's society was associated with the fourth roundhouse of the Ponca in Indian Territory.

In 1983 a ceremonial drum believed to have been made about 1880 for the use of the Pa-data Women's Society was transferred to four contemporary Ponca women. David Jones, a tribal elder who had inherited the drum, selected the women as the new owners. Descended from chiefs, they were described as the first members of the Scalp Dance Society since the 1920s. A ceremony, held to transfer the drum, included opening prayers, blessings with an eagle feather, an explanation of the drum's purpose, the performance of a traditional dance around the drum, a feast, and concluding prayers. Over a century old, the drum had both Ponca and Osage keepers during its long history. The ceremonial drum, placed in retirement, was later loaned to the Marland Estate Museum in Ponca City, Oklahoma.

WOMEN'S SONGS *Iroquois* A series of important songs associated with the growth of life and supporting the crops. The songs are performed during Corn Planting, CORN SPROUTING, and Corn Ripening Ceremonies.

WOOD, THOMAS *(c. 1711–1778)* Physician and Church of England missionary. Born in New Jersey, Wood practiced medicine in New York, in Philadelphia, and with a New England regiment before he decided to turn to religious work. Seeking ordination in the Church of England, he traveled to England in June 1749. He was ordained on September 4th as a deacon and five days later as a priest. Upon his return to America later that year, he began serving a mission in New Jersey at New Brunswick and Elizabethtown under the auspices of the SOCIETY FOR THE PROPAGATION OF THE GOSPEL (SPG). In 1751 he requested that the SPG transfer him to Nova Scotia, leaving the following year on his own. Based at Halifax, he traveled to other parts of the region on missionary tours. Wood was named chaplain of a garrison in 1855 and of Halifax's first House of Assembly in 1859, the same year he became vicar of St. Paul's Church. In 1764 he moved to Annapolis Royal, where it is believed that he continued his missionary tours. A linguist who knew several European languages, Wood had begun studying Micmac earlier with the assistance of Abbé Pierre Maillard. In 1764 he began working on a translation of the Book of Common Prayer and a Micmac grammar. By September 4, 1766, he reported to the SPG that he had completed the first volume of the grammar and had started the second and final volume. In 1769 he indicated that he had visited Native communities on the Saint John River. His ministry included both Native and non-Native people in the region. Wood died on December 14, 1778, at Annapolis Royal, Nova Scotia. He was married to Mary Myers, and the couple had five children.

WOODEN LANCE (Apiatan, Ah-pea-taw, Apheatone) *(c. 1860–1931) Kiowa* PEYOTE leader and head chief of his people. Born about 1860, Wooden Lance's ancestry included a grandmother who had been a Lakota captive. During the GHOST DANCE OF 1890, he accepted an invitation to the Pine Ridge Reservation in South Dakota to meet his Lakota relatives and to find out whether reports of the new doctrine were true. Hoping that the religion's belief in a reunion with deceased relatives and friends would enable him to see a child he had recently lost, he left to search for the rumored messiah, WOVOKA. Wooden Lance was sent as a delegate by Kiowa leaders, and funds were raised to meet the expenses of his trip. Before leaving for the north in September 1890, most of the tribe assembled to see him off, and a ceremony of blessing was performed over him by the principal men. He went first to Pine Ridge and then traveled to Fort Washakie in Wyoming

and met with Northern Arapaho and Shoshone. After finding out the route to the Paiute, he left for Nevada, where he met with the Ghost Dance leader WOVOKA. An interview with him was disappointing, as he was convinced that Wovoka was a fraud. On his way home, Wooden Lance stopped at Fort Hall, Idaho, to write his people of his findings. Upon his return he debated SITTING BULL, the Arapaho apostle of the Ghost Dance, at a council held at Anadarko agency in Oklahoma on February 19, 1891. He later received a medal from President William H. Harrison for reporting against the doctrine.

After the turn of the century Wooden Lance was identified as a peyote leader. It has been speculated that he practiced peyotism earlier and that it may have contributed to his rejection of the Ghost Dance religion. Besides serving as a principal chief and spiritual leader, Wooden Lance held a COURT OF INDIAN OFFENSES judgeship until losing the position because he practiced polygamy. He died on August 8, 1931, in Oklahoma. His Kiowa name also appears as Ah-pea-taw and Apheatone, among other variants.

WOODENLEGS, JOHN, SR. (Morning Star) *(1912–1981) Cheyenne* President of the Northern Cheyenne NATIVE AMERICAN CHURCH, leader of traditional ceremonies, Northern Cheyenne Chief, and Tribal Council president. Woodenlegs was born to Fannie Wolf Voice and Thomas Woodenlegs (also Twin) in 1912. A descendant of both Suhtai and Cheyenne ancestors, he began his membership in the Native American Church at an early age. He later became active in a number of leadership roles. Woodenlegs began serving as President of the Northern Cheyenne Native American Church about 1946, continuing in that capacity until 1975. Besides being a PEYOTE ROADMAN, he held numerous other offices. He served as president of the Northern Cheyenne tribal council between 1955 and 1968, fighting against federal Termination policies that were aimed at ending the trust status of Indian lands during his tenure. In 1962 he also became a member of the Chief's Society. Other affiliations included the Northern Cheyenne Research and Human Development Association and the War Dancers Society. Woodenlegs was named to national boards as well, including President Lyndon B. Johnson's Commission on Rural Poverty. He was also affiliated with the Association on American Indian Affairs, serving as a field worker. In 1974 he fasted at NOAHA-VOSE, or BEAR BUTTE, while the SACRED BUFFALO HAT was being renewed.

WOODY, JACK *Peyotist* (See TAKES GUN, FRANK; *PEOPLE V. WOODY.*)

WOOLSEY, THOMAS *(1818–1894)* Methodist missionary at Fort Edmonton and other posts. He was born in

Lincolnshire, England, and after approximately 15 years of service to the Methodist Church in England, Woolsey traveled to North America in the early 1850s. He was ordained in London, Ontario, in 1855, along with HENRY BIRD STEINHAUER, an Ojibway missionary. Woolsey was sent to Fort Edmonton, Alberta, to fill a position vacated by ROBERT TERRILL RUNDLE, his brother-in-law. He reopened the Pigeon Lake Mission and used it as his headquarters as he visited Indian groups on his circuit. In 1860 Woolsey established a new post to the northeast at Smoky Lake, referred to as "Smoking Lake." Three years later he, JOHN MCDOUGALL, and Henry B. Steinhauer established Victoria (later called Pakan) mission on the North Saskatchewan River. McDougall, an assistant to Woolsey for two years, later wrote of their work together. Woolsey's missionary efforts in the region ended in 1864. After traveling to England, he worked at positions in Quebec and Ontario until his retirement in 1885. Woolsey died in Toronto in 1894.

WORCESTER, SAMUEL AUSTIN *(1798–1859)* The missionary to the Cherokee who is best known for his role in *Worcester v. Georgia,* the landmark 1832 case in which the U.S. Supreme Court ruled against the claims of sovereignty over the Cherokee Nation by the state of Georgia. Born to the Reverend Leonard and Elizabeth Hopkins Worcester on January 19, 1798, in Worcester, Massachusetts, he was reared in Peacham, Vermont. He attended the University of Vermont, where his uncle, Samuel Austin, was president, and graduated in 1819. A few years later, in 1823, Worcester graduated from Andover's theological seminary. He married Ann Orr of Bedford, New Hampshire, on July 19, 1825, and a short time later, on August 25, 1825, he was ordained a minister at Park Street Congregational Church in Boston. He then left for the Brainerd Mission in Tennessee, where he served as a supervising missionary among the Cherokee for two years. In 1827, Worcester oversaw the production in Boston of type for printing the Cherokee syllabary invented by Sequoyah. The same year he was transferred to the tribal capital in New Echota, Georgia, where he continued his missionary work and translated biblical passages from the Greek to Cherokee. In 1828 he helped establish the *Cherokee Phoenix,* the first American Indian newspaper, to which he often contributed, and he collaborated on biblical translations with ELIAS BOUDINOT.

At the height of pressures to remove the Cherokee west to Indian Territory (present-day Oklahoma), Worcester and other missionaries, including ELIZUR BUTLER and JAMES JENKINS TROTT, were arrested in 1831 for violating a Georgia law forbidding non-Indian residency in tribal territory without pledging allegiance to the state and obtaining a license. Convicted and sentenced to four years at hard labor,

all of the missionaries except Worcester and ELIZUR BUTLER accepted pardons. Wanting a test case on the Cherokee-state conflict, they appealed to the U.S. Supreme Court, which later heard the case. Chief Justice John Marshall wrote the opinion in 1832, the landmark decision fundamental to federal Indian law. President Andrew Jackson's support of the state of Georgia resulted in Cherokee removal despite the legal victory.

Shortly after Worcester's release from prison on January 14, 1833, he prepared to move to Indian Territory with the Cherokee people. He arrived there in May 1835 and began the work of rebuilding in the new location. Assisted by the carpentry skills he had learned in prison, Worcester established the Park Hill mission, which became the largest of its kind in Indian Territory. He continued to publish Cherokee-language materials, including biblical passages, hymn books, and the *Cherokee Almanac* on what was likely the first printing press in the area. He also organized a number of organizations, such as temperance and Bible societies. His first wife, with whom he had a daughter named Ann Eliza, died on May 23, 1840. He married Erminia Nash, his second wife, on April 3, 1841. Worcester died on April 20, 1859, and was buried near Park Hill. His daughter, ANN ELIZA WORCESTER ROBERTSON, was also a missionary and translator.

WORLD RENEWAL CEREMONIAL CYCLE *Chilula, Hupa, Karok, Tolowa, Wiyot, Yurok* Annual cycle of rituals in the spring and fall with the purpose of renewing the world, maintaining order, ensuring an abundance of acorns and other foods, plants, animals, fish, securing assistance from spirits, and preventing natural disasters like floods and earthquakes. It is believed that the rites were established by the Immortals at the time of creation, and the teachings were incorporated into language, customs, and rituals of people. The rites are carried out by a priest, or formulist, of each local group at certain localities to which the performances are inseparably linked and restricted. The priests, who are purified before and after the rites, perform a series of ritual acts going from one sacred spot to another while reciting long ritual narratives. People believe that by repeating acts and procedures established by the Immortals in proper ritual order, at specified spots indoors or outdoors, the earth's resources will continue. The priest also kindles a new fire and eats acorns or salmon ceremonially. Death and rebirth of the world are reenacted in the rebuilding of sacred structures (sweathouses, ceremonial houses, dance arenas), which the priest oversees, the creation of sacred fires, and the erection of a sand pile on which the priest stands.

Each group near a major fishing ground stages its version of the world renewal rituals. As salmon progressed up the Klamath River, for example, the performances were given in succession from the mouth of the river to the upper portions. Although there were and are many local variations of ceremonial details, these rituals and dances share important elements. Nearly every occasion requires a ritual formulist to recite ancient stories and ritual formulas and to visit sacred sites. The formulas are spoken in sections before spots marking the abode of spirits. The ceremonies are accompanied by the performance of one or both of two major public dance cycles, the WHITE DEERSKIN DANCE and the JUMP DANCE, held for one or two and up to 10 to 16 days, providing occasions for the wealthy to display the property on which their positions rest. Each dance has its own steps, songs, and regalia. There are various first fruits ceremonies (ACORN FEAST) tied to a ceremonial calendar and specific locations. Dance hosts need wealth, power, and networks of wealthy friends to organize the dances. The hosts borrow or own requisite ceremonial regalia used by dancers and resources to provide food for feasts.

WOVOKA (Wagud, "Wood-cutter," Jack Wilson, etc.)

(c. 1856–1932) Northern Paiute (Numu, Paviotso) The prophet who founded the GHOST DANCE OF 1890. Born about 1856 near Walker Lake in present-day Esmeralda County, Nevada, he was the son of TAVIBO (also Numu-tibo'o), a visionary and leader. Known as Wovoka or Wuvoka from his youth, he later took the name of his paternal grandfather, Kowhitsauq ("big rumbling belly"). Wovoka was eventually influenced by a neighboring white farmer, David Wilson, and Wilson's family, who gave him the name Jack Wilson. Wovoka later worked on the family's farm and, when he was in his 20s, married Tumma, who became known as Mary Wilson.

Wovoka's great revelation occurred on January 1, 1889, during an eclipse of the sun. He first heard a "great noise," then lost consciousness. When he revived, he announced that he had been taken to the other world, were he had seen the Creator and people who had died. Wovoka was given a number of powers there, including five songs for weather control, invulnerability to weapons, political responsibility, and prophecies. The Creator instructed Wovoka to return to his people and to instruct them to live in peace without warfare, lying, or stealing. They were to work and to live in peace with the whites. If they obeyed these instructions, they would be reunited with family and friends in the other world, where there would be no sickness, old age, or death. Wovoka taught a sacred dance, known to the Northern Paiute as *nanigukwa*, "dance in a circle," which was to be performed at intervals for five consecutive days.

Out of Wovoka's experience of death and rebirth, the religious practices of his family and tribe, and his exposure to the Presbyterian beliefs of the Wilsons, evolved the Ghost Dance religion, which quickly spread to other tribal groups.

Wovoka, the Northern Paiute prophet who founded the Ghost Dance of 1890. *National Anthropological Archives, Smithsonian Institution.*

Emissaries representing more than 30 tribes traveled great distances to visit him and to learn more of his teachings, often returning home filled with messages of hope for their people. Some of the visitors from the Plains included KICKING BEAR, PORCUPINE, SHORT BULL, SITTING BULL (Arapaho), and WOODEN LANCE. As the religious movement spread, it took on features unique to individual tribal groups. The Ghost Dance was opposed by government agents and missionaries, and efforts to suppress the movement ended in tragedy among the Lakota. Federal troops opened fire on Big Foot's band at Wounded Knee in South Dakota on December 29, 1890, killing men, women, and children.

In the aftermath of the events on the Northern Plains, Wovoka continued to receive correspondence from Ghost Dance adherents. Assisted by Ed Dyer, a store owner who served as his secretary, the Paiute prophet mailed sacred red ocher, eagle or magpie feathers, Stetson hats, and other clothing he had worn to those who had made requests and sent money. He also traveled to distant reservations, served as a shaman and healer, sought land on the Walker River Reservation in Nevada and continued to believe in his political and spiritual powers. Wovoka spent the last 15 years of his life at the Yerington Indian Colony in Nevada. Before he died he prophesied that an earthquake would occur if he reached the other world again. Wovoka died at his home on September 29, 1932. Other names for the prophet included Wevokar, Wopokahte, Cowejo, Koit-tsow, Quoitze Ow, Jackson Wilson, and Jack Winson. He was also referred to as Tamme Naa'a, "Our Father," and the Messiah.

WRAPS HIS TAIL (Wraps-up-his-tail or Cheez-tah-paezh) *(d. 1887) Crow*   A medicine man who led a demonstration against the government in 1887. While participating in the Cheyenne SUN DANCE in the summer of that year, he was given a medicine saber by the Cheyenne and took the name Sword Bearer. On his return home, he acquired a following among the people who believed in his spiritual powers. Besides asserting that he was invulnerable to enemy bullets and other weapons, Wraps His Tail promised that prosperity would return to the Crow. Dissatisfied with government domination and with the government's agent, he led a number of warriors against the Crow Agency on September 30, 1887. The agent sent for government troops and ordered Wraps His Tail's arrest, but he successfully evaded capture for more than a month. Wraps His Tail was shot and killed by Firebear, a Crow policeman, on November 5, 1887. Native informants reported the appearance of a red flame above his grave after his burial. Sometimes referred to as "The Prophet," his name also appears as Wraps-up-his-tail and as several variations of Cheez-tah-paezh.

WRIGHT, ALFRED *(1788–1853)*   Presbyterian missionary to the Choctaw people; founder of Wheelock Mission in Indian Territory (present-day Oklahoma). Wright was born in Columbia, Connecticut, on March 1, 1788, and was graduated from Williams College in 1812 and Andover Seminary in 1814. A short time after his ordination as an evangelist in 1819, he began working among the Mississippi Choctaw under the auspices of the AMERICAN BOARD OF COMMISSIONERS FOR FOREIGN MISSIONS (ABCFM). When missionary activities were disrupted during the Removal period, Wright returned to New England in 1830. He later accompanied Choctaw people on their journey west and arrived in Indian Territory after a long delay caused by illness and other problems. Wright organized a church on December 9, 1832, and established a day school the following year.

He was assisted by his wife, Harriet Bunce Wright, who served as a missionary and teacher. Besides her work as the first principal of Wheelock Academy, she contributed to Wright's numerous Choctaw-language publications. Alfred Wright served as a minister, physician, and translator at Wheelock Mission until his death on March 31, 1853.

WRIGHT, ALLEN (Kiliahote or Kilihote, "Let's Kindle a Fire") *(1825–1885) Choctaw*   Choctaw minister who served as principal chief of his people between 1866 and 1870. Born in Attala County, Mississippi, on November 28, 1825, Kiliahote was orphaned early and taken in by the Reverend CYRUS KINGSBURY, a Presbyterian minister, who gave him the name Allen Wright, after ALFRED WRIGHT, an early missionary to the Choctaw. After his conversion to Christianity and education in local schools, such as the Choctaw Nation's Spencer Academy, Wright was selected for further schooling in the east. An excellent student, he first attended a school in Delaware and then entered Union College in Schenectady, New York, where he received a degree in 1852. Three years later, in 1855, he graduated from Union Theological Seminary in New York City. Ordained as a Presbyterian minister in 1856, Wright returned to Indian Territory to work with his own people. He was later elected to public office, serving in the Choctaw House of Representatives, the Senate, and then as treasurer. During the Civil War, he was in the Confederate army for a short time in 1862. In 1866, as a delegate sent to Washington, D.C., to negotiate a new treaty between the Choctaw, Chickasaw, and the U.S. government, he was influential in wording the terms of the agreement. One of his suggestions was that Oklahoma, from *okla* "red" and *homma* "people," be the name for the region. During his absence as a delegate, Wright was elected principal chief of the Choctaw Nation, then reelected in 1868. Besides achieving recognition as a religious and political leader, Wright was known as a linguistic scholar. His knowledge of languages included Choctaw, English, Latin, Greek, and Hebrew. His *Chahta Leksikon,* or Choctaw dictionary, was published in 1880. He also translated the Choctaw and Chickasaw constitutions, legal codes, and several hymnals. Before his death on December 2, 1885, in Oklahoma, Wright completed a translation of the Psalms from Hebrew to Choctaw. He was married to Harriet Newell Mitchell, a missionary from Dayton, Ohio, with whom he had eight children. His son FRANK HALL WRIGHT also became a missionary.

WRIGHT, ASHER *(1803–1875)*   A Congregational missionary among the Seneca of New York from 1831 until his death in 1875. Wright was born in Hanover, New Hampshire, and was educated at Dartmouth College and Andover Theological Seminary. After his 1831 ordination, he began working as a missionary to the Seneca on the Buffalo Creek Reservation under the auspices of the AMERICAN BOARD OF COMMISSIONERS FOR FOREIGN MISSIONS (ABCFM). He married Laura Sheldon, after his first wife died, in Vermont on January 21, 1833. After mastering the Native language, Wright began efforts to translate religious and educational works. He obtained support from his sponsors for a printing press equipped with the type for a Seneca orthography he had devised. The Mission Press, which he established in 1841, published the first books printed in Buffalo, New York. Wright's publications included *The Mental Elevator,* a journal with Scripture translations and other writings published in 19 issues ending on April 15, 1850. Laura completed a reading book in 1836 and assisted him in translating a hymnal. From 1837 to 1845, when the Seneca struggled to protect their territory from the Ogden Land Company, Wright was instrumental in securing 1842's "Compromise Treaty," under which the Allegany and Cattaraugus Reservations were to be retained by the tribe. Besides his own writings on the Seneca, Wright contributed information about the tribal group to the anthropologist Lewis Henry Morgan. Wright's wife LAURA MARIA SHELDON WRIGHT was also a missionary.

WRIGHT, FRANK HALL *(1860–1922) Choctaw* Presbyterian minister who founded missions in Indian Territory (present-day Oklahoma). He was born on January 1, 1860, to Harriet and Allen Wright at Boggy Depot in Indian Territory. After receiving private tutoring from missionary teachers, he attended Spencer Academy in the Choctaw Nation. He then completed studies at Union College in Schenectady and at the Union Theological Seminary in New York City (1885). After marrying Addie Lilienthal of Saratoga, New York, he returned to the Choctaw Nation to work among his people. He later went back to the East; where he was stricken with tuberculosis while working as an evangelist. During his recuperation he conducted missionary work in Indian Territory under the auspices of the Women's Executive Committee of the Reformed Church. After founding the Comanche-Apache mission, he traveled to Segar Indian Agency, where he began working among the Cheyenne and Arapaho people and established the Columbian Memorial Mission. In 1917 he received a doctor of divinity degree from Westminster College in Fulton, Missouri. Wright died at Muskoka Lakes in Ontario, Canada, on July 16, 1922.

WRIGHT, LAURA MARIA SHELDON *(1809–1886)* A Congregational missionary to the Seneca in New York. Laura was born in 1809 in St. Johnsbury, Vermont. After attending the Young Ladies' School she taught for six years at nearby Barnet and Newbury. She married ASHER WRIGHT, already a missionary among the Seneca, on January 21, 1833, in Barnet. The following day they left for Asher's post on the Buffalo Creek Reservation, studying the Seneca language on the way. She later assisted her husband in producing instructional materials and religious works. A primer she prepared, the first of their bilingual textbooks, was published in Boston in 1836. Other publications followed, including a speller, a bilingual journal, and a hymnal. One of their assistants at the press was Nicholas H. Parker, a member of a prominent Seneca family, who became an interpreter. After the Seneca lost their Buffalo Creek Reservation during struggles with the Ogden Land Company, the Wright's reestablished their mission near Cattaraugus Creek in 1845. Besides taking in orphans left by an 1847 typhoid epidemic, the couple later founded the Thomas Asylum for Orphan and Destitute Indian Children and assumed codirectorship of the shelter. Wright also founded the Iroquois Temperance League. After her husband died in 1875, she lived at the home of Nicholas H. Parker until her own death in 1886.

WUWUCHIM CEREMONY *Hopi* A 16-day ceremony in November in which Hopi ritually supplicate for germination of all forms of life. Four societies participate, the ONE HORN, TWO HORNS, FLUTE, and Wuchim. There are kiva rites and a public dance on the concluding day of the ceremony. During the ceremony, young men are initiated into one of the four sacred societies that ensures the proper operation of the ceremonial cycle, gives them adult status, and qualifies them to dance as kachinas or to take part in the winter solstice ceremony. These initiation rituals dramatize the emergence of the Hopi from the underworld and prepares the novices for positions in the underworld after death. During the ceremony, the Hopi dead are invited to return to their villages, and a road is kept open for them to enter. In a Closing of the Roads ceremony, the roads leading to the villages are sealed off to other people. Wuchim Society members formally tease the members of the MARAW SOCIETY, the women's organization, as the women do the men during their ceremony. In some villages, the Wuwuchim both closes and opens the Hopi ceremonial cycle.

Y

YAQUI CEREMONIALISM Yaqui religion of the 20th century encompasses beliefs and practices derived both from their ancient spiritual traditions and from Roman Catholicism. Yaqui have combined these beliefs into a two-part universe, one part represented by the town and church, whose dwellers are mortal, and the other by the *HUYA ANIYA,* the Yaqui spirit world and source of spiritual power, whose dwellers are immortal. The Yaqui have integrated the *huya aniya* and town/church world in ritual expressions. Every Christian ceremony also requires the participation by ceremonialists whose power is derived from the *huya aniya.* For example, a PASCOLA dance is performed at each important religious event on the Christian calendar. Further, the PAHKO, or fiesta, involves both church groups and Pascola dancers. These linkages of church and Yaqui spirit world integrate Christian and Native religious traditions. A distinctive feature of Yaqui ceremonialism is that Yaqui worship does not require people to go to church. Rather, the church goes to the people. The Pahko, the institutional arrangement through which this action is carried out, is a joint religious ceremony conducted by the church organization and a household, which becomes the church itself during a Pahko. Yaqui emphasize a dual division in their ceremonial year. Winter and spring constitute one season and summer and autumn the other. The seasonal dichotomy is expressed in people's attitudes, music, ritual action, and the different ceremonial performers that dominate each season. During winter and spring, the helmet-masked Chapayeka dominate every occasion at church or at private homes, and a solemn and repressive mood, taboos, and restrictions pervade the towns. During summer and autumn, Matachin dancers dance in ceremonies and create a pleasurable, relaxed mood.

In Yaqui towns, there are five authorities (*ya'uram*) or sharply defined jurisdictions in which a particular kind of authority is exercised: civil affairs, military affairs, church affairs, affairs of the patron saints of the town, and activities connected with Lenten and Holy Week ceremonial (WAEHMA). The term *ya'ura* refers to individuals vested with the authority, implying that the men who exert authority are inseparable from the authority itself.

Church Authority

The most complex of the town's organizations, the church authority is concerned with relations between the townspeople and the SANTORA, or spiritual residents of the church building. The organization is composed of several groups, including the Maestros-Kopariam, Temahtim, the Kiyohteim, and Matachinim. At the top of the church hierarchy are three senior officials, the eldest in church affairs, the Maestro, Temahti, and Kiyohtei, the first two always male and the last female.

Maestro (**Maestro, Maehto**) The members of the ruling triumvirate, who are religious leaders and teachers. The Maestros read sacred texts (prayers, sermons, parts of the Mass, or the Mass for the dead) and sing hymns and other portions of the Catholic liturgy. In the church hierarchy, the senior Maestro, who has a prestigious position in a Yaqui town, is prepared to take the leadership role in

340

church ritual formerly assumed by a missionary. The Maestros are aided by the Kopariam, who are female singers.

Temahtim These members of the ruling triumvirate take care of the church building, its male icons, and the money collected in the church's name. They also serve as assistants to the Maestros in regular services.

Kiyohtei These members of the ruling triumvirate are responsible for the care of female images in the church, altar cloths, and all other textiles used in church altar decoration. They manage the female ceremonial participants as well.

Below these three groups is the second level of hierarchy.

Church Governor The church governor coordinates all activities of the church groups at every church service or Pahko. He manages the activities of Matachin Dance Society (see below) and its musicians, synchronizing them with other church activities.

Pihkan Ya'ut A highly specialized official, he performs the duties of catechist and instructor in Yaqui Christian Church doctrine. He teaches and maintains the knowledge of the standard Catholic prayers, translated into the Yaqui language during the 1600s. As a teacher and repository of doctrine, he forms strong relationships with individual townspeople and children.

Matachin Dance Society This church organization of as many as 40 or even more dancers in a town is under the direction of the church governor, whose services are dedicated to the church and who represent the good forces against the evil of the Chapayeka. Led by their dance master, the Monaha, the Matachinim wear headdresses called *sewa* ("flowers"), made of brightly colored crepe paper or cloth, usually red, and colored skirts, and carry gourd rattles and wands called *palma,* trident-shaped frames decorated with feathers. They carry a statue of Mary, their patroness, in a box whenever they go to a household to carry out their part of church services, and they observe exacting discipline to please their patroness at all times. They dance to music played by violinists and guitarists at household ceremonies, vespers, and other ceremonies at the church. Three to six dancers, called *malinche,* usually very young boys who are newly dedicated members of the Matachin organization, wear long skirts until they graduate to full membership. Matachin dancers dominate the greater part of the ceremonial year, dancing from May until January the following year. The Matachin Dance, the most sacred of Yaqui dances, is a sacred ritual, a form of group worship. The dance takes place simultaneously with prayers and chants before church or household altars. The dance honors Mary and ensures the continuance of her blessings. The Matachin dancers remain in eclipse through the Waehma season until Holy Saturday, when the Passion of Christ is reenacted, and they participate in the downfall of the Infantry (see below),

who represent the betrayers of Christ. The flowers on the Matachin headdresses, which to the Yaqui symbolize the blood of Christ, defeat the Judases. The Matachin Dancers are under orders to the Kohtumbre (Customs Authority) during the Waehma ceremonial. During Waehma, the Matachin Dance Society also dances and leads processions.

Customs Authority (Kohtumbre Ya'ura)

One of five well-defined authorities in a Yaqui town, this Yaqui ceremonial organization is ritually the dominant authority in a Yaqui town and sponsors and directs the Waehma, the Yaqui version of the Christian religious drama the Passion. It is in charge of the Easter ceremony and all ceremonial events taking place during Lent, both in plazas and in households. Members of this authority only appear in ceremonial roles during the Waehma season (Lent and Holy Week) and carry out the action of the dramatic narrative of the Waehma. The groups within the authority are the Horsemen Society and the Infantry, composed of the Soldiers of Rome and the Chapayekas. The groups are organized in military fashion, with officers and soldiers.

During Lent, the Kohtumbre does penance and prays for all people, and guards the most sacred customs of the Yaqui. During Holy Week, it takes possession of the church and eliminates civil and military authorities through symbolic acts. Indeed, all ceremonial groups are under orders to the Kohtumbre during Lent until its ritual defeat during the great ceremonial battle on Holy Saturday morning. The Kohtumbre societies sponsor household fiestas throughout Lent and are known by the Spanish term *fiesteros* (fiesta hosts) or by the Yaqui term *pahkome* (fiesta givers). The Kohtumbre members perform manual labor associated with ceremonies, account for all money, patrol the village for violations of Lenten taboos, and punish offenders. They also have special functions in the death ceremonies of members and their families whether or not they occur during Lent. Kohtumbre ritual objects include lances or swords, red and blue flags, and CHAPAYEKA MASKS. The ceremonial labor of individual Kohtumbre members is regarded as the hardest of all ceremonial labor, especially the roles of Chapayekas.

Horsemen Society (**Kabayum, Caballeros, Cavalry**) The dominant group in the Customs Authority, organized along military lines, with captains, lieutenants, sergeants, corporals, and flag bearers. The ritual role of the society is to guard Jesus from his persecutors during the Waehma. Under vow to Jesus, the horsemen wear no distinctive regalia, but carry lances and swords; one carries a blue flag, their most important insignia, signifying good.

Infantry (**Fariseo, Pharisee**) Representing the people who persecuted and executed Christ, the Fariseos ritually enact the pursuit, capture, and crucifixion of Jesus. Ritually subordinate to the Horsemen Society, the other organization with the Customs Authority, the Infantry are the focus of interest in the dramatic narrative of the Waehma. The ritual head of the Fariseos is Pontius Pilate, an office held by several people at the same time. Pilate sits or stands apart from the active arena of command during the ceremony but is deferred to and consulted with in difficult matters. Jesus is regarded as the actual head of the Fariseo Society and members are under vow to Christ for three years or often for life.

One part of the Infantry is called the Soldiers of Rome. Sometimes called foot soldiers, they represent the worst kind of evil. Organized militarily, the top command consists of boys and men who perform unmasked. Their role is to promote and supervise participation of individuals in the Waehma. Their flag is red, the color associated with the land of the dead. On Holy Saturday, the Soldiers of Rome are stripped of their evil power in ceremonial battle with the church group, the Matachin dancers, a Deer Dance, and the Pascolas, who unite in "killing" them with flowers. Afterwards, the Soldiers undergo a kind of rebaptism back into the world of good men.

The Chapayekas, the other part of the Infantry, who are under the command of the Soldiers of Rome, are masked ceremonial performers most commonly called chaps or Judases. Clad in blankets and wearing a belt of deer-hoof rattles and leg rattles of cocoons, with helmet masks covering their heads down to their necks, they spend most of their time clowning in foolish but threatening ways. Their duty is to enforce behavior taboos. Compelled by vows of ritual silence, they communicate through gesture by shaking deer (or pig) hoof rattles and two sticks. They use their left hands and do sacred things backward. Their clowning activities and pantomine (which contrast with the Pascolas dancers) are shockingly blasphemous and irreverent. They do hundreds of things that no ordinary Yaqui would do. The Matachin Dance Society, Deer Dancer, and Pascola dancers unite in "killing" the *fariseos* with flowers, a symbol of Christ's blood.

Pahkome (*fiesteros*)

One of the five well-defined authorities in a Yaqui town, the Pahkome burn the dead during summer and autumn seasons, maintain the town's continuing obligations to its patron saint each year, and at the annual fiesta enact the triumph of Christians over Moors in a ritual battle. Of limited influence in town affairs, compared with the other four authorities, the Pahkome are regarded as fulfilling some of the most arduous duties for the town. They manage and administer the annual SAINT'S DAY FIESTA, the most complex of the various Pahkos. They divide the town into two competing companies, organize two separate, simultaneous fiestas in the town plaza, and oversee the ritual resolution of the mock battle. There are two distinct groups of Pahkome, the Reds and the Blues, symbolized by different-colored wooden crosses, during the Saint's Day celebration.

Military Society (Bow Leaders, Coyotes)

One of five well-defined authorities in the Yaqui town government, the Bow Leaders, or Officers, have served Yaqui communities for centuries as a military society defending towns. Membership in this military organization became a sacred obligation. During the 19th century, when the society integrated with the church sodalities of the town, it became a ceremonial sodality like those that constituted the integrated units of the church. Today, the Coyotes have many religious duties. They are visible during certain Pahkos, ceremonial fiestas when Yaquis gather to perform religious rituals that combine their Christian faith with Native elements. On these occasions, Coyotes dance and perform burlesques to special songs. By singing and dancing they also perform their duty as stewards of the Yaqui homeland. They have many obligations to the church and other ceremonial activities throughout the year and participate in rituals at Sunday services in Yaqui churches. They protect the altar during the ritual of the MUHTE and lead the KONTI procession each Sunday, carrying the image of their patroness, the Blessed Virgin, the Virgin of Guadalupe. They act like guardians during ceremonials to keep drinking and fighting out of the plaza or the household patio where a ceremonial is taking place. Initiations take place in the church, with sponsorship of a godparent. The Military Society is under the authority of the Kohtumbre, Customs Authority, during the Lenten season and the Waehma.

YEHASURI ("Not Human Ones," Wild Indians) *Catawba* Dwarf-like creatures of traditional Catawba belief. These forest spirits were known to kidnap children, to tie people by the hair to trees, to play with baby clothing left outside to dry, to braid the manes of horses, and to cause other mischief and even death. Their diet was believed to consist of acorns, roots, fungi, turtles, and tadpoles. Precautions taken against the spirits by the Catawba included rubbing tobacco on the head, taking clothing inside at night, and sweeping away children's tracks from the yard before nightfall. These tiny creatures are also called Wild Indians in English.

YEI *Navajo (Dineh)* The Navajo (Dineh) name for deities who emerged from lower worlds before the creation of the human race and appeared as helpful mentors as soon as humans appeared. They are HOLY PEOPLE who are speechless and who may change their forms at will. Before the *yei* people left for homes to which they were assigned, they made face prints of themselves in white bead, turquoise, abalone, and jet but directed humans to reproduce their faces in buckskin. Buckskin YEIBICHAI MASKS, painted white, blue, red, or black, imitate the original jewel face prints. The *yei* are represented in human form in sacred paintings made in connection with curing ceremonies and by the masked impersonators in public performances like the NIGHT WAY CEREMONY. The *yeis*, both in SANDPAINTINGs and as masked beings, are believed to visit the home of the patient in person. *Yeis* prefer hours after sunset until dawn, but they also perform in daylight and sandpaintings of them are made only in daylight. Believed to be benevolent to humans, they perform over patients to remove causes of indisposition. Among Navayo ceremonies that require the appearance of masked impersonators are the Mountain Way, Big God Way, Plume Way, and Coyote Way.

YEIBICHAI MASKS *Navajo (Dineh)* Rectangular, roundhead, or face masks worn by impersonators representing the *YEI* people. They contain the spiritual life and powers of the spirits they represent. Made of unwounded buckskin, their manufacture is regulated. They must be cut and sewn during a NIGHT WAY (Yeibichai) CEREMONY, then inducted for public use at a second ceremony. At this ceremony, every mask is colored and feathered properly, and after this, pollen is strewn through the eyes and the mouths of the masks. They are colored anew for every dance, and trimmings are removed after every public performance. The masks belong to medicine men who conduct Yeibichai ceremonies, and they must be treated with respect and handled with proper prayers and ceremony. If used incorrectly, disaster can result. (See also MASKS.)

YELLOW HAND (Ohamagweia, Ohamagwaya) *(c. early 1760s–?) Comanche.* A SUN DANCE leader and Shoshone chief. Yellow Hand, said to be related to the guide and interpreter Sacajawea, joined the eastern Shoshone people and introduced the Sun Dance to them in about 1800. He instructed them in the Comanche or Kiowa form of the ceremony. It is believed that the Sun Dance came to him in a vision. Besides serving as a Sun Dance leader, he was also recognized as a Shoshone chief in 1820. Yellow Hand's Shoshone band received a visit from PIERRE JEAN DESMET, the Catholic missionary, in 1840. At that time the chief is said to have instituted stricter laws against stealing. Yellow Hand's descendants maintained leadership of the Shoshone Sun Dance for more than a century. JOHN TREHERO, Yellow Hand's great-grandson, introduced it to the Crow people in 1941. Trehero believed that Yellow Hand was a Crow and that the ceremony he originated among the Shoshone came from the Crow's Beaver Dance. He is also known as Ohamagwaya.

YELLOWTAIL, THOMAS (Medicine Rock Chief) *(1903–?) Crow* Medicine man and SUN DANCE chief of the Crow. Yellowtail was born on March 7, 1903, near Lodge Grass, Montana. His family's surname came from a shortened version of his father's name, "Hawk with the Yellow Tail Feathers." Yellowtail, a member of the Whistling Waters clan, was born during the reservation era. As a youth, he was influenced by elders who had participated in the traditional way of life on the Plains. When Yellowtail was six years old, he was given the name Medicine Rock Chief by Chief Medicine Crow, a renowned war chief and holy man among the Crow. As a child, Yellowtail was also adopted into the Sacred Pipe Society of his people. Years later, in 1924, he was adopted into the Tail Feather Society as well. Both traditional societies originated with responsibilities for sacred activities.

About 1971, after Yellowtail had participated in the Sun Dance for nearly 30 years, he was chosen by the Shoshone holy man JOHN TREHERO to succeed him as Sun Dance chief. Trehero had reintroduced the Sun Dance among the Crow in 1941 at the request of WILLIAM BIG DAY. Nearly 90 and ready to retire, Trehero transferred his medicine powers to Yellowtail and assisted him until he was able to conduct the sacred work on his own. Yellowtail's Sun Dance religion includes SWEAT LODGE purification, the VISION QUEST, daily prayers with the pipe, and the actual Sun Dance ceremony. According to Yellowtail, the Sun Dance is much more than a three- to four-day ceremony. Other religious activities must take place throughout the year, including daily prayers, monthly prayer meetings, and four outdoor ceremonies at the Sun Dance site.

Yellowtail married his wife, Susie, on April 27, 1929, and they raised many children, including three of their own. In 1952 the couple traveled to Europe, North Africa, and the Holy Land on a Native American dance tour sponsored by the United States State Department. In 1970 they were jointly named outstanding American Indian of the Year at the All-American Indian Days in Sheridan, Wyoming. Yellowtail's wife, who died in 1981, was inducted into the Montana Hall of Fame in 1987 and a biography on her life is planned. In 1984 Yellowtail chose John Pretty on Top to succeed him as Sun Dance chief of the Crow. Two years later Pretty on Top, who prayed with the SACRED PIPE, represented American Indians at a world prayer meeting held by Pope John Paul II in Italy. Yellowtail told his life story to his adopted son, Michael Oren Fitzgerald, and it was published as *Yellowtail: Crow Medicine Man and Sun Dance Chief* in 1991.

YOANIA *Yaqui* The term refers to the Yaqui homeland and way of life before Christianity. It is the spiritual essence of the *HUYA ANIYA,* the ancient source of all great Yaqui traditions and powers. Yaquis believe the *yoania* to be visible under certain conditions in visions or dreams, in distant places, in caves or in secret places. A person with an earnest desire to see *yoania* and extraordinary courage to survive ordeals attains success. Participation is voluntary and the reason an individual desires to experience the *yoania* is to acquire skills or special gifts associated with it.

YONAGUSKA ("Drowning-Bear," derived from "The Bear Drowns Him," Yonagusta) *(c. 1759–1839) Cherokee* Prominent peace chief and prophet among the Eastern Band of Cherokee Indians whose oratory was said by other leaders of his day to be unsurpassed. The adopted father of Colonel William Holland Thomas, the legal and business agent to the Cherokee, he lived a short distance from present-day Bryson City, North Carolina, before moving to Oconaluftee. After the removal of the Cherokee to Indian Territory (present-day Oklahoma), Yonaguska and a band of his people remained in their eastern homeland and, assisted by Thomas, settled on land near Soco Creek, in North Carolina.

Later in life, when he was about 60 years old, the leader became ill and went into a trance. Mourned as dead by his people, Yonaguska regained consciousness at the end of 24 hours and announced that he had gone to the spirit world. Besides seeing and talking with departed friends and relatives, he reported that he had spoken with the Creator, who had given him a message to share with the people. Awed by his experience, his followers listened to every word. Yonaguska, who stopped drinking and organized a temperance society, influenced others by his message and example. He also had Thomas write out a pledge banishing whiskey from among his people, and it was signed, not only by the chief, but by council members.

Although Yonaguska and his people were pressured to move to Indian Territory, the leader and prophet was opposed to Removal and resisted all efforts to persuade him to leave. He stated that the Cherokee could only be happy in the home where nature had put them and that they were safe from aggression there. Yonaguska counseled his people to have friendly and peaceful relations with whites, but he maintained his own faith and was suspicious of Christian missionaries. After the Bible had been translated into the Cherokee language, he refused to allow it to be read to his people until first listening to a reading himself. After hearing some of it, he commented: "Well, it seems to be a good book—strange that the white people are not better, after having had it so long."

Shortly before dying, Yonaguska was carried, as he requested, to the Soco Creek town house, built under his supervision, and spoke to his people for the last time. After recommending Thomas as chief and repeating his warning against removal to Indian Territory, the leader died. His death, in April 1839, occurred a short time after the Cherokee removal to present-day Oklahoma. Besides his two wives, Yonaguska's family included a daughter, Katalsta, who became a potter. The prophet's name also appears as Yonagusta.

YOUNG, EGERTON RYERSON *(1840–1909)* Methodist missionary at Norway House, a post of the Hudson's Bay Company on Lake Winnepeg's northern end, and at other mission stations in Canada. Young was born in Crosby, Upper Canada, and attended the provincial normal school in Toronto. After serving as a schoolmaster for several years, he was ordained to the Methodist ministry in 1867 and was sent to Norway House in present-day Manitoba the following year. At Norway House he repeated the agricultural experiments attempted by JAMES EVANS, who had established missions in the region in the 1840s and became known for his linguistic work among the Cree people. Young remained in the region until 1876, when he returned to Toronto and served as a missionary at other stations until his retirement in 1888. He then authored a number of publications based on his experiences in the north, including *By Canoe and Dog Train Among the Cree and Saulteaux Indians* (London, 1890), *Stories from Indian Wigwams and Northern Camp-fires* (London, 1893), and a compilation of Native stories entitled *Algonquin Indian Tales* (1903). Among his works of fiction were such titles as *Three Boys in the Wild North Land, Summer* (1896), *Winter Adventures of Three Boys in the Great Lone Land* (London, 1899), *The Children of the Forest* (1904), and *The Battle of the Bears* (1907). Young's family included a son of the same name who was born at Norway House in 1869, entered the Methodist ministry, and also authored books of northern stories.

YOYOUNI (YO-YONAN) *(?–1917) Wanapam* The son and successor of SMOHALLA, the dreamer-prophet from the Priest Rapids area of the Columbia River in Washington State. Yoyouni, who also had the name Tolookhowit as a youngster and became known as Little Smohalla, was the prophet's only son. The leader instructed Yoyouni and his cousin, PUCK HYAH TOOT, in the sacred ways of their people, and they both became priests. After Smohalla died in 1895, they were left to carry on his teachings. During a serious illness when the people were locked in by snow and ice, Yoyouni was guided to a distant medicine dance by a raven. By the time the five-day ceremony ended, he was strong enough to sing and dance. The people knew then that his spiritual powers were strong. Yoyouni's life was cut short by illness in 1917. During the winter of that year he, Puck Hyah Toot, and other tribal members went hunting for deer or elk to use in a midwinter ceremony. While the group was trying to reach home during a blizzard, Yoyouni became ill and died. As dreamer-prophets were known to return to life with messages from the spirit world, many people attended his funeral. He was buried on December 22, leaving Puck Hyah Toot to continue the sacred ways. Yoyouni was married to Willulami of Rock Creek.

YUWIPI A Lakota term generally used to refer to Yuwipi lowanpi, a nighttime curing ceremony conducted in a darkened room by a medicine man, Yuwipi wicasa, who has been bound and wrapped like a mummy. According to Lakota holy man JOHN (FIRE) LAME DEER it is a sacred word with many meanings. *Yuwi* means "to bind, to tie up." *Yuwipi* is also the term for tiny, sacred stones gathered from anthills for use in ceremonies and is another name for Tunka, an ancient, rocklike spirit. Another definition is given by the anthropologist William K. Powers, who points out that the spirits who arrive during the course of the ceremony are often called *yuwipis.* A person seeking help with a problem, such as an illness or the disappearance of a loved one, generally initiates the ceremony by approaching a Yuwipi medicine man with a pipe filled with tobacco to request assistance. If agreement is reached, preparations begin. The person seeking help, or the sponsor, is required to provide food for a feast following the ceremony and to prepare for the Yuwipi as directed by the medicine man.

An account of a contemporary Yuwipi ceremony indicates that it includes the following features. It can be held in any large room where the furniture has been removed and the windows, doors, and mirrors have been covered to make certain that no light penetrates while the ritual is in progress. Sacred sage is spread on the floor. Tobacco is put into small squares of cloth from the four sacred colors (black, red, yellow, and white) to make small bundles that are then strung together. This string is used to form a rectangle within the room. The area inside the rectangle is the sacred place where the medicine man lies bound and wrapped. Participants sit outside the string against the walls of the room. After the string is in place, four flags of cloth in the same four colors are put at the corners of the rectangle. According to Lame Deer, some Yuwipi medicine men use green and blue flags as well. These symbolize the earth and sky. A staff, half red and half black with a white stripe dividing the two and an eagle feather tied to the top, is placed between the black and the red flags. The colors are symbolic of day and night, and the eagle represents power and wisdom from above. Also on the staff is the tail of a special deer, *tahca topta sapa,* which represents the unity of the universe. Two, sometimes four, gourds, or rattles, containing tiny sacred stones are put at the sides of the altar. *Yuwipi* ceremonies, according to Lame Deer, must have tobacco offerings, the flags, the staff, the altar, the gourds, and most importantly the SACRED PIPE. A kettle with ritual dog meat and a container of spring water are also placed within the rectangle.

After the room is purified with burning sweet grass and participants put sage in their hair or behind an ear to attract the spirits, the ceremony can begin. The Yuwipi man is tied up, using rawhide, his arms behind his back. Then he is wrapped in a star quilt, formerly a buffalo robe, and tied with seven knots in the rawhide thong. Tying has to be done correctly, without mistakes, to avoid endangering the holy man. As Lame Deer states in his autobiography, "This is tying us together, ending the isolation between one human being and another; it is making a line from man to the Great Spirit. It means a harnessing of power. The man is tied there so that the spirit can come and use him. It pulls the people together and teaches them." After the tying is done, the Yuwipi man is placed on the floor, face down, and those present concentrate on their prayers. Drumming, singing and praying begin. According to Lame Deer, spirits arrive as bright sparks of light: "They come from above and from beneath, making the walls and the floor shake and tremble. They come as voices, little voices without bodies or mouths, nonhuman voices which we can understand all the same." When the ceremony ends and the lights are back on, the Yuwipi man is seen sitting unwrapped and untied. After talking with the participants, he prays with the sacred pipe, then passes it around clockwise for each person to smoke. The ceremony ends with a feast and a drink of pure water. In addition to John (Fire) Lame Deer, other Yuwipi men included in this volume are FRANK FOOLS CROW and GEORGE PLENTY WOLF.

Z

ZEISBERGER, DAVID *(1721–1808)* Member of the Church of the United Brethren, or Moravians, who served as a missionary to Indians in Pennsylvania, New York, Ohio, Canada, and Michigan for more than 60 years. Born in Zauchtenthal, Moravia, on April 11, 1721, Zeisberger's first years of mission work, 1744 to 1755, were devoted to studying Iroquoian languages and serving as an emissary and interpreter. After the French and Indian War curtailed these efforts, he began establishing mission towns among Algonquian people, starting with Christian converts from the Mahican and Lenni Lenape, or Delaware, tribes. After 1763 he lived in Delaware towns, where his missionary activities included studying the Native language, translating religious works, and teaching literacy. He was successful in converting PAPOUNHAN there but became the enemy of the Munsee prophet WANGOMEN.

In 1771 he followed the Native people farther west, building a church at Schonbrunn, the first beyond the Ohio River. Although four villages were established, war was again disastrous to his efforts. In 1781 he was arrested by British authorities who accused him of revolutionary sympathies. During the following year, while he was absent, American troops killed nearly 100 Christian Indians from Gnadenhutten and Salem and burned their villages. Zeisberger followed Native refugees to Canada, where he founded the town of Fairfield on the Thames in Ontario in 1792, to Michigan, and again to Ohio. Because so much of his work was destroyed by war and the onslaught of whites through Delaware land, his legacy is primarily literary. Besides translating numerous religious works into the Delaware language, he wrote a primer in that language. He also wrote grammatical studies of Onondaga and Delaware and an ethnographic treatise. His publications include *Essay of a Delaware Indian and English Spelling Book* (Philadelphia, 1776), *A Collection of Hymns for the Use of the Christian Indians* (Philadelphia, 1803), *Sermons to Children* (Philadelphia, 1803), *The History of our Lord and Saviour Jesus Christ* (New York, 1821), and *Diary of David Zeisberger* (Cincinnati, 1885). Zeisberger died on November 17, 1808, in Goshen, Ohio. (See also ETTWEIN, JOHN; GRUBE, BERNHARD ADAM; HECKEWELDER, JOHN; POST, CHRISTIAN FREDERICK.)

ZINZENDORF, NIKOLAUS LUDVIG *(1700–1760)* Leader and philanthropist of the Church of the United Brethren, or Moravians, who initiated missionary work among Native groups. Zinzendorf was born into a noble, wealthy Austrian Lutheran family on May 26, 1700. He studied law at Wittenberg from 1716 to 1719 and later served as a royal counselor in Dresden and as a squire. By 1722 he possessed an estate, which he used to house Protestants from Bohemia and Moravia. Within five years they had revived the Unitas Fratrum, or the Church of the Brethren, as an organizational structure. Zinzendorf served as preacher, as well as patron, of a community called Hernhut, and after 1737 he became the bishop of the Moravians. He arrived in America in 1741 to initiate missionary efforts and to oversee efforts started by his church as early as 1734. In an effort to unite German Protestants, he dispensed with his titles and began working as a preacher in Pennsylvania. His efforts to convert Lutheran and Reformed adherents to the Moravian Church were for the most part unsuccessful. In 1742 Zinzendorf made three trips to Delaware (Lenni Lenape) and Iroquois communities, starting Moravian missionary work that was to endure until the end of the century. Zinzendorf returned to Europe on January 9, 1743, and continued his ministry in England and Germany until his death.

ZUNI CEREMONIALISM The foundation of Zuni ceremonalism is the collective force of people participating in a series of great public rituals closely correlated with growth, maturing, and harvesting of grain. There is an elaborate ritual life of interrelated ceremonial societies, each devoted to the worship of groups of spirits and each having a priesthood, rules for membership, a body of sacred ritual, sacred objects, special places of worship, and a calendric cycle of ceremonies starting and ending with the winter solstice. The activities of these societies are meant to bring individuals and groups into harmony with the universe and to assure fertility, growth, and harvest of corn.

The Zuni ritual year is divided into two halves by the winter and summer solstices, midwinter to midsummer and midsummer to midwinter. The winter ceremonies primarily are concerned with medicine, war, and fertility, and the summer ceremonies are concerned with rain and crops. At the solstices, there is a convergence of these various activities in honor of the sun. Ceremonies take place outdoors in plazas and indoors in kivas, or ceremonial chambers, of religious organizations or individual homes. The annual round of ceremonies includes dancing, drumming, singing and chanting of ancient texts, masking regalia, body painting, corn pollen sprinkling, puppetry, clowning, curing, feasting, smoking, and racing. (See Subject Index for Zuni ceremonies included in this volume. See also ITIWANA.)

ZUNI SALT LAKE *New Mexico* One of the most sacred of all lakes to the Navajo (Dineh). Located in a flat crater of an extinct volcano, it is reputed to be the home of Salt Woman, one of the Holy People who traveled around the country leaving deposits of salt wherever she rested until she reached this lake and settled here. Navajo, Hopi, and Zuni as well as other tribes have made annual pilgrimmages to gather SALT, which is highly valued for ceremonial purposes.

FURTHER READING

GENERAL TITLES

Albanese, Catherine L. *Nature Religion in America: From the Algonquian Indians to the New Age.* Chicago: University of Chicago Press, 1990.

Allen, Paula Gunn. *The Sacred Hoop.* Boston: Beacon Press, 1986.

Andrus, Cecil D., Chairman, Federal Agencies Task Force. *American Indian Religious Freedom Act Report, P.L. 95–341.* Washington, D.C.: U.S. Department of the Interior, 1979.

Arden, Harvey. "An Indian Cemetery Desecrated: Who Owns Our Past?" *National Geographic,* March 1989, 376–393.

Arden, Harvey, and Wall, Steve. *Travels in a Stone Canoe: The Return to the Wisdomkeepers.* New York: Simon & Schuster, 1998.

Axtell, James, ed. *The Indian Peoples of Eastern America: A Documentary History of the Sexes.* New York: Oxford University Press, 1981.

———. *The Invasion Within: The Contest of Cultures in Colonial North America.* New York: Oxford University Press, 1985.

Bartlett, Richard H. *The Indian Act of Canada.* 2d ed., Saskatoon, Saskatchewan, Canada: University of Saskatchewan, Native Law Centre, 1988.

Beck, Peggy V., and Walter, Anna L. *The Sacred: Ways of Knowledge, Sources of Life.* Tsaile, Arizona: Navajo Community College Press, 1977.

Benedict, Ruth Fulton. *The Concept of the Guardian Spirit in North America.* American Anthropological Association Memoirs, no. 29. 1923. New York: Kraus Reprint Corporation, 1964.

Bierhorst, John. *The Mythology of North America.* New York: William Morrow and Co., 1985.

Biographical Dictionary of Indians of the Americas. 2 vols. Newport Beach, Calif.: American Indian Publishers, 1983.

Bopp, Judie; Lane, Phil; et al. *The Sacred Tree: Reflections on Native American Spirituality.* Lethbridge, Alberta, Canada: Four Worlds Development Press, 1984.

Brown, George W., ed. *Dictionary of Canadian Biography.* Vol. I, 1000–1700. Toronto: University of Toronto Press, 1966.

Brown, Vinson. *Voices of Earth and Sky.* Happy Camp, Calif.: Naturegraph Publishers, 1974.

Brumble, H. David, III. *American Indian Autobiography.* Berkeley: University of California Press, 1988.

Bullchild, Percy. *American Indian Genesis: The Story of Creation.* Berkeley, Calif.: Ulysses Press, 1998.

Burland, Cottie. *North American Indian Mythology.* Rev. ed. New York: Peter Bedrick Books, 1985.

Capps, Walter, Holden, ed. *Seeing With a Native Eye.* New York: Harper and Row, 1976.

Collins, John James. *Native American Religions: A Geological Survey.* Native American Studies, vol. 1, Lewiston, N.Y.: Edwin Mellen Press, 1991.

Cooper, Thomas W. *A Time Before Deception: Truth in Communication, Culture, and Ethics.* Santa Fe: Clear Light Publishers, 1998.

Crozier-Hogle, Lois, and Wilson, Darryl Babe. *Surviving in Two Worlds: Contemporary Native American Voices.* Edited by Jay Liebold. Austin: University of Texas Press, 1997.

———. *For This Land: Writings on Religion in America.* New York: Routledge, 1999.

Deloria, Vine, Jr. *God Is Red.* New York: Dell, 1973. Deloria, Vine, Jr.

Dockstader, Frederick J. *Great North American Indians: Profiles in Life and Leadership.* New York: Van Nostrand Reinhold, 1977.

Dooling, D. M., and Jordan-Smith, Paul, eds. *I Become Part of It: Sacred Dimensions in Native American Life.* New York: Parabola Books, 1989.

Eastman, Charles A. *The Soul of the Indian.* Boston: Houghton Mifflin, 1911.

Echo-Hawk, Roger C., and Echo-Hawk, Walter R. *Battlefields and Burial Grounds: The Indian Struggle to Protect Ancestral Graves in the United States.* Minneapolis: Lerner Publications, 1994.

Edmunds, R. David, ed. *American Indian Leaders: Studies in Diversity.* Lincoln: University of Nebraska Press, 1980.

Fiddler, Chief Thomas, and Stevens, James R. *Killing the Shamen.* Moonbeam, Ontario, Canada: Penumbra Press, 1985.

Gill, Sam D. *Native American Religions: An Introduction.* Belmont, Calif.: Wadsworth, 1982.

———. *Native American Religious Action: A Performance Approach to Religion.* Columbia: University of South Carolina Press, 1987.

Gill, Sam D., and Sullivan, Irene F. *Dictionary of Native American Mythology.* Santa Barbara, Calif.: ABC-CLIO, 1992.

Green, Rayna, and Mitchell, Nancy Marie, comps. *American Indian Sacred Objects, Skeletal Remains, Repatriation, and Reburial: A Resource Guide.* Washington, D.C.: American Indian Program, National Museum of American History, Smithsonian Institution, 1990.

Grinnell, George Bird. *When Buffalo Ran.* Norman: University of Oklahoma Press, 1966. (Originally published by Yale University Press in 1920.)

Hagen, William T. *Indian Police and Judges: Experiments in Acculturation and Control.* New Haven: Yale University Press, 1966.

Harrod, Howard L. *Renewing the World: Plains Indian Religion and Morality.* Tucson: University of Arizona Press, 1987.

———. *Becoming and Remaining a People: Native American Religions on the Northern Plains.* Tucson: University of Arizona Press, 1995.

Heth, Charlotte, ed. *Native American Dance: Ceremonies and Social Traditions.* Washington, D.C.: National Museum of the American Indian, Smithsonian Institution with Starwood Publishing, 1992.

Hodge, William. *A Bibliography of Contemporary North American Indians.* New York: Interland, 1976.

Horse Capture, George P., ed. *The Concept of Sacred Materials and Their Place in the World.* Cody, Wyoming: Buffalo Bill Historical Center, 1989.

Hudson, Charles M., ed. *Black Drink: A Native American Tea.* Athens: University of Georgia Press, 1979.

Hultkrantz, Åke. *The Religions of the American Indian.* Berkeley: University of California Press, 1967.

———. *Belief and Worship in Native North America.* Edited by Christopher Vecsey. Syracuse: Syracuse University Press, 1981.

———. *The Study of American Indian Religions.* Edited by Christopher Vecsey. New York: Crossroad, 1983.

———. *Native Religions of North America: The Power of Visions and Fertility.* New York: Harper and Row, 1987.

Irwin, Lee. *The Dream Seekers: Native American Visionary Traditions of the Great Plains.* Norman: University of Oklahoma Press, 1994.

———. ed. "To Hear the Eagles Cry: Contemporary Themes in Native American Spirituality." Special Issue, *American Indian Quarterly,* vol. 20, nos. 3 & 4 (Summer and Fall 1996). Parts 1 and 2.

———. ed. "To Hear the Eagles Cry: Contemporary Themes in Native American Spirituality." Special Issue, *American Indian Quarterly,* vol. 21, no. 1. (Winter 1997). Part 3.

Johnson, Sandy. *The Book of Elders: The Life Stories of Great American Indians.* New York: HarperCollins Publishers, 1994.

Leeming, David Adams, and Page, Jake. *The Mythology of Native North America.* Norman: University of Oklahoma Press, 1998.

Jorgenson, Joseph G. *The Sun Dance Religion.* Chicago: University of Chicago Press, 1972.

Lincoln, Kenneth, and Slagle, Al Logan. *The Good Red Road: Passages into Native America.* San Francisco: Harper and Row, 1987.

Littlefield, Daniel F., Jr., and Parins, James W. *A Biobibliography of Native American Writers, 1772–1924.* Metuchen, N.J.: Scarecrow Press, 1981.

Lurie, Nancy Oestreich. *North American Indian Lives.* Milwaukee: Milwaukee Public Museum, 1985.

Lyons, William S. *Encyclopedia of Native American Healing.* New York: W.W. Norton and Company, 1996.

McCoy, Ronald. *Circles of Power.* Flagstaff: Museum of Northern Arizona Press, 1984.

Mark, Joan. *A Stranger in Her Native Land: Alice Fletcher and the American Indians.* Lincoln: University of Nebraska Press, 1988.

Matthiessen, Peter. *Indian Country.* New York: Viking Press, 1984.

Mending the Circle: A Native American Repatriation Guide. New York: American Indian Ritual Object Repatriation Foundation, 1996.

Michaelsen, Robert. S. "'We Also Have a Religion': The Free Exercise of Religion Among Native Americans." *American Indian Quarterly 7,* no. 3 (Summmer 1983):111–142.

———. "The Significance of the American Indian Religious Freedom Act of 1978." *Journal of the American Academy of Religion 52, no. 1 (March 1984):19–115.*

Mihesuah, Devon A., ed. "Repatriation: An Interdisciplinary Dialogue." In Special Issue, *American Indian Quarterly,* vol. 20, no. 2 (Spring 1996).

Miller, Dorcas S. *Stars of the First People: Native American Star Myths and Constellations.* Boulder, Colo.: Pruett Publishing, 1997.

Mills, Antonio, and Slobodin, Richard, eds. *Amerindian Rebirth: Reincarnation Belief Among North American Indians and Inuit.* Toronto: University of Toronto Press, 1994.

Milne, Courtney. *Sacred Places in Native North America: A Journey of the Spirit.* New York: Abbeville, 1995.

Nabokov, Peter, and Easton, Robert. *Native American Architecture.* New York: Oxford University Press, 1989.

NARF Legal Review. Boulder, Colorado: Native American Rights Fund.

Paper, Jordan. *Offering Smoke: The Sacred Pipe and Native American Religion.* Moscow: University of Idaho Press, 1988.

Penn, W.S., ed. *The Telling of the World: Native American Stories and Art.* New York: Stewart, Tabori & Chang, 1996.

Powers, William K. *Beyond the Vision: Essays on American Indian Culture.* Norman: University of Oklahoma Press, 1987.

Price, H. Marcus, III. *Disputing the Dead: U.S. Law on Aboriginal Remains and Grave Goods.* Columbia: University of Missouri, 1991.

Price, Monroe E. *Law and the American Indian.* New York: Bobbs-Merrill, 1973.

Prucha, Francis Paul. *A Bibliographic Guide to the History of Indian-White Relations in the United States.* Chicago: University of Chicago, 1977.

———. ed. *Documents of United States Indian Policy.* Second Edition, Expanded. Lincoln: University of Nebraska Press, 1975.

———. *Indian-White Relations in the United States: A Bibliography of Works Published 1975–1980.* Lincoln: University of Nebraska Press, 1982.

Roberts, Sir Charles G. D., and Tunnell, Arthur L. *Canadian Who Was Who, 1875–1937.* Toronto: Trans-Canada Press, 1938.

Rutledge, Don (with Rita Robinson). *Center of the World: Native American Spirituality.* North Hollywood, Calif.: Newcastle Publishing, 1992.

St. Pierre, Mark, and Long Soldier, Tilda. *Walking in the Sacred Manner: Healers, Dreamers, and Pipe Carriers—Medicine Women of the Plains Indians.* New York: Simon & Schuster, 1995.

Sarris, Greg. *Mabel McKay: Weaving the Dream.* Berkeley: University of California Press, 1994.

Seton, Ernest Thompson, and Seton, Julia M. *The Gospel of the Redman.* Santa Fe, N.M.: Seton Village, 1963.

Snake, Reuben, as told to Fikes, Jay C. *Reuben Snake: Your Humble Serpent.* Santa Fe: Clear Light Publishers, 1996.

Stefansson, Vilhjalmur. *Greenland.* New York: Doubleday, 1947.

Steltenkamp, Michael F. *The Sacred Vision: Native American Religion and Its Practice Today.* New York: Paulist Press, 1982.

Story, Norah. *The Oxford Companion to Canadian History and Literature.* Toronto: Oxford University Press, 1967.

Sullivan, Lawrence E., ed. *Native American Religions, North America.* New York: Macmillan, 1987.

Surtees, Robert J. *Canadian Indian Policy: A Critical Bibliography.* Bloomington: Indiana University Press, 1982.

Thompson, Stith. *Tales of North American Indians.* Cambridge: Harvard University Press, 1929.

Underhill, Ruth M. *Red Man's Religion: Beliefs and Practices of the Indians North of Mexico.* Chicago: University of Chicago Press, 1965.

U.S. Commission on Civil Rights. *Religion in the Constitution: A Delicate Balance.* Clearinghouse publication no. 80. Washington, D.C.: U.S. Commission on Civil Rights, 1983.

U.S. Congress. Senate. Select Committee on Indian Affairs. *American Indian Religious Freedom. Hearings Before the United States Senate Select Committee on Indian Affairs on S.J. Res. 102.* 95th Cong., 2d sess., February 24 and 27, 1978.

U.S. Congress. Senate. Select Committee on Indian Affairs. *Native American Grave and Burial Protection Act; Native American Repatriation of Cultural Patrimony Act; and Heard Museum Report. Hearing Before the Senate Select Committee on Indian Affairs on S. 1021 and S. 1980.* 101st Cong., 2d sess., May 14, 1990.

U.S. Congress. Senate. Select Committee on Indian Affairs. *Religious Freedom Act Amendments. Hearing Before the Senate Select Committee on Indian Affairs on S. 1124.* 101st Congress, 1st Session, September 28, 1989.

U.S. Fish and Wildlife Service. *Endangered Species Act of 1973; As Amended through the 100th Congress.* Washington, D.C.: U.S. Department of the Interior, 1988.

———. *Administration of the Marine Mammal Protection Act of 1972: January 1, 1988–December 31, 1988.* Report of the Department of the Interior. Washington, D.C.: U.S. Department of the Interior, 1989.

Van Doren, Charles, ed. *Webster's American Biographies.* Springfield, Mass.: Merriam, 1974.

Vecsey, Christopher, ed. *Handbook of American Indian Religious Freedom.* New York: Crossroad, 1991.

———. *Imagine Ourselves Richly: Mythic Narratives of North American Indians.* New York: Crossroad, 1988.

———. ed. *Religion in Native North America.* Moscow: University of Idaho Press, 1990.

Waldman, Carl. *Atlas of the North American Indian.* New York: Facts On File, 1985.

———. *Encyclopedia of the Native American Tribes.* New York: Facts On File, 1988.

———. *Who Was Who in Native American History: Indians and Non-Indians from Early Contacts through 1900.* New York: Facts On File, 1990.

Walker, Deward E., Jr., ed. *Systems of North American Witchcraft and Sorcery.* Anthropological Monographs no. 1. Moscow: University of Idaho, 1970.

Wall, Steve. *Wisdom's Daughters: Conversations with Women Elders of Native America.* New York: HarperCollins Publishers, 1993.

———. *Shadowcatchers: A Journey in Search of the Teachings of Native American Healers.* New York: HarperCollins Publishers, 1994.

Wall, Steve, and Arden, Harvey. *Wisdomkeepers: Meetings with Native American Spiritual Elders.* Hillsboro, Oregon: Beyond Words Publishing, 1990.

Wallace, W. Stewart. *The Macmillan Dictionary of Canadian Biography.* Toronto: Macmillan Co. of Canada, 1963.

Williams, Walter L. *The Spirit and the Flesh.* Boston: Beacon Press, 1986.

Williamson, Ray A. *Living the Sky: The Cosmos of the American Indian.* Norman: University of Oklahoma Press, 1984.

Yarrow, H. C. North American Burial Customs. Edited by V. LaMonte Smith. Ogden, Utah: Eagles's View Publishing, 1988. (Reprint. Smithsonian Institution Bureau of American Ethnology Report, 1879).

MISSIONARIES

Anderson, Owanah. *Jamestown Commitment: The Episcopal Church and the American Indian.* Cincinnati: Forward Movement Publications, 1988.

Baierlein, E. R. *In the Wilderness with the Red Indians: German Missionary to the Michigan Indians, 1847–1853.* Translated by Anita Z. Boldt and edited by Harold W. Moll. Detroit: Wayne State University Press, 1989, 1996. (Originally published in German by Justus Naumann's Buchhandlung, Dresden in 1888).

Battey, Thomas C. *The Life and Adventures of a Quaker Among the Indians.* Norman: University of Oklahoma Press, 1968.

Berkhofer, Robert F. *Salvation and the Savage: An Analysis of Protestant Missions and American Indian Response, 1787–1862.* Lexington: University of Kentucky Press, 1965.

Bowden, Henry Warner. *Dictionary of American Religious Biography.* Westport, Conn.: Greenwood Press, 1977.

———. *American Indians and Christian Missions: Studies in Cultural Conflict.* Chicago: University of Chicago Press, 1981.

Boyd, Robert. *People of the Dalles: The Indians of Wascopam Mission: A Historical Ethnography Based on the Papers of the Methodist Missionaries.* Lincoln: University of Nebraska Press, 1996.

Carlson, Laurie Winn. *On Sidewalks to Heaven: The Women of the Rocky Mountain Mission.* Caldwell, Idaho: Caxton Printers, 1998.

Christopher, Brett. *Positioning the Missionary: John Booth Good and the Colonial Confluence of Cultures.* Vancouver: University of British Columbia Press, 1998.

Coleman, Michael C. *Presbyterian Missionary Attitudes toward American Indians, 1837–1893.* Jackson: University Press of Mississippi, 1985.

Costo, Rupert, and Costo, Jeannette Henry, eds. *The Missions of California: A Legacy of Genocide.* San Francisco: Indian Historian Press, 1987.

Cross, F. L., ed. *The Oxford Dictionary of the Christian Church.* London: Oxford University Press, 1974.

Delfeld, Paula. *The Indian Priest: Philip B. Gordon, 1885–1948.* Chicago: Franciscan Herald Press, 1977.

Donnelly, Joseph, P. *Wilderness Kingdom: Indian Life in the Rocky Mountains: 1840–1847. Journals and Paintings of Nicolas Point S. J.* Chicago: Loyola University Press, 1967.

Drury, Clifford Merrill. *Henry Harmon Spalding.* Caldwell, Idaho: Caxton Printers, 1936.

———. *Elkanah and Mary Walker: Pioneers Among the Spokanes.* Caldwell, Idaho: Caxton Printers, 1940.

Goodbird, Edward. *Goodbird the Indian: His Story: Told by Himself to Gilbert L. Wilson.* St. Paul: Minnesota Historical Society Press, 1985. (Reprint.)

Grant, John Webster. *Moon of Wintertime: Missionaries and the Indians of Canada in Encounter Since 1534.* Toronto: University of Toronto Press, 1984.

Graves, W. W. *Life and Letters of Fathers Ponziglione, Schoenmakers, and Other Early Jesuits at Osage Mission.* St. Paul, Kansas.: By author, 1916.

Hamilton, Raphael. *Marquette's Explorations.* Madison: University of Wisconsin Press, 1970.

Harrod, Howard L. *Mission Among the Blackfeet.* Norman: University of Oklahoma Press, 1971.

Haury, David A. *A Guide to the Mennonite Library and Archives.* North Newton, Kansas: Bethel College, 1981.

Hu-DeHart, Evelyn. *Missionaries, Miners, and Indians: Spanish Contact with the Yaqui Nation of Northwestern New Spain, 1533–1820.* Tucson: University of Arizona, 1981.

Jackson, Leroy F. *Enmegahbowh—A Christian Missionary.* Bismarck: State Historical Society of North Dakota, 1908.

Jenson, Andrew. *Latter-Day Saint Biographical Encyclopedia.* Salt Lake City: Western Epics, 1971. Originally published by the Andrew Jenson History Company, 1901, 1914.

Kelsey, Rayner Wickersham. *Friends and the Indians, 1655–1917.* Philadelphia: Associated Executive Comittee of Friends on Indian Affairs, 1917.

Kessell, John. *The Missions of New Mexico Since 1776.* Albuquerque: University of New Mexico, 1980.

———. *Mission of Sorrows: Jesuit Guevavi and the Pimas, 1691–1767.* Tucson: University of Arizona Press, 1970.

Kidwell, Clara Sue. *Choctaws and Missionaries in Mississippi, 1818–1918.* Norman: University of Oklahoma Press, 1995.

Lee, George P. *Silent Courage: The Autobiography of George P. Lee.* Salt Lake City: Deseret Book Company, 1987.

McLoughlin, William G. *Cherokees and Missionaries, 1789–1839.* New Haven, Conn.: Yale University Press, 1984.

———. *Champions of the Cherokees: Evan and John B. Jones.* Princeton: Princeton University Press, 1990.

Milner, Clyde A., II. *With Good Intentions: Quaker Work among the Pawnees, Otos, and Omahas in the 1870's.* Lincoln: University of Nebraska Press, 1982.

Milner, Clyde A., II, and O'Neil, Floyd A. *Churchmen and the Western Indians 1820–1920.* Norman: University of Oklahoma Press, 1985.

Moore, James T. *Indian and Jesuit: A Seventeenth Century Encounter.* Chicago: University of Chicago Press, 1982.

Morrison, Dane. *A Praying People: Massachuset Acculturation and the Failure of the Puritan Mission, 1600–1690.* New York: Peter Lang Publishing, 1995.

Mulhall, David. *Will to Power: The Missionary Career of Father Morice.* Vancouver: University of British Columbia, 1986.

Nock, David A. *A Victorian Missionary and Canadian Indian Policy: Cultural Synthesis vs Cultural Replacement.* Published for the Canadian Corporation for Studies in Religion. Wilfrid Laurier University Press, 1988.

Noll, Mark A., et al., eds. *Eerdmans' Handbook to Christianity in America.* Grand Rapids, Michigan: William B. Eerdmans, 1983.

O'Brien, Jean M. *Dispossession by Degrees: Indian Land and Identity in Natick, Massachusetts, 1650–1790.* New York: Cambridge University Press, 1997.

Osgood, Phillips Endecott. *Straight Tongue: A Story of Henry Benjamin Whipple, First Episcopal Bishop of Minnesota.* Minneapolis: T. S. Dennison, 1958.

Perkins, Cornelia Adams; Nielson, Marian Gardner; and Jones, Lenora Butt. *Saga of San Juan.* San Juan County, Utah: San Juan County Daughters of Utah Pioneers, 1957.

Peterson, Jacqueline (with Laura Peers). *Sacred Encounters: Father De Smet and the Indians of the Rocky Mountains West.* Norman: University of Oklahoma Press in association with the De Smet Project, Washington State University, 1993.

Pitezel, John H. *Life of Rev. Peter Marksman, An Ojibwa Missionary: Illustrating the Triumphs of the Gospel Among the Ojibwa Indians.* Cincinnati: Western Methodist Book Concern, 1901.

Rahill, Peter J. *The Catholic Indian Missions and Grant's Peace Policy, 1870–1884.* Washington, D.C.: Catholic University of America Press, 1953.

Reese, Linda Williams. "Christianity for the Kiowas" in *Women of Oklahoma, 1890–1920.* Norman: University of Oklahoma Press, 1997.

Roark, Harry M. *Charles Journeycake: Indian Statesman and Christian Leader.* Dallas: Taylor, 1970.

Ronda, James. P., and Axtell, James. *Indian Missions: A Critical Bibliography.* Bloomington: Indiana University Press, 1978.

Ruby, Robert. H., and Brown, John A. *Myron Eells and the Puget Sound Indians.* Seattle: Superior, 1976.

Schultz, Jack M. *The Seminole Baptist Churches of Oklahoma: Maintaining a Traditional Community.* Norman: University of Oklahoma Press, 1999.

Scott, Benjamin, and Neslund, Robert. *The First Cathedral: The Episcopal Community for Mission.* Faribault, Minnesota: Cathedral of Our Merciful Saviour.

Scott, Rev. E. C., D.D., ed. *Ministerial Directory of the Presbyterian Church, U.S. 1861–1941.* Austin, Texas: Von Boeckmann-Jones, 1942.

Shea, John Gilmary. *History of the Catholic Missions Among the Indian Tribes of the U.S., 1529–1854.* New York: E. Dunigan and Brother, 1854.

Simmons, William S., and Simmons, Cheryl L., eds. *Old Light on Separate Ways: The Narragansett Diary of Joseph Fish 1765–1776.* Hanover, N.H.: University Press of New England, 1982.

Smith, Donald B. *Sacred Feathers: The Reverend Peter Jones (Kahkewaquonaby) and the Mississauga Indians.* Lincoln: University of Nebraska Press, 1987.

Sweet, William Warren. *The Congregationalists. Vol. III of Religion on the American Frontier 1783–1850.* New York: Cooper Square Publishers, 1964.

Tanner, Rev. George Clinton. *Fifty Years of Church Work in the Diocese of Minnesota 1857–1907.* St. Paul: Committee of Church Work in the Diocese of Minnesota, 1909.

Terrell, John Upton. *The Arrow and the Cross: A History of the American Indian and the Missionaries.* Santa Barbara, Calif.: Capra Press, 1979.

Tinker, George. *Missionary Conquest: The Gospel and Native American Cultural Genocide.* Minneapolis: Fortress Press, 1993.

Vecsey, Christopher. *On the Padres' Trail* (American Indian Catholics, vol. 1). Notre Dame, Ind.: University of Notre Dame Press, 1996.

———. *The Paths of Kateri's Kin* (American Indian Catholics, vol. 2). Notre Dame, Ind.: University of Notre Dame, 1997.

———. *Where the Two Roads Meet* (American Indian Catholics, vol. 3). Notre Dame, Ind.: University of Notre Dame, 1999.

Warkentin, A., ed. *Who's Who Among the Mennonites.* North Newton, Kansas: by editor, 1937.

Warkentin, A., and Gingerich, Melvin, eds. *Who's Who Among the Mennonites.* North Newton, Kansas: Bethel College, 1943.

Wedel, Waldo R., ed. *The Dunbar-Allis Letters on the Pawnee.* New York: Garland, 1985.

Whipple, Henry Benjamin. *Lights and Shadows of a Long Episcopate.* New York: Macmillan, 1899.

Whitehead, Margaret. *They Call Me Father: Memoirs of Father Nicolas Coccola.* Vancouver: University of British Columbia, 1988.

PROPHETS AND RELIGIOUS MOVEMENTS

Aberle, David F. *The Peyote Religion among the Navajo.* Chicago: University of Chicago Press, 1982 (1966).

Aberle, David F., and Stewart, Omer C. *Navajo and Ute Peyotism: A Chronological and Distributional Study.* Boulder: University of Colorado Press, 1957.

Anderson, Edward F. *Peyote: The Divine Cactus.* Tucson: University of Arizona Press, 1980.

Barber, Bernard. "A Socio-Cultural Interpretation of the Peyote Cult." *American Anthropologist* N.S. 43, no. 4, pt. 1 (October-December 1941):673–675.

Barnett, H. G. *Indian Shakers: A Messianic Cult of the Pacific Northwest.* Carbondale and Edwardsville: Southern Illinois University Press, 1957.

Daniels, Edwin. *Ghost Dancing: Sacred Medicine and the Art of J. D. Challenger.* New York: Stewart, Tabori, & Chang, 1998.

d'Azevedo, Warren L. *Straight with the Medicine: Narratives of Washoe Followers of the Tipi Way.* Berkeley, Calif.: Heyday Books, 1985.

Dobyns, Henry F., and Euler, Robert C. *The Ghost Dance of 1889 Among the Pai Indians of Northwestern Arizona.* Flagstaff: Prescott College Press, 1967.

Du Bois, Cora. *The Feather Cult of the Middle Columbia.* General Series in Anthropology 7. Menasha, Wisconsin: George Banta, 1938.

———. *The 1870 Ghost Dance.* Anthropological Records, vol. 3, no. 1 Berkeley: University of California Press, 1939.

Edmunds, R. David. *The Shawnee Prophet.* Lincoln: University of Nebraska Press, 1983.

Herring, Joseph B. *Kenekuk, The Kickapoo Prophet.* Laurence, Kansas: University of Kansas Press, 1988.

Hittman, Michael. *Wovoka and the Ghost Dance.* Carson City, Nevada: The Grace Dangberg Foundation, 1990.

Kehoe, Alice Beck. *The Ghost Dance: Ethnohistory and Revitalization.* New York: Holt, Rinehart and Winston, 1989.

La Barre, Weston. *The Ghost Dance: Origins of Religion.* Garden City, N.Y.: Doubleday, 1970.

———. *The Peyote Cult.* Norman: University of Oklahoma Press, 1989.

Lesser, Alexander. *The Pawnee Ghost Dance Hand Game.* Madison: University of Wisconsin Press, 1978.

Meighan, Clement W., and Riddell, Francis A. *The Maru Cult of the Pomo Indians: A California Ghost Dance Survival.* Los Angeles: Southwest Museum, 1972.

Miller, David Humphries. *Ghost Dance.* Lincoln: University of Nebraska Press, 1959.

Mooney, James. *The Ghost Dance Religion and Wounded Knee.* New York: Dover, 1973. (Reprint from 1896 publication).

Mount, Guy, comp. and ed. *The Peyote Book: A Study of Native Medicine.* Arcata, Calif.: Sweetlight Books, 1987.

Oesterreich, Shelley Anne, comp. *The American Indian Ghost Dance, 1870 and 1890: An Annotated Bibliography.* Westport, Conn.: Greenwood Press, 1991.

Petrullo, Vincenzo. *The Diabolic Root: A Study of Peyotism, the New Indian Religion, Among the Delawares.* New York: Octagon Books, 1975.

Ruby, Robert H., and Brown, John A. *Dreamer-Prophets of the Columbia Plateau.* Norman: University of Oklahoma Press, 1989.

Siskin, Edgar E. *Washo Shamans and Peyotists: Religious Conflict in an American Indian Tribe.* Salt Lake City: University of Utah Press, 1983.

Smith, Hulton, and Snake, Reuben, comps. and eds. *One Nation Under God: The Triumph of the Native American Church.* Santa Fe: Clear Light Publishers, 1996.

Smith, Rex Alan. *Moon of Popping Trees.* New York: Crowell, 1975.

Spier, Leslie. *The Prophet Dance of the Northwest and Its Derivatives: The Source of the Ghost Dance.* General Series in Anthropology I. Menasha, Wisconsin: Banta, 1935.

Stewart, Omer C. *Ute Peyotism: A Study of a Cultural Complex.* Boulder: University of Colorado Press, 1948.

———. *Peyote Religion: A History.* Norman: University of Oklahoma Press, 1987.

Thornton, Russell. *We Shall Live Again: The 1870 and 1890 Ghost Dance Movements As Demographic Revitalization.* Cambridge: Cambridge University Press, 1986.

Trafzer, Clifford E., ed. *American Indian Prophets.* Sacramento: Sierra Oaks, 1986.

Walker, Paul Robert. *Spiritual Leaders.* (American Indian Lives Series). New York: Facts On File, 1994.

Wallace, Anthony F. C., *The Death and Rebirth of the Seneca.* New York: Knopf, 1970.

TRIBAL

Albers, Patricia, and Medicine, Beatrice. *The Hidden Half: Studies of Plains Indian Women.* University Press of America, 1983.

Alvarez, Michelle. "Mount Shasta: A Question of Power." *News From Native California,* vol. 8, no. 3 (Winter 1994/95): 4–7.

———. "An Ongoing Threat to Our Sacred Places: More News on the Status of Mount Shasta." *News From Native California,* vol. 8, no. 4 (Spring 1995): 18–19.

Amoss, Pamela T. *Coast Salish Spirit Dancing: The Survival of an Ancestral Religion.* Seattle: University of Washington Press, 1978.

Annerino, John. *Apache: The Sacred Path to Womanhood.* New York: Marlowe and Company, 1998.

Arden, Harvey, comp. *Noble Red Man: Lakota Wisdomkeeper Matthew King.* Hillsboro, Oreg.: Beyond Words Publishing, 1994.

Bad Heart Bull, Amos, and Blish, Helen. *Pictographic History of the Oglala Sioux.* Lincoln: University of Nebraska Press, 1968.

Bahr, Donald M.; Gregorio, Juan; Lopez, David; and Alvarez, Albert. *Piman Shamanism and Staying Sickness (Ká:cim Múmkidag).* Tucson: University of Arizona Press, 1974.

Bailey, Garrick Alan, ed. *The Osage and the Invisible World: From the Works of Francis La Flesche.* Norman: University of Oklahoma Press, 1995.

Baird, W. David. *The Quapaw Indians: A History of the Downstream People.* Norman: University of Oklahoma Press, 1980.

Balikci, Asen. *The Netsilik Eskimo.* Garden City, N.Y.: Natural History Press, 1970.

Bancroft-Hunt, Norman, and Forman, Werner. *People of the Totem: The Indians of the Pacific Northwest.* Norman: University of Oklahoma Press, 1979.

Barrett, S. A. "Ceremonies of the Pomo Indians." *University of California Publications in American Archaeology and Ethnology* vol. 12, no. 10, Berkeley: University of California Press, 1917.

———. *The Dream Dance of the Chippewa and Menominee Indians of Northern Wisconsin.* New York: AMS, 1979. (Reprint of 1911 work.)

———. "The Wintun Hesi Ceremony." *University of California Publications in American Archaeology and Ethnology* vol. 14, no. 4 (March 1919): 437–488.

Basso, Keith H. *The Cibecue Apache.* New York: Holt, Rinehart and Winston, 1970.

———. *The Gift of Changing Woman.* Bureau of American Ethnology, Bulletin 196, pp. 113–173. Washington, D.C.; Government Printing Office, 1966.

Bean, Lowell John. *Mukat's People: The Cahuilla Indians of Southern California.* Berkeley: University of California Press, 1972.

Bean, Lowell John, and Blackburn, Thomas C., eds. *Native Californians: A Theoretical Perspective.* Socorro, N.M.: Ballena Press, 1976.

Bear Heart (with Molly Larkin). *The Wind is My Mother: The Life and Teachings of a Native American Shaman.* New York: Clarkson N. Potter, 1996.

Black Elk, Wallace, and Lyon, William S. *Black Elk: The Sacred Ways of a Lakota.* San Francisco: Harper and Row, 1990.

Blackburn, Thomas. *Flowers of the Wind: Papers on Ritual, Myth, and Symbolism in California and the Southwest.* Socorro, N.M.: Ballena Press, 1977.

Blaine, Martha Royce. *The Ioway Indians.* Norman: University of Oklahoma Press, 1979.

———. *The Pawnees: A Critical Bibliography.* Bloomington: Indiana University Press, 1980.

Blau, Harold. "Dream Guessing: A Comparative Analysis." *Ethnohistory* 10, no. 3 (Summer 1963): 233–249.

Boas, Franz. *Kwakiutl Ethnography.* Edited by Helen Codere. Chicago: University of Chicago Press, 1966.

———. *The Religion of the Kwakiutl Indians, Part II. Columbia University Contributions to Anthropology,* Vol. 10. New York: Columbia University Press, 1930.

Bowers, Alfred W. *Mandan Social and Ceremonial Organization.* Chicago: University of Chicago Press, 1950.

———. *Hidatsa Social and Ceremonial Organization.* Bureau of American Ethnology, bulletin 194. Washington, D.C.: U.S. Government Printing Office, 1965.

Boyd, Doug. *Rolling Thunder.* New York: Dell, 1974.

Boyd, Maurice. *Kiowa Voices: Ceremonial Dance, Ritual and Song.* Fort Worth: Texas Christian University Press, 1981.

Brightman, Robert. *Grateful Prey: Rock Cree Human-Animal Relationships.* Berkeley: University of California Press, 1993.

Brown, Jennifer S. H., and Brightman, Robert. *"The Orders of the Dreamed": George Nelson on Cree and Northern Ojibwa Religion and Myth, 1823.* St. Paul: Minnesota Historical Society Press, 1988.

Brown, Joseph Epes. *The Sacred Pipe: Black Elk's Account of the Seven Rites of the Oglala Sioux.* Norman: University of Oklahoma, 1953.

Brugge, David M., and Frisbie, Charlotte, eds. *Navajo Religion and Culture: Selected Views.* Papers in Anthropology 17. Santa Fe: Museum of New Mexico Press, 1982.

Bullchild, Percy. *The Sun Came Down: The History of the World as My Blackfeet Elders Told It.* San Francisco: Harper and Row, 1985.

Bunzel, Ruth. "Introduction to Zuni Ceremonialism." Bureau of American Ethnology, 47th annual report. Washington, D.C.: Government Printing Office, 1932.

———. "Zuni Katchinas." Bureau of American Ethnology, 47th annual report. Washington, D.C.: Government Printing Office, 1932.

Bushnell, David I., Jr. *Burials of the Algonquian, Siouan, and Caddoan Tribes West of the Mississippi.* Bureau of American Ethnology, bulletin 83. Washington, D.C.: Government Printing Office, 1927.

———. *Native Cemeteries and Forms of Burial East of the Mississippi.* Bureau of American Ethnology, bulletin 71. Washington, D.C.: Government Printing Office, 1920.

Callahan, Alice Anne. *The Osage Ceremonial Dance I'n-Lon-Schka.* Norman: University of Oklahoma Press, 1990.

Campbell, Janet, and Sam, Archie. "The Primal Fire Lingers." *The Chronicles of Oklahoma* 53, no. 4 (Winter 1975–1976):463–475.

Capron, Louis. *The Medicine Bundles of the Florida Seminole and the Green Corn Dance.* Bureau of American Ethnology, bulletin 151, Anthropological Papers, no. 35. Washington, D.C.: U.S. Government Printing Office, 1953.

Casagrande Joseph B. "John Mink, Ojibwa Informant." In *In the Company of Man: Twenty Portraits of Anthropological Informants,* edited by Joseph B. Casagrande. New York: Harper and Row, 1960.

Catlin, George. *O-Kee-Pa: A Religious Ceremony and Other Customs of the Mandans.* Lincoln: University of Nebraska Press, Bison Book, 1976.

Chafe, Wallace L. *Thanksgiving Seneca Rituals.* Bureau of American Ethnology, bulletin 183. Washington, D.C.: Government Printing Office, 1961.

Chahta Hapia Hoke: We Are Choctaw. Philadelphia, Miss.: Mississippi Band of Choctaw Indians, 1981.

Champs, Flavia Waters. *The Matachines Dance of the Upper Rio Grande: History, Music, and Choreography.* Lincoln: University of Nebraska Press, 1983.

Choate, H. S. *The Yaquis: A Celebration.* Tucson: University of Arizona Press, 1997.

Collier, John. *On the Gleaming Way: Navajos, Eastern Pueblos, Zunis, Hopis, Apaches, and Their Land; and Their Meanings to the World.* Chicago: Sage Books, 1949, 1962.

Collier, John, and Moskowitz, Ira. *Patterns and Ceremonials of the Indians of the Southwest.* New York: Dutton, 1949.

Collins, June. *Valley of the Spirits: The Upper Skagit Indians of Western Washington.* Seattle: University of Washington, 1974.

Colson, Elizabeth. *The Makah Indians: Study of an Indian Tribe in Modern American Society.* Manchester, England: Manchester University Press, 1953.

Colton, Harold S. *Hopi Kachina Dolls With a Key to Their Identification.* Rev. ed. Albuquerque: University of New Mexico Press, 1959.

Conetah, Fred A. *A History of the Northern Ute People.* Fort Duchesne, Utah: Uintah-Ouray Ute Tribe, 1982.

Cooper, John M. *The Gros Ventres of Montana: Part II Religion and Ritual.* Edited by Regina Flannery. Washington, D.C.: Catholic University of America Press, 1956.

Copway, George. *The Traditional History and Characteristic Sketches of the Ojibway Nation.* Toronto: Coles, 1972 (Originally published in London, 1850).

Crow Dog, Mary, and Erdoes, Richard. *Lakota Woman.* New York: Grove Weidenfeld, 1990.

Crummet, Michael. *Sun Dance: The 50th Anniversary Crow Indian Sun Dance.* Helena and Billings, Montana: Falcon Press Publishing, 1993.

Cushing, Frank Hamilton. *Zuni Fetishes.* Bureau of American Ethnology, 2d annual report. Washington, D.C.: Government Printing Office, 1883.

Daugherty, Richard D. *The Yakima People.* Phoenix: Indian Tribal Series, 1973.

DeLoria, Ella. *Speaking of Indians.* Vermillion: University of South Dakota, 1979. (Reprint.)

DeMallie, Raymond J., ed. *The Sixth Grandfather: Black Elk's Teachings Given to John G. Neihardt.* Lincoln: University of Nebraska Press, 1984.

DeMallie, Raymond J., and Parks, Douglas R., eds. *Sioux Indian Religion.* Norman: University of Oklahoma Press, 1987.

Dempsey, Hugh A. *Charcoal's World.* Lincoln: University of Nebraska Press, 1979.

———. *Red Crow, Warrior Chief.* Saskatoon, Saskatchewan, Canada: Western Producer Prairie Books, 1980.

Densmore, Frances. *Chippewa Customs.* Minneapolis: Ross and Haines, 1970. (Reprint of 1929 work.)

———. *Mandan and Hidatsa Music.* Bureau of American Ethnology, bulletin 80. Washington, D.C.: U.S. Government Printing Office, 1923.

———. *Teton Sioux Music.* New York: Da Capo Press, 1972. (Reprint of 1918 work.)

Dewdney, Selwyn. *The Sacred Scrolls of the Southern Ojibway.* Toronto: University of Toronto Press, 1975.

Dial, Adolph, and Eliades, David K. *The Only Land I Know: A History of the Lumbee Indians.* San Francisco: Indian Historian Press, 1975.

Dooling, D. M., and Jordan-Smith, Paul. *I Become Part of It: Sacred Dimensions in Native American Life.* New York: Parabola Books, 1989.

Dorsey, George A. "How the Pawnee Captured the Cheyenne Medicine Arrows." *American Anthropologist* 5, no. 4 (October–December 1903):644–658.

———. "The Osage Mourning-War Ceremony." *American Anthropologist* 4, no. 3 (July–September 1902):404–411.

———. *Traditions of the Arikara.* Washington, D.C.: Carnegie Institution of Washington, 1904.

Dozier, Edward P. *Hano: A Tewa Indian Community.* New York: Holt, Rinehart and Winston, 1966.

———. *The Pueblo Indians of North America.* New York: Holt, Rinehart, and Winston, 1970.

Drucker, Philip. *Cultures of the North Pacific Coast.* San Francisco: Chandler, 1965.

———. *Northern and Central Nootkan Tribes.* Bureau of American Ethnology, bulletin 144. Washington, D.C.: U.S. Government Printing Office, 1951.

Dusenberry, Verne. *The Montana Cree: A Study in Religious Persistence.* Uppsala, Sweden: Almqvist and Wiksell, 1962.

Dutton, Bertha P. *The Pueblos: Indians of the American Southwest.* Englewood Cliffs, N.J.: Prentice-Hall, 1975.

Eargle, Dolan H., Jr. *The Earth Is Our Mother: A Guide to the Indians of California, Their Locales and Historic Sites.* San Francisco: Trees Company Press, 1986.

Edmunds, R. David. *The Potawatomis: Keepers of the Fire.* Norman: University of Oklahoma Press, 1978.

Eggan, Fred. *Social Organization of the Western Pueblos.* Chicago: University of Chicago Press, 1950.

Erdoes, Richard. *Crying for a Dream: The World Through Native American Eyes.* Sante Fe: Bear and Company, 1990.

———. *The Sun Dance People.* New York: Knopf, 1972.

Ewers, John C. *The Blackfeet: Raiders on the Northwestern Plains.* Norman: University of Oklahoma Press, 1958.

———. *Plains Indian Sculpture.* Washington, D.C.: Smithsonian Institution Press, 1986.

Fahey, John. *The Kalispel Indians.* Norman: University of Oklahoma Press, 1986.

Farr, William E. *The Reservation Blackfeet, 1882–1945: A Photographic History of Cultural Survival.* Seattle: University of Washington Press, 1984.

Fenton, William N. *The False Faces of the Iroquois.* Norman: University of Oklahoma, 1987.

———. *Iroquois Eagle Dance: An Offshoot of the Calumet Dance. With An Analysis of the Iroquois Eagle Dance and Songs by Gertrude Prokosch Kurath.* Bureau of American Ethnology, bulletin 156. Washington, D.C.: U.S. Government Printing Office, 1953.

———. "Masked Medicine Societies of the Iroquois." In *Smithsonian Institution Annual Report for 1940,* 391–430. Washington, D.C.: U.S. Government Printing Office, 1941.

———. *An Outline of Seneca Ceremonies at Coldspring/ Longhouse.* New Haven: Yale University Press, 1936.

———, ed. *Symposium on Local Diversity in Iroquois Culture.* Bureau of American Ethnology, bulletin 149. Washington, D.C.: U.S. Government Printing Office, 1951.

———, and Gulick, John, eds. *Symposium on Cherokee and Iroquois Culture.* Bureau of American Ethnology, bulletin 180. Washington, D.C.: U.S. Government Printing Office, 1961.

Feraca, Stephen E. *Wakinyan: Contemporary Teton Dakota Religion.* Browning, Montana: Museum of the Plains Indian, 1963.

Ferguson, Erna. *Dancing Gods: Indian Ceremonials of New Mexico and Arizona.* Albuquerque: University of New Mexico Press, 1931.

Fewkes, J. Walter. *The Snake Ceremonial at Walpi.* Journal of American Ethnology and Archaeology, vol. 4, Hemenway Southwestern Archaeological Expedition. Boston: Houghton Mifflin, 1894.

Finger, John R. *The Eastern Band of Cherokees, 1819–1900.* Knoxville: University of Tennessee Press, 1984.

Fitzgerald, Michael Oren. *Yellowtail, Crow Medicine Man and Sun Dance Chief: An Autobiography.* Norman: University of Oklahoma Press, 1991.

Fitzhugh, William W., and Crowell, Aron. *Crossroads of Continents: Cultures of Siberia and Alaska.* Washington, D.C.: Smithsonian Institution Press, 1988.

Fitzhugh, William W., Kaplan, Susan A. *Inua. Spirit World of the Bering Sea Eskimo.* Washington, D.C.: Smithsonian Institution Press, 1982.

Fletcher, Alice C. "The Hako: A Pawnee Ceremony." *Twenty-Second Annual Report of the Bureau of American Ethnology to the Secretary of the Smithsonian Institution 1900–1901.* Part 2. Washington, D.C.: U.S. Government Printing Office, 1904.

———. "Star Cult Among the Pawnee—A Preliminary Report." *American Anthropologist* 4, no. 4 (October–December, 1902):730–736.

———. "Wakondagi." *American Anthropologist* 14, no. 1 (January–March, 1912): 106–108.

Fogelson, Raymond D. *The Cherokees: A Critical Bibliography.* Bloomington: Indiana University Press, 1978.

Foster, Kenneth E. *Navajo Sandpaintings.* Navajoland Publications Series 3. Window Rock, Arizona: Navajo Tribal Museum, 1964.

Foster, Michael K. *From the Earth to Beyond the Sky: An Ethnographic Approach to Four Longhouse Iroquois Speech Events.* National Museum of Man Mercury Series, Canadian Ethnology Service, paper no. 20. Ottawa: National Museum of Canada. 1974.

Fowler, Loretta. *Shared Symbols, Contested Meanings: Gros Ventre Culture and History, 1778–1984.* Ithaca, N.Y.: Cornell University Press, 1987.

French, Laurence, and Hornbuckle, Jim. *The Cherokee Perspective.* Boone, N.C.: Appalachian Consortium Press, 1981.

Frey, Rodney. *The World of the Crow Indians: As Driftwood Lodges.* Norman: University of Oklahoma Press, 1987.

Frisbie, Charlotte Johnson. *Kinaalda: A Study of the Navaho Girl's Puberty Ceremony.* Salt Lake City: University of Utah Press, 1993.

———. *Kinaaldá: A Study of the Navajo Puberty Ceremony.* Middleton, Conn.: Wesleyan University Press, 1967.

———. *Navajo Medicine Bundles or Jish: Acquisition, Transmission, and Disposition in the Past and Present.* Albuquerque: University of New Mexico Press, 1987.

———, ed. *Southwestern Indian Ritual Drama.* Albuquerque: University of New Mexico Press, 1980.

Frisbie, Charlotte J., and McAllester, David P., eds. *Navajo Blessingway Singer: The Autobiography of Frank Mitchell, 1881–1967.* Tucson: University of Arizona Press, 1978.

Geertz, Armin W. *Hopi Indian Altar Iconography.* Leiden, Netherlands: E. J. Brill, 1987.

———. *The Invention of Prophecy: Continuity and Meaning in Hopi Indian Religion.* Berkeley: University of California Press, 1994.

Geertz, Armin, and Lomatuway'ma, Michael. *Children of Cottonwood: Piety and Ceremonialism in Hopi Indian Puppetry.* Lincoln: University of Nebraska Press, 1986.

Gibson, Arrell M. *The Chickasaws.* Norman: University of Oklahoma Press, 1971.

Gilbert, William Harlen, Jr. "The Eastern Cherokees," *Anthropoligical Papers, Numbers 19–26.* Bureau of American Ethnology, bulletin 133, paper 23. Washington, D.C.: U.S. Government Printing Office, 1943.

Gilman, Carolyn, and Schneider, Mary Jane. *The Way to Independence: Memories of a Hidatsa Indian Family, 1840–1920.* St. Paul: Minnesota Historical Society Press, 1987.

Goldman, Irving. *The Mouth of Heaven: An Introduction to Kwakiutl Religion and Thought.* New York: Wiley, 1975.

Goulet, Jean-Guy. *Ways of Knowing: Experience, Knowledge, and Power among the Dene Tha.* Vancouver: University of British Columbia, 1998.

Griffin, Robert, and Grinde, Donald A., Jr. *Apocalypse of Chiokoyhikoy: Chief of the Iroquois.* Quebec: Les Presses de L'Université Laval, 1997.

Grim, John A. *The Shaman: Patterns of Religious Healing Among the Ojibway Indians.* Norman: University of Oklahoma Press, 1983.

Grinnell, George Bird. *By Cheyenne Campfires.* Lincoln: University of Nebraska Press, 1971. (Reprint of 1926 work).

———. *The Fighting Cheyennes.* Norman: University of Oklahoma Press, 1956. (Reprint of 1915 edition.)

———. "The Medicine Wheel." *American Anthropologist* vol. 24 (1922): 299–309.

———. *Pawnee, Blackfoot and Cheyenne.* New York: Scribner, 1961.

———. *When Buffalo Ran.* Norman: University of Oklahoma Press, 1966. (Originally published by Yale University Press in 1920).

Haile, Berard. *Head and Face Masks in Navaho Ceremonialism.* St. Michaels, Arizona: St. Michael's Press, 1947.

———. *Navaho Sacrificial Figurines.* Chicago: University of Chicago Press, 1947.

Hallowell, Alfred I. *The Role of Conjuring in Saulteaux Society.* New York: Octagon Books, 1971.

Harper, Kenn. *Give Me My Father's Body: The Life of Minik, the New York Eskimo.* Iqaluit (Frobisher Bay), N.W.T.: Blacklead Books, 1986.

Harrington, M. R. *Religion and Ceremonies of the Lenape.* New York: AMS Press, 1984 (1921).

Heizer, Robert F., ed. *Some Last Century Accounts of the Indians of Southern California.* Ramona, Calif.: Ballena, Press, 1976.

Heizer, Robert F., and Whipple, M. A., comps. and eds. *The California Indians: A Sourcebook.* 2nd ed. Berkeley: University of California, 1971.

Hewitt, J. N. B. *Iroquoian Cosmology.* 2 parts. Part 1: Bureau of American Ethnology, 21st annual report, 127–339. Washington, D.C.: U.S. Government Printing Office, 1903; Part 2: Bureau of American Ethnology 449–819. 43d annual report, Washington, D.C.: U.S. Government Printing Office, 1928.

———. *Orenda.* Bureau of American Ethnology, bulletin 30. Washington, D.C.: U.S. Government Printing Office, 1910.

Highwater, Jamake. *Ritual of the Wind: North American Ceremonies, Music, and Dance.* New York: Van Der Marck, 1984.

Hill, W. W. *An Ethnography of Santa Clara Pueblo, New Mexico.* Edited by Charles H. Lange. Albuquerque: University of New Mexico Press, 1982.

———. *Navajo Salt Gathering.* Anthropological Series vol. 3, no. 4. Albuquerque: University of New Mexico Press, 1940.

Hillerman, Tony. "Sacred Ground." *National Geographic Traveler* 6, no. 3 (May–June 1989):44–59.

Hoebel, E. Adamson. *The Cheyennes: Indians of the Great Plains.* New York: Holt, Rinehart and Winston, 1960.

Hoffman, Walter James. *The Midewiwin's or 'Grand Medicine Society' of the Ojibwa.* Bureau of American Ethnology, 7th annual report, 1885–86. Washington, D.C.: U.S. Government Printing Office, 1891.

Holler, Clyde. *Black Elk's Religion: The Sun Dance and Lakota Catholicism.* Syracuse: Syracuse University Press, 1995.

Holm, Bill. *Crooked Beak of Heaven: Masks and Other Ceremonial Art of the Northwest Coast.* Seattle: University of Washington Press, 1968.

Horse Capture, George, ed. *The Seven Visions of Bull Lodge.* Ann Arbor, Michigan: Bear Claw Press, 1980.

Howard, James. *The Canadian Sioux.* Lincoln: University of Nebraska Press, 1984.

———. *The Plains Ojibwa or Bungi: Hunters and Warriors of the Northern Prairies with Special Reference to the Turtle Mountain Band.* Lincoln, Nebraska: J. & L. Reprint, 1977 (Reprint).

———. *Shawnee: The Ceremonialism of a Native American Tribe and Its Cultural Background.* Athens: Ohio University Press, 1981.

Howard, James, Le Claire, Peter; et al. *The Ponca Tribe.* Bureau of American Ethnology, bulletin 195. Washington, D.C.: U.S. Government Printing Office, 1965.

Howard, James, and Lena, Willie. *Oklahoma Seminoles: Medicines, Magic, and Religion.* Norman: University of Oklahoma Press, 1984.

Howard, James, and Levine, Victoria Lindsay. *Choctaw Music and Dance.* Norman: University of Oklahoma Press, 1990.

Hunter, Helen Virginia. *The Ethnography of Salt in Aboriginal North America.* Philadelphia: 1940.

Iliff, Flora Gregg. *People of the Blue Water: A Record of Life Among the Walapai and Havasupai Indians.* New York: Harper and Brothers, 1954.

Inter-Tribal Council of Nevada. *NEWE: A Western Shoshone History.* Reno: Inter-Tribal Council of Nevada, 1976.

———. *NUMA: A Northern Paiute History.* Reno: Inter-Tribal Council of Nevada, 1976.

———. *NUWUVI: A Southern Paiute History.* Reno: Inter-Tribal Council of Nevada, 1976.

———. *WA SHE SHU: A Washo Tribal History.* Reno: Inter-Tribal Council of Nevada, 1976.

Jenness, Diamond. *The Carrier Indians of Bulkley River, Their Social and Religious Life.* Bureau of American Ethnology, bulletin 133, Anthropological Papers, no. 25, 471–586. Washington, D.C.: U.S. Government Printing Office, 1943.

Jilek, Wolfgang G. *Indian Healing: Shamanic Ceremonialism in the Pacific Northwest Today.* Surrey, British Columbia, Canada: Hancock House, 1982.

Johnston, Basil H. *The Manitous: The Spiritual World of the Ojibway.* New York: HarperCollins Publishers, 1995.

———. *Ojibway Ceremonies.* Lincoln: University of Nebraska Press, 1990. (1982, McClelland Stewart).

———. *Ojibway Heritage.* New York: Columbia University Press, 1976.

Johnstone, Bernice Eastman. *California's Gabrielino Indians.* Los Angeles: Southwest Museum, 1962.

Jones, David E. *Sanapia: Comanche Medicine Woman.* Prospect Heights, Ill.: Waveland Press, 1984. (Holt, Rinehart and Winston, 1972).

Jones, Peter. *History of the Ojebway Indians: With Especial Reference to Their Conversion to Christianity.* Freeport, New York: Books for Libraries, 1970. (Reprint of 1861 publication).

Jones, William. *Ethnography of the Fox Indians.* Bureau of American Ethnology, bulletin 125. Washington, D.C.: U.S. Government Printing Office, 1939.

Kan, Sergei. *Symbolic Immortality: The Tlingit Potlatch of the Nineteenth Century.* Washington, D.C.: Smithsonian Institution Press, 1989.

Kelly, William H. *Cocopa Ethnography.* University of Arizona Anthropological Papers no. 29. Tucson: University of Arizona Press, 1977.

Kelly, Roger; Lang, R. W.; and Walter, Harry. *Navajo Ritual Human Figurines: Form and Function.* Santa Fe: Museum of Navajo Ceremonial Art, 1972.

Kilpatrick, Alan. *The Night Has a Naked Soul: Witchcraft and Sorcery Among the Western Cherokee.* Syracuse: Syracuse University Press, 1997.

Kilpatrick, Jack Frederick, and Kilpatrick Anna Gritts. *Run Toward the Nightland: Magic of the Oklahoma Cherokees.* Dallas: Southern Methodist University Press, 1967.

King, J. C. H. *Portrait Masks from the Northwest Coast of America.* New York: Thames and Hudson, 1979.

Kleivan, Inge, and Sonne, B. *Eskimos: Greenland and Canada.* Leiden, Netherlands: E. J. Brill, 1985.

Kluckhohn, Clyde. *Navaho Witchcraft.* Boston: Beacon Press, 1944.

Kluckhohn, Clyde, and Leighton, Dorothea. *The Navaho.* Rev. ed. New York: American Museum of Natural History, 1962.

Kluckhohn, Clyde, and Spencer, Katherine. *A Bibliography of the Navaho Indians.* New York: Augustin, 1940.

Kniffen, Fred B.; Gregory, Hiram F.; and Stokes, George A. *The Historic Indian Tribes of Louisiana.* Baton Rouge: Louisiana State University, 1987.

Kroeber, A. L. *The Arapaho.* Lincoln: University of Nebraska Press, 1983. (Reprint.)

———. *Ethnology of the Gros Ventres.* New York: AMS Press, 1978. (Reprint of 1908 work.)

———. *Handbook of the Indians of California.* Bureau of American Ethnology, bulletin 78. Washington, D.C.: U.S. Government Printing Office, 1925. Reprint. New York: Dover Publications, Inc., 1976.

———. *Walapai Ethnography.* American Anthropological Association Memoirs no. 42. Menasha, Wisconsin: 1935.

———. "World Renewal: A Cult System of Native Northwest California." *Anthropological Records 13,* no. 1 (1949):1–156.

———. "The World Renewal Cult of Northwest California." In *The California Indians: A Sourcebook.* 2d ed. Berkeley: University of California, 1971.

Kurath, Getrude Prokosch. *Dance and Song Rituals of Six Nations Reserve, Ontario.* Bulletin 220. Ottawa: National Museum of Canada, 1968.

———. *Iroquois Music and Dance: Ceremonial Arts of Two Seneca Longhouses.* Bureau of American Ethnology, bulletin 187. Washington, D.C.: U.S. Government Printing Office, 1964.

Kurath, Getrude P., and Garcia, Antonio. *Music and Dance of the Tewa Pueblos.* Santa Fe: Museum of New Mexico, 1970.

Ladd, Edmund J. "Zuni Religion and Philosophy." In *Zuni El Morro, Past & Present Exploration,* Annual Bulletin of the School of American Research. Santa Fe: School of American Research, 1983.

Laird, W. David. *Hopi Bibliography: Comprehensive and Annotated.* Tucson: University of Arizona Press, 1977.

Lake, Robert G., Jr. *Chilula: People from the Ancient Redwoods.* Washington, D.C.: University Press of America, 1982.

Lame Deer, John (Fire), and Erdoes, Richard. *Lame Deer, Seeker of Visions.* New York: Simon and Schuster, 1972.

Landes, Ruth. *Ojibway Religion and the Midewiwin.* Madison: University of Wisconsin Press, 1968.

———. *The Prairie Potawatomi: Tradition and Ritual in the Twentieth Century.* Madison: University of Wisconsin Press, 1970.

Lang, Julian. "Traditional Tobacco Use in Northern California: A Special Report." *News From Native California,* vol. 9, no. 3 (Spring 1996):26–38.

Lange, Charles H. *Cochiti: New York Pueblo: Past and Present.* Austin: University of Texas Press, 1959.

Laughlin, William S. *Aleuts: Survivors of the Bering Land Bridge.* New York: Holt, Rinehart and Winston, 1980.

LaViolette, Forest E. *The Struggle for Survival: Indian Cultures and the Protestant Ethnic in British Columbia.* Toronto, Canada: University of Toronto Press, 1973.

Levy, Jerrold E. *In the Beginning: The Navajo Genesis.* Berkeley: University of California Press, 1998.

Levy, Jerrold; Neutra, Raymond; and Parker, Dennis. *Hand Trembling, Frenzy Witchcraft, and Moth Madness: A Study of Navajo Seizure Disorders.* Tucson: University of Arizona Press, 1987.

Librado, Fernando. *The Eye of the Flute: Chumash Traditional History and Ritual.* As told to John P. Harrington. Edited by Travis Hudson et al. Santa Barbara, Calif.: Santa Barbara Museum of Natural History, 1977.

Linderman, Frank B. *Pretty-shield: Medicine Woman of the Crows.* Lincoln: University of Nebraska Press, 1972. (Reprint.)

Loeb, E. M. *The Crow Indians.* Lincoln: University of Nebraska Press, 1935.

Loftin, John D. *Religion and Hopi Life in the Twentieth Century.* Bloomington: University of Indiana Press, 1991.

Lurie, Nancy Oestreich. *Mountain Wolf Woman: Sister of Crashing Thunder.* Ann Arbor: University of Michigan Press, 1961.

McCleary, Timothy P. *The Stars We Know: Crow Indian Astronomy and Lifeways.* Waveland Press, 1997.

McFeat, Tom. *Indians of the North Pacific Coast.* Seattle: University of Washington Press, 1966.

McLoughlin, William G. *The Cherokees and Christianity, 1794–1870: Essays on Acculturation and Cultural Persistence.* Walter H. Conser, Jr., ed. Athens: University of Georgia Press, 1994.

McNeley, James Kale. *Holy Wind in Navajo Philosophy.* Tucson: University of Arizona Press, 1981.

McTaggart, Fred. *Wolf That I Am: In Search of the Red Earth People.* Norman: University of Oklahoma Press, 1984. (Reprint).

Mails, Thomas E. *Fools Crow.* New York: Doubleday, 1979.

———. *The People Called Apache.* Englewood Cliffs, N.J.: Prentice-Hall, 1974.

———. *Secret Native American Pathways: A Guide to Inner Peace.* Tulsa, Okla.: Council Oaks Books, 1988.

———. *Sundancing at Rosebud and Pine Ridge.* Sioux Falls, S.D.: Center for Western Studies, 1978.

———. *Sundancing: The Great Sioux Piercing Ritual.* Tulsa: Council Oak Books, 1998.

Marquis, Thomas B. *The Cheyennes of Montana.* Algonac, Michigan: Reference Publications, 1978.

Martin, Marlene. "Iroquois False Face Masks." *Indian Notes,* 8 (1972): 12–167. New York: Museum of the American Indian.

Matthews, Washington. *The Night Chant, A Navaho Ceremony.* American Museum of Natural History Memoir no. 6. New York: 1902.

Merriam, Alan P. *Ethnomusicology of the Flathead Indians.* Chicago: Aldine, 1967.

Meyer, David. *The Red Earth Crees, 1860–1960.* Mercury Series. Ottawa: Canada, National Museums of Canada, National Museum of Man, 1985.

Michelson, Truman. *Notes on the Fox Wapanowiweni.* Smithsonian Institution, Bureau of American Ethnology, bulletin 105. Washington, D.C.: U.S. Government Printing Office, 1932.

Miller, Jay. *Shamanic Odyssey: The Lushootseed Salish Journey to the Land of the Dead.* Menlo Park, Calif.: Ballena Press, 1988.

Miller, Jay, and Eastman, Carol M. *The Tsimshian and Their Neighbors of the North Pacific Coast.* Seattle: University of Washington Press, 1984.

Modesto, Ruby, and Mount, Guy. *Not for Innocent Ears: Spiritual Traditions of a Desert Cahuilla Woman.* Arcata, Calif.: Sweetlight Books, 1980.

Mooney, James. *Calendar History of the Kiowa Indians.* Washington, D.C.: Smithsonian Institution Press, 1979. (Reprint from 1898 publication.)

———. "Cherokee Mound-Building." *The American Anthropologist,* vol. 2 (April 1889): 167–171.

———. *Myths of the Cherokees and Sacred Formulas of the Cherokees.* Nashville: Charles Elder, 1972. (Reprint of the 7th and 19th Bureau of American Ethnology reports.)

Morgan, William. "Human Wolves Among the Navajo." *Yale University Publications in Anthropology,* no. 11. New Haven: 1936.

Moriarty, James Robert. *Chinigchinix: An Indigenous California Indian Religion.* Los Angeles: Southwest Museum, 1969.

Murie, James R. *Ceremonies of the Pawnee.* Edited by Douglas R. Parks. Lincoln: University of Nebraska Press, 1989. (Reprint).

Nabokov, Peter. *Indian Running.* Santa Barbara, Calif.: Capra Press, 1981.

Neihardt, John G. *Black Elk Speaks.* Lincoln: University of Nebraska Press, 1961. (Reprint from 1932.)

Nelson, Eunice. *The Wabanaki: An Annotated Bibliography.* Cambridge, Mass.: American Friends Service Committee, 1982.

Newcomb, Franc Johnson. *Hosteen Klah: Navaho Medicine Man and Sand Painter.* Norman: University of Oklahoma Press, 1964.

Newcomb, Franc Johnson; Fishler, Stanley; and Wheelwright, Mary C. *A Study of Navajo Symbolism.* Papers of the Peabody Museum of Archaeology and Ethnology, Harvard University, vol. 32, no. 3 (1956).

Newcomb, Franc Johnson, and Reichard, Gladys A. *Sandpaintings of the Navajo Shooting Chant.* New York: Augustin, 1937.

Newkumet, Vynola Beaver, and Meredith, Howard L. *Hasinai: A Traditional History of the Caddo Confederacy.* College Station: Texas A & M University Press, 1988.

Norman, Howard. *Where the Chill Came From: Cree Windigo Tales and Journeys.* San Francisco: North Point Press, 1982.

Olden, Sarah Emilia. *Shoshone Folk Lore: As Discovered from the Rev. John Roberts, A Hidden Hero, on the Wind River Indian Reservation in Wyoming.* Milwaukee: Morehouse, 1923.

Olson, R. L. "Quinault Indians." *University of Washington Publications in Anthropology* 6, no. 1 (November 1936): 1–194.

Opler, Morris Edward. *An Apache Lifeway: The Economic, Social, and Religious Institutions of the Chiricahua Indians.* Chicago: University of Chicago Press, 1941.

Ortiz, Alfonzo, ed. *New Perspectives on the Pueblos.* Albuquerque: University of New Mexico, 1972.

———. *The Tewa World: Space, Time, Being and Becoming in a Pueblo Society.* Chicago: University of Chicago Press, 1969.

Oswalt, Wendell H. *Alaskan Eskimos.* San Francisco: Chandler, 1967.

Ourada, Patricia K. *The Menominee Indians: A History.* Norman: University of Oklahoma Press, 1979.

Overholt, Thomas W., and Callicott, J. Baird. *Clothed-in-Fur and Other Tales: An Introduction to an Ojibwa World View.* Lanham, Maryland: University Press of America, 1982.

Painter, Muriel Thayer. *Yaqui Beliefs and Ceremonies in Pascua Village.* Tucson: University of Arizona Press, 1986.

Paper, Jordan. "From Shaman to Mystic in Ojibwa Religion." *Studies in Religion* 9(1980):185–199.

Parezo, Nancy. *Navajo Sandpainting: From Religious Act to Commercial Act.* Tucson: University of Arizona Press, 1983.

Parlow, Anita. *A Song From Sacred Mountain.* Lakota Nation, S.D.: Oglala Lakota Legal Rights Fund, 1983.

———. *Pueblo Religion.* 2 vols. Chicago: University of Chicago Press, 1939.

Perrone, Bobette; Stockel, H. Henrietta; and Krueger, Victoria. *Medicine Women, Curanderas, and Women Doctors.* Norman: University of Oklahoma Press, 1989.

Peters, Russell M. *The Wampanoags of Mashpee.* Jamaica Plain, Mass.: Indian Spiritual and Cultural Training Council, 1987.

Petersen, Karen Daniels. *Plains Indian Art from Fort Marion.* Norman: University of Oklahoma Press, 1971.

Peterson, Natasha. *Sacred Sites: A Traveler's Guide to North America's Most Powerful Mystical Landmarks.* Chicago: Contemporary Books, 1988.

Pflug, Melissa A., and Irwin, Lee. *Ritual and Myth in Odawa Revitalization: Reclaiming a Sovereign Place.* Norman: University of Oklahoma Press, 1998.

Pond, Doreen "Walking Woman," and McDonald, Arthur L. *Cheyenne Journey: Morning Star, Our Guiding Light.* Santa Ana, Calif.: Seven Locks Press, 1996.

Pond, Samuel W. *The Dakota or Sioux in Minnesota As They Were in 1834.* St. Paul: Minnesota Historical Society Press, 1986. (Reprint.)

Powell, Jay, and Jensen, Vicki. *Quileute: An Introduction to the Indians of La Push.* Seattle: University of Washington Press, 1976.

Powell, Father Peter John. *People of the Sacred Mountain.* Two vols. San Francisco: Harper and Row, 1981.

———. "Power for Blessing: Sacred Rock Medicines." In *To Honor the Crow People*. Edited by Father Peter J. Powell. Chicago: Foundation for the Preservation of American Indian Art and Culture, St. Augustine's Center for American Indians, 1988.

———. *Sweet Medicine: The Continuing Role of the Sacred Arrows, the Sun Dance, and the Sacred Buffalo Hat in Northern Cheyenne History*. Two vols. Norman: University of Oklahoma Press, 1969.

———. *The Cheyennes, Ma?heo?o's People: A Critical Bibliography*. Bloomington: Indiana University Press, 1980.

Powers, Marla N. *Oglala Women*. Chicago: University of Chicago Press, 1986.

Powers, William K. *Oglala Religion*. Lincoln: University of Nebraska Press, 1975.

———. *Sacred Language: The Nature of Supernatural Discourse in Lakota*. Norman: University of Oklahoma Press, 1986.

———. *Yuwipi: Vision and Experience in Oglala Ritual*. Lincoln: University of Nebraska Press, 1982.

Powers, William K., and Powers, Marla N. "Putting on the Dog." *Natural History* 95, No. 2 (February 1986):6–16.

Radin, Paul. *The Autobiography of a Winnebago Indian*. New York: Dover, 1963 (1920).

Ray, Carl, and Stevens, James. *Sacred Legends of the Sandy Lake Cree*. Toronto, Canada: McClelland and Stewart, 1971.

Ray, Dorothy Jean. *Eskimo Masks—Art and Ceremony*. Seattle: University of Washington Press, 1967.

———. *Primitive Pragmatists: The Modoc Indians of Northern California*. Seattle: University of Washington Press, 1963.

Red Sky, James. *Great Leader of the Ojibway: Mis-quona-queb*. Edited by James R. Stevens. Toronto, Canada: McClelland and Stewart, 1972.

Regina v. *Machekequonabe,* 28 O.R. 309, Ontario Divisional Court, Armour C.J., Falconbridge and Street JJ (8 February 1897).

Reichard, Gladys A. *Navaho Medicine Man Sandpaintings*. New York: Augustin, 1939. Reprint. New York: Dover, 1977.

———. *Navaho Religion: A Study of Symbolism*. 2 vols. Bollingen Series 18. New York: Pantheon Books, 1950. Reprint: Princeton: Princeton University Press, 1990.

———. *Social Life of the Navaho Indians, With Some Attention to Minor Ceremonies*. New York: Columbia University Press, 1928.

Relander, Click. *Drummers and Dreamers*. Caldwell, Idaho: Caxton, 1956.

Rhodes, Robert. *Hopi Music and Dance*. Occasional Papers (Music and Dance Series), vol. 3, no. 2. Tsaile, Arizona: Navajo Community College Press, 1977.

Rice, Julian. *Black Elk's Story: Distinguishing Its Lakota Purpose*. Albuquerque: University of New Mexico Press, 1991.

———. *Before the Great Spirit: The Many Faces of Sioux Spirituality*. Albuquerque: University of New Mexico Press, 1998.

Ridington, Robin, and Hastings, Dennis (In'aska). *Blessing for a Long Time: The Sacred Pole of the Omaha Tribe*. Lincoln: University of Nebraska Press, 1997.

Ritzenthaler, Robert E., and Ritzenthaler, Pat. *The Woodland Indians of the Western Great Lakes*. Milwaukee: Milwaukee Public Museum, 1983.

Roediger, Virginia M. *Ceremonial Costumes of the Pueblo Indians: Their Evolution, Fabrication, and Significance in the Prayer Drama*. Berkeley: University of California Press, 1941.

Roessel, Ruth. *Women in Navajo Society*. Rough Rock, Navajo Nation, Arizona: Rough Rock Demonstration School, 1981.

Roscoe, Will. *The Zuni Man-Woman*. Albuquerque: University of New Mexico Press, 1991.

Rountree, Helen C. *The Powhatan Indians of Virginia: Their Traditional Culture*. Norman: University of Oklahoma Press, 1989.

———. *Pocahontas's People: The Powhatan Indians of Virginia Through Four Centuries*. Norman: University of Oklahoma Press, 1990.

Ruby, Robert H., and Brown, John A. *A Guide to the Indian Tribes of the Pacific Northwest*. Norman: University of Oklahoma Press, 1986.

Salisbury, Neal. *The Indians of New England: A Critical Bibliography*. Bloomington: Indiana University Press, 1982.

Samek, Hana. *The Blackfoot Confederacy 1880–1920: A Comparative Study of Canadian and U.S. Indian Policy*. Albuquerque: University of New Mexico Press, 1987.

Sandner, Donald. *Navaho Symbols of Healing*. New York: Harcourt Brace Jovanovich, 1979.

Sandoz, Mari. *Crazy Horse*. Lincoln: University of Nebraska Press, 1961. (Reprint from 1942).

Schlesier, Karl H. *The Wolves of Heaven: Cheyenne Shamanism, Ceremonies, and Prehistoric Origins*. Norman: University of Oklahoma Press, 1987.

Schuster, Helen H. *The Yakimas: A Critical Bibliography*. Bloomington: Indiana University Press, 1982.

Scully, Vincent. *Pueblo: Mountain, Village, Dance*. 2nd ed. New York: Viking Press, 1975.

Seguin, Margaret. *The Tsimshian: Images of the Past/Views for the Present*. Vancouver, British Columbia, Canada: University of British Columbia Press, 1984.

Simmons, Marc. *Witchcraft in the Southwest: Spanish and Indian Supernaturalism on the Rio Grande*. Lincoln: University of Nebraska Press, 1974.

Slotkin, James S. *The Menominee Powwow*. Milwaukee: Milwaukee Public Museum, 1957.

Smith, Andrea Lee. *Sacred Sites, Sacred Rites*. New York: American Indian Community House/National Council of the Churches of Christ in the USA, 1998

Smithson, Carma Lee and Euler, Robert C. *Havasupai Legends: Religion and Mythology of the Indians of the Grand Canyon*. Salt Lake City: University of Utah Press, 1994.

Smithsonian Institution Traveling Exhibition Service. *The Year of the Hopi: Paintings and Photographs by Joseph Mora,*

1904–06. New York: Rizzoli International Publications, 1979.

Sneve, Virginia Driving Hawk. *They Led A Nation: The Sioux Chiefs.* Sioux Falls S.D.: Brevet Press, 1975.

Snow, John. *These Mountains Are Our Sacred Places: The Story of the Stoney Indians.* Toronto, Canada: Samuel-Stevens, 1977.

Speck, Frank G. *Catawba Texts.* New York: AMS Press, 1969. (Reprint from 1934.)

———. *Ethnology of the Yuchi.* Atlantic Highlands, N.J.: Humanities Press, 1979. (Reprint from 1909).

———. *Midwinter Rites of the Cayuga Long House.* Philadelphia: University of Pennsylvania Press, 1949.

———. *Oklahoma Delaware Ceremonies, Feasts and Dances.* New York: AMS Press, 1980 (1937).

———. *Tutelo Spirit Adoption Ceremony: Reclothing the Living in The Name of the Dead.* Harrisburg: Pennsylvania Historical Commission, 1942.

Speck, Frank G., and Broom, Leonard. *Cherokee Dance and Drama.* Norman: University of Oklahoma Press, 1983. (Reprint from the University of California, 1951.)

Spicer, Edward, ed. *Perspectives on American Indian Culture Change.* Chicago: University of Chicago Press, 1961.

———. *The Yaquis: A Cultural History.* Tucson: University of Arizona Press, 1980.

Spindler, George D. *Sociocultural and Psychological Processes in Menomini Acculturation.* Berkeley: University of California Press, 1955.

Spindler, George D., and Spindler, Louise. *Dreamers Without Power: The Menomini Indians.* New York: Holt, Rinehart and Winston, 1971.

Standing Bear, Luther. *My People the Sioux.* Lincoln: University of Nebraska Press, Bison Book edition, 1975.

Steinmetz, Paul B., S. J. *Meditations with Native Americans: Lakota Spirituality.* Santa Fe, N.M.: Bear and Company, 1984.

———. *Pipe, Bible, and Peyote Among the Oglala Lakota: A Study in Religious Identity.* Knoxville: University of Tennessee Press, 1990.

Stevenson, Matilda Coxe. *Zuni Indians: Their Mythology, Esoteric Fraternities, and Ceremonies.* Bureau of American Ethnology, 23rd annual report. Washington, D.C.: U.S. Government Printing Office, 1904.

Stewart, Omer C. *Indians of the Great Basin: A Critical Bibliography.* Bloomington: Indiana University Press, 1982.

Stott, Margaret A. *Bella Coola Ceremony and Art.* Canadian Ethnology Service Paper no. 21. Ottawa: National Museum of Canada, 1975.

Sturtevant, William, gen. ed. *Handbook of North American Indians.* Vol. 4: *History of Indian-White Relations,* 1988; Vol. 5 *Arctic,* 1984; Vol. 6: *Subarctic,* 1981; Vol. 7: *Northwest Coast,* 1990; Vol. 8: *California,* 1978; Vol. 9: *Southwest* (Pueblo peoples), 1980; Vol. 10 *Southwest* (non-Pueblo peoples), 1983; Vol. 11: *Great Basin,* 1986; Vol. 15: *Northeast,* 1979. Washington, D.C.: Smithsonian Institution Press.

Swan, Daniel C. *Peyote Religious Art: Symbols of Faith and Belief.* University of Mississippi Press, 1998.

Sweet, Jill D. *Dances of the Tewa Indians: Expressions of a New Life.* Santa Fe, N.M.: School of American Research Press, 1985.

Tanner, Adrian. *Bringing Home Animals: Religious Ideology and Mode of Production of Mistassini Cree Hunters.* New York: St. Martin's Press, 1979.

Tanner, Helen Hornbeck, ed. *Atlas of Great Lakes Indian History.* Norman: University of Oklahoma Press, 1987.

———. *The Ojibwas: A Critical Bibliography.* Bloomington: Indiana University Press, 1976.

Tax, Sol. *Indian Tribes of Aboriginal America.* Chicago: University of Chicago Press, 1952.

Tedlock, Dennis, and Tedlock, Barbara, eds. *Teachings from the American Earth: Indian Religion and Philosophy.* New York: Liveright, 1975.

Thomas, Chief Jacob (with Terry Boyle). *Teachings from the Longhouse.* Toronto: Stoddart Publishing, 1994.

Thomas, David Hurst, ed. *A Blackfoot Source Book: Papers by Clark Wissler.* New York: Garland Publishing, 1986. (Reprint).

———. *A Great Basin Shoshonean Source Book.* New York: Garland Publishing, 1986.

Tooker, Elisabeth. *The Indians of the Northeast: A Critical Bibliography.* Bloomington: Indiana University Press, 1978.

———. *The Iroquois Ceremonial of Midwinter.* Syracuse: Syracuse University Press, 1970.

———, ed. *Iroquois Culture, History, and Prehistory.* 1965 Conference on Iroquois Research. Albany: New York State Museum and Science Service, 1967.

———. *Native North American Spirituality of the Eastern Woodlands: Sacred Myths, Dreams, Visions, Speeches, Healing Formulas, Rituals, and Ceremonials.* Mahwah, N.J.: Paulist Press, 1979.

Trenholm, Virginia Cole. *The Arapahoes, Our People.* Norman: University of Oklahoma Press, 1970.

"Tribute to James Mooney, Cherokee Ethnologist." *Journal of Cherokee Studies 7,* No. 1 (Spring 1982): special issue.

Trigger, Bruce G. *The Huron: Farmers of the North.* New York: Holt, Rinehart and Winston, 1969.

Tucker, Toba. *Hodinonshonni: Portraits of the Firekeepers, the Onondaga Nation.* Syracuse: Syracuse University Press, 1999.

Tyler, Hamilon A. *Pueblo Gods and Myths.* Norman: University of Oklahoma Press, 1964.

Uintah-Ouray Ute Tribe. *A Brief History of the Ute People.* Fort Duchesne, Utah: Uintah-Ouray Ute Tribe, 1977.

———. *The Ute People.* Fort Duchesne, Utah: Uintah-Ouray Ute Tribe, 1977.

———. *Ute Ways.* Fort Duchesne, Utah: Uintah-Ouray Ute Tribe, 1977.

Underhill, Ruth M. *Papago Indian Religion.* New York: Columbia University Press, 1946.

Unrau, William E. *The Emigrant Indians of Kansas: A Critical Bibliography.* Bloomington: Indiana University Press, 1979.

———. *The Kansa Indians: A History of the Wind People, 1673–1873.* Norman: University of Oklahoma Press, 1971.

Upham, Warren, and Dunlap, Rose Barteau, comps. *Minnesota Biographies 1655–1912.* St. Paul: Minnesota Historical Society, 1912.

Vander, Judith. *Songprints: The Musical Experience of Five Shoshone Women.* Urbana: University of Illinois Press, 1988.

Vecsey, Christopher. *Traditional Ojibwa Religion and Its Historical Changes.* Philadelphia: American Philosophical Society, 1983.

Vennum, Thomas, Jr. *The Ojibwa Dance Drum: Its History and Construction.* Washington, D.C.: Smithsonian Institution Press, 1982.

Vestal, Stanley. *Warpath: The True Story of the Fighting Sioux Told in a Biography of Chief White Bull.* Lincoln: University of Nebraska Press, 1984 (1934).

Vizenor, Gerald. *The People Named the Chippewa.* Minneapolis: University of Minnesota Press, 1984.

Voget, Fred W. *The Shoshoni-Crow Sun Dance.* Norman: University of Oklahoma Press, 1984.

Walker, James R. *Lakota Belief and Ritual.* Edited by Raymond J. DeMallie and Elaine A. Jahner. Lincoln: University of Nebraska Press, 1980.

Warren, William W. *History of the Ojibway Nation.* Minneapolis: Ross and Haines, 1957.

Waters, Frank, and Fredericks, Oswald White Bear. *Book of the Hopi.* New York: Penguin Books, 1977. (Reprint of 1963 edition.)

Weltfish, Gene. *The Lost Universe: Pawnee Life and Culture.* Lincoln: University of Nebraska Press, Bison Book edition, 1977.

Weyer, Edward Moffat. *The Eskimos: Their Environment and Folkways.* New Haven: Yale University Press, 1932.

Wilson, Gilbert L. *Buffalo Bird Woman's Garden: Agriculture of the Hidatsa Indians.* St. Paul: Minnesota Historical Society Press, 1987.

Witthoft, John. *Green Corn Ceremonialism in the Eastern Woodlands.* Ann Arbor: University of Michigan Press, 1949.

Whitman, William. *The Oto.* New York: AMS Press, 1969 (Reprint).

Wildschut, William. *Crow Indian Medicine Bundles.* New York: Museum of the American Indian, Heye Foundation, 1960.

Wood, Raymond, and Liberty, Margot, eds. *Anthropology on the Great Plains.* Lincoln: University of Nebraska Press, 1980.

Wright, Barton. *Kachinas of the Zuni.* Flagstaff, Arizona: Northland Press, 1985.

———. *This Is a Hopi Kachina.* Flagstaff: Museum of Northern Arizona, 1965.

Wright, Muriel H. *A Guide to the Indian Tribes of Oklahoma.* Norman: University of Oklahoma Press, 1951.

Wyman, Leland C. *Blessingway.* Tucson: University of Arizona Press, 1970.

———. *Southwest Indian Drypainting.* Albuquerque: University of New Mexico Press, 1983.

Wyman, Leland C., and Kluckhohn, Clyde. "Navaho Classification of Their Song Ceremonials." In American Anthropological Association. *Memoirs,* no. 50. Menasha, Wisconsin, 1938.

Yetter, Bob. *Badger-Two Medicine: The Last Stronghold, Sacred Land of the Grizzly, Wolf, and Blackfeet Indian.* Missoula, Mont.: Rocky Mountain Front Advisory Council, 1992.

Young, David; Ingram, Grant; and Swartz, Lise. *Cry of the Eagle: Encounters with a Cree Healer.* Toronto, Canada: University of Toronto Press, 1989.

SUBJECT INDEX

BIBLE TRANSLATORS

Arch, John
Boudinot, Elias
Bushyhead, Jesse
Byington, Cyrus
Copway, George
Davis, John
Dukes, Joseph
Egede, Povl
Eliot, John
Evans, John
Foreman, Stephen
Freeman, Bernardus
Gahuni
Garrioch, Alfred Campbell
Hall, Charles L.
Hall, Sherman
Goodbird, Edward
Horden, John
Hunter, James
Jacobs, Peter
Jones, Evan
Jones, John Buttrick
Jones, Peter
Kirby, William West
Kohlmeister, Benjamin
McDougall, John
Mason, Sophia Thomas
Mayhew, Experience
Morgan, Jacob
Nesutan, Job
O'Meara, Frederick Augustus
Onasakenrat, Joseph

Osunkhirhine, Pierre Paul
Perryman, James
Perryman, Thomas Ward
Petter, Rodolphe
Petter, Bertha
Pond, Gideon
Pond, Samuel
Rand, Silas
Riggs, Stephen Return
Roberts, John
Robertson, Ann Eliza
    Worcester
Robertson, William Schenck
Sergeant, John
Spaulding, Henry Harmon
Steinhauer, Henry Bird
Watkins, Edwin Arthur
Worcester, Samuel Austin
Wright, Asher

CEREMONIAL GAMES/RUNNING

Bowl (Peach Stone) Game
Ceremonial Relay Race
Ghost Dance Hand Game
Kickstick Race
Lacrosse
Ritual Football Game
Single Pole Ball Game
Snowsnake
Stickball Game
Stick Game Dances

CEREMONIES BY TRIBE AND REGION

ALGONQUIAN
Shaking Tent

APACHE
Ceremonial Relay Race
Deer and Antelope
    Ceremonies
Hair-Cutting
    Ceremony
Holiness Rite
Long Life Ceremony
Lightning Ceremony
Little Rite
Mountain Spirit Dancers
Putting on Moccasins

ARAPAHO
Sun Dance

ARIKARA
Sun Dance

ASSINIBOINE
Fool's Dance
Sun Dance

ATHABASCAN
Stick Dance

BELLA COOLA
Memorial Potlatch
Winter Ceremonial

BLACKFEET
All-Smoking Ceremony
Black-Tailed Deer Dance
Dance for the Spirits
    of the Dead
Stick Game Dance
Sun Dance

CADDO
Drum Dance

CAHTO
Kuksu Religion

CALIFORNIA
Bear Dance
Doctor's Dance
Ghost Dance of 1870
Hesi Ceremony
Jump Dance
Kuksu Religion
White Deerskin Dance

CHEROKEE
Cementation or Reconciliation
    Festival
Exalting or Bounding Bush
    Feast
First New Moon of Spring
    Festival
Foundation of Life
Great New Moon Feast
Green Corn Feast
Mosquito Dance

364

CEREMONIES

Deer and Antelope
Ceremonies
First Catch Ceremonies
Hunting Ceremonials
Hunting Dance
Sedna Ceremony
Wakan Feast
Whale Feast

CURING CEREMONIES

Animal Dances
Bathing
Black-Tailed Deer Dance
Blackening
Bowl (Peach Stone) Game
Buffalo Ceremony
Catch-the-Stone Ceremony
Curing Ceremonials, Apache
Curing Ceremonials, Keresan
Pueblos
Curing Ceremonials, Zuni
Dark Dance
Dream Guessing Rite
Enemy Way
Evil Way
Father Dance
Feast to the Dead, Iroquois
Feather Dance, Iroquois
Girl's Puberty Rite, Western
Apache
Hanbleceya
Holiness Rite
Holy Way Ceremonies
False Face Ceremony
Husk Face Ceremony
Iruska
Life Way Ceremonies
Mountain Spirit Dance
Navajo Curing Ceremonies
Night Way
Picofa Ceremony
Remaking Rite
Shaking Tent
Snake-Antelope Ceremony
Snow-Snake
Spirit Dance Ceremonial
Stick Game Dance
Striking-a-Stick Dance
Sweat Lodge Ritual
Traveling Rite
War Dance, Iroquois
War Dance, Navajo
Yuwipi

FERTILITY AND PLANT
PROPAGATION
CEREMONIES

Basket Dance
Bread Dance
Busk
Chelkona
Cloud Dance
Corn Dance
Hopi Dance
Kachina Dances
Ritual Football Game
Shalako
Sun Dance

FIRST FOODS, FOOD
HONORING AND
HARVEST CEREMONIES

Acorn Feast
Bean Ceremony
Berry Festival
Bread Dance
Corn Dance
Cranberry Day
First Catch Ceremonies
First Salmon Rites
Green Corn, Iroquois
Green Corn Ceremony,
Oklahoma Seminole and
Creek
Green Corn Dance, Shawnee
Harvest Festival, Iroquois
Harvest Festival for Crops,
Zuni
Our Life Supporter Dances
Peace Dance
Root Feast
Round Dance, Great Basin
Strawberry Festival
World Renewal Ceremonial
Cycle

MASKED CEREMONIES

Animal Dances
Apache Ceremonialism
Bladder Festival
Chapeyeka Masks
Dancing Societies
False Face Ceremony
Girl's Puberty Rite, Western
Apache
Hamatsa Dance
Holiness Rite
Hopi Ceremonialism
Hunting Ceremonials
Husk Face Society

Kachina Dances
Koko
Mask
Masquerade Festival
Messenger Feast
Mountain Spirit Dancers
Night Way Ceremony
Niman Kachina Ceremony
Pascola Dancer
Powamu Ceremony
Shalako Ceremony
Winter Ceremonial, Kwakiutl
Winter Ceremonial, North
Pacific Coast
Yaqui Ceremonialism
Yeibichai Masks
Zuni Ceremonialism

MEMORIAL AND
MOURNING
CEREMONIALS

Bladder Festival
Chinigchinix Religion
Condolence Ceremony
Death Feast
Family Condolence Rite
Feast for the Mourners
Feast to the Dead, Huron
Feast to the Dead, Inuit
Feast to the Dead, Iroquois
Ghost Keeping Ceremony
Giveaway Dance and
Ceremony
Iroquois Ceremonialism
Memorial Potlatch
Mourning Anniversary
Ceremony
Mourning Ceremony, Cocopa
Mourning Ceremony,
Diegueno
Mourning Ceremony,
Havasupai
Mortuary Cycle
Requickening Address
Roll Call of the Chiefs
Stick Dance
Tenth Day Feast

NEW FIRE CEREMONIES

Big House Ceremony
Busk
Cementation or Reconciliation
Ceremony
First New Moon of Spring
Festival
First Salmon Rites

New Fire Ceremony, Hopi
New Fire Ceremony, Zuni
Preliminary Green Corn
Feast
Stirring Ashes Rite
World Renewal
Ceremonial Cycle

RAIN CEREMONIES

Animal Dances
Chelkona
Flute Ceremony
Gallo Pull
Hopi Dance
Kachina Dances
Kuksu Religion
Lightning Ceremony
Prayerstick Festival
Rain Ceremonial
Ritual Football Game
Saguaro Festival
Shalako
Snake-Antelope
Ceremony
Striking-a-Stick Dance
War Dance

THANKFULNESS
CEREMONIES

Anointing Sacred Pole
Ceremony
Bean Ceremony
Bush Dance
Busk
Feather Dance, Iroquois
First Food Observances
Green Corn, Iroquois
Hanbleceya
Harvest Festival, Iroquois
Harvest Festival for Crops
Iroquois Calendrical
Ceremonies
Iroquois Ceremonialism
Longhouse Religion
Midwinter Festival
Oakah Dance
Our Life Supporter Dances
Peach Dance
Personal Chant
Raspberry Ceremony
Seed Planting Ceremony
Spring Rite
Stirring Ashes Rite
Strawberry Festival
Sun and Moon Ceremony
Sun Dance

INDEX

Page numbers in **boldface** indicate main articles. Page numbers in *italics* indicate illustrations. Page numbers followed by m indicate maps.